AEQ.

DN

# BEAUTY IN HISTORY

## Books by Arthur Marwick

The Explosion of British Society 1914–1962 (1963; revised and expanded
edition for the period 1914–1970, 1971)

Clifford Allen: The Open Conspirator (1964)

The Deluge: British Society and the First World War
(1965; new edition 1973)

Britain in the Century of Total War: War, Peace and Social Change
1900–1967 (1968)

The Nature of History (1970; 3rd edition in preparation)

War and Social Change in the Twentieth Century: A Comparative Study of
Britain, France, Germany, Russia and the United States (1974)

The Home Front: The British and the Second World War (1976)

Women at War 1914–1918 (1977)

Class: Image and Reality in Britain, France and the USA since 1930 (1980)

(Editor) The Illustrated Dictionary of British History (1980)

British Society Since 1945 (1982, revised and expanded edition
in preparation)

Britain in Our Century: Images and Controversies (1984)

(Editor) Class in the Twentieth Century (1986)

(Editor) Total War and Social Change (1988)

# BEAUTY IN HISTORY

Society, politics and personal appearance
*c.* 1500 to the present

## Arthur Marwick

with 124 illustrations

Thames and Hudson

This book is dedicated jointly to Marc Ferro,
distinguished historian, and to my daughter, Louise.

© 1988 Arthur Marwick

All Rights Reserved. No part of this publication may be reproduced
or transmitted in any form or by any means, electronic or mechanical,
including photocopy, recording or any information storage and
retrieval system, without permission in writing from the publisher

Typeset by Q-Set, Hucclecote, Gloucester
Printed and bound in the German Democratic Republic

# Contents

# Preface and Acknowledgments

As with all of my books, this one is intended as a dialogue with my readers, not as an attempt to browbeat them into accepting my particular interpretation. To make lucid arguments possible, I state clearly my definitions, my assumptions and the questions I am trying to answer. Readers may prefer other definitions, may wish I had asked different questions; but if they are forced to think carefully about their own assumptions (even if, in the end, these are reinforced), or are stimulated into pursuing further enquiries of their own, then this book will have achieved a valuable purpose. Some readers will find that much of what I say conforms with their own experiences of the human world in which we live; others will be shocked to find that this book challenges a fundamental orthodoxy of our time about the nature of human affairs, the orthodoxy which holds that all matters relating to human society, instead of having an independent 'real', 'essential', or 'universal', existence, are in fact constructed by society; and that, to take the subject matter of this book, as society changes so what is considered beautiful in human beings changes. My position is that just because many aspects of human life *are* socially constructed that does not necessarily mean that *all* are. Orthodoxies should always be subject to challenge, never taken as read.

The main themes of this book emerged slowly over the years of my researches and differ almost totally from the few scrappy ideas I outlined for my publishers at the beginning of the enterprise, the one fixed point being my conviction that the whole question of the implications of human beauty (male and female) in the real lives of actual human beings (as distinct from studies of representations, or images, of beauty) had never been properly explored. The study of human beauty, it seems to me, falls outside, or across, conventional studies of social inequality. In so far as the beautiful (again, male and female) have advantages denied to the rest of us, the rest of us are disadvantaged. This does not mean that I take a 'traditionalist' or 'conservative' view of society: though my account is primarily analytical and historical I do suggest how the facts of personal beauty (as I perceive them) may be reconciled with the proper objective of enabling each individual to realize the full portential of her or his particular combination of personal attributes.

Historians have generally been more successful in describing the looks of male personages than of female ones (rather as medieval painters give highly individual characteristics to male saints and donors, while often painting the Madonna and female saints in highly stylized forms). Try to get a clear impression of the personal appearance of Madame de Pompadour, or Ninon de Lenclos, or Nell Gwyn (or Bonnie Prince Charlie, for that matter), and a search of the literature will bring only vagueness and confusion; as for Georgiana, Duchess of Devonshire, you'll find that the same insubstantial description is simply handed down from book to book. Using visual and written sources, this book attempts, among many, many other tasks, to establish clear ideas about what real people really looked like. But it is concerned not just with the great and the bad. Did the peasant's son with a pretty face stand a better chance of rising to be a footman than his less well-favoured brothers? How about actors and actresses? How about shop assistants, male and female?

This book covers a long span of time, starting with a brief summary of the classical and medieval periods, before beginning detailed analysis in the sixteenth and seventeenth centuries. The basic theme is that while beauty itself has not *significantly* changed, the *value* placed on it has. Now, never before have I produced a book which extends outside my own area of specialization, the twentieth century. Yet, whatever the limits of my own specialist knowledge, I have always maintained that the whole of our human past, not just that immediately behind us, is of interest and relevance. This book is an attempt to vindicate that fundamental principle. I start with the obsession we have today with human beauty, and ask: 'Was it always so?' I was, I believe, taught medieval and early modern history in a good department (that of Edinburgh University – where, also, I was well instructed in the history of art), even if many, many years ago, and I have, I hope, mastered the most recent, and most relevant, secondary reading. Above all, I would insist that my themes have emerged unprompted from the primary material, most of it of a type not much studied by other researchers. As part of my belief in the dialogue with the reader, my sources, of course, are cited, and frequently extensively quoted from.

However, happy is the historian who has friends much cleverer than he is himself. I could never have got off to the rapid start I did without the initial guidance of Open University colleagues Erika Langmuir, Catherine King, Lucille Kekewich and Anne Laurence. Along the way very vital specialist help has been provided by Tony Lentin and Jim Moore. During the time I was researching at the Hoover Institution at Stanford, California, I was given much help and encouragement by Peter

Dignan, Lewis Gahn, Theory Berger, Joseph Berger and John Petersen. I owe a special debt to Peter Stansky of the History Department, Stanford University, and would also like to thank Jim Sheehan and Carl Landauer for their helpful comments. During my stay in the Bay Area I delivered early versions of my thoughts on beauty to the History Departments at both the University of California at Berkeley and at Stanford. I am grateful for the wide range of comments which I received, some of them most helpfully critical. I'd like to express special thanks to Sheldon Rothblatt at Berkeley. Having given papers in many other places and also, I fear, spent an awful amount of time in informal conversation on the subject of beauty, I am unable to record all of those who have most helpfully contributed to the development of my thinking. I would, however, like to single out John Jacob, Curator of Kenwood House, for specialist advice on portraiture, Douglas and Madaleine Johnson, Irene Sorlin, Joan Bellamy and Henry Cowper.

I have been particularly lucky in the help I have received from librarians and curators. First of all, I must single out Tony Coulson, Media Librarian at the Open University, who, while being the model professional, has gone far beyond the call of professional duty in tracing reproductions back to their original sources, in acquiring slides for me, and in guiding me through the morasses of attribution and misattribution. Then I must thank my good friend Agnes Petersen of the Hoover Institution, generous as always with advice and comfort, and with whom I have been in touch right up to the compilation of this preface. In the Hoover Institution Archives Elena Danielson, together with her assistants, provided perfection in the way of service to a researcher on a most abstruse topic. Molly Tuthill was most considerate in giving me access to such as was possible of the Ronald Reagan collection. In the Special Collections and University Archives of the Stanford University Libraries I also received immaculate service from Carol Rudisell, Sara Timby and Margaret J. Kimball, and from all the staff working there. In the General Reference Section of the Green Library at Stanford Jim Knox went out of his way to provide me with vital initiatory bibliographical guidance. Coming nearer home, I must record with thanks the special assistance of Jack and Ann Flavel at the Bodleian Library and of Geoffrey Marsh at the Museum of London.

It has never been my practice to distinguish between male and female colleagues. However, given the nature of this book, and the sorts of reactions to which my topic has already given rise, it is probably worthwhile stressing how many women, often acting in their professional capacities, have been involved in the final shaping of *Beauty in History*. Kay Syrad, formerly a research student at the Open University, provided me at an early stage with important bibliographical information. It was my hope that she would read and comment on the entire text of the book. After four chapters (of a very early draft), however, she gave up in disgust, and wishes it to be made clear that she totally dissociates herself from my book. I was deeply sad about this, but feel bound to record that I found her criticisms of these first four chapters quite extraordinarily helpful. The entire text has been read by Martine Brant. The professional editor supplied by my publishers was a woman whose editorial comments were extremely helpful. Large parts of an early draft were typed by Pat King, and all of the later drafts by Gill Wood; I am grateful to both for helpful comments, and to Gill Wood for many thoughtful suggestions. In my audience at Stanford was Margaret Gelatt, who described herself unjustly, but all too typically, as 'only a secretary in the Civil Engineering Department', but who gave me both encouragement and useful bibliographical information. The page proofs were read by Holly Jones. To all of these, my heartiest thanks.

Nevertheless, I have now to give special mention to Pierre Sorlin, of Paris, and Dan Leab of New York. Both of these have gone meticulously through my text, word by word, sentence by sentence. Pierre subjected me to an almost frightening examination in his Paris flat, revealing both my deep ignorance in many areas, and our irreconcilable differences upon certain key assumptions. Dan Leab, with enormous patience, provided lengthy and learned annotations. No thanks of mine can possibly repay their devoted labours.

Now I must turn to the prosaic, but fundamental, matter of acknowledging the generosity of copyright holders in allowing me to make use of copyright material: to Lord and Lady Monson for permitting me to quote from a letter from the 6th Baron to his son from the Monson Papers in the Lincoln County Record Office; to Patricia Anderson Liedtke for permission to use Melville Anderson and Charlena Van Vleck material from the Anderson Papers in the Department of Special Collections and University Archives, the Stanford University Libraries; to Evelyn F. Gardiner and Janet Nicoleau for permission to quote from the Mary Hallock Foote Papers in the same department. I should like to thank the Hoover Institution Archives for making it possible for me to use a number of important collections (listed in my sources), the National Library of Scotland for the James Gall Journal and the Robert Graham Diaries, and the Trustees of the Imperial War Museum for access to the Anne Meader Diary. I have made strenuous efforts to trace all copyright holders, but if in any instance I have failed to make due acknowledgment I shall be glad to put the matter right as quickly as possible.

None of this would have been possible without financial support. My first, and biggest, debt is to the Hoover Institution, Stanford, California, which in giving me a Visiting Scholarship for 1984/85 enabled me to make my first really serious attack on the problems involved in my study. Then, I would like to thank the Ecole des Hautes Etudes en Sciences Sociales in Paris, for the post of Directeur d'Etudes Invité in May 1985 which enabled me to launch forays into the French sources; my personal debt to Marc Ferro is represented in the dedication of this book. Further grants from the Open University Research and Overseas Travel Committees and from the Open University Arts Faculty Research Committee enabled me to continue the momentum thus so well established. To all my financial sponsors a most grateful thanks.

Securing exactly the right visual reproductions for this book, and situating them in exactly the appropriate places in the text, have raised considerable logistic problems. I should like to thank my publishers for their efficiency and sensitivity in handling these and other problems.

This preface has contained many names. I suspect that a majority of them may remain in intellectual opposition to several of the main contentions of this book (which, as I have said, challenges much which is widely accepted in current thinking). I mention these names, not in any way to implicate them in the results of my insistence on going my own way, but simply as an expression of very profound gratitude. One thing more. Consciousness of ill looks, or of physical handicap, causes much human suffering. At times I have had to ask myself whether it is not the height of insensitivity, not to say downright bad taste, to dwell upon, and analyse, matters of personal appearance. But then historians are perennially associated with distasteful topics: massacres and wars, for instance. I have tried to write a book which faces matters as they are, not as we would like them to be; but my hope is that, all in all, it may contain not only much of interest, but also much good cheer.

# 1 Beauty: *Only* Skin Deep, but in the Eyes of *All* Beholders

The starting point of this book is today. All around us lies the evidence that our civilization, as it exists now, has an intense preoccupation with personal appearance and gives a very high rating to human beauty. Whether on the bill-boards which line our streets and stations, in the glossy magazines which jostle for position on bookstalls and in the newsagents, or during the regular assaults of the television commercials on our own living rooms, we see that the received method of marketing products of every type is to associate them with a beautiful human being, whether male or female. Mikhail Gorbachov is certainly not beautiful, and his wife is perhaps no more than pretty, but, on their first visit to the West, an inordinate amount of space was devoted to their youthful (relatively) and fashionable (again relatively) appearance, largely no doubt because of the inspiriting contrast with the crumbling decrepitude exhibited by Soviet leaders of the immediately preceding years.

When commentators refer to the decrepitude of President Reagan it is not usually of his appearance that they are speaking; indeed, for over twenty years it was the 'youthfulness' of Reagan's appearance which drew most attention. Reagan's opponent in the 1984 Presidential election, Walter Mondale, was not thought to possess much in the way of personal beauty; but a great deal of space had been devoted to the good looks of Mondale's defeated rival for the Democratic nomination, Gary Hart. In different ways, for different reasons, and with various levels of exactitude, there has been much comment on the personal appearance of former French Socialist Prime Minister Laurent Fabius, of Mayor of Toulouse Dominique Baudis, of British Cabinet Ministers Cecil Parkinson and John Moore, of would-be leader of a new force in British politics, David Owen, of Italian Prime Minister Giovanni Goria, and of US presidential aspirant Jack Kemp. New Zealand's overweight Prime Minister David Lange underwent a dangerous stomach bypass operation in order to reduce himself to a more comely appearance; one is tempted here to draw a comparison with an American president at the beginning of the century, William Howard Taft, who though fat and unprepossessing saw no need to moderate his consuming passion, gluttony.

While it was scarcely a matter for surprise or special note that enormous attention should be devoted to the appearance of the young and lovely Princess Di, there was significance in the intelligence that the caterers for the Washington reception accorded to the Princess and her husband early in 1986 had been instructed to ensure that all serving staff of both sexes came up to the standard of looks set by the Princess.[1] Waiters and waitresses catering to the ordinary nine-to-five hordes would continue to be the normal ill to moderately favoured lot; but for the elite only the most beautiful would do. From the sixties onwards jobs had multiplied in advertising, modelling and public relations, but these were spheres with a bottom-line requirement for good looks. Even in more traditional branches of business, appearance, for men as well as women, was being weighed in the scale against such old-fashioned virtues as social background, education and ability.[2] Since at least the early seventies feminists had been protesting against what they saw as the male oppression involved in the categorization of women by their looks; but whatever the protests, by the eighties it was very evident that, in a no doubt wicked world, looks did indeed count for a great deal. Everywhere stress was laid on the close association between success and good looks.

In the novels which feminist writers wrote about adventurous and successful women, these women were nearly always strikingly beautiful, either born so, or rendered so through the deliberate commissioning of plastic surgery.[3] In other novels by women writers it was the beauty of the male which received most attention.[4] At the end of the previous century, George Bernard Shaw had mocked the ludicrous appearance of fat and ageing opera stars singing passionately in romantic opera, suggesting that the only thing for the spectators to do was to lie back in their seats with their eyes shut. In the eighties, as well as being able to sing, opera stars are often also beautiful; that is the expectation of audiences, particularly audiences composed, as opera audiences mainly are, of the rich and the successful. Research into the responses to, and the consequences of, the possession of beauty is now almost routine in the psychology departments of many American universities. As the British weekly paper *New Society* commented in summing up some recent findings of this research, the trend seemed to be towards increasing discrimination against the less well favoured: the article was neatly headed, 'Uglies' Lib'.[5]

I am not arguing that today politicians and businessmen are assessed largely on their looks, nor that it is impossible for a woman to achieve success in the modern world unless she is beautiful. Clearly the many other qualities which go to make up an individual's total personality still carry great weight, fortunately for the organization of human affairs. In such matters as love and marital choice, personal idiosyncrasies and predilections are still of very great importance, fortunately for the survival of the human race. All I am saying is that, in all aspects of contemporary life, beauty is openly recognized as having a very high value. Defining personal appearance as an 'autonomous status characteristic', the American sociologist Joseph Berger places it alongside the other 'status characteristics', such as social background, education and race, by which we rate the people we bump into, associate with, hire, promote or fire.[6]

Beauty can be described as an 'autonomous' or indeed 'independent' characteristic because, so the argument goes, when we give a high rating to a person who is beautiful, we are doing so essentially because of the beauty itself; we may well believe, as many people do, that a beautiful person is lucky, congenial, will attract clients, please colleagues and generally be highly successful, but we do not automatically assume that a beautiful person will be particularly virtuous or specially talented. Conversely, though we may perceive a person to be both virtuous and talented, or, for that matter, well educated, or of high social status, we will not confuse these qualities and characteristics with beauty. Beauty is a physical attribute, distinct from morality, or intelligence, or any other quality: it is autonomous.

It is true that in ordinary speech we do use the word 'beauty' in different and sometimes contradictory ways: thus someone might say 'he's not particularly good looking but he is a beautiful person'. 'Beautiful' here is being used in an almost spiritual sense, referring to a combination of qualities which could not be pinned down very quickly or precisely; in this phrase it is the adjective 'good looking' which relates to the notion of beauty as an autonomous characteristic. Many readers, no doubt, will prefer this 'spiritual' or 'moral' use of the word 'beauty'. It is no part of my purpose to lay down rules as to how that haunting and potent word should be used. I merely signal clearly now that the beauty which is discussed in this book is beauty of personal appearance, physical beauty, the beauty intimately related to sexual attractiveness (and in that sense, I suppose, not totally autonomous, though clearly autonomous in the sense of not being in any way related to moral qualities).

There can be little disagreement that the world we live in today is not a particularly spiritual one: the beauty which is used to market men's and women's fashions, chocolates, shampoo, package holidays and sometimes even politicians, is not truth or spirituality, or intellect, but simply itself, a quality held in very high esteem by our society.

This notion of beauty, that it is purely physical, an autonomous characteristic to be ranked along with social position, wealth, education, race, etc., I shall term, for the purposes of this book, the 'modern' notion of beauty. It is the opposite of the notion which holds that beautiful people are inherently virtuous and identified with truth and the divine, and vice versa, that the divinely virtuous are inevitably beautiful, which I shall term the 'traditional' notion of beauty. Taken to its logical conclusion, as it was in the Middle Ages, and much much later, this notion held further that ugly people are inherently vicious and evil, and vice versa, that the vicious and evil are inevitably ugly. A classic statement of the 'modern' view is to be found in Sir Kenneth Dover's study *Greek Homosexuality* (1977), itself a classic monument to the modern sensibility in matters which previous generations were unable to approach with sense or sensibility: 'I apply the term "beautiful" only to physical appearance or to colour or sound; for me the phrase "beautiful soul" has no meaning.'[7]

But let me, for the moment, stick with the main point, the preoccupation with, and high evaluation of, beauty in today's world. Was it always so? If the present is my starting point, that, in effect, is the question which gets my book moving, a book which, as the subtitle makes clear, seeks to explore the social and political implications of personal appearance from, roughly, the sixteenth century to the present. I say 'roughly' because, in the one chronological direction, I do have issues to raise about Greek and medieval evaluations of beauty, while in the other, my serious study relating to actual named individuals begins only in the seventeenth century for the simple reason that before then the evidence is grossly inadequate; however, in the early sixteenth century, particularly in some of the Italian Renaissance cities, there are important discussions which hint at elements of a 'modern' appraisal of beauty, so that is the chronological starting point I have chosen to incorporate in my title.

In attacking my initial question, first in the libraries and archives and then in my study and in front of various academic audiences (with frequent returns to the libraries and archives), striving to bring often intractable material into a coherent and persuasive analysis, three major themes have slowly, though not usually steadily, emerged. The first theme is that throughout the ages there has indeed been a recognition, by some individuals at least, of beauty as an autonomous characteristic of great potency, of great power to enrapture or disturb; or, at the very minimum, there has been recognition by some people, in some places, at some points in time that personal appearance is one of the most immediate and most important characteristics which we register in our ordinary encounters with other people. However, while this awareness of the potency of beauty and of the important differences that are to be found in the personal appearance of different individuals has always existed, it has been very largely weakened or overlaid by what I am calling the 'traditional' view of beauty which, stemming from Platonic philosophy and the canons of the Christian church, has represented beauty not as an autonomous characteristic, but as an essentially moral quality associated with the divine. This theme, then, deals with the interplay between, on the one side, how people did sometimes instinctively respond to personal beauty and, on the other, the prevailing orthodoxy which involved a low valuation of what was thought of as 'mere' beauty – as distinct from 'true' beauty, a divine gift – and which anyway was ranked well below wealth and social position. Mainly this theme stresses how for so many centuries beauty, compared with its evaluation today, ranked (in public morality if not necessarily in actual behaviour) fairly low in the list of desirable attributes.

My second theme concerns the question of how, and when, the traditional view associating beauty with other moral and intellectual qualities came to be superseded by the notion of beauty as an autonomous characteristic with a high value of its own. There is great danger in using adjectives such as 'traditional' and 'modern', a danger, in particular, of seeming, or indeed becoming, simplistic or deterministic. I shall hope to make clear in the course of this book the complex set of circumstances and attitudes which I see as characterizing 'traditional' society and, therefore, giving rise to the traditional evaluation of beauty, and I shall specify in detail the particular features of 'modern' society which I believe to be relevant to the emergence of the notion of beauty as an autonomous characteristic of high value.

Political scientists, and historians, have sometimes used the word 'modernization' to define the processes by which traditional, non-industrial societies have been transformed into the high-technology, mass–consumption societies of today. Arguably both the words 'modern' and 'modernization' have been used, and abused, in such a facile and question-begging way that it is better to do without them. Personally, I think they can still form a useful shorthand if one is at pains at all times to specify exactly what one has in mind. But the reader can certainly ignore the concept of modernization if he or she prefers, for I shall in fact spell out in detail the processes and facets of change relevant to the changing evaluation of beauty; my list will not necessarily cover all those items usually included in definitions of modernization, and will include some items very significant with regard to the question of beauty, but not usually given prominence in discussions of modernization. Above all, I must stress that I do not see any predetermined or linear development between the traditional appraisal of beauty and the modern one: as I have already suggested, at all times there were individuals who reacted to beauty in what is, in my technical language, a 'modern' way, just as today there are many who still prefer the 'traditional' outlook; at all times, there are confusions and conflicts. I shall in particular be drawing attention to the very modern-sounding attitudes to beauty which surfaced strongly in the early sixteenth century but then sank beneath the distress, violence and turbulent acquisitiveness of evolving early modern society.

None the less, to assist the reader who is unfamiliar with the notion of modernization, and to encapsulate the way in which I see the changing *evaluation* (not, of course, changing *standards*) of beauty as being closely related to changing social and economic circumstances, I am going to quote here a representative example of the original, and perhaps rather banal, conception of 'modernization', dating from the 1960s when the term first came into general usage:

Historically, modernization is the process of change towards those types of social, economic, and political systems that have developed in Western Europe and North America from the seventeenth century to the nineteenth and have then spread to other European countries and in the nineteenth and twentieth centuries to the South American, Asian, and African continents.[8]

Recent writers have stressed the significance of the sixties themselves as a decade of critically accelerated modernization;[9] as it happens, this new emphasis fits in well with one of the central contentions of this book, that there was an International Cultural Revolution (of great significance for the evaluation of beauty) in that very decade.

However, let me return directly to my second theme, which, as I have indicated, is concerned with how the high evaluation of beauty today came to replace the ambivalent attitudes of earlier times. As I see it, a key precondition for the emergence of a perception of beauty as an autonomous characteristic is that individual human beings should have opportunities to compare and contrast the appearance of a wide range of other human beings. Where, as in many peasant communities, choice is severely limited in regard to members of the opposite sex actually encountered, then judgments about beauty are simply not possible. One of the great historical transformations which can, but doesn't have to be, subsumed under the term modernization is *urbanization*: with the growth of towns human beings become more mobile, mix and mingle with each other, and have new opportunities to compare and contrast different types of personal appearance. Closely associated with the first full industrial stage of urbanization was the revolution in transport, first facilitating further mobility within countries, subsequently developing into the extensive international travel which is such a noteworthy feature of our own age: opportunities to compare and contrast multiply; not least of the implications of jet setting is the prospect of encounters with the beautiful. The growth of the mass media of communication made possible, in the early nineteenth century, a rather unsatisfactory study of engraved, and then photographic, images of the beautiful, but led ultimately to the television and video systems which bring highly naturalistic images of a variety of the world's most beautiful people into almost every home.

Save perhaps for the very rich and privileged, people in pre-industrial 'traditional societies' generally suffered from deficiency diseases, deformities, malnutrition and, as a consequence of the first and third of these, and of special significance in regard to the appraisal of beauty, had rather weak sexual appetites. I shall deal with the interrelationship between beauty and sexuality in the next chapter, but here I shall simply assert that as sex drives increase in intensity and as sex becomes far more than a routine activity for creating the family which will provide essential labour and support in old age, discrimination in sexual choice, and therefore in appreciation of beauty, increases.[10] The process accelerates as, through contraception, sex is divorced from procreation, and then from marriage.

Modernization theorists almost always refer to the German sociologist Max Weber and his notion of *Entzauberung*, which literally means 'demagification' (though sociologists, in the confusing manner which sometimes seems to be one of their most obvious characteristics, usually say 'disenchantment'): the point Weber was making was that a critical aspect of the emergence of modern society has been the dethronement of traditional shibboleths, superstitions and conventions. Integral to this development has been a questioning of Platonic and theocratic notions of beauty and the advancement of secular and rational ones. In traditional societies there were no elections, as we understand the term; there were no electorates for politicians to appeal to. Only in democracies, and, above all, in democracies with television, could the question of the personal appearance of political candidates become an issue. Contrary to what is often argued, greater freedom and new roles for women have also contributed to the emergence of the modern evaluation of beauty: women active in society offer enhanced opportunities for comparison and choice, while at the same time women themselves begin to judge men as men had, prevailing orthodoxies notwithstanding, tended to judge women – by appearance.

My second theme, then, essentially comprises a study of how, and when, these different processes came to take effect in modifying assessments of the value of (mere) beauty. The different processes took effect at different times: their impact varied between countries, and between social classes. Changes towards a more modern appraisal were often accompanied by others reinforcing traditional concerns. There were some noteworthy, though not necessarily enduring, developments during the Renaissance. There were further important developments in the classic period of industrialization and entrepreneurial organization in the nineteenth century. But traditional attitudes remained very strong. My final contention in exploring this second theme will be that the sustained and triumphant challenge to traditional views of beauty came only in the 1960s, the time, as some have it, of accelerated modernization, or, as I put it, of the International Cultural Revolution.

In summarizing my second theme I have been speaking of changes in conventions and attitudes. My third theme is concerned with investigating the histories of certain individuals with a view to establishing what effects, if any, their personal appearance had on their lives, public and private, and also with looking at certain occupational groups to see whether, within them, good looks conferred any special advantages.

Personal appearance taken as an autonomous characteristic (if personal appearance, or beauty, becomes confused with other personal qualities serious study becomes impossible) is evaluated both within the broad historical context just outlined, and against other variables, including the obvious ones of wealth and social status, but also including personal qualities such as intellect, integrity, dedication, and so on. I shall not argue that beauty alone maketh the man or the woman, but will simply attempt to assess the significance of beauty as against other qualities and characteristics; I shall also consider the implications of contingency or sheer luck.

Stripped to essentials, this book takes the line that beauty is itself, not something else. Beauty is a surface, purely physical phenomenon; it is *not* more than skin deep. But neither is it something which is merely in the eye of the beholder. Beauty would not have the potency and value it undoubtedly has, were it not that in fact it is very widely recognized; beauty is what is perceived as beauty in the eyes of large numbers of beholders. Almost every book written concerned with any aspect of beauty has insisted that standards of beauty vary from age to age;[11] personally I do not believe that this is so and shall hope to substantiate that assertion, as well as the others made here, in chapter two. The fashionable orthodoxy of our time decrees that every facet of human activity is a product of society, is 'socially constructed'. Now the root idea here is perfectly sound (as even the most conventional of historians have accepted for generations), *provided it is applied with care and discrimination*. It is a central argument of this book that as society has changed, so the manner of defining beauty and the value placed on physical beauty have changed, *but* that the perception or definition of physical beauty itself (my main concern) has changed rather little. Notions of physical beauty, I believe, are the product of an immensely long period of biological and social evolution (as is human sexuality itself) and in their essence (as distinct from minor fluctuations in convention) not subject to 'short-term' change, that is change directly related to shifts in the economic structure or ideological imperatives of society. Quite possibly notions of beauty in non-Western cultures have evolved in different ways; I am not qualified to pronounce on that, though I would just note in passing that Western perceptions of what is physically beautiful, perhaps regrettably, now appear to have a very wide currency. My quarrel with the 'sociology of knowledge' approach, the approach which declares everything socially constructed and that, in all its aspects, 'humanness is socio-culturally variable',[12] is that it pushes a sensible idea to absurd extremes, mechanistically applying an inappropriately 'short-term' formula, and grossly exaggerating the significance of relatively minor differences in fashion and convention. That sexuality is socially constructed (in the 'short-term' sense) is a claim made by Michel

Foucault and his many followers. In *Sex, Politics and Society*, Jeffrey Weeks notes that:

some cultures have seen no connection between sexual intercourse and conception. Some cultures have made little distinction between heterosexual and homosexual forms, concentrating rather on the age or class of the partner; our culture has made the distinction of prime social significance. In some societies, sex is a simple source of pleasure, a key to the glorification of the erotic arts; in others it is a source of danger and taboo, of mortification of the flesh.[13]

Yet presumably Dr Weeks would accept as a quite unconstructed fact that there *is* a connection between intercourse and conception, and that there *are* differences between vaginal, anal and intercrural intercourse. As so often, there is a refusal to see the universal wood for the exotic differences of flower and foliage; sexuality itself is confused with regulation of sexuality and with the particularities of sexual conduct. And it is staggering that all these learned books on sexuality have little or nothing to say on the phenomenon of physical attraction. Anyway, if human beauty is as I define it, then it can scarcely be 'socially constructed'. The faith, of course, is that if only one could change society then these distinctions, grossly unfair as they certainly are, would disappear. For myself, I think it better to face up to the perhaps bitter truth that distinctions of physical appearance, to a very substantial degree, are biological and inborn (insisting, however, that human beings are possessed of many other appealing qualities which have nothing to do with beauty, rigorously defined).

Such an assertion runs counter to almost all recent feminist writing. I must, therefore, repeat again that my book concerns beauty and personal appearance in men as well as in women. Feminists would like to believe that as women achieve freedom and equality, the tyranny, as they see it, of judging women by their looks will come to an end. I, on the contrary, believe that as women have achieved greater freedom and greater equality still greater stress has been placed on the importance of looks, particularly, of course, looks in men. It is argued that notions of beauty are essentially political, part of the male plan to subjugate women. All the complicated talk of politics and power struggles and male conspiracy and oppression seem to me to miss the simple heart of the matter: the sheer uncomplicated joy of going to bed with a beautiful woman. I see no reason to believe that there is not an exact analogue for women, bed being a place for shared pleasure, not politics or conquest. With respect to both men and women, beauty has got a deal more to do with the quest for pleasure than with that for power. My earnest hope is that this book should not seem, or, more important, that it should not be, sexist, but just level headed and clear sighted, though, naturally, as any book must be, fallible in many areas.

Anyway, let it be recorded here that my own work has benefited enormously from the various feminist writings on beauty and on fashion which have appeared in the last few years, even though it has seemed to me that too often fashion and beauty have been confused with each other. Thus, if in the course of this book I engage critically with such writers as Robin Tolmach Lakoff and Raquel Sherr, Susan Brownmiller, Lois Banner, Jan Marsh, Valerie Steele and Nancy C. Baker, that is because their deep and thought-provoking scholarship has drawn me directly into argument.

The plan of the book is simple. In the next chapter I elaborate on the points I have just been making, setting out fully my basic assumptions and explaining my methodology. In chapter three I examine the 'traditional' view of beauty and the ascendancy it asserted right through to the end of the eighteenth century, while at the same time I consider the challenges to this view raised by a number of individuals in the early sixteenth century, particularly in the urban centres of Renaissance Italy. In chapter four I turn to my third theme and attempt, within the context (roughly from the sixteenth to the end of the eighteenth century) set out in chapter three, to assess the significance personal appearance itself had in the life experiences and life chances of various real living individuals and occupational groups. Chapter five looks at how the traditional view was partially undermined by the great transformations of the nineteenth century, but stresses the resilience, despite the emergence of some 'modern' elements, of traditionalism. Chapter six again looks at the actual realities of how personal appearance affected peoples' lives, this time for the period of the nineteenth century. Chapter seven, in concentrating on the twentieth century, brings all three themes together, looking at how far a more 'modern' view was beginning to take hold in the period up to 1960, and at what effects, if any, this had on individual life experiences and life chances. Chapter eight deals with that period of cataclysmic transformation which I term the International Cultural Revolution, showing what the bases of this 'revolution' were, and how the old evaluation of beauty was overturned. Chapter nine is a short conclusion dealing with society since the 1960s. My first task is, in the next chapter, to show why I believe so much of the received wisdom about the nature of beauty is quite ill-founded.

# 2 Darwin, Freud, Feminism and Fashion

## 1 *Beauty, Fashion and Self-Presentation*

It is commonplace that many important words have several different meanings. This is true of such notorious semantic hot potatoes as 'civilization', 'culture', 'ideology' and 'class'. It is also true of 'beauty'. In English the substantive 'beauty' is the root word; for the adjective, signifying being possessed of the quality of beauty, a more elaborate word is needed, 'beautiful'. In French, German and Italian it is the other way round: *beau* (feminine *belle*), *schön* and *bello* (feminine *bella*, both sometimes shortened to *bell'*) are the root words: it is the substantive, meaning the quality which is possessed, which requires the more elaborate *la beauté*, *die Schönheit*, or *la bellezza*. In the three Continental languages the adjective can have wider and less specific meanings than the English 'beautiful' and can signify 'fine', or 'elegant', or even something like 'excellent'. In English the complication is, as so often, that there are several different adjectives: for example, 'handsome', 'pretty' and 'good looking', and in American English 'cute'. On the whole, and among most (though not necessarily all) English speakers, the word 'pretty', as applied to human beings, has come down in the world: once it signified a highly complimentary appraisal of a woman's appearance; now, while still very much a term of praise and admiration, it tends to indicate something less than true beauty.

Oddly, through a deliberate irony typical of the cultural revolution of the 1960s, 'pretty' when used to describe a man is often a more marked compliment than when applied to a woman. The French equivalent, *jolie*, on the other hand, has retained most of its force as entailing a very high compliment to a woman's personal appearance. As with all difficult words, much depends on the context: sometimes I have felt it proper to translate *jolie* as 'beautiful'. *Jolie laide*, properly used, can never mean beautiful (*une laide* being a person who is plain or ugly); sometimes, however, the phrase is used with the connotation of unorthodox beauty: one of the sub-themes of this book is that modern society is much more open to the many varieties of beauty than was traditional society. In nineteenth-century Britain, 'handsome' was quite frequently deployed in praising a woman's appearance when we would now probably say 'beautiful'; in current usage it is probably still more customary to call a man 'handsome' rather than 'beautiful', while, as noted, there is no analogous problem in the Continental languages. In this book, the concern of which is, after all, European-based Western culture (including the USA), not Great Britain alone, I take the line that it is part of the 'modern' conception of beauty to apply the word 'beautiful' to both men and women: for my purposes, when a man is described as 'handsome' that is equivalent to his being described as 'beautiful'. It may be noted anyway that referring to his own painting of the 1850s, *Work*, Ford Madox Brown described its central character as a 'young navvy in the pride of manly health and beauty'.[1] Whether 'good looking', 'cute', 'gorgeous', 'smashing', and so forth, are to be construed as 'beautiful' will, as with *jolie*, depend on the context.

My concern is with beauty in human beings, though obviously the word can be, and is, used in respect of other phenomena: one may speak of beauty in art, or of a beautiful poem, or of a beautiful view. It was part of the traditional understanding of beauty that there ought to be one all-embracing definition which would include all applications of the word including that to human beings. This misguided pursuit of a universal definition, like so many of the activities of philosophers, simply added to the confusions and ambivalences about the nature of human beauty. Leaving aside the question of whether 'beauty' is not in fact a somewhat inadequate concept for describing something as complex as a poem or painting, I'll merely make the obvious, but frequently neglected, point that for a serious study of the significance of *human* beauty what is needed is a clear understanding of what is meant by *human* beauty: other possible uses of the word just aren't relevant.

But even if we stick strictly to the question of beauty in respect of human beings, there are a number of ambiguities to be dealt with. The heading 'Beauty' encountered in our magazines and newspapers almost always signals, not a discussion of whether David Owen is more beautiful than Gary Hart, or Farrah Fawcett than Princess Di, but advice on cosmetics, diet, dress and fashion. 'Beauty' here is being used in a technical or colloquial sense: what is really meant is 'self-presentation'. This book makes a rigorous distinction between beauty, which I take to be the natural characteristics of the face and form with which one is born, or more accurately, into which one grows in late adolescence and early adulthood, and self-presentation or grooming, the 'beauty' of the women's magazines. Of course, there are significant interconnections. Fashion in dress in a particular era, for example, may tell us something about how high or how low an evaluation is being placed on 'natural' or 'inherent' beauty; so also may the use of wigs, powders, patches and paints. The issues are far from uncomplicated, but it may be that in eras where clothing conceals and seriously distorts the natural lines of the human body relatively low esteem is attached to natural beauty, whereas the revealing fashions of the 1920s, or of the 1960s, for example, may indicate a rise in the value of natural beauty. Similarly, in some eras cosmetics may be used to conceal natural features and in others to draw attention to them. It is self-evident that, save perhaps in ages where fashion decrees a very high level of artificiality, those whose endowment of natural beauty is already high will be most successful in achieving, through their application of cosmetics and exploitation of fashion, the form of self-presentation most desired. But true beauty needs neither clothes nor make-up; the beautiful man, or the beautiful woman, is the one who, stark naked, is at his or her best. When the small boy cried out that the Emperor had no clothes the Emperor was seen to be just an ordinary man; beauty at least, even if desperately unequal and cruelly unfair, needs neither insignia of rank nor robes of office. The beauty, then, whose social and political significance throughout the ages it is the purpose of this book to assess, must be distinguished from self-presentation, fashion and grooming. But because of the inevitable interconnections I shall have to give some attention to these matters, and indeed among my most valuable primary sources for changes in the value attached to 'true' or natural beauty are the guides to grooming and fashion, which are far from being the least among the offspring of the invention of the printing press.

So, a few preliminary reflections on fashion and cosmetics. Some feminists have presented both as being part of the male conspiracy against women: patriarchal society, the argument runs, insists that women's lives only have meaning in relationship to men, and that the only real success for a woman is to be desired by men; this desirability is achieved through observing the whims of fashion and applying the latest cosmetics – and here, for good measure, the further argument can be introduced that the profits go entirely to capitalistic male *couturiers* and manufacturers. Many male writers, on the contrary, and this is a continuing theme throughout the period of Western history we will be studying, have maintained that the real conspiracy lies in reducing all women to a common artificiality, unreasonably withholding from male eyes the lovely faces, legs, bottoms and breasts of the truly beautiful, making it possible for the plain and the ugly to pass themselves off as presentable in terms of the fashion of the day, and denying the fastidious male the opportunity to discriminate between the former and the latter (till, too late, the implication usually is, he finds himself bedded and up against the naked truth).

The most striking early example of this point of view is to be found in the *Utopia* of Sir Thomas More, written in the first decade of the sixteenth century and published (in the original Latin) in 1518; the English translation of Ralph Robynson was published in 1551. The More of the first years of the century was a lusty, hard-living critic of the conventions and pieties of his day, the embodiment of that Renaissance humanism which entailed a rekindled interest in classical civilization, an emphasis on rational thought and a glorification of the life of the flesh lived with gusto in the full glare of civic society. More was writing at a time when deformity and ugliness were considered signs of inherent evil. The people of his Utopia are infinitely more clear headed and sensitive. 'To mocke a man', they believe (I cannot resist the evocative charm of the Robynson translation), 'for his deformitie, or for that he lacketh anye parte or lymme of his bodye, is counted great dishonestie and reproche, not to hym that is mocked, but to hym that mocketh.' Should one partner in a marriage subsequently become deformed, then 'there is no remedy but patience', for 'they judge it a greate poynte of crueltie that any body in their moste nede of helpe and comforte, shoulde be cast off and foresaken'.[2] All that said, More makes it clear that 'naturall bewtie and comliness' are very highly valued, noting that even 'wise men' are much concerned with 'the endowments of the bodye'.[3] The people of Utopia thus have a very simple custom: before a man can marry he must see his wife-to-be completely naked, just as the woman must also be shown the husband-to-be in his nakedness:

> . . . in cheusyng wyfes and husbandes they observe earnestly and straytelye a custome whiche seemed to us very fonde and folysh. For a sad and honest matrone sheweth the woman, be she maide or widdowe, naked to the wowere. And lykewise a sage and discrete man exhibyteth the wowere naked to the woman.[4]

There can be no question that the procedure described here was merely a kind of medical inspection; the context, with its emphasis on 'bewtie' and 'the endowements of the bodye', makes it clear that such an innocently public-spirited reading would entirely miss the point. The point is that More objected to costume that concealed the body, as he objected also to cosmetics ('payntinges').[5]

It had become a platitude by the time of the eighteenth-century Enlightenment to maintain (quite erroneously and absurdly) that clothes had been invented by the ugly to conceal their defects. In the early nineteenth century a careful guide was offered to British men as to how, despite the voluminous apparel which concealed even a woman's face, they could pick out the pretty from the plain.[6] Alphonse Karr, a mid-century French intellectual, had the ordinary man expostulate before the heavily made-up woman of the time: 'Madame, uncover your face a little so that one can see if you are pretty.' The American music critic and Darwinian 'philosopher' whose name truly was Henry Theophilus Finck (though if it had not been, one might have had to invent it) declared fashion 'the hand-maid of ugliness', arguing that it was a device of the ugly majority for compelling the beautiful minority to conceal their charms.[7] The most sophisticated expression of this general point of view came from the French scholar Marcel Braunschvig, author of *Women and Beauty*, published in 1919. Fashion, he said, substitutes a false conception of beauty for the real thing:

In the eyes of many beauty is confused with elegance, which is simply conformity to the latest demands of fashion. From this many aberrations in taste follow: luxurious grooming leads an ugly woman to be judged beautiful, while the beauty of a woman wearing an unfashionable costume passes unnoticed. Dress has constituted a beauty by conventions which often supersede true beauty. The majority of women believe that this is to their advantage; for, lacking true beauty, so rare, a woman always has the money to procure the beauty which can be bought.[8]

Theodore Zeldin, in his famous social history of France published in the late 1970s, improved on this, noting that men 'implied, and also wrote, that most women were ugly', adding that 'women clearly believed this':

The great attraction of fashion was that it diverted attention from the insoluble problems of beauty and provided an easy way – which money could buy – of at any rate approximating outwardly to a simply stated, easily reproduced ideal of beauty, however temporary that ideal.[9]

The baleful tone of misogyny is all too apparent in many of these quotations. My purpose is not in any way to endorse them, but to cast doubt on any notion of fashion being imposed by men on women. Other accounts represent fashion, and changes in fashion, as being directly related to social, economic and even political circumstances. But, as recent work has brought out, the matter is rather complex. Anne Hollander does concede something of the masculinist view I have just been detailing at length when she writes: 'without clothes bodies show the amazing irregularity of human nakedness, an untidy, unpredictable diversity of all kinds, at odds with the conception of an ideal – even an ideal of variety'.[10] But in essence the desire to dress up which, as soon as the most rudimentary needs are met, goes far beyond, in men as well as women, the simple need to keep warm, is an expression of fundamental artistic and dramatic instincts akin to those which have led to music making, art and drama at both popular and elite levels.[11] In general, changes in fashion are to be explained in the same way as changes in artistic styles. There are connections to be made with the historical context, but fashion also has a logic of its own which, in a highly simplified way, can be represented as: innovation, exaggeration, reaction. There is a sexual element in fashion, at its simplest the wish to appear appealing before others, though modesty and concealment may as often be the determinants as overt eroticism; the pat explanation of fashion changes as having reference to 'changing zones of erotic attraction' (meaning feet, wrists, breasts, legs, etc.) is no explanation at all (Why do the zones change? Do they anyway?, etc.).

Even among the very poor, fashions do change, and wherever the resources are available the popular classes will be seen striving to emulate the elites.[12] Only a minuscule minority seek to set fashions, and only a still very small minority to be modish; but even those who protest against the very idea of fashion find that just to look normal, they have to change, because as fashion changes so does the perception of what is normal.[13] Now, lest I be misunderstood, let me repeat that I am speaking here entirely of fashion, of dress, not of beauty as I am defining it. A truly beautiful person in outmoded dress will look slightly odd, but he (or she) will still also look truly beautiful.

For almost two centuries the most colourful and spectacular aspects of fashion have been confined to the female sex. But it would be quite wrong to think that the instinct upon which fashion is based is utterly alien to men. As is well known, in earlier eras male fashion was very colourful and striking; there has been something of a revival, though in fact a rather modest one, over the last thirty years or so. What is often missed is that even when dull and colourless, male fashion has always had its little rules and foibles, and its little changes, which the well-dressed man would ignore at his peril. Cosmetics, it is true, though far from unknown among men, have always been more heavily and more lavishly used by women. The sexual element is again not negligible: the wearing of make-up serves many purposes, some profoundly and mundanely utilitarian, but it does also give a signal, a signal of the intention to look and be attractive. What it has been socially acceptable for women to wear in the way of cosmetics has varied from generation to generation. Men have often been among the strongest denouncers of the wearing of make-up. In some periods cosmetics were quite definitely associated with sexual looseness and prostitution. Now that some men (though, it must be added, still a small minority) openly wear cosmetics, there is perhaps no great boldness in suggesting that making up is also (like fashion in dress) part of a deep need for dramatic self-presentation nurtured in Western society (and seemingly in other societies as well). However, it does seem to be an activity that is thought by both women and men to be on the whole more appropriate to the former than to the latter, men having other distinctive devices for establishing their image.

Susan Brownmiller, one of the leading figures in the twenty-year climacteric of feminism, is determined not to acquit men of the crime of imposing a certain conception of femininity on women, yet admits, with a pleasantly mocking wit, that much of the impulse comes from women themselves. A new hairstyle, she recognizes, can give a woman a 'psychological uplift'. She notes that on the matter of make-up and fashion many of her feminist friends became 'back-sliders':

I think my friends returned to dresses because they felt life was getting gray without some whimsical indulgence in the feminine esthetic . . . On bad days I mourn my old dresses . . . One cannot take on a new identity by changing trousers.

Then her delicious punch line:

> . . . in our time the teenage girl has pined and begged for her first grownup pair of high-heeled shoes. To put them on and to try the first few wobbly steps is to enter a new life. The forward pitch of the knees and the backward thrust of the buttocks, which startles the young initiate, magically induces a leggy, stilted walk which, she will hear, is deeply provocative and a delight to behold. From this point on, whenever she puts on her heels she will be set apart from the rest of the species, children and men who walk and run and climb with natural ease.[14]

Almost the whole of chapter two of volume two of Simone de Beauvoir's *The Second Sex*, the bible of post-war feminism, is taken up with fashion and cosmetics and is highly critical of them, alleging that they confirm women's position as sex objects. Yet there is one sentence which suggests in a much more profound way what the true significance of making up and dressing up may be to a woman: 'to care for her beauty, to dress up, is a kind of work that enables her to take possession of her person, as she takes possession of her home through housework, her persona then seems chosen and created by herself'.[15] The simple historical point can certainly be made that although women today enjoy far greater freedom than they did at the time when Simone de Beauvoir was writing, they have, if anything, gone in for a far more extensive use of cosmetics. There is, to say the least, no simple correlation between subjugation and preoccupation with fashion and grooming.

The most persuasive account I have read occurs in Dr Vernon Coleman's introduction to a book he wrote with his wife, essentially as an exposure of the abuses and corruption of the 'beauty' industry. In the foreword Dr Miriam Stoppard states candidly (and many other distinguished women have written in similar terms): 'I love cosmetics. I love the plethora of products that allows me to paint, disguise, camouflage, accentuate and define.'[16] 'After all,' writes Dr Coleman, putting the view from the outside,

> half the population is female, and I have increasingly come to realise that the vast majority of women wear at least some make-up. Men simply haven't realised this because they never see the women with whom they don't share bathrooms in their naked faces.
>
> It is a curiously unnerving discovery, but it shouldn't be thought that all this art is employed entirely to dupe and mystify men, since women clearly enjoy making themselves up as much for each other and for themselves as for men. Most women have a routine whereby they apply a minimum of disguise every morning – either foundation, mascara or lipstick – and without it they feel unhappy. It can work as a mood-changer. For instance, part of the enjoyable anticipation of a party or an evening out is reflected in more time spent creating more elaborate effects with face paint, while at the other extreme when a woman is feeling low she may go out and buy a new lipstick or eye-shadow, or have a haircut to cheer herself up.

Doubtless men would enjoy using cosmetics too, if society approved and their equivalent bathroom time weren't spent removing their beards. At various periods in the past men have been quite as artfully decorated, and male punks today must enjoy using make-up as much for the same reasons women do as for the sake of shocking the conservative elements in society.

We all admire good skin and bone structure, but few of us have them; even fashion models apparently have flaws they are neurotic about. Make-up is a device which enables women to enhance their good features and cover up those which are unfashionably unattractive. It can allow fair heads to compete with brunettes with eye lashes that emphasise their eyes; it can provide the girl without hollow cheeks with at least the semblance of them; it can cover up teenage acne, signs of worry, ill-health and age to some degree. In all, it helps women feel less vulnerable – something we all try to hide in various ways.

Dr Coleman then goes on to stress the importance of looks in modern life as suggesting the possession of other qualities as well, such as intelligence, charm, sympathy and confidence (this does not impinge on the autonomy of beauty; beauty may, within limits, suggest other qualities, but it is not being maintained that beauty *is* intelligence, still less deep spiritual truth).

Make-up will therefore indirectly create the impression that a woman possesses these qualities. Men seek the same facades in other ways – by the choice of cars and clothes. Probably they have less of a feeling of vulnerability anyway. It will be interesting to see whether more men take to make-up as the Women's Movement grows and more women leave theirs off.[17]

Much of this is borne out, rather touchingly, in a brief opinion survey conducted in San Francisco in January 1985. Various women at the Bank of America headquarters were asked whether they ever left the house without make-up.

Not if I can avoid it. In the summer with a little sun and a few freckles I look okay, but in the winter I look like a peeled potato . . .

No. If I would see somebody I would know I'd die. They always see me with make-up and they'd see a difference.

Only to the corner Seven Eleven [i.e. local mini-market].

Only they know what I really look like because you never know when you'll meet Mr Wonderful and make-up makes me look like I have eyes.

Yes, as long as I am hiding behind my sunglasses. I look better with it because I'm blonde and make-up enhances my eyelashes and eyebrows. I look pretty hairless without it.[18]

This discussion of fashion and cosmetics has been necessary for a number of reasons. Not least of these is my desire to make it clear that, although I do make a firm distinction between the natural beauty with which this book is basically concerned and questions of grooming and self-presentation, I am in no way hostile to a preoccupation with fashion or an indulgence in cosmetics; indeed I see these activities as a normal part of social life as it has evolved from the very earliest times. Having made it clear that they are not what I mean by beauty, I must now look more closely at what I do mean by beauty.

I mean beauty of face and of form, or 'figure' as we usually say in contemporary English (raising, incidentally, yet another linguistic problem since *figure* in French over the centuries can mean either 'figure', or, more usually in recent French, 'face'). Many commentators would say that the sense of what constitutes beauty of face and form changes. I believe that beauty is, with minor qualifications, unchanging. I say 'with minor qualifications' because I recognize that all matters relating to human beings are subject to social influences. But there is all the difference in the world between being 'socially constructed' and being 'socially influenced' (more especially when the influence is of minor degree). In any age there are conventions and prejudices which will affect perceptions of beauty; compared, however, with the central physical or biological fact of beauty, these are minor. Thus, in jargon, beauty is a universal, or, more precisely, to take account of the minor social influences, a *relative universal*. That is to say that, while there are slight shifts in preferences and preconceptions, fundamentally someone who in the sixteenth century was regarded as being beautiful would, if travel through time were actually possible, also be so regarded in the twentieth.

But to get it exactly right, I must elaborate slightly: beauty, I believe, is a *relative universal*, but, and this is absolutely crucial, *in many types*. It is on this point that most previous commentators have gone wrong, in that they have drawn their evidence exclusively from paintings, sculpture, fashion plates and literary fancies, without looking at the real behaviour of actual living people. It is perfectly true that artists in any particular era tend to seize upon one particular *type* of beauty and concentrate solely on it in their paintings, as do the fashions and conventions of *self-presentation* projected by whatever social elite happens to hold a dominant position. But just because one type of beauty has been favoured by the prevailing artistic canon or by the latest twist of fashion this does not necessarily mean that flesh-and-blood human beings going about their business, applauding favourites, appointing servants, jumping into bed, cheering actors and actresses, getting married, are blind to all the other types of beauty. This book, in exploring the significance of human beauty, is concerned not with abstractions and formulations relating to the Virgin Mary, gods and goddesses, or the heroes and heroines of invented romance, but with the behaviour of living human beings. Thin aesthetic-looking men are not more beautiful than broad-shouldered rugged men; beautiful thin men are more beautiful than ugly rugged men, and vice versa. Blondes are not more beautiful than brunettes; beautiful brunettes are more beautiful than ugly blondes and vice versa. Buxom women are not more beautiful than slim women. Properly proportioned buxom women with beautiful faces are more beautiful than scrawny slim women with plain faces; properly proportioned slim women with beautiful faces are more beautiful than ill-proportioned buxom women with plain faces. Ugly men with fashionable haircuts are uglier than beautiful men with unfashionable haircuts. There was, true, a fashion in the fifteenth and sixteenth centuries for shaven foreheads in women. Not quite our taste: but the confrères of Piero della Francesca and the compatriots of Queen Elizabeth could recognize, as we can, that a beautiful woman with a shaven forehead was beautiful, and an ugly woman with a shaven forehead was not.

I have, I hope, offered a sufficient variety of examples to kill stone dead any notion that I am talking solely of what is called 'the Greek ideal of beauty'. If the phrase is to mean anything, then (with regard to women) it must mean the style of beauty of the Venus de Milo with her noble body and somewhat sexless and insipid face, the nose dominating the chin, a beauty repeated in many of the Madonnas of Raphael and in the nymphs and shepherdesses of Boucher, and then later in the soft porn of the nineteenth century (both versions being quite sexy). The variety I am speaking of goes far beyond Greek stereotypes.

These points seem breathtakingly obvious; yet how much agonizing goes into trying to establish their opposite! Let me take some recent examples. Paul Newman, Steve McQueen, Paul McCartney, David Bailey, George Best, Michael York, Sydney Poitier, Sean Connery, Connery's son, Jason Connery, are, or were, all beautiful; but each is a very different type (pick the Greek!). Gina Lollobrigida (Italian star, dark, large breasts), Samantha Fox (British pin-up, blonde, large breasts), Twiggy (noted for her slim figure), and Monica Vitti (very different) are all beautiful, but scarcely Greek (short of the suffocating argument that everyone beautiful is 'Greek' and everyone else, however ugly, represents some kind of non-Greek beauty). One of the most empty contentions, paraded over and over again, is that Twiggy was beautiful only because fashion decreed skinniness to be beautiful. In the sixties, as now, there were very many skinny women who were not in the least beautiful. Twiggy was beautiful because her figure was perfectly proportioned and because she had an astoundingly lovely face. Fashions certainly do change, but a Twiggy in any era would have the same devastating impact on living human beings as she had when she first went among them in the 1960s. (The notion that Twiggy was desirable because 'androgynous' – i.e. both girl and boy – is so absurd as not to be worth considering, as is the theory that what is, incorrectly, termed 'androgyny' is the most highly attractive physical characteristic; Twiggy is discussed in chapter eight, and 'androgyny' in chapter nine). Let me, finally, on this business of Greek ideals of beauty add that, applying my definition of beauty as a relative universal, I would maintain that among the Arab, Indian and (above all) Chinese peoples are to be found a higher proportion of beautiful individuals than in most Western societies, today, as in the past.

Now, it is part of my overall thesis that beauty as an autonomous characteristic and, as I have just been arguing, relative universal (in many types), was less appreciated in past centuries than it is now. While, without doubt, we have our own fixations and rituals, these earlier centuries were burdened to a crushing degree by the weight of superstition, tradition and convention. But to recognize the existence of conventions and prejudices which, of course, *are* socially constructed, and to recognize the fact that such conventions and prejudices *could* lead to a failure to recognize certain types of beauty, is not to accept that beauty itself, in its different types, is socially constructed (in the sense in which the phrase is generally used). Since I mentioned Twiggy just now, I should make it clear that I do recognize that notions of what constitutes fatness have changed over the years. In past ages those who could afford to certainly ate excessively and unwisely; partly this was due to sheer gluttony, partly, perhaps, to the need to keep warm in open-plan castles, on blasted heaths, or while riding into the wind. What *all* the sources make irrefutably clear is that at no time was fatness itself considered to be beautiful: even Rubens (the Flemish artist ineluctably associated in the minds of the vulgar with paintings of fat women) decreed that the body of a woman must be 'neither too thin or skinny, nor too large and fat'.[19] Central to beauty as a universal is a sense of proper proportions, though, I agree, the perception of what precisely constituted these proportions could vary, but not to anything like the extent that is sometimes maintained by proponents of the thesis that beauty is socially constructed. Perhaps I should deal here with the oft-repeated contention that in certain cultures fatness in women is actually prized, because it connotes good living and therefore wealth and status. Though it is not relevant to my own discussion of Western society, I would point out (since the issue is of general relevance to my main arguments) that prizing a physical characteristic because it connotes wealth and status is not the same as, indeed it is the opposite of, prizing beauty. In my view, cultures which value fatness are cultures which in fact value wealth and status above human beauty.

In any age a person's behaviour will, in greater or lesser degree, be affected by prevailing conventions; but, I am arguing, when it comes to appreciating human beauty, conventions (in Western society, at any rate) are very far from omnipotent. In earlier ages clear complexions were specially valued, in comparison, say, with shapely noses or chins; this was because, for all sorts of reasons to do with health and nutrition, blemished faces were very common. For much of the nineteenth century there was a convention that red-headed women could not be beautiful, very largely, I think, because red hair was associated with freckled faces. However, a normal, lusty young man, in this case the nineteen-year-old Englishman James Salter of Tolleshunt D'Arcy, attending the Lewes Ball in December 1859, while affected by the convention was not blinded by it: 'singularly enough, I did not see one girl pretty enough to attract or detain the eye beyond the first glance, and another prodigy was that, of the most passable, three red-headed girls stood first, both as regards dancing and looks'.[20] Convention, too, favoured the buxom, as against the Twiggies. Yet our friend Finck (to be discussed in chapter five), who quite definitely had an eye for female beauty, fell in love with an extraordinarily beautiful girl (we have her photograph) with, as he commented, 'no figure worth talking about'.[21] Sarah Bernhardt, in the era when plump faces and ample bosoms were allegedly the ideal of feminine beauty, was also slim and girlish: that stopped no one from lusting after her astonishing beauty. In evaluating beauty we should not, as all previous writers have done, look simply at what painters *painted*, or fashion writers *decreed*, nor even at one or two individual beauties (actresses and music hall stars, say) and what was *said* about them; we must look at what people actually *did*.

## 2 *Beauty and Sex*

So far, apart from referring to a certain harmony of proportions, I have scarcely defined this universal beauty. Let us proceed by actual historical example. Look, throughout the ages, at rich and powerful men, and look at the women they have chosen to consort with. There, in general, the odd exceptions apart, you will find beautiful women in their various types. Identifying beautiful men is perhaps not quite so simple. It is an obvious fact that there have been very few rich and powerful women, absolutely free in their personal choice of men, unconstrained by the need to find a protector or breadwinner. However, if we look, in the past, to Catherine the Great, and if, with greater certainty, we look to rich and influential women of today, such as Angela Lansbury or Joan Collins, we can, by looking at the men these women choose, identify beauty in men in its various types. Beautiful women are the women that wealthy and powerful men choose; beautiful men are the men that wealthy and powerful women, given freedom from all other constraints (as, for instance, Elizabeth I of England was not), choose.

Now let me depart from history into the world of imagination (though not fantasy). Imagine that we hire a hall, the sort of hall that might be used for morning assembly in a sizeable school. Into this hall we place two hundred men and two hundred women. First the men go up onto the platform, giving plenty of time for the women to study them, then they come down and mingle on the floor, not making conversation but simply ensuring that all of the women have the chance to study them closely. The process is then repeated, the men having the opportunity to study the women. This completed, the women are asked to vote for the ten most beautiful men, and the men are asked to vote for the ten most beautiful women. There will, of course, be some highly personal, even idiosyncratic choices; but, as a wealth of empirical psychological study (discussed in chapter eight) indicates, a very definite decision would emerge as to who, among the men, appeared as beautiful to a majority of women, and who, among the women, appeared as beautiful to a majority of men.

The question asked, I should stress, would be 'Who is beautiful?', not 'Who would you like to marry?' Obviously, marital choices are based on many other considerations. We have, as I have suggested, the factor of personal idiosyncrasies and personal psychological imprinting. Many people are genuinely attracted to members of the opposite sex who are quite definitely not beautiful. We have the undoubted fact of love, which may well be inspired by many qualities other than beauty. We also have the point that people must accommodate to the choices which are actually open to them. On the whole, as ordinary observation, apart from a certain amount of systematic psychological research, suggests, the beautiful, or certainly the powerful, consort with the beautiful. The less beautiful soon find that there is little point in pursuing the unattainable. Thus everyone makes adjustments, and the human race continues. In many cases, particularly with regard to the choices made by women, other constraints operate. As already noted, for much of the past women have had to be severely practical in their choice of mates. This is all extremely important in human behaviour, but it is not directly relevant to what constitutes beauty. Beauty, I am saying, is the choice of the majority; beauty is the choice one makes when one is totally free of all constraints and all psychological quirks (unreal conditions for the vast majority at any point in time). Many women, I understand, deliberately shun outstandingly beautiful men because they are aware of the dangerous power such beauty possesses. When in a psychological experiment (discussed more fully in chapter eight) they were presented with beautiful dance partners (without having to make any effort or run any risk of rejection) both men and women (though the women slightly less positively than the men) wanted to continue the relationship thus initiated, citing physical attraction as the overwhelming reason. But when subjects were faced with real-life obstacles, and the possibilities of rejection, the pursuit of sheer beauty was seriously qualified.[22] What people want is beauty; what they recognize they are likely to get is something less than that.

Many will find what I am saying here utterly unacceptable. Thus, I wish at this point to consider an important book on the subject by two contemporary feminists: *Face Value: The Politics of Beauty* by Robin Tolmach Lakoff and Raquel L. Scherr. Lakoff and Scherr are seemingly uncompromisingly entrenched in a position opposite to the one I have just taken up:

> To begin our search for 'beauty' by assuming any universality in its representation is to court disillusion. A choice made by one artist at one time bears no necessary relation to that of another artist, at another. Today's essential ingredient is yesterday's irrelevancy; another culture's necessity our superfluity. And at least, even as we are smarting from our failure to uncover comforting all-time truths or generalisations about the nature of feminine beauty, we will see that this failure in itself is a worthwhile discovery: that beauty is not located in any specific physical attribute, but rather in the aggregate of physical and less tangible traits that a particular time esteems.[23]

Ignoring their transparent disingenuousness (the authors are certainly not 'smarting' and the last thing they would find 'comforting' would be 'all-time truths' about feminine beauty), let us note that the evidence for these contentions is entirely traditional: that of artistic representations. From there the authors go on, very sensibly, to remark that no woman would 'be accounted beautiful, or be anyone's model of Venus (or Eve, or the Virgin Mary) if she does not also have certain basic attributes of physical attractiveness'. Some of these 'basic attributes' are identified: 'a nose must fit the face; it must not be large, or hooked, nor, for true beauty, very small and snub'; 'the figure must not be ridiculously obese, nor painfully thin, nor must any part of it be out of proportion'.[24] Having made these extremely important points, which, despite the authors' wish to argue to the contrary, clearly *support* the idea of beauty as a universal, they then insist that all else is purely subjective. There is, they conclude, 'no universal agreement':

> Any ten people, asked about the movie-star sensation of the moment, will cover the spectrum of responses, from 'nothing special' to 'spectacular', with everything in between.[25]

Ten, perhaps, is a rather small sample: take a hundred and I think you would in fact get the sort of congruence I have already suggested. More critically, though we all like to express idiosyncratic personal choice when confronting the famous, the fact is that a person normally has to be beautiful before ever becoming a 'movie-star sensation' in the first place. The real dividing line is between those who become 'sensations', and those who are already ruled out because they don't have 'certain basic attributes of physical attractiveness'. How much, in fact, is the 'all else' which is 'purely subjective'? What Lakoff and Scherr *demonstrate* (rather than *assert*), it seems to me, is that beauty is universal, being dependent on 'basic' (i.e. universally recognized) attributes; the subjective aspects, in reality, relate to rather minor details.

To further their argument about the subjectivity of beauty the authors then propose a number of 'oppositions', or contradictions, in views about beauty. In an agreeably sensuous paragraph, 'neat' beauty is posed against 'wild' beauty:

> Is beauty chaotic or controlled? Should we expect a neat cap of hair, short, close to the face but off it, sleek or tightly curled; pale eyes, porcelain skin; clothing simple, efficient, fitting close but not overly revealing, not flying in the wind? Or tendrils of hair whipping across the brow into the eyes, untrammelled – nature's triumph over art; dark snapping eyes, blood-red lips, generously wide; a 'hectic flush' on the cheeks; clothing clinging in places, or perhaps flying in the breeze, not in any rapport with the body, but as free as its wearer?[26]

I, however, would again suggest that beauty lies not in either 'neatness' or 'wildness', and that the question is not whether a woman is 'neat' or 'wild', but whether she is beautiful. I will add (anticipating a later stage in my argument) that 'wild' beauty will often signal availability to the male, while 'neat' beauty can appeal to that most profound of male desires, to transform the neatest and most composed of women into the most wildly and distraughtly passionate. A few pages later, and we are actually being asked 'is any blonde more beautiful than any brunette?'[27] Presumably a reference back to the earlier discussion of 'basic attributes' could have produced the answer that a blonde with 'a large or hooked nose' could not possibly be more beautiful than a brunette with a nose to 'fit the face'.

Lakoff and Scherr discuss the fact that 'a man remains attractive to women until a much greater age than a woman to men'.[28] Their handling of this undoubtedly distressing matter has an elegiac sensitivity not found in all feminist writings on the subject. To some feminists it is all a matter of social convention and attitude; change society, it is suggested, and then young men would happily bunk down with older women; or, it is said, it's really just a matter of the poverty of language, there being no female equivalent, for example, for the notion of the distinguished-looking older man. Angie Dickinson, successful, influential, wealthy, middle-aged Hollywood actress, famous for her affairs with men much younger than herself, put a practical perspective on the matter when she revealed that she was well aware that her young men did not find her particularly sexually desirable but hoped that she could help them in furthering their film careers, usually leaving her as soon as they felt she had served *that* purpose.[29] The relationship between beauty and age will be discussed shortly; meantime I shall note, not for the only time in this book, that what we might wish beauty to be is not necessarily the same as what beauty actually is.

It is the failure to see that most men are more interested in the pursuit of pleasure than the pursuit of power which undermines the declared thesis of the book (one, in fact, not very thoroughly developed), that beauty is political: 'the prospect of being considered beautiful is a

political instrument held over women: a promise, a threat';[30] 'women
. . . are controlled by the tyranny of looks, by the threat of having
approval, and with it power, withheld'.[31] Not being sexually attractive is
a problem a lot of people have, including men, but to call this 'political' is
to stretch that word into meaninglessness. Lakoff and Scherr are very
careful not to place the blame on men; indeed, in an echo of some of the
sources already quoted with regard to women's use of make-up, they
ask: 'Do women suffer to be beautiful less for men's sake – and more for
reasons (whatever they might be) of their own?'[32] The final plea is that
'the criteria for good looks in women must no longer be so dis-similar to
the criteria we use for men'. In so far as this is addressed to women, as it
appears to be, it is a very humane aspiration. But there do seem to me to
be two problems. First, it is really not open to women to decree what
men shall find beautiful in women. Secondly, the question of looks is
being confused with the way in which men are often, to a much greater
extent than women, rated highly on qualities which have nothing to do
with looks. It will not help to call ugliness beauty; what is needed is to
recognize beauty clearly for what it is, something very important, but
something which can be placed alongside other qualities, such as
intelligence or kindness, so that one can say honestly, and with genuine
admiration, of a person that they are not particularly beautiful, but that
they are intelligent and kind.

Traditionally, the endeavour of philosophers has been to produce a
definition of beauty which would apply not just to human beings, but
which would be of total validity, including art, poetry, music and
philosophy itself. Learned studies of beauty, therefore, tended to separate
beauty, which was good and truthful, from that which stimulated the
sexual appetite, which was to be condemned. But writings related more
directly to the realities of human existence, for all their ambivalence and
pious moralizing, usually hinted quite strongly at one thing, the very
thing, it would seem safe to assume, that prompted the ambivalence and
moralizing in the first place: that beauty is in some way closely related to
sexual desirability. It did not require Darwin or the Darwinists to
propose that if you wanted to have beautiful children you had best seek
out a beautiful partner: Shakespeare, after all, had begun the Sonnets
with:

> From fairest creatures we desire increase,
> That thereby Beauty's rose might never die . . .[33]

Darwin thought that ideals of beauty did vary, though he cited the
contrary view of the famous explorer and womanizer, Captain Burton,
who insisted 'that a woman whom we consider beautiful is admired
throughout the world'.[34] Frankly, Burton knew a great deal more about
male–female relationships than the feeble and sexually timid Darwin.

The latter, at any rate, was clear that it was on the basis of the relevant ideal of beauty that those with a choice, both male and female, selected their sexual partner. It was Darwin's disciples who more strongly emphasized the notion that physical beauty represented all the highest qualities of humanity and that it was therefore in the interests of the survival of the race for individuals to seek out beautiful partners. Their work rapidly degenerated into the sort of eugenist and openly racist statements which have given attempts to isolate the autonomous and universal qualities of beauty something of a bad name ever since. Some things said were simply silly, if at times amusing. Finck, like many other nineteenth-century pundits (including Ruskin), thought brunettes more dynamic than blondes. He also thought (perhaps with some reason) that it was only ugly men who needed to conceal themselves behind beards.[35] By his own theories of sexual selection, blonde women and bearded men would be extinct by the 1980s. As we shall discover later, his views on blondes were sharply altered when he met a very beautiful one.

In the later nineteenth century, particularly in France, the direct connection between personal beauty and the arousal of strong sexual desire began to be openly stated, though often the latter continued to be represented as a most unfortunate by-product of the former. Others, however, argued that it was the very sexual instinct itself which gave rise to notions of the aesthetic, that, and this had been suggested earlier in the century by Arthur Schopenhauer, what we desire is union with our ideal. The French philosopher Lucien Bray, in a very Darwinian study of the origin and evolution of aesthetic sensibility (a book only marginally concerned with human beauty), argued that, 'among superior organisms, the struggle for survival, in its sexual aspects, is the principal, if not the only source of beauty, and, arising from that, of the sentiment and idea of beauty'.[36] Others again argued that we naturally wish to possess beautiful objects and thus wish sexually to possess beautiful human beings. Freud wrote less on the subject than might have been expected. 'There is to my mind', he wrote in a footnote in *Three Essays on the Theory of Sexuality*, 'no doubt that the concept of "beautiful" has its roots in sexual excitation and its original meaning was "sexually stimulating".' A few pages later he added the view that 'the quality of beauty' attaches 'to certain secondary sexual characteristics'.[37] There was a more lingering passage in his *Civilization and its Discontents*:

The enjoyment of beauty has a peculiar, mildly intoxicating feeling. Beauty has no obvious use; nor is there any clear cultural necessity for it. Yet civilization could not do without it. The science of aesthetics investigates the conditions under which things are felt as beautiful, but it has been unable to give any explanation and origin of beauty, and, as usually happens, lack of success is concealed beneath a flood of resounding and empty words. Psycho-analysis, unfortunately, has scarcely anything to say about beauty either. All that seems certain is its derivation from the field of sexual feeling. The love of beauty seems a perfect example of an impulse inhibited in its aim. 'Beauty' and 'attraction' are originally attributes of the sexual object. It is worth remarking that the genitals themselves, the sight of which is always exciting, are nevertheless hardly ever judged to be beautiful; the quality of beauty seems, instead, to attach to certain secondary characteristics.[38]

Taking the three quotations together, and ignoring the perhaps not completely helpful notion of 'an impulse inhibited in its aim', the implication seems obvious: the person who is recognized by many as being sexually exciting is a beautiful person. However, there is another way of looking at the matter which, in fact, was first stated explicitly, almost a hundred years previously, by the French writer and novelist Henri Beyle, better known as Stendhal. Stendhal's famous sentence is so often misquoted in English that it is necessary to set it out both in its context and in the original French. In his *On Love*, completed in 1822, Stendhal included a chapter entitled 'Beauty Dethroned By Love'. The argument was that a man, knowing that the woman he loves is certain to go to bed with him, will prefer that woman to a much more beautiful one about whom he has no such certainty. He continues: 'if one thus comes to prefer and to love *ugliness*, it is because in this case ugliness is beauty'. The famous sentence then occurs as a footnote to this remark: 'La beauté n'est que la *promesse* du bonheur.'[39] This is best translated, I believe, as 'Beauty is no more than the *promise* of a good time', though 'Beauty is only the *promise* of happiness' would be acceptable; what Stendhal did not write is: 'Beauty is the promise of happiness.'

Stendhal is writing about the supremacy of love (and no one, certainly not I, will argue with his theory). Love, he says, 'dethrones' beauty. The person we love becomes beautiful, even if actually ugly, for 'in this case ugliness is beauty'. Now it may be that Freud was saying the same thing in less romantic terms, that the person an individual finds sexually exciting is beautiful to that individual. The trouble with all this is that it amounts to no more than a variant on the proposition that beauty is in the eye of the beholder. Now it may well be true that love does dethrone beauty and makes an ugly person seem beautiful; but to all other observers that person remains ugly; beauty is dethroned for the individual in love but remains in existence for everyone else. If there is to be a definition of beauty at all, it has to be a definition that is valid for large numbers of people; if ugliness can become beauty then words have no fixed meanings. In fact we know very well from everyday experience, let alone psychological experiments, that, give or take the odd minor personal preference, human beings in the mass do agree over the minority among them who are beautiful. So all that one can, with certainty, learn from Stendhal and Freud is the sense of an association between the beautiful and the sexually exciting. Of course, the plain, or the ugly, are, as we also know from experience, sexually exciting to certain individuals. The beautiful are those who are immediately sexually exciting to almost all members of the opposite sex (and sometimes to members of their own sex as well). Personally, I think Stendhal would have been wiser to have written what he is often thought to have written: 'Beauty is the promise of happiness.'

But registering the association between sexual excitation and beauty is not the same as declaring sexuality, whether sublimated or not, the root of aesthetics. The fact is that nobody, including Freud, knows whether it is or not. What is indisputable from historical evidence and everyday perception is that human beings are born with deep aesthetic instincts, giving rise to drama, poetry, song, popular and high art, fashion in costume, and many, many other activities and artifacts. These instincts are more fully developed in some individuals than others, in some societies than others, among certain classes than others. Given reasonable material conditions, somewhat above the stressful routine of survival, subsistence and procreation, human beings make aesthetic judgments about their environment, indulge in activities which are not purely functional or merely 'animal'. Given the chance, that is to say, a certain amount of mobility, a certain amount of genuine choice, they apply aesthetic judgments to other human beings. Even children do this, as we know from psychological experiments,[40] and from our own experience (I recall that my daughter at the age of four dismissed the perfectly agreeable, though certainly not well-favoured, lady who ran a local restaurant as 'holl'ble, ugly' and that she decisively selected Richard Chamberlain as her favourite among the Four Musketeers). That children are sensitive to beauty suggests to me that it is a universal rather than something socially constructed. We don't need to postulate sublimated sexuality. We can simply register the point that children like good-looking people, both other children and adults; they like playing dolls' houses, or trains, or going for walks with beautiful people. Adults like beautiful people and like to associate with them, converse with them, etc., etc. This applies with respect to women and women, men and men, as well as in more manifestly sexual relationships. In the various types of relationship there are different intensities of liking and appreciation, but for most people the most intensive type of relationship is a sexual one, and, of course, aesthetic instincts are at least as much involved here as they are in other human activities. We like to talk to and associate with a beautiful person; naturally, if we have the chance, we like to go to bed with a beautiful person.

To sort out properly the relationship between beauty, desirability and sexual pleasure, we must distinguish between the initiation and the continuation of a sexual relationship, and between arousal and satisfaction. Beauty certainly creates arousal (which, of course, is essential to satisfaction) and is the most direct, non-verbal signal indicating the likelihood of pleasure (Stendhal rephrased). When it comes to realization of pleasure (satisfaction), and to continuation of a relationship, then it is a matter of beauty enhancing the aesthetic dimension of a sexual relationship (does one wish to contemplate one's partner, or does one wish to bury one's head in the pillow?). All this is very well known, which, of course, is why the rich and powerful, who can make choices, almost invariably have beautiful sexual partners. In any relationship, as I have stated several times, many other factors come into play; but surely of any single factor, beauty is the most potent.

If a more thorough statement on the relationship between the aesthetic impulse, sex and human beauty is required then I prefer the pronouncement of the British Freudian Havelock Ellis, in his *Studies in the Psychology of Sex*, published in the first decade of this century:

We need not even be concerned to make any definitive assertion on the question whether our ideals of sexual beauty have developed under the influence of more general and fundamental laws, or whether sexual ideas themselves underlie our more general conceptions of beauty. Practically, so far as man and his immediate ancestors are concerned, the sexual and the extra-sexual factors of beauty have been interwoven from the first. The sexually beautiful object must have appealed to fundamental physiological aptitudes of reaction; the generally beautiful object must have shared in the thrill which the specifically sexual object imparted. There has been an inevitable action and reaction throughout.

Actually one could almost forget Freud and the Freudians. Many earlier writers, including the great eighteenth-century Scottish philosopher David Hume (of whom more in chapter four), had clearly stated the relationship between beauty and sexuality.[41]

Beauty (in human beings) is always perceived as sexually desirable, though everything that is sexually arousing is not necessarily beautiful. This allows for the existence of such potentially erotic qualities as (in men) height or strength, and (in both sexes) voice, demeanour, or self-presentation. It also helps to dispose of Freud's point about the genitals not usually being considered beautiful, though the sight of them tends to be sexually arousing. In any case, it might actually be more accurate to say that the genitals set within the entire context of a beautiful body and a beautiful face can be seen as part of the total beauty; one breast taken in isolation, or even a nose cut off from the rest of the face, would be unlikely to seem beautiful.

There has, however, been another quite persistent theory about the relationship between the genitals and human beauty, linked also to the traditional doctrine that women are the beautiful sex and that the concept of beauty does not apply to men. In his *The Nature of Love: Essay on the Sexual Instinct* (1903), Rémy de Gourmont summed up the essence of the theory:

The superiority of feminine beauty is real; it has one unique cause: unity of line. What makes woman more beautiful is the invisibility of her genital organs. Sex, which is sometimes an advantage, is always a burden and always a blemish; it exists for the sake of the race, not for the individual. With the human male, and precisely because of his upright posture, the sex organs are the most noticeable and visible feature, an obstacle to the eye, like a rough obstruction on a flat surface, or a sharp break in a smooth line. The harmony of the feminine body is therefore geometrically much more perfect, above all if one considers the male and the female at the height of sexual desire, at the moment when he presents the most intense and the most natural expression of life. The woman then, all her movements being interior, or visible only by the undulation of her curves, preserves her full aesthetic beauty, while the man seems suddenly to regress towards the primitive condition of animality, appears diminished, devoid of all beauty . . .[42]

This somewhat overwrought account is highly typical of one aspect of what I term the 'traditional' concept of beauty. My concern in discussing beauty is with the reactions and behaviour of human beings as they go about normal social life, where judgments are made on the basis of the face and the (clothed) figure and not usually on a display of nudity, least of all 'at the height of sexual desire'. Further, it should be stressed that any argument which maintains that *all* women are more beautiful than *all* men flies so obviously in the face of observed experience as to be totally absurd.

Earlier I spoke of two hundred men selecting the ten most beautiful women, and two hundred women choosing the ten most beautiful men. I assumed that both men and women would react in broadly the same way in the assessment of members of the opposite sex. Now, in fact, some empirical studies employing very much the selection process I have just described have suggested that men and women do not react in quite the same way. Men come much closer to unanimity in choosing the beautiful women, while women will produce a much wider range of choices.[43] It may be that the differences are inherent: that women are naturally more flexible in what they consider to be beautiful in a man, or that beauty as such does not rate as highly with them so that, in making judgments, other factors are brought in; it may be that women are wiser than men and realize that judgments based purely on physical beauty are not necessarily rational ones.

Some scientists would argue that the processes of human evolution and sexual selection (including the latest stages during the development of Western civilization) have produced marked differences in sexuality in men and women, and therefore in appraisals of physical attractiveness. Donald Symons writes: 'Physical characteristics, especially those that correlate with youth, are by far the most important determinants of women's sexual attractiveness. Physical characteristics are somewhat less important determinants of men's sexual attractiveness; political and economic prowess are more important; and youth is relatively unimportant.'[44] Symons, like many of the nineteenth-century Darwinians, links physical beauty in women with the power to reproduce beautiful and healthy children and thus continue the evolutionary process. 'I have tried to show', he writes,

that the ultimate cause of the greater importance of female than male physical attractiveness is easily explained by the nature of reproductive competition during the course of human evolution: a female's reproductive value can be assessed more accurately from her physical appearance than a male's reproductive value can. Human females compete with one another in the currency of physical attractiveness because that is primarily what males value . . . A woman's physical attractiveness is significant not only in heterosexual interactions that result in sexual intercourse, but in almost any heterosexual interaction in which male sexual interest can be advantageous to the woman or to her employer.[45]

Symons then continues with a very clear statement of the modern evaluation of beauty (in women at any rate) as an autonomous status characteristic: 'Thus women employers are likely to be no less concerned than men about the physical attractiveness of their female employees, since they recognize that beauty is a tangible economic asset.' He adds, perhaps rather grudgingly: 'Of course this is true also of male employees, but to a markedly lesser extent.'[46] (My own comment, which will be elaborated on later, is that it very much depends on what type of male employment one is talking about.)

Our notion of human beauty, it seems to me, is our notion of what a human being ought to look like. Given freedom from all constraints, what we would like to unite with sexually is a most nearly perfect specimen of our species. Again, with Havelock Ellis, I do not see any need to try to specify which comes first, beauty or sexuality; there is an impenetrable interrelationship between them. What we find most desirable is most beautiful; what is beautiful we wish to possess. I prefer the phrase 'most nearly perfect specimen' to 'ideal specimen' because of the ambiguities inherent in the word 'ideal'. I also believe that any analogies from the animal kingdom applied to human beings are deeply suspect; our evolution and acculturation has proceeded over thousands of years in highly distinctive circumstances. However, there may be something to learn from the way in which we perceive beauty in animals. As Georges Bataille, French connoisseur of the erotic, has suggested, 'animals are more or less beautiful as they more or less resemble the ideal specimen of the kind';[47] that is, of course, beautiful to us the human spectators, not to other animals.

To all but the most inveterate cat haters, the domestic cat usually presents an image of beauty; there is, perhaps, something in feline grace which puts one in mind of feminine grace. Yet we have all seen cats that we would regard as ugly, whether through old age and over-indulgence, some desperate fight with the local tom, or accident of birth; we find this cat ugly because it departs from the as nearly perfect as possible specimen of cathood that we have in mind. Let me repeat that I am talking about cats as they appear to us; it seems pretty certain that animals have no sense of aesthetic appreciation of each other, though virile males will most certainly win the females, and all will probably shun the sick and malformed. However, just as a beautiful cat is a cat which looks like what we think a cat ought to look like, so a beautiful person is one as like as possible to what we think a human being ought to look like; there is not one type, but each type appears as close to perfection as possible.

Now what are the characteristics of this perfection? It is frequently asserted in the literature, I believe with reason, that we expect human beings to look human and not in any way like members of the animal kingdom; this is particularly so in regard to our nearest ancestors in the animal kingdom, the apes – to be ape-like is very definitely not to be beautiful. Georges Bataille has proposed that an important element in 'assessing the beauty of a man or woman' is that 'the further removed from the animal is their appearance, the more beautiful they are reckoned'. He continues: 'Any suggestion of the animal in the human form is unquestionably repugnant, and more particularly the anthropoid shape is found disgusting.'[48] Perhaps I should say at this point that I find the conclusion to which Bataille then leads (that the essence of the human sexual instinct is the befoulment of beauty) foul, disgusting and utterly stupid, just as I totally reject the racist conclusions of much Darwinian and eugenist work. However, the basic points I have cited seem sensible and are supported elsewhere in the literature where, for instance, it is often pointed out that a proper chin and a distinctive, free-standing, as it were, yet not over-large nose, are both attributes not possessed by animals, and absolutely essential to the notion of human beauty.[49] There are no precise mathematical measurements of beauty (though it has long been one aspect of the traditional approach to beauty to try to produce them). The notion of a two thirds–one third ratio for chin to eyes and eyes to hairline does not work for many manifestly beautiful people, while probably fitting many who are palpably plain. While harmony and proportion are called for, absolute regularity is not; it is the very faintly exaggerated feature, the eyes slightly out of line, say, which can give the ultimate sexual enhancement to a beautiful face. Eyes, of course, are important, but do not alone create beauty. An Arab woman can be most seductive behind her yashmak, then utterly disappointing when her nose is revealed (though, as already stated, a high proportion of Arab women *are* very beautiful). Hair can be a great attraction, 'a beauty', as might be said in Victorian English, but does not itself make beauty. Chekov says it all when he has Sonya cry out that 'when a woman is plain, she is always told "You have beautiful eyes, you have beautiful hair" . . .'[50]

Once or twice already the idea has surfaced that to be beautiful a
woman must be youthful, but that this is not a crucial matter in regard to
a man. While in this study I am particularly anxious to avoid fashionable
and trite appeals to the paramountcy of immediate cultural and environ-
mental factors, I am equally anxious not to fall into the snare of
biological determinism. However, undoubtedly the perpetuation of the
human race was served by the division of a woman's life into stages, so
that after she ceases to be fertile and fully sexually active, she still has a
long period in which she can rear her children; while the point has little
validity in an over-populated world, there was a time when it was in the
interests of the continuance of the race that the male could go on
impregnating females very late into his own life cycle. At the other end
of the scale there is the biological fact that females mature more quickly
than males and that, for obvious reasons, a female has reached the peak of
her growth by the time she is capable of bearing children. Thus
Darwinians, and others, have put forward such calculations as that
women are at the peak of their beauty between the ages of eighteen and
twenty-five, and men between twenty-eight and thirty-five; these figures come from Finck, who was thirty-three at the time.[51] The stipula-
tion of precise ages is absurd, but the point remains that in regard to both
sexes an appearance of youthfulness, however exactly that is interpreted,
would seem to be a necessary component of beauty. If we look at the
matter negatively, which sometimes seems to be necessary in trying to
define beauty, we can say that anything which suggests sexual infertility
or impotence, or, even worse, draws attention to mortality, is very
definitely not beautiful and would most likely be regarded as ugly.
(None of this is to deny that it is perfectly proper in everyday speech to
talk of there being a form of beauty appropriate to each stage in the life
cycle, from babyhood to old age.) Bodily and facial hair are usually
acceptable in males. In our culture they are generally not acceptable in
females: whether this is related to animal and mortality taboos is
impossible to say, but this seems to me a reasonable speculation. One
characteristic with which we are all familiar and which certainly con-
demns a girl, and most probably a boy as well, to being regarded as, at
best, plain is that look of somehow being old before one's time, of not
possessing even in childhood the qualities of youthfulness.

So, in talking of beauty, I am talking of sexual attractiveness, of
characteristics of face and figure which fit harmoniously together, of
having a nose and chin and other features which suggest near perfection
in humanity, and in no way suggest simian or animal qualities, of
youthfulness or at least (in a man) an appearance of virility. Consider for
a moment the well-known phenomenon that a man or a woman at a
distance will often seem quite beautiful, well shaped and apparently with
a face pleasantly and characteristically human; as that person comes into
close vision, we begin to perceive all kinds of imperfections – a sagging

waistline, perhaps, or a thick nose, or a wrinkled brow. This seems to me to confirm that we do have a general notion of what a human being should look like, which may be met by a person too distant to be seen properly; at close range we detect all the blemishes which prevent most people from being beautiful.

There is another similar phenomenon. As we all know, most people tend to look better full face than in profile. This may be because in full face some of the most potent human characteristics are in evidence, particularly the eyes and the mouth. But it is in profile that the shape of the nose becomes more clearly delineated, as also the balance between the forehead, nose and chin: these are often the features and the relationships which finally determine whether a person conforms to what we feel he or she ought to be or belongs to the mere common run of humanity. All of this is very general. One could write several books based on the descriptions of beautiful people to be found in both literary and historical sources. Yet I have become increasingly struck by how difficult it is to give a meticulous description of individual beauty. We believe in the beauty of Gwendolen (in *Daniel Deronda*), or of Trollope's Lizzie Greystock, it seems to me, more through the effects they have on other people (a phenomenon we are all familiar with) than through any painstaking descriptions by the authors. Beauty is that entirely physical phenomenon which has a profound effect on other people.

I have said much about beauty because, alas, it is by the beautiful that we set our standards. But this book is about personal appearance; and human beings certainly don't just divide into the beautiful and the not beautiful. Actually, in all forms of historical discourse the drawing of firm boundary lines is extremely difficult, whether between ethnic types, social classes, or historical periods. So also with different levels of physical attractiveness. Broadly what I have in mind is a fourfold division, but with a multitude of individuals and types who manifestly cross the boundaries (the man with the beautiful face, but a distressingly puny body; the *joli(e) laid(e)* – male as well as female; the lovely girl with the terrible legs). First we have the *beautiful*, who are a tiny minority: perhaps, today, around five per cent of the male and female population between the ages of twenty and forty in any Western country. Then there are the *personable*, perhaps up to about a third of the same population – those who definitely have some of the characteristics of beauty and who have a strong chance of doing well in the realm of self-presentation. (My numbers are crude and impressionistic and have no serious scientific basis. It may be worth noting that Victorian commentators, who were certainly energetic travellers and assiduous observers, thought that while the very highest quality of beauty was to be found solely among a tiny minority of women, the proportion of personable men was higher than that of personable women;[52] this is not, however, an issue of great significance to the main themes of this book.) Then we have what I am simply going to call the *ill favoured*, probably rather more than half of the population just defined, and ranging from individuals who, in all sorts of ways, because, say, of particular personal qualities, are widely recognized among those who know them to possess considerable sexual attractiveness, to individuals who, in a not unfriendly way, will be thought of as homely, to those who are termed plain, to those who are, if honestly appraised, thought to be ugly. Finally there are those who suffer from some significant physical deformity.

In many contexts, as I shall hope to show during this book, the crucial distinction is between being personable and being definitely ill favoured; I shall later be illustrating the point with a contrast between two nineteenth-century female writers, who both adopted male pseudonyms – George Sand, the French writer who was personable enough to achieve quite striking success in her own personal mode of self-presentation, and George Eliot who was quite definitely plain and desperately aware of it. Among recent American politicians I think it could fairly be said that Adlai Stevenson and Hubert Humphrey were definitely ill favoured; General Eisenhower (with the boyish look which was often remarked upon) and Jimmy Carter, in different ways, were personable; J. F. Kennedy, John Lindsay and, in his days as Governor of California, Ronald Reagan, were all good looking, that is to say, in my usage, *beautiful*.

In concluding this section, I want to make a further set of distinctions which help to explain the inconsistencies and ambiguities in human attitudes and behaviour with respect to personal appearance. In discussing people's ideas of beauty and their reactions to it, or what they take it to be, we must first of all distinguish what I am going to call *private inclination* (Symons speaks of 'sexual emotions',[53] but I don't think this term very clearly expresses what he means) from what people actually do or say openly: private inclination (or sexual emotions) would determine our actions (or experiences) if we were totally free of all constraints and conventions. But, of course, in any society there exist what I will refer to as *public mores* (the second of my distinctions which, for example, define what forms of sexual behaviour are socially acceptable, or what evaluation should be placed on beauty as against other characteristics, or indeed what qualities should be regarded as beautiful). My third category is *actual behaviour*, which above all is what I want to study in this book. Actual behaviour is piggy-in-the-middle: a compromise between what we would really like to do and what we are actually permitted to do – together of course with what, given our own limitations, we are actually able to do. I shall not be making particularly overt use of these distinctions but I do believe that they are helpful in resolving certain manifest puzzles in regard to the relationship between beauty and sexual behaviour.

## 3 *Beauty Studied Systematically*

Most histories of beauty depend very heavily upon the representations of artists and argue, say, that because Cranach painted Eve this way, Raphael his Madonnas that way and Titian his female figures from Greek mythology in yet another way, this shows the manner in which standards of beauty change and are indeed socially constructed. But, as I have already said, there is little evidence to support the assumption that just because painters concentrated on one particular style of beauty that was the only style that princes, courtiers, merchants and all real living people in a position to make choices recognized. There is a further problem: it is too readily assumed that every painting of a woman by every artist must be intended to be beautiful, and (this is perhaps the more critical point) was widely accepted as such by a majority of contemporary viewers. At the very least, before reading off from a painting conclusions about concepts of beauty, we have to have information on both the artist's intentions and on contemporary reactions. I have already mentioned the difficulties writers face in describing a beautiful individual: given that at the heart of human beauty lies the element of

1 Venus and the Three Graces, Sandro Botticelli, *c.* 1480s

sexual appeal, it is not necessarily easy for painting, essentially a static art form, still less for sculpture, with its coldness, hardness and lack of colour variations, to render that beauty.

Painters in past centuries were often concerned to render such qualities as holiness or spirituality, nobility and dignity. It is, I believe, profoundly significant that Botticelli was in his own day, and has been since, one of the most controversial of all painters of women. His women have a stunning beauty and sexiness which speaks directly to us today (as the publishers of Lakoff and Scherr undoubtedly appreciated in choosing the cover for *Face Value*). Some of Botticelli's paintings were burned by the pietistic monk Savonarola, undoubtedly because of the manner in which his women truly were disturbingly beautiful; learned critics in the nineteenth century, made uncomfortable by these same women, argued that the models were in fact tubercular – a complaint also raised against the women represented in Pre-Raphaelite paintings who projected a similar sexuality.[54] The eighteenth-century British portrait painter Sir

2 *Theory*, Sir Joshua Reynolds, *c.* 1779

3 *John the Baptist*, Leonardo da Vinci, *c.* 1509

Joshua Reynolds aimed at a consciously dignified style even with his most beautiful female subjects. They tend, therefore, to lack sensuality, though curiously we can get a very clear sense of the uninhibited notion of beauty of the time from Reynolds's renderings of such abstractions as Theory and Justice – again they speak directly to us, as the universal quality of (sexual) beauty always must, and demonstrate that there was *not* a particular eighteenth-century canon of beauty, expressed in the academic art of the time.

There is, thus, a too ready assumption that because a painting is acknowledged to be a great painting, and because it also contains a

4 *The Broken Jug*, Jean-Baptiste Greuze, *c.* 1770

woman, then that woman must be, and must be intended to be, beautiful. Leonardo da Vinci's portrait of the lady who may have been Madonna Lisa Gioconda is without doubt, in artistic qualities and profundity of expression, everything it has always been held to be. But the face is not that of a beautiful woman; the face in fact is practically identical with that in Leonardo's painting of St John the Baptist. Leonardo was almost certainly a homosexual: we have absolutely no need to believe that the Mona Lisa, marvellous painting though it is, in any way represents an ideal of female beauty held by the heterosexual men of the time. On the other hand, paintings of no great artistic merit can contain indisputably beautiful women: the paintings of Greuze provide important support for my contention that a woman desired for her beauty in the late eighteenth century would be so desired today – *The Broken Jug* is no masterpiece, but what a lovely young woman it portrays.

That, perhaps, is not an especially impressive, or novel, piece of analysis. The rather more important problem that has to be attacked, if I am to maintain the idea of beauty as a relative universal, is the work of Peter Paul Rubens. Some art critics whom I greatly respect would argue that Rubens's women actually are beautiful and that it is only because we look at them wrongly that we get the sense of their being grossly overweight.[55] I think it has to be admitted that both in our own eyes, and judged by the types of women being painted just before, and just after Rubens, and indeed by other artists at the time of Rubens, his women are too fat to be beautiful. If it were true, as is often maintained, that these women (they are not real women, of course, but a painter's representation of women) were widely accepted at the time as an ideal of feminine beauty, then my arguments about the relative universality of beauty would be seriously damaged.

What I am going to suggest is that in Europe as a whole (Rubens was an international painter renowned throughout Europe) these women were not widely so regarded, and that indeed to see them as ideals of beauty is to misconceive Rubens's own objectives. Let me start with Rubens's own treatise entitled *The Theory of the Human Figure*. This work is based on Greek theories of art and on the careful study of surviving Greek statues. It is overwhelmingly devoted to the male figure, which is said to be based on the cube and the triangle. 'The male form', Rubens writes, 'is the true perfection of the human figure.'[56] In chapter three there is a section on antique statues, with some brief

5 *The Judgment of Paris*, Peter Paul Rubens, 1639

references to statues of woman, who differs 'from man in that she is more apprehensive and more feeble, because her centre of gravity, which passes through the middle of the throat, does not correspond exactly and perpendicularly with the centre of equilibrium which ought to be found in the middle of the back of the leg, as it is in man . . .'[57] Only chapter seven, the last one, is devoted entirely to 'the proportions of the woman'. Rubens writes:

The elements of the human figure are different in man and in woman, in that in man all the elements tend towards perfection, as in the cube and the equilateral triangle: in woman, on the contrary, everything is more feeble and smaller. From which it happens that, in woman, the perfection is less, but the elegance of forms is greater: in place of the cube which is enfeebled in the figure of woman, there is a parallelogram . . . From that one can infer that, with regard to the perfection of forms, woman takes second place after man . . . the idea of the beauty of man having been created perfect, as it probably existed in Adam and in Christ.

Rubens then moves on to 'the perfection of the various parts of the body of a woman'. He says that the body must not be 'too thin or too skinny, nor too large or too fat, but with moderate *embonpoint*, following the model of the antique statues'.[58]

Rubens, then, was concerned to paint women (and men) as in antique statues, and he considered women to be less beautiful than men. I will return shortly to more of Rubens's aims as a painter, but it is important also to consider his personal circumstances. He was himself handsome and a great success in the world both as a diplomat and as a painter. In 1609, at the age of thirty-two, he married Isabella Brandt, who was eighteen. The double portrait which Rubens did of himself and his young bride is a charming one; Rubens is the handsome dashing figure, his wife youthfully enticing enough, but plumpish and with a round, personable face, rather than a strikingly beautiful one. From the available Flemish womankind, Rubens had, as everyone does, made *his* choice. The marriage was without doubt a happy and loving one. By Isabella he had one girl and two boys, but then in 1626 she died. One famous letter survives of Rubens's reflections on her death:

Truly I have lost an excellent companion, whom one could love – indeed had to love, with good reason – as having none of the faults of her sex. She had no capricious moods, and no feminine weakness, but was all goodness and honesty. And because of her virtues she was loved during her lifetime, and mourned by all at her death. Such a loss seems to me worthy of deep feeling, and since the true remedy for all ills is Forgetfulness, daughter of Time, I must without doubt look to her for help. But I find it very hard to separate grief for this loss from the memory of a person whom I must love and cherish as long as I live.[59]

Now there is no mention in this of Isabella's beauty; this may tell us something of Rubens's perception of his wife, or it may simply be in

6 *Double Portrait with first wife* (Isabella Brandt), Peter Paul Rubens, 1609

keeping with the elegiac tone of the letter. In any case, as will be argued in the next chapter, beauty was not necessarily a quality singled out openly in the seventeenth century as being of particular importance.

Just over eight years later, Rubens did decide to marry again, this time choosing Hélène Fourment, a girl of sixteen with a remarkable resemblance to Isabella, whose niece indeed she was; Rubens was fifty-three. The several portraits of Hélène show her as having even more of a pudding face than Isabella, and show also that she very quickly became obese.

7

7 *Portrait of Hélène Fourment* (the artist's second wife), Peter Paul Rubens, *c.* 1630–32

I think we can take it that Rubens, personally, liked fattish women; I think it can also be said that he became fixated on a particular facial type and perhaps also that he did not look for, and possibly did not expect to find, particular distinction of feature in a woman's face. That, *as a painter*, he could register more distinguished and appealing features is brought out in his famous painting (in the National Gallery, London) of Hélène's sister, Suzanne, known as *Le Chapeau de Paille* (*The Straw Hat*). In his great mythological paintings filled with women who, both in their heavy limbs and rather boring faces, tend to be reminiscent of Isabella or Hélène, was not Rubens following his own personal predilections, shaped, of course, by what he believed to be the proper way of representing the human form, rather than offering widely acceptable representations of female beauty?

It should be remembered also that one of his most famous commissions was the cycle (in the Louvre) on the life of Marie de' Medici, who was herself a heavy and rather plain woman. Rubens did his best with her, but maybe it was tactful to surround her with other female figures built on a similar scale. These are probably minor points compared with the overall artistic problems of composition and scale; in particular, in the Baroque style which Rubens himself was helping to develop, massive proportions were required. Beyond that, Rubens was immensely preoccupied with the texture of flesh, and the play of light upon it. For artistic purposes, he needed considerable expanses of rather ponderous flesh.

True, there are contemporary expressions of praise for the beauty of the women represented in Rubens's paintings and, above all, admiration for Hélène.[60] When the Cardinal-Infante Ferdinand bought a *Judgment of Paris* for his brother, the King of Spain, he accompanied it with a letter which remarked that 'the Venus in the centre is a very good likeness of his wife who is certainly the handsomest woman to be seen here'.[61] Probably I am overdoing it if I suggest that this has something of the force of the comment by the British Conservative politician R. A. Butler on the then Prime Minister, Anthony Eden, that 'he's the best Prime Minister we've got'. But what I am confidently arguing is that Rubens's women were not intended by Rubens to be beautiful in the sense in which I am using the term, and that, furthermore, while his women may well have been representative of a type which predominated in the Flanders of the day, they were not throughout France, Italy and England universally considered representative of the highest female beauty.

Let me conclude this argument by quoting from an art historian who confesses to finding much of Rubens's work 'arousing' and describes *The Rape of the Daughters of Leucippus, The Toilet of Venus, The Three Graces* and *Hélène Fourment in a Fur Wrap* (more often regarded as a masterpiece of obesity) as masterpieces of erotic art.[62] In trying to deal with the current view that Rubens's woman are too bulky, this critic, Keith Roberts, offers 'a word . . . in Rubens's favour'. This 'word' would seem to support my own contentions:

Even now, very few women have figures as trim as Brigitte Bardot's. Undress any crowd of Saturday morning shoppers in one of the main shopping streets of Europe and the effect would probably be depressing and more 'Rubensian' than one might have imagined. A more important point is that in saying 'I hate Rubens's fat women' one is mentally taking them out of the picture and seeing them as real figures in the real world; but the degree of illusion Rubens creates through his brilliant painting of skin is, first and last, an *artistic* illusion.

What is really significant about Phoebe and Hilaria in *The Rape of the Daughters of Leucippus* is not their bodies, judged as female bodies in this or any other situation, but their *poses* in this particular composition . . . How the figures might have looked in other situations, or in life, was totally irrelevant.[63]

My case rests: Rubens as the painter of an everyday crowd of Saturday morning shoppers, Rubens as the creator of great pictorial compositions, is fine; this is not the artist painting, as so often alleged, the seventeenth-century ideal of beauty.

I have already briefly mentioned the reactions aroused by the pronounced sex appeal of some Pre-Raphaelite models. Recently, in a lively and scholarly work, Dr Jan Marsh has argued that in reality two of the Pre-Raphaelite 'beauties', Lizzie Siddall and Jane Burden, were actually rather plain, and that their 'beauty' was 'constructed' by Gabriel Rossetti and the Pre-Raphaelites.[64] Dr Marsh meticulously presents the visual evidence, but as I hope to show in chapter six, this evidence is open to other interpretation. At this stage I simply want to drive home the point that careful scrutiny and assessment of both visual and written documentation is needed both before assumptions are drawn about past standards, and before conclusions are reached about what people looked like.

My concern is essentially with identifiable individuals (a portrait of 'An Unknown Young Man' is not much more helpful to me than a painting of the Virgin Mary) or with coherent occupational groups (such as servants, prostitutes, film stars or shop assistants). When discussing ordinary individuals or occupational groups I have usually been entirely dependent on written sources, which is unsatisfactory, though not, I believe, debilitatingly so; from the mid-nineteenth century onwards some private collections do contain family photographs. Famous individuals are usually commemorated in portraits, though of varying reliability. My procedure has been to try wherever possible to check the visual sources against the various written ones. My methods are those of the pragmatic historian.[65] Of portraits, I have asked the following questions: Is it authentic? What allowances may be made for the conventions in which the painter was operating, and what for flattery? In general I have assumed that an artist would be more likely to err on the side of flattery than its opposite, but I have also had to remember that standards of gravity and decorum may have precluded any attempt to bring out the sexual attractiveness of the sitter – often it was more important to bring out the qualities of dignity, status and wealth. Finally, many reputed beauties only achieved high status, and the distinction of having a portrait painted, in their later years, so that the only surviving portraits may not do justice to the beauty they possessed in their youth.

Written sources, as all historians know, have many traps as well. Often tributes to someone's personal beauty reveal themselves as mere conventional flattery; many commentators turn out to be prejudiced and idiosyncratic in their assessments. In general I have sought the evaluations of *l'homme moyen sensuel* (or of *la femme moyenne sensuelle*); Horace Walpole (under-sexed and highly idiosyncratic) and Casanova (over-sexed and utterly undiscriminatory) are less reliable than, say, H. T. Finck or George Eliot.

Establishing what individuals really did look like was one task, assessing the implications of this another. For the latter I have used such biographical materials as are available. We know a lot about the famous, though not consistently so; we know little about the humble. There has been no possibility of systematic statistical analysis. Yet this study is far from mere impressionism. My controls are provided by my three major themes, spelled out in the previous chapter, and in particular the second one, which provides a framework of the development from a 'traditional' evaluation of beauty to a 'modern' one from thorough empirical research of the traditional sort; my biographical excursions are then constantly checked against it.

There is a further point. Although most of my extended biographical discussions are of those exceptional, or, more exactly, fortunate, people whose lives have been richly recorded, frequently my most important conclusions have been drawn from their early lives; the early lives of the ultimately famous often do not differ significantly from those of others of similar social background and so have a more representative quality than might at first be thought. For instance, Nell Gwyn, known in the history books as a mistress of Charles II, started out life as a hawker of fish; she then became an orange seller in the theatre (a highly coveted position); from there she progressed to the stage, becoming a comic actress of considerable renown. Now if we cut the biography off there and ignore the subsequent royal connection we have an outline of a career that was far from untypical – we can in fact see the possibilities that were open to a good-looking girl of very humble origins. Similarly with Rodolpho Guglielmi. In New York at the end of the First World War without cash or contacts, he exploited his dashing Italian good looks to become a gigolo, moving up from third-rate tea dances to exclusive clubs. If we forget that Guglielmi eventually (and to a degree fortuitously) became Rudolph Valentino we have a nice encapsulation of the prospects open to penniless male beauty. There are many other examples in the pages which follow. Where I discuss occupational groups my material, ipso facto, is of general relevance.

This chapter has set out the assumptions upon which this study is based, and the methods employed in it. Now I must proceed to the first steps in establishing the long transition from the 'traditional' evaluation of beauty to the 'modern' one. The next chapter deals with traditional society, yet brings out some anti-traditional ideas expressed in the urban societies of the later Renaissance.

# 3 Beauty, Provoker of Thieves: Ancient Athens to *c.* 1800

## 1 *The Classical and Medieval Traditions in their Pre-Industrial Context*

Never a learned book on beauty but one must start with the Dialogues of Plato, working one's way through to Burke, Schopenhauer, Schiller, Emerson and Ruskin, just as there is never a book on social class but one must first be stuffed full of what Marx said, and then what Weber said, and what Durkheim said, and (if one is particularly unlucky) what Lenin said. It is no part of the purpose of this book to chronicle what philosophers of beauty, however illustrious, have said about their subject; they are of interest only in so far as their perceptions have entered into the framework governing the actions of real people. In the history of ideas it has been conventional to contrast medieval thought with classical thought, and then to postulate a revival of classical ideas during the Renaissance. My concern, however, is with the mix of ideas and social and economic constraints operating from the sixteenth century onwards, which determined evaluations of the significance of beauty. I shall first state what I take that mix to be, before proceeding briefly to look chronologically at some of the individual components.

First, there are the fundamental social, economic and medical facts, the vital statistics, in the very widest sense, we might quite properly say. From classical times till at least the late nineteenth century the over-whelming majority of the inhabitants of the West (in this book basically France, Britain and, eventually, the United States, with some references to Italy in the Renaissance period) scratched a living from the land. They were mobile neither geographically nor socially: the peasant lived, worked, married and died within his own community. For neither man nor woman was there much choice in the way of sexual partners: the notion of choosing someone because of their superior personal appearance was an almost meaningless one. Standards of nutrition and health were low and so also, therefore, were sex drives: marriage was overwhelmingly a matter of stern practicality rather than of sexual gratification. Again, therefore, personal appearance was scarcely a matter of great concern.

Even had private inclination existed, without the chance to travel, without the chance to move up in society, the opportunity for comparison, and therefore for selection, scarcely existed. With illness, mortality and early decrepitude everywhere in evidence, an overwhelming priority was the rearing of (comparatively) healthy children for continuance of the family and, probably more pressingly, support when earning powers failed. The imperatives, then, were far other than those of sexual aesthetics.[1]

For those who existed above bare subsistence level, a long series of categories from successful peasants, yeomen, artisans, shopkeepers, merchants, all through the ranks of the different systems of land holding, up to dukes, princes and monarchs, there operated, secondly, a set of imperatives which may perhaps be termed 'cultural'. Even for the highest born, life was brutish and potentially short: every sinew had to be stretched towards maintaining and, if possible, improving the family fortunes. For the better off there were no doubt some opportunities for (if male) seeking out real choices in the way of sexual partners and (if female) for considering such choices even if, in the end, most decisions were imposed ones. But in marriage considerations of wealth and status had to reign supreme.

Thirdly, we come to the (as far as actual behaviour was concerned) inextricably intertwined heritage of classical thought and pagan superstition, which held that a person of beauty was automatically a person of moral virtue. This certainty, however, was somewhat confused and weakened by the admittedly less certain proposition that someone who was morally virtuous must, ipso facto, be beautiful, though the latter could be invalidated by the greater certainty that someone who was manifestly ugly or deformed was quite surely evil; it was, in short, part and parcel of common knowledge that a person's character was closely related to their physical appearance. This structure of beliefs and values affected the lower sections of those sufficiently above subsistence level to have some concern with personal appearance; revulsion against deformity and manifest ugliness affected even the lowest strata. Among the elites judgments were sometimes clouded, even if private inclination remained intact, by the philosophical conception of beauty, which tried to assimilate human beauty to the beauty to be found in art, poetry, music and religion: thus again the disposition was away from evaluating beauty as purely physical and sexual and towards associating it with moral and spiritual qualities.

Linked to this imperative, 'ideological' as we might term it, was another, mainly the creation of dogmatic Christian religion, but partly fostered by the lessons of lived experience within the constraints and necessities already described. It was not in reality difficult for those sufficiently well heeled and highly sexed to observe, indeed they could scarcely avoid doing so, the intimate relation between beauty and the arousal of sexual desire. Thus the servants of a church morbidly preoccupied with what it saw as the evils of sexuality railed against such beauty, while prudent parents could see that lust for a beautiful face or body could be totally disruptive of careful schemes for enhancing the family position. 'Beauty', as Shakespeare so resonantly put it in a line to which I shall return shortly, 'provoketh thieves sooner than gold.' If, then, the third imperative decreed that beauty was only truly so if supported by moral purity and spiritual and intellectual worth, the fourth held that 'mere' beauty should be shunned as a snare and dangerous temptation.

Two final points, of perhaps slightly different character, complete this sketch (in six points) of the traditional perception of the nature of beauty. The first of these, *fifth* in the total sequence, was that beauty was the distinguishing and defining characteristic of women, with very little relevance in the assessment of men – this view did not, of course, hold sway in ancient Athens, and it was never totally dominant in the centuries which followed – it being an inescapable concomitant of traditional attitudes that they are inconsistent and self-contradictory. However, in so far as the notion was a widespread one, its implications were that if all women were inherently beautiful then there could be no meaning to distinctions of beauty as between one woman and another and, equally, if beauty was not an attribute of men there could be no point in comparing the personal appearance of one man with that of another. I have already discussed the notion of women as *the* beautiful sex and some of the more asinine theorizing lying behind it. But as part of a widely effective framework of ideas it was probably based on two interrelated and in many respects highly practical assumptions. The first assumption was of the greater lustfulness of males compared with the supposed sexual passivity of uninitiated females: thus women who aroused, or increased, or were at any rate the object of, lust were in that sense (which, of course, contradicts the moral view of beauty) the beautiful sex. The second assumption was that men were the active sex while (this would only be strictly true for the better-off sections of society) women existed solely to inspire men to valiant deeds, to be decorative and to provide, in their persons, suitable prizes for victorious males. I will just remark in passing that these are assumptions which have been under increasingly heavy fire in the modern period, leading eventually to the destruction of the traditional framework of ideas associated with them.

The second of my two final points (the *sixth* point in all) is that pre-modern societies were highly authoritarian, deeply respectful of convention, custom and received wisdom. It would be unhistorical to imply that our own society does not have its own rituals and conventions, but it is broadly true that the process of *Entzauberung* or demagification (discussed in chapter one) in the modern era has resulted in the rise of individualism, the growth of scepticism and the spread of rationality. (No doubt there have been many losses as well: my purpose is not to present some naive account of alleged 'progress'.) While, even in the long era dominated by the traditional framework of ideas (lasting at least till the onset of industrialization), those with eyes to see were falteringly aware of beauty as a universal in many types, the force of convention and the appeal of contrivance were strong, so that purity and whiteness of skin were too highly praised, darkness of colouring and minor blemishes too strongly condemned, and the mannerisms and affectations of the mighty too slavishly imitated. When convention is all powerful, true beauty is weak (though never, of course, utterly without effect).

Now, having set the frame, let me look chronologically at some of the detail, starting with Plato's various – and rather scattered – pronouncements on beauty. Ancient Athens was in many respects a vicious society, founded it could almost be said on the twin institutions of slavery and capital punishment (and death by the swallowing of hemlock was, contrary to what is often believed, a most unpleasant one).[2] The enduring appeal of ancient Athens is that the bright young men of its elite addressed themselves to questions of human existence in all its ramifications which have remained on our agenda ever since. Plato (427–347 BC) was primarily a political animal, preoccupied with the questions of how the good life should be achieved and how the individual within the community should be governed. In Athens those dramatic instincts which lie deep in human nature and gain other outlets in shaping the development of fashion were expressed in drama and in political debate. Plato's chosen form, in which he explored his great questions, was the dialogue. In many of the dialogues the leading figure is Socrates (469–399 BC), Plato's revered teacher; many of the other characters had a genuine historical existence; a few seem to have been invented. The words, and probably much of the thought, are almost certainly those of Plato and are usually thus attributed, as they will be here. The major discussions of beauty are contained in the *Georgias*, the *Greater Hippias*, the *Phaedras* and the *Symposium* (or Banquet). The intention in the *Greater Hippias* would seem to be to set up Hippias so that the superficiality of his comments is exposed as Socrates goes on to reveal deeper and more subtle truths. Personally, I am very taken by Hippias' response to Socrates' question, 'What is beauty?': I find an impressively modern ring in Hippias' answer, 'A beautiful young lady is a beauty.'[3] However, striking a bell that was to go on vibrating into the 1960s, Socrates trumps that with: 'Is not the most beautiful of mortal women plain when compared with the perfect and unfading beauty of the immortal Gods?' Socrates then, in a famous, but to me somewhat inconsistent line, suggests that 'the useful and the effective directed to the achievement of a good end, are the beautiful'.[4]

It is in the *Phaedras* that one finds the core of the Platonic view of beauty which, in all its poignant ambivalence, formed the basis of the conception of beauty held for around two millennia. True beauty,

Socrates says, is, together with the wise and the good, a part of divinity. But there is also 'mere bodily beauty' and, Socrates laments, it is ordained:

that all men, even the wisest, shall be the slaves of corporeal beauty . . . Base souls, almost wholly embruted in sense, love, almost as brutes do, rushing in to enjoy and beget . . . but all noble human souls see in the loved object the more or less complete realization of that particular type of excellence, the lines of which were stamped into their souls during their celestial career in the train of the chariots of the gods in heaven.[5]

The idea that beyond mere bodily beauty there exists true, divine beauty and that the beautiful, the true and the good are only different manifestations of one eternal divine perfection is repeated in the *Symposium*. Here there is, as it were, a dialogue within a dialogue, when Socrates reports on the interchange he has had with the wise woman Diotima of Mantinea. Why this character, almost certainly fictional, should have been introduced is not clear; both Plato and Socrates were generally contemptuous of the intellectual powers of women, but it may be that, as Sir Kenneth Dover conjectures, Plato wanted independent support for his propaganda on behalf of homosexuality.[6] Anyway, it is in the reported words of Diotima that we have the famous passage about the ladder or series of ascending stages which leads from earthly beauty to absolute beauty.

For he who would proceed aright in this matter should begin in youth to seek the company of corporeal beauty; and first, if he be guided by his instructor aright, to love one beautiful body only – out of that he should create fair thoughts; and soon he will of himself perceive that the beauty of one body is akin to the beauty of another; and then if beauty of form in general is his pursuit, how foolish would he be not to recognise that the beauty in everybody is one and the same! And when he perceives this he will abait his violent love of the one, which he will despise and deem a small thing, and will become a steadfast lover of all beautiful bodies. In the next stage he will consider that the beauty of the soul is more precious than the beauty of the outward form; so that if a virtuous soul have but a little comeliness, he will be content to love and tend him, and will search out and bring to birth thoughts which may improve the young, until he is compelled next to contemplate and see the beauty in institutions and laws, and to understand that the beauty of them all is of one family, and that personal beauty is a trifle; and after institutions his guide will lead him on to the sciences, in order that, beholding the wide region already occupied by beauty, he may cease to be like a servant in love with one beauty only, that of a particular youth or man or institution, himself a slave mean and narrow-minded; but drawing towards and contemplating the vast sea of beauty, he will create many fair and noble thoughts and discourses in boundless love of wisdom, until on that shore he grows and waxes strong, and at last the vision is revealed to him of a single science, which is the science of beauty everywhere.[7]

8 Greek vase depicting Ganymede, the legendary figure described in Homer's Iliad as 'the most beautiful of mortal men' and whose beauty excited the desire of Zeus himself; early 5th century BC

This ascent from earthly to absolute beauty, Diotima concludes, should govern the lives men should live.

Human beauty, then, is little compared with the beauty of the Gods; earthly beauty is nothing compared with divine beauty. As Greek sculptors showed, the beauty of the Gods was not in character different from that of human beings, but to achieve it, one had to take the best features from many different human beings. As there were Gods and Goddesses, so divine beauty had male and female forms. Greek sculpture, in both forms, represented not the beauty which aroused brutish instincts to enjoy and beget, but divine beauty.

This book does not accept the notion of divine beauty (while accepting that the concept of such beauty may well have been real enough to the Athenians and to subsequent generations); it is concerned purely with corporeal beauty. Clearly we must be wary of assuming that the representations of Greek sculpture are representations of what Athenians coveted in the way of bodily beauty. In fact, as was revealed in the words attributed to Diotima just quoted, where the powerful male Athenian sought beauty was not in the likes of the Venus de Milo, but in young men. The true Athenian pin-up is perhaps Ganymede, in one of the numerous naturalistic representations of this, of course, mythical figure. In the *Charmides*, whose central political topic is that of moderation, we

8

get a quite staggering insight into what powerful, middle-aged Athenians really thought constituted beauty.

Socrates is the narrator; he tells of how he was in the palaestra of Taures after a considerable absence from Athens. He asks 'about the present state of philosophy, and about the youth . . . whether any of them were remarkable for wisdom or beauty, or both'. Critias speaks of 'the great beauty of the day' – Charmides. Charmides enters and

at that moment, when I saw him, I confess that I was quite astonished at his beauty and stature; all the company seemed to be enamoured of him; amazement and confusion reigned when he entered; and a second troupe of lovers followed behind him. That grown-up men like ourselves should have been affected in this way was not surprising, but I observed the boys and saw that all of them, down to the very smallest, turned and looked at him, as if he had been a statue . . . Chaerephon called me and said: What do you think of the young man, Socrates? Has he not a beautiful face?
Most beautiful, I said.
But you would think nothing of his face, he replied, if you could see his naked form: he is absolutely perfect.
And to this they all agreed.
Ye Gods, I said, what a paragon if only he has one other slight addition!
What is that? said Critias.
If he has a noble soul . . .
He is as fair and good within as he is without, replied Critias.
Then before we see his body, should we not ask him to strip and show us his soul? . . .

When Charmides comes and sits beside Socrates his powers of conversation flee:

I caught sight of the inwards of his garment and took the flame. Then I could no longer contain myself. I thought how well Cydias understood the nature of love, when, in speaking of a fair youth, he warns someone 'not to bring the faun in the sight of the lion to be devoured by him', for I fear that I had been overcome by a sort of wild-beast appetite.[8]

This should not be written off as undiluted hypocrisy, even if there does seem to be more than a touch of wanting to have your crumpet and philosophize about it too. Clearly Plato (or Socrates) believed deeply in the distinction between the noble beauty of the soul and the wickedly tempting beauty of the body. All I want to point out here is that, for all the reluctance, there is a clear recognition of beauty in the modern, sexual (in this case homosexual) sense; and, secondly, that insistence upon the distinction between earthly and noble beauty, within the further insistence upon there being an absolute beauty embracing everything, including institutions, science and noble thoughts and discourses, leads to the appalling muddle which has bedevilled the study of human beauty ever since. The muddled and apparently hypocritical notion of beauty went hand in hand with the relegation of women to a thoroughly subordinate status, and a contempt for real wives, mothers and daughters (as distinct from Goddesses). The emergence of the modern conception of beauty, to which so many feminists take exception, was to depend, not on the continued subordination of women, but upon their increasing liberation.

To their Roman, and medieval successors, the Greeks transmitted their ambivalences about human beauty though not, on the whole, their homosexuality. While Athenian males had relegated their womenfolk entirely to the private sphere of home and kitchen and only applauded beauty contests among young males, leaving beauty contests among girls entirely for female audiences,[9] the Romans did allow their women some part in social life and applauded young women acrobats and other performers dressed in the scantiest of 'bikinis'.[10] The traditional factor that runs right through, of course, is that corporeal beauty, where recognized, is something essentially for males to admire, whether it be in other males or in females. In medieval Europe, as a consequence of majority male preferences, the ideology (that is to say, the version publicized in literature and art) of beautiful women as the inspiration of male action and heroics became established. Beauty certainly was considered a valuable asset in medieval monarchs, and the medieval romances do not entirely neglect male personal appearance, but the emphasis is on stature and strength, and also on such personal qualities as nobility and valour, rather than on distinction of feature. In the words of the American scholar Walter C. Curry, where the heroic male is concerned, 'the poet never leaves us in doubt as to the great stature, enormous strength, long sinewy arms, broad square breast and shoulders, together with a small waist and retreating stomach. His legs are long, with thighs thick and strong; and in general appearance he is more like a giant than a mere knight.' His eyes are generally blue in colour, 'with the fierce, proud glance of a falcon; and when his helmet is removed, his golden hair falls down over his shoulders in long curls'.[11] Curry points out that while heroines are invariably blonde, a 'broader taste' is shown in descriptions of men, who may also have various shades of darker hair. 'In portrayals of manly beauty,' Curry concludes, 'comparatively small space is given to the presentation of the personal appearance alone. On the other hand, the poet never tires of heaping up epithets in his attempts to delineate the noble and wise character of his hero and to show forth his manly virtues.' In introducing his hero Thomas Randolph, the poet Barbour requires a full twenty-two lines to catalogue his virtues of prowess, loyalty and honour, while his personal appearance can be dealt with in three:

> He weas of mesurabill stature,
> And portrait weill at all mesur,
> With braid visage, pleasand and fair.[12]

Although much more detail is given on the personal attributes of heroines, it is highly stereotyped.

. . . the type of feminine beauty praised by the poets in their catalogs of charms, is, without an exception, a blonde, whose hair is golden or like gold wire, eyes sparkling bright and light blue in color, cheeks lily-white or rose-red, forehead broad and without wrinkles, red lips, white evenly set teeth, long snow-white arms, and white hands with long slender fingers. Her figure is small, well rounded, slender and graceful, with a small willowy waist as a prime standard of excellence. The skin is everywhere of dazzling whiteness, rivalling the finest silk in softness; and the lower limbs are well formed and as white as milk, with small white and shapely feet.[13]

In the later Middle Ages (and on into the sixteenth and seventeenth centuries) there were standard summaries of what was held to constitute beauty in a woman: first there are seven essential qualities, then nine, then eighteen, and then the elaborate and very popular thirty, grouped in threes: three to be long – hands, legs and hair; three to be white; three to be pink; three to be round; three to be narrow, and so on . . . Clearly the magic was as much arithmetical as sensuous.[14] We are very short of biographical information for the Middle Ages, but it would certainly be unwise to conclude that even those men who were in a position to make choices exclusively favoured blondes, or went around ticking off the long items, the pink ones, the round ones, etc. On the point that beauty was felt to be a characteristic of women rather than men, however, the evidence is sound. This is borne out further by the fact that there are very few descriptions of ugly women in medieval literature and that where they exist their purpose is usually to bring out the beauty of the heroine.[15] Overall, what we have is a very strong emphasis on the conventional and even the artificial, an emphasis which precludes a proper appreciation of natural beauty in its many forms. Absolutely central is the association between looks and character: in the romances, the villains, from the devil upwards, are all extremely ugly.[16] From classical times there had been treatises on physiognomy translated, retranslated, and hawked around medieval Europe, treatises which reinforced the contempt and cruelty habitually shown towards the physically ill favoured and deformed. *Certeyne Rewles of Phisnomy* (a fourteenth- or fifteenth-century translation from the Arabic) tells us that: 'ye face that es playne with outen rounde hilles, signyfies a strydiefull man, truandous wrongewyse and unclene . . . Grete lippes are token of a folische man.'[17]

The theory, then, was that beauty went with goodness and godliness: along with their conventionalized physical attributes, heroines always have a string of oft-recurring and rather bland epithets applied to them: worthy, godly, virtuous, gentle, meek.[18] But, of course, even in the most ritualized society, reality keeps breaking in. With its strong

9 *Temptation of St Antony*, Henrick Met de Bles (known as 'Il Civetta'), mid–16th century: if we glance down to the lower right we can see what was thought to be genuinely tempting. The breasts and stomachs are highly tactile; the faces are sweet, if rather stereotyped, and easily distinguishable from that of Madame to the left

(official) hatred of sexual pleasure, the Christian church was overly aware of the sinful temptations besetting a beautiful woman since, even if she was inherently virtuous, she would be the object of persistent attentions from desirable males to a degree not encountered by her less well-favoured sisters. Through to at least the early seventeenth century writers with the approved ideological stance present the same sort of conflicting and hypocritical utterances as can be found today in the tabloid press: within a few pages a writer can define beauty as goodness, attack it for arousing lust, and then proceed to dwell lubriciously on the unseen intimate beauties of a woman's body. The stylistic trick used by medieval painters to give an almost tactile sense of physical intimacy was to paint palpably round stomachs (the 'bellies' so lovingly described in the literature). The proper place to look for an image of physical beauty is in a painting where the women really are meant to be tempting.

Gabriel de Minut's *Of Beauty* (1587), dedicated to Catherine de' Medici, contains within its full title its purpose 'to signify that what is naturally beautiful is also naturally good'. In one of the essays there is a description of one of the great reputed beauties of sixteenth-century France (on whom, however, we have little detail), la belle Paule.

Although we are told that she is completely free of the vice which renders ugly the most beautiful person, Minut does insist on how corporeal beauty can, in the context of someone with a black soul, give rise to 'the pollution and contamination of vice and ordure'.[19] A slightly later work by David de Flurance Rivault refers to the beauty which rules over our affections, dominates our will and enslaves our liberty, causing unbelievable desires, excesses of passion and fires of sensuality.[20] Minut praises la belle Paule precisely because she has to fight over and over again, 'a hundred plus a hundred times', he says, to defend her honour; she therefore merits the crown of glory far more than a woman who is not thus tempted.[21] Quite palpably, though, he clearly relishes the thought of those beautiful women who, being tempted, succumb, weeping crocodile tears over 'the poor hymen totally broken and torn'.[22] Then comes his description of the physical attributes of la belle Paule.[23] In the usual conventional way we have descriptions of her forehead, eyes, eyebrows and nose – hers we learn is perfect, and the further information is thrown in that according to Aristotle different shapes of nose indicate different types of personality. The ears, chin, throat and so on are described, and the mouth, interestingly, is compared to that of a handsome young man. Then we come to the breasts (he uses the respectable, but sensual *tetin*), which Minut describes as 'fine', while noting that we don't get to see or touch them. There is much on the thighs and the buttocks, but these we can only guess at since we cannot see them. Then the belly is lovingly described 'with the entry which babies come through'. But this entry is accessible only to one person, the many others who lusted after it having been bravely fought off, so that, says Minut, 'we may decorate and embellish this zone of the very centre of which we are now speaking . . . the Temple dedicated to Venus'.[24] But by the last page of the book we are back to an insistence that beauty and all moral qualities are interrelated, with the final words: 'beautiful is good, and good is beautiful'.[25]

## 2 New Perceptions of Beauty in Late Renaissance Urban Society

The set of ideas and prejudices about beauty that I have just been discussing persisted for many centuries, which indeed is why I have been able to take some of my examples from the sixteenth and early seventeenth centuries. The Renaissance did not entail any sudden reversal of attitudes. The main function of this section in the broad unfolding of my chronicle of change from traditional to modern evaluations of beauty is to show how in very particular circumstances a congruence of some of the factors which collectively make up modernization (to use that term of convenience) could give rise to the expression of 'modern' thoughts about the nature and significance of beauty. This section serves also to reinforce the caution that there is no absolute linear development from 'traditional' to 'modern', and, above all, to reveal once again that whatever the obfuscations of ideology, and whatever the social and economic constraints, certain truths about beauty keep breaking through.

There was, as I have said, no sharp break with the past. Art and philosophy, culture and behaviour continued to be pervaded and dominated by religious categories and religious modes of thought and expression. The single, central, indisputable feature of what Italians themselves at the time recognized as the 'Renaissance' was the revival (or 'rebirth') of classical learning. Inevitably there was a re-emphasis on Platonic ideas. Yet, in the early part of the sixteenth century a debate was initiated in which, whatever the surface formalities, a challenge was mounted to both Athenian and medieval evaluations of human beauty. This challenge was related both to the general ideas of Renaissance humanism (as expressed, for example, in More's *Utopia*) and to the special features of urban culture in such city states as Florence, Venice, Mantua and Urbino; the general ideas and the special features affected only a privileged elite; and very shortly the position of that elite was undermined as the French invaders marched into Northern Italy.

The city states (though not exclusively urban, being closely integrated gith their *contado*, or rural hinterland) offered a unique urban environment in which comparisons and choices could be made between attractive members of the opposite sex, and a unique form of courtly life wherein questions of beauty and sexual attractiveness were openly discussed: the whole process was greatly enhanced by the considerable mobility which existed between these North Italian cities. Secondly, the humanist thought which was at full strength at the beginning of the sixteenth century, while not to be identified with secularism, certainly encouraged hedonism and the belief that 'pleasure is the proper purpose of every human act'. As early as 1430 Lorenzo Valla had written that 'pleasure is the true good'. Bringing our central topic back into focus, he had then continued, 'what is sweeter, what more delectable, what more adorable, than a fair face?', recommending that in summer beautiful women should go lightly clad or clad not at all.[26] Thirdly, in the Italian city states were gathered the finest artists, and the finest collections of paintings; how beauty should be painted was an important matter for discussion; aesthetic standards were high and could actually be applied in the pursuit of sexual pleasure. Finally, among the privileged of Florence and Urbino, Mantua and Venice, Ferrara, Siena and Lucca women were less trammelled by conventions and stereotypes than they had been in medieval courts and castles; questions of male beauty came into the reckoning, as well as the more traditional ones of male valour. Feminist historians have queried whether 'women had a Renaissance' at all, a very reasonable question to ask; but arguments that women actually had greater freedom in the age of the troubadours, based as they are entirely on the romances and other literary fancies, and a rather special reading of them at that, seem to me quite perverse.[27] Indubitably, the position of women, even in circles where 'modern' ideas about beauty were being canvassed, remained very much one of dependency. Yet, if the reputation of Urbino had been built by Duke Federigo di Montefeltro, the dominant figure at the end of the fifteenth century was Elisabetta di Gonzago from Mantua, wife of Federigo's son, Guidobaldo, who was himself incapacitated by gout. In running the brilliant court society of Urbino, Elisabetta was assisted by her lady, Emilia Pia.[28] During the discussions of beauty he conducted at Prato with the women of nearby Florence, Agnolo Firenzuola went out of his way to insist that he believed women to be the equals of men; the very insistence suggests that the view was not very widely held, but the words Firenzuola used strongly indicate that he, the primary proponent in the late Renaissance period (as we shall see) of modern ideas about beauty, was totally sincere in his belief in the abilities of women. To him it is manifest that, 'you ladies are not less noble than we men, that you are as wise, as apt for things learned, moral and speculative, as ingenious in mechanical acts and knowledge as we; and that the same powers and essential habits dwell in your minds as well as ours'.[29]

The confrontation between the Platonic and the modern view of beauty can be seen at its sharpest in a too-much-neglected section of the fourth book of *Il libro de cortegiano* (*The Book of the Courtier*) by Count Baldesar Castiglione, which was based on real conversations held on four evenings during March 1507 in the palace of Urbino (under the general sponsorship of Elisabetta and immediate chairwomanship of Emilia Pia), though undoubtedly much edited and revised before eventual publication in Venice in 1528. Thereafter it became one of the most influential of all sixteenth-century books, there being, for instance, an English translation by Sir Thomas Hoby in 1561.[30] The discussion is opened by the Platonist Pietro Bembo, humanist scholar and, much later, Cardinal of Rome. He begins (I use the Hoby translation, with phrases from the original Italian where there may be ambiguity; more modern translations seem to me not always to get things quite right) by distinguishing between the beauty which applies to all things 'framed in good proportion' and the rather more interesting subject, now the immediate topic for discussion, the beauty 'that we meane, which is onlie it, that appeareth in bodies, and especially in the face of mann' (that is, 'in the face of human beings', *nei volti humani* in the original), proceeding immediately to a moving invocation of the power of this beauty (in both males and females) to arouse sexual love. To understand fully the passage (which I shall quote *in extenso* in a moment), one has to be aware that the phrase 'mens [sic] eyes' (*gli occhi humani*) means the eyes of both males and females, that the 'it' immediately preceding, the 'him selfe' following (after 'imprinteth') and the 'him' (last word of the quotation) all refer to the quality of beauty, and that the 'her', twice repeated, refers to *anima*, the soul (of a man or a woman). Beauty, then,

moveth thys fervent covetinge which we call love, we will terme it an influence of the heavenlie bountifulness, the whiche for all it stretcheth over all thyngs that be created (like the light of the Sonn) yet when it findeth out a face well proportioned, and framed with a certain livelie agreement of severall colours, and set furth with lightes and shadowes, and with an orderly distance and limites of lines, therinto it distilleth it self and appeareth most welfavoured, and decketh out and lyghtneth the subject where it shyneth wyth a marveylous grace and glistinge (like the Sonne beames that strike against beawtifull plate of fine golde wrought and sett wyth precyous jewelles) so that it draweth unto it mens eyes [*gli occhi humani*] with pleasure, and percing through them imprinteth him selfe in the soule [*s'imprime nell'anima*], and wyth an unwonted sweetenesse all to stirreth [*tutta la comove*] her and delyteth, and settyng her on fire maketh her to covett him [*lei desiderar si fa*].[31]

Then comes the conventional moralizing (hypocritical also, since Bembo's own life fully demonstrated his own carnal interest in female beauty):

When the fool then is taken with covetting to enjoy this beauty as a good thing he falleth into most deep errors and judgeth the body i.e. in whyche Beawtye is discerned, to be the principall cause thereof: whereupon to enjoye it, he reckoneth it necessarye to joigne as inwardlye as he can with that bodye, whyche is false.

Our senses, says Bembo, are the cause of wretchedness; beauty, he concludes, is always good. At this, a minor figure, Morello, expostulates that he has seen many beautiful women of a most ill inclination, cruel and spiteful, and that beauty in women in fact makes them proud, and pride makes them cruel. Re-emphasizing the sexual element, another courtier, Count Ludovico, smilingly replies that they probably seemed cruel to Morello 'because they content you not with it that you would have' (*perche non vi compiacciono di quello, que vorreste*). This gives Federigo Fregoso (courtier, diplomat and scholar) the opportunity to put most succinctly the case for the autonomy of beauty (in men as well as women). Beautiful women, he says, have caused wars; then he continues:

There be also manye wicked men that have the comlinesse of a beautiful countenance, and it seemeth that nature hath so shaped them, because they may be the redier to deceive, and that this amiable looke were like a baite that covereth the hooke.[32]

After this sane appraisal (which, however, I should stress, was far from completely original, similar phrasing being detectable in earlier literature)

Bembo has the last word, returning us totally to the old superstition: 'Beawtie is a face pleasant, merrie, comelye and to be desired for goodnesse: and Foulness is a face darke, uglesome, unpleasant and to be shonned for yll.'[33]

But there were other persuasive opponents of tradition (including, as we have already noted, from Northern Europe, Sir Thomas More; a little later there was Montaigne).[34] Pride of place, however, must go to Firenzuola's *Dialogue on the Beauty of Women*, first published in 1548. Of a number of similar works from the sixteenth century, this most unambiguously presents the notion of beauty as an autonomous (essentially sexual) characteristic. Over a period of several years Firenzuola had been providing at Prato lectures on and discussions of the nature of beauty, and his book, like *The Book of the Courtier*, is a record, again no doubt suitably polished and embellished, of actual conversations with real participants who in this case, however, are concealed behind fictitious names, Firenzuola himself taking the name of Celso Selvaggio.[35] There is an agreeable informality and naturalism about the discussions which indicate that one is indeed in touch with real people expressing genuine opinions. Firenzuola (under his pseudonym of Celso) constantly expresses amused irritation when, just as he is talking about the shape of female breasts, the women go out of their way to conceal their own. At one point he expostulates to Madonna Selvaggia as she pulls a scarf over the upper part of her bosom: 'if only you suffered others to see it!' He recognizes that few women have all the attributes of perfection and says wisely to Madonna Amororrisca: 'albeit you may not have all the complete parts of perfect and measured beauty, it is enough that you have such as, in the opinions of others, earn you the place of the fairest of the fair'. For her part, Madonna Amororrisca makes a little joke, saying that after Firenzuola's comments, 'henceforth I shall deem myself deformed'. Some of these qualities of informality and naturalism are apparent in Nicoló Franco's *Dialogue on Beauty* (1542) and Lodovico Domenichi's *The Nobility of Women* (1549), both of which deal with real living contemporaries and not simply abstractions, and, to a lesser degree, *The Book of the Beautiful Woman* (1554) by Federigo Luigini and *The Chief Beauties of Women* (1566) by Nicoló Campani.[36] Rather different are the books simply designed to instruct painters on how to achieve the effects of perfect beauty, such for example as the famous work of Giovan Giorgio Trissino.[37] Even Firenzuola's *Dialogue* provides some elements of this kind of instruction, which I do not consider directly relevant to this study, but in fact he does pleasantly distance himself from such abstract discourse when he says: 'there are many other measurements which, however, are of no importance and as Nature even rarely conforms to them, we will leave them to the painters, who, with a stroke of the brush more or less, may lengthen or shorten them as seems good to them'.[38]

Although the exchanges from *The Book of the Courtier* already studied referred to beauty in both men and women, a previous discussion in the same book had stressed the medieval precept which, I do not deny, continued to hold sway in most circles throughout the Renaissance and for a long period thereafter: 'Me thinke well beawty is more necessarie in her then in the Courtier, for (to saye the truth) there is a great lacke in the woman that wanteth beawtie.'[39] The very fact that all of the books I have mentioned indicate in their titles that their prime concern is with the beauty of women shows how firmly their authors were constrained by existing convention; I do, however, want to bring out the extent to which beauty is treated as being pertinent to men as well as to women. In Firenzuola's *Dialogue* Madonna Lampiada actually asks for clarification as to whether, in speaking of beauty, Celso is speaking of men or of women. Celso responds first with the classical fable (recounted by Plato) of the original double human creatures, half-male, half-female, each with two heads, four legs, etc., which being divided into separate males and females thereafter sought reunion with each other (homosexuality being a result of the fact that some of the original creatures were all-male or all-female). As Celso tells it, the fable emphasizes the strongly sexual element in beauty, and he reinforces this by saying that it is proper for women to contemplate the beauty of men and for men to contemplate the beauty of women, concluding that when (in their dialogues) 'we are speaking of beauty in general, we mean your beauty, and our beauty', but then adds that the particular concern will be with what he calls the more delicate beauty of women.[40] In their discussions of the proper proportions of the body both Firenzuola and Franco refer as much to men as to women. Firenzuola says that the stature or form of a *man* may be contained in a square, subsequently remarking that 'what is said of a man is likewise to be understood of a woman in this, and in all other measurements'.[41]

Franco says that he will mainly be talking about beautiful women, but refers to the *corpo humano* in saying that arms and legs outstretched are in proportion to the head and other parts of the body.[42] With that refreshing practicality to which I have already referred Firenzuola observes along the way that a shapely nose is as important for a man as it is for a woman,[43] while Franco has a brief discussion of the proper styling of the beard.[44] Furthermore the first part of Franco's work actually concludes with glorifications of the beauty of two men, Alfonso Davalo and the French king Charles V. However, it has to be admitted that there is both a continuance of the medieval tradition in that other qualities such as strength, diligence and intellect are integrated into the descriptions of physical features, and a strong element of sheer flattery.[45] Domenichi is entirely conventional in declaring that women are more beautiful than men, but he does recognize that certain physical characteristics in men will be attractive to women.[46]

'Delight',[47] Firenzuola says, 'is the end of every human act.' While, obviously, there is nothing new in his retelling of Plato's myth about the double humans, nor in his evocation of the sexual power of beauty, what is significant is that beauty and sexual gratification are presented as good ends in themselves, without any need to link one to godliness and condemn the other. For beauty, he says, 'we see a man forget himself; and on beholding a face graced with this celestial gift, his limbs will quake, his hair stand on end, and he will sweat and shiver at the same time'[48] (again this is not an original observation; it has its roots in classical literature). Firenzuola is in agreement with Sir Thomas More (and many other men throughout the ages) in being opposed to the fashions, the paddings and the cosmetics which conceal the true attributes of natural beauty. Men like himself are not fooled: 'when Art is not aided by Nature it can do little; and that little is unsuccessful, and few are they who do not discern it'.[49] Health, he says, and the emphasis is a brisk modern one, 'gives a clear and lively colouring'.[50] Beauty, this natural attribute, this 'celestial gift' is very much *not* something merely in the eye of the beholder, a matter of subjective judgment:

When we speak of a beautiful woman we mean one whom all alike admire, and not this one or that one only; thus Nova, so ill-favoured as she is, appears most pleasing in the sight of her Tomaso, albeit she is as uncomely as she possibly can be . . . a lady fair in all points, like yourself, must necessarily be pleasing to all, as you are; *albeit few are pleasing to you*, as I know full well.[51]

The phrase I have italicized (Celso is addressing the gorgeous Madonna Selvaggia) brings out again Firenzuola's recognition that women too can be fussy about beauty in the opposite sex. In medieval romances lack of looks in women, and certainly downright ugliness, was scarcely mentioned; ugliness was something confined to evil male figures. High Renaissance high society was discriminatory in the extreme; the works I have just been discussing openly declare not merely what an advantage it is for a woman (in particular) to be good looking, but what a disadvantage to be ill looking. Firenzuola quotes a male contemporary whose view was that no matter how many beautiful women there were at a ball, the sight of one ugly one would ruin his evening.[52] Generally good taste prevented overt descriptions of ugliness, but from *The Nature of Love* (1531) by Mario Equicola d'Areto we learn that, 'ugliness consists in having long feet, flat breasts, a big nose and small white eyes'. There is a rather more elaborate account by Campani:

Feet like clodds of earth, above them two fat legs straight and hung like vine poles, knees as large as whole onions; the body large and flat as a straw mat and hanging like a sail-cloth; the ribs like a grid iron; the bosoms like a pair of bellows; the arms long and thin, the hands appearing like rakes; the neck as stretched as that of the stork; the mouth wide as a cavern; the teeth like locusts, the nose long and curved like the beak of the woodcock; the eyes like those of a civet cat, each ear looking like a cradle.[53]

Now it is no part of my purpose to suggest that this is a particularly naturalistic or persuasive description, still less that there is anything admirable about penning such descriptions in the first place. All I want to stress is that just as beauty, in these accounts, is not in any way associated with moral qualities, so here ugliness is not in any way associated with the lack of them. In these various quotations we have for the first time, at least since the Roman era, a clear expression of the autonomy of personal appearance, unmixed with any Platonic or religious moralizing. On the whole, in the centuries to follow, such a view, as far as public mores were concerned, was to be firmly subjugated to a reiteration of more traditional views. None the less, actual *behaviour* in the more sophisticated Western courts, and among self-confident aristocrats, would quite often conform to the tenets so cheerfully enunciated by Firenzuola. The next section, however, returns to the mistrust of, and ambivalence about, beauty.

## 3 *The Persistence of Traditional Attitudes*

The attitudes towards beauty which, in all their ambiguity, dominated the succeeding centuries are, as one might expect, most neatly encapsulated in one Shakespearian line. At the end of act I of *As You Like It* (written in the closing years of the sixteenth century), Celia and Rosalind decide to flee from the court of the wicked uncle who has usurped the throne.

| | |
|---|---|
| *Rosalind.* | Why whither shall we go? |
| *Celia.* | To seek my uncle in the forest of Arden. |
| *Rosalind.* | Alas! What danger will it be to us,<br>Maids as we are, to travel forthe so far?<br>Beauty provoketh thieves sooner than<br>gold! |
| *Celia.* | I'll put myself in poor and mean attire,<br>And with a kind of umber smirch my face;<br>The like do you; so shall we pass along,<br>And never stir assailants.[54] |

The line 'Beauty provoketh thieves sooner than gold' captures both the power of beauty and, through the association with thieves, its dangerous, even disreputable, quality. In Shakespeare's time, of course, both Rosalind and Celia were played by young male actors. Only from the 1660s were female roles on stage consistently and continuously played by women. This in itself was an important, if relatively small, step in a more candid evaluation of beauty in both sexes. There then came to be a different kind of resonance about the disguises adopted by Rosalind and Celia. A gorgeous actress would be no less fetching for having a besmirched face nor, still less for, as in Rosalind's case, being dressed as a page boy. Popular Restoration and eighteenth-century plays frequently contained a part (for actresses who specialized in this role) which required the adoption at some point of masculine disguise: this provided the opportunity for the actress to show off, and the audience to appreciate, the shape of her legs.[55]

Naturally, the perception of beauty as a desirable commodity in its own right did not suddenly disappear with the collapse of the Italian city states: in secure, affluent environments (for example the courts of Louis XIV and Louis XV, or the great houses of some of the most eminent English aristocrats) beauty could be an autonomous characteristic of great value to its possessor. But the publication of dialogues openly praising sexual beauty ceased; mistrust and moralizing took over.[56]

For almost all sections of society in the seventeenth and eighteenth centuries life was too serious for beauty to play a significant role. For families at the top of the social scale, as also in the relatively comfortable middle, the most pressing requirement was the consolidation or improvement of social status, and the acquisition of a beautiful spouse did not automatically secure that. Even where personal considerations were taken more fully into account, matrimonial compatibility was more highly prized than sexual attractiveness. This is, in itself, a highly sensible attitude, but the sense is usually swamped in quite frenetic denunciations of the evils of sexual beauty.

Sense, and sensitivity, are two of the strongest characteristics of the eighteenth-century English novelist and magistrate Henry Fielding. Squire Allworthy in Fielding's *Tom Jones* was all in favour of marriage being founded on love: he regarded as equally undesirable parental compulsion, avarice for a great fortune, snobbery for a title and lust for a beautiful person. In what Fielding, as author, disarmingly terms All-worthy's 'Sermon' there is some double-tracking, Allworthy opening and – as we shall see – closing with the formal morality of the time:

For surely we may call it a Profanation to convert this most sacred Institution into a wicked Sacrifice to Lust or Avarice: and what better can be said of those Matches to which Men are induced merely by the Consideration of a beautiful Person, or a great Fortune?

However, Allworthy then immediately continues, matching morality against self-awareness: 'To deny that Beauty is an agreeable Object to the Eye, and even worthy of some Admiration, would be false and foolish', admitting that, 'It was my own good Fortune to marry a Woman whom the World thought handsome, and I can truly say I liked her better on that Account.' But then intemperate moralizing takes over:

to make this the sole Consideration of Marriage, to lust after it so violently as to overlook all Imperfections for its Sake, or to require it so absolutely as to reject and disdain Religion, Virtue and Sense, which are Qualities, in their Nature, of much higher Perfection, because an Elegance of Person is wanting: this is surely inconsistent with a wise Man or a good Christian. And it is perhaps being too charitable to conclude that such Persons mean anything more by their Marriage than to please their carnal Appetites, for the Satisfaction of which, we are taught, it was not ordained.[57]

The unwitting testimony here is that, whatever might be said in sermons, there were, as always, those with a sharp and determined eye for 'Elegance of Person'.

In Fielding's poem 'Advice to a friend on choosing a wife' there are some moving lines:

A tender Heart, which while thy Soul it shares,
Augments thy Joys, and lessens all thy Cares . . .

Soon, however, the language becomes quite intemperate, and there is a gross confusion between beauty and artifice:

Of Beauty's subtle Poisen well beware;
   Our hearts are taken e'er they dread the Snare:
Our Eyes, soon dazzled by that Glare, grow blind,
   And see no Imperfections in the Mind.
Of this appriz'd, the Sex, with nicest Art,
   Insidiously adorn the outward Part.
But Beauty, to a mind depraved and ill,
   Is a thin gilding to a nauseous Pill;
A cheating Promise of a short-liv'd Joy,
   Time must this idol, Chance may soon destroy.

And then at the end we have the moralizing:

Fond of thy Person, may her Bosom glow
   With Passions thou hast taught her first to know.
A warm Partaker of the genial Bed,
   Thither by Fondness, not by lewdness led.[58]

Nothing could speak louder than this equation of beauty with lewdness.

Quite a balanced view was shown by Miles Coverdale, Bishop of Exeter, in the sixteenth century. He argued that a spouse should be chosen for true riches of mind, body and, of course, temporal substance; but he did have the grace to add that 'if beside these, thou foundest other great riches (beauty and such like gifts) . . . thou has the more to thank God for'.[59] However, his near contemporary Philip Stubbes, perennial critic of society and its morals, was probably more in tune with public mores when he complained of feckless marriages, with a boy not caring whether he had sufficient funds as long as 'he have his pretty pussy to huggle with all'.[60]

In *Women in Stuart England and America*, Roger Thompson tells us that 'passion, alias infatuation, alias lust' was seen throughout the seventeenth century 'as a noxious ingredient, rather than a pre-requisite yeast' (for successful marriage) and that 'sex and mere looks' were considered 'special snares'.[61] Throughout the seventeenth and eighteenth centuries, as Lawrence Stone points out, it was strongly urged that sexual desire was not a proper motive for marriage. The wisdom and the fears and prejudices of the day were well summed up by Mrs Mary Astell, prolific commentator on proper and improper behaviour, in *Some Reflections on Marriage* of 1700. Choice in marriage, she says quite reasonably, should be 'guided by Reason', as against what, rather heatedly, she calls 'Humour or brutish Passion'. What, she asks, 'do Men propose to themselves in Marriage?', and quickly answers: 'What will she bring is the first enquiry. How many Acres? Or how much ready Coin?' Mrs Astell, a true daughter of her time, does not altogether disapprove, 'for Marriage without a Competency . . . is no very comfortable condition'. A few pages later comes an immensely rich passage, shot through with witty cynicism and heavy mistrust of beauty:

But suppose a man does not Marry for Money, though for one that does not, perhaps there are thousands that do; let him Marry for Love, an Heroick Action, which makes a mighty noise in the World, partly because of its rarity, and partly in regard of its extravagancy, and what does his Marrying for Love amount to? There's no great odds between his Marrying for the Love of Money, or for the Love of Beauty, the Man does not Act according to Reason in either Case; but is governed by irregular Appetites.

Finally there is, as with Fielding later, that refusal to believe that beauty can exist independently of powder and paint, plumpers, wigs and elaborate dress – understandable enough in an era when artificial convention often mattered more than natural beauty: 'Beauty with all the helps of Art is of no very lasting date, the more it is help'd the sooner it decays, and he who only or chiefly chose for Beauty, will in a little time find the same reason for another choice.'[62]

Throughout the sixteenth and seventeenth centuries in England, both Catholic and Puritan writers warned against basing marriage on beauty or wealth.[63] For the period 1680 to 1760 Dr Peter Borsay (admitting to considerable simplification) has summed up marriage among the middle and upper classes as follows: 'the woman brought wealth and the man status; a woman was as beautiful as she was wealthy, a man as handsome as he was superior'. He also quotes 'An Epistle to a Friend' from the *Tunbridge and Bath Miscellany* for the year 1714:

With scorn Clodalia's haughty face we view,
    The deadn'd aspect, and the sordid hew,
Her wealth discover'd gives her features lies,
    And we find charms to reconcile our eyes . . .[64]

Beauty, or in this case its absence, *is* recognized to exist; but against social status or wealth, beauty is not highly regarded, and discovery of a woman's wealth will readily lead to a modification of the estimate of her beauty.

At the bottom of society, the struggle for existence, as throughout the Renaissance period, was so intense that there was little time for the contemplation of beauty in either sex. 'Certainly', the American social historian Edward Shorter tells us, 'physical attractiveness was relatively unimportant.' He cites the peasants of Baden, who warned, 'you look at the money bag not at the face'. Charles Perron, the historian of the Franche-Compté, tells us that, in a bride, beauty was a very subordinate quality, 'if not actually more feared than desired', and in addition to the succinct 'you can't eat beauty with a spoon' he cites two other sayings:

When one has a beautiful wife, one has no fine pigs – Why? – Because the pigs, instead of eating, spend all their time staring at her;

and

It is better to say: Ugly, let us have supper than to ask: Beauty, what do we have for supper?[65]

In any case, as Professor Olwen Hufton reminds us about eighteenth-century France: 'a woman or man who was not pockmarked, who did not suffer from a vitamin-deficiency disease, or from a congenital defect was in a small minority'.[66] Well into the next century matters were even worse on the other side of the Alps, as the anonymous author of a 'Journal of a tour . . . in the year 1824', and seeker after natural beauty, lamented:

The frequent and appalling objects of misery which here present themselves, are however a serious antidote to the enjoyment of the fine scenery of this part of the country – Goiterous and idiotic persons, are dreadfully numerous and tho' we had occasionally them on the other side of the Alps, yet nowhere did they assume so horrible an aspect as in this valley.[67]

Without doubt human beauty, wherever and whenever it could be found, throughout asserted its power, even if wise virgins of both sexes preferred to ignore it; the very weight of the denunciations by preachers and social moralists makes the point. But fashion and philosophy appear to have supported the preachers.

I have already said something about the relationship between fashion and the relative values placed on natural beauty. Fashions, male and female, changed markedly at intervals throughout the sixteenth, seventeenth and eighteenth centuries, broadly in step with the rise and decline of the Baroque in the arts. But the general objective was the achievement of a certain conventionalized image, in which the less well favoured could approximate to the better favoured, and the most favoured would scarcely be able to shine in their full natural splendour. A courtier in the reign of Louis XV complained that the heavy use of rouge made it difficult to distinguish one lady from another, adding that 'they quench every feeling of desire in men, whose one wish was to flee from them'. Philip Dormer Stanhope (fourth Earl of Chesterfield), in *The World*, the weekly 'paper of entertainment' which ran between 1753 and 1756, wrote of 'this heinous crime of self-painting', which he found to be 'extremely epidemical'. The 'inferior class of women' used 'a sort of rough cast, little superior to the common lath and plaister', the 'generality of women of fashion . . . a superior stucco, or plaster of Paris highly glazed, which does not require a daily renewal', while only ladies 'not only of the first rank, but of the most considerable fortunes' could afford the 'transcendent and divine powder' made from pearls 'with an exquisite varnish superinduced to fix it'. As have many other men in every era, he remarked that while the ladies 'flatter themselves' that the artifice 'is not discoverable', he begged 'leave to assure them' that it was 'immediately discovered by the eye at a considerable distance'. Unendearing to the eye, such plasters and powders apparently also had an unpleasant smell and 'when warm upon the face . . . had the most nauseous taste imaginable'. In his reactions Stanhope is, of course, exceptionally fastidious, and, in his wit, malicious. He delicately concluded (in the vein of Sir Thomas More or Alphonse Karr) that the overall effect may not have been sexually very enticing: 'offensive to three of the senses, it is not, probably very inviting to the fourth'.[68] With the heavy use of powder, men and women were, effectively, concealed behind masks; powder on the hair, and, of course, even more on wigs, helped to obliterate some of the obvious distinctions between youth and age. The poem *Mundus Muliebris: or The Lady's Dressing Room Unlock'd* of 1690 (possibly written by Mary Evelyn), while highly satirical in tone, notes some of the elaborate artifices resorted to by women in the late seventeenth century. A 'Fop-Dictionary' at the end elucidates the various devices. Plumpers are 'certain very thin, very round, and light Balls to plump out, and fill up Cavities of the Cheeks . . .' The various false additions to the coiffure are listed as follows: the *Choux* – 'the great round Boss or Bundle'; *Crushes* – 'certain smaller Curls, placed on the Forehead'; *Confidants* – 'smaller *Curles* near the Ears'; *Passagers* – 'are Curl'd Locks next the Temples'; *Berger* – 'a plain small Lock'; *Tour* – 'an artificial Dress of Hair on the Forehead'; *Meurtriers* – 'murderers, a certain Knot in the Hair, which ties and unites the Curls'; *Creve-Coeurs* – 'the two small Curl'd Locks at the Nape of the Neck'.[69] All told, wigs, powdered hair, false curls and knots, paint and beauty spots, ostrich feathers, elaborate hats and all the excesses of male and female costume thoroughly submerged natural attributes and put a high premium on money and leisure in comparison with innate beauty.

Philosophers (male) disapproved of fashion and artifice and were at one with poets, preachers and advice writers in denigrating 'mere' beauty. I have already quoted from the French authors Gabriel de Minut (writing at the end of the sixteenth century) and David de Flurance Rivault (writing at the beginning of the seventeenth century): the former's discourses on beauty, while indulging a certain amount of lubricity (as well as much pedantry), are devoted to the proposition that goodness and beauty are the same.[70] The series of discourses by Flurance, somewhat misleadingly entitled *The Art of Beautifying*, are dedicated to the propositions that wisdom beautifies the face and that the body is an outward projection of the qualities of the soul. Of all the qualities that make life pleasant and which further human happiness, he says, the first are honour and beauty. The King (at this juncture Henry IV) is responsible for honour, while the Queen (to whom the book is dedicated) provides the beauty; there is a close affinity between honour and beauty.[71] As already observed, Flurance does recognize the sexual lure of beauty, but conjures this away through the 'sacred paradox' that it is really wisdom that makes the face beautiful; it is when wisdom is lacking that the evil aspect of beauty suborns the true one. The three characters of beauty, corresponding with the three graces, are spirit, body and voice. Through a wealth of classical and scriptural quotation, some discussion of the physical appearance of different races, a brief catalogue of the different physical characteristics of human beings, he proceeds remorselessly to his conclusion, which was also his initial assertion, that wisdom is the mother of beauty, and that wisdom beautifies the face just as the face of a beautiful person reveals wisdom.[72]

Yet it was also in France that some of the most rational, if, usually, rather masculinist, comments were made, particularly during the period of intense religious, political and intellectual conflict of the seventeenth century in which embattled libertarians (such as the playwright Molière) refused to echo the orthodoxies and the slavish flattery of Church, Nobility and Monarchy, by which the multitude were pinioned. Pierre de Bourdeilles, Seigneur de Brantôme, actually lived between 1534 and 1614, but his memoirs were not published till 1666. His descriptions of beauty are limited by the arithmetical formulae of the Middle Ages, but in discussing love he was able to confine himself to physical qualities (leaving out moral and intellectual ones), debating the relative merits of touch, appearance and voice. He gave a very impressive assessment of 'mere' physical beauty:

Certainly, since sight and the eyes are the first to attack in the battle of love, we have to avow that they provide enormous pleasure when they bring into our vision something fine and rare in beauty. Well! where is there anything in the world one can see which is more beautiful than a beautiful woman.[73]

La Bruyère (1645–96) described love as something which is born suddenly, without reflection, out of beauty: 'a feature of beauty tranfixes us', he wrote; 'and while it takes years to establish friendship, a beautiful face or a lovely hand can achieve far more in a single moment'.[74] Like the Italian Renaissance writers already quoted he was highly conscious of, though deeply cynical about, the appeal to women of masculine beauty: 'A vain, indiscreet, garrulous and vulgar man, who speaks confidently of his faith and of others with contempt, impetuous, haughty, conceited, lacking in morals and probity, with a crippled mind, bad judgment and free imagination, he needs nothing more in order to be thoroughly adored by women than to have a beautiful face and a fine figure.'[75] 'A beautiful face', he says, speaking now of women, 'is the finest of all spectacles.' Again the masculinist cynicism is apparent in recognition of the sexual appeal, and therefore power, of the girl-woman (what the French call *la beauté du diable*); he comments that he'd like to be 'a beautiful girl from the age of thirteen to the age of twenty-two' but that after that age to become a man.[76] Individual French authors continued to produce thoughtful, deeply felt utterances on human beauty, but the received view, both in France and in the rest of Europe, was as the Chevalier de Méré put it: 'Ladies who dream more of being beautiful than of being agreeable, are badly advised; if they are beautiful that is the worst possible basis in the world for love.' This may seem rational enough, but then Méré becomes almost hysterical in maintaining that striking physical beauty 'is almost always false' and leads to 'disgust'.[77] John Aubrey, in his very brief 'brief life' of Eleanor Radcliffe, Countess of Sussex (who died in 1666, 'of ', according to Aubrey, 'the Pox'), describing her as 'as great a beauty as any in England', cites her solely as 'a great and sad example of the power of Lust and Slavery of it'.[78]

In one version or another, however, these *were* the attitudes which dominated, in Britain, in Germany, and in the USA. Anthony Ashley Cooper, Lord Shaftesbury (1671–1713), is now seen by historians as a very important figure in the formulation of cultivated taste in eighteenth-century Britain. His views on beauty, which he expressed a good deal less succinctly than did Shakespeare's Celia, stand well for what had been widely held previously, but was now actually set down among the canons of good taste. Shaftesbury was concerned to reject what he called 'Romantick Passion' and encourage 'refine'd Contemplation'. In a rather cunning twist on an old argument he recognizes the immediate appeal of beautiful places as well as beautiful faces but rejects both as merely aspects of romantic passion. Thus, he says, there is no more reason 'to fear these *Beautys* which strike a sort of *Melancholy*, like the Places we have nam'd [such as woods, rivers, seashores], or like the solemn *Groves*. No more shall I avoid the moving Accents of soft *Musik*, or fly from the *enchanting Features* of the fairest *Human Face*.'[79] He acknowledges 'certain powerful FORMS in *Human* Kind, which draw after 'em a Set of eager *Desires*, *Wishes* and *Hopes*'; but these are in no way suitable 'to your rational and refined Contemplation of *Beauty*. The Proportions of this *living Architecture*, as wonderful as they are, inspire nothing of a *studious* or *contemplative* kind.' He is interested, he says, in 'a nobler Love than such as common Beautys inspire', and later he says it is not love but hunger which is excited by beauty. One should not, he declares, be 'captivated by the Lineaments of a fair Face, or the well-drawn Proportions of a human Body'. The very essence of his argument is that we have to cultivate taste; only thus can we appreciate Divine Beauty. The upshot is nothing very novel: 'beauty . . . and good . . . are still one and the same'.[80] Finally, in the age-old rebuttal of mere sensuality:

The *Beautiful*, the *Fair*, the *Comely*, were never in the *Matter*, but in the Art and Design; never in *Body* it-self, but in the *Form* or *Forming Power* . . . Never can the *Form* be of real force where it is uncontemplated, unjudg'd of, unexamin'd and stands only in the accidental Note or Token of what appeases provok'd Sense, and satisfies the brutish Part . . .[81]

The principles of contemplation, of good taste, of judging carefully and examining cautiously, predominate in British thought in the eighteenth century; thus, the portraits even of beautiful women have that dignified quality to which Reynolds aspired, and lack sensuality and romantic appeal. William Hogarth's *Analysis of Beauty* (1743) is essentially a somewhat austere guide for artists; nor does Edmund Burke in *A Philosophical Enquiry into the Origin of our Ideas on the Sublime and Beautiful* (1756), with his rather odd list of 'the qualities of beauty' ('to be comparatively small', 'to be smooth', 'to have variety in the direction of the parts', 'to have these parts not angular, but melted as it were into each other', 'to be of a delicate frame', 'to have its colours clear and bright' but not 'glaring', and, if 'glaring' to 'have it diversified' with other colours),[82] take us much further into the real world of living people. He does refer to 'handsome men' and 'beautiful women', declaring that 'both sexes are undoubtedly capable of beauty' (though the female more so than the male), but his search, this interesting blow against traditionalism apart, is once more for a sublimity beyond mere physical beauty.[83] Even the more probing *philosophes* of the French Enlightenment do not offer much of an alternative. If Voltaire could see that beauty was not a divine universal, he still used the term to cover literature as well as personal appearance. To him beauty was absolutely relative: hence the famous pronouncement:

Ask a toad what is beauty . . . he will answer that it is his female with two huge round eyes coming out of her tiny head, large flat mouth, yellow belly and brown back.

A tragedy cheered in Paris would be jeered in London; 'what is proper in Japan is improper in Rome; what is in fashion in Paris is out in Peking'.[84]

A different strand of traditional thought was given enormous reinforcement by one of the most famous of all eighteenth-century publications within the realm of personal appearance. *Essays on Physiognomy*, by the Swiss pastor Johan Lavater, were published in Zurich in 1775. Rapidly translated from the original German into the other main European languages, they enjoyed a tremendous vogue, seeming to show that there was a valid empirical basis for the notion, deeply rooted in the uncultivated human psyche, that appearance and character are firmly interrelated. Such a publication, enjoying such popularity, marked a sharp setback to any concept of the autonomy of beauty. In the meantime Friedrich Schiller added his weight to the old doctrine that true beauty must be separated from the sensuous instinct, which is to be deplored.[85]

For the direct application of these often rather academic notions to everyday life at most levels of society we can turn to a Scottish moralizer whose works tended to go through many editions, Henry Home (Lord Kames). 'The sense of beauty', he wrote,

does not tend to advance the interests of society . . . Love . . . arising from a sense of beauty, loses, when excessive, its sociable character: the appetite for gratification, prevailing over affection for the beloved object, is ungovernable, and tends violently to its end, regardless of the misery that must follow. Love in this state is no longer a sweet agreeable passion: it becomes painful, like hunger or thirst, and produceth no happiness but in the instant of fruition. This discovery suggests a most important lesson, that moderation in our desires and appetites, which fits us for doing our duty, contributes at the same time the most to happiness: even social passions, when moderate, are more pleasant than when they swell beyond proper bounds.[86]

Such precepts governed the everyday advice offered, in particular, to young women. They may or may not have found it consoling. 'People, to be beautiful, should endeavour to be virtuous; and should avoid Vice, and all the worst Sort of Passions, as they would fly Deformity. I wish the more beautiful Half of the human Creation, in particular, were thoroughly sensible of this great Truth; "that the readiest way to be beautiful, is to be good".'[87] Thus wrote the Reverend Joseph Spence under his pseudonym of Sir Harry Beaumont in 1752. 'Would you be fair? – BE GOOD', this was the advice contained in some verses by the Reverend Dr John Cosens, addressed first to the ladies of Britain, and then in 1788 to the ladies of the newly independent American colonies:

Mere beauty *is not happiness*
    But fatal to itself; – in power
It gleams the meteor of an hour;
    For one it guides to joy and light,
It plunges ten in Stygian *night*.[88]

That is how, while in fact admitting the power of beauty, the upholders of public morals in the seventeenth and eighteenth centuries sought to dismiss it: by calling it *mere* beauty, or external beauty, or (as with Shaftesbury) '*common* beauty', or some such other damning adjective designed to separate it off from the real article, sublime or divine beauty.

Yet if external beauty was officially scorned, the rituals of fashion and make-up commanded much attention, and thus there was quite a market for guides to self-presentation and cosmetics. A work of 1760 repeats points made in earlier works (beauty manuals, anyway, tend to copy from each other). First of all the full title is itself of interest:

THE ART OF BEAUTY or a Companion for the Toilet in which the CHARMS OF THE PERSON Are Considered and Explained Under the Several Heads of SHAPE, FEATURES, AND COMPLEXION. To which are added, EASY, SAFE, and CERTAIN METHODS, of Attaining EXTERNAL BEAUTY. Being an entire New Work, written by a late Eminent English Physician at the Russian Court. An absolute necessary for every Woman that would either become, or continue Handsome.

The fundamental point to be made is that, constrained by the prevailing mistrust of beauty and of attempts to simulate beauty, such guides had in effect to apologize for their existence and excuse themselves on the grounds of the frailty of human nature. The *Ladies Dictionary* of 1694 had conducted a long discussion over whether 'beautifying' was permissible at all, concluding guardedly that, provided it was 'for honest purposes', we 'see no reason to forbid it', it 'not being proved a sin'.[89] The preface to *The Art of Beauty* was still more hesitant:

Altho' piety, modesty, virtue, good sense, and ingenuity, ought to be the chief objects of every woman's attention; yet since the frailty of human nature inclines men, rather to listen to their senses than their judgment, it must be allowed an innocent at least, if not a necessary care in the fair Sex to cultivate beauty.[90]

Since this is a practical work, for use by real people, it does offer a definition of beauty of greater persuasiveness (to me at least) than any we have encountered from philosophers preoccupied with the notion of divinity. It is a definition which, one or two conventions apart, supports the idea of the relative universality of beauty.

I say that the form of an entire body, that can be considered as beautiful, ought to please our eyes by its extent. If persons be too big, or too little, too fat or too lean, we cannot like them; because there is not a certain resemblance or proportion between them and us, or between the generality of mankind.[91]

Fair skin is described as perfection, brown or yellowish skin, or skin covered with freckles, is defined as ugly;[92] however, the guide also remarks (and here clearly there has, in our century, been a change in fashion) that skin that appears tawny may be so only through too much exposure to the weather.[93] The universalist definition then continues:

The number of parts that compose an entire body is so determined, that it neither can increase nor diminish, without a remarkable deformity. Imagine a man with two noses and one eye; would not such a face appear very strange; for we see, that the want of the eye-brows, a wen on the forehead, a wart, a pimple, or any such excrescence, makes a very disagreeable impression.

BEAUTY consists in the disposition of the parts. Ill ranged teeth, or locks of hair slovenly placed upon the forehead, render the whole countenance so odd, that it cannot please, let the other parts be ever so handsome.

There ought to be an exact proportion between all the parts; for what seems more ridiculous, than a great head upon a small body, and a small nose upon a large face?

The definition further calls for perfect texture, for the absence of baldness, pimples and pockmarks. Then, rather sensibly, 'our Sense of Smelling ought to be Satisfied in the enjoyment of those things we account to be beautiful'. An agreeable voice is also identified as a component of beauty.[94]

So, in this final section of this chapter, I have endeavoured to show that there was some recognition of the universal aspects of beauty, while I have mainly concentrated on the persistence of traditional constraints, however phrased, upon the appreciation of 'mere' or 'external' beauty. One particularly strong convention was that of women being the beautiful sex. This, ironically, is forcefully brought out by a pioneering feminist tract published in 1751, *Beauty's Triumph or the Superiority of the Fair Sex invincibly proved*. The point is really made in the main part of the title just quoted; but to clinch it, the title continues by undertaking among other things to show that women's minds 'be as much more beautiful than the Men's as their Bodies'. The continuance of that sentence, finally, reveals that even to radicals, beauty and virtue in women are closely related: 'and that, if they had the Same Advantages of Education, they would excel their Tyrants as much in Sense as they do in Virtue'.[95]

# 4 Personal Appearance and Life Experiences, *c.* 1600–*c.* 1800

## 1 *Beauty's Potential*

Henry IV, King of France, was assassinated in 1610; his murderer was tortured with molten lead, boiling oil, and finally torn apart by four horses. There followed the first of the three regencies which were to punctuate French history during the next 180 years, open incitement to rebellion in a country divided by religion and not yet a consolidated nation state. In England, civil war broke out in 1642 and the King, Charles I, was beheaded in 1649. By this time the bitter internecine strife, known as the Fronde, had broken out in France. By 1653 it had faded away, one of its more popular leaders suffering the fate of many common criminals in being broken on the wheel. Brutality, insecurity, famine and plague continued to afflict vast numbers in both countries, but under Louis XIV (ruling in his own right from 1654 and passing into his dotage in the first decade of the new century) France established cultural ascendancy over the whole of Europe. England's restored monarch, after 1660, was in many respects a client of the French 'Sun King'. Political and social stability, menaced at times by the Jacobite threat, but accompanied by steady economic growth, came to Britain (the Scottish and English parliaments had been united in 1707) only after the installation of the Hanoverian dynasty in 1714. France, under yet another regency, then under Louis XV (1723–74), retained its eminence in arts and letters, though the British contribution to the philosophical and historical writing of the Enlightenment was far from negligible. However, a series of wars drove home the point that Britain, governed by its great landed families, and a few commercial ones, was, in political and economic power, eclipsing the France of absolute monarchy and stiff-necked nobility.

We have noted the recognition, and the distrust, of the power of beauty in these centuries. What actual significance could personal appearance have when monarchs and great lords ruled by inheritance and ordinary life was pervaded by violence and insecurity? For monarchs of both sexes marital choices were strictly limited by reasons of state; but a powerful or popular monarch, particularly if in matrimony he (or she) had served the strategic and diplomatic interests of the nation, was in a strong position to defy routine incantations against lust. For a good-looking young woman, to be mistress of Louis XIV was a legitimate aspiration; however, to be openly acknowledged, a woman had to be of noble birth, and, anyway, a king might choose his mistresses for other qualities than physical beauty, might he not? By the late seventeenth century both Paris and London were substantial cities, utterly different in scale and character from any other town in either country. Here were growing new service trades, shops in particular where – who knows? – a fine figure and agreeable countenance might be considered assets by a prospective employer. With regard to service in a more basic sense, might not a good-looking personal secretary, or an array of handsome footmen, be valuable symbols of status? The theatre was now firmly established in both countries, with doubts as to whether it was proper for women to perform on the stage finally allayed; would not looks be an obvious advantage, even a prerequisite here?

Paris was a centre of intellectual and cultural exchange after a style to which London could scarcely lay claim. At the heart of Parisian intellectual life were the foregatherings in certain private houses of the leading scholars and wits of the time, presided over by hostesses whose names today are as well remembered as those of many wits and most scholars. What did it take to establish a salon, become a *salonière*? – beauty, wit, intellect, managerial skills? Were *salonières* simply courtesans? What power, if any, did a famous courtesan possess? As contemporaries observed, there was, for women, a descending scale of callings involving the granting of sexual favours, running from courtesan in the original sense of 'lady of the court' right down to the common street prostitute. What part did personal appearance play in all this? In what ways, if any, were good looks an advantage?

## 2 *Kings, Queens and Favourites*

As Jacqueline Boucher has pointed out, the physical appearance of a monarch undoubtedly was a matter of note, and a good presence, if not necessarily good looks, was an asset. Dr Boucher quotes a Venetian report of 1546 on Francis I of France: 'His appearance is completely royal, so that, without ever having seen his face or his portrait, on seeing him one would say instantly: it's the King. All of his movements are so noble and so majestic that no prince could equal him.' [1] However, given that, even in the times of greatest upheaval, some claim to royal blood was an essential qualification, it cannot be claimed that looks played much part in the winning of thrones. Louis XIV was a striking figure, Charles II even more so. Louis XV, known as *le bien-aimé* (or 'the well beloved') was undoubtedly very handsome, which seems to have contributed to the popularity he enjoyed in the first part of his reign, although perhaps also to the indolence which, together with his general lack of decisiveness and moral fibre, rendered his reign a most unfortunate one for his country. William of Orange was ill formed and quite unprepossessing, a word which can accurately be applied also to the Hanoverians.

But, already by the end of the sixteenth century, the role of the influential royal mistress was firmly established. As far as one can tell from the inadequate evidence, Diane of Poitiers, mistress of Francis II, was not very beautiful, though she was celebrated for the youthful appearance she preserved into old age.[2] Though constrained by the mincing conventions of the School of Fontainebleau, the portrait in the Louvre of Gabrielle d'Estrées (mistress of Henry IV) with one of her sisters, bosoms fully exposed, clearly does suggest a woman of great physical attractiveness, an impression more than confirmed by a contemporary drawing (in the Bibliothèque Nationale) of her as she looked in 1592 when she was around nineteen. The titillating boldness of the Louvre portrait hints at much, but not all, of Gabrielle's story, which was one of the brutality and enticements of royal power as well as of a beautiful woman exploiting her charms to the full.[3] Henry of Navarre, in

10

11

10 *Gabrielle d'Estrées and her sister in the bath*, School of Fontainebleau, *c.* 1590. Gabrielle is on the right

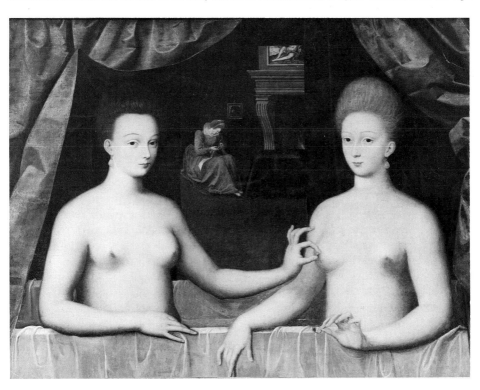

11 *Gabrielle d'Estrées,*
drawing, Anon., *c.* 1592

face of two other powerful factions, established himself as Henry IV of
France in 1589. A brave and highly competent soldier, he was a man of
phenomenal energy who devoted himself to consolidating his kingdom,
travelling its length and breadth waging battle and siege, and to hunting,
gambling and wenching. He wrote romantic, passionate letters; often the
same letter to several women simultaneously. He was thirty-seven when
he met, and fell in love with, Gabrielle, who was then engaged to the
handsome and youthful Roger de Bellegarde; she did not immediately
take to Henry, who was faun-like in appearance, worn by illnesses
largely brought on by his various excesses, though, as an English
observer reported of him over ten years later, 'his colour [was] fresh and
youthful, his nature stirring and full of life, like a true French man';[4] even
for these unhygienic times his bodily stench was noteworthy. The king
put pressure on Bellegarde; the d'Estrées family put pressure on Gabrielle;
she herself understood well enough the privileges and perquisites of
being chief royal mistress – and indeed she was soon hugely enjoying, as
Professor Buisseret neatly puts it, playing 'the dizzy blonde' at Henry's
court.[5] She was created Duchess of Beaufort and exercised much
influence over royal policy; her family gained all the preferment they had
schemed for. She gave Henry two sons and a daughter, and, without
doubt, he personally hoped to marry her; but such a marriage would
have thrown wide open again the whole question of the succession to the

throne. It was a hazardous life in any case, and Gabrielle, not yet thirty, died of convulsions after giving birth to a fourth, stillborn child.

Royal marriages were made in a different way. Henry was already heavily in debt to the Medici family, 'the bankers of Europe',[6] so marriage to the Princess Maria de' Medici, daughter of the Grand Duke of Tuscany, seemed an eminently rational proposition. Neither prospective spouse had met the other, but the dowry was huge, and a secure and respectable succession seemed a near certainty; so a marriage by proxy took place in Florence. Yet when Maria did finally arrive in France, Henry was (for the moment) genuinely delighted with his twenty-seven-year-old virgin bride. The British diplomat Winwood put all his professional skill into his description of her: 'She is of comely stature, and for her beauty, the commendation which she seemeth most to affect (for she doth use no Artifice) is *forma uscovici*'[7] – she was well shaped to be a wife and mother, or, in other words, as portraits demonstrate, she was fat and plain. Virtue, status and wealth were prized qualities in a queen; Henry was soon disporting himself with his rather more attractive mistresses. Still, the great cycle of paintings of the life of Marie de' Médicis (as she had now become) by Rubens, also in the Louvre, show that, however plain, a woman born the right pawn in the dynastic game would never want for flattery. Marie survived her husband and remained a central political figure in strife-torn France, reigning as regent from

12 *Mme de Montespan*, Pierre Mignard, *c.* 1670s

1610 to 1614. In the seventeenth century, royalty counted for more than beauty.

Louis XIV also did his dynastic duty, marrying the daughter of Philip IV, King of Spain, Maria Teresa, who was short, fat and ugly. Her status as daughter of the King of Spain had made Maria Teresa Queen of France, but there was no possibility of her holding the King's attention. The *maîtresse déclarée* (or *maîtresse en titre*) for most of the 1660s was a shy, reticent girl of, by court standards, low social status (she was from the minor nobility and had suffered the double blow, not so much that first her father, then her father-in-law, had died, but that before doing so each had amassed substantial debts), Louise de la Vallière, who had come to the court as a maid of honour to the King's sister-in-law, Henrietta of England. By the second half of the decade, as contemporaries remarked, Louise de la Vallière was being strongly challenged for the King's favour by a woman four years older than herself, Madame Françoise de Montespan.[8] By birth Madame de Montespan was a Mortemart, one of the oldest families of France. By the end of the decade she had supplanted Louise. The two best-known portraits of Madame de Montespan are by mediocre artists (one literally unknown, the other, Henri Gascar, so nearly unknown as makes no difference), which may explain the bland, sexless, sub-Venus de Milo appearance in both. The portrait by the highly competent Mignard shows a very striking and sensual woman. Two well-known renderings of Mlle de la Vallière, both enamels by Jean Petitot, suffer from the medium and also, again, from being in the Grecian mode. But for their sense of vivacity and freshness, they beat the mediocre Montespan portraits hands down.[9] The truly lovely portrait of Louise, the Jean Nocret in the Museum of Versailles, renders her by about the same margin more beautiful than the Mignard Montespan.

But is this satisfactory evidence as to the relative beauty of the two women? The written testimony is far from conclusive, though, on balance, it favours Madame de Montespan. What is clear is that the latter was lively, witty and strong willed in a way Mlle de la Vallière was not; also that she made a quite determined and calculated bid to oust Louise and become chief mistress. The Prince de Condé said of Mme de Montespan in November 1666 that 'no one could have more spirit or more beauty';[10] an Italian gentleman at court, Primi Visconti, lyricized over her 'blonde hair, large azure blue eyes, well-formed aquiline nose, vermilion mouth, beautiful teeth', making, 'in a word, a perfect face'.[11] Was it perhaps the notability of the Mortemarts that was being admired, or did Mme de Montespan more closely fit the courtly convention of the time? (This was a time, I have noted, when conventions in beauty were of considerable importance, though that doesn't mean everyone was taken in by them.) There were many comments on the fresh beauty of Mlle de la Vallière,[12] but the famous one by the Abbé de Choisy hits off the impression that Louise stood outside the pale of courtly convention:

13 *Louise de la Vallière*, Jean Nocret, *c.* 1660s

she is not, he says, 'one of those perfect beauties that one often admires without loving'[13] (a delicate way, I surmise, of referring to someone who fulfils the arithmetic but has no real sex appeal). The boring magistrate Olivier Lefèvre d'Ormesson, keeper of a massive journal, found Louise 'not at all beautiful', but skinny (she was certainly thin), with a long face and nose too wide at the bottom[14] (this actually agrees with the fetching Nocret portrait). But d'Ormesson, who had been scorned by the King, was a supporter of the Queen. He later refers to Mme de Montespan's power, but not at all to her looks[15] (because he disliked her too? Or because they were not so remarkable – I don't know).

My opinion is that Louis, with so much choice on easy offer, could see beyond the conventions which bound sycophantic observers and appreciate a more unusual (and more truly sexual) beauty. What he also appreciated, I must stress (since I want to bring out the balance between beauty and other qualities in affecting a person's life chances), was the fact that Louise was a magnificent horsewoman; she was, in fact, something of a tomboy (a characteristic at odds with the seventeenth-century courtly image of womanhood), and, from a childhood accident, resulting from a dangerous jumping game practised with her brother, she always had the very faintest suspicion of a limp.[16] For many months after Françoise, who, in the fashion of *les précieuses* of the day, had adopted the name of Athénaïs, had openly launched her campaign Louis remained devoted to Louise and utterly indifferent to Mme de Montespan.[17] But in the end her spirit, wit, determination and confidence won out over Louise, who twice retired to a convent, being, the first time, deliberately brought back and openly cherished by Louis, who created her duchess and recognized their daughter, Marie-Anne. Determination and personality, aided probably by status and convention, at last prevailed; Louise now retired finally to a life of piety. Eventually at fifty-two Louis fell for Marie Angélique de Fontanges, an eighteen-year-old maid of honour to Henrietta. Every piece of evidence shows that she was outstandingly beautiful, though apparently rather stupid.[18] As soon as she became pregnant Louis made her a duchess, but the child was stillborn and she herself never recovered. There were always hazards attached to careers based on the granting of sexual favours.

But of all the women associated with Louis XIV, the one best known to history is Madame de Maintenon. In the 1650s and 1660s this lady, known as Madame Scarron, had moved in intellectual and even libertarian circles; well known for her strict virtue, she was even then, as a Mignard portrait suggests, no more than personable. A comment of Barillon de Montangis is perhaps more revealing of a particular attitude towards the link between beauty, poverty and temptation than a factual statement about her appearance: 'I have known the lady since the time when she was Madame Scarron and her very glance inspired respect. One was constantly amazed that such beauty, charm and poverty could be combined with virtue.'[19] Madame Scarron first attracted the attention and gratitude of the King by assuming responsibility for the children he had by Madame de Montespan; she in fact proved an excellent surrogate mother, and the King gave her the estate of Maintenon, so that she became the Marquise de Maintenon. As her niece observed, Mme de Maintenon was welcomed by the Queen: unlike the three women first discussed, she posed no threat.[20] In middle age, as the country was shaken by a series of poison scandals, the King turned towards a kind of evangelical religiosity, reinforced by the death of the Queen in July 1683. The prim and deeply religious Madame de Maintenon, three years older

than Louis, matched his mood exactly. She had been establishing a
stronger and stronger hold over him, and at some stage, possibly even as
early as 1683, they were secretly married. As is well known, the whole
tone of the latter years of Louis' reign was pervaded by the puritanism of
Madame de Maintenon. It can scarcely be argued that looks played any
great part in her triumph.

However, if we look back across the Channel to the court of Charles II
matters are more straightforward; in that environment beauty certainly
brought rewards. Charles's first mistress after the Restoration was

14 *Barbara Villiers*, Sir Peter Lely, *c.* 1663

Barbara Villiers, Mrs Palmer. Charles created Palmer Earl of Castlemaine so that Barbara could have the rank of Lady Castlemaine. Financially she did well out of Charles (or, more accurately, the public purse), and she was able to ensure a secure future for her children. She was undoubtedly a woman of strong personality and great spirit, not only greatly influencing Charles, but taking a number of other lovers even while she was his mistress. But the foundation of her career was the astonishing Villiers good looks (an earlier, male, Villiers will be discussed shortly). Lely painted her many times; the portrait reproduced as Ill. 14 is known to have been done before 1664,[21] when the artist was still giving careful individual attention to his most important clients. Contemporaries spoke of her as 'the finest woman of her age', or 'by far the handsomest of all King Charles's mistresses, and, taking her person everyway, perhaps the finest woman in England in her time'.[22] The success in life of a Barbara Villiers depended upon her power, through physical appearance, to fascinate powerful men, including the King of England.

4

The wider meaning of such power can be seen in the reactions of Samuel Pepys, civil servant and celebrated diarist. Pepys, who had sailed to France in connection with the arrangements for the Restoration, a cultured man, inquisitive about the many facets of human experience, travelling about in Westminster and London and sometimes to Cambridge, was a good representative of *l'homme moyen sensuel* (he can be contrasted with his friend and fellow diarist, John Evelyn, who was gloomy and puritanical in outlook). In Whitehall, seeing Lady Castlemaine, he 'glutted' himself 'with looking on her', the 'only she', as he put it on another occasion, 'I can observe for true beauty'. Several years later he confesses to the best dream he ever had when with Barbara in his bed he 'was admitted to use all the dalliance I desired with her'. Most significant of all is the reflection, after seeing her at the theatre, that though he knows 'well enough she is a whore' – and it must be stressed that he did recognize this; beauty was not here being confused with morality or truth – because of her beauty he is ready to think the best of her and even to pity her.[23] There was no possibility, of course, of Lady Castlemaine becoming Queen of England. In accordance with the dynastic imperatives we have already noted, in 1662 Charles married Catherine of Braganza, once more, as portraits do not conceal (one suspects the artists of not trying very hard), a dumpy and unattractive woman. Despite the installation of the new Queen, Barbara Villiers was made a lady of the bedchamber and exercised influence over ministerial appointments in a way that the Queen simply did not.[24]

Other beautiful women at the court served as mistresses to the King and were not unrewarded but, by force of both beauty and character, Lady Castlemaine retained her pre-eminence. It was possible, it must be insisted, to refuse the King; and it must be added that while clearly the

15 *Portrait of Charles II*, studio of John Michael Wright, *c.* 1660–65

crown itself provided the seductive magic, one element in Charles's
successes with women was his own striking physical appearance, as well
perhaps as his general good humour and graciousness. While Louis XIV
was short, Charles was six feet two inches tall, a very considerable height
for that age. His swarthy, sexual looks are familiar from portraits;          15
Madame de Motteville's description of him as a young man matches the
portraits and hits off that sort of male appearance which, while definitely
not beautiful, certainly has impact: 'well-made, with a swarthy complexion agreeing well with his fine black eyes, a large ugly mouth, graceful
and dignified carriage, and a fine figure'.[25] Upon the arrival at court of
the young Frances Stuart, Charles became infatuated with her; she was

described by Pepys as 'the greatest beauty I ever saw I think in my life', at first giving her precedence over Lady Castlemaine, but then (in keeping, I would say, with the visual evidence) reversing that judgment.[26] She did not succumb to the King and eventually eloped with her cousin, the Duke of Richmond.

The early career of Nell Gwyn tells us much about the relationship between looks and social mobility outside the exceptional and limited ambit of royalty, and will be taken up shortly in my discussion of ' "Show-biz", Selling, Service and Sex'. However, let me start off by admitting that there is no certainty as to what Nell Gwyn really looked

16 *'Nell Gwyn'*, studio of Sir Peter Lely, *c.* 1675. There are reasons for doubting whether this really is Nell Gwyn

like. There was a time when curators of art galleries happily paraded any number of 'Nell Gwyns'; now the poor historian risks being crushed to death in the stampede to deny that *any* portrait could possibly be of that particular seventeenth-century person. The trouble is that over the centuries the habit developed of indiscriminately pinning the name 'Nell Gwyn' on any and every female portrait dating from the later seventeenth century. A further problem arises from the procedures followed in the studio of Peter Lely. Already by 1661, when this Dutch-born artist was appointed Court Painter to Charles II, Lely had developed a technique of over-emphasizing the lower part of the eyelid which, when sensitively done, gave his sitters a slumberingly sensuous look. But soon 'Lely' portraits, often in several copies, were being manufactured at great speed by his many assistants. The well-known and much-reproduced portrait sold as a postcard and slide by the National Portrait Gallery, London, dates from the mid-1670s when the eyelid trick had become an ugly mannerism producing protuberant eyeballs; the short curls and shepherdess style (the lamb on the right is the giveaway) were stereotypes employed on dozens of other sitters. R. B. Beckett has questioned whether the portrait is actually of Nell at all[27] – certainly it has to be doubted whether this not overly appealing representation can be taken as a good likeness.

16

Nell, the humble tart who consorted with royalty, has not been well served by the British establishment. To the unprepossessing image purveyed by the National Portrait Gallery must be added the insult offered by the Dictionary of National Biography:

She appears to have been low in stature and plump, to have had hair of reddish brown. Her foot was diminutive, and her eyes when she laughed became all but invisible.

The source for this is the highly dubious *Memoirs of the Life of Eleanor Gwinn* published in the middle of the eighteenth century.[28] In any case the jibe about the smallness of her eyes is, of course, utterly inconsistent with the over-prominence given to them in the National Portrait Gallery 'Lely', and the total impression is much at odds with Samuel Pepys's repeated emphasis on her 'prettiness', Madame D'Aulnoy's admiration of her figure, and the fact that on stage she could successfully represent herself as a male gallant. Because there is so much emphasis on her wit, her vivacity and her gaiety, it may be wise to conclude that she was highly personable rather than ravishingly beautiful, but near enough to beauty for her appearance indeed to have been a crucial asset. In the straightforward engraving by Henri Gascar, Nell is, of course, no longer in first youth. It is known that James, Duke of York, possessed a portrait of Nell as a reclining nude (which he kept behind a sliding panel) but it cannot now be established that the *Venus Reclining with Cupid* by Lely is this portrait, which, such is the labyrinth we have entered, has variously

17

18

17 *Nell Gwyn and her two sons,* engraving, Henri Gascar, mid-1670s

18 *Portrait of Nell Gwyn and the Infant Duke of St Albans* (sometimes also catalogued as *Venus Reclining with Cupid* since there are gaps in the history of the provenance of this painting), Sir Peter Lely, 1671

been sold as 'Nell Gwyn' and as 'Barbara Villiers'.[29] Personally, I am inclined to follow Beckett in seeing this as a likely Nell Gywn; after all, even if links in the chain are missing, we do know that such a painting of her *was* painted. If this luscious nude genuinely is Nell, then it establishes a case that she really was beautiful, rather than merely highly personable.

By 1667 Nell Gwyn was an established comic actress and had become briefly the mistress of Lord Buckhurst. Charles already had on his team of lady friends an actress from the Duke's Theatre, Moll Davis; late in 1667 he recruited Nell. Both actresses, in their different ways, were good-looking (or certainly personable) women, but Nell Gwyn clearly had other qualities which enabled her to remain a favourite of the King's till his death in 1685. In dedicating her play *The Feign'd Curtizans* to Nell, the female dramatist Aphra Behn wrote:

Besides all the charms, and attractions, and powers of your sex, you have beauties peculiar to yourself – an eternal sweetness, youth, and air which never dwelt in face but yours. You never appear but you gladden the hearts of all that have the fortune to see you, as if you were made on purpose to put the world into good humour.[30]

Marie Catherine, Baronne D'Aulnoy, was a sharp and not over-romantic observer of the English court, her memoirs being published within ten years of Charles's death. Of Nell Gwyn she commented: 'There are few people who do not know that she was an actress whom the King loved more for her wit than the attractions of her person; not but what she had a very pretty figure, and her spirits were such that it was difficult to remain long in her company without sharing her gaiety.' Madame D'Aulnoy gives a fine description of Nell taking over proceedings at a court ball and moving everyone out onto the lawns while the faint-hearted slipped away.[31]

Nell Gwyn played an important part in the life of Charles II, but as a former actress, of still humbler origins, she could not be *maîtresse en titre*. That role, as Charles tired of Lady Castlemaine (though she continued to enjoy public benefits, receiving a title as Duchess of Cleveland in 1670), was to go to Louise de Kéroualle, twenty-one-year-old daughter of an ancient and venerable Breton family and maid of honour (yet another one!) to Charles's sister, Henrietta, Duchess of Orleans. Charles had met her previously in France, and now, with the death of the Duchess of Orleans in 1670, she was sent to England as maid of honour to Queen Catherine. Louise had a baby face and haughty aristocratic manners. It took Charles a year to seduce her. According to Brian Masters, 'Louise's one overwhelming advantage was her beauty';[32] in itself, this was true, but it seems that she was also able to provide the style and comforts Charles desired in a principal mistress or, in effect, alternative Queen. Of course, in attempting to make these assessments of qualities other than physical beauty we are never dealing with constants: Charles now was

19

19 *Louise de Kéroualle, Duchess of Portsmouth,* engraving after Sir Peter Lely, *c.* 1680s

older, though by no means in the sort of condition that turned Louis XIV towards Madame de Maintenon. The shared feature in all of the women who found favour with Charles II was undoubted physical beauty.

Louise's son by Charles was legitimized as Charles Fitzroy, Duke of Richmond, and she herself in 1673 became Duchess of Portsmouth. Briefly her position was shaken by the arrival of a woman who, even more than Barbara Villiers, had used her personal beauty to lead a life as liberated as was possible for any woman in that age. Hortense Mancini was the niece of the great French statesman Mazarin. Sensitive perhaps to the dangerous emotions her great beauty aroused, he married her to the Marquis de la Meilleraye, making over to him a substantial fortune and the title of Duc de Mazarin. Unfortunately the newly created duke was quite mad, a sad punishment, though an appropriate one, some no doubt thought, for great beauty. Hortense escaped and boldly travelled all over Europe, skilfully exploiting the devastating effect she had on men. Her first great love was the Duke of Savoy, with whom she spent three years. The second was Charles (she arrived in England in 1675), fascinated by her personal appearance and intrigued by what a hostile contemporary described as her 'experienced and well travelled Lust'.[33] But this affair was in full flood for only three months, after which Hortense simply joined the team with a suitable pension till the end of her days, while the Duchess of Portsmouth was restored as principal mistress, her main rival thereafter the popular Nell Gwyn. Mobbed in Oxford by a crowd who mistook her for the hated Catholic royal mistress, Nell put her head out of the coach window, saying: 'Pray, good people, be civil; I am the Protestant whore.'[34]

Charles II had secretly converted to Rome; he was succeeded by his brother James II, who was completely open, and indeed, from the point of view of his subjects, over-enthusiastic in his Catholicism. It was actually Charles's witticism that James's mistresses were all ugly and must have been prescribed for him as a penance by his confessors. The legend was perpetuated by the great Protestant families (the Whigs), who resented both his religion and his rejection of their attempts to assert their influence through parliament, and who finally ensured his overthrow in favour of William of Orange and Mary. Catherine Sedley is usually said to have been rather plain, with a long nose, a big mouth, a cast in her eye and a scrawny figure. She does not look at all unattractive in the portrait from the Lely factory but, of course, in face of the written evidence one cannot go on this alone. What this written evidence tells us is that she was a woman of immense wit, high spirits and vigorous unconvention- ality.[35] One can presume that it was these qualities of personality, together with an at least presentable appearance, which endeared her to James. Certainly there was nothing wayward in his taste, and his two other principal mistresses, Susan Lady Belasyse and Elizabeth, Countess of Chesterfield, both matched in beauty any of the mistresses of the new King's late elder brother. It remains to be remarked that William, the dedicated upholder of the Protestant cause, had nothing in the way of looks to commend him. Both Mary his wife, and Anne her successor, were attractive when young, but Anne very rapidly deteriorated.

The women we have been discussing seem to have done well from their beauty. The more highborn of Charles's mistresses were raised in status and were able to provide security for their offspring. Nell actually did rather well also, Charles supporting her in her great extravagances, and creating their first son Duke of St Albans; his deathbed request, 'Let not poor Nelly starve', was more than faithfully discharged by his brother James II, who settled much money and a fine house, Bestwood Park, Nottingham, on her. Charles's very first mistress, however, Lucy Walter, came nearer to fulfilling that part of popular lore which charges that beauty can only bring unhappiness (she certainly demonstrated one truism: better an ugly old king than a handsome young claimant). She had given birth to the son, James (later Duke of Monmouth), who was one of Charles's own favourites, but she herself lost all contact with him and died a miserable death in 1658 at the age of around twenty-eight.

This draws our attention to an important point, one of the keys to this long chapter. One cannot predict that a person born beautiful will automatically enjoy happiness and success. What one can predict is that their lives are likely to be different from those led by the less comely. For good or ill they will draw attention to themselves; they will have, or will seem to have, opportunities not open to others: whether these opportu- nities are real or not, what is made of them will depend on other personal qualities, and on circumstance. Beauty, as the title of the chapter indicates,

affects life *experiences* rather than necessarily life *chances*. This is brought out rather sharply by the careers of certain male beauties of the period.

Let us go back to the reign of James I, and to 1614 when James, then forty-seven, met George Villiers, then aged twenty-two. Villiers was an extraordinarily handsome and highly sexed young man, quite ready to exploit James's rampant homosexuality. Villiers's physical presence gave him power over women and also heterosexual men; but now, of course, it was the King's favour which counted most. Villiers established himself at the centre of a web of patronage which brought good profits to himself. In 1616 he was appointed Master of the Horse, dubbed a Knight of the Garter and created Viscount Villiers. The following year James conferred on him an earldom, giving this charming explanation to the Lords of the Counsel:

I, James, am neither God nor an angel, but a man like any other. Therefore I act like a man, and confess to loving those dear to me more than other men. You may be sure that I love the Earl of Buckingham more than anyone else, and more than you who are here assembled. I wish to speak in my own behalf, and not to have it thought to be a defect, for Jesus Christ did the same, and therefore I cannot be blamed. Christ had his John, and I have my George.[36]

Buckingham shortly became a marquis and then, eventually, a duke, receiving the only dukedom granted outside the blood royal between 1485 and 1660. Buckingham meantime captivated the entirely hetero-sexual heir to the throne, Charles (later Charles I). As well as charm, Buckingham had much skill and cunning, but in devising the scheme

20 (left) *Portrait of George Villiers, Duke of Buckingham, with his family*, after Gerard Honthorst, 1628

21 (right) *Portrait of Henri D'Effiat, Marquis de Cinq–Mars*, Anon., 1640

whereby he and Charles went to Spain in search of a Spanish consort for Charles he showed how far arrogant self-confidence could outrun political judgment. The scheme was a humiliating fiasco; none the less, even after the accession of Charles I in 1625 Buckingham remained the single greatest influence in the kingdom. But for arrogant beauty, Nemesis was at hand: to wide rejoicing, Buckingham was assassinated in 1628.

Something very close to an action replay took place a decade later in France, though on a perhaps more heroic scale. Under the regency of Marie de' Médicis and, more critically, in the early years of the reign of Louis XIII, the man who steadily concentrated power in his own hands was Richelieu. A bishop, and later cardinal, in the Roman Catholic church, Richelieu imposed no unreasonable constraints upon his sexual instincts, which were entirely heterosexual. None the less, and there is nothing odd about this, he warmed to the delicately featured Henri D'Effiat, created the Marquis de Cinq-Mars. As part of his campaign to dominate the sickly Louis XIII Richelieu pushed Cinq-Mars forward as a court favourite and Louis was completely captivated by this young man whose real talents, in fact, lay in the direction of seducing women: Marion de Lorne, reputed Paris's most beautiful courtesan at the time (see p.129), was madly in love with him, arousing the King to deepest jealousy, and Cinq-Mars's mother to bringing accusations of rape and seduction against Marion.[37] Like Buckingham before him, Cinq-Mars came to feel himself all-conquering and invulnerable. In 1641 he joined in a conspiracy involving the Spanish government to assassinate his former

21

patron, Richelieu, and take over power in Paris. Cinq-Mars and his cronies were no match for the Cardinal's espionage system, which practically lived up to its legendary reputation. Nemesis once again had overtaken overweening male beauty: Cinq-Mars was executed.

Three dead swallows do not make a winter; still, let us look at the third in the gorgeous, tragic trio. The early pages of Madame D'Aulnoy's memoirs of the English court are dominated by Charles's illegitimate son by Lucy Walter, James, Duke of Monmouth. As portraits show, he had inherited the beauty of his mother; Madame D'Aulnoy wrote:

> One could not have known the Duke of Monmouth without singing his praises. Of all men in the world he was one of the most perfectly made: he bore on his face a character of grandeur corresponding to that of his birth; he was brave to the point of intrepidity; and when he served in France and other foreign countries, it was agreed that he could not have been surpassed in valour: the care lavished on his education already found in him a subject who had received the most favourable gifts from nature. He danced so wonderfully that one could cease neither to watch him nor to admire him. There has never been a more gallant man, and his heart was always divided between love and glory.[38]

Monmouth, as Madame D'Aulnoy admiringly tells us, had many mistresses; but men also admired his beauty. His friend Lord Bruce called him 'most charming both as to his person and engaging behaviour'; 'of charming countenance', said another courtier;[39] 'none so beautiful, so brave, as Absalom' (i.e. Monmouth), wrote the poet Dryden.[40] Monmouth lived the seventeenth-century equivalent of the life of a public-school rowdy (on one occasion he callously ran through with his sword a watchman come to halt a brothel brawl), interspersed with hectic periods of soldiering. Yet he had the magic gift of gaining the sympathy and support of his social inferiors, a gift greatly aided by personal beauty but not created by it alone. He won a striking victory over rebelling Scottish Covenanters in 1679, and then good repute for the clemency he showed to the defeated. Monmouth was uncompromisingly Protestant, an important consideration for all those who feared the accession of the openly Catholic James.

Charles II died unexpectedly in February 1685, to be succeeded unopposed by James. Monmouth resigned himself to what seemed likely to be a long exile in Brussels. Yet within months (on 11 June to be precise) Monmouth had landed at Lyme Regis on the Dorset coast to head a rebellion against James. Though he rallied considerable support in the West Country, he was soon defeated and, on 11 July, beheaded on Tower Hill as a traitor. To get these events, and the place of Monmouth's looks in them, into perspective, we have to go back to 1680 when the Earl of Shaftesbury, seeing the possibility of making Monmouth the puppet of the Whig grandees who wished to exclude James from the throne, deliberately organized for him an almost royal 'progress' through the West Country; looks *were* important here (as Shaftesbury undoubtedly realized): Monmouth could only gain in popularity through being shown off. Shaftesbury died in 1681, but Whig conspirators both in London and in exile continued to work on Monmouth; so much success had come to him so easily that he was readily persuaded, which is not to say that genuine political and religious conviction (as well as personal ambition) was not also involved. Monmouth was perfectly qualified to raise a movement of the poor to middling interests in the West, but lacked both the organizational skills and the bold decisiveness (he fumbled any chance of seizing Bristol) to lead them to victory.[41] Had he done so, he would, of course, be one of the heroes of British history. I am not, therefore, attributing his failure and sad end to his beauty; I am saying that it was an important factor in the actual course his life took. Consider: had Lucy Walter's son been born ugly, would there have been a Monmouth's Rebellion?

It is a relief to turn to a man whose start in life, on which he founded his future great success, was almost certainly due to his physical beauty. John Churchill's career began in service to James, while he was still Duke of York. At twenty-one John Churchill, with his slim elegant figure, brilliant grey-green eyes, long eyelashes and long fair hair, almost merits the adjective 'pretty', save that the word is too weak for the powerful impact he undoubtedly had on those around him. It was at this age that he was taken up by Barbara Villiers, now twenty-nine and Duchess of Cleveland. Although Charles himself acknowledged her daughter Barbara, born in 1672, the father was almost certainly Churchill.[42] The proposition that John Churchill owed the financial security, upon which

23

22 *James, Duke of Monmouth*, after William Wissing, *c.* 1683

23 *John Churchill, Duke of Marlborough*, attributed to John Closterman after John Riley, *c.* 1685–90

he built his subsequent glorious career, to the loving generosity of Barbara Villiers is based on the testimony of the fourth Earl of Chesterfield, writing to his son in 1748, but seems plausible (the receipt for the annuity certainly exists, and there would not appear to be any other possible source for the purchasing price than Barbara Villiers, known to have been very generous towards those with whom she was enamoured). While the Dutchman Van Goslinger said that 'except for his legs which were thin', Churchill was 'one of the handsomest men ever seen',[43] Chesterfield, largely from spitefulness, had more to criticize than Churchill's legs, but his recognition of the physical 'graces' carries conviction:

Of all the men that ever I knew in my life (and I knew him extremely well), the late Duke of Marlborough possessed the graces in the highest degree, not to say engrossed them; and indeed, he got the most by them, for I will venture (contrary to the custom of profound historians, who always assign deep causes for great events) to ascribe the better half of the Duke of Marlborough's greatness and riches to those Graces. He was eminently illiterate; wrote bad English, and spelled it still worse. He had no share of what is commonly called *parts*; that is, he had no brightness, nothing shining in his genius. He had, most undoubtedly, an excellent good plain understanding, with sound judgment. But these alone would probably have raised him but something higher than they found him which was page to King James the Second's Queen. There the Graces protested and promoted him; for, while he was an Ensign of the Guards, the Duchess of Cleveland, then favourite mistress to King Charles the Second, struck by those very graces, gave five thousand pounds, with which he immediately bought an annuity for his life, of five hundred pounds a year, of my grandfather, Halifax, which was the foundation of his subsequent fortune. His figure was beautiful, but his manner was irresistible, by either man or woman . . . he could refuse more graciously than other people could grant; and those who went away from him the most dissatisfied as to the substance of their business, were yet personably charmed with him, and, in some degree, comforted by his manner.[44]

Marlborough the great general and national hero obviously called on a vast number of other qualities than those of mere personal appearance. The only point being suggested here is that Marlborough's beauty brought him the financial security upon which he was able to build his political and military career, and that that security might well not have come in any other way. Indeed it seems possible at this stage to venture the generalization, perhaps an obvious one, that beauty has its most critical effects in the early stages of a career, other qualities then becoming increasingly important; but between getting a start and not getting a start there can sometimes be the whole difference.

Marlborough's victories laid the basis for the gathering ascendancy of Britain over France, though a series of eighteenth-century wars and desperate colonial struggles had still to be fought. These fell within the period of the Hanoverian monarchs. None of the first three Georges had any claim to good looks, and the fact that neither their wives nor their mistresses were physically very appealing either raises some interesting thoughts:[45] George II's Queen, Caroline of Anspach, was the best of the bunch, pleasant looking, but no beauty; his mistresses, at least the ones who lasted any length of time, scarcely came up to this standard, the two main ones being rather plain; George I's two mistresses after he came to the throne at the age of fifty-four were quite definitely plain; George III's wife, Charlotte of Mecklenburg-Strelitz, was so manifestly ugly that the King's bouts of madness, Professor Sir John Plumb has suggested, may have been due to the strain of having sexual relations with her.[46]

Is the key to the contrast between the record (in bringing beauties to court and to bed) of Charles II (and indeed James II) and that of the first three Georges to be found in the considerable physical appeal of the former as compared with the latter or, perhaps, in the discriminating tastes of the former as against the latter? There is probably something in both points. The Georges tended to be creatures of habit, preferring what was conveniently accessible to making the effort that Charles sometimes expended on his conquests. But, above all, and it is here that we have a close fit with what was suggested in the previous chapter, the Georges looked for suitability in their women – they had to be of proper social status; and the Georges were not attracted by the exciting or the strong willed. Perhaps the point can be most economically made by reference to the way in which, on the insistence of his close personal adviser, the very handsome Lord Bute, George III, while still a Prince, meekly abandoned his infatuation for the beautiful fifteen-year-old daughter of the Duke of Richmond. There was, thus, a very sharp contrast between the court of the Hanoverians and the court of Louis XV in France. But there was also a contrast between the tastes and behaviour of the dull and dowdy Georges and that of some of the leading English aristocrats whose influence on public affairs had no analogue in absolutist France. We will leave the English peerage till the next section, and turn now to the court of Louis XV.

Perhaps we should start off with the observation that Louis XV, Louis the well beloved, was genuinely good looking, taller than Louis XIV and much prettier than either Louis XIV or Charles II. His Queen, the Polish Princess Maria Leczinska, was plain; but then so were his first two mistresses, for Louis was indolent, easily led, conventional by instinct and ready to settle for what was easily to hand. In fact, his first three mistresses, one at a time, one after the other, each lasting several years, were sisters, all daughters of the same leading court figure, the Marquis de Nesles, giving rise to contemporary jokes about whether this moving from one sister to another represented the utmost constancy or its opposite.[47] First was the eldest daughter, Louise-Julie de Mailly, aged twenty-four in 1734 when the relationship began, and notoriously plain.

Louise-Julie was already married, a convention Louis always insisted on, partly no doubt to ensure that any children need not necessarily be attributed to him. Louise-Julie lasted five years and was then replaced by the equally plain second daughter, wife of the Marquis de Vintimille du Luc; she, sadly, died in September 1741. There was a fifth sister, now aged twenty-four, Marie-Anne, widow of the Marquis de la Tournelle. Marie-Anne was actually rather pretty, perhaps even beautiful; maybe this gave Louis confidence in himself, for his later mistresses were all to be at least personable. As well as being good looking, the Marquise de la Tournelle was a strong and imperious woman who got more out of Louis than either of her two sisters, in particular the title of Duchesse de Châteauroux. Louis took the new Duchess with him to join his army at Metz in one of the campaigns of the Austrian Succession War. However, Louis himself fell gravely ill and, timid soul that he was, and surrounded by priests declaring the evils of his sexual conduct, he renounced Marie-Anne. But obviously he did not attribute the recovery which followed to this renunciation, since he proceeded at once to recall her. But before the lovers could be reunited she, tragically, died of pneumonia on 8 December 1744, at the age of twenty-seven.

Foreigners had been shocked by the plainness of Louis' first two mistresses; but all three had one indispensable characteristic: they were of noble birth. With the next two and most famous mistresses, known to history, respectively, as Madame de Pompadour and Madame Du Barry, we come to the real heart of some of the main issues this study is intended to explore. Neither was of noble birth, but the former was extremely rich and had powerful connections and an exceptionally good education, while the latter was extremely poor, dependent on the charity of the church for her education and, in fact, a classic instance of the woman whose sole asset is her looks. But what of the looks of Jeanne Antoinette Poisson, born in Paris in 1721, later the Marquise de Pompadour? We enter a swamp of sentiment, fantasy and misattribution as treacherous as that guarding the true physical appearance of Nell Gwyn, even though in this case we have a dozen or more thoroughly authenticated portraits. As the great Pierre Gaxotte put it in response to his own question, 'First of all what did Madame de Pompadour look like?': 'Simple question to which, right from the start, it is not easy to reply.'[48] There are, as he says, portraits or sculptures in abundance, by Nattier, Boucher, Carl Van Loo, La Tour, Cochin, Drouais, Lemoyne and Pigalle; yet still one remains puzzled. There are many genuine-sounding tributes to her beauty, though also some critical comments. We are all familiar with the Boucher portraits, very regal, very dignified, but showing a woman whose face is too pinched, whose nose is just slightly too beaky and chin just slightly too weak to be beautiful. Now, the portrait reproduced as Ill.26 dates from about 1750, most of the well-known Bouchers being from this period when Madame de Pompadour

26

24 *Mme de Pompadour*, Carl Van Loo, 1740s. Presumed to be a youthful portrait, possibly before she became Mme de Pompadour

25 *Mme de Pompadour as Diana*, Jean-Marc Nattier, 1748

was reaching the peak of her power, but passing the peak of her physical attractiveness. Perhaps one should look for earlier portraits; perhaps, anyway, Boucher for some reason or another failed to capture an exact likeness – possibly because he deliberately sought regal dignity rather than sexual charm. Some early portraits which have been reproduced in biographies of La Pompadour are of doubtful authenticity (for example the anonymous *La Jardinière du Bien-Aimé*[49]); certainly there is a most enticing youthful sexiness in the Carl Van Loo portrait which Alfred    24
Leroy used on the cover of his *Madame de Pompadour et son temps* and a certain direct appeal in the Nattier portrait of 1748 in St Omer. But the    25
Nattier clearly indicates the same nose and chin as later Bouchers, and even in the Van Loo one can see that behind *la beauté du diable* the features are not quite beautiful. Thus I would conclude that while the Bouchers fail to convey the sex appeal of the younger Pompadour, they are accurate in respect of her facial characteristics.

Of course, there is one further possibility (in two alternative formulations), the one favoured by the academic orthodoxy which this book challenges: that Pompadour's looks, though not beautiful in our eyes, exactly met the convention of beauty of the time (or, alternatively, whatever she actually looked like, painters rendered her in the form of the ideal beauty of her time, that ideal, again, being different from our own). There is one insuperable obstacle to this thesis, in whichever version. Boucher painted hundreds of legendary and pastoral scenes featuring naked or nearly naked young women, Athenian in features,    27
though far more luscious than any Raphael Madonna, and also some

portraits of lovely young women in similar style. Here, clearly, was the contemporary ideal of beauty, and it does not differ one whit from one of the types which we find beautiful today. If Boucher had wished to paint Pompadour as a 'conventional beauty' he would have painted her like one of his goddesses, nymphs or shepherdesses. He did not: thus we can be pretty sure that Boucher, Nattier, and the rest, did render fairly accurate representations of Madame de Pompadour. From these we can see that she was an attractive woman with an agreeably oval face, but

26 *Mme de Pompadour*, François Boucher, *c.* 1750

27 *Venus*, François Boucher, *c.* 1750

slightly undistinguished features; she comes very high up in that level of
looks which I have termed 'personable'. (Occasionally, even in scholarly
works, one of Boucher's luscious females is presented as 'Mme de
Pompadour' – just as, once upon a time, so many Lelys sailed under that
flag of convenience, 'Nell Gwyn'. Thus there is a ravishing 'Pompadour'
in Anne de Marnhac's excellent *Femmes au bain*, but since the painting,
'From a private collection', is attributed to 1758, when Pompadour was
thirty-seven, credulity is strained to breaking point.)[50]

Some foreign observers of the French court expressed, or affected,
surprise at her lack of looks – but they may well have been prejudiced.

The Marquis d'Argenson, who was definitely not well disposed towards her, described her as 'snow white, rather badly made'.[51] Yet there is plenty of testimony on the other side, much of it from before she became royal mistress, and certainly not to be written off as sycophantic flattery. The Duc de Luynes said she was 'very beautifully shaped and very lovely to look at';[52] Hénault, President of the Court of Appeal, said she was 'one of the loveliest women he had ever seen';[53] and the Comte de Cheverny described her as a woman 'whom every man would like to have had as a mistress . . . beautifully shaped . . . every feature regular'.[54] The best-known description is that of Georges Leroy, lieutenant of the hunt at Versailles. Leroy may perhaps be suspected of flattery since the account is paired with a somewhat fulsome one of Louis XV himself. Still, his words should be left to speak for themselves. The Marquise de Pompadour, he said,

was taller than the ordinary, slim, curvaceous, supple, elegant; her face well matched her figure, a perfect oval, with beautiful hair more like chestnut than blonde, large enough eyes, adorned with lashes with the same colour, her nose perfectly shaped, charming mouth, very beautiful teeth, and the most delicious smile; the most beautiful skin in the world gave the greatest brilliance to all of her features. Her eyes had a particular charm, because there was some uncertainty as to their colour, they did not have the sharp brightness of black eyes, the tender langour of blue eyes or the particular finesse of grey eyes, their indeterminate colour seemed to render them suitable for all kind of seductiveness and to express successively all the impression of a dynamic spirit; the play on the face of the Marquise de Pompadour was infinitely varied, but one never saw any discordance between her features; all contributed to the same goal, which presumes a spirit which was in complete control of herself; her movements were in accord with all the rest, and the complete ensemble of her person seemed to establish the exact nuance between the last degree of elegance and the first degree of nobility.[55]

Personally, I am struck by the emphasis (at the end) on deportment and (earlier) on facial expressiveness. Cheverny speaks of the 'fire', 'spirit' and 'brilliance' of her eyes. He also says that: 'She absolutely extinguished all the other women at the Court, although some were very beautiful',[56] which *may* imply that, for all his plaudits, he recognized that she was not 'very beautiful'. If we take the almost universal tributes to her expressiveness and dynamism, along with the assertion of her brother, Abel, that no portrait ever did justice to her,[57] and the portraits themselves, we may be able to firm up a conclusion. This would be that, although personable rather than beautiful, she had a spirit and vivacity which could at times render her very attractive. She also had, as I shall discuss in a moment, some most seductive talents. In the letter by Hénault just quoted, he continues immediately: 'She plays music perfectly, she sings with all the gaiety and tastefulness possible, knows a hundred songs, acts in comedy at Etioles in a theatre as fine as that of the opera.' One further fact may be illuminating: as a child Jeanne Antoinette was frequently ill. Conceivably there is a link here with both the intense expressiveness she could show and the pinched and peaky look of her face in repose.

However, I now want to argue that without extreme good fortune in birth and upbringing Mademoiselle Poisson would neither have been able to develop these talents to the full, nor have been in a position to exploit either them, or her qualities of vivacity and personableness. Jeanne Antoinette's father acquired considerable wealth as steward to two influential brothers, one a court banker, the other a provisioner to the army. But in the turbulent world described at the beginning of the chapter no one was secure, and following his implication in a financial scandal, Monsieur Poisson was sentenced to death and had to flee the country. Eventually he was pardoned and able to re-establish his influential position, but meantime the four-year-old Jeanne Antoinette was taken under the wing of the powerful and wealthy Monsieur le Normant de Tournehem. It was he who provided her with the best education then available, so that she developed into an immensely cultivated young woman, a lively conversationalist and brilliant musical performer. He also provided her with a husband in the form of his nephew Charles-François Paul le Normant de Tournehem or le Normant d'Etioles, as he now styled himself, whose reluctant agreement may suggest that he found her less than irresistibly beautiful. The marriage took place in March 1741, when she was nineteen. With the husband came a substantial independent income, an elegant Paris address, the Château d'Etioles in the Forest of Sénart and the fine-sounding name of Madame d'Etioles. At Etioles she built her own theatre, where she became famous for her dramatic and musical presentations. In Paris she was to be seen in the salons and at supper parties.

The events which followed are explicable only as part and parcel of a deliberate campaign by Madame d'Etioles to establish herself as mistress to the King, a campaign she waged with courage and resourcefulness. Louis regularly went hunting in the Forest of Sénart, so, to attract his attention, she took to following the hunt in a brightly coloured chaise. She adopted the same procedures in Paris, where she would ensconce herself at the theatre in full view of the King. The final opportunity came in 1745 when a series of masked balls were held in honour of the marriage of the Dauphin. Under cover of the festivities Madame d'Etioles succeeded in luring the essentially rather timid Louis into her bed. Shortly she was acknowledged as *maîtresse en titre* and given the title of Marquise de Pompadour. After the fashion of such promotions, she had her brother created Marquis de Marigny and appointed Director-General of Buildings. Effectively, for almost twenty years, till her death on 15 April 1764, she was Queen of France. Because of Louis' indecisiveness and weakness of character she had much influence over affairs of state and choice of ministers – almost entirely for the worse. On the other hand, as a cultured, educated and talented woman, she played a leading part in maintaining the high aesthetic standards of the court. The platform for her success was the wealth and security bestowed on her, partly by her father, mainly by her guardian; without it she could never have pursued her audacious objectives. To achieve them she had not had to develop a prior tactic of granting sexual favours, as an ambitious poorer woman would have had to do. Indeed, I doubt whether, if born poor, she could have followed such a policy in the first place, her looks simply not being exceptional enough. On the other hand, while her many talents were essential to her establishing herself as a much-talked-about woman, she could not have attracted the King's attention without looks which, though falling short of beauty, were highly personable: her strategy would not have been a viable one for a plain woman.

That the King should have taken a bourgeoise as *maîtresse en titre* was quite shocking, though so cultured were Pompadour's graces, and so regal was her style, that criticism was muted. The woman who eventually took her place and reigned as *maîtresse en titre* till the King's death came from an altogether lower social position, a fatherless child from the provinces. For the poor, the only social services were those provided by the church and Jeanne Bécu received a solid religious education. At fifteen she was given employment as a companion to the widow of a *fermier-général* (tax collector). The first description we have of her is at age sixteen when we are told 'she was already built to ravish; a figure both lithe and noble; an oval face as if drawn with a paint brush; large eyes, clearly set apart, with that slumberous glance, which made them a constant invitation to love; lovely mouth; small feet; hair so abundant that I could not have held it in my two hands'.[58] The writer concludes by remarking that from this exterior impression he could deduce everything else about her. With such looks, and such immediate sex appeal, there were two obvious career openings for Mlle Bécu: she could go into the theatre (where, however, the pay was tiny or non-existent), or she could serve in an elegant shop, patronized by richer Parisians always on the look out for beautiful potential mistresses. Bécu, at the age of seventeen, in fact took employment as a *vendeuse* at the elegant fashion shop Labille, in rue Neuve-des-Petits-Champs. Jeanne Bécu attracted enormous attention, and her potential was appreciated by at least two commercial specialists in female beauty: Madame Gourdan, a well-established procuress, and Jean Du Barry, always known, accurately, as 'le Roué'. Jeanne, now calling herself Jeanne Beauvarnier, because it sounded grander, became the mistress of Du Barry, who was not so much interested in his own pleasure as in the hard cash value of such an outstanding beauty. The police were interested as well, and in their

28 *Mme Du Barry*, Germain-Jean Drouais, *c.* 1771

journal of 19 December 1764, two inspectors reported of Mademoiselle Beauvarnier: 'she is a person nineteen years old, tall, well-made and of distinguished appearance, with a most lovely face'.[59]

She could not attract the attention of the King with quite the elegant panache shown by Madame d'Etioles, but she deliberately made visits to Versailles, positioning herself so as to be noticed by him. Here there is no question but that beauty, pure (though that is scarcely the right word) and simple, was the sole, unalloyed element in the chemistry which followed. The King, now fifty-eight, did notice Jeanne and instructed his valet de chambre to find out more about her. Jean Du Barry acted as the middleman, making his expected profit for his pains; as the King found Jeanne Beauvarnier in all respects to his pleasure, Du Barry, in fulfilment of the King's sense of the proprieties in the matter, had Jeanne married to his own brother, Count Guillaume Du Barry, in July 1768. In April 1769 Madame Du Barry was formally presented at the Court of Versailles and, as noted, remained the King's principal mistress till his death in 1774; her lower-class origins and lack of aristocratic graces meant that she continued to be a subject of scandal to a degree that had never been the case with Madame de Pompadour, and it is significant that she was never elevated beyond the title which, for convenience, she had already acquired as the Comtesse Du Barry.

Du Barry, in almost every way, represents the central notion of beauty as itself, not something else: she pioneered the greatest simplicity of dress, making absolutely the most of her natural attributes, and, to the great vexation of older women, she put no powder on her hair. The earlier portraits, taken with the wealth of written testimony, suggest that, of her own particular type, Du Barry was quintessentially beautiful. She was found so by the much-travelled Austrian diplomat, the Prince de Ligne, whose is the sort of testimony one really values since at one point he remarks that 'there are countries where one cannot find one single pretty woman. There are just not enough of them in the whole world.'[60] The Comte d'Espinchal, who saw her at the opera ball, unmasked as she, with good reason, liked to be and, again characteristically, dressed entirely in simple white, declared: 'Never have I seen anyone more beautiful than this heavenly woman as she was that night.'[61] Perhaps the most impressive account of all is that of a simple supplicant at the royal court, a Monsieur de Belleval:

Madame Du Barry was one of the loveliest women at the court, where there were many, and quite definitely the most seductive because of the complete perfection of her entire body. Her hair, which she usually wore without powder, was most beautifully blonde, and it was in such profusion that she hardly knew what to do with it. Her blue eyes, wide open, were both caressing and frank . . . She had a delicate nose, a small mouth and a skin of stunning whiteness. The upshot was that I was very quickly under her spell, and almost forgot the purpose of my visit to the court because of the ravishing sensation I derived just from looking at her.[62]

It would be wrong to ignore the personal qualities which Madame Du Barry did possess. She was high spirited and cheerful, learned to speak French correctly and was a brilliant storyteller. Obviously, she suited the King perfectly in his declining years. But she had no security for the future, and with the King's death she was forced into a not very comfortable retirement, still occasionally visited and praised by former admirers. Her associations with the old regime were nevertheless too evident, and under the Terror she was dragged from her seclusion: understandably her spirit cracked and she died a sad, undignified death at the guillotine. The message does not need to be underlined that there was often little security for a woman whose social ascent was dependent upon granting sexual favours to powerful men. However, that message must be set within the context of societies which, even for the most powerful men, could be cruel and uncertain: whilst stability was only slowly being established in Britain, Louis XV himself almost succumbed to an assassination attempt.

Let us conclude this section by considering what happened when the boot was on the other foot. By the time of the Georges and Louis XV, Russia was playing an important part in the diplomatic and military affairs of Europe. For over fifty years, with only the slightest interruption, the Russian empire was ruled by two strong-willed women: the Empress Elizabeth, and the Empress Catherine II, Catherine the Great.[63] At the Russian court, did beautiful men have the advantages of a Pompadour or a Du Barry, or were other qualities demanded by the imperial rulers? Neither Elizabeth nor Catherine, if truth be told, was what could be termed beautiful: both, however, were striking, indeed commanding, so one would certainly put them above the boring Georges and perhaps somewhere approaching the category of Charles II. (I would surmise that, without the magic of royalty, Charles II would still have been pretty successful with women. Because of their strong personalities and undoubted sensuality both Elizabeth and Catherine would probably have had many lovers, but without the imperial crown the choice would have been rather more restricted.)

Elizabeth, daughter of Peter the Great, achieved the throne through a well-conceived bloodless coup against her female cousin, the Regent Ann. She had had a number of not particularly distinguished lovers when the equivalent of a *maîtresse en titre* appeared in the form of Alexis Razumovsky. Razumovsky was of even lower social status than Madame Du Barry – he was a Ukrainian peasant. Clearly he was a man of sense, patience and skill, but above all he was handsome in the most virile way. Elizabeth created him Prince and field marshal. As Razumovsky grew older, Elizabeth kept him on the strength but added three very handsome younger men, Shuvalov, Kachinersky and Beketov.

In the gothic half-light of Russian imperial intrigue it was not altogether astonishing that the daughter of Peter the Great should achieve the throne. Catherine, born Princess Sophia Augusta Frederika of Anhalt-Zerbst, a minor German princess without money or (in her youth, certainly) looks, scarcely seemed a candidate for any great destiny, let alone the imperial throne of Russia. Elizabeth, however, for romantic reasons of her own, chose a basically German prince, grandson of Peter the Great, as her heir, naming him Grand Duke Peter Fedorovich; Elizabeth also decided that the Princess Sophia was the proper wife for the Grand Duke. Sophia and her mother were summoned to Russia. In her memoirs, written up of course much later, Catherine gives this perhaps not inaccurate (once you have read it carefully) first description of Elizabeth:

There, on the threshold of her state bedchamber, the Empress appeared before us. Certainly, it was quite impossible on seeing her for the first time not to be struck by her beauty and the majesty of her bearing. She was a large woman who, in spite of being very stout, was not in the least disfigured by her size nor was she embarrassed in her movements; her head, too, was very beautiful.

Most succinctly, Catherine recorded of Razumovsky: 'He was one of the handsomest men I have ever seen in my life.' Of the Grand Duke Peter, Catherine noted:

I cannot say that I either liked or disliked him . . . but to tell the truth I believe that the Crown of Russia attracted me more than this person. He was sixteen, quite good-looking . . . but small and infantile, talking of nothing but soldiers and toys. I listened politely and often yawned, but did not interrupt him and he enjoyed talking to me for long periods of time. Many people took this for affection.[64]

But shortly the Grand Duke caught smallpox and Catherine remarked, 'he had become horrid to look at'. The Grand Duke was a feeble creature and in so far as the activities of the kings we have been discussing were excused because in doing their dynastic duty they had married unattractive wives, so in the same way the young Sophia, who had converted to the Russian orthodox church and taken the name of Catherine, could be excused for looking for a rather more personable lover than her husband.

30        The first was Serge Saltikov (how reliable the much-reproduced portraits of Catherine's lovers are, I am unable to say); 'unfortunately', as Catherine later wrote, 'I could not help listening to him; he was handsome as the dawn; there was no one to compete with him in that, not at the Imperial Court, and still less at ours. Nor was he lacking in intelligence, or the accomplishments, manners, and graces which are a prerogative of the *Grand Monde*, but especially of the Court.'[65] Saltikov was Catherine's chamberlain. Of Catherine herself it would perhaps be fair to say that from being an ugly duckling she, as she filled out, 29        achieved a certain impressive statuesque quality. Certainly her next lover, the Polish Count Stanislaus Poniatowsky, wrote in enraptured

29 *Catherine the Great*, Alexander Roslin, 1775

fashion of his first impressions: 'With her black hair, she has a dazzlingly white skin, the liveliest colouring, her very eloquent big blue eyes, rolling and eloquent, very long dark lashes, a Grecian nose, a mouth which seemed to ask for kisses, perfect arms and hands, a lissom figure, though on the large rather than the small side, a lively gait which was nevertheless of the utmost nobility . . .'[66] Poniatowsky was generally thought to be one of the best-looking men of his time, though Catherine herself commented on his extreme short-sightedness[67] (which may of course have affected his judgment of her).

In 1759 Catherine turned to Gregory Gregorievitch of the powerful Orlov family. The classic perfection of his features was commented upon by both men and women, as also the virile strength of his body. Orlov was a Barbara Villiers, with rather more power: he had his pick of all the most beautiful young women at court (he was twenty-five, Catherine thirty), while he treated Catherine in a very casual way. At this stage, of course, she was not yet Empress and Orlov himself was a very powerful figure. Catherine, however, was preparing herself carefully for her future role as Empress: she was both far better informed and inherently far more intelligent than anyone else at court.

On the afternoon of Christmas day 1761, the Empress Elizabeth died. The Grand Duke Peter became Tsar Peter III. By now estranged from his clever and highly sexed wife, he hoped to be able to get rid of her and establish as Empress his homely mistress, Elizabeth Worontsov, with whom he felt at ease. Actually he assisted Catherine's cause by making blunder after blunder. The first quality Catherine showed was cool, calculating courage; second, she showed sensitivity and skill in choosing her moment. Undoubtedly her physical presence counted for much, but it is unclear that her sexual favours to Orlov made much difference. She had the support of the Guards regiments and personally led them against Peter, who abdicated without bloodshed. Again we get a sharp reminder of the world with which we are dealing: on 5 July 1762 Peter was murdered.

As Empress, Catherine could fully indulge her tastes in men. Orlov remained her principal lover till 1772. If one runs through the list, the qualifications clearly were beauty and youth. It is true that her long-term lover after Orlov, Gregory Potemkin, was all of thirty-five years old, but then she was forty-five. Potemkin was large and dramatic rather than beautiful, being very dark, with an aquiline nose, and by the time his relationship with Catherine got going he had lost an eye (probably due to a neglected abscess) and he had also developed a facial tic. She wrote to him as 'My beauty, my marble beauty',[68] but obviously, like Pompadour, he had other qualities than the purely physical, and she kept up her correspondence with him long after she was devoting herself almost exclusively to handsome young soldiers. In the late sixties there had been

31    the gorgeous twenty-seven-year-old Plato Zubov, whom she showed

30 *Serge Saltikov*, print, Anon., *c.* 1750s          31 *Plato Zubov*, print after Johann Baptist Lampi, *c.* 1800

off publicly as a man would show off a beautiful girlfriend. For two years in the early seventies there was the handsome Guardsman Alexander Vasilikov. In 1775 there began the most famous period when she had a series of beautiful young soldiers, each one appointed to a post as Adjutant General, and each one around twenty-three at the time of his appointment.

Very, very few women indeed find themselves in a position anything like that of Catherine the Great. She had achieved that position in part by the decision of another woman, the Empress Elizabeth, but ultimately through her own intelligence, courage and hard work (not least in learning the Russian language and Russian ways): personal beauty did not enter into it, and she could never have made a career as a Du Barry or even as a Barbara Villiers. She is of interest for our purposes in showing what could happen when a woman did have freedom and power; her lovers can be put alongside George Villiers, Cinq-Mars, James, Duke of Monmouth and John Churchill as examples of men who, for a period of time at least, derived definite advantages from *their* looks.

## 3 *Eminent Women*

If young women in the seventeenth and eighteenth centuries had had the sorts of forms young people today have to fill in, stating their aim in life or intended occupation, very few, probably, would have written 'Mistress of the King'; we have been dealing with an almost infinitesimal minority of the minority who at any time constitute the beautiful women of the age. There are lessons of general relevance to be learned from the

experience of monarchs and their favourites, but it is time to move
beyond the world of the royal paramour.

In this age of La Fontaine, Molière and Racine there were a number of
women eminent in the social and literary scene; all seem to have had a
commanding presence, that is to say, they were certainly personable, but
essentially they derived their positions from other qualities. Letter
writing was a highly developed craft in the seventeenth century, when
those who hungered for news relied more on private correspondence
than on any form of printed journal. Best known and most quoted of all
seventeenth-century letter writers is Marie de Rabutin-Chantal, Marquise
de Sévigné.[69] Witty and humane, Madame de Sévigné is an endearing
figure and was clearly much admired by those who knew her. Animation,
vivacity, graciousness are the characteristics most often emphasized in
descriptions of her; she was not beautiful. Left a widow at an early age by
her 'gallant' (i.e. promiscuous) husband, she led a blameless life, devoted
to her daughter, who was not always prompt in responding to her letters.

However, as it happens, Madame de Sévigné's daughter, Françoise-
Marguerite, *was* held by contemporaries to be a striking beauty. Unfortunately, as so often, no portraits survive from the youthful period
during which she captivated the royal court. In the Mignard portrait she
is a sedate married lady, but enough provocative charm survives, I think,
to give credence to the written accounts. We may note the benefits she
derived, the tribulations she suffered, and the fact that, unlike her
mother, she is practically unknown to history. From 1663 to 1665,
between the ages of seventeen and nineteen, she enjoyed three seasons of
glory. In the ballet performed at the royal court in the presence of the
King it was the custom for beautiful young women of noble birth to take
important roles. Françoise-Marguerite danced along with Mademoiselle
de Saint-Simon, subsequently the Duchesse de Brissac, and with a trio of
soon-to-be-famous ladies we have already met, Louise de la Vallière,
Françoise-Athénaïs de Mortemart (shortly Madame de Montespan), and
Henrietta, sister of the future Charles II. In some verses, the choreo-
grapher Benserade expressed the sense of sexual power and danger which
contemporaries were always aware of in the sheer physical beauty
possessed by Françoise-Marguerite:

Already that beauty makes one fear its power
And exposes us to extreme dangers,
She is just entering into the age where one begins
To distinguish the wolves from the shepherds.[70]

The writer of the court gazette, Loret, after, naturally, praising the
beauty of the other dancers, was specially flattering in his description of
Françoise-Marguerite: 'young', 'brilliant', 'with ravishing features', she
had through her 'lovely endowments' charmed every heart; spectators

32 *Mme de Grignan (Mlle de Sévigné)*, Pierre Mignard, *c.* 1680

were 'overwhelmed with wonder' in admiring 'her dancing and her beauty'. Her mother's cousin, Bussy, who was no flatterer, termed her 'the most beautiful girl in France', and the Marquis de Tréville said that she could 'set the world on fire'. In February 1664 Françoise-Marguerite was again invited to dance at the royal court in 'the Ballet of the Concealed Loves'. With her danced Madame de Montespan and two other beautiful ladies of the court. The masculine roles were taken by the King himself, his brother, the Marquis de Ranson and the Marquis de

Villeroy; alongside were the best professional actors, actresses and dancers of the day. Loret included some verses in his gazette of 16 February:

I thought to commit an idiocy
In forgetting that lovely,
That virgin Sévigny,
Object of infinite merit.
Certainly I who have twice seen her
Endowed with many charms
And with a truly rare beauty
At the Ballets of his Majesty,
If someone came to say to me,
It might be the King our Sire:
Have you ever seen anything sweeter?
I would reply firmly: No.[71]

Within the ambience of the court it was very flattering to say of a girl that she was worthy of becoming the mistress of the King; but for persons as fastidious as Madame de Sévigné and her daughter, it was also embarrassing. Madame de Sévigné, it has to be added, refused to forswear the friendship of persons Louis regarded as enemies. Had Françoise-Marguerite shown the complaisance of the other beauties involved in the ballets, things would quite certainly have been different; in fact, after 1665 she did not again dance at the royal court. To her mother what all this furiously signalled was that she must have her daughter securely married as quickly as possible. Several possibilities were canvassed, but all fell through. It seems that Françoise-Marguerite, properly conscious of her outstanding beauty, was not willing to be paired off with someone she did not herself fancy, even though her mother was beginning to despair (such was the convention of the time) that at over twenty her daughter might already be on the shelf. It is possible also that, while resistant to the importunities of the King, Françoise-Marguerite was confused by the attentions of royalty and all the rumours these aroused, so that she felt bound to keep her options open as long as possible. As the historian Roger Duchêne has summed up: 'one could not with impunity be young, beautiful, in the public gaze, complimented and invited by the king. It became all the more urgent to see her married.'[72]

This Madame de Sévigné achieved in January 1669, when her daughter was married to François Adhémar de Monteil, Comte de Grignan, who at thirty-six had already buried two wives. Madame de Sévigné explained to her cousin Bussy:

The most beautiful girl in France is marrying, not the most beautiful boy, but one of the most honourable men in the kingdom . . . All his wives have died to give place to your cousin, and even his father and his son by an extraordinary turn of fortune, with the result that being even more rich than he was before, and finding himself besides, by his birth and by his establishments and by his fine qualities, exactly as we would wish him to be we did not bargain at all as one usually does.[73]

So unsuitably old was Françoise-Marguerite felt to be at twenty-two that in the marriage act her age was entered as eighteen; however, as with so much in the areas with which we are concerned, convention was stronger than reality, and the subtraction of five years from a bride's age was nothing uncommon. Apparently Françoise-Marguerite was so unable to conceal the terror she felt upon her wedding night that the failure of its consummation became the subject of gossip and ribald song. Sung to the tune of 'The Cat has Stolen my Cheese', one version went:

He has brought only a rat to my rooftop,
Wicked Tom cat, says Sévigné.
Not being amused, I left him alone
Following the advice of my beloved mother.
Alas! this Tom cat fuming with rage
Got no more than a smell of my cheese.[74]

It was the fate of beauty to attract such ribaldry. However, the marriage seems to have developed into a happy one; so in the end one can say that the woman called the most beautiful girl in France, despite a few upsets, had her few years of glory followed eventually by long-term security. But, having refused to ally her looks to complaisance, she had not, for all her beauty, 'set the world on fire'.

Françoise-Marguerite de Sévigné was an innocent; that could certainly not be said of the two women whose fame (for totally different reasons) almost rivals that of her mother or Madame de Maintenon: Marion de Lorne and Ninon de Lenclos (or Lanclos). We have no contemporary portrait of Marion de Lorne, though (the fact is probably significant in itself) several of Ninon de Lenclos; however, there is just about enough written evidence for some instructive comparisons between the two friends who are France's most famous courtesans of the seventeenth century.

Marion de Lorne was born into the nobility, her father being Monsieur de Lon, Seigneur de l'Orme, Baron de Baye, counsellor of the King and treasurer of France in Champagne.[75] Marion was given a good education, qualifying her for religious orders which, in view of her background and qualifications, would have meant a career of considerable status as well as relative security. However, her astonishing good looks (all the sources are agreed on this, though, as I have said, there is no visual corroboration) changed her destiny. Seduction, it is true, might be the fate of almost any girl, but only someone of Marion's looks would have won the attention of the notoriously handsome, highly practised seducer Jacques Vallée Des Barreaux (who later found another vocation in the writing of religious verse). Marion had a child by Des Barreaux, but fortunately she had money, and when her father died she moved with her mother to Paris, where they settled in an elegant house in the Place Royale (now the Place des Vosges).

Marion, who could charm with her outstanding talents as a musician as well as with her looks, and was literate and well educated, established herself as a courtesan of class. Her principal lovers were all notable, wealthy and influential figures, but none was part of the great intellectual and cultural ferment of the time, so that the names do not mean much today. All in all, there were seven or eight men with whom she had serious relationships,[76] including Cinq-Mars, with whom she was undoubtedly deeply in love. These relationships all had their financial rewards, but in addition there was a much larger number of men whose role was that of mere client. Marion de Lorne had several children but her standard of living was affluent enough for these not to be an embarrassment. We know that she was a brunette and was said to have had the body of Aphrodite; she was described by Saint-Evremont (male) as 'the marvel of her age'.[77] She clearly enjoyed life to the full, spending extravagantly, attending all festive occasions (she was not, however, a part of the royal circle) and everywhere being lauded as undisputed queen. Another contemporary account tells us:

The room was brightly lit
And one spoke of rare beauties
And above all that beauty
By which every heart is enchanted,
The lovely Marion de l'Orme,
In an arm chair, not on a bench,
Mobbed with lovers at her feet,
To whom she was causing torment.[78]

Given her extravagance, it is hard to be absolutely certain, but de Lorne probably accumulated enough wealth to enable her to live through a tranquil middle age. In fact she died at thirty-seven before her looks had fully faded.

While the principal biographer of Ninon de Lenclos, Emile Magne, has very gallantly sought to maintain Ninon's legendary status as a great beauty, the evidence is against him.[79] Magne rightly pointed out that the authors of the two most important pieces of contemporary evidence who claimed that in *physical appearance* Lenclos was greatly inferior to de Lorne did not see her personally till she was in her forties; in my view, however, it is reasonable to assume that in making their judgments both Tallement de Réaux and Somaize would have taken into account what others reported on both Ninon and Marion as they were in their earlier years. Magne refers to a portrait of Lenclos in the Museum of Brussels, but this really shows her to be no more than personable in appearance.

33

33 (left) *Portrait of Ninon de Lenclos*, Anon., mid-17th century

34 (above) *Portrait of Ninon de Lenclos* (authenticity doubted by some authorities), Anon., mid-17th century

The portrait in the Museum of Versailles, which Magne does not accept as fully authenticated, though Ninon de Lenclos' name is actually on the canvas, does share facial characteristics with the Brussels portrait, but is considerably less flattering. The portrait in the Museum of Marseilles shows Lenclos in her later years and certainly suggests that she was well preserved (essential for a practising courtesan). Given the visual evidence, it is possible to take at face value the judgments of Tallement and Somaize. The former wrote, 'as for beauty she never had a great deal, but she always had plenty of spirit', while Somaize declared:

34

As for beauty, although she is well enough schooled in what it takes to inspire love, it must however be admitted that her mind is more attractive than her face and that many would escape her toils if they confined themselves just to looking at her.[80]

Two references to Lenclos in novels, both written by women, scarcely back up Magne's assertion that they bring out her beauty, as distinct from her many other fine qualities: she appears in Madeleine de Scudéry's *Clélie* as Clarisse: 'Clarisse . . . is capable of pleasing everybody by a certain natural way which gives her grace . . . She has a tender and sensitive heart, she will cry with afflicted friends: she is generous and constant . . . ' In Angélique Petit's *L'Amour échappé* Ninon is Pithie: 'Nobody ever danced better than Pithie; she plays the lute in a fashion which charms all who hear . . . when she has to be serious and to speak of lofty things, she does so admirably . . . In a word, the capital . . . should consider its self fortunate to have such an illustrious girl.'[81]

Ninon de Lenclos was born in 1623 (or possibly in 1620) into the lesser nobility of Touraine. Her father was driven into exile after committing a murder. She was, however, left a sufficient sum of money to enable her to purchase an annuity to give her a comfortable living for life. What she did not have was a dowry to tempt potential husbands, but since she showed such independence of character from an early age it is questionable whether she ever really wished to take a husband. She seems to have entered fairly knowingly into her first sexual relationships and, through her high spirits, her intelligent conversation, her great musical gifts and her skills in the arts of love, she quickly established herself as a favourite of almost all the leading men of the age (and she had the good opinion of women as well). According to Tallement, she made a distinction between her 'favourites', to whom she abandoned herself (M. de Sévigné was one for a time), her 'payers', whom she mocked, and her 'martyrs', whom she teased. Ninon perfectly combined the roles of courtesan and *salonière*, the one reinforcing the other. She was received and exercised some influence at the court; Richelieu may have been her lover. As she achieved fame as a courtesan, as a hostess and as a person of intellect and influence she, in effect, became, to use a modern word, a celebrity. Anybody who was somebody, or wanted to become somebody, wished to be able to boast of knowing Ninon, or, better, if a man, of having slept with her. The 'celebrity effect' is an important one and can sometimes lead to those who are not really beautiful being reputed as such (celebrity in women may have something of the same sexual impact as power is said to have in men). The matter, and also the contrast with de Lorne, is well expressed in the slightly ambiguous account given by the eighteenth-century writer Dreux de Radier, who, of course, was drawing on the recollections and writings of others, not on his own personal experience:

One would never have been attracted to Marion if she had not been beautiful; it was her first merit. It was only the second of Ninon's, and without beauty she would have had a host of admirers; one almost forgot her personal attraction in favour of her mind, her character, and her conversation. But in Marion one saw only a charming creature, who had sprightliness and playfulness because of her beauty.[82]

Within Ninon's circle were Molière, de Bayle, Saint-Evremont and quite probably Pascal. She was an author herself, and she was a leading light in the libertarian, anti-authoritarian intellectual movement of the period. Her outspoken scepticism led to her being confined in a convent for a time by Mazarin, Richelieu's successor as most influential minister. However, she lived well into her eighties, well preserved (this *is* an important point), and she had lovers almost to the end. Asked how she managed to preserve her looks, she replied: 'That's because I don't like cards, wine or women.' Ninon de Lenclos has earned the approbation of Simone de Beauvoir:

the French woman whose independence seems . . . the most like that of a man is perhaps Ninon de Lenclos, seventeenth-century woman of wit and beauty. Paradoxically, those women who exploit their femininity to the limit create for themselves a situation almost equivalent to that of a man . . . Free in behaviour and conversation, they can attain – like Ninon de Lenclos – to the rarest intellectual liberty. The most distinguished are often surrounded by writers and artists who are bored by 'good' women.[83]

Ninon, to repeat, was not beautiful; rather she was personable – much in the manner that Catherine the Great was personable. Ninon had many other talents, and she achieved celebrity and even some influence, if not real power. The parallel with Catherine the Great is a worthwhile one. Both started with, or in Catherine's case had wished on her, considerable social advantages; both, yet, had to work for what they attained, Catherine taking the more considerable risks, but then being possessed of the unique magic of the imperial crown. Both were definitely advantaged compared with Queen Christina of Sweden, who was short, slightly hunchbacked and marked by smallpox. Ninon did not have the beauty of Marion de Lorne, who undoubtedly profited immensely therefrom, but through qualities of character and intellect, was certainly the more famous figure both then and subsequently.

The truly great age of the salons is the eighteenth century, *le siècle des lumières*, the century of the Enlightenment, and the full golden age is that of the thirty years after 1750 – the years of brilliant and sustained criticism of the authoritarianism and irrationality of the *ancien régime*. There was no career in the eighteenth century quite like that of Ninon de Lenclos. A few *salonières* led, or had led (many salons were dominated by ladies of quite advanced age), lives rich in sexual experience; a number, mainly through having contracted unrewarding arranged marriages, had slightly irregular sexual liaisons; some were solidly respectable. On the whole, the famous *salonières* of the eighteenth century are not, as a group, striking for their beauty.

Marie de Vichy Chamrond (born 25 September 1697), who became the Marquise du Deffand, certainly led a full voluptuous life, including being briefly the mistress of the Regent, Philippe d'Orléans; she must have had her physical attractions but we simply don't know whether or not she was beautiful.[84] The presumption must be not. A passage on Madame du Deffand in her late twenties from the journal of a female contemporary, Rose Delaunay, concentrates on other qualities:

We saw around this time the arrival at Sceaux of the Marquise du Deffand. She gave me an intimation of graces one cannot resist. No one had more spirit nor was so natural in the possession of it. This sparkling fire which animated her penetrated to the depths . . . She possessed to a supreme degree the talent of producing verbal character sketches, and the sketches, livelier than the originals, led one to know their subjects better than the closest intimacy with them would have done. She gave me a completely new idea about this style of writing in showing me several sketches which she had written.[85]

The Comtese de Boufflers was a personable, but never beautiful woman, separated from her husband and mistress of the Prince de Condi. Both she and the Marquise du Deffand were born into high social status, and the Duchesse de Maine (who was quite good looking) and the Duchesse de Berri (who was not, but who ran the most aristocratic of all the salons) into still higher. Judging from such portraits as there are, the only true beauty was the Marquise de Tencin, whose salon was the least intellectual and the most licentious, and dated from before 1750.[86]

More interesting and instructive are the cases of Madame Geoffrin, who, born in 1700, belonged to the same generation as the three famous hostesses just mentioned, had a husband, but no title or noble *particule* ('de'), and Mlle Julie de Lespinasse, who had the *particule*, was still relatively young during the golden age of the salon (having been born in 1732), but had no husband. François Geoffrin was the ultimate bourgeois, a wealthy glass manufacturer who, at the age of forty-eight, took a wife, Marie Thérèse Rodet, whose appeal was probably more her extreme youth (she was fourteen) than any distinction of looks; her father had been a valet at the royal court. Geoffrin could readily provide the wherewithal for lavish entertaining, but had no interest in the world of wit and intellect. More, he lived to the age of eighty-four. Only with his death in 1749 was Mme Geoffrin able to realize to the full her ambition of providing dinners for the intellectual giants of the day, such as Montesquieu, Helvétius, d'Holbach, and Diderot and D'Alembert, editors of the *Encyclopédie*, together with most of their famous contributors. At fifty she was a plain woman, plainly dressed in prim, almost spinster-like fashion.[87] The very reticence and sexlessness was a strength: her dinner parties, held in the afternoon, were deeply serious and highly moral, intended for men only, without any distraction of flirtation or amorous interchange.

Character, patience, dignity, integrity and deep commitment were her key qualities (at the request of Poniatowsky, she even made the hazardous journey to Poland).[88] Strangely, she had won the respect of Mme de Tencin, who, as it happened, died in the same year as M. Geoffrin, and the geniuses who had gone to Mme de Tencin's for amusement now came to Mme Geoffrin's for education. If any one woman made a signal contribution to the twenty-five-year (1751–76) production of the thirty-five volumes of the *Encyclopédie*, the Enlightenment dictionary of universal knowledge, it was the prim, even prissy, Mme Geoffrin.

She had at least one other great achievement: she made a protégée of the young Julie de Lespinasse, who thus became the only other woman to be present at the afternoon salons held at the Geoffrin home on rue

35 *Julie de Lespinasse*, Louis Carmontelle, 1760

St Honoré. Julie de Lespinasse was illegitimate, and, though cherished by her mother, had in adolescence no prospects other than entering a convent. Extremely intelligent, she had the lively charm that often goes with that, but she was not particularly pretty. Through family connect-  35 ions she did encounter Mme du Deffand, who was so taken by her intelligence and charm that she persuaded Julie to join her in Paris.[89] Julie attracted the admiration of, among others, Mme du Deffand's friend Hénault, who informed her: 'Though not actually beautiful, you are distinguished-looking, and attract attention.'[90] D'Alembert expressed a genuine personal devotion, in sentiments familiar from my previous chapter: 'I shall say of your appearance what, it seems to me, impresses everybody, that you have much nobility and grace in your entire bearing, and, what is preferable to a cold beauty, much expressiveness and spirit in all your features.'[91]

Jealous perhaps of the admiration her fortuneless protégée was arous-ing, Mme du Deffand provoked a quarrel with her; Julie, anyway, was much more attracted to the austere ambience of Madame Geoffrin's salon. Mlle de Lespinasse's presence there was greatly welcomed – 'she inspired us all', wrote Marmontel[92] – but she also began holding evening salons of her own, from 5 pm to 8 pm in her house on rue de Belle Chasse. What little money she owned had gone into the purchase of life annuities. She had no dowry; she was illegitimate: thus she was not sought in marriage by any member of the nobility. She was not beautiful, and so unlikely to be courted by a rich bourgeois. However, D'Alembert showed himself devoted to her and it may be that the critical factor here was that she was not herself very strongly attracted to him.

In the autumn of 1765 Julie caught the fearsome disease by which, it is said, one French woman in four in those days was permanently disfigured, smallpox. D'Alembert despaired that she might die; she did recover, but with her eyesight seriously weakened, her health impaired and, the dread of so many women, such agreeable cast of countenance as she had possessed totally destroyed. Julie herself, of course, was fully aware of her disfigurement, as is clear from her own references to it, references which, however, in keeping with her fortitude and high spirits, are amazingly infrequent. The faithful D'Alembert was alone in writing (to their common friend, the Scottish philosopher David Hume): 'She is a good deal marked by the small-pox, but not the least in the world disfigured.' It was this brave judgment which de Lespinasse's Edwardian biographer Camilla Jebb described as 'touchingly characteristic of a sex most unjustly charged with inconstancy and an excessive regard to external appearances'.[93] The critical point is that the disfigurement in no way interrupted de Lespinasse's brilliant career at the soul of Enlightenment Paris.. She had in no way lost her vivacity and charm, her qualities of sympathy and understanding, and her powers of wit and intellect. She still had the devotion of D'Alembert, but her own comment on herself was: 'It does not matter what one does, when one is thirty years old, and, to use fine language, *ravaged by disease.*'[94]

Two romantic, though non-physical (almost), affairs were to follow.[95] First there was an encounter in Paris with the Spanish Marquis de Mora. As Mora was forced by his family to return from Paris to his posting in the Spanish Army, this was one of those romances largely conducted by letter, thus being both intense and recorded for posterity. Then at a garden fete on 21 June 1772 Julie met the even more glamorous Comte de Guibert, eleven years her junior and then enjoying a great success in respect of his preliminary 'Discourse' to his *General Essay on Tactics*, which was a powerful plea for social and political reform. In his funeral eulogy for Julie, Guibert declared: 'her plainness had nothing repulsive about it, at the first glance; at the second one had accustomed oneself to it, and as soon as she started speaking one forgot it'. He had not met her till she was thirty-eight, but 'her figure was still noble and full of grace'. But above all, he said, in quintessentially 'traditional' language, what distinguished her was her expressiveness of feature (*la physionomie*) – 'that vital charm without which beauty is only cold perfection'.[96]

Again separation may have provided an essential ingredient. With Guibert off on his travels, Julie overwhelmed him with passionate letters, while at the same time keeping up her loving correspondence with Mora. On Guibert's return in February 1774 (she was now forty-one) the relationship intensified.[97] Mora, meantime, had resigned from the Spanish Army and, though dying of tuberculosis, was endeavouring to make his way back to Julie in Paris. In fact he died at Bordeaux. Guibert married the sixteen-year-old Alexandrine de Courcelles, a very lovely girl, as we can see from the portrait by Greuze. Still at the height of her reputation as a great conversationalist and hostess, Julie de Lespinasse died on 22 May 1776, not yet forty-four.

The relationship between wealth and beauty in social mobility; the way in which wealth can render beauty inessential; the power of personal qualities other than beauty: all these are illustrated in the histories of two *salonières* of the later eighteenth century, Madame Necker, and her daughter, Madame de Staël. Susan Curchod was the daughter of a Swiss Calvinist clergyman, well educated, undoubtedly beautiful, but poor. She attracted the young Edward Gibbon, till his father laid interdict on any possibility of marriage. Rising members of the bourgeoisie seemed to better, and were probably better able to, appreciate beautiful wives than the nobility. Mademoiselle Curchod married the Swiss banker Jacques Necker, one of the richest men in Europe, who became Louis XVI's Director of the Treasury. In the previous chapter I discussed some of the ambiguities and confusions about beauty, and the conventions that sometimes matched with, and sometimes did not match with, actual behaviour. In 1771 the Abbé Galiani expressed one aspect of the matter in recalling to Madame Necker 'that fearful and ever memorable evening when I was declared a monster because I dared say what everybody else thought. I said that I like men only for their money, and Monsieur Necker is rich; I said that I liked women only for their beauty, and you are beautiful.'[98]

Alas, in looks, their daughter Anne-Louise-Germaine favoured the father rather than the mother.[99] Madame de Charrière, whose *Caliste* Germaine had read twenty times by the age of twenty, thought her plain and this was the, strictly accurate, verdict of most women. The same Edward Gibbon who had admired her mother described her as 'wild, vain, but good-natured and with a much larger provision of wit than beauty'. However, as her subsequent life was to demonstrate indisputably, she had her attractions for many men. The Comte de Guibert, seducer of the disfigured, middle-aged Mademoiselle de Lespinasse, declared: 'Her great dark eyes are alight with genius. Her hair, black as ebony, falls around her shoulders in wavy locks. Her features are marked

rather than delicate . . . She has that which is more than beauty. What variety and expressions in her face! What delicate modulations in her voice! What perfect harmony between thought and its utterance!'[100] She developed an ample bosom, and almost everyone found her eyes striking; otherwise, as portraits show, her complexion was swarthy, her lips were thick and her nose was too prominent.

36

37     There now enters one of those men whose primary, if not only, qualification is his good looks. Eric-Magnus, Baron de Staël, was an attaché to the Swedish ambassador in Paris, Count Creuz. Because of his looks he was something of a favourite with the Swedish King Gustavus III, and through his popularity with the Parisian ladies he managed to make ends meet in Paris, though personally very poor. Creuz informed Gustavus: 'Monsieur de Staël leads a very busy life. He is very well received at Court, and all the young women of France would tear my

36 (left) *Mme de Staël*, crayon drawing, Anon., *c.* 1785

37 (right) *Baron Eric-Magnus de Staël*, Westmuller, 1783

eyes out if I did not show great concern for him. Madame de La Marck and Madame de Luxembourg would exterminate me.' Subsequent letters noted that, 'Comtesse Jules de Polignac feels a tender friendship for him', and that, 'Madame de Boufflers loves him like a son.'[101] De Staël even had private access to Louis XVI's queen, Marie Antoinette, something which Creuz himself was not able to obtain. Gustavus was prevailed upon, with Necker putting up the hard cash, to give de Staël a life tenure on the ambassadorship in Paris. On that basis a marriage contract with Germaine was agreed to: Necker had not so much lost a daughter, he had gained a son-in-law with beauty, a title and a post of high social status.

Madame de Staël was a woman of considerable talent and great creative energy, probably France's most distinguished woman of letters in the Revolutionary and Napoleonic eras. She had great self-confidence, a powerful personality, a liberated psyche and strong sexual appetites.

38 *Mme Récamier*, Jacques-Louis David, 1800

No doubt she was proud of her handsome husband. When she first saw the tall, awkward Benjamin Constant his appearance, she admitted, 'filled me with an insurmountable physical repulsion'.[102] But she had a daughter by him, as she had two sons by the Comte de Narbonne, in addition to the three children she bore her husband. With her father's immense riches behind her, with her own literary talent, with her strong personality and brilliant wit, she established unchallenged eminence as literary hostess and *salonière* in the period which followed that of Madame du Deffand and Julie de Lespinasse, the period which embraced the last years of the *ancien régime*, the Revolution, the Napoleonic era and the Bourbon restoration.

There was, indeed, only one real challenger, that very beautiful Madame Récamier to whom, as is well known, Madame de Staël wrote 'I would give half of the wit with which I am credited for half of the beauty you possess.'[103] Juliette Bernard was scarcely into her teens when her good looks were being widely remarked upon. Having no money of her own, though her mother had been the mistress of a rich banker, Jacques-Rose Récamier, she was highly vulnerable. It seems likely that Récamier thought Juliette was, or at least might be, his own daughter. At any rate, in the interests of securing her position she was married to him at the age of fifteen, he then being forty-two. It was common knowledge that the marriage was not consummated. If her husband's wealth provided the basis, Juliette's beauty was undoubtedly one of the prime attractions of her salon; but the testimony is unanimous that she was a gracious and sympathetic hostess, testimony all the more impressive since she held tenaciously to her virginity. Juliette Récamier was no rival to Germaine de Staël in wit and literary flair, but she monopolized attention as a beauty whom painters loved to paint and whose complete simplicity of dress exposed the empty pretentiousness of *les merveilleuses*, the elaborately over-dressed ladies of the 1790s.

38

Madame Récamier had her setbacks, particularly when her husband went bankrupt: that she managed to re-establish her place in the Paris scene must be largely attributed to her beauty. Although at times men were attracted away from Madame de Staël in her direction, she led nothing of the former's active sex life. At the age of thirty she was engaged to Prince August of Prussia, but the engagement came to naught; it has been suggested that the Prince was impotent.[104] Passionate love did not come to her until the age of forty when her famous affair with Chateaubriand, who was nine years her senior, began. Apart from the astonishing beauty of her youth, which certainly helped to launch her on her particular career, Madame Récamier was remarkable in the way in which she preserved her looks: a drawing of her by Gérard in 1829 when she was fifty-two makes her look like a young woman in her twenties; and similar thoughts are even stirred by a medallion of 1846. Here we have a woman whose life experiences were basically determined by her beauty, but whose success and popularity were as great as they were only because of her warm personal qualities; other factors, both personal and external (she lost the favour of Napoleon for a time), brought reverses of fortune, unhappiness, and for a long period (it seems likely) a deep sense of unfulfilment.

The only English woman who can be directly compared with those French sponsors of philosophy, social criticism and good conversation is Georgiana, Duchess of Devonshire. In the sophisticated, talented gatherings she brought together at Devonshire House in the 1770s we have the closest thing to the salons of the *lumières*. Furthermore Georgiana led what the distinguished author of the eighteenth-century volume in the *Oxford History of England* has termed 'a beauty chorus of aristocratic ladies'[105] in charming lower-class citizens into supporting the Whig leader Charles James Fox at Westminster (where the franchise was remarkably wide) in the general election of 1784. How beautiful was the Duchess?: the problems are similar to those encountered with La Pompadour and with Nell Gwyn. Let me state at this point that it is no part of my purpose to bludgeon readers into accepting my conclusions as to what particular historical figures looked like, and how that relates to the significance or otherwise of a particular sort of looks. Frankly, the evidence in regard to Georgiana could be interpreted in a number of ways. Summarizing, her most recent biographer says she 'was not especially beautiful in the classic sense'.[106] In a retrospective reflection on 'one of the most distinguished females of high rank whom the last century produced' Nathaniel Wraxall declared (rather as others had done of Ninon de Lenclos) that 'her personal charms constituted her smallest pretension to universal admiration'; unlike that of two renowned beauties of the day (to be discussed shortly), Elisabeth and Maria Gunning, her beauty, he said, did not 'consist . . . in regularity of features and faultless formation of limbs and shape'; instead 'it lay in her irresistible manners and the seduction of her society'.[107] Horace Walpole decreed her 'a phenomenon' who 'effaces all without being a beauty'.[108] Fanny Burney, who admired her disposition and character, 'did not find so much beauty in her as I expected'.[109] On the other hand, the actor David Garrick, whose leading ladies (also to be discussed shortly) were among the most beautiful in the land, was quite unequivocal: 'Her Grace of Devonshire is a most enchanting, Exquisite, beautiful Young Creature. Were I five and twenty I could go mad about her, but as I am past five and fifty I would only suffer martyrdom for her.'[110] The elderly Mrs Delany found her 'handsome' and indeed Walpole's initial impression had been of 'a lovely girl, natural, and full of grace'.[111] Portraits by Reynolds and Gainsborough show a remarkable congruence, and, in my

39 *Portrait of Georgiana, Duchess of Devonshire, as Diana*, Maria Cosway, 1782

THE DUTCHESS CANVASSING FOR HER FAVOURITE MEMBER.

40 *The Duchess Canvassing for her Favourite Member*, political cartoon, Dent, 1784. This is actually one of the harshest caricatures of Georgiana, Duchess of Devonshire, but as in other cartoons her appealing looks are clearly contrasted with the less appealing ones of the Duchess of Portland

view, present a decidedly beautiful woman: I take this to be confirmed by the portrait of Georgiana as Diana by the female artist Maria Cosway, reproduced as Ill.39. Now, it may be that all this, contrary to the case I have been making throughout this book, indicates that while Georgiana looks beautiful to us, she did not meet the (it can be argued, rather different) taste of her own day. My version would qualify that, maintaining the notion of beauty as a relative absolute. There is no doubt that Georgiana was perceived as physically immensely attractive, while evidently she did not match the rather limited canons exemplified by the Gunnings. There was also an unfashionable redness in her hair. The tributes that we do have to her looks suggest, as ever, that such canons did not have absolute force. Georgiana, of course, was a highly controversial figure. Of sixty-two satiric prints relating to the Westminster election, published between 29 March and 29 April, thirty-six featured the Duchess. Now if it really had been held by a large number of people (as distinct from a handful of aesthetes and pedants) that she had definite faults of face and figure, these undoubtedly would have been caricatured; in fact the Duchess is rendered in such a way as to make her sexual allure ('beauty', as I understand the term) her most distinctive feature. She was also the subject of several popular ballads, including 'The Piccadilly Beauty'.[112]

   I believe, then, that the Duchess of Devonshire was beautiful, though

39

40

this was not fully appreciated by those of this still 'traditional' age who upheld convention in looks, one of the marks of 'traditionalism' in the evaluation of beauty. Obviously she had many other qualities which contributed to her intellectual and social eminence. But to be brought into the Westminster campaign, and to create the stir she did, she had to be at least personable, and, on the visual evidence, she was much more than that. The career of Georgiana, Duchess of Devonshire, hostess, supporter of political liberty, celebrity but also (unloved by her husband), gambler and philanderer, illustrates both the power in the wider society of unconventional beauty (readers may also feel that it once again demonstrates the 'celebrity effect') and the inability of the ideologues of eighteenth-century high society to evaluate it properly. Of course it also shows the value placed on qualities of character and intellect as well as on status and wealth. In the wielding of political influence only one other woman, earlier in the century, seems to rank with Georgiana. This was Sarah Churchill, wife of the first Duke of Marlborough. Sarah was born in the aristocracy, her husband only raised into it. Without her beauty she would not have captivated the beautiful and upward-moving John Churchill, whose suit at first she rather contemptuously dismissed. All her assets came together in making her the most formidable woman in early eighteenth-century England.[113]

## 4 'Show-biz', Selling, Service and Sex

Each individual is born with a different mix of potential assets: wealth, status, education (many being born without all three), looks (few being born really beautiful), musical or other talent, qualities of personality and character. Evidently the greatest opportunities to cash in on looks lay with women, which does not mean, of course, that the majority of women were advantaged (it may, indeed, mean that the less well favoured were positively disadvantaged). For a woman, cashing in on her looks essentially meant the granting of sexual favours. Given the overriding concern of the time with wealth and status, there were few instances of direct transition from rags to riches. In the exploitation of beauty, a careful, though necessarily fairly rapid, step-by-step strategy was needed.

The profession above all others which demanded no obvious qualification of status, or wealth, but in which a good personal appearance was definitely an asset, was that of the theatre. (The phrase 'show-biz' is, of course, utterly anachronistic, but I have used it deliberately to highlight an element which continues, grows and mutates right through to the age of film and television; service and selling are eternal, but also assume new forms and new significance in the 'modern' and contemporary periods.) For a woman, going on stage could simply be a planned first step towards attracting the attention of some rich protector; for a successful theatrical career, dramatic talent, as well as looks, was required (it has to be remarked that many leading male actors had little or no claim to personal beauty). However, even if Nell Gwyn had never been taken up by Lord Buckhurst, let alone Charles II, her early career would still be a model of social mobility, strongly dependent on looks, of very wide applicability. Born (in 1650) into a completely destitute family, Nell's first employments, as a child, were as a street hawker of fish, and then as a servant girl in a brothel.[114] Nell gained the coveted position as an orange girl in the newly opened King's theatre because of her personable appearance; but she distinguished herself, and consolidated her position, by demonstrating in brilliant degree the wit and power of repartee which were expected in this job. Wit, but still mainly looks, gained Nell's promotion to the stage itself. To hold her place on stage, she had to show, as she did, great talent for comedy (for tragedy she had little bent). Pepys hit off her various talents with his usual acuity: 'Pretty witty Nell' he called her; seeing her at her lodging door in Drury Lane on May Day 1667, he remarked that 'she seemed a mighty pretty creature'; seeing her dressing herself backstage, he described her as 'very pretty, prettier than I thought'; appraising her performance in Dryden's *The Mayden Queen*, he declared: 'So great a performance of a comical part was never, I believe, in the world before as Nell doth this, both as a mad girle and then most and best of all, when she comes in as a young gallant; and hath the notions and carriage of a spark the most that ever I saw any man have.'[115] But talent could probably not have triumphed unsupported by the granting of sexual favours. From the start of her stage career Nell was the mistress of the leading actor, Charles Hart (a great-nephew of Shakespeare), who provided her dramatic training and who arranged for her to be taught to dance by another actor, John Lacey.

In France in the seventeenth century it was on the whole the players of minor, and usually unpaid, parts who aimed to move quickly to the role of courtesan or kept woman. Let us look closely at La Champmeslé, great tragedienne and supreme interpreter of Racine. She was born into a family of middling prosperity and no social status in Rouen in 1642. She had had one husband before seemingly settling permanently into a theatrical career and marrying a fellow actor, Champmeslé.[116] Her advantages were sheer talent, a marvellous voice and the ability to play the most passionate parts with complete authenticity, allied to a figure and appearance which seen on stage were perfectly acceptable to audiences: Madame de Sévigné, a great admirer of her acting, said that she was ugly when seen close up, with small round eyes and a poor complexion. 'It is', wrote de Sévigné, 'the player not the play that one comes to see. I went to *Ariane* only to see her. That tragedy is feeble . . . But when La Champmeslé appeared, one could hear a murmur, everybody was ravished and moved to tears by her despair.'[117] For seven years

Racine and La Champmeslé were lovers, though often the relationship seemed more like a marriage of convenience than a love match. During the same period La Champmeslé had four or five other lovers, including the apparently inevitable Charles de Sévigné.

The greatest figure in eighteenth-century British theatre is David Garrick (1717–79), a pupil of Dr Johnson's at Lichfield, whose theatrical career began in 1740 and who from 1747 was joint manager of the Drury Lane theatre. Garrick wrote, acted, managed, directed and brought a new naturalism and a new professionalism to the theatre. From the 1740s we have these descriptions of him: 'a very sprightly young man, neatly made and of an expressive countenance, and most agreeable and entertaining manners'; 'little Garrick, young and light and alive in every muscle and every feature'.[118] An account late in his life refers to his 'brilliant, piercing eyes'. From the various portraits we can see that he was comely, but not strikingly beautiful. However, many of the other dominant figures in the theatre of the day were scarcely even personable, whatever the roles they played might seem to demand. The rival whom Garrick effectively eclipsed, Quin, was now old and paunchy, but even in youth had never been handsome.

Garrick had difficulty in finding, and retaining, actresses of the quality he desired, sometimes because of meanness, and even jealousy, on his side. His favourite in the earlier years was Mrs Mary Ann Yates, a classic beauty and highly talented actress. She, however, moved to Edinburgh. Her own appraisal of her qualities, and their worth, comes out neatly in her reply to Garrick's determined effort to get her back: 'On considering every circumstance in my situation here, and my novelty, to say nothing of my beauty I think I cannot in conscience take less than £700 a year for my salary. For my clothes (as I love to be well dressed, and the characters I appear in require it), I expect £200.'[119] In fact, the agreement arrived at was £750 plus an additional £50 per annum for two years.

Garrick's other female star at this time was Mrs Abington (the former Fanny Barton). Fanny Barton's story is the proverbial one of beauty providing the springboard and talent the wings for a girl to soar from penury to a secure and respected celebrity (without commerce with royalty, or even nobility). Fanny Barton was born sometime in the 1730s, her mother dying when she was young (though at what age exactly is not certain). As a child she earned pennies selling flowers (which earned her the nickname of 'Nosegay Fan'), singing or reciting in public houses, or simply running errands. Sometime she wangled a way into the private rooms of better establishments, doing recitations from a tabletop, 'her efforts and beauty winning the reward of a few pence from her auditors'.[120] While still very young she apparently became a servant in the house of a milliner in Cockspur Street, where, displaying an aptitude for learning, which was one of her characteristics, she acquired the beginnings of a knowledge of dress and fashion, and also of French. It was almost inevitable that she should also have worked as a prostitute; presumably her good looks meant that her earnings were better than average. The Victorian gloss on this part of her life was:

Fanny underwent many painful and ignoble experiences, that her early days were miserable, squalid and vicious, but that she strove after a better life. She may not be judged with severity, at least the circumstances of her condition must be remembered in passing sentence upon her, and something of the evil of her career must be charged to the heartlessness of the world in which she lived. [121]

The striving can scarcely be doubted since at some stage she developed not just a facility in French, but an ability to converse in Italian. She then seems to have been in service to some kind of relation; after breaking away from this, she eventually, in the early 1750s, sought to put her natural and acquired talents to use by turning to a career in the theatre. In 1754 or 1755 she appeared at the Haymarket, where her immediate success suggests that she did indeed have great natural talent. She came to the attention of Garrick, who presented her first appearance at Drury Lane on 29 October 1756. Meantime she was taking music lessons from a trumpeter in the Royal Service, James Abington. This showed dedication and involved sacrifice since, not being of the tiny minority of top-of-the-bill stars, she was poorly paid: career pressures and economic circumstances may explain why by September she had become Mrs Abington.

Garrick offered her neither opportunities nor good wages, so she moved to Dublin. A critic there described her as 'more womanly than Farren [Elizabeth Farren, see below], fuller, yet not heavy'. [122] A contemporary engraving after Gosway certainly shows her to have a fine bosom and a plump, wide face, with a shapely nose in proportion, big eyes and a smallish, but very sexy mouth; indeed, whether by design of the artist or not, an appealing physicality is projected. If we are fully to understand the rise of Fanny Barton this is a far more relevant portrait than the well-known, but much later, 'dignified' one by Reynolds. Abington became jealous of both her success and her many admirers; finally she made him regular payments in exchange for accepting full separation. She now took as lover the elderly but rich member of parliament for Newry. Again there is a choice piece of Victoriana: 'This connection, brought about through an approving choice of the mind on both sides, rather than the gratification of any other wish, the pleasure arising from this intercourse became gradually so intense, that he delighted in no company so much as her's, each was a great and irresistible attraction to the other . . .' [123] He died, leaving a settlement on her which, as surely as the Villiers gift had provided for Churchill, provided her with the financial platform upon which she could display her talents, and, as surely, was earned through the lure of sexual beauty. Beauty gave her security, but it was talent that gave her fame: Garrick now offered her £5 a week to

41

42

41 (left) *Fanny Barton*, engraving, *c.* 1755, reproduced in *Life of Mrs Abington*, 1888

42 (right) *Mrs Abington as Miss Prue in Congreve's 'Love for Love'*, Sir Joshua Reynolds, 1771

return to Drury Lane (far short, though, of what he paid to get Mrs Yates back).

The tale can now be taken up by Thomas Davies in his *Memoirs of the Life of David Garrick*, published in 1780.

I need not recall to the reader's mind the great delight which Mr Garrick gave to the audience in Don John . . .

But Mr Garrick, some years after, in Mrs Abingdon, met with a Constantia who disputed the palm of victory with him. She so happily assumed all the gay airs, peculiar oddities, and various attitudes of an agreeable and frolicksome madcap, that the audience were kept in constant good humour and merriment, which they recompensed by the loudest applause, through all the several scenes in which she acted . . .

Like another Oldfield, or Cibber, she receives visits from, and returns them to, ladies of the most distinguished worth, and the highest rank. Her taste in dress is allowed to be superior, and she is often consulted in the choice of fashions by her female friends in high life; but as it would be absurd to confine her merit to so trifling an accomplishment, she cannot be denied the praise of engaging and fixing the regard of all her acquaintance by her good sense, elegance of manner, and propriety of conduct.[124]

Cutting through the stilted rhetoric of the day, one can simply note that Mrs Abington through the 1760s and 1770s was established as a brilliant player of a range of comic parts, as a leader of fashion, and as a welcome visitor in high social circles.

In 1782, still at the height of her popularity, though now perhaps fifty

or more, she fell out again with Garrick and so moved to Covent Garden, where her successes continued; at Drury Lane her place was taken by Elizabeth Farren. Three major contemporary sources attest to the stir created by the life of Eliza Farren. First, the *Memoirs of the Present Countess of Derby (Late Miss Farren)* by 'Petronius Arbiter', which, published in 1797, went through five editions in that year at the price of 1s.6d; second, a response to this critical account published in the same year and entitled *The Testimony of Truth to Exalted Merit: or a Biographical Sketch of the Right Honourable the Countess of Derby in Refutation of a False and Scandalous Libel*; and a satirical and critical poem, *Thalia to Eliza*,

43 *Elizabeth Farren,*
engraving, Anon., *c.* 1780

published in 1789. The second document has as its frontispiece an
engraving of her, showing a cheeky, sexy, not statuesque face, with
bright eyes, pointed nose, sensuous lips and rounded chin; by my
definition, which applies to living and breathing human beings, not to
statues, she counts as beautiful.

43

Eliza Farren was born in 1759 into a family of strolling players then
operating in the north-east. Her father died when she was very young;
Eliza, with her elder sister Kitty, was put on the stage. According to the
hostile 'Memoirs', Eliza as a little girl carried the drum which was the
means by which strolling players attracted their audiences; this seems
perfectly likely, though the 'Testimony' strove to deny that the future
Countess ever did anything so undignified.[125] Eliza was evidently
talented, as well as good looking, and she was taken under the wing of
Mr Joseph Younger, patentee of the Liverpool theatre, where she was
launched on a successful and more respectable acting career. Through
Younger's commendation to Colman, manager of the Haymarket
theatre in London, in 1777 Farren moved to the capital, where she mainly
played tragic parts. However, when Mrs Abington made her move to
Covent Garden, Eliza took over her role as leading comic actress. An
interesting, but priggish contemporary criticism gives a fair insight into
her talents of many sorts; it also expresses the conventional wisdom that
a woman should be plumpish – but, whatever the conventional wisdom,
we have a clear case of a thin woman who was in fact immensely
appealing both to audiences and to influential admirers:

Her figure is tall but not sufficiently muscular; were it little more *embonpoint*, it would be one of the finest the Theatre can boast. Her eyes are lively, her face handsome, and very capable both of comic and sentimental expression. But she has lately fallen into an error in the use of these gifts, which, if she is ambitious of true praise, it is incumbent on her immediately to correct. She is too playful, too free in the management of her countenance, and frequently not only understands too soon, but more than is consistent with the character. In real life, if any gentleman is audacious enough to utter a *double entendre*, every lady of good sense is careful to give no intimation of knowing its indelicate meaning, but continues the conversation in its direct and innocent construction.[126]

These manifold talents attracted much attention, including that of the high-living and predatory Whig leader Charles James Fox. Interestingly, even the hostile 'Memoirs' do not allege that Eliza became the mistress of Fox or of anyone else. Instead, a humorous account, again indicating that Eliza was unfashionably thin and suggesting that Fox – who was more than fashionably fat – had highly conventional tastes, is provided of how Fox lost interest. In her second season she had a 'breeches part' (that is, a part largely played in male attire, thus showing off an actress's legs and bottom), that of Charlotte in Colman's comedy *The Suicide*.

But her appearance in this was so different from what it had been in other characters, and she looked to so much disadvantage in breeches, that the passions of the MAN of the PEOPLE were completely cooled by seeing her, and after exclaiming, 'D-n it, she has no prominence either before or behind – all is a straight line from head to foot; and for her legs, they are shaped like a sugar loaf' – he gave up the pursuit for ever.[127]

A footnote suggests that a certain peer, 'whose *propensities* were then much talked of, on seeing her Ladyship perform in *The Suicide*, declared, "she looked like a fine *awkward growing Boy*, and would make a charming companion – in *breeches*"'.

It may well be that with her eyes fixed on significant social promotion, Eliza did indeed take care to avoid any suggestion of sexual experience. The Whig leader was succeeded as principal admirer by the elderly Earl of Derby. With the Countess still alive, Eliza was given an understanding that she could consider herself the *expectant* Countess of Derby. And, true enough, Eliza Farren made her last stage appearance on 8 April 1797, preparatory to her marriage to the Earl of Derby on 8 May of the same year. The criticisms made of Eliza are actually curiously feeble. She is accused, once successful, of living grandly, Petronius Arbiter alleging that she 'changed from the homely fair of a *Shoulder of Mutton* in a *brown dish*, for the *luxuries* of an *elegant table*'.[128] The satirical poem is supposed to represent the criticisms of Mrs Abington ('Thalia');[129] but in fact Mrs Abington had no reason whatsoever to reproach Eliza. Both poem and memoirs mainly speak of ingratitude and meanness to former associates.

Miss Farren, it is being snobbishly asserted, was no gentleman; clearly her ascent into the peerage was upsetting. It was an age highly suspicious in its attitude towards beauty, perhaps above all towards unconventional beauty. Beauty, talent, sexy wit and perhaps also a determined guardianship of her 'virtue' had brought Eliza a quite enormous jump in social status. In the perspective of history, Fanny Barton and Eliza Farren are not remembered at all as actresses but as examples of a not negligible phenomenon, that of women whose personal charms brought them social promotion.

The greatest English actress of the eighteenth century, the one who is remembered in history as such, appeared only towards the end of Garrick's reign. But I will venture the judgment that without her strong and distinctive features she would never have stepped from her provincial touring company into the pages of history. She was performing with her company at Cheltenham when a number of aristocrats in the audience, who had come expecting some hilarity at the expense of incompetent mummers, were so struck by her that they wrote to Garrick. Garrick immediately sent out his talent spotters and one of them, the Reverend Henry Bate, caught up with the company at Worcester. In his report Bate said of Mrs Siddons that her face 'is the most strikingly beautiful for stage effect that ever I beheld'.[130] In fact Mrs Siddons was so nervous in her first performances in London that she was not a great success. She therefore moved to Bath, where she steadily built up an immense reputation, laying the basis for her eventual triumph in London. She soon became the sole dominating figure, holding that position till, at the age of sixty-seven, she retired in 1812. We have, of course, many portraits of Sarah Siddons, so that we need have no doubt of her intelligent, individualistic, but inescapably, deeply sensual beauty.

44

The only French name that one can put alongside that of Sarah Siddons is that of Claire-Josèphe Levis de la Trude, always known as La Clairon. It would be ridiculous to build a whole national comparison on two actresses, though the point has surfaced already in this study: in France, given a personable appearance striking enough when seen on the stage, an actress who remained in the profession, as distinct from using it as a stepping stone to courtesanship, was valued above all for intelligence and dramatic intensity. Edwige Feuillère, a great French star of the twentieth century, to whom, perhaps, the same phrase could also be applied, described La Clairon as 'pretty and gracious rather than beautiful'.[131] We cannot, in fact, be sure as to her appearance: the presumed portrait by Maurice-Quentin de la Tour in the Musée Antoine Lecuyer in Saint Quentin shows a fine, intelligent face, but one which is definitely not beautiful. As to her reputation as the greatest tragic actress of the eighteenth century, there can be no doubt.

So far I have been talking of a handful of named actresses and a couple

44 *Sarah Siddons*, portrait in chalks, John Downman, 1787. Her strong nose was not universally approved in the eighteenth century

of actors, taking them as representative of certain general truths, but not pretending that they indicate the experience of the hundreds of men and women who in some way or another sought a livelihood through the theatre. The simple point remains: theatre was a showcase for women who had that autonomous characteristic called beauty. What happened to them then depended on other factors, personal and external. Much the same could be said of the young women who took employment in the shops which developed in the seventeenth and eighteenth centuries to meet the needs of fashionable ladies. There was only one Du Barry, but others used the same occupation to gain their first introductions to rich and influential men, though no doubt they also encountered imposters who brought a disastrous pregnancy rather than social or economic gain.

The career of Kitty Fisher demonstrates both the potency of beauty and what I have termed the 'celebrity effect'; it is also suffused with that sense of tragedy insisted upon in so much of the folklore about beauty being no real blessing for a woman. Born in Soho in London in 1738 she was, in recognition of her looks, apprenticed to a milliner. She came quickly to the attention of London's leading gallants and had a succession of increasingly famous lovers. Like Ninon de Lenclos (though in place of Ninon's intellectual powers she simply had sheer beauty) she became a celebrity, desired almost as much for that as for her sex appeal: twice she was painted by the best-known artist of the age, Sir Joshua Reynolds.    45
For six years she was, as London's leading beauty, at the centre of the aristocratic social scene though not, however, considered quite eligible

45 *Kitty Fisher as Cleopatra*, Sir Joshua Reynolds, *c.* 1759

for marriage into the aristocracy. Then suddenly she fell ill, due, it has been said, to over-use of the highly poisonous cosmetics of the day. She retired from high society, marrying humble John Norris. Within five months, at the age of twenty-nine, she was dead.

The overwhelming number of pretty women who became salesgirls of one sort or another did not become celebrities, though, one hopes, they usually lived longer than Kitty Fisher. Ned Ward, pioneer investigative writer, who began his *London Spy – The Vanities and Vices of the Town Exposed to View* in 1698, described the New Exchange as 'this seraglio of fair ladies', and noted that 'the chiefest customers . . . were beaux', and that they 'were paying double price for linen gloves or sword-knots, to the prettiest women, that they might go thence and boast among their brother fops what singular famous and great encouragement they had received'.[132] Earlier Pepys had reflected on his paying the glove seller Doll twenty shillings for one pair, 'she is so pretty, that, God forgive me, I would not think it too much'.[133]

We know of no male Kitty Fishers, but perhaps not sufficient attention has been paid to the way in which shops catering mainly for women often found it advantageous to employ good-looking young men. Since, in general, it was less easy for a rich woman to take a lower-class lover than it was for a rich man to take a lower-class mistress, the prospects for sharp social promotion were not great for handsome young shop assistants – still, relatively comfortable employment in a city shop was a distinct improvement upon the furious struggle for subsistence permanently waged in the lower reaches of the metropolis, as in the towns and villages. The appearance and style of some shop assistants are referred to by Mrs Mary Manley in her *Female Tatler* (1709):

This afternoon some ladies, having an opinion of my fancy in cloaths, desired me to accompany them to Ludgate-hill, which I take to be as agreeable an amusement as a lady can pass away three or four hours in. The shops are perfect gilded theatres, the variety of wrought silks so many changes of fine scenes and the Mercers are the performers in the Opera . . . dished-out creatures; and, by their elegant address and soft speeches, you would guess them to be Italians.[134]

On a shopping expedition the fictional character Evelina (in Fanny Burney's novel of that title) observes that 'there seems to be six or seven men belonging to each shop'. 'And such men!', she adds. Real-life shop assistants at the London Bridge drapers Flint and Palmer's had their hair curled, powdered and starched each morning before appearing in front of their customers. Just into the next century Robert Southey wrote of male shop assistants as 'engaging'.[135]

The cultural hegemony which France established in the seventeenth and eighteenth centuries was perhaps felt less in Britain than in the rest of Europe. But Britain too was in thrall to the world of dress and fashion. By the middle of the eighteenth century the shops on rue St Honoré were exporting their products to all corners of the Western world. Most famous of the eighteenth-century couturières was Marie-Jeanne Bertin, whose rise in the social world matches that of many of the actresses and courtesans we have been discussing. She came from a modest family in Abbeville in Picardy (though she herself was actually born in nearby Amiens, in 1744), her grandfather an artisan carpet maker, her father an *agent de la sécurité publique*, a policeman in fact. From modest sufficiency the family were plunged into real poverty when her father, already seventy-two although Marie-Jeanne was only seven, died. As soon as possible she was apprenticed to a dressmaker in Abbeville. The incredible natural flair that she showed from the start is one of these things we can never really explain, though we know them to exist.[136]

As well as flair, Mademoiselle Bertin had those highly developed business abilities which certain women often reveal if they are given a chance to use them. She did so well in Abbeville that she was able to move to Paris, though to the unfashionable rue de Gesvres. However, in 1773, at the age of twenty-nine, she moved to the heart of the fashion world in rue St Honoré itself, where her business was established under the sign 'Au Grand Mogol'. Her clientele included many of those leaders of society we have already discussed, the Marquise de Boufflers, for example, many crowned heads abroad, above all from the Russia of Catherine the Great, and also Georgiana, Duchess of Devonshire. Mademoiselle Bertin had arrived in rue St Honoré in good time for the accession of Louis XVI and Marie Antoinette: she was introduced to the latter by one of her most influential customers, the Duchesse de Chartres.

In physical appearance, let it now be revealed, Marie-Jeanne Bertin was plain. But then her success lay in pleasing women, not men; and pleasing anyway through her creations, not her person. Already by the time of her introduction to Marie Antoinette she was a celebrity by virtue, as Madame Campan put it in her *Mémoires*, of 'the total change which she introduced into the appearance of French ladies'.[137] But it was her good fortune that Marie Antoinette intended both to be a leader of fashion and to support the French fashion industry: Mlle Bertin was the perfect instrument and in consequence was granted many signs of favour. On one occasion when the royal cortège passed down rue St Honoré the Queen saluted Mademoiselle Bertin as she stood on her balcony with her thirty female assistants: the whole cortège repeated the royal sign of favour. Then Marie Antoinette had her dress designer designated 'Minister of Fashion', and Bertin took an apartment in Versailles itself. These arrangements for a number of reasons did not meet with the approval of Madame Campan:

One could say that the admission of a *marchande de modes* into the residence of the Queen was followed by harmful results for Her Majesty. The craft of the shop keeper, received inside the court in violation of the custom which without exception kept persons of this class at a distance, made it easy for the Queen to adopt a completely new style for each single day.

Everyone wanted, immediately, to have the same appearance as the Queen, to wear the feathers and garlands to which the beauty of the Queen, which was then at its most stunning, added an infinite charm. The expenses of young ladies were enormously increased; mothers and husbands grumbled; several giddy creatures went into debt and there were angry family scenes, several households were estranged or on bad terms, and it was widely put around that the Queen would ruin all the ladies of France.[138]

At the height of her prosperity Mlle Bertin had the satisfaction of setting up in the world her niece and nephew. Using all her intelligence and resourcefulness, she managed to survive the Revolution, though somewhat impoverished thereby: in that sense her talent served her better than Mme Du Barry's beauty ultimately served her.

From one great service trade, shopkeeping, it is appropriate to turn to another, domestic service. Servants formed a sizeable social group, from eight to thirteen per cent of the population in French towns at the end of the seventeenth century; most households which could afford domestic service at all simply had one servant, usually female. Male servants were more often found in the larger households. In the earlier part of the period the main concern was over their honesty, for servants were generally regarded as belonging to the 'dangerous' classes so much feared by those striving to establish a respectable living and life style.[139] But as we move into the eighteenth century it is clear that for ambitious families elegant and presentable male servants are important status symbols. The connection between the employment of male servants and ostentatious ornamentation was recognized in Lord North's tax of 1777 of a guinea per male servant for a year; and it was at this time that the word 'flunky' came into use.[140] For beautiful young men there were openings as footmen and valets; as with male shop assistants there was little likelihood of meteoric elevation through sex appeal, though Dr Cissie Fairchilds has shown that, with their good looks, fine clothes and sophisticated manner, male servants often did marry up: with daughters of artisans and shopkeepers, or even surgeons and schoolmasters and, sometimes, merchants.[141] At least they ran no danger of being cast into the streets seven months pregnant. Using the statements which the *ancien régime* required of all unmarried mothers, Dr Fairchilds has also shown how, apart altogether from unscrupulous employers, female servants were often seduced by their male counterparts: 'menservants were usually handsome, because they were hired to look well in livery, and their fine clothes and sophisticated manner might well turn a woman's head'.[142] Dr Sarah C. Maza has noted some special opportunities for 'a few educated, well-groomed and presentable' women as well as men,[143] but, on the whole, domestic service seems one of the professions which bears out Henry Fielding's observation that 'beauty was the greatest fortune for a man and the greatest misfortune for a woman'.[144]

One celebrated escapee from domestic service was Emma Lyon, who later became, successively, mistress of Sir Harry Fetherstonehaugh (at the age of sixteen), mistress of the Honourable Charles Greville, and mistress, then wife, of Greville's uncle, Sir William Hamilton, British Minister Plenipotentiary in Naples. Her celebrated affair with Admiral Nelson is of less interest to this study than her remarkable social progress. She was born in Cheshire, probably in 1765, daughter of a blacksmith. Unfortunately we do not know the vital stages by which she

46 *Emma Hamilton*, George Romney, *c.* 1785

moved into gentry circles. She had a job locally as an under-nursemaid, then her mother, who had herself moved to the great metropolis, got her a post as nursemaid in London (a crucial geographical move). She may then have moved to Mrs Kelly's very high-class brothel, which was possibly the central stepping stone, but we don't know for sure. We do

46    know, from the many Romney portraits, that she possessed, as Sir William (long before he had any notion of marrying her), and almost everyone else, perceived, 'exquisite beauty'.[145]

For the overwhelming majority of women *the* career was marriage, whatever other drudgery in field, farm, domestic workshop, or shop might also be involved. Now, as we have seen, both men and women were thought deeply unwise to make a marriage choice on the basis of personal appearance. We have noticed some of the occupations through which women of humble background could hope to win for themselves the economic support of a male. Women of the respectable classes did not enter such employment, but simply occupied themselves with grooming and displaying, ready to join in the serious business of the marriage market. The 'serious' must be stressed: the large majority of marriages even in aristocratic circles in England, and almost all in such circles in France, were based on the conventions of social status and careful appraisals of wealth. Beauty was a threat, beauty had power: power to break conventions, power to overthrow the proper ordering of society.

Let us turn to the poor but honest Gunning sisters, Elizabeth and Maria. Despite the frequent attributions of their great beauty to their

Irish ancestry, they were in fact born in England, but brought up in Ireland, where their father established himself as a member of the very minor gentry.[146] Unfortunately he was a spendthrift, so the family home had to be sold up. But the Gunning status was sufficient, and the mother sufficiently knowledgeable and astute, for her to be able to wangle a small government pension for the family. She then brought the two sisters back to England and – it is as simple as that – put them on display. (Many of the better-known portraits of the sisters are stiff and formal, stressing status but lacking in allure; occasionally, as in the mezzotint of    47 Elizabeth by Finlayson after Catherine Read, one gets a clear sense of what all the fuss was about: contemporaries are unanimous in their praises.) One could say that the sisters now led *careers* as beauties, not after the style of Kitty Fisher, of course, but with great care to keep reputation and everything else intact. Again the celebrity factor comes in, aided in this case by there being the two of them: one beauty was always interesting, two beauties together were remarkable. One young aristocrat who took a connoisseur's interest in beautiful women was the handsome roué James Duke of Hamilton, so great an interest, in fact, that (appreciating their rarity) he was prepared to marry one. There is nothing very romantic about the story. He had first of all proposed to Elizabeth Chudleigh, whose fame as a beauty was only subsequently

47 *Portrait of Elizabeth Gunning,* Francis Cotes, 1751. Through the rather dignified pose, one can see something of the allure captured in the popular mezzotint mentioned in my text

rivalled by the scandal she involved herself in as the bigamous Duchess of Kingston; but as she was already secretly married, Hamilton turned towards her great rivals in the beauty ratings, the Gunning girls who, wrote a contemporary, neatly summarizing the less conventional aspect of the business of marriage, 'had luckily brought their stock in trade to a market, where beauty frequently fetches an excellent price'.[147]

Such cynical frankness (so at odds with the ideology of the valueless-ness of mere beauty) was not appropriate in public: the official version was entrusted to a young member of the Hamilton family who, anonymously, produced a pamphlet of rhyming couplets in honour of the marriage of Elizabeth to Hamilton.[148] It deserves extensive quotation as neatly bringing together the points I made in the previous chapter about the ambiguities and confusions surrounding beauty and this actual, flesh-and-blood instance of the power of beauty. The poem begins:

When *Beauty* spreads her Glories to View,
Our wond'ring Eyes the radiant Blaze pursue;
Enraptur'd we behold the pleasing Sight,
And lose ourselves in *infinite Delight*;
*Unruly Passions* urge us to possess
The richest Treasure of a Mortal's Bliss.
But when *strict Virtue* guards the charming Fair
With Prudence arm'd, and Chastity severe;
Aw'd and chastiz'd by such superior Powe'r,
We stand at Distance, and almost adore.
Long of the GUNNINGS – both *divinely Fair* –
Unrival'd shorn in *Beauty's* glorious Sphere . . .

Some lines later, this section concludes:

Strange is the Powe'r of Beauty to controul
Our rugged Humours, and our Passions rule.

Later come some social and moral reflections:

Thus when a GUNNING shews her charming Face,
*All other* Beauties *unregarded pass*
The Noble *Hamilton* confess'd his Flame,
A Name recorded in the Books of Fame!
In vain high Titles and an antient Blood,
The Lawness of his *Choice* proclaim aloud.
Small Fortune, but no Titles grace the Fair,
Her honour'd Father but a rural 'Squire;
Her greatest Portion in herself remains,
Virtue and Beauty and refined Sense;
Things in this Age but of a small Regard,
*When Wealth's the Idol so ador'd and fear'd.*

The gen'rous Peer, regardless of his Blood,
Thinks it no *Stoop* to love the Fair and Good.
Virtue, tho' e're so low, commands Respect,
And Beauty never passes with Neglect . . .

Subsequently, the poem turns to the, as was then widely believed, Irish
origins of the Gunnings, and to the virtues of the Irish, managing a nice
blow at rue St Honoré along the way:

They [i.e. the Irish] Nature's Dictates wisely do pursue,
Live by her Laws, and as she bids they do.
By foreign Fashions they are not disguis'd,
What Heaven gives, by them is choicely priz'd.
Their sense is native, so their Beauties too,
And artless Love within their Bosoms glow.

After more in similar vein, a couplet,

How oft have we been arrogantly told,
That perfect Beauty's cast in *English* Mould,

prefigures an interesting piece of anti-racism, as a prelude to a return to
old tunes; the first line which follows is addressed to England's own
'arrogant beauties':

No more, ye Fair, on your Perfections stand,
For Beauty flourishes in every Land.
Ev'n Negros, so distasteful to the Sight,
Produce their Beauties eminently bright.
Exactest Symmetry their Persons form,
And glowing Graces all their Features warm.
Wit and good Sense are equally their Due,
Their Colour only differs them from you:
And what is Colour but a tinctur'd Skin,
Tho' black without, yet all is fair within;
Tis' *Virtue gives a Beauty to the Face,*
The fairest Form may be without a Grace;
The Rose and Lily, now in fragrant Bloom,
Sickness or Age will wither and consume . . .

The poem says it all, the sexual power of beauty being recognized in the
opening lines, only then to be thoroughly tangled up in a series of high-
sounding and contradictory assertions.

The more private aspects of marriage will be alluded to in the next
section. Meanwhile I want to conclude my discussion of marriage as a
career with one of the most famous of all marriages, that between
Napoleon and Josephine, and, more importantly, with the earlier life of
Josephine, which once again illuminates the relative unimportance of

beauty (in this case in eighteenth-century France) when family connections and inheritance are at stake. Marie-Josèphe-Rose (later Josephine) de Tascher de la Pagerie, the eldest of three daughters, was born in Martinique in June 1763. The family belonged to the ancient country gentry of France and still had excellent connections there, but had fallen on hard times – Josephine's father was a struggling sugar planter. There was talk of a marriage alliance with Alexandre de Beauharnais, son of the powerful Marquis de Beauharnais. Although the Beauharnais had not actually seen any of the daughters, the choice had fallen on the second daughter, Josephine being considered, as the Marquis explained, too old:

I would have very much desired that your eldest daughter were several years younger. She would certainly have had the preference, since I have been given an equally favourable picture of her, but must declare to you that my son, who is only seventeen and a half, finds that a young lady of fifteen is of an age too close to his own.[149]

The middle sister died, and Alexandre, who was anxious to lay hands on the inheritance which would become his on marriage, calmly agreed to the youngest, at this time eleven-and-a-half; her father wrote of her that 'health and gaiety of character are combined with a figure that will soon be interesting'.[150] However, mother and grandmother united in defence of the child, so the choice at last passed to Josephine. The Marquis had the banns published in Martinique, wisely leaving a blank where the document of authorization specified the name of the bride. The engaged couple had their first meeting in Brest in October 1779. A long letter from Alexandre to the Marquis mentions many other matters before coming round to his intended: 'Mademoiselle de la Pagerie will perhaps seem less pretty to you than you expect, but I believe I can assure you that the honesty and sweetness of her character will surpass whatever people have been able to tell you about her.'[151] Alexandre got the marriage he needed and his inheritance, and continued his relationship with his mistress, Mme de Longpré. He and Josephine were legally separated in 1785.

It was ten years later that Josephine, now a widow of thirty-one, met Bonaparte, who was twenty-five. Josephine had never been beautiful, but she now had great poise and self-confidence, and, as the Duchesse d'Abrantès later wrote, 'was still charming at this period . . . Her teeth were frightfully bad, but when her mouth was shut she had the appearance, especially at a few paces distant, of a young and pretty woman.'[152] Several portraits, among them one by Gros, show her as distinctly personable. Napoleon was pale, thin and awkward looking. He afterwards recalled:

One day when I was sitting next to her at table, she began to pay me all manner of compliments on my military qualities. Her praise intoxicated me. From that moment I confined my conversation to her and never left her side. I was passionately in love with her, and our friends were aware of this long before I ever dared to say a word about it.[153]

Two weeks after their first meeting Napoleon was appointed Commander-in-Chief of the Army of the Interior. They could well have drifted apart: it was Josephine who took the initiative in writing to him. Even after they were married they were necessarily much apart; she may have had one affair, but she certainly became an excellent wife to the Emperor. But fate is unfair in many other matters than the distribution of beauty. Josephine failed to produce a son, a necessity if Napoleon's dynastic ambitions were to be fulfilled. Napoleon divorced her in 1809, and she died a lonely woman in 1814.[154]

Unbending moralists would probably describe many of the careers followed by the women discussed in this chapter as prostitution. But this study assumes that sexual exchanges, whether overtly physical or not, are going on all the time in life as it is actually lived. The profession or occupation I am now concerned with is that of the common prostitute, or, in the French of the day, *la fille publique*. By the definitions I am applying, Nell Gwyn at thirteen was not a prostitute, she was an orange girl; Ninon de Lenclos was never a prostitute, she was a courtesan and *salonière*; no label, certainly not that of prostitute, is quite appropriate to Mme de Pompadour. Women of noble birth, women with great wit, or intellect, or musical talent do not usually become prostitutes; women with great beauty hope to become something more than mere prostitutes. Sebastien Mercier in his *Tableau de Paris* of 1781 liked making moral points, but he was concerned also with sociological accuracy; he did not miss the real social and economic distinctions. 'There are in Paris thirty thousand *filles publiques* and around ten thousand, more discreet, who are *entretenues* [kept women], and who from year to year pass to different hands.'[155] On courtesans he writes:

one calls by that name those who, always covered in diamonds put their favours to the highest bidder, without sometimes having more beauty than the poverty-stricken who ply their trade at the lowest price. But caprice, cunning, trickery, a touch of art or of inspiration put an enormous distance between two sorts of women who in fact have exactly the same goal.[156]

The critical point here is the 'enormous distance' separating the common prostitute, whether operating in a brothel or on the streets, from the others. It is undoubtedly true, as Antonia Fraser has pointed out, that 'women who supported themselves as manure-gatherers, salt-spreaders and the like (not the pleasantest of jobs) might well envy the financial rewards of prostitution'.[157] On the other hand, good looks might be a contributory cause to a woman's downfall in the first place, leaving her with no choice but to go into prostitution. *Harris's List of*

*Covent Garden Ladies* of 1793 tells us of a beautiful servant, employed in a 'gentleman's family' who, on walks, attracted the attention of a 'gentleman of the law', who invited her to his chambers:

The sequel it were needless to relate: she was debauched and after deserted by her betrayer. The consequence of which was, having lost her place, and being destitute of a character, she was obliged to have recourse to her beauty for subsistence.[158]

This publication, as also *Ranger's Impartial List of the Ladies of Pleasure in Edinburgh* of 1775, gives insights into the importance of personal beauty to a prostitute and its relationship to other desired qualities. In discussing another Covent Garden lady, Harris declares that 'Beauty . . . is generally looked upon as the first and chief requisite; and next to it, an agreeable conversation.' What this lady has, however, is 'good nature'; but then 'her favours may be had on very moderate terms'.[159] The seduced servant, on the other hand, being 'at that time one of the finest women upon the town', 'accordingly made one of the best figures from the emoluments of her employments'.[160] There is an Edinburgh girl of sixteen whose 'youth and beauty procure her a great many admirers'; another young lady is not pretty, but 'makes a tolerable livelihood'.[161] Descriptions of appearance are usually quite meticulous: the ill favoured can expect half-a-guinea, while a 'beautiful lady' newly arrived in London from Wales charges five guineas.[162] In the Scottish guide musical talents and the ability to be a congenial drinking companion are also prized attributes, and in the London guide the epithets 'well bred' or 'well educated' indicate high prices. Both guides, as is the custom in such publications, and often in identical language, stress the skill in the arts of love of their subjects: however, since this skill is allowed to every single one, it scarcely amounts to a characteristic upon which discrimination between different prostitutes could be based. Self-evidently, very many prostitutes cannot have been at all beautiful, and obviously various professional skills were important, at least among the brothel- or home-based ones featured in these lists.

That beauty was a most important asset for the woman who hoped to do particularly well is clear from the open attention paid to it, and from some of the more ambiguous and even downright offensive (in our eyes) comments. Of one Edinburgh lady it is reported: 'Beauty is not the only requisite of love, there is a certain mode of behaviour that renders even deformity pleasing; which this lady possesses in every degree.' Of another: 'This lady is a fit person to grace a table, being pretty fat and comely, she is a good Winter-piece; and, indeed, upon the whole, very agreeable.' Of a third: 'If it was not for this Lady's inordinate desire for the sport of Venus, she would certainly never have followed the game, as she does not possess one outward accomplishment to recommend her.'[163] On the customer's side, as Antonia Fraser has neatly put it, 'it was a case of striking a balance between what his purse could afford and what his sensibilities could stand'.[164] But if a woman were to derive real advantage and significant social promotion from her looks then she had to get out of common prostitution as quickly as possible before it destroyed them (Emma Lyon, if she ever was a prostitute, had escaped by the time she was sixteen). The seduced servant of the Covent Garden list did do well for a time as a kept woman, but when her protector died 'she was compelled to have recourse to a more general commerce, in which she has not been so successful as before'. Although the guide concluded that 'she may, nevertheless, still be pronounced a very good piece, and a desirable woman', the reasons for her diminished success (and, evidently, hope of escape) were clear:

chagrine added to the usual irregularities accidental to her profession, has diminished those charms which were before so attracting; her face is now rather bloated, and she is grown somewhat masculine in her person.[165]

For all prostitutes the risks were high, particularly from venereal diseases and pregnancy. The prostitute could not insist that her customer wear 'armour': if he did, it was to protect himself against disease. The normal contraceptive method, a sponge soaked in alcohol, was not very effective.

We come to a fundamental proposition in this analysis of beauty, sex and social success. If a woman were to sell sexual favours and retain some kind of security, or attain further social advancement, she had to get into a level of society where she could have pregnancies without sabotaging her entire career. One route was across the gap and into the world of kept women and courtesans: on the whole the better looking were more likely to achieve this, but the overwhelming majority, including the truly beautiful, failed, never really having had a chance in the first place. The other route was to become a brothel keeper (like the celebrated Mrs Hayes in mid-eighteenth-century London, who, reputedly, retired worth £20,000);[166] here high initial earning power, immense good luck and some managerial ability would be necessary.

Male prostitution (and above all child prostitution) for male customers was not a glamorous business. Male prostitution for female customers, however, was a much more select affair and here men with the right attributes, which might include beauty of face and form, could add to their economic, and even improve their social, prospects. Alas, it is not known whether this advertisement from the *Nottingham Weekly Courant* of 26 November 1717 was genuine or merely a spoof:

Any able young Man, strong in the Back, and endow'd with a good Carnal Weapon, with all the Appurtenances thereunto belonging in good Repair, may have Half A Crown per Night, a Pair of clean Sheets, and other Necessaries, to perform Nocturnal Services on one Sarah Y-tes, whose Husband having for these 9 Months past lost the Use of his Peace-Maker, the unhappy Woman is thereby driven to the last Extremity.[167]

To what profession should we allocate Casanova, who spent much time in eighteenth-century England? Casanova, in fact, could appropriately be described as a con man: he lived off his quick wits, his plausibility and his flair. He had nothing in the way of good looks, so in one sense his life demonstrated how, in a man, mental agility could outweigh absence of physical appeal.[168] His large number of 'conquests', for knowledge of which we are almost entirely dependent on his own memoirs (which undoubtedly contained a certain measure of fantasy), was due to his overpowering, and probably sexually ambivalent, drive; he was little concerned with either beauty or relationships: as a lover he does not really compare with Cinq-Mars, Monmouth, or John Wilkes, who was even uglier than Casanova, and to whom we turn towards the end of this chapter.

I have mainly been talking of the beautiful and the personable and of the successes they attained. We have encountered one or two people who were plain, and even disfigured, who none the less enjoyed considerable success. What did it mean to be manifestly ugly, or deformed? Some made a sort of profession out of misfortune by becoming beggars. But without doubt the whole cast of early modern society was to be inconsiderate to the extent of cruelty towards the truly ill formed. Women in the seventeenth century, though not in the eighteenth, ran the risk of being identified as witches. It may be that those who are very successful with their pen, but are not actually seen by those who read their books, can afford to be ill favoured, as was Mlle de Scudéry. How far was this true of the spectacularly misshapen, and highly celebrated, Augustan poet, Alexander Pope? A victim of Pott's disease, Pope was a dwarf of four feet six inches, crippled by arthritis. In his own poignant words he referred to 'this long Disease, my life'. It may be that some of the passion which drove him on to success as a poet and writer derived from his deformity. But though contemporaries had to recognize his genius, it cannot be said that in general they behaved well towards him. Official recognition of his merit, and the religious tolerance of Catholicism granted to many others, were withheld from him. His private life was scarcely happy. Professor Pat Rogers has written that 'his overstrained attitude to sex, mingling boyish smut with elaborate gallantry, must derive from feelings of being unattractive, if not grotesque, to the women he desired'.[169]

## 5 *The Private Sphere*

Were beautiful people in the seventeenth and eighteenth centuries happier than those not so well favoured? Of course, it is impossible to make a complete separation between the private sphere and the public: while many individuals seemed content to live out their lives in the station to which it had pleased God to call them, others engaged desperately in the struggle for social promotion. As we have seen, the widely proffered advice was that private happiness would not be found in the pursuit of beauty. In examining such evidence as there is, one is immediately brought up against the infinite variety, and constantly changing character, of human mood and response, and against the strange and unpredictable force of human love. Nevertheless, I can definitely show: an *awareness* of beauty, *evaluations* of it (as against other qualities) and *reactions* to it (and its absence), which add substance and detail both to my overall contentions and to the broad historical survey of attitudes presented in chapter three.

What Thomas Turner, a prospering shopkeeper in the mid–eighteenth century in East Hoathly, near Lewes in Sussex, hoped for from marriage was companionship and someone to run his household: his diary evidently served a useful function in enabling him to record his despair over the way in which his hopes were not being fulfilled. 'Oh!', he exclaimed in his entry for Saturday 30 August 1755, 'what a happiness must there be in a married state when there is sincere regard on both sides and each party truly satisfied with each other's merit.' But, he continued, 'it is impossible for tongue or pen to express the uneasiness that attends the contrary'. Miserably, he notes the many quarrels between himself and his wife, constantly agonizing over where he has gone wrong. After another quarrel he states, on the first day of the new year, his reasons for having married: 'I was neither instigated to marry by avarice, ambition, nor lust. No, nor was I prompted to it by anything; only the pure and desirable sake of friendship.'[170] Such motives, of course, coincided exactly with the advice handed out by preachers and publicists; perhaps the very rationality of the approach was what was ruining the marriage. At no time is there any reference to his wife's looks, yet in February 1756, after another quarrel, he describes her as 'so infinitely dear to me' and 'the charmer of my soul'. In October he states that given his chances over again he would still make the same choice.[171]

One cause of marital friction may have been his wife's poor health. In 1761 she died. There are many lamentations over her loss and tributes to her qualities as a wife, tributes very much in keeping with the notion of marriage as a rational partnership in which one certainly did not marry for 'lust'. First he declares that 'She was undoubtedly superior in wisdom, prudence and economy to most of her sex and I think the neatest and most cleanest woman in her person I ever beheld.'[172] Eighteen months later he is lamenting that he cannot find another woman to compare with her: 'I shall never have a more virtuous and prudent wife than I have already been possessed of.'[173] A year after that he declares that 'I have never spent hardly one agreeable hour in the company of a woman since I lost my wife, for really there seem very few whose education and way of thinking is agreeable and suitable with my own.'[174] The notion of the wife's role in the business of marriage comes through in the lamentation of 10 November 1763: 'No one but a servant to trust the care of my concerns to or the management of my household affairs, which are now all confusion. My affairs abroad are neglected by my confinement at home . . .' Clearly this is all deeply felt, though in fact Turner's shop was continuing to prosper. But most significant of all is the latter part of the very first entry lamenting his wife's death: 'I think words can convey but a faint idea of the pleasure and happiness that a husband finds in the company of a virtuous, prudent and discreet woman, one whose love is founded not on the basis of sensual pleasures but on the more solid foundation of friendship and domestic happiness, whose chief delight is to render the partner of her bosom happy.'[175]

When, at last, another woman does enter his life the first reference to her (Monday 19 March 1764) is entirely laconic: 'I dined on the remains of yesterday's dinner. At home all day; posted my day book. Molly Hicks drank tea with me. In the even wrote my London letters. Very little to do all the day.' Five days later, however, the entry is much more enthusiastic and once again gives us an insight into the qualities Turner looked for in a wife:

After tea my brother Richd and I took a walk (Molly Hicks, my favourite girl, being come to pay Mrs Atkins a visit in the even, went home to her father's, and I along with her, my brother going with her companion for company.) We came back about 8.10. This is a girl I have taken a great liking to, she seeming to all appearances to be a girl endued with a great deal of good nature and good sense, and withall so far as hitherto come to my knowledge is very discreet and prudent.[176]

Molly was in fact working as a servant to a local JP, not an unusual occupation for a girl from, say, the artisan or smallholding class, and one which was reckoned as an excellent training for marriage. Only with the very last entry do we learn that she does have excellent financial prospects: thus his earlier assertion that along with lust, avarice and ambition were no part of his motivation in seeking a wife, may not have been completely candid. On the evening of Good Friday, 5 April 1765, he met Molly by appointment and walked home with her where, the weather being excessively bad, he stayed with her till past five o'clock in the morning. One presumes that no sexual activity took place.

The comment next day, the comment perhaps of a man lacking total confidence in himself and recalling the turbulence of his previous marriage, is: 'In the even very dull and sleepy; this courting does not well agree with my constitution, and perhaps it may be only taking pains to create more pain.'[177] There is no direct reference to an engagement, but just over a week later an entry in the diary, mentioning that after dinner on Sunday 14 April he set out to pay Molly Hicks a visit, refers to her as 'my intended wife'. He spent the afternoon (dinner being a midday meal) 'with a great deal of pleasure, it being very fine pleasant weather and my companion very agreeable. I drank tea with her and came home about 9.30.'[178] Then, in a long entry, he considers how news of his intentions will be treated in the world, 'some likely condemning, others approving my choice'. But since the world cannot judge 'the secret intentions' of his mind and may censure him through not knowing his true motives, he decides he will set down 'what are really and truly my intentions and the only motive from which they spring', which, he adds, 'may be of some satisfaction to those who may happen to peruse my memoirs'. In his statement he refers first to the general role of marriage, moving quickly to his own personal loneliness. He then goes on to enumerate the qualities of his intended:

. . . as to the motives which spur me on to think of marriage, first I think it is a state agreeable to nature, reason and religion and in some manner the indispensable duty of Christians. For I think it is the duty of every Christian to serve God and perform his religious services in the most calm, serene and composed manner, which if it can be performed more so in a marriage state than a single one, it must then be an indispensable duty. Now as to my present situation, my house is not at all regular, neither is there any family devotion performed in that serious manner as formerly in my wife's time, nor have I one friend in the world; that is, I have not anyone whom I can thoroughly rely upon or confide in. Neither have I anyone to trust the management of my affairs to that I can be assured in their management will be sustained no loss. I have not one agreeable companion to soften and alleviate the misfortunes incident to human nature. As to my choice I have only this to say: the girl I believe as far as I can discover is a very industrious, sober woman and seemingly indued with prudence and good nature, and seems to have a very serious and sedate turn of mind. She comes of reputable parents and may perhaps one time or other have some fortune.[179]

Then comes the only reference to her personal appearance (and also to his own): 'As to her person I know it's plain (so is my own), but she is cleanly in her person and dress (which I will say is something more than at first sight it may appear to be towards happiness).' There is then a discreet comment on her figure which, presumably, had remained fairly well concealed from him in her voluminous clothing: 'she is I think a well-made woman'. Immediately he passes on to other qualities, and finally back to his overall aims in marriage:

As to her education, I own it is not liberal, neither do I think it equals my own, but she has good sense and a seeming desire to improve her mind, and, I must in justice say, has always behaved to me with the strictest honour and good manners, her behaviour being far from the affected formality of the prude, nor on the other hand anything of that foolish fondness too often found in the more light part of the sex.

Then he describes what he terms his 'real intentions'; they are:

of marriage and of the strictest honour, having nothing else in view but to live in a more sober and regular manner, and to be better able to perform my duty to God and man in a more suitable and truly religious manner, and with the grace of the Supreme Being to live happy and in a sincere union with the partner of my bosom.

It is perhaps worth commenting that though the diary from time to time, with some regret, mentions bouts of drinking, there is no suggestion that Turner had sought sexual adventures during his years of loneliness. Comment must also be made upon his dislike of 'foolish fondness', that is to say, excessive show of affection; this thoroughly eighteenth-century notion may perhaps have played a part in his difficulties with his first wife. That there *is* affection on his side seems clear; a few days later he admits to spending a delightful evening, 'nothing wanting to make it so except the company of my dear Molly and an easy mind'.[180] The following Sunday, 28 April 1765, he once more stays the greater part of the night with her, coming home about 4.40 am. Then he seriously injures his leg, and the fondness issue comes up again: 'At home all day; my leg very painful. In the even my intended wife and her sister called to see me and sat with me some time. This may possibly be imputed to the girl as fondness, but I must do her the justice to say I esteem it only as friendship and good manners. For I have never met with more civil and friendly usage from anyone of the fair sex than I have from this girl.'[181] As the wedding drew near, Turner succumbed to a fever (psychosomatic, one can't help suspecting), and for fourteen days after the wedding (which took place on 19 June) he suffered intermittently. At this point the diary ends, suggesting that Turner now felt himself settled, if not necessarily completely happy, though he states himself 'happy in my choice', continuing: 'I have, it's true, not married a learned lady, nor is she a gay one, but I trust she is good natured, and one that will use her utmost endeavour to make me happy, which perhaps is as much as it is in the power of a wife to do.' Then, alas, I am rather sorry to say that his last words, entirely in keeping with the ethic of the time, are on her economic prospects: 'As to her fortune, I shall one day have something considerable, and there seems to be rather a flowing stream.'[182]

Turner's diary makes no mention of the procreative function of marriage, though this might simply have been due to personal reticence, particularly since his first marriage was in fact childless (as also, it transpired, was his second). But the production of children to continue the family line, provide labour and ensure support in old age was, as we have seen, a very strong motive behind marriage, which often meant that robustness rather than beauty was what was sought. From roughly the same period, in France, the account (somewhat dramatized) given by the novelist Rétif de la Bretonne of the courtships of his father, a humble clerk, indicates sensitivity to beauty while overwhelmingly demonstrating the influence of employers and parents, and above all of considerations of status and wealth, in marital choices.

Perhaps the single most interesting feature in Turner's comments is the emphasis on cleanliness, which really does remind us of the age we are dealing with; when such elementary considerations were to the fore, beauty was an unreal luxury. But just once in a while we get a fascinating single glimpse of personal preferences. Such a glimpse is offered by the advertisement placed by a country gentleman, 'fifty-two years of age next July, but of a vigorous, strong and amorous constitution', in the *Daily Advertiser*; he was looking for a wife:

Tall and graceful in her person, more of the fine woman than the pretty one; good teeth, soft lips, sweet breath, with eyes no matter what colour, so they are but expressive; of a healthy complexion, rather inclined to fair than brown; neat in her person, her bosom full, plump, firm and white; a good understanding without being a wit, but cheerful and lively in conversation, polite and delicate of speech, her temper humane and tender, and to look as if she could feel delight where she wishes to give it . . . She must consent to live entirely in the country, which, if she likes the man, she will not be unwilling to comply with; and it is to be hoped she will have a heart above all mercenary views and honest enough not to be ashamed to own she loves the man whom she makes her choice. She must not be more than fourteen years, nor less than seven years, younger than the gentleman.[183]

The upper age limit of forty-five suggests that the breeding of children was not a consideration. However, clearly the woman had to be personable, and there is an agreeable, and tasteful, stress on sexual 'delight'.

Now it would be absurd to suggest that marriage was a guarantee, or a condition, of happiness for a woman in the eighteenth century. Repeated pregnancies and births were a dreadful burden, so that sometimes wives were pleased rather than otherwise when their husbands did take mistresses and fathered children elsewhere. Nevertheless, all contemporary evidence suggests that, such were the attitudes, conventions and economic realities of the time that to remain unmarried was a likely cause of unhappiness for a woman. It would be quite inaccurate to suggest that the plain were the ones who did not get married (we have Thomas Turner's testimony to the contrary), but there is evidence to support the commonsense guess that matters were stacked against the ill favoured. The author of the *Tableau of Paris* commented sourly on the avarice for dowries which led, he alleged, to marriage being out of favour. Even more acid was his comment on the plight of the many young women who had neither fortune nor an attractive personal appearance: those with beauty, he declared, should be auctioned off to provide dowries for those without.[184]

The knowledge of being ill favoured could certainly bring bouts of unhappiness to men. Dudley Ryder, a shopkeeper's son who, through the prosperity of his father's business, was already moving in gentlemanly social circles, had a keen eye and a sharp concern for female beauty, as well as a full measure of sensuality: drink could temper the former and increase the latter. Of one social occasion he remarked: 'There were some few pretty ladies enough but nothing very extraordinary.' After another social occasion he 'was very warm with drinking wine and had a mighty inclination to fill a whore's commodity'.[185] Joining in the social round at Bath he was smitten by Sally Marshall, the 'most celebrated beauty' there. 'She had something so very agreeable in the cast of her countenance and features of her face as troubled me very sensibly when I first saw her.'[186] But in comparison with his handsome friend Samuel Powell, he saw himself as having no chance with Sally, remarking miserably on: 'My littleness and want of beauty, ill complexion, not being merry company nor gay and diverting'.[187] Whatever personal unhappiness there may have been, and Ryder remained single for another twenty years, his social ascent was not obstructed: eventually he became a peer and Lord Chancellor. In his forties, he married, and the marriage seems to have been happy enough.

As far as one can ever judge these things, David Hume, the celebrated Scottish philosopher and leading *lumière*, led a happy and fulfilled life, depending, however, upon what weight one gives to the probability that he died a virgin (encounters with prostitutes always being a possibility). Hume certainly had the enlightened intellectual's sensitivity to female beauty and, indeed – as already noted – was fully aware of the connection between beauty and sexual arousal: it seems that early in life he courted a beautiful young woman of good family, but was rejected.[188] He himself was certainly far from ugly and indeed in natural inheritance was not ill favoured. At age eighteen he was tall for his times, being just under six feet (however, in eighteenth-century eyes height could seem an oddity rather than an advantage); he was very thin, though quite pleasant looking. But Hume very quickly ran to fat, and by his thirties he was presenting a large, ungainly and even comical appearance. A seventeen-year-old student, a great admirer of the philosopher James Caulfeild, later Lord Charlemont, gave a slightly overdrawn account of Hume at thirty-seven:

Nature, I believe, never yet formed any Man more unlike his real Character than David Hume. What added greatly to the natural Awkwardness of Hume was his wearing an Uniform, which He wore like a Grocer of the Trained Bands . . . The Powers of Physiognomy were baffled by his Countenance, neither cou'd the most skilful in that Science pretend to discover the smallest Trace of the Faculties of his Mind in the unmeaning Features of his Visage. His Face was broad and fat, his Mouth wide, and without any other Expression than that of Imbecility. His

48 *David Hume,* medallion by James Tassie from a drawing by C. N. Cochin, 1764

eyes vacant and spiritless, and the Corpulence of his whole Person was far better fitted to communicate the Idea of a Turtle-eating Alderman than of a refined Philosopher . . . Tho' now near fifty years old He was however strong and healthy, but his Health and Strength, far from being advantageous to his Figure, instead of manly Comeliness, had only the Appearance of heavy Clumsiness and coarse Rusticity.[189]

The exaggeration of the age has been pointed out by Hume's distinguished biographer, E. L. Mossner, who very properly draws attention to Alan Ramsay's portrait of 1754 showing a 'not unhandsome' face with 'a high forehead, long straight nose, heavy dark brown eyebrows, grey-blue eyes, generous but sensitive and essentially diffident mouth',[190] but it would seem that the general image Hume projected was that of both ungainliness and of being old before his time.

It is through Caulfeild that we know of a special humiliation Hume suffered in Turin in 1748. Being told by Caulfeild of a beautiful twenty-four-year-old Countess, Hume requested that introductions be arranged. Caulfeild gives his own motivation as being 'an ardent Wish . . . that the Choice of my Heart shou'd be admired by a Man whom I so highly esteemed'. Hume was captivated and paid daily visits to the Countess throughout the following months: embarrassed, the Countess informed Caulfeild that she had 'made a compleat Conquest of the great Philosopher'.[191] Caulfeild attributed this to female vanity, remonstrating with the Countess: 'If my Friend were only armed by his Philosophy, I shou'd think that perhaps a weak Shield against your Charms; But Age is usually an Armour of Proof, and, however You may resemble Venus, I am sure that neither his Figure nor his Manner are those of Adonis.' To prove her point the Countess prevailed upon Caulfeild to eavesdrop on a meeting between Hume and herself. Mossner provides a vivid account:

Hidden behind the curtain that same evening, the youthful intriguer witnessed a scene from a Restoration comedy. He saw his 'old fat Philosopher' enter the room, plump down on his knees before the Countess, and protest his passion. Panting, sighing, groaning, Hume managed to bring forth after considerable effort, 'Ah, Madame, j'étouffe avec l'amour. Chère, Chère Dame, je suis désolé – abîmé – anéanti!' [desolate, ruined, annihilated]

'Oh! pour *Anéanti*,' replied the lady with more wit than charity, 'ce n'est en effet qu'une Opération très naturelle de votre Système.' She then ordered him to rise to his feet.

In his hiding place Caulfeild, with 'too much Vanity to be jealous,' was vastly entertained with Hume's endeavours to embrace the knees of the Countess. 'The picture of old, ugly, blubbering, fat, ungainly Passion' well nigh forced him into open laughter. 'Silenus on his Knees to one of the Graces,' he mused, 'or a Bear making Love to an Italian Greyhound wou'd be Objects ridiculous enough. But neither Silenus nor the Bear are Philosophers.' After toying with her unwanted love for a few moments more, the Countess assumed 'the most serious Air of Resentment' and curtly dismissed him. He left the room 'in a Burst of blubbering Affliction, Tears trickling down his flabby Cheeks.'

The account is colourful – and people do not, of course, speak in capitals – but the gist seems to be correct and Hume's problems became fairly common knowledge among his British colleagues, so that his humiliation was far from entirely private. However, sixteen years later, when Hume was quite definitely passing on towards old age, he had astonishing and gratifying successes among the most beautiful women of Parisian society. 'Mr Hume is the darling of all the pretty women here', Madame de Verdelin wrote to Rousseau, and much to his own amazement Horace Walpole, arriving in Paris in the autumn of 1765, had to confirm the same point.[192] Hume, recognized now as one of the greatest figures of the Enlightenment, was, no doubt, old and personally unattractive enough to be no threat: thus he could be pampered and petted. But it may not be true that he was completely neutered: when he was sixty there was talk of a possible marriage to Nancy Orde, then in her twenties – though certainly nothing came of this.[193] The experiences of David Hume make no general point save the obvious, but best not totally forgotten one, that in personal interchanges looks matter and are much remarked upon.

There is no space to belabour the point, but it may be noted that most of the unhappiness and much of the wayward behaviour of the poet Oliver Goldsmith was caused by his consciousness of his own ugliness:

'Look at that fly with a long pin stuck through it!', a passing bully once shouted.[194] Samuel Johnson's weird appearance is well known. His friends did not refrain from commenting on the matching oddity of the wife twenty years older than himself he married when twenty-six. Garrick spoke of her as 'very fat, with a bosom of more than ordinary protuberance, with swelled cheeks of florid red, produced by thick painting, and increased by the liberal use of cordials'.[195] True, she brought the needy Johnson a dowry of £600. But after her death he clearly missed her; and little hope had he of winning another spouse.

In discussing the importance of looks one must always be aware of the force of the counter-imperatives of power. Beautiful women, as we have observed, could often be at the mercy of powerful men, and in this one area at least, the sex roles were not necessarily very dissimilar. Dudley Ryder, lamenting his own lack of looks, was also given to comparing his misfortune with the good luck of the well-favoured Samuel Powell. It was from Powell that Ryder received information about certain goings on at the University of Oxford: 'he has been told that among the chief men in some of the colleges sodomy is very usual and the master of one college has ruined several young handsome men that way, that it is dangerous sending a young man that is beautiful to Oxford'.[196]

But let me finish this section with the paradigmatic story of the beautiful woman to whom, in a world where the odds were heavily loaded against women, beauty brought little happiness. Having begun chapter four with the French cultural hegemony established in the seventeenth century, it is appropriate for me now, as we move again into the last quarter of the eighteenth century, to cross the Atlantic to the colonial town of Philadelphia, just then at the heart of the revolution against British rule. Nancy Shippen was famous as 'a belle and beauty of Philadelphia during the closing years of the American revolution'.[197] The one visual representation we have of her, in a miniature attributed to Benjamin Trott, is not entirely satisfactory. The relationship of her head to her shoulders and bust is awkwardly realized, suggesting a lack of competence on the part of the painter himself, so that we can perhaps discount the apparently slightly puffy face and accept instead the good nose, sensual lips, large blue eyes and deeply potent expression of sadness which pervades the whole. If, in recording that she did incontrovertibly have a series of distinguished suitors, I also mention that she was the daughter of a very rich doctor and leading social figure in Philadelphia, this simply means that the good fairy had brought all three gifts to her cradle: wealth, status and beauty.

Of her many suitors, her very strong preference was clearly for Louis Guillaume Otto, Comte de Mosloy, the dashing French representative in Philadelphia who, as can be seen from the miniature by Jukes, painted in London in 1801, had features of highly refined beauty. Otto was an eligible enough suitor, though he fell slightly outside the normal pattern for an aspiring colonial family; in an almost classic example of marriage as an integral part of the serious business of improving wealth and status, Nancy's father insisted that she marry Colonel Harry Livingston from a famous, and rich, New York family. Livingston had served with distinction and great bravery in the Revolutionary war; he scarcely fulfilled, however, the qualities of compatibility and reliability in marriage which moralists and preachers stressed, but which family match makers evidently ignored. Her husband's infidelities and the open knowledge of his various illegitimate children decided Nancy, still apparently pining for Otto, to leave her matrimonial home and return to her parents; it was at this point that she began her *Journal Book*, which is the basic source for her life. The main characters are concealed behind pseudonyms and in the following extract, dated 'May 10, 10 at night', 'Lord B' is her husband:

Miserable all day – in consequence of a letter from Lord B. He tells me – O what is it that bad he does not tell me! but what affects me most is his accusing me of infidelity. Wretched Unhappy man – Nothing but your being jealous, and treating me ill in consequence of that jealousy, shou'd have tempted me to leave you – and now you say I left you because I loved another. – Had you not deceived me by so often swearing you loved me to distraction I shou'd not have been the wretch I am. O I am wretched indeed! and the father too of my sweet baby – I am almost distracted.

Three days later she reads some advice on matrimonial problems by Madame de Maintenon and decides to transcribe this into her *Journal Book*, which she does two more days later:

*May 15* – 10 in the morning – I sit down to write now what I intended to write the day before yesterday. I hope I shall not be disturbed. My baby lies asleep in the Cradle before me – I will write till she awakes –

Do not hope for perfect happiness; there is no such thing in this sublunary state. Your sex is the most exposed to suffer, because it is always in dependence; be neither angry nor asham'd of this dependence on a husband . . .

Do not hope that your union will procure you a perfect peace: the best Marriages are those where with softness and patience they bear by turns with each other . . .

Do not expect the same degree of friendship that you feel: men are in general less tender than women; and you will be unhappy if you are too delicate in your friendship . . . In sacrificing your own will, pretend to no right over that of a husband: men are more attached to theirs than Women, because educated with less constraint.

They are naturally tyrannical; they will have pleasures and liberty, yet insist that Women renounce both: do not examine whether their rights are well founded; let it suffice to you that they are established. They are masters, we have only to suffer and obey with a good grace.

'Thus far Madame de Maintenon must be allowed to have known the heart of man', Nancy agrees, but then, one is deeply relieved to find, reacts strongly against the gloomy moralizer of the late years of Louis XIV's reign:

I cannot agree with her that Women are only born to suffer and to obey – that men are generally tyrannical I will own, but such as know how to be happy, willingly give up the title of master for the more tender and endearing one of Friend. Equality is the soul of friendship: marriage, to give delight, must join *two minds*, not devote a slave to the will of an imperious Lord.[198]

Alas, her father's will and the social constraints of the time gave her little chance to act out these sentiments. In order that her daughter should benefit from the favour and wealth of the Livingston family, she had to agree to give her up. To no avail, in fact, since in 1797 the daughter (Peggy), at the age of sixteen, fled from the Livingstons to return to her mother; but Nancy, in a condition – understandably enough – of chronic distrust of her parents, and now shunned by Otto, was already in decline and moving into the state of melancholia in which she lived out the last forty hopeless years of her life. She had tried to secure a divorce, but that enterprise was doomed since her parents took Livingston's side in the matter.

## 6 *Politics*

In suggesting a possible relationship between that complex web of historical developments which may, for convenience, be termed 'modernization' and the growth of a perception of beauty as an autonomous status characteristic, I mentioned, as two important elements of modernization, the growth of representative government and the development of mass communications. The idea is that with a wide electorate, and ultimately, of course, with an electorate principally addressed by means of television, the external appearance, and therefore immediate appeal, of politicians comes to mean more and more. Only in Britain and her American colonies (I shall take up the American story in chapter six) was there anything approaching representative government in the period currently under consideration; the only means of visual communication of any significance was that of political caricature. We have already witnessed the impact particularly beautiful men, such as Buckingham, Cinq-Mars, Monmouth, even Lord North, could have in the realm of high politics. In the narrow world of eighteenth-century representative politics, it can be said right away, personal appearance counted for very little.

The one successful political leader who stands out in eighteenth-century Britain as having something in the way of a genuine popular following is William Pitt the Elder, subsequently Earl of Chatham, known to contemporaries as 'The Great Commoner', and described a century later by the *Dictionary of National Biography (DNB)* as 'pre-eminently the most striking figure on the English political stage during the eighteenth century'. All *DNB* biographies of leading political figures, drawing upon contemporary testimony and portraits, conclude with a formal section on the subject's personal appearance. With Pitt the Elder, the first emphasis is placed upon his voice, the biographer quoting from Butler's *Reminiscences* of 1824: 'his voice was both full and clear, his lowest whisper was distinctly heard; his middle tones were sweet, rich, and beautifully varied; when he elevated his voice to its highest pitch, the house was completely filled with the volume of sound'. As we shall find again, a good voice and an imposing presence are the most important personal qualities for a politician and for some time to come far outweigh considerations of mere beauty. The *DNB* biographer tells us that 'Chatham's figure was tall and imposing, with the eyes of a hawk, a little head, a thin face, and a long aquiline nose. He was scrupulously exact in his dress . . .' We also learn that 'his vanity was excessive, and he delighted in pomp and ostentation'.[199]

Pitt, then, was personable, but far from good looking. One of the other great popular figures of the eighteenth century, John Wilkes, was quite definitely ugly. Sir Joshua Reynolds put it thus: 'his forehead low and short, his nose shorter and lower, his upper lip long and projecting,

49 *Caricature of John Wilkes,*
William Hogarth, 1763

50 Prince Charles Edward Stuart, portrait in oils based on the pastel by Maurice-Quentin de La Tour first exhibited at the Paris Salon, 1747

his eyes sunken and horribly squinting'.[200] The caricature by Hogarth is one of the best known in eighteenth-century political caricature. Of it, Wilkes himself said: 'It must be allowed to be an excellent caricature of what nature has already caricatured.'[201] The Reverend Dr Alexander Carlyle, in his *Autobiography*, spoke of Wilkes's 'ugly countenance', but added that he was 'a sprightly and entertaining fellow'.[202] Wilkes did in fact take pains, through walking and riding, to preserve his good figure. He was dynamic, eloquent and, though direct in expressing his sexual interest in women who appealed to him, impeccable in manners. As the great and courageous campaigner against Lord North and George III, he attracted attention and won much favour. Politically he was successful, winning one of his most important battles against the government when the judiciary declared general warrants illegal; he was also extremely successful with women, it being said that his other qualities very quickly obliterated his face. In the politics of the day not only was it not essential to have good looks, but lack of them, provided other qualities were present, was clearly no serious handicap.

But let us not then fall into the error of thinking that looks in men were not noticed, were of utterly negligible importance. The very sobriquet of Prince Charles Edward Stuart, leader of the Jacobite Rebellion of 1745, should alert us against that. Looks gave him something of the popularity which attended upon Monmouth, but whereas Monmouth's looks may actually have affected events, birth and cause would undoubtedly have made 'Bonnie Prince Charlie' an active claimant to the throne even if he'd been born a hunchback. Just exactly how

49

50

good looking the prince really was is, as so often, a matter of dispute. As Donald Nicholas showed in his classic study, *The Portraits of Bonnie Prince Charlie* (1973), many of the best-known portraits are incompetent copies of copies, and many that are reproduced show him as a boy rather than a young adult. It was Nicholas's considered judgment that 'except perhaps for the portrait of him by La Tour, the Prince could not be called handsome'. For myself, I am prepared to back the judgment and talent of La Tour and find Charlie indeed bonnie, and I have reproduced a 50 contemporary copy of the original La Tour pastel of 1747. For a few months, after the Battle of Prestonpans, Prince Charles Edward lorded it in Edinburgh as the heroic cynosure. Looks, I am sure, were very much part of the overall image, though they were really rather wasted since the Prince, poor fellow, had no taste for beautiful women, even though they threw themselves at him.[203] His career, and legend, say much for the fact that, whatever ideology might exist about beauty being the prerogative of women, male beauty has always been of interest; on the political significance of beauty they say no more than that his looks contributed to his popularity and helped establish his precise identity – they certainly did not materially affect the course of history.

Hugh Smithson, the *DNB* boldly tells us, 'was the handsomest man of 51 his day',[204] and the Gainsborough portrait deliberately shows off his gorgeous legs – very important as a setting for the Order of the Garter. Silver spoons dropped by the dozen into the mouth of Smithson, yet it was surely his sex appeal that swept him into the marriage (strongly opposed by the bride's family) which led to him becoming first Duke of Northumberland in the new creation. He was born in 1715 in Yorkshire. In 1729 he succeeded his grandfather, Sir Hugh Smithson, as fourth baronet of Stanwick, Yorkshire. Eleven years later he inherited property in Middlesex from another relative, Hugh Smithson, Esq., of Tottenham. He became High Sheriff at York in 1738 and MP for Middlesex in 1740. This was also the year in which he made his brilliant marriage. Elizabeth Seymour was daughter of Baron Percy and granddaughter of the sixth Duke of Somerset (who strenuously opposed the marriage). On the death of the sixth Duke, Lady Betty's father was created Earl of Northumberland, with the succession to Smithson and his heirs by Lady Betty. Smithson succeeded in 1750 and in the same year assumed, by Act of Parliament, the name and arms of Percy. 'For the next thirty years Northumberland and his wife figured prominently in social and political life.'[205] In 1766 Smithson (now Percy) was created Duke of Northumberland. He had the face, the figure and the legs for it.

But, of course, it was social position that really counted. For those with it, like Catherine the Great, beauty was not especially important, though it was almost always better to be personable than plain, or worse. For the woman of lowly birth, beauty *could* be a passport to quite striking social advancement, though the risks were great and the strategy had to

51 *Hugh Smithson, 1st Duke of Northumberland*, Thomas Gainsborough, exhibited 1783

be carefully articulated. For men of lowly birth beauty could lead to comfortable, if not usually very elevated, positions. The actual patterns of the exploitation of beauty sharply differed between women and men: for women sexual transactions were inevitably involved; for men this could be, but was not necessarily so. Beauty was noticed and sought after, and it affected the experiences of individuals, but it still rated well below the primary autonomous status characteristics of the traditional world, social position and wealth: thus the social and political implications of personal appearance were still firmly circumscribed.

# 5 Beauty and the Growth of Entrepreneurial Society *c.* 1800–*c.* 1905

## 1 *Industrialization and Social Relations in Britain, France and the USA*

In chapter one I referred to those aspects of the development of modern society which, I believe, have ultimately resulted in the dethronement of traditional estimates in favour of an enhanced evaluation of beauty as an autonomous characteristic. They were: industrialization, urbanization, higher living standards, secularization, the advance of rationality at the expense of the mystic and the religious, greater equality between the sexes, better health, stronger sex drives and the notion of sex detached from procreation and indeed marriage. Central to my thesis is the notion that only when people have the opportunity to make choices and comparisons can they make a genuine evaluation of personal appearance. For rich and powerful males such opportunities had long existed, but it was only with the processes of industrialization touched off in the late eighteenth century that the possibility arose of such choices being extended to large numbers of the population.

Industrialization came first to Great Britain, though it then developed rather more spasmodically than some of the older textbooks have suggested. Within all three Western countries the exploitation of steam power meant that transport improved quite significantly around the mid-nineteenth century and in the immediately following decades. The impulse towards enterprise, innovation and what, of course, lies behind both of these, profit-taking, was strongly marked well before that, while the great industrial towns and cities of Britain and the USA, with their internal transport systems, newspapers and cheap facilities for reproduction of photographs, only assumed in the later part of the century the shape they were to hold till the 1960s. Urbanization, though not technological and entrepreneurial innovation, came more slowly in France, where many large industrial complexes were sited in quite remote country areas.

However, as far as industrial, technological and commercial phenomena are relevant to the question of beauty, the three countries essentially went through the same experience: living standards and health improved, middle-class groups prospered, while at the same time there were areas of the most severe deprivation and the continued incidence throughout all classes of physical deficiency and deformity. Recent research has challenged the stereotype of the sexual passivity of respectable women in nineteenth-century Britain and the USA,[1] and it is probably in the prospering business and professional groups that there was a growth in the appreciation of sex as an integral part of the good life (and, therefore, of course, according to my argument, a greater appreciation of personal appearance).

It is a part of popular wisdom in the Anglo-Saxon countries that the French are by nature especially preoccupied with questions of fashion, grooming, and so on, though whether a greater interest in self-presentation (on the part of both males and females), even if genuine, necessarily means a higher evaluation of natural beauty is far from certain. What the evidence (philosophical and other treatises on beauty, practical guides to beauty and grooming, etc.) suggests is that broadly the same changes in attitudes towards beauty took place in France as in Britain and the USA. However, there is one important contextual difference. In France an intellectual tradition of scepticism in the face of authority and convention and of rational appraisal of human behaviour is apparent in the seventeenth century, and again during the Enlightenment. Such a tradition exerted real influence through journalism, pamphleteering and the production and consumption of novels, and continued to grow in strength throughout the nineteenth century, effectively eclipsing the views on beauty peculiar to the more devout and puritanical members of the Catholic church. In Britain and the USA, on the contrary, public mores for the major part of the nineteenth century were dominated by the pieties of evangelical Christianity. Of course, the philosophical tradition stemming from both Plato and the medieval church was far from impotent in France; but it was the British and American upper classes, especially through the educational establishments known as public schools in England, and as boarding schools in the USA, who deliberately propagated an amalgam of Greek and Christian ideas.

Here, then, are elements which run counter to the processes of modernization, and which are distinctive to each society. With regard to the United States, large areas were affected by the ethics and the aesthetics of the frontier, where often the struggle for survival left little scope for the appreciation of personal beauty. The insecurity of a nation perched between the high civilization of New York, or Boston, or New Orleans, and life lived at the very fringes of primitivism, can be seen in the highly conventionalized codes of morality and behaviour established on the East Coast, particularly in Boston. Such codes usually cut across an appreciation of natural beauty. It would, I believe, be a mistake to take the physical qualities of those women who found employment as dancers

in cattle towns, frontier encampments and gold-rush saloons as necessarily representative of a considered American judgment on what
constituted beauty in women.

Among middle-class women in Britain and the USA, though probably
less so in France, where the Catholic church had considerable influence,
knowledge of contraception spread relatively widely in the second half of
the nineteenth century. Thus (though strictly within marriage, save for
all but a few very daring women) sex and procreation were now set
slightly apart. Among English aristocrats in the first part of the century,
and at the court of Louis Napoleon in the 1850s and 1860s, affairs, and
conceptions, outside of marriage took place more or less openly, as they
also did in the circle of the British Prince of Wales (later Edward VII); but
on the whole the public orthodoxy in the later part of the century was
very much one of fidelity within marriage, involving a heavy taboo on
illegitimacy. Again these are conditional constraints upon the free
appraisal of beauty. But for all that Christian religion in its various forms
was fundamental to society of the time (though not for the teeming
masses in Britain's industrial slums, as the devout discovered to their
horror), the nineteenth century is a crucial era in the advance of rational
and scientific thinking with regard to questions of sex and personal
appearance. I have already discussed the views of the Darwinians and the
Freudians; in fact more 'scientific' approaches to sex and beauty are
apparent well before Darwin's work was published. Mistaken as all were
in some respects, these approaches did offer a challenge to the traditional
association of beauty with morality and truth – though, as we shall see,
such ideas persisted with great tenacity.

Did women gain greater equality with men in the nineteenth century?
On the one hand, one has to look very critically at stereotypes of the
Victorian woman as totally passive and dependent, as the 'angel in the
house'; on the other, one should avoid any assumption that the emancipation of women is an inevitable concomitant of the laws of progress and
must have been greatly assisted by the economic and social transformations of the nineteenth century. The most important point, it seems to
me, is that the role and status of women was a matter of open discussion
and debate in the second half of the nineteenth century. Previously only a
few voices had spoken out against the subjection of women; now men, as
well as women, argued that they should have rights as citizens. Committed novelists such as George Eliot expressed the disabilities under which
women suffered; uncommitted ones like Anthony Trollope remarked on
the ways in which young women at mid-century enjoyed greater
freedom than they had done a generation or two before.[2]

But the inescapable fact remains that in 1900 women were still very
much in a subordinate position. However, changes can be seen in the
establishment of married womens' property rights, and of the right of
women to vote (in local elections in Britain, in state elections in parts of

the USA), in the trade union activism of some women and, above all, in the views being expressed by women on all aspects of relations between the sexes (privately in letters for the most part, but also sometimes publicly).

And here we come to the truism that if we are seriously to consider changes in the position of women, we also have to consider changes affecting men. In the next section I shall look at romanticism and the rise of what has been called 'affective individualism', involving the argument that greater mobility, greater security and a new sensibility fostered by certain philosophers and poets were challenging earlier ideas about marriage being essentially a matter of stern practicality in which personal inclination was relatively unimportant. The essential point is that through the nineteenth century there was greater scope, for women as well as men, to express personal choices in regard to the selection of a mate. As these choices are made, the 'traditional' assumption that beauty pertains only to women and that it is unimportant whether or not a man is beautiful is subjected to severe scrutiny. However, it should be stressed that in many rural areas choice remained as restricted as ever.

Immediately relevant is the question of clothing and fashion. In the early nineteenth century male and female clothing became differentiated as never before. While women continued to dress in elaborate, colourful and often extravagent ways, male costume became increasingly sombre and plain, most obviously featuring trousers which, on the whole, managed to conceal the shape of the leg, and coats or jackets which gave no special emphasis to manly shoulders, or a virile chest. Hats continued to be worn but not in any profusion of variety or colour; rather than individuality, the type of hat worn indicated class, occupation, or occasion. Yet it would be wrong to assert, as it often has been, that a new mould was established which remained unbroken for the next century and a half. Male fashion did change, though usually in small and subtle ways; there grew up an elaborate code of what could, and more important, what could not, be worn on particular occasions. But the essential distinction between the sexes was abundantly clear. Commerce, business and the professions flourished (if not without much risk taking and many bankruptcies); aristocrats discreetly adapted to the new sources of profit. The new form of dress, suitable for urban man, was also influenced by the developing English aristocratic ideal of gentlemanly understatement. Male dress suggested hard work, solidity, respectability, continuity. Only bohemians and soldiers stood out; the fact that both groups were widely held to have instant sex appeal for women reveals that the respectable civilian male was deliberately opting out from this aspect of self-presentation. It almost seemed that the eighteenth-century assertion of the primacy of practical considerations in marriage was being reinforced, with men wishing to stress their role as steady investors and reliable breadwinners rather than dashing suitors or passionate lovers. More distinctly than ever before it was being made clear that it was women's role to dress up; that it was women's role to 'be beautiful', in the sense of 'making efforts at elaborate self-presentation'.

For, of course, women's fashions in the nineteenth century were very far from showing off natural attributes. There had, in fact, been a strong move in that direction at the end of the previous century when, in the aftermath of the French Revolution and during the search for what were thought to be classical ideas of dress (as well as classical ideas of politics), there was a reaction against the elaborate artificialities of the eighteenth century and an attempt to recreate the simple flowing robes of classical Rome. Indeed, in 1790s Paris among certain leaders of revolutionary fashion (or rather, of one revolutionary fashion – not all male politicians approved) there flourished a style sexier than anything to appear again before the twentieth century, with breasts bared and diaphanous fabrics clinging to the legs. The empire line which, as it were, celebrated Napoleon's declaration of himself as Emperor of the French, was not so revealing, though it retained classical simplicity and some respect for the natural contours of the female body. In Britain breasts were never so fully revealed, but in a more or less restrained way the fashionable followed the decrees of Paris.

For most of the nineteenth century, however 'natural' a fashion might appear, it generally concealed layers of starched petticoats which restricted the physical activities a woman could undertake and also imposed a heavy burden of time and care as she prepared herself to meet the world. Some feminists have argued that fashion has always been designed to restrict and constrain women and to keep them in a passive and dependent position. For some fashions and some societies, there is undoubtedly truth in this, but it seems basically an unsatisfactory theory which, as feminist writing so often does, actually underestimates the extent to which women exercised initiative and choice within those areas where it was possible for them to do so. Whether that theory, or any other theory for that matter, is correct or false is not relevant to the main concerns of this book; fashion is important here only in so far as it indicates how natural beauty was evaluated and how far beauty and self-presentation were thought to be matters exclusive to women. As always, there were men who expressed impatience with female fashion, and their wish that women would show more of their natural form and employ less in the way of padding and disguise; others, of course, strenuously upheld the current conventions of women's dress and spoke pompously about what was 'charming' and 'becoming', and fulminated against what went beyond 'modesty'. There is also a long and ignoble tradition of masculine mockery of women, of their 'silliness' and alleged absurdities of dress.

In 1796 an English provincial newspaper had commented: 'It is an extraordinary circumstance that although there are scarce two women alike yet all adopt the same mode of dress; and the fat short woman imagines, when she has tied her girdle under her arms, that in dress and graceful shape she can vie with those who are elegantly formed by nature.'[3] A decade later another male writer was expressing his appreciation of the new fashion (sometimes described as the 'naked fashion'), though he did feel that, 'in the midst of this praise I must be permitted to make an observation; and that is, some thoughtless females indulge in the licence of freedom rather too far, and show their persons in a manner offensive to modesty'. His substantive comment was:

The ladies have at length, much to their honour, thrown aside those hateful attempts to supply Nature's deficiencies or omissions, the false breasts, pads and bottoms; and now appear in that native grace and proportion which distinguishes an English-woman: the Hair, cleansed from all extraneous matter, shines, in beautiful lustre carelessly turned round the head in the manner adopted by the most eminent Grecian sculptors; and the Form appears through their snow-white draperies in that fascinating manner which excludes the least thought of impropriety.[4]

Different men, obviously, had different personal views; the documents must always be read with that simple point in mind. None the less, I want to bring out that the documents do suggest a growing recognition of the economic potential of women's fashion and grooming in a highly commercial, entrepreneurial society. As newspapers developed in the early nineteenth century and sought to increase their readership, they eschewed mockery and took more and more to straight reporting of London and Paris fashions, interspersed with only the occasional admonitory note, as in an article 'On Taste in Female Dress' published in 1817 in the provincial newspaper already quoted (the *Chester Chronicle*). This declared dress to be 'the natural finish to beauty'; without it, 'a handsome woman is a gem, but a gem that is not set'. The writer then re-establishes his *gravitas* by declaring that in some respects he entertains 'a perfectly philosophical contempt of dress' but adds that he will 'not shrink from the avowal that, in the contemplation of a beautiful woman, elegantly and tastefully attired, I have at all times enjoyed a pleasure of no vulgar cast'. His conclusion nicely balances the various assumptions and developments I have been discussing:

The love of dress is natural to women. This has been seen and attested in all ages and in all countries of the world, in the most savage as well as in the most polished states. It is a laudable, a useful, and interesting propensity; but it requires to be chastened and regulated by the hand of taste, by a sense of the beautiful in nature, of the correct and harmonious in art.[5]

After the relatively 'natural' lines of the first decade of the century ('natural' is a dangerous word, as is 'simple' – simplicity in one aspect of dress could be accompanied by fantastic elaboration in another: in a hat, say, exuberantly festooned with flowers and feathers), the most obvious fashion development related to the female bottom, ranging from padding, to small ribbed constructions, to the expansive crinoline of the 1850s. Such constructions had been seen before, as in the farthingale of Elizabethan times, and in eighteenth-century high fashion, but generally these gave width to the body, while the crinoline most palpably jutted out to the rear. What complex of circumstances created this fashion it would take a foolhardy historian to define. Obviously, the crinoline enabled women of diverse shapes and sizes to achieve one universal silhouette signifying the essence of womanhood. In it women seemed to glide rather than walk, suggesting that they possessed nothing so carnal as legs. It created space around a woman, suggesting virginal untouchability. This effect was heightened by the prim, oval bonnet, usually known as a 'coal scuttle', introduced to London earlier in the century by the Russian Baroness Oldenburg. Two contrasting stories about the Baroness hit off exactly my central point about fashion. One version said that she was so beautiful that everybody copied her bonnets; the other said that she was so ugly that the bonnets were designed to hide her face.[6] As the century moved towards its end dress followed more naturally the lines of the body, but a body always constrained and prodded by the harsh magic of the corset. Head gear became ever more elaborate. Although respectable women could not use cosmetics in any way that showed, throughout the nineteenth century artifice easily outplayed naturalness. On the whole, fashion continued to be consistent with a traditional rather than modern appraisal of beauty.

Greater geographical mobility and the expansion of travel facilities and opportunities were a facet of nineteenth-century society of particular significance for the main themes of this book. The Grand Tour of the eighteenth century had been undertaken only by aristocrats. Now such products of a lower order of society as Charles Dickens travelled far further afield. Dickens toured first in the United States (1842) before, two years later, making the journey to Italy. In the USA he found that collectively the women of Boston were 'unquestionably very beautiful' and those of New York 'singularly beautiful', while on the tiresome river-boat journey to Cincinatti he picked out one individual beauty.[7] His sensitivity to various types of ugliness is strongly expressed in his description of the Italian tour: he found the young women of Genoa 'not generally pretty', the priests 'repulsive', and he shortly encountered 'a monstrous ugly Tuscan'. But he also remarked upon a 'handsome' friar, a 'savagely good-looking' postilion, and many 'beautiful' or 'handsome' women.[8] Over a decade earlier, Thomas Hamilton from Edinburgh had travelled widely in the United States. Subsequently he allowed himself the indulgence of two published volumes in which to describe his experiences.[9] Hamilton wrote on such topics as his 'presentation to the

President', the 'manners of the higher orders', 'aristocratic feeling', the 'character of the people', the 'climate of the United States', 'barbarism in language', and 'Broadway'; but by page fourteen of the first volume he has turned to the 'beauty of the women', and he subsequently discusses the 'ladies of New York', the 'ladies of Boston', and the (female) 'quadroons' and 'creoles' of New Orleans.

Baltimore, he notes, 'is celebrated for hospitality, and the beauty of its women'; he can, he adds, 'bear testimony to the justice of its reputation for both'. The ladies of Baltimore 'are remarkable for personal attraction':

indeed, I'm not aware that, in proportion to the numbers assembled, I have ever seen so much beauty as in the parties of Baltimore. The figure is perhaps deficient in height, but sylphlike and graceful; the features are generally regular and delicately modelled, and the fair Baltimoreans are less remarkable than American ladies usually are for the absence of a certain fullness and grace of proportion, to which, from its rarity, one is led perhaps to attach somewhat too much value as an ingredient of beauty.

From this somewhat graceless remark he descends further:

The figure of an American lady when past the first bloom of youth, presents an aggregate of straight lines and corners altogether ungraceful and inharmonious. There is an overweening proportion of bone, which occasionally protrudes in quarters where it certainly adds nothing to the general charms of the person. The result is, perhaps, a certain tendency to *scragginess* ...[10]

The same thought obtrudes upon his consideration of the ladies of New York where, he says, he has 'observed many countenances remarkable for beauty, among the more youthful portion of the fair promenaders', but then adds that 'unfortunately beauty in this climate is not durable'.

At one or two-and-twenty the bloom of an American lady is gone, and the more substantial materials of beauty follow soon after. At thirty the whole fabric is in decay, and nothing remains but the tradition of former conquests, and anticipations of the period, when her reign of triumph will be vicariously restored in the person of her daughter.

The fashions of Paris reach 'even', as he puts it, to New York. Announcing himself 'something of a judge in such matters', Hamilton then claims that he can pronounce ex cathedra 'that the ladies of New York are well dressed, and far from inelegant'. He adds that the average of height 'is certainly lower than among my fair countrywomen: the cheek is without colour, and the figure sadly deficient in *en-bon-point*'.[11]

In New Orleans, his first concern is with the low standard of morals; after that he turns to the 'coloured women' or 'quadroons':

I have heard a great deal of the beauty of these persons, but cannot profess having been at all smitten with their charms. One often meets a fine figure among them, but rarely a fine countenance. The skin is dingy, and the features are coarse. Something of the negro always remains – the long heel – the woolly hair – the flat nose – the thick lips – or the peculiar form of the head.

But the Creole ladies, on the other hand, struck him as 'handsome':

They too are dark, but their complexion is clear not clouded, like that of the quadroons. Their figure is light and graceful, and with fine teeth, and an eye, large, dark, and bright, they must be admitted to possess quite as much attraction as the New Orleans gentlemen deserve. The effects of this enervating climate however are visible enough. The Creole ladies speak with a sort of languid drawl; their motions want energy and briskness, and the efficacy of their charms might perhaps be increased by a little more animation. [12]

Hamilton was quite convinced of the gross inferiority, compared to that of Britain, of the American climate (and the disastrous consequences thereof) and he was led from this observation to a general condemnation of the appearance of the American population as a whole:

The heat in summer is that of Jamaica; the cold in winter that of Russia. Such enormous vicissitudes must necessarily impair the vigour of the human frame; and when we take into calculation the vast portion of the United States in which the atmosphere is contaminated by marsh exhalations, it will not be difficult, with the auxiliary influences of dram-drinking and tobacco-chewing, to account for the squalid and sickly aspect of the population. Among the peasantry, I never saw one florid and robust man, nor anyone distinguished by that fullness and rotundity of muscle, which everywhere meets the eye in England. [13]

A snobbish and chauvinistic commentator, then; but one who – and this is what I want to bring out – clearly felt that a commentary on the personal appearance of the women he encountered was an important element in his tour. However, Hamilton does also comment on the personal appearance of President Jackson (though these comments must be considered alongside the ungracious ones on older American women):

General Jackson is somewhat above the middle height, spare, and well formed. Though he has probably numbered more than the years specified by the Psalmist as forming the ordinary limit of human life, no symptom of decrepitude is visible in his air or motions. His hair, though nearly white, is abundant, and on the upper part of the head bristles up somewhat stiffly. The forehead is neither bald nor expansive, though by no means deficient in height. The head, like that of Sir Walter Scott, is particularly narrow in the region of ideality. The countenenance of General Jackson is prepossesing; the features are strongly defined, yet not coarse; and, even at his advanced age, the expression of the eye is keen and vivid. [14]

As middle-class readers with money to spend on books became increasingly numerous and as the publishing industry expanded, more and more travel books were published (particularly in Britain), a large number of them betraying this same interest in the appearance of all, or some, of the female population of the countries visited. Many of these books formed a part of the great scientific enterprise of accumulating information, which will be discussed in the next section. In their private diaries too, men recorded their impressions of the women they encountered. Genuine admiration, racial stereotyping and acknowledgment of the continuing almighty power of wealth combine in an entry from the diary kept by Captain James E. Bouldu of his journey from Missouri to California in 1849–50. The Captain has arrived at a ranch in California and is sitting beside a young lady who is to be married in a few days:

She was a Beautiful girl for a Spaniard – much more delicate than most of them – a considerable tinge of the Indian and Spaniard but quite dark though her features are delicate, figure trim and fine hair black as a raven black eyes and white teeth but with all this she like all the rest of her race has no animation or sprightly appearance which spoils all her beauty ... [her father is] said to be worth 2 or 3 millions of Dollars ... this hides her inanimation ...[15]

Travellers were aware that female beauty was not always to be spotted in the most obvious places. Another voyager to California at the same period, while in Durango, Mexico, one Thursday in April 1849, after spending the afternoon at a cock fight, went to church at night where he 'saw some of the prettiest women that I ever saw anywhere'.[16]

With men, private inclinations in the matter of female beauty were not wildly different from their published reflections on the same matter. Men had much greater freedom and opportunity to travel than women had. But, and there is a double thrust to my argument here, as the century advanced some women (though still in a rather limited way) did have greater opportunities to travel further and more frequently than ever before, and so had new opportunities to observe and respond to the many varieties of male beauty. These might be recorded in private letters and journals; they were not usually published in the manner of a Thomas Hamilton or a Sir Richard Burton.

American women, as Dickens noted, travelled widely and unchaperoned. Mary Hallock, at the age of twenty-two, was quite accustomed to travelling alone by boat between her home up the River Hudson and New York City. To a friend she described one return journey: 'the boat was pervaded by lovers. They were very funny but there was besides something rather grand in their supreme and utter indifference to public opinion. But I found myself after the way of the world more interested in the well-dressed and handsome lovers than the plain and awkward ones.'[17] It is a characteristic of traditional ideals of beauty that they are largely derived from purely verbal and fictional sources, while the modern appraisal of beauty is based on actual living, moving people, even if these are seen only on film or television. Mary Hallock refers her friend to 'Clive's blond beauty' in *The Newcomes* by Thackeray:

I confess to a weakness for the beauteous Clive; he is one of a series of ardent generous gallant youths of whom I have been very fond at various stages of my novel-reading career. Quentin Durward was about the first and had the least intellect of any of them but even he with his honest heart, strong arm and comely face was more satisfactory than our melancholy subtle modern Hamlets, old before their time, and weary of the world.[18]

After her marriage in 1875, Mary Hallock Foote moved to California. She described her impressions of some of the powerful men she encountered in San Francisco:

Mr Hague is very handsome and has great harmoniousness – he never jars – I fancy his calm philosophy conceals a gentle cynicism – but it is not evident – Mr Ashburner is prematurely gray, with keen dark eyes which give distinction to the otherwise plain countenance – Mr Janin is dark and strong jawed – very black, troubled-looking eyes – I speak of the men first because at the dinners and evenings they talked to me and because they were rather more remarkable than the women.[19]

The experiences of more famous women such as George Sand and George Eliot will be recounted in the next chapter. Let us now go straight to the beginning of the new century to note how, travelling alone on an ocean liner between Britain and New Zealand, Katherine Mansfield (aged seventeen) registered her reactions to the presence of one beautiful male:

The first time I saw him I was lying back in my chair, and he walked past. I watched the complete rhythmic movement, the absolute self-confidence, the beauty of his body, and that [the next word is marked as *illegible* in the version of the journal published much later by her husband, but presumably the word is 'longing' or 'desire', or 'excitement', or something similar] which is everlasting and eternal in youth and creation stirred in me. I heard him speaking. He has a low, full, strangely exciting voice, a habit of mimicking others, and a keen sense of humour. His face is clear cut, like the face of a statue, his mouth completely Grecian. Also he has seen much and lived much and his hand is perfectly strong and cool. He is certainly tall, and his clothes shape the lines of his figure. When I am with him a preposterous desire seizes me, I want to be badly hurt by him. I should like to be strangled by his firm hands.[20]

But for present purposes there is much illumination to be derived from works intended for immediate commercial publication. One great arena of entrepreneurial opportunity for the publisher was that of advice on beauty and grooming. I shall be returning to grooming guides in the final section of this chapter; here my main purposes are to explore further two issues: the question of how far beauty continued to be treated as essentially a female concern, and comparisons and contrasts between French, British and American attitudes. Actually the two issues come together in the, no doubt not unexpected, fact that, while the overwhelming majority of the grooming guides of all three countries do concentrate on women, it is in France that most serious attention is given to male self-presentation. Guides for respectable French women are as full of inconsistency and bland reassurance as all such works have to be; but there is sometimes more openness on the matter of sexuality than is ever found in nineteenth-century British or American guides. Approving reference is often made to the great French courtesans of the past, such as Ninon de Lenclos or Marion de Lorne – British guides do not invoke Nell Gwyn or Barbara Villiers – and French works are more likely to recognize that women, as well as men, are capable of promiscuity and sexual infidelity. French discussions on beauty and grooming, in short, do share some of the perceptions advanced so vigorously by the French Realist novels of the early and middle nineteenth century. Stendhal, as we saw in chapter two, in effect argued that it was more important to a man that a woman should be immediately sexually available to him than that she should be beautiful. With Balzac and others, he broke with the venerable tradition that a heroine must, by virtue of being a heroine, be beautiful; novels now suggested that a woman, even if plain or old, could still be passionate, active and loved.[21] I do not want to make too much of this; but to summarize, the implication of much French writing is that since it is only given to a few women to be truly beautiful anyway, in life as actually lived by the majority it is more important to strive to be attractive rather than beautiful. Anglo-Saxon writings tend to stress the value of what they call 'beauty', but then beauty, it often turns out, is being taken (with much inconsistency and double thought) to include moral as well as physical qualities.

To concentrate now on the particular issue of whether beauty was thought to pertain to women alone, let us consider a fascinating French publication of 1825, *The Secret of Conquering Women and Holding Their Affections*, a book which, as far as I know, has no equivalent in Britain or the USA. The book is not, as might be expected, a guide to the arts of seduction. Its clear premise, and in this it is very much in the traditional mould, is that it is important for a man to make a sensible marriage; thus the book offers advice to men both on how to make themselves pleasing to women and also on how to choose an appropriate wife. It is 'modern' only in its insistence on the value of a good appearance to men, and on the power of beauty in women. Discussing first 'The Art of Pleasing' the book begins with 'Physical Qualities', remarking that they are the ones which come into play most immediately and the ones whose effects are the most involuntary. A tall stature, regular features, good proportions exercise from the start an almost irresistible power, which, the book continues, in an interesting anticipation of evolutionist theory on this subject, comes from an instinct natural to all beings to tend towards preserving the beauty of the species. In love there is always an element of personal vanity: a woman is flattered to captivate a man whom her rivals find beautiful. Evidently anxious not to lose the custom of readers whose stature falls short of the desirable, the author then adds the reassurance typical of almost all works on personal appearance: those who are short can often make up for this by their grace and vivacity; if a man is well proportioned one can forget that he is small. But it is not possible to console all customers: beauty is a matter of proportion, and a fat man is as disagreeable to the eye as an extremely thin one; however (and perhaps this is a sop to the fat) thinness is less suited to love.[22]

After these introductory, and perhaps slightly arbitrary, opinions, the book settles down to practical advice on care of the hair, the mouth, the teeth, the eyes and the eyebrows. With regard to the mouth it is recognized frankly that a man with a sweet-smelling mouth will be most likely to invite kisses; fine teeth are the finest ornament. This highly rational section concludes with the admonition that an indispensable quality for pleasing women is cleanliness and that in this area excess is quite permissible.[23] Then ineluctably we move to 'moral qualities'. With this extended aphorism we are right back in the heart of traditionalism:

The mind [the French *l'âme* does not distinguish between 'mind', 'spirit', or 'soul'; to suit the tone of the book I have chosen the most secular translation] is truly the man; without it the purely physical appearance has no charms; it beautifies every feature through giving them their expression . . . the mind is everything; without it there is no eloquence, no talent, no true beauty . . . with a sensitive mind one is beautiful, with a dull one the most regular features will give birth only to the most ephemeral passions.

This concluding phrase, at least, is consistent with the opening statement that good looks are most immediately effective in arousing a response. But the conclusion to this section is that 'ugliness is no longer a fault in a man who is courteous and engaging'.[24]

The section on how to retain a woman's affections sets out, in a way nineteenth-century books of this sort in English would not do, to explain woman's basic nature: 'all of them desire a man of birth, fortune, and beauty [*un beau physique*]'. There then follows a warning, again reminiscent of the preachings of the seventeenth and eighteenth centuries: beauty in a woman is often destructive of the happiness of a husband; a lovely woman always has many admirers, who will usually succeed in ruining his peace of mind since it is rare for a beautiful woman not to succumb to temptation. Beauty, then, is not a quality which a man should look for in a wife. In fact – and here there is an interesting departure from the usual advice of the eighteenth century, one that reaffirms that it is the physical side of marriage which is under contemplation – a quality much more precious to a husband's happiness is health: without health there will only be loathing and disgust, for physical attraction cannot exist without health. The final pages of this section are more conventional, though continuously obsessed by women's potential for infidelity. Qualities of the heart are more important than wealth; adultery results from young women marrying rich old men: 'A man who is much older than his wife, whatever his other qualities, must expect to be deceived.'[25] But poverty should be avoided; that is to say, if a man is poor he shouldn't marry. If he does marry he should marry someone of the same social status; otherwise he risks humiliation.

A still more noteworthy work, of exactly the same period, is the *Code of the Toilet, Complete Manual of Elegance and Hygiene, Containing the Laws, Rules, Applications and Examples of the Art of Caring for One's Person, and of Dressing with Taste and Method* by Horace Raisson, which had gone through five editions by 1829. This book is that genuinely remarkable artifact, a thoroughly unisex guide to beauty and grooming (albeit, it is slightly sexist in that, in general terms, it is addressed to 'men of the world'). Yet in almost all respects this book has the true ring of the nineteenth century about it. It is a sermon in support of the absolute essentiality of devoting care, time and orderliness to one's grooming. Upon those who have natural beauty there falls the heaviest responsibility to cherish and conserve it. Beauty is 'the most precious, as it is the most perishable, of items in the world in which we live'.[26]

Raisson offers fascinating testimony to developments in the evaluation of beauty particular to his era and country; but, more important, he is a star witness to my case that at all times there have been penetrating observers able to see that whatever the public mores, whatever the dictates of fashion and convention, natural beauty has always had significance. His commercial objective, of course, is to equip his readers, male and female, to cut an acceptable figure in the society of their day. He does say (in seeming contradiction of the point I have just made) that beauty is a matter of convention and that it varies in character depending on period and context; but he then continues that it always entails an idea of grace and harmony and, further, that we are naturally predisposed to believe that a beautiful person possesses a natural gift and precious qualities.[27] The nineteenth century rings through in his declaration that even the most perfect beauty will gain a new sparkle from orderliness, and from care in presenting it in exactly the most appropriate way: 'one can accept ugliness, but negligence, never'. He declares that the era of make-up is passed, that true appeal lies in a soft and fresh pallor. He signals a peculiar nineteenth-century affectation when he declares 'what a misfortune to have red hair', while implicitly recognizing the absurdity of that prejudice when he asks rhetorically, 'hasn't red hair for ten centuries been regarded as the most beautiful?'[28]

He allows wigs 'to be respectable', but then asks: 'may one not however smile at the pretension of those youthful old men, who hide a forest of grey hair beneath a wig of Adonis?'[29] Chapter ten deals with the care and styling of the beard. However, maintaining the unisex tone, towards the end of the chapter a sentence begins, 'As for the ladies . . .', there following some advice on the disposal of superfluous hair. It may at first sight seem strange that the unisex approach continues into the discussion of dress, given that it was at this very time that male and female costume were becoming so distinctly differentiated from each other. In fact Raisson's comments bring out that however great the differences, men and women do share common objectives of self-presentation. According to Raisson, 'elegance, lightness, and suppleness of figure constitute one of the qualities essential to beauty; one's manner of dressing contributes to showing off to the best advantage this quality if one possesses it, and to simulating it if one does not'. He then pronounces that for both elegance and health one needs clothing which embraces and clings exactly to the figure and the buttocks, so that particular attention must be given by women to the corset, and by men to the belt of their trousers. At the same time a certain erectness of posture is essential to both men and women; however, it is for women only that he recommends metal stays.[30]

Yet Raisson has nothing to say on features peculiar, and essential, to feminine beauty, features which figure prominently in all later nineteenth-century books on beauty: the breasts. Instead, he pays interesting attention to the arms, claiming that while beautiful arms are important to a woman, for a man they are among the foremost elements in his grace and general appearance. When he does turn particularly to women he again shows his ability to penetrate beneath the temporary conventions of fashion to one of beauty's universal truths. In spite of the fashion for plumpness, he counsels women to stay slim: 'guard preciously your slimness, beautiful ladies, and console yourselves with the thinness of your figure, the lightness and elasticity of your step, and the comfort of your clothes . . .'[31]

Towards the end of the book there is a practical section on the preparation of such beauty aids as cleansers and oils; he is, as we remarked, against the use of powders and paints. It is the fact that for most of the nineteenth century cosmetics did go out of fashion; it would probably be wrong, however, to attribute that to a belief in natural sexual beauty, rather than to a somewhat prudish association of cosmetics with loose sexual morality. Raisson himself has a conclusion on 'Morality', in which he warns in particular against excesses in, for example, such matters as tight corsets. Raisson's final sentence again combines elements of nineteenth-century entrepreneurial society and elements of universal truth: 'One's *toilette* is founded on cleanliness, not on indolence; inevitably it must favour beauty, but above all it is health that it must affirm and develop.'[32]

From France in the early part of the century, then, there is clear evidence that beauty and care over personal appearance are not simply regarded as the prerogative of women alone. It may be recalled (from chapter three) that British beauty manuals of the eighteenth century were almost exclusively directed towards women, and were excused on the grounds of the frailty of human nature (in essence, the frailty of men who too often judged women not, as by prevailing public mores they ought to have done, by their mental and moral qualities, but by their external appearance). There is a very marked change in the British manuals of the first half of the nineteenth century which adumbrate the attitudes towards preoccupation with self-presentation which were to dominate the later part of the century. The tone is matter of fact, rational, even scientific: it is obviously sensible that individuals should take care of their personal appearance. Since the activity is straightforward and sensible there is no reason why males should be excluded; several of the manuals do indeed, in a general way, address both sexes, though the assumption clearly remains that grooming is a matter of much greater significance to women. *The Book of Health and Beauty or the Toilette of Rank and Fashion* of 1837 announces in its subtitle that it is offering 'a variety of select recipes for the dressing room of both sexes'. *The Toilette: or A Guide to the Improvement of Personal Appearance and the Preservation of Health* of 1854 plunges straight in with a scientific disquisition on the nature of human hair, both male and female. It then notes that: 'There is no more attractive ornament to the handsome features of a man, or the lovely face of a woman, than a fine set of teeth', adding that there is no pain more acutely distressing than toothache. In contrast to the eighteenth-century concession to human 'frailty', the 1837 work declares that 'a rational desire to improve and beautify the surface of the body' is 'no frivolous pursuit'. The tone is utterly unapologetic, down to earth and practical. This desire to beautify 'excites as much interest and is productive of as beneficial consequences, as the exertions of many *pseudo*-philosophers, who devote the toil of years to arrange their notions in certain systematic forms, but who are not fortunate enough to attain the great object of their labours'. Then, still more positively, the virtues of moderation, the active life, health and empiricism are invoked: the authors have had many opportunities of observing 'that the desire of beauty, when restrained within moderate bounds, may prove a source of virtuous and laudable pursuits, and may also be greatly instrumental to the preservation of health'. Thus, having noted the harm done by false recipes, they are now offering a list of 'empirical preparations'. Despite the subtitle and despite the general claim that the book demonstrates that 'beauty and health are inseparable companions', it is in fact almost exclusively addressed to women; only one brief chapter contains 'Directions for Easy Shaving'.[33] *Female Beauty* (1857) by Mrs Walker (wife of the physiologist) made no pretence of aiming at men; but its break with the notion of 'frailty' was equally sharp: 'a due attention to . . . Regimen, Cleanliness, and Dress, is a proof of love of order, regularity of conduct, and habits of cleanliness; and it therefore produces a favourable impression on those who observe it'.[34]

The manifest assumption behind eighteenth-century manuals was that women beautified themselves to gain the approval of men. In essence the assumption has not greatly shifted in the classic Victorian doctrine of beauty as a woman's duty. Yet, interestingly (in respect of my contention that a link exists between female emancipation and the modern evaluation of beauty), in arriving at this doctrine, *The Toilette: A Dressing-Table Companion* (1839) premises (inaccurately, of course) that 'in all European nations woman is made and treated as the equal and companion of man'. This position is founded on woman's superiority in 'the combined beauties of mind and body': the preservation of this superiority 'is not only a duty which she owes to herself, but likewise to society at large'. Thus, 'it is a duty of the greatest importance that the various parts of our beautifully constructed frames, should meet daily attention which they so much require, particularly from the female sex . . . who are destined not only to become the companion of man, but likewise the mother of his children'.[35]

An increasingly dominant theme in this age of science, sewerage, and concern for public health, is embodied in the title of a work by Robert Dick, MD, *The Connexion Of Health And Beauty* (1857). The tocsin of duty is sounded again: health is essential to those charms of person which every woman 'ought, perhaps, always to exhibit'. Males just about scrape in: 'We need scarcely here observe, that for those of the male sex, who are desirous of being distinguished by a fine personal appearance, many, or all of the rules and directions about to be given will be found useful.'[36] A brief guide entitled *The Art of Beautifying and Improving the Face and Figure*, of 1858, moves us beyond duty and into the entrepreneurial era and the cool evaluation of beauty: 'Every person is aware of the importance of good personal appearance with both the sexes; good looks in a man, and comeliness and beauty in a woman, influence both their fortunes and happiness in life.'[37] Several themes come together in Arnold J. Cooley's exhaustive study *The Toilet and Cosmetic Arts in Ancient and Modern Times with a review of the different theories of beauty and copious allied information, social, hygienic, and medical*, of 1866, a book aimed at small shopkeepers desirous of mixing their own cosmetics for sale, as well as at individual readers (presumed to be male). The Creator, says Cooley,

has not merely endowed man with an instinctive care of personal cleanliness, but has also implanted in his bosom a feeling of self-pride, or rather say, of self-respect, which, when controlled by reason and good taste, incites him to a laudable, but not an excessive attention to those *duties* and particulars which it is my desire to enforce and explain. (my italics)

At one point Cooley far outbids any claim I might myself make for the significance of my subject: 'A mere notice of the influence of personal beauty alone, on individuals and on society, in all ages of the world, would embrace the whole history of the human race.' But at once he's back to the provoking of thieves: 'It has, perhaps, owing to the lawless passions and vices of mankind, been productive of more contention than has been caused by ambition, and more misery than has been occasioned by avarice and gold.'[38]

After the 1860s, and still more towards the end of the century, there is a great expansion in the number of beauty books produced, almost all of them, as we shall see, directed quite unambiguously at women. This parallels an expansion in the printing industry generally, and a considerable rise in the production and distribution of newspapers. The latter is in itself an important development, for newspapers began to carry stories, and pictures, of famous beauties, Lillie Langtry, say, or Lillian Russell, or Sarah Bernhardt. Thus again people's notions of beauty were extended, their powers to make comparisons and contrasts, if only of photographs, expanded: at least the photographs were of real people, not the invented figments of romance. One must also take into account technological developments of earlier in the century. Critical improvements in the mass production of engravings took place in the 1820s and 1830s. Probably the single type of subject matter most widely distributed as a result was that of attractive young womanhood: often publishers managed to combine an ostensible educational purpose with a little mild pornography.

*Finden's Tableaux of National Character, Beauty and Costume* (1843) could, said its publisher, only be offered on the mass market because of modern inventions in the art of engraving. A work of such merit was 'formerly within the reach of the affluent only'. The book's main selling point was its sixty-one beautiful illustrations; these, however, were accompanied by 'original tales in prose and poetry', specially written by 'the Countess of Blessington, Miss Mitford, L. E. L, Mrs S. C. Hall, Allan Cunningham, Barry Cornwall, Leigh Hunt, and others of the most popular authors of the day'.[39] Whatever the titles of the 'Tableaux', they all managed to feature women in positions of prominence, and usually in states of undress titillating for mid-Victorian times. Within beauty as a relative universal, as I have said, greater or lesser weighting will be given to cultural conventions in different eras. Despite their alleged different nationalities, all the women here have similar features: in the classical style of Greek statues, as reinterpreted by Raphael, they tend to be round faced, with big foreheads and gentle chins, and maidenly, almost simpering, expressions; they do none the less conform to a recognizable type of sexually attractive beauty. In 'Greece – The Wounded Patriot', the attention is monopolized by two young women in this style. In 'Georgia – The Two Sisters', we get both a naked breast and a naked

52 'Arabia', engraving from *Finden's Tableaux of National Character, Beauty and Costume*, 1845

back. The trick to both 'The Romaunt Of The Page' and 'The Ministral Of Provence' is that both the Page and the Minstrel are women in men's clothing so that – rare treat for Victorian men – we get a good view of their legs. In 'Scotland – Sir Allan And His Dog', Sir Allan is, in fact, in the middle distance, viewed from the rear: the foreground is commanded by two of the usual young ladies.[40] Similar 'Athenian' types were featured 52 in a later volume (1845) of the same publication.

Productions such as *Finden's Tableaux* demonstrated beauty unconfined by crinoline or coal-scuttle bonnet, but they also reinforced a stereotype of facial beauty. Engravings, and then photographs, of real, breathing, beautiful women, particularly actresses, circulated widely in the later decades of the century. However much women might conceal themselves behind the trappings of fashion, young men were being presented with new standards of female beauty against which to make comparisons and contrasts.

In concluding this sketch of the general factors which gave rise to the specific developments to be examined in the other two sections of this chapter, I must re-stress the depressing, indeed tragic, features of the age. For all the growth in Gross National Product brought by industrialization, for all the bounce of the entrepreneurs, for all the concern for public health and personal hygiene, the ordinary inhabitants of all three societies – British, French and American – were a prey to harsh working conditions, debilitating sickness, congenital deformity and sudden death.

One product of commercial expansion was the rise of the commercial traveller. A source from 1847, probably slightly fictionalized, shows one commercial traveller in a rather more sympathetic light than that usually cast on him by tradition and suggests the kind of hazards which prevented a working woman from preserving youth and beauty. Among the *Sketches from the Life of a Commercial Traveller* by Throne Crick is one of 'A Waitress At An Hotel', describing her 'unintermitting occupation, distending the muscles, increasing the size of the ankle and width of the foot, while ascending and descending a flight of steps from the kitchen to traveller's room and bar, and back again into the kitchen . . .' But her

neat and cleanly appearance, and invariable good humour, constantly cheer us; for although her once rosy tinged and healthy looking cheek is now blanched, and has long lost its colour in our service, it has not lost its power to charm. Yet although her spirit may be willing, her flesh is evidently weak, and indicates not only unceasing labour by day but wearing, tearing fatigue by night.[41]

Unwittingly, many beauty guides bring out just how prevalent were ugliness of feature and deformity of body and limb. References to plainness are not frequent, but when they come they are often couched in degrees of matter of factness, resignation, or callousness. References to nose machines for dealing with ill-formed noses are almost grisly. Recommendations of the use of shoulder braces give an insight into endemic physical weakness:

Excellent teachers of physical training say the will alone should be used to force oneself to stand straight. This is true of a person in perfect health. But round shoulders often result from weakness of sedentary pursuits, against whose influence it is useless to struggle; and I would not debar any half-invalid from the luxury of the support given by a strict pair of braces.

Another extract highlights the prevalence of one particular deformity:

A crooked leg is a matter for surgical treatment; and in these days of curative ingenuity, with steel braces it will be but the work of a few months to bring the most awkward limb into shape. Those who have seen the wonders wrought with deformed children who have crooked limbs and bodies will consider it a simple matter to bring a partial disfiguration under control.[42]

Despite the optimistic tone, optimism is not the sentiment one is left with.

No matter how perfectly formed, how beautiful a child or young man or woman might be, everywhere the risks of fatal disease were high. In her journal entry for 17 November 1834, Eugénie de Guérin lamented the death in her village of a beautiful young woman, who left an unweaned baby, remarking that, 'One speaks only of illness and death . . . It is the malign fever which carries out its ravages, as in every year.'[43] The reality of childhood death in Middle America at mid-century is brought home most movingly by this letter from one young girl to another (I have not altered the punctuation and spelling, nor supplied the two missing words; the recipient, Charlena Van Vleek, later Mrs Melville Anderson, was eleven or twelve at this time – presumably this was the age too of the writer):

Ellington April 23rd 1865

My dear friend Charlena

It has been a long time since I heard from you. I am well and guess all the other scholars are well. I heard that you have been sick but are better, and that Wilma was dead. I was sorry to hear such news. But there is sorrow all around here. I presume you heard that our school mate Nora Manley was dead. She was taken sick the 29th of March and died the 8th of April at twenty minutes past twelve o'clock. I saw her the day before she died she could hardly breath and her were swollen very large she died at noon the next day. She now sleeps by the side of Eunice. She gave away her things she gave me her doll and she gave Laura a book I shall always remember Nora by the doll Mrs Manley had Nora's likeness taken after she died don't you remember Charlena how you and used to talk about her we did not think how soon she would be remembered with the dead.

There have many others died among them are Jason Manely and Lobby Grant. I presume you heard all about Jason Manelys death. I wish you could come out here to school this summer it seems as though the schoolhouse will be like a prison.

We made sugar this season and if you will come out here I will give you a small cake of sugar though I don't know as it would be much of a treat. I wish you lived on your old place so that you and I could rove about in the woods and find may flowers as we used to I have found a few may flowers this season but it seems no one to enjoy them Nora and I used to find them but she has gone and you and I used to and you have moved away Laura is my only school mate now. I guess you cannot read this that I have written so I will not write anymore

From your friend<br>Annie Kethrol[44]

In the wider sweep of human concerns, when death, disease and deformity are still widespread, there must obviously be a limit to the significance which one can place on the beauty of adults lucky enough to survive in good health and reasonable living standards.

## 2 *Romanticism, Science and the Consolations of Religion*

At the beginning of the eighteenth century, in laying down the canons of taste which became part of the mainstream of public thought through-out the century, Anthony Ashley Cooper, Lord Shaftesbury – as we saw – was very critical of what he called 'Romantick Passion'. Romantics, of course, exist in any age, but historically the term Romanticism or 'The Romantic Movement' is generally used to refer to those poets and artists, working around the beginning of the nineteenth century, who reacted against the calculated, tasteful, dignified standards of eighteenth-century society and against the manifestations of the industrial society which sprang out of eighteenth-century rationality and accumulation. The Romantics sought release from the pains of the present by looking to the past, or to the future, or to nature; they believed in the rights of individuality and the passionate expression of feeling.

Broadly defined as an historical phenomenon, Romanticism can be taken to include, for instance, John Constable, the Suffolk painter, best known for his freely executed and passionately felt landscapes. Constable's skies are usually dramatic. They are not, as might be thought, the products of frenetic bursts of romantic inspiration. Constable, in fact, spent hours in the meticulous study and recording of cloud formations, in scientific study one might almost say. The word 'science' was just beginning to come into widespread use and still held most of its older connotation of 'systematic body of knowledge'; the word scientist was not invented till the 1830s. At this time, therefore, there was not necessarily any sharp distinction between scientific activities and artistic activities, nor necessarily any incompatibility between science and Romanticism. Indeed an important task of this section is to show how Romantic and scientific impulses came together to give a greatly enhanced evaluation of human beauty, as expressed in H. T. Finck's *Romantic Love and Personal Beauty* of 1887 (in which, very early on, the author makes the connection most self-consciously by remarking that Romantic love is not much older than the telegraph). But let me stress again that there is no simple linear development from 'traditional' to 'modern' attitudes towards beauty. Romantic sensibilities on beauty (far from consistent in any case) are not modern sensibilities; certain matters which were the subject of rigorous scientific enquiry are quite at odds with the conception of beauty as an autonomous characteristic.

In the earlier part of the nineteenth century there was, in particular, an enormous vogue for what was thought to be the scientific study of physiognomy, with large numbers of books being published on the subject in the wake of many reissues of Lavater's famous work.[45] Robert Owen, factory owner and social reformer, had great faith in the subject, as did, later in the century, the eminent thinker Herbert Spencer. Physiognomy had a notable influence on creative writing in France and Germany. Those who, during act two of the opera *La Bohème*, are moved by Rudolfo's *Mimi è una civetta . . . ma ho paura, Mimi è tanto malata* ('Mimi's a flirt . . . but I'm afraid, Mimi is so ill') might be taken aback by the description provided by her original creator, Henry Murger, in *Scènes de la Bohême*, set in the 1840s (both Mimi and Musette were courtesans, whose actual prototypes will be discussed in the next chapter). Mimi's features, Murger wrote:

took on, in certain moments of boredom or temper, an almost ferocious brutality from which a physiologist [*sic*] would perhaps recognise the indications of a thorough-going egotism or of a total lack of human sensitivity.

Murger punished Mimi far more severely than did Puccini: told, in error, that she is already dead, Rudolfo – luxuriantly bearded, but prematurely bald, according to Murger – fails to keep his promise to visit her in hospital so that she dies in utter loneliness and despair. The Bohemians then go on to become successful participants in the world of entrepreneurial money-making.[46] Theories that good looks reflect moral qualities and that ugliness is an indicator of evil seem obviously to run counter to the modern conception of beauty. However, Dr Roy Porter, with all his usual elegance and wit, has recently argued that our modern high evaluation of beauty is simply an extension of nineteenth-century physiognomy, whereas eighteenth-century fashion was the enemy of physiognomy in that it concealed the true expressiveness of feature through which the physiognomist could divine character.[47] Personally, I see highly artificial fashions and physiognomy as going hand in hand in distracting attention from the true value of natural beauty. In any case, in spite of being incorporated into the fashionable subjects of phrenology, craniometry, and then physical anthropology and racial theory, physiognomy was pretty thoroughly discredited by the later part of the century, though elements of it continue to surface in popular works. It may be recorded that as early as 1806 the *Gentleman's Magazine* was happy to declare it 'fallen into oblivion',[48] and that a (rather exceptional – and anonymous) guide to beauty of 1826 presented the 'modern' view as trenchantly and unambiguously as any Firenzuola or Dover:

Even the knowledge of vicious or improper conduct in a beautiful woman does not make us consider her to be . . . deprived of all her beauty. It may, and ought to, diminish our respect for her; but though we know her to be abandoned to every sort of crime and indecorum, we cannot withhold our testimony to the beauty of her form and complexion, which, in many cases, is so powerful as even to overcome our detestation of her guilt.

The argument continues:

there are, perhaps, a greater number of females of plain and homely appearance, who have health, and innocence, and intelligence, and gaiety, and delicacy, and vivacity, than of those called beauties, who have these qualities and dispositions – The truth is, we make a marked distinction between a lady who is beautiful, and one who is amiable.[49]

This is both an instance of the rational approach which was increasingly to dominate scientific endeavour and possible testimony to the growing strength of private inclination over the public morality of which Henry Fielding had been such a dedicated upholder.

The scientific impulse was seen most commonly in a desire to reduce all subjects (including beauty) to systems of classification or laws. *Kalogynomia, or the Laws of Female Beauty,* by T. Bell, MD, first published in London in 1821, is, among other things, noteworthy for its very detailed anatomical drawings of the male and female sex organs. With respect to these there is a special note at the beginning of the book explaining how these plates, which 'should not be carelessly exposed either to Ladies or to Young Persons', have been stitched up separately:

As the work is a scientific one, and calculated both by its mode of construction and by its price for the higher and more reflecting class of readers, and as the plates above enumerated are also entirely scientific and anatomical, the Publisher might have dispensed with this precaution; but he is anxious that these readers should have it in their power to obviate the possibility of the careless exposure of such anatomical Plates: they are therefore detached from the work, and may be looked up separately.[50]

Bell argues, not very convincingly, that there are three types of female beauty; what he really means is that there are three female anatomical types. He does, however, argue that there is just one universal standard of beauty admired by all, by which he clearly means the Grecian type. His insistence that beauty is essentially related to sex has a modern ring to it, though it might be commented that the book seems to be more about the physical than the aesthetic aspects of sex.

The book ends with a 'Catalogue Raisonné of defects of female beauty', and these turn out to relate to physiological functions, such as gestation, parturition and the 'sexual embrace', rather than to beauty of feature or form. It is as a preliminary to this catalogue that he provides his list of 'indications, by which the Kalogynomist, who happens to follow a female in the street, or on the promenade, may be aided in determining whether it is worth his while to glance at her face in passing',[51] from which I have already briefly quoted in chapter two. The list, in slightly expanded form, is repeated by Alexander Walker (author also of a book on physiognomy) in his *Beauty, Illustrated Chiefly by an Analysis and Classification of Beauty in Women*, first published in London in 1836. Highly popular – there was a fifth edition in 1892 – Walker's book is very much a scissors-and-paste effort: despite its scientific veneer, it therefore repeats most of the traditional contradictions and confusions on the subject of beauty, paying no heed to the trenchant modernism expressed ten years earlier in the anonymous guide of 1826. 'Goodness and beauty in women', says Walker in a tone somewhat different from that in which the advice on how to spot beauties in the street is given, 'will be found to bear a strict relation to each other; and the latter will be seen always to be the external sign of the former'.[52]

Early 'scientific' writings, then, pointed to no consensus about the nature and evaluation of beauty; neither did the utterances of the Romantics, nor their behaviour. The Romantic cult of the beauty of nature in all its untamed wildness was very different from the code of tasteful restraint laid down by Shaftesbury and eighteenth-century arbiters of the beautiful, and both verbal and visual portraits of human beings in the Romantic era throw dignity to the winds, showing beauty as sex appeal; but when Keats spoke of 'the mighty abstract Idea of beauty I have in all things',[53] or Shelley of the 'Spirit of Beauty, that dost consecrate / with thine own hues all thou dost Shine upon / Of human thought or form',[54] they were nearer to Shaftesbury and to Plato than to any notion of the autonomy of beauty. The ideas and the poetry of Keats were not well known in his own time, but to many Victorians the last words on beauty were those of the last stanza of 'Ode on a Grecian urn':

Beauty is truth, truth beauty, that is all
Ye know on earth, and all ye need to know.

For a couple of generations now, literary scholars have been pointing out that these lines are spoken, not by Keats, but by the urn, and that we must not assume that they express Keats's own personal views on the subject.[55] Be that as it may, their importance for changing, or in this case unchanging, evaluations of beauty is that, in the Victorian period, they were used as supporting testimony to the Platonic outlook. On the other hand, a rather different utterance of Keats's has achieved almost as much fame, a purely private one which became known to the Victorians with the publication of the first collection of his letters. As we have no letters from her to him, we can only imagine the remonstrance from Fanny Brawne, the young woman to whom he shortly became engaged, to which the following was the reply:

Why may I not speak of your Beauty, since without that I could never have love'd you? I cannot conceive any beginning of such love as I have for you but Beauty. There may be the sort of love for which, without the least sneer at it, I have the highest respect and can admire it in others: but it has not the richness, the bloom, the full form, the enchantment of love after my own heart.[56]

The respect is for the love described by Fielding; but the full, rich, romantic passion is only aroused by the outward beauty which Fielding had affected to detest. Such too was the view of Shelley, discussing 'sentimental love' and the proper conditions for a sexual relationship (in words, however, not published till 1931, and even then only in an edition of a hundred copies):

. . . the person selected as the subject of this gratification should be as perfect and beautiful as possible, both in body and in mind; so that all sympathies may be harmoniously blended, and the moments of abandonment be prepared by the entire consent of all conscious portions of our being; the perfection of this intercourse consisting, not perhaps in a total annihilation of the instinctive sense, but in the reducing it to as minute a proportion as possible, compared with the higher faculties of our nature, from which it derives its value.[57]

Being both well connected and extremely good looking, Shelley had    53
*choices* (an important sub-theme of this book) not open to Keats and was in a far better position to practise the precepts of Romantic passion. On the other hand, his life, from his student days, when he published his

53 *Shelley*, Amelia Curran,
1819

pamphlet *The Necessity for Atheism* and eloped with the beautiful servant girl Harriet Westbrook, till his death, several beautiful women later, in the Gulf of Poets, Italy, could also serve as a homily on the text of beauty as a dangerous snare and delusion. The Romantic concern was with love rather than marriage, with personal inclination rather than social or familial calculation. It did not inexorably entail an exalted status for beauty, but articulated a special preoccupation with beauty of personal appearance. The domesticated version, the counterpart of 'truth beauty, beauty truth', was rendered (in prose), long after both Keats and Shelley were dead, by one of the most sensitive and lyrical of Romantic poets, Leigh Hunt, who declared

we find beauty itself a very poor thing unless beautified by sentiment . . . unless she has a heart as well as a face, and is a proper good-tempered, natural, sincere, honest girl, who has a love for the people . . . Mere beauty [we are back to that eighteenth-century phrase] ever was, and ever will be, a secondary thing, except in fools . . .

It turns out, however, that mere beauty is not being dismissed after all: 'the most fascinating women are those who can most enrich the everyday moments of existence . . . beauty is little without this. With it, she is indeed triumphant.'[58]

The 'triumphant beauty' is beauty in women, the traditional conception. Yet Romanticism as a Europe-wide movement did place on centre stage the notion of the Romantic hero who, if not necessarily beautiful, was always striking in appearance. Shelley clearly took personal appearance to be a consideration for both partners in the sexual embrace, and he himself had the perfect looks for a Romantic hero. However, the first vigorous and sustained presentation of the case that the male could appeal to the female purely on the grounds of looks and sexual prowess, and not on those of economic security and social promotion, was already embodied in the career of Lord Byron, who was being lionized while still a student in 1802. It would almost be proper to say of Lord Byron that he was the first (heterosexual) male pin-up in history, save for the awkward fact that many of the women who wrote or fantasized about his beauty had never even seen a picture of him, let alone pinned it above their pillows. Still, the fundamental facts were that he *was* very beautiful and that his beauty was much commented on and swooned over. That it was *his* beauty and not someone else's that attracted so much attention was due in part to his reputation as a poet and lover – another instance of the celebrity effect; and, while he scarcely offered social or economic security, his title undoubtedly had its own appeal. To these qualifications I must add the further one that among women who did actually meet him personally, a quality many found most arousing was his voice. 'The tones of Lord Byron's voice were always so fascinating, that I could not help attending to them', said the novelist Amelia Opie, adding that it was

54 *Byron in Ottoman costume*, Thomas Phillips, 1813

'such a voice as the devil tempted Eve with; you feared its fascination the moment you heard it'. At a small evening party, Jane Porter, author of *The Scottish Chiefs*, was distracted 'by the most melodious Speaking Voice I had ever heard. It was gentle and beautifully modulated. I turned round to look for the Speaker, and saw a Gentleman in black of an Elegant form . . . and [the continuation is noteworthy] with a face I shall never forget.'[59] The face ('so beautiful a countenance I scarcely ever saw', said another contemporary) was entirely nature's bounty; but the elegant form Byron achieved through a deliberate, if eccentric, slimming campaign: hot baths, copious draughts of vinegar, violent exercise. This, together with his use of curlers, points up the explicit promulgation of male beauty. His deformed foot interfered not at all with the beauty, merely adding the requisite romantic edge to it[60] (in a former age, though, this deformity might have been seen as a sign of evil).

One part, then, of the Romantic legacy was an emphasis on natural beauty and its sexual associations; another was faith in the importance of personal choice in sexual matters. Exercise of personal choice in matrimony was in any case becoming more widespread with the growth of what historians have termed 'affective individualism', though this was mainly an urban rather than a rural phenomenon. Possibly it was among the urban working classes, where lads and lasses had little in the way of inheritance to bother about, that freedom of choice was first most widely practised. Undoubtedly the notion did grow throughout all classes,[61] a higher regard being paid to personal appearance. Of course, social and economic pressures could still bear heavily in the other direction. The advice tendered by Lord Monson to his son in the 1850s strikes a judicious middle:

I hope to heavens you will not marry entirely for money. It is a sacrifice that would be dreadful and which nothing would justify. If you could meet with a very nice girl indeed her being an heiress would be no objection . . . I do not see why a little money or even a good deal is to prevent love. It would certainly be very desirable that the young lady of your choice should have something. But I would rather it was less with a nice girl, than more with the contrary.[62]

Freedom of choice, and therefore, perhaps, a high evaluation of beauty was probably greatest in the United States,[63] while French commentators, still apparently assuming that in some earlier age matters had been different, openly lamented the small part beauty played in marriage choices compared with mercenary calculations. The French literary and historical scholar Alphonse Karr in the 1850s, speaking particularly of the middle classes, declared that 'it is today an accident, a sort of prodigy when a man marries a woman solely because she is beautiful'. Beauty, he continued, 'in our time of mercenary preoccupations has fallen in value'.[64] In fact, as I shall show later in this chapter, beauty was going up in value, though certainly it had not yet come near to attaining the esteem it was to be accorded in the late twentieth century. Of course the dice was loaded differently for the two sexes, and it seems rather unfair of another French intellectual, Paul Diffloth, at the beginning of the new century, in his lament about decadence and the devaluation of beauty, to complain that beautiful girls preferred rich men, rather than young beautiful ones. As for men, it was not that they were unmoved by beauty, but simply that other calculations were more important: 'there is not a man who does not feel the power of beauty and does not desire the possession of a perfect body, but if the heart had, at the time of Pascal, reasons of which reason knows nothing, in our own time, cold reason dominates feeling demonstrating to men the inconvenience of unions based on reasons of the heart'.[65] The real significance of these lamentations lies in their assumption that mere beauty *ought* to be valued above other more practical considerations.

Meantime science was offering reasons of its own for placing a high value on beauty. Darwin, as we saw, was contradictory in some of his utterances, but the general tenor of theories of sexual selection (and these, as we have also noted, considerably pre-dated Darwin) was that it was through the selection of beautiful mates that the quality of the race was improved. The races that thus cultivated beauty, it was implied, were the superior races. The great mass of information which the Victorians (and their French and American counterparts) assiduously accumulated from their prodigious travels was often paraded in support of such views. The Count of Gobineau, who had been French Minister in

Persia, Greece, Brazil and Sweden, stated in 1854 that 'of all human groups, those belonging to the European nations and to their descendants are the most beautiful'. To be totally convinced of this, he said, all you had to do was to compare the various types spread out across the globe. Beauty is both an absolute and a necessity: the white race is superior in beauty to all the others who, among themselves, differ in beauty by the extent to which they are closer or further from the white model. Thus, apart from any qualities of intelligence, civilization, etc., there is an inequality of beauty among human groups, a logical, explicable inequality, which is permanent and indelible. Gobineau's standards, of course, were those of Western civilization, the subject of this enquiry. Not everything he said was totally prejudiced. He thought that the most successful results from the point of view of beauty arose from marriages between whites and blacks. In support he cited the powerful charms of mulatto and quadroon women, dismissing in comparison Russian and Hungarian women whom he saw, utterly inaccurately, as products of a union between the yellow and white races.[66]

Almost all race theory, and much of eugenics, was nasty in both assumptions and conclusions. Together they probably did little more than reinforce existing prejudice, but the theory of sexual selection is important in connection with this present study in that it stressed the physical and sexual aspects of beauty, rather than any alleged association with truth or morality. The major pioneer of eugenics, Francis Galton, had his more charming side. He had a special pocket 'registrator' with which to record 'the percentage of attractive, indifferent, and repellent looking women he met in his walks through the streets of various towns with the object of forming a "Beauty-Map" of the British Isles'. He never completed the project, though he did reach the conclusion that London had the most, and Aberdeen the fewest beautiful women of the towns he had observed.[67]

Sexual selection was brought together with Romanticism in a most striking way by a young German–American, Henry Theophilus Finck. Despite the improbable name, and despite the inevitable constraints imposed by the culture in which he lived, Finck is, as a good example of *l'homme moyen sensuel*, worthy of some credence in his pronouncements on beauty. His life, furthermore, exemplifies that mobility I see as enabling increased comparison and appraisal of personal appearance. Both his father and his mother came from near Stuttgart in Germany, but they did not actually meet until they both found themselves part of a German–American settlement in Bethel, Missouri. He was an apothecary and a gifted amateur violinist. Henry was born in 1854; when his mother died a few years later his father moved the family to Oregon, travelling via Panama. In the predominantly German community of Aurora Mills, Henry, with the assistance of Christopher Wolf, a graduate of Göttingen, nurtured his ambition to traverse the entire width of America in order to study at prestigious Harvard. The young Finck supported himself on scholarships, and in 1876 he graduated with highest honours, having majored in philosophy and psychology, and also taken classes in music. On borrowed money he travelled to the first Bayreuth festival, with commissions to do reports for a couple of American journals. He wintered in Munich, returned briefly to the US, then spent three more years on a scholarship in Berlin, Vienna and Heidelberg. He changed his middle name, Gottlob (after his mother's distinguished brother, Professor Fink of Tübingen), to its nearest Anglo-Saxon equivalent, Theophilus. Disappointed in his hopes of an academic career, he established himself as a music critic and popular lecturer. As can be seen from the photograph in his autobiography, Finck was a very good-looking young man, and it is clear that, no doubt with the decorum suited to the age, he took a lively interest in attractive young women.[68] Although he was subsequently to bring out books on Chopin, Wagner, Grieg and Schubert, his first book was, in the language of the time, a 'philosophical work', *Romantic Love and Personal Beauty*. Published in two volumes in 1887, it was immensely successful in both the USA and Britain.

So successful was it in fact that Finck's thoughts turned towards marriage. Continuing his extensive travels (his appraisals of beauty in *Romantic Love and Personal Beauty* were based partly on his own travels and partly on the many other travel and anthropological books of the time to which I have already referred), he met in Spain a certain Mr Curry 'and his niece Virginia a girl of dazzling beauty', who made such an impression on him that he decided to make her a present of the one copy of his book which he had with him. Virginia was a blonde; embarrassingly, as may be recalled from chapter two, Finck, in this same book, had declared brunettes vastly superior to blondes. Finck's response towards Virginia's blonde beauty demonstrates once again just how feeble are conventions about what constitutes beauty in face of real beauty of whatever type. Understanding well that Virginia was scarcely going to be entranced by the views on blondes he had expressed in the very book he was intending to give to her, he had a 'happy thought': 'I gave her the book after writing in it following her name; Please remember that the chaper on "brunettes versus blondes" was written before I had seen you.' In fact he didn't marry her, 'nor did I marry one of half-a-dozen other beauties who had temporarily dazed me'.[69]

The woman he did marry was called Abbie Helen Cushman. His description of their first meeting both shows that the processes of getting acquainted with a beautiful woman don't change much and also suggests that, whatever the conventional mode of expression, it is not so much beautiful eyes as the eyes of a beautiful woman which thrill. Abbie was at a concert in New York in the company of Nellie Learned, managing editor of the *Evening Post,* who was known to Finck. 'One glance and I hastened to sit right behind them, casually as it were. I was introduced to Abbie and the first glance of her dark merry eyes stabbed my heart . . .' Abbie was only seventeen and the marriage did not take place for another four years. His comments on Abbie at twenty-one again show (as with Sarah Bernhardt) the absurdity of the notion that men in the nineteenth century could not appreciate beauty in women who were not buxom: 'She had no figure worth talking about at that time, being slight as a school girl, which makes it the more remarkable that I, a born sensualist if ever there was one, should have fallen so madly in love with her.' Not remarkable at all when one looks at the slim beauty in the photographs reproduced in Finck's autobiography. It was, Finck continued,

55

a genuine romantic love: eye love, face love, soul love. And she has a mind as well as a soul. Music was her passion, and her preferences were usually the same as mine. Soon she began to help me with my critical work and after a few years she could write so cleverly in my style that few could detect the author.[70]

The autobiography, of course, was written many years later. But we probably have here as good a personal and 'real' a definition of the romantic, affective individualism of the nineteenth century as in Keats's letter to Fanny Brawne or Shelley's 'Discourse'. We also see how male centred this conception was, and how far women still were from the kind of independence which I have stressed as being closely associated with the full emergence of a genuinely modern evaluation of beauty.

55 Abbie Helen Cushman
Finck, photograph, *c.* 1890

Now, I have spent some time on Finck's biographical details, partly because of the evidence they offer in support of fundamental themes in this book, partly because they provide the context within which to evaluate his attempt to combine Romanticism and Darwinism. Much of what was said by the early nineteenth-century Romantics did not, on examination, appear to differ greatly from what had been said by Platonists and medieval romancers, though it did differ from the conventional wisdom of the seventeenth and eighteenth centuries in stressing the importance of individual preferences in love and marriage. At first sight, some of Finck's pronouncements do not seem so different either. But the crucial point in Finck's book, and in what was coming to be widely believed among the wealthier classes (hence Finck's excellent sales figures), is the bringing together of beauty, love and the future of the race. Finck does not regard personal beauty as completely autonomous, though he does give it an evaluation far above anything to be found in systematic earlier writings. He is not essentially valuing beauty because of any connotations of morality or godliness, but because beautiful people embody the highest achievements of humankind, physical and cultural, and are thus best fitted to continue the further evolution of the race: beautiful people marrying beautiful people will produce beautiful children.[71] But there is nothing prescriptive or viciously racist about all this. Finck values very highly qualities of individualism and sensibility, and thus at all times stresses the importance of individual choice. Also, the fundamental scientific principle which informs the whole work is that of 'crossing': it is marriage between different racial types which helps create beauty; intermarriage within one race or community leads to decadence and ugliness. Finck recognizes the astounding beauty achieved by some Jewish people. Undoubtedly, the emphasis is masculinist, but Finck is quite unequivocally saying that beauty is important in men as well as in women, and he rejects the convention that by definition and function women are the beautiful sex. He is a supporter of women's rights as these were understood in the 1880s.[72] Although there is, of course, dogmatism, the work is mainly characterized by a warm, commonsense sensitivity to the world as it really is or had become by the later nineteenth century: 'if you tell twenty of your male acquaintances that you have been introduced to a young lady, nineteen of them will ask immediately, "is she pretty?". No reporter ever writes about a girl murdered by a tramp or burnt in a house, without describing her as a model of beauty, in order to double the reader's interest and quintuple his pity.'[73]

Finck was a man of great intellectual and cultural sensitivity, and could be characterized as a snob. However, it is a major contention of this book that human beauty only becomes fully appreciated when material standards rise and there is time and opportunity for aesthetic appraisal. Responding to the argument that beauty is all a matter of taste, Finck declares: 'Precisely. Of good taste and bad taste.'[74] In a later work Finck developed this line of thought further with a series of pungent (and in the ears of our own day, provocative) similes:

If a peasant who has never had an opportunity to cultivate his musical sense insisted that a certain piano was exquisitely in tune and had as beautiful a tone as any other piano, whereas an expert musician declared that it had a shrill tone and was terribly out of tune, would anybody be so foolish as to say that the peasant had as much right to his opinion as the musician? Or if an Irish toper declared that a bottle of Chambertin, over which French epicures smack their lips, was insipid and not half as fine as the fusel-oil on which he daily got drunk, would not everybody agree that the Irishman was no judge of liquors, and that the reason why he preferred his cheap whiskey to the Burgundy was that his nerves of taste were too coarse to detect the subtle and exquisite bouquet of the French wine? . . . Most men of science know so much less about matters of beauty than about everything else in the world. They labor under the delusion that the sense of beauty is one of the earliest products of mental evolution, whereas their own attitude in the matter affords painful proof that it is one of the latest. They will understand some day that a stearyopygous 'Hotentot Venus' is no more beautiful because an African finds her attractive, than an ugly, bloated, blear-eyed harlot is beautiful because she pleases a drunken libertine.[75]

I do not wish to hide behind the nineteenth-century presence of Henry Theophilus Finck: this passage expresses exactly, if colourfully, some of the basic assumptions on which this book is based.

However, the task here is not to praise or criticize Finck, but to relate his ideas to the changing evaluation of beauty and to the changing economic, social and intellectual context which is the prime mover in these changes. He believed in evolution, sexual selection, crossing, health and fitness, and, bound in with all that, his notion of a Romantic Love which 'always urges the choice of a mate who approaches nearest to the ideal type of Beauty'. Taken together this leads him to reject the eighteenth-century scheme of the calculated, or arranged, marriage:

In future ages, when aesthetic refinement will be more common, and Romantic Love, its offspring, less impeded by those considerations of rank and money and imaginary "prudence" which lead parents to *sacrifice the physique and well being of their grandchildren* to the illusive comfort of their sons and daughters (in marriages of reason) – what an impetus will then be given to the development of Personal Beauty! Refined mouths and noses, rosy cheeks, sparkling eyes, plump and graceful healthy figures, now so lamentably rare, will then become as plentiful as blackberries in the autumn.[76]

Finck, like every other human being, was a product, and therefore a captive, of his age. He confuses beauty with love and with the attractiveness of the entire physique and personality; there appears something of that contradiction which we have encountered so many times before when he says that intellectual qualities are required for complete personal beauty. But Finck is 'modern' in appreciating that a new evaluation of beauty different from traditional evaluations is emerging, even if he is neither clear nor rigorous in establishing what that beauty is; and, although his form of expression is deeply Victorian, with Freud and Havelock Ellis, and the French Darwinians, he does perceive the link between beauty and sexuality. The quotation which follows is again from the 1899 work, *Primitive Love and Love Stories*:

the sense of personal beauty is neither a synonym for libidinous desires nor is it based on utilitarianism. It is practically a new sense, born of mental refinement and imagination. It by no means scorns a slight touch of the voluptuous, so far as it does not exceed the limits of artistic taste and moral refinement – a well-rounded figure and 'a face voluptuous, yet pure' – but it is an entirely different thing from the predilection for fat and other coarse exaggerations of sexuality which inspire lust instead of love.[77]

Finck felt that truly beautiful men had no need of the crutch of facial hair; sophisticated beauty guides from the seventeenth century onwards had indicated that facial hair on a woman was the very antithesis of beauty (though, apparently, in Italian *peasant* society a light moustache was sometimes seen as a sign of beauty in a woman). The Darwinians and post-Darwinians directed attention to the question, a vexed one in the later twentieth century, of bodily hair. The general argument (which I touched on in chapter two) was that among human features thought most beautiful were those which sharply distinguished human beings from animals, or, perhaps more accurately, that any features which reminded one of a particularly gross animal would definitely be considered ugly. The argument then seems to have been, though it was by no means a convincing or consistent one, that female humans are distinguished from female animals by not having hair on the face or over the entire body. Such, of course, was Victorian fashion and propriety that the only part of the female body usually likely to be glimpsed was the arms. Finck, in fact, recorded his aversion to hair on a woman's arms. The German anatomist Stratz set down the view that among attractive features in a female were absence of hair on the body, and sparse hair in the armpits; as a scientist, Stratz was aware that complete absence of hair in the armpits was extremely unlikely. Havelock Ellis agreed with Stratz.[78] Fashion and custom in the twentieth century have led to more and more of the female body being exposed and it became the practice for women to remove hair from both legs and armpits. Obviously, by the definitions offered in chapter two, this must be accounted an aspect of grooming, as distinct from natural beauty. However, it may be, as the Darwinians were suggesting, that behind this convention of our own time, the era of autonomous beauty, there lie deep instincts related to the aesthetics of sexuality.

That is to look too far ahead for the moment. Instead, consideration must now be given to other, more traditional, forces strongly at work in the mid- and later nineteenth century. Despite the challenges of science, strong religious belief pervaded most aspects of life in the three countries we are studying. The conventional piety was directly to link beauty and 'virtue': thus, in her journal entry on the ravages of 'malign fever', and, in particular, the death of a young mother, Eugénie de Guérin refers to the latter, in one breath as it were, as 'the most beautiful, the most virtuous in the parish'.[79] Among the two most influential writers and counsellors on all aspects of social life were Ralph Waldo Emerson, essayist and poet, born in Boston in 1805, and John Ruskin, author, artist and social reformer, born in London in 1819. Emerson was credited with developing a 'new religion'; Ruskin declared his mother's daily Bible readings to have been 'the one essential part of all my education'.[80] Both were fundamentally Platonists, committed to a definition of beauty which would embrace poetry, art, nature, intellect and behaviour, and dismissive of the human beauty which was merely sexually appealing. Emerson, without great originality, declared that 'beauty is Truth'.[81] Ruskin thundered against Renaissance principles of art which tended to:

the setting of Beauty above Truth, and seeking for it always at the expense of truth. And the proper punishment of such pursuit – the punishment which all the laws of the universe rendered inevitable – was, that those who thus pursued beauty should wholly lose sight of beauty.[82]

Ruskin made many admirable pleas on behalf of the working man and his right to the good things of life, but it was characteristic of a particular type of Victorian pontification that in support of his dubious, if not nonsensical, proposition about Renaissance art, 'all the laws of the universe' should be invoked.

The general influence of evangelical Christianity as well as the individual influence of Ruskin can be seen in the light fiction of the time. The novel *The Beauty and Her Plain Sister* (1865) is a highly moral, highly religious tale in which Grace, a very plain girl of thirteen, is deeply conscious of the horrible contrast between her fate and that of her elder sister, the beautiful Georgie; but, in fact, she learns that this is a false consciousness and through her deeply pious governess she takes up visiting the poor and learns to be happy. It may be noted, however, that the novel does not pretend that in physical terms the truth is any other than that Georgie is beautiful and Grace is ugly; it is not, in other words, pretended that Grace's moral worth in any way actually changes her physical appearance.[83] As I have observed before, traditional discussions are always deeply confused and ambiguous on this point. *The Book of Home Beauty* (New York, 1851), though in lavish format, 'with twelve portraits of American ladies from drawings by Charles Martin, Esq.',[84] is not, as might appear, a guide to grooming, but a moralizing piece of light fiction. The portraits, actually, are on the respectable side of the soft pornography which forms one of the best sources for the contention that, within the Western tradition, beauty is a relative universal, deeply sexual in character.

The preface opens in the conventional way, insisting that all pleasant and good thoughts are akin to beauty; in the book itself the characters spout poetry and improving thoughts at each other (many culled from Ruskin). Early in the book, a middle-aged male character, Mr Aldis, showing off his astronomical knowledge to the young married women who accompany him, declares that on near view the planet Venus is ugly.

'You cannot deny that beauty is sometimes a disadvantage,' said Mrs Marston. 'Oh, my dear Madam,' said Mr Aldis, discomforted at being thus pushed from the pinnacle whence he meant to have dispensed a shower of pretty compliments, 'what a sentiment! Beauty a disadvantage!'
'Yes,' said Mrs Marston, in her quiet way, 'unless coquetry is commendable. Beauty certainly makes a great many coquettes.'
'Do you think so!' exclaimed Mrs Berry; 'I must say I have fancied that security of pleasing preserved some pretty women from these unhandsome efforts to attract interest which constitute coquetry. Certainly some of the plainest women I have known have been among the vainest!'
'Unless we believe beauty to be the result of mere accident,' observed Mr Berry, 'we have a right to expect good qualities where we find it, though Nature's fitness may in all cases be marred, in a great degree, by untoward circumstances. I intuitively look for goodness where I see beauty.'
'That is rather a hard doctrine for us plain people,' said Mrs Whipple.
'I hardly know any plain people,' replied Mr Berry, not taking the bait; 'for the darkest complexion, the most oblique nose, the worst marking with small-pox, does not make an ugly face for me. I can discern the original beauty through all those. It is only when the structure of the face is bad that I find it absolutely devoid of beauty, and behind such faces I confess I never look for goodness, though culture and grace may do much.'[85]

In the ensuing discussion it is generally agreed that beauty is indeed in the eye of the beholder and that any two dozen men would all make their own individual choices (which would seem to be contrary to the more realistic philosophy upon which the twelve portraits, of manifest appeal to almost any two dozen men, were selected). Ten pages later, the discussion centres on the possibilities of loving a plain woman, an admission after all that plainness does exist. All then approve a quotation from Ruskin to the effect that beauty and morality are intertwined. In the conclusion to the book readers, reasonably enough after so many contradictory utterances, are left to decide for themselves, but the authorial suggestion is that 'Beauty and Virtue are a twin growth.'[86]

There is more than a touch of this pietistic vision in Dickens. The beautiful girls are almost always self-sacrificing and virtuous; the exceptions are simply self-indulgent and bad at household management, or, as with Estella in *Great Expectations*, subject to a deliberately warped upbringing. But in the great naturalistic novels of Trollope, George Eliot and Thomas Hardy, while beauty's power is recognized, it is never automatically associated with virtue. Gwendolen in *Daniel Deronda* is superbly described, principally through the effects that she creates on others, but there is never any suggestion that she is anything other than self-centred and selfish; much the same is true of Lizzie Greystoke in Trollope's *The Eustace Diamonds*. More daringly, in such novels there is recognition, though usually through minor characters, that 'being good' (the advice offered in the eighteenth century) provides no effective compensation for being plain. The full-scale study of the miseries and vulnerability of a plain woman in *Washington Square* (1881), by the London-based American novelist Henry James, was exceptional. And the undeceived realism conveyed by Chekov's *Uncle Vanya* in Sonya's lament was, when presented in the West shortly before the First World War (*Uncle Vanya* the play was first performed in Moscow in 1899), almost shocking: 'Oh, how awful it is that I am not beautiful! How awful it is! And I know I am not, I know it, I know it! . . . Last Sunday, as people were coming out of church, I heard them talking about me and one woman said: "She is a sweet generous nature, but what a pity she is so plain . . ." Plain . . .'[87]

The new forces of the nineteenth century, then, did not lead to a new consensus about the role and status of beauty. Further new forces became increasingly important towards the end of the century, including a new phase of urbanization, the rise of the labour movement, the growth of the women's movement and of socialism: none would seem to be very closely related to the questions at issue, save that both socialism and the womens' movement might be expected to resist the suggestion that there is any inherent value in physical beauty. In fact, the most relevant socialist tract, *News From Nowhere* (1893) by William Morris, is deeply ambivalent. Does it really show that a better-organized society will produce more beautiful people, or does it simply show that, as a healthy male, Morris had something of a preoccupation with beautiful women? As the narrator admits, on first encountering women in Morris's society of the future, he naturally looked at them very attentively, finding them 'at least as good as the gardens, the architecture, and the male men'.

As to the women themselves, it was pleasant indeed to see them, they were so kind and happy-looking in expression of face, so shapely and well-knit of body, and thoroughly healthy-looking and strong. All were at least comely, and one of them very handsome and regular of feature.[88]

Here, incidentally, we have a simple definition of beauty as involving regularity of features, and perhaps also a recognition that socialism could never produce more than happiness, good health and comeliness, beauty continuing to be the attribute of the relatively rare individual. Morris's idea of beauty also seems to involve youthfulness of appearance: a contrast is drawn between these women of the future, 'skin smooth as ivory', lips red as roses, 'beautiful arms . . . firm and well-knit from shoulder to shoulder', and Morris's contemporaries, even the young ones, and above all the idle rich ones, with 'wretched little arms like sticks' and 'thin lips and peaked noses and pale cheeks'. No wonder, it is concluded with a somewhat incomplete charity, 'they bore ugly children for no one except men like them could be in love with them, poor things!'[89] Thomas More, in his *Utopia* of almost four hundred years earlier, had recognized that even the wisest of men are greatly influenced by the beauties of the body. Unwittingly, *News from Nowhere* reveals exactly the same thing about William Morris. Sex is explicitly present as well. The people of this future society believe that:

a child born from the natural and healthy love between a man and a woman, even if that be transient, is likely to turn out better in all ways, and especially in bodily beauty, than the birth of the respectable commercial marriage bed, or of the dull despair of the drudge of that system. They say, Pleasure begets pleasure.[90]

By the end of the century, it was no longer axiomatic for mere corporeal beauty to be scorned as a dangerous provoker of unreflecting lust (though many influential figures, including Ruskin, seemed to be close to that position); instead the possible links between physical beauty and legitimate procreation were being openly contemplated.[91]

## 3 Beauty, Duty and Entrepreneurial Values, c. 1875–c. 1905

There always had been recognition of the power and significance of beauty, but never on the scale represented in the sheer volume of beauty manuals and guides published in the last decades of the nineteenth century.[92] None of these works is free from the contradictions and ambivalences inherent in traditional perceptions of beauty, yet together they mark the culmination of a qualitative change in the evaluation of beauty. Beauty had become *respectable*: respectable in a manner closely related to the social values of the time, which include duty, moral exhortation, work, enterprise and individualism, together with faith in the new levels of 'progress' and 'culture' believed to have been attained thereby, and which, rejecting the Byronic ideal of male beauty, call for ornamentality in the female and discreet appearance in the male.

The works themselves come in various types, from slim pamphlets to complete books, sometimes specially written, sometimes composed of pieces published earlier in a periodical. But all are marked by a discursiveness in the discussion of the nature of beauty and its significance. This self-consciousness, indicating that the intense preoccupation with personal appearance is recognized as new and problematic, is in contrast with the matter-of-fact tones of our own time when it is taken for granted that personal appearance is a matter of importance. Some of the national differences already identified are still apparent,[93] but on the whole the market has become an international one, with French works appearing in English, and English-language works, whether originated in Britain or the USA, often being published on both sides of the Atlantic. The authors are usually women – society beauties, professional writers on various topics, including etiquette and fashion, pioneers in the realm of 'beauty treatment', even purveyors of cosmetics, potions and corsets; there are a few male medical writers and one or two French practitioners of 'beauty medicine' or teachers in 'beauty schools'. Writers vary in their personal idiosyncrasies, in the weight they place on moral qualities, and the degree of realism with which they address the problem of ugliness, but the entire range offers a remarkably clear view of the nature and importance of beauty as widely understood at the end of the nineteenth century.

The most elaborate expression of the idea that a new attitude towards beauty had come into being in the late nineteenth century occurs in a substantial volume published in New York in 1899, *The Woman Beautiful*, by Ella Adelia Fletcher:

It is not so very long ago that there existed a certain prejudice – a sort of aftermath of Puritan influence – against the endowment of physical beauty, it being looked at askance as a dangerous gift. And neither girl nor woman could have devoted the thought and time to personal care which is now thought necessary without being charged with the heinous faults of vanity.[94]

Nature, says Mrs Fletcher, in Darwinian, or rather Finckian vein, 'is making perpetual efforts to attain perfection and beauty'; 'more and more in *our generation* [my italics] are we coming to a realization that Beauty's mission should be an exalted one . . .'[95] For '[us] fortunate women whose lot is cast in the closing years of this wonderful century'[96] the emphasis must be on 'the *culture* [my italics] of perfect womanhood, to which more time and rational thought are being given in our own day than since the period of the ancient Greeks'. An awful warning is offered by 'certain classes, oftener seen abroad than in this country, who, from an unwise manner of living, change from delicate, refined beauties, in their teens, to grossly coarse women before they reach the age of forty'.[97]

Similar points had been touched on two decades earlier in a series of articles in *St Paul's Magazine*, which formed the basis of another substantial work, *The Art of Beauty* (1878), by Mrs H. R. Haweis, author among other things of *Chaucer for Children* (what an exquisite task of bowdlerization that must have been!). The '*culture* of personal beauty', she wrote, 'and, *in our age*, especially of female beauty, is of the first interest and importance'.[98] The 'pain of ugliness' is felt by 'those whose taste has been *cultivated* by having beautiful things always about them . . .'[99] While one of the first in this era to give open approval to the judicious (or, let us say, cultivated) use of facial cosmetics, she was none the less contemptuous of the decadent past:

I should be very sorry were the corrupt fashion of the eighteenth century to return, in which a woman was considered only half dressed till her natural complexion was concealed; and hence many a lovely cheek and lip be disguised at the bidding of those who had no beauty to lose.[100]

Harriet Hubbard Ayer, a considerable beauty, as we can see from the photographs published in her book, was married at sixteen, then subsequently had to make a career for herself as a beauty consultant. She addressed *Harriet Hubbard Ayer's Book* to the 'thorough-bred daughter of the nineteenth century'[101] and expressed contempt for the 'old-fashioned', 'absurd' and 'demoralizing' idea that a woman should resign herself to the decrees of Providence and take no care of her personal appearance.[102] 'Modern woman' must accept 'that she is accountable to herself, as well as to her family for every wrinkle, for her middle-aged figure, triple chin, scant locks, toothless mouth, bent back, and general invitation in her appearance to Time to do his worst . . .'[103]

*Harriet Hubbard Ayer's Book* contains before-and-after photographs to demonstrate the success of her courses of beauty treatment: 'I do not advance theories, but demonstrated facts in what I have to say.'[104] The belief in empiricism and science, detectable in the beauty guides from the first half of the century, continued unabated. The British professor Boyd Laynard, in *Secrets of Beauty, Health, and a Long Life*, invokes 'the great laws of health' and 'strict attention to the smallest details relative to diet and regimes'.[105] Baronne Staffe expresses faith in 'the Science of Rhinoplasty', which 'has made such progress that it is possible to modify, even to change, the shape of the nose'.[106] The American Annie Wolf, author of *Pictures and Portraits of Foreign Travel* and *Pen Pictures of London Society*, insists in *The Truth about Beauty* (New York, 1892) that there 'is a science which may be successfully pursued toward physical perfection'.[107]

What these, and the host of slighter volumes, all declare unambiguously is the importance and value of beauty and therefore (their main witting purpose) the legitimacy of a preoccupation with beauty, and of the desire to simulate it by every means. The first line of argument is that, for a woman, a preoccupation with beauty is entirely natural. Mrs Humphry, 'Madge' of the periodical *Truth*, and author of *Manners for Men* and *Manners for Women,* in her *How to be Pretty though Plain* (1899), made the introductory assertion, 'Girls that are merry and wise know perfectly well that to be pretty is the natural desire of the girlish heart', but later in her pamphlet adds some reasoned support:

There is every excuse for a girl to wish to be pretty. If she opens a book of poems, or a novel, she finds beauty bepraised and ugliness condemned. If she looks in at a picture gallery, or gazes at the photographs in a shop window, she finds the handsomest faces selected to be hung on the line. At the opera or theatre she sees the attention excited by a lovely face. In the park she watches with appreciation the pretty faces and observes that others do as well. Wherever she goes, in fact, the great truth, that the pretty are among the most sought after things on earth, is made patent for her.[108]

Mrs Fletcher used very similar words, remarking that a girl soon realizes 'that Beauty's path through life is a sort of rose-bordered one, a royal progress'.[109] Mrs Hubbard Ayer simply recorded that 'from babyhood the secret aim of every little girl is to be beautiful'.[110] Any element of egocentricity that might seem inherent in this argument was dispelled by the further one that beauty gives pleasure to others: 'the immortal worth of beauty', says Mrs Haweis, 'lies in the universal pleasure it gives',[111] 'the conquest of beauty', declares the French beautician Dr P. Marrin, 'is one of the most noble occupations of our existence'.[112]

Echoing some of the political rhetoric of the age, Mrs Haweis chooses her words carefully when she declares 'the culture of beauty' (not beauty itself) to be 'the natural right of every woman'.[113] A similar thought is expressed by the American author Teresa H. Dean in the preface to the British edition of her *How to be Beautiful* (1890):

all women, all over the world, wish to know how to be beautiful. There is absolute unanimity on this point. In all other matters, on the other hand, there is diversity of sentiment: there are women who want to vote, or who don't want to vote; who want to marry, and who don't want to marry; some who believe in peace, and some who believe in war; some who favour total abstinence, and some who prefer the moderate use of stimulating liquors; but all women, with one accord, believe that they ought to be, must, and *can* be beautiful. One has no pessimism to contend with in this direction; there is abundant faith, in even the most ill-favoured of her sex, that she can be beautiful if she tries. The application of the proper means will effect the desired result.

Mrs Dean adds that she attributes the enormous commercial success of the American edition of her book to this universal female aspiration.[114]

The break with the morality of the past implicit in these statements of the legitimacy of beauty, and the awareness of it, is most sharply brought out by Mrs Haweis's combative: 'It is not "wicked" to take pains with oneself'; and, 'it is *not* a sin or a folly to long, as every woman longs, to be lovely'.[115] The assessments of the actual value of beauty are not new (Mrs Haweis asserts that 'the power and sanctity of physical as well as moral beauty, has been recognized in all ages'[116]), but are made with a new insistence and force, in which, although the advice is being tendered to women, there is a strong suggestion that beauty is relevant to business and professional success. The traditional aspect, that attention to personal appearance is necessary to attract and hold a man, is widely expressed, but some writers go further. 'Want of beauty', says H. Ellen Browning in *Beauty Culture* (1898), 'always "handicaps" a woman, whatever her vocation in life may be.'[117] A very full assessment is provided by Boyd Laynard (speaking of women as much as men):

Next to character, the face is the most important factor in forming the circumstances that go to make up our lives. Friendships are generally first formed by the attraction of the face, long before character is discerned; and how many of these acquaintanceships afterwards ripen into love.

Apart from the advantages in regard to matrimony, Laynard continues,

good looks are often of value in fighting the battle of life. In many professions and businesses, it frequently happens that those persons with the most attractive and intelligent faces are chosen to fill positions in preference to other applicants, who, perhaps may be more capable, but are not so prepossessing in appearance. In numerous walks of life, men and women discover the fact that their face has, indeed, much to do with their fortune.[118]

A rather more general assessment of the disadvantage of lack of looks was put forward by Mrs Haweis in arguing that ugliness often makes a woman ill tempered, and is a burden, ill understood by herself or her friends, which has pernicious effects on her moral character[119] (an ealier age had argued the other way round, that a defective character caused ugliness).

What all of these manuals and guides are in effect saying (sometimes quite explicitly) is that there are two kinds of beauty. Such a position, though different from that which holds beauty an autonomous universal, marks an important stage towards clearing up some traditional confusions. *Sylvia's Book of the Toilet* (1886) makes a bold lunge in the direction of the autonomous view in declaring 'Handsome is as handsome does' an 'untrue proverb', continuing,

Beauty is a great gift. Those who possess it should cultivate and embellish it as they would any other talent bestowed upon them. Those who have it not will perhaps learn, from the advice tendered in the following chapters, how to make the best of whatever share of comeliness they possess.

It is the sincere wish of the authoress that both these classes may find instruction and occasionally amusement in perusing her pages.[120]

Arthur Lefèbvre, professor at the Universal Academy of Coiffure in Paris, put it more explicitly and succinctly: 'there are two sorts of beauty, that which one receives from nature and that which one knows how to give oneself'.[121]

Naturally, a major concern of the writers of beauty literature is with the second type (they wouldn't have much of a market otherwise). Another very important concern was with showing women how to preserve their youth, it being, as we have seen, a contention (not altogether ill founded) that in less civilized eras and societies women deteriorated rapidly. The central message is that such concerns represent both the legitimate and the achievable. The most striking feature of the discussions of how beauty and youth are to be simulated is the open admission that artifice is the name of the game (recognition, in effect, that the second sort of beauty is not real beauty at all). There are, however, differences of view as to exactly how the second sort of beauty is to be achieved, with many writers stressing the importance of personality, cheerfulness, etc., in attaining an attractive exterior.

Before looking at the question of artifice, I want to emphasize the significance given in these works of the late nineteenth century to a judicious attention to the preservation of youth. The second chapter of *Harriet Hubbard Ayer's Book*, 'The Art of Remaining Young', is, in her vaunted empirical spirit (courtesans hitherto having been banned from English-language works), supported by references to Diane de Poitiers, Juliette Récamier and Ninon de Lenclos, and photographs of Sarah Bernhardt at fifty-nine and the opera *diva* Adelina Patti at fifty-four. The lady of Baronne Staffe's *The Lady's Dressing Room* is a married lady 'defending her beauty against the attacks of time and the fatigues of life'.[122] The Baronne is one of the frankest in identifying the artifice behind this defence, counselling that its secrets should at all costs be kept from the husband.[123] In *The Beauty Secrets of a Parisienne* the Marquise de Garches openly avows that these secrets are tricks to make the best of what one has and to hide one's faults.[124]

The less admirable features of the age show themselves in the particular prescriptive tone of much of the advice. Book after book, pamphlet after pamphlet, rams home the doctrine of women's *duty* to be beautiful. Not many went as far as to say explicitly that men could be ugly while it was an obligation for women to be beautiful, as Dr Monin of Paris did, but practically every publication had a phrase about beauty being a woman's duty.[125] A fascinating variation is that it is a woman's *business* to be beautiful.[126] But it was all very well saying every woman had a right to the cultivation of beauty: the harsh corollary was that 'no woman has a right to be ugly'.[127] Even scriptural authority might be invoked: 'if you read your Bible carefully you will see that the priests talk of the beauty of Jewish women. Sometimes receipts [sic] are also to be found in the Holy Book, as in the case of Esther, who was bathed or rubbed with myrrh and frankincense, which are both skin-tighteners, and make the flesh firm and soft at the same time.'[128] There is much moral exhortation: 'She must not give herself up as hopeless, as many a plain girl does.'[129] The woman 'who wilfully neglects her personal appearance is deserving of the severest censure'.[130] Harriet Hubbard Ayer speaks of 'the sin of dowdiness'.[131] In fact the work ethic applies to women as much as to any aspiring office boy: hard work, as well as willpower, are frequently cited as essential factors in the cause of beauty, the French sources being particularly explicit, with one making it clear that working girls must be prepared to rise an hour earlier each morning.[132]

Where the literature is strong and clear, and surely deserving of credit for performing a useful service, is in the almost universal assertion that healthy habits and a healthy diet are essential prerequisites for showing oneself off at one's best.[133] There is also a certain clarity about what constitutes beauty (of the first sort) or what characteristics enhance appearance. All discussions start from the idea of regularity and harmony of features.[134] 'Sylvia' listed 'several kinds of beauty':

(a) Beauty consisting of regularity of feature
(b) Beauty consisting of good colouring and youthful freshness, called by the French, *beauté du diable*
(c) Beauty of expression
(d) Beauty consisting of some or all of these, so skilfully mingled that the partial absence of any one is compensated by the addition of a fair share of another
(e) Beauty consisting of the three first types, producing absolute perfection, and very rarely seen, luckily for the world.[135]

Laynard described 'prettiness' as 'something almost indefinable that attracts the attention and charms the eye of the casual observer . . . for instance a clear complexion, bright sparkling eyes, and a well-shaped nose'.[136] 'A Professional Beauty' stressed the need for a soft, smooth, young-looking face.[137] 'An MD' identified 'purity of complexion, luxuriance of hair, whiteness and regularity of teeth, clearness of eye, and suppleness and grace of figure'.[138] Mrs Haweis had some clear-headed comments to make on the vexed question of waists:

The reason why a small waist is a beauty is because, when it is natural, it goes together with the peculiar lightness and activity of a slenderly built figure. All the bones are small, the shoulders and arms *petite*, and the general look is dainty and graceful.

The reason why tight-lacing is ugly, is because it distorts the natural lines of the figure, and gives an appearance of uncertainty and unsafeness.[139]

The perfect requiem for foundation garments that fail!

As well as Firenzuola, or Lakoff and Scherr, our writers knew the significance of the nose, 'the most prominent feature of the face, and when crooked, deformed, or otherwise unsightly, the whole countenance suffers considerably'.[140] Much optimism was expressed over the efficacy of nose machines, which, worn at night, exerted pressure on the offending bone and gristle (the science of rhinoplasty meant no more than the wearing of this infernal gadget). One of the more honest accounts admitted: 'It is a process that should not be resorted to unless there is a positive deformity, as it is very tedious, somewhat painful, and decidedly unpleasant, and then there is a risk that the new-shaped nose may not suit the old face.'[141] Many guides indicated that the only hope was if the treatment were applied by mothers to their unfortunate daughters from infancy.[142]

In regard to care of the skin most guides offered recipes for creams and cleansers, sometimes recommending off-the-shelf products. Avoidance of very hot water and hard water was advocated, along with other suggestions, such as the bandaging of raw veal onto the face at night.[143] 'Nothing is uglier than to see a woman with hair on her face',[144] and it was not wanted on neck or arms either. Plucking or, more hesitantly, electrolysis, were recommended.[145] Advice about regular care of the teeth was eminently sensible, though one French writer had the idea that the nicotine and carbon released by smoking were beneficial; however, since smoking made the breath disagreeable, she ruled that a woman 'will always abstain' from smoking.[146] Overtly there was a hostility towards dyeing the hair, described as both 'pernicious' and 'immoral': since, however, means were always suggested,[147] one can take it that there was covert approval for a practice which, where openly perceived, suggested loose living and prostitution. The use of readymade curls, and even full coiffures, was fully approved.[148]

Because so much of the rest of the body was concealed, feet loomed large – they should, of course, be small – as objects of attention. Only *The Ugly Girl Papers*, in this period, actually supported the binding of the feet; other authors conselled against this barbarity, but even while favouring fresh air and exercise, felt it necessary to advise against too much walking, which 'enlarges the feet'.[149] All works stress the importance of a good figure, some pointing out that it is a more lasting asset than a good face.

It is so impossible to be graceful without a good figure, that really one cannot take too much trouble to attain that end. No young girl's room is complete without a reclining board on which she ought to be made to lie for an hour or two at a time. If this plan were to be more universally adopted we would see fewer round backs and crooked shoulder blades.[150]

Remedies for more extreme cases I have already mentioned in section one. Undoubtedly the conventional view was that 'extreme thinness is a much more cruel enemy to beauty than extreme stoutness'.[151] But there really was little favour for the latter either: 'It is very nice to see a woman round and plump, but when plumpness becomes positive obesity then it is no longer a beauty'; 'obesity is the enemy of beauty and incompatible with it'; 'Even the prettiest face loses some of its attraction when it is accompanied by a heavy, bulky figure, fat out of all proportion to the head and face.'[152] The French Dr Marrin expressed the view that the most serious complaint in regard to the size of the breasts was 'an excess of volume' because of the difficulty of preserving the proper shape.[153] The admirable feature of almost all guides was their stress on the value of fresh air and exercise, though the exact amount of the latter was in contention. At one extreme tennis, riding, gymnastics and long walks of two or three hours (the feet no doubt could look after themselves) were recommended, while at another only 'gentle athletic exercise' was advised, lawn tennis being decreed 'rather vehement for the average woman'.[154]

Views on the effects of exposure to the sun were not as unanimous as is sometimes suggested. Undoubtedly one purpose of hats and veils was to screen out the sun, and the balance of opinion was certainly against running any risk of acquiring freckles, or anything in the nature of a suntan. Such patent remedies as Rowland's Kalydor claimed to eradicate freckles and tan, as well as pimples, spots and discolouration.[155] Yet there was the contrary view that 'sunshine has a most beneficial effect' or, indeed, that its benefit 'cannot be too greatly emphasised',[156] and generally the tenor of all advice is towards looking sparkling and glowing rather than exhibiting the pallor once, in theory at least, much praised. The silly taboo on freckles (and their association with red hair) did remain strong:

Freckles are not pretty, and they are practically there to stay. The freckles of red-haired women are conspicuous during the day, but they do not show much, sometimes not at all, by gaslight.

A red-haired, freckled girl too often lacks sufficient contrast beween eyebrows, eyelashes, and skin to give her a clean-cut look.

I think in such cases it is a woman's duty to darken the eyebrows and lashes. This can be done with little trouble and is imperceptible. The complexion of the red-haired girl is her most serious drawback.

It lends itself to untidiness, so the victim must be especially careful to keep it looking clean and well cared for.

If the red-haired girl has an oily skin she must be careful of her diet, avoiding all greasy and stimulating food, and in addition she must use an astringent lotion and a very little fine powder.[157]

Creams and cleansers, herbal remedies and treatments figure conspicuously. Earlier in the century universal anathema had been pronounced against powders and paints, an attitude which was partly a reaction against eighteenth-century high artificiality, but which probably owed more to evangelicalism than to a deep belief in naturalness. Inevitably, given the intense preoccupation with personal appearance, the last quarter of the nineteenth century was characterized by the creeping return to respectability of cosmetics. After her denunciation of 'the

corrupt fashion' of the eighteenth century, written originally as early as
the middle 1870s, Mrs Haweis, recognizing that 'the face is always
exposed', thus demanding 'at least as much attention as the rest of the
person', allowed that 'cosmetics have their use as well as their abuse'.
However, we are only at the very beginning of a period of change, for
she has to advise that powder and paint are still not regarded as
respectable: she favours their use *where necessary to conceal defects* and
makes the surely telling point that they are as justified as tight lacing or
padding.[158] Our 'Professional Beauty' summarizes the state of the art and
the social code which governed it at the end of the next decade:

The use of rouge and pearl powder seems to have become more fashionable now
than it has been for many years . . . I have seen girls who are certainly not more
than seventeen or eighteen with their faces painted and very badly done into the
bargain. It would be so much better to try to correct the faults of the face with a
little more care and art without covering the *whole* of it with a *mask* of paint. I
have seen some hideous specimens lately of painted women who think they are
objects of beauty, instead of which they have made themselves objects of
ridicule.[159]

Cosmetics clearly are in use, and have never been more so for several
centuries, says one source.[160] But the 'Professional Beauty' expresses the
slightly uneasy orthodoxy now emerging: 'I do not wish to speak out
against the use of rouge and pearl powder, but merely to point out to
those who use them that they must be used with extreme care and not
abused!' Duty is the clinching argument: 'as I have before remarked', a
woman 'ought to do everything within reason to make herself beautiful'.
Yet the concluding line is: 'For those who can possibly do without, I say,
Do not begin to paint the face . . .'[161] By the end of the century it is clear
that two broad conventions obtain, though they are evidently not fully
observed. One is that cosmetics are not needed by the young woman
under thirty, while, writes Mrs Hubbard Ayer, they are fully justified
thereafter.[162] The other is that a distinction should be drawn between
what may be worn during the day and what is more acceptable in the
evening: 'In order for day-time make-up [*maquillage*] to be successful, it
must be invisible, giving the illusion of reality.'[163] That really drives
home one of the main points I am making: this preoccupation of late-
nineteenth-century entrepreneurial society was oriented towards a high
evaluation of natural beauty. Heavy, 'artificial' use of cosmetics triggered
a different code, signalling open sexual availability. All this, I should
quickly add, was linked to a thoroughly inflexible attitude on the crucial
significance of dress, and of dressing as fashion decreed. The frankest
statement, and one which takes me directly into my next topic, commercialism, is that of the 'Professional Beauty': 'Perfect taste and plenty of
money combined are what we must possess before we can hope to be
well dressed.'[164]

The same author has already counselled against using home-made face powders: 'Much better buy them from the best perfumers in London and Paris.'[165] If one were to comb through the literature constantly seeking overt commercial motivation one would be disappointed. The larger more elaborate books often contained no advertisements; on the other hand periodicals are full of them (hairdressing, manicure, chiropody, face massage, corsets, creams and powders, etc., etc.), and some of the shorter pamphlets contain more advertising than editorial matter.[166] Madame Bayard owned her own dress shop at 7 Southampton Street, off the Strand in London, marketed various potions and creams, and published advice on 'beauty', including *Toilet Hints or How to Preserve Beauty, and How to Acquire It* (1883). As well as the commercial ethic, she also believed in the desirability of plumpness:

Ladies who wish to become plump without being stout, and have a complexion like milk and roses, cannot do better than drink the new tea that is now all the rage in Paris, I mean *Serkys* – which can be had at this office. By *continually* drinking this tea, instead of the usual tea, you will soon acquire a full bust and a complexion on which Time will not set its ugly finger. Drink it with milk and sugar like any other tea. You must not expect wonders at first, but persevere and you will be pleased with the result.

Realism (of a sort) then floods in: ladies who are still dissatisfied are recommended to turn to porter (that dark, rich style of beer also known as 'stout').[167]

Although this period was one of real (though very modest) advances in the status (married women were enabled to own property in their own right; better-off women could sit on local councils) and consciousness (suffrage societies developed in most of the major towns) of women, it was manifestly one in which the traditional view that beauty was a woman's responsibility and prerogative was re-emphasized. At its most rigid this orthodoxy postulated that it didn't matter if a man was ugly or that 'one scarcely preoccupies oneself with the beauty of a man'.[168] Some books do incorporate references to male grooming, recognizing, say, 'that men would also like to know how to become beautiful',[169] though these are usually of a rather incidental nature. Dr Marrin, in his title, claimed to be addressing men (first) and women (second), but most of the book is about women. *Sylvia's Book of the Toilet* was a 'Ladies' Guide to Dress and Beauty' *with* a 'Fund of Information of Importance to Gentlemen'. Here, as in other discussions, the emphasis was almost exclusively on the hair, or lack of it, on head and face, and on dress. As the final few pages in a pamphlet basically addressed to women put it, before going on to a discussion of baldness, dandruff and greyness: 'The expression of a man's face depends largely on the cut of his beard, moustache, whiskers, and hair.'[170] 'Sylvia', perhaps, revealed a deeper level of perception:

Every handsome man must, at some period of his life, however free he may be from vanity, regret that the fashion of wearing the masculine hair and beard during the reigns of Charles I and Charles II has not lasted down to his own time. Then a man had some chance to look picturesque, while in our own day, the most beautiful of manly countenances is seen at a certain disadvantage with close-cropped hair, over a stiff collar and under a still more stiff and impossible hat.

She then pointed out that despite the extreme (and boring, she obviously thought) shortness, there were different stylistic possibilities: partings at the side, or down the middle, hair swept back or in a fringe, falling about in various directions, or arranged with all the lines of the hair running in the same direction.[171] But on clothes she despaired: 'Modern masculine attire leaves a man no choice. He must dress as other men . . .'[172] More precisely, as another author put it, 'a gentleman never indulges in extremes. He dresses unobtrusively yet correctly.'[173]

But even from these references we can see that, as in other ages, men's looks, and particularly good looks, were noticed and did have significance, whatever the superficial orthodoxy might maintain. A 'Society Beauty' expressed the sexual element more explicitly than was usual in declaring that 'male beauty' was needed 'in the race for some prized woman', while Marrin openly claimed that women were sexually excited by male beauty.[174] And, of course, given the nature of employment opportunities between the sexes, there had to be recognition of the commercial value of beauty for men as well as women. I have already quoted Laynard on the relationship between face and fortune; referring explicitly to men, 'Sylvia' observed: 'the cultivation of an attractive appearance has its value, even from a business point of view'.[175]

Faith that beauty is indeed more than skin deep, that beautiful features must connote virtue and moral worth, died hard. Mrs Hubbard Ayer tried to escape from a purely traditional rendering by 'proving' beauty and virtue to be synonymous on the grounds that 'purity' and 'temperance' were essential to the preservation of a woman's beauty after her early thirties.[176] Most writers remained deeply troubled that beauty could so often be 'dangerous' and give rise to 'evil', that is to say, arouse lust rather than the spirit of truth and heavenly contemplation.[177] Of course, it was the first type of beauty, 'natural' beauty, which did this, not the 'beauty' inspired by duty and achieved through hard work. Some writers glossed over the problem; others resorted to the traditional series of flat contradictions. The prize must go to Annie Wolf, whose continued belief in physiognomy and touching faith in the beginning-of-the-century pin-up is worthy of note as we come to the end of this chapter: 'For all Lord Byron's unhappy life, his sensual gift of verse, and the unsavoury gossip attaching to his personality, so God-like a physiognomy could not have been the mark of a completely debauched and debased mind.'[178] After first declaiming the apparently unambiguous (if dubious) proposition that, 'visible beauty is the outward sign of interior worth; and, depend upon it, the countenance that is sublimely beautiful is only the semblance [i.e. representation] of an illuminated mind',[179] she managed in the space of half-a-dozen pages to reel off the following confusing and self-cancelling utterances:

Beauty is a boon that should be utilized as any other of God's gifts . . .

Unusual beauty is often accompanied by licentious proclivities . . . we find no beauty of countenance complete without the amorous curve of the lips; the love-light flashing from the eye . . .

The world's beauties are seldom happy in their domestic relations . . . rare beauty, like rare genius, is sure to experience desolation, disapproval, and loneliness . . .

The chief advantage of beauty is power . . . 'More women have attained honour for their beauty, than for all other virtues beside' [a saying of Lucian's quoted with approval] . . . though plain women detract [sic] it, and pulpits expostulate against it, like liberty, the influence of beauty will live until the stars turn backward in their orbits.[180]

Writers who wished to gain acceptance, and a readership, could not pronounce beauty autonomous, even if they were able to recognize it as such. But one who could was an anonymous and rather unpleasant satirist (one of his jibes was that women should give up dancing before dancing gave them up),[181] whose persistent tone was that of someone forcing outrageous truths upon a resistant audience. I close this chapter with a statement which ranks alongside those of Firenzuola and Federigo Fregoso as one of the major pre-twentieth-century presentations of aspects of the 'modern' perception of beauty – one, of course, not generally accepted at the time:

People not infrequently betray an invincible dislike to acknowledging that certain things are, so long as they feel a moral conviction that they ought not to be . . . Now a great many persons have the strongest repugnance to conceding any force to what they are accustomed to call accidental advantages. Beauty, it is asserted, is nothing more than an accident . . . Like the rain of heaven, it falls on the just and the unjust alike, and in larger proportion, it is alleged, to the latter than to the former. It will be seen that we are treating of Beauty proper, beauty which would be beauty in all ages, and in that sense a joy forever; not that other so-called Beauty, that loathesome counterfeit to be had of Madame Rachel, purchased at the hairdresser's for seven-and-sixpence, or compressed into a little box of pigments fetched from Rue de la Paix. The Beauty of which we speak is, we freely allow, as complete an instance of accident as anything that can be named . . . The possession of it unquestionably predestines certain people to the enjoyment of much bliss in this world, and the want of it equally entails upon certain others much private weeping and a fair amount of public gnashing of teeth.[182]

# 6 Personal Appearance and Life Experiences, c. 1800–c. 1905

## 1 Context and Variables

The biographical material studied in chapter four made it clear that in any assessment of the significance in public or private life of an individual's personal appearance, we have to consider the particular historical circumstances, the class context, other personal qualities, and the influence of sheer luck, or contingency. Chapter five established the major historical developments leading to some changes in attitudes towards, and estimates of the value of, beauty, though we saw that many traditional confusions and ambivalences remained. Liberal democratic sentiment, the forces of Romantic individualism and the imperatives of entrepreneurial capitalism had helped during the nineteenth century to create an ideological context in which it was firmly held to be the responsibility of each individual woman to make the most of her appearance, but the period was certainly not one of universal democracy. Rights of citizenship were most widely diffused in the American Republic, yet even here for much of the nineteenth century there were restrictions on the right to vote. In Britain there was a series of Representation of the People Acts, but even in 1914 two-fifths of all adult males still did not have the franchise. Forms of government changed sharply in France, the Napoleonic Empire being followed by a restored autocratic monarchy, which, after the revolution of 1830, gave place to a 'constitutional' monarchy responsive to the interests of the high bourgeoisie. The revolution of 1848 established a republic, quickly followed by the coup d'état of Louis Napoleon which led to the Second Empire. Only after 1870 was there a (relatively) stable republic with universal manhood suffrage. Overall the scope for a politician to make a popular appeal on the basis of looks was very limited, though there is a prima facie case for taking a close look at Louis Napoleon. Apart from a few states in the United States towards the end of the nineteenth century, nowhere did women have the vote; generally restrictions on women's freedom of choice and expression remained considerable.

Despite their revolutionary traditions, both France and the United States resembled Britain in having recognizable class structures. Aristocratic influence was strongest in Britain, and the aristocracy remained at the core of the consolidated upper class of older and newer elements which emerged by the end of the century. In France and the USA, too, disproportionate power rested in the hands of an upper class (even if, in the USA, there was much more social and geographical mobility than in either of the two European countries). Accordingly there were privileged males who, without necessarily having to do very much to justify it, exercised great power, and were thus both in a strong position to exploit women (they also exploited other men – though in a different way) and were, as it were, targets for ambitious women who perceived in them a means towards social advancement and high living. Extreme manifestations of this syndrome were to be found at the court of the notoriously predatory Louis Napoleon and in the entourage of Edward, Prince of Wales, who exercised his princely 'rights' with all the aggressive selfishness of, and a good deal less charm than, a Louis XV or Charles II. In the Prince's Britain, however, the public morality was that of 'purity' and continence in sexual matters. This was even more the case in the United States; and, indeed, in France the forces of Catholic morality were still very strong. In all three countries there was pride in what were seen as the cultivated, progressive qualities of society, and a horror of such relics of barbarity as unrestrained sexuality, usually associated with the very lowest classes in the urban slums. Standards of what constituted respectable behaviour, particularly for a woman, were strict. Yet the restoration of republican values did not much alter the actual life chances of beautiful women able to establish themselves in Paris – during *la belle époque* (roughly the last two decades of the nineteenth century and the first years of the twentieth) probably even more beautiful women were living well from the sale of their bodies than had been the case during the Second Empire. But, if it was a woman's duty to be beautiful, could a beautiful woman exploit her looks without having to utilize her sexuality? If she did grant sexual favours, could she remain respectable? – in Paris, in France, in Britain, in the USA? These questions, all directly related to beauty's potential, are newly pressing in the period we are now studying.

## 2 *Public Life*

In my introductory chapter I referred to the way in which, in the late twentieth century, the personal appearance of politicians and the effect this might have on their political success was becoming a matter for comment and concern. If the origins of this development are to be found anywhere they must surely be in the most open and democratic of nineteenth-century Western societies, the United States of America. It would thus seem worthwhile to take a look at the men who achieved the office of president in this period. Fortunately the two standard American biographical dictionaries, the *Dictionary of American Biography (1928– )*, for the entire period, and *Appleton's Cyclopaedia of American Biography (1888–1889)*, for most of it, like the British *Dictionary of National Biography*, always comment if the subjects are felt to be particularly good looking, or, alternatively, distinctly ill favoured, and *Appleton's Cyclopaedia*, in addition, carries engravings. There are, in any case, portraits of some sort for all of the presidents; and, of course, there are vast amounts of additional biographical information.

Right away it can be stated that the first twenty-four presidents from George Washington, immediately after the Revolution, to William Howard Taft, just before the First World War, were not a particularly handsome bunch. Washington, certainly, was impressive, if not quite beautiful, in figure and countenance, but his accession depended manifestly upon achievement, as vanquisher of the British and founding father of the Republic, not on appearance. Adams ('in person . . . plain, florid, and somewhat corpulent . . . the typical John Bull'),[1] Jefferson ('not prepossessing in appearance'),[2] Madison ('never impressive in person'),[3] Harrison, Taylor ('muscular and stocky'),[4] Fillmore, Buchanan, Grant, Hayes, Garfield, Arthur, Cleveland, Harrison, McKinley and Taft (overweight and unprepossessing) were plain or worse. So also Lincoln (of whom more in a moment) and Theodore Roosevelt, for all his energetic efforts to overcome the effects of his asthma and defective vision. Jackson ('an impressive countenance'), Van Buren, Tyler and Polk (though he 'possessed little personal magnetism') were all personable, with Van Buren (the 'little magician') having a certain charisma (which is to be distinguished from looks however) as an orator and an instinct for immaculate self-presentation.[5] What all have in common are Protestant British, or (in two cases) Dutch, names and origins, though they do come from quite a variety of social and geographical backgrounds, with aristocratic influence waning after the beginning of the nineteenth century, and upper-class influence asserting itself at the beginning of the twentieth. Reputations for military prowess (Washington, Jackson, Harrison, Taylor and Grant), or the oratorical skills of a lawyer, are clearly helpful. The conclusion is inescapable that looks played no significant part in the elections of American presidents up to the First World War. However, I have missed out one president (a particularly ill-fated one, as it happens: apart from his appalling incompetence, he suffered the trauma of seeing his only son killed in a railway accident) who was indisputably beautiful and youthful looking: Franklin Pierce. 56 Pierce was a conservative Democrat lawyer, an unexpected, compromise candidate, product of a deadlocked Democrat convention.[6] It may be that it is in such circumstances, when a candidate without any strong characteristics but with a certain bland appeal is required, that personal appearance does become important.

56 Franklin Pierce,
engraving, *c.* 1840, from
*Appleton's Cyclopaedia of
American Biography*, Vol. V,
1888

Let us go back to Lincoln, the effect his looks had upon himself and upon others, and the question of the relationship between looks and charisma. Lincoln was certainly aware of his own appearance, which can be described as odd, or striking, but certainly never as beautiful as that word has been defined in this book; practitioners of the new photographic art posed and lighted him in many dramatic ways, but the physical essence of the man, it seems to me, comes through accurately in the relatively straightforward portrait reproduced as Ill. 57. Both of the major biographical sources have much to say on his personal appearance. First the *Cyclopaedia*:

Mr Lincoln was as unusual in personal appearance as in character. His stature was almost gigantic, six feet and four inches; he was muscular but spare of frame, weighing about 180 pounds. His hair was strong and luxuriant in growth, and stood out straight from his head; it began to be touched with gray in his last years. His eyes, grayish brown, were deeply set, and were filled, in repose, with an expression of profound melancholy, which easily changed to one of uproarious mirth at the provocation of a humorous anecdote told by himself or another. His nose was long and slightly curved, his mouth large and singularly mobile. Up to the time of his election he was clean-shaven, but during his presidency the fine outline of his face was marred by a thin and straggling beard.

The twentieth-century account is more extensive:

The Lincoln of the Prairies was a man of marked individuality. Standing six feet four, with uncommon length of arms and legs, his figure loomed in any crowd, while the rugged face bespoke a pioneer origin and early life of toil and poverty. In a head not over large each feature was rough and prominent. In contrast to the round full-cheeked Douglas [Lincoln's Presidential rival], Lincoln's face showed deep hollows and heavy shadows. The craggy brow, tousled hair, drooping eyelids, melancholy gray eyes, large nose and chin, heavy lips, and sunken, wrinkled cheeks produced an effect not easily forgotten. A wide variety of qualities is revealed in his portraits, which give the impression of a character whose depth is not readily sounded – a personality in which conflicting hereditary strains were peculiarly blended. Those who have described him from life dwell upon the contrast between the seeming listlessness of the face in repose and the warmth of the countenance when animated with conversation or public speech. The trappings of the man intensified the effect of crudeness. In a day of grandiose adornment Lincoln's habiliments departed as far from the Godey fashion plate as did his mid-western speech from the sophisticated accents of the East. The battered stovepipe hat stuffed with papers, the rusty ill-fitting coat, the ready-made trousers too short for the legs, the unpolished boots, the soiled stock at the neck, the circular cloak in winter or linen duster in summer, the bulging umbrella and hard-used carpet-bag, gave an entirely upremeditated effect of oddity, the man's appearance being apparently of no more concern to him than the food which he seemed to eat without tasting.[7]

57 Abraham Lincoln, photograph, Alexander Heller, 1860

His very carelessness of dress may suggest that he felt his features and form simply not worth the attention of good grooming. He referred in public to his 'poor lean, lank face', and there was one story about his appearance he particularly liked to tell (apocryphal, no doubt, but highly revealing of his image of himself). Splitting rails one day, he claimed, he was yelled at by a passing stranger. Looking up, Lincoln found the stranger aiming a gun at him, declaring that he had promised to shoot the first man he met who was uglier than himself. After scrutinizing the stranger's face closely, Lincoln declared, 'if I am uglier than you, then blaze away'.[8] Lincoln made a socially advantageous but, from the point of view of personal happiness, disastrous marriage. He was not successful with women, possibly because of some self-consciousness over his appearance, and led what must be accounted an unfulfilled sex life.[9] Yet, a young Southern woman is reported as saying: 'His face is certainly ugly, but not repulsive; on the contrary, the good humor, generosity and intellect beaming from it, make the eye love to linger there until you almost find him good-looking.'[10] What comes through most strongly in the written testimony is the way in which his appearance was transformed once he began speaking and became animated. According to Horace White, editor of the *Chicago Tribune*: 'The dull, listless features dropped like a mask. The eyes began to sparkle, the mouth to smile, the whole countenance was wreathed in animation, so that a stranger would have said, "Why, this man, so angular and somber a moment ago, is really handsome."' Another male contemporary declared Lincoln 'the homeliest man I ever saw'; yet, Lincoln's face, he said, 'brightened, like a lit lantern, when animated'. In action, Lincoln had enormous appeal; he had charisma. That apart, he was always striking. After seeing him for the first time, William Howard Russell, correspondent of the London *Times*, wrote: 'it would not be possible for the most indifferent observer to pass him in the street without notice'.[11] Lincoln made his way 'from log cabin to White House' by energy, dedication and considerable talent (he was a highly respected and successful lawyer); in the electoral arena his striking appearance and charisma were undoubtedly positive assets. But he was not beautiful, nor, apparently, sexually very appealing. This is a case of an ugly man with other personal qualities, including even physical ones (such as great height), having enormous success in public life (though, it may be surmised, suffering a deprived private life).

Beauty of face and form may be a source of appeal to a wider public, or it may, of course, be an enticement to a patron. In British politics for the major part of the nineteenth century the latter would seem to be a more important consideration than the former. Most renowned for looks among Victorian ministers was Henry John Temple, Viscount Palmerston, the dominant figure in British politics from 1850 to 1865. In the main body of the entry, the *DNB* speaks of the young Palmerston as having had 'the advantage of a strikingly handsome face and figure',

58 *Palmerston*, Thomas Heaphy, 1802

which, the writer continues, 'afterwards procured him the name of "Cupid" among his intimates'.[12] The basic reason for Palmerston's success was that he was an aristocrat, groomed for office from very early years: his way was smoothed for him by his guardian, Lord Malmesbury, and there is no reason at all to believe that this had anything to do with Palmerston's looks or sex appeal. As an aristocrat, Palmerston was able to take his MA without examination, 'by right of birth', then, entirely through patronage and influence, was returned for a pocket borough; already the influence of his guardian had secured him a post as a Lord of the Admiralty. Not long after getting into Parliament, Palmerston was appointed Secretary at War, a post in which he then remained for nineteen years. Palmerston's career had got off to an early start; he was in a post he liked; he could afford to relax and enjoy life. During his early years at the War Office he was admitted to Almack's, the exclusive club run by a group of aristocratic ladies who were very particular about the men they admitted to membership; several of these ladies were Palmerston's mistresses. Undoubtedly Palmerston was enjoying life; and the opinion of Lord Shaftesbury was a fairly common one: 'on first acquaintance I could see nothing in him of the statesman, but a good deal of the dandy'.[13]

Palmerston's most recent biographer describes him as: 'tall, dark and handsome . . . about five feet ten, with a fresh complexion, dark hair and magnificent blue eyes (though lacking a few teeth from hunting accidents, occasionally inclining to over weight, and with a definitely receding hairline)'. His appearance can be confirmed from his portraits, particularly the dashing early one by Heaphy, and from the later statement of the painter Benjamin Haydon that 'his nose is small, forehead fine, and he is handsome'.[14] In 1839, at the age of fifty-five, Palmerston married one of his mistresses, now fifty-two, the Countess Cowper, whose late husband had himself been reputed one of the handsomest men in London. The marriage was a happy one, which did not prevent Palmerston from continuing his amorous adventures. As Victorian Britain reached its high point in confidence and optimism, Palmerston's brand of assertive patriotism endeared him to politicians and public opinion. It is not surprising that, in a time of fragmented party politics and shifting alignments, this still handsome figure should assume supremacy. Palmerston was born to his opportunities; his good looks simply facilitated the nonchalance with which he let them fall into his lap. They enabled him to lead a particularly full social and sexual life and contributed to the relaxed attitude which inclined a nineteenth-century biographer to comment on 'the tardiness with which Lord Palmerston reached political prominence'.[15] But then, in fact, everything, including the prime ministership, fell into place for him.

For an early nineteenth-century aristocratic insider like Palmerston, good looks were simply an additional bonus. For Benjamin Disraeli, son of a Jewish man of letters and accordingly something of an outsider in the Tory Party, they were rather more important. Speaking of an early speech (1837, when Disraeli was thirty-three) in the House of Commons, the *Dictionary of National Biography* refers to 'the thin, pale, dark-complexioned young man, with long black ringlets and dandified costume'.[16] Twice further on the same page the impression made by Disraeli's appearance is remarked upon; it was, if not beautiful, certainly personable and, partly through dint of dress, striking. Commenting on Disraeli's later unwillingness to take up votes for women (though he was not unfriendly in principle to the idea), his most recent authoritative biographer has said that Disraeli himself stood most to gain by such an extension of the franchise.[17] Disraeli was certainly attractive enough, as well as distinguished and dynamic enough in both his literary and political careers, to marry in 1839 the extremely wealthy widow Mrs Windham Lewis. It was with her fortune that he was able to set himself up as the country gentleman, probably the most crucial single stage in his career towards prime ministership, the devotion of Queen Victoria and an earldom. Looks here were relevant in the negative sense. Had Disraeli been manifestly ugly, a John Wilkes, say, it is unlikely that his in many ways remarkable career would have evolved as it did. But Disraeli's personal charm was essentially exerted over a relatively small circle and, for all his sponsorship of the concept of Tory democracy, we cannot cast him into the same category as the present-day politician anxious to cut the best possible figure on television.

Looks were an added grace for Palmerston, an important blessing for Disraeli; they could have been ruinous for a handsome, lower-class would-be politician late in the century. David Lloyd George was born in 1863, son of a schoolmaster who returned to his farming roots in north Wales, dying while David was still very young, so that he was brought up by his uncle, a master shoemaker. His brother describes him as 'a good-looking youth with a vivacious manner and a ready wit', and his nephew tells us that 'he had realised early in life how attractive he was to women'. The entry in the *Dictionary of National Biography* (by top civil servant Thomas Jones) is more circumspect, stating simply, 'his charm was irresistible'.[18] The best evidence is photographic. The small north Wales town of Criccieth in which Lloyd George grew up was dominated by Non-Conformist morality, and an ambitious young man eager to make his way upwards in the world had to observe constraints unknown to Lord Palmerston. Rebuked by his sister for his flirtations, the young Lloyd George recorded in his diary (17 June 1880) his own intention to exert self-discipline:

59

I am rather seriously disposed to give up these dealings; this I know, that the realization of my prospects, my dreams, my longings for successes, are very scant indeed unless I am determined to give up what, without mistake, are the germs of the 'fast life'. Be staunch and bold and play the man. What is life good for unless some success, some reputable notoriety be obtained. The idea of living for the sake of living is almost unbearable – it is unworthy of such a superior being as man.

But the risks of disreputable notoriety were considerable. 'Blast these malicious gossips', is an entry of a few years later.[19] To his further irritation, his uncle took to spying on his evening activities. Treading a careful path, the young Lloyd George showed himself a man of distinct promise in the solicitors' office where he worked, while establishing a reputation as a fiery and effective public speaker in the Liberal cause. He paid court to Maggy Owen, only daughter of a well-off and rather superior family, whose members saw themselves as gentlemen farmers rather than mere working farmers; eventually, against the initial resistance of the

59 David Lloyd George, photograph, 1898

family, he married her on 24 January 1888. For the time being, solid respectability was fully established. Just over two years later David Lloyd George was elected Liberal member of parliament for the Caernarvon Boroughs. Safely based in London (which his wife hated, and from which she subsequently departed for long periods in Wales), and steadily rising in political reputation or, to use his own word, 'notoriety', he found discretion more crucial than abstinence. In 1910 began a long relationship with Frances Stevenson, the beautiful secretary less than half his age, whom eventually, after the death of his wife, he married. Though at all times Lloyd George had many enemies, not a word of this relationship was ever referred to in the press. Status and looks, in a man, were a devastating combination; but the latter without the former could still be an ambivalent gift.

What of beauty and public life in France? Revolutionaries, it would seem, do not need to be beautiful – no more so, anyway, than ordinary run-of-the-mill politicians: Louis Blanc, the leading socialist figure of 1848, was under-sized and unimpressive in appearance. For charisma (not, as I have already stressed, necessarily the same thing as beauty) we have to turn to Louis Napoleon, elected President of the new republic in 1848, who declared himself Prince President in his coup d'état of 1851 and was subsequently ratified Emperor in a national plebiscite. Napoleon III's greatest asset was carrying the name, and being a nephew, of the great Napoleon. He was also a man of considerable personal courage, had a certain animal magnetism, and cut a dashing figure on a horse. Beaky-faced, he was certainly far from good looking. The narrative which follows gives a nice insight into the relative values of status and beauty in nineteenth-century Europe. Napoleon was desperately anxious to underpin his position and establish himself as a true monarch by contracting a marriage alliance with one of the European royal families, in particular with that of the most powerful nation of the day: his plan was to marry Queen Victoria's niece, Princess Adelaide. But since the British Queen scarcely concealed her view of Napoleon as a despicable

60

60 *Louis Napoleon,*
Hippolyte Flandrin, 1861–62

61 *Bust of Empress Eugénie*, Jean-Baptiste Carpeaux, *c.* 1850

upstart, the Emperor was forced to turn from royalty to beauty, going against the advice of his most influential advisers.[20] The woman who, at the age of twenty-six, became the Empress Eugénie had been born in Granada in Spain. Tutored by her mother, she had just enough in the way of resources and connections to have established herself as an international beauty, at home in Parisian high society, as well as in the company of the British aristocracy (at a reception given by Lady Palmerston in the spring of 1849 she was described as 'a vision of youth and beauty'),[21] and among the prodigiously wealthy Rothschilds, through whom she had been introduced to Louis Napoleon. She had indeed used the greatest skill and the greatest self-discipline to ensure that her beauty (not shown off to advantage in the well-known Winter-halters, which make her look dumpy in the regal style of Queen Victoria, but perceivable in the portrait bust reproduced in Ill.61) brought her the highest possible social status.

61

And so we return to the role of female beauty. Certainly, in the areas of social promotion and political power, female beauty (allied to good fortune and an appropriate strategy) combined to achieve greater signifi-cance than male beauty. This rather obvious truth is highlighted by the manner in which biographies of even the plainest presidents make frequent references to the beauty of their wives.[22] Still, much further down the social scale male beauty was increasing in value in certain areas, as we shall see in the next section.

## 3 *Careers*

It continued to be true, as it had been in the seventeenth and eighteenth centuries, that if a woman founded a career on her personal appearance this almost certainly entailed the granting of sexual favours, whereas such was not necessarily the case in respect of the handsome men who secured posts as shop assistants or servants (though, of course, in some cases homosexual relationships might be involved). The women who moved sharply upwards in the social scale did so through favours granted to a relatively small number of influential or powerful men. Social promotion and social esteem were largely achieved through *personal* relationships, though, of course, the maintenance of esteem within the peer group which the woman joined depended in part on her widely admired beauty, and, of course, on any other personal qualities she might possess. Women who granted (or, perhaps, more accurately, were forced to grant) sexual favours on a wide, impersonal basis, unless they made the break to better things in good time, would not appear as striking social successes (they would remain 'common prostitutes'), though they might, if lucky, make a reasonably comfortable living. Good-looking men who did well out of their personal appearance essentially did so through *display* of their beauty (to house guests, potential customers, etc.); this also was relatively *impersonal*. For good-looking men making a career out of their looks, sexual activity was usually (the court of Catherine the Great provided the paradigmatic exception) incidental to social success, whereas for the good-looking woman it was central to it. However, while this section will inevitably reiterate the hard core of this truism, it also seeks, together with section six, to bring out the very slight, but significant, shift to a situation where women could achieve success and esteem in various walks of life on the basis of looks alone, without sexual transactions necessarily being directly involved. As it became openly asserted that it was a woman's duty to be beautiful, so women who were truly beautiful became models to be widely admired. As shops became bigger and more numerous, as new creations in costume and fashion competed with each other, requiring to be shown off and advertised, as photographs circulated and attracted adulation, as families striving to establish themselves in the upper class sought cohorts of servants who would do them credit in all departments, so the opportunities for beautiful women to *display* themselves, and to larger and more *impersonal* audiences, increased, as did the rewards adjoined thereto. This shift hints at the modern perception where good looks in both men and women are highly esteemed without having to involve a sexual exchange.

At the same time, whatever the ideological emphasis on beauty as a feminine attribute, an expanding economy meant expanding opportunities for the exploitation of male beauty. The first successful department store entrepreneur in the United States was Alexander Turney Stewart, whose emporium in New York City was completed in 1846. Stewart's very deliberately and positively catered to women: 'he chose his salesmen for their "gentlemanly" manners and pleasing appearance'; each customer was greeted at the door by the general manager who 'assigned her, if she desired, a special salesman who escorted her through the store'.[23] In the journal of Louis Fissner, a Prussian Jew employed as a clothing shop salesman in Newburyport, Connecticut, in the 1850s, there is a definite preoccupation with personal appearance. On 14 April 1854, he notes the arrival of a new salesman from Boston: 'he is good looking but in my opinion he will stay but a short time'.[24] Henry Mayhew, the London journalist, tells us of dress shops in the 1860s with 'fifty gentlemen behind the counters';[25] the fine appearance necessary is suggested in Ill.62. John Bird Thomas, writing of his experiences as a shop boy in the 1870s, records the importance of a good appearance even in ordinary grocers' shops. He had been advised that 'a good appearance and plenty of cheek will get you anywhere'. But apparently careful attention to dress was not enough, genuine good looks being an important requirement: 'I think that dressing up better helped because when I applied in answer to advertisements I generally got an interview, but there were so many taller and better looking applicants that all that happened was that they took my name and address and "would let me know".'[26]Perhaps the best summary of the relatively secure but also, of course, relatively menial prospects in this area for the handsome lad is provided by a satirical cartoon of 1881: 'Yes, Madam?' enquires a shopwalker of a customer entering the shop; the Lady replies, 'I want something handsome and cheap'; 'Certainly, Madam', replies the shopwalker, 'Mr Jones, step forward.'[27]

62 Farmer and Rogers' 'Great Shawl and Cloak Emporium', Regent Street, engraved advertisement, 1866, showing elegant male shop assistants

In chapter four I discussed the change in attitude towards male servants (apparent by the later eighteenth century) from seeing them as members of the dangerous classes to appreciating them as display objects. As old families grew wealthier by wise collaboration with industrial enterprise, and new families pushed their way in amongst the old, the premium placed upon what was considered the cultured display of elegant, appropriately dressed male servants greatly increased. Speaking of the mid-nineteenth century, Merlin Waterson, author of the standard history of an English country house, writes: 'At grander country houses the first requirement of a footman, groom or coachman was that they should have the physique to show their liveries off to advantage.'[28] In her thorough study, *The Rise and Fall of the Victorian Servant*, Pamela Horn has written that, 'Personal appearance was very important for any boy aspiring to the position of footman or page in a large household, for only the tall and well-built were considered.' She adds that 'wages often related to height, with the tallest men or boys receiving the highest pay'.[29] Similar considerations weighed heavily as the American upper class of the late nineteenth century developed in self-consciousness. 'Among the "smart set" of the post-1870s', writes the historian of *Americans and their Servants* in the period 1800–1920, 'an imposing looking butler was a must. A "good" five-foot three-hundred-pound, balding butler was impossible.'[30]

Even in the later eighteenth century, it will be recalled, female servants were not intended for display. However, by the later nineteenth century, it was becoming a matter of prestige to have personable female servants: 'no one wanted a squat, thickset chambermaid; tall, comely ones were required in wealthy homes'. There was at least a chance now of a good-looking girl getting a position, principally for the attractiveness of her appearance and for display to envious guests, rather than for satisfying the desires which that appearance aroused. Of course the beautiful servant still ran special risks: either of being seduced by one of her masters, or of being sacked as a potential temptation to a growing son.[31] But the main point stands and is confirmed, as will be seen in a moment, by developments in the world of the female shop assistant. Being a servant was no wonderful achievement with respect to conditions of work, earnings or status. But it was seen by working-class and lower-middle-class men, by shopkeepers, tradesmen, peasants and farmers as an excellent preparation for the duties of a wife.[32] Given that marriage remained the basic 'career' for most women, a comely girl who got a good post thereby was twice blest in the marriage stakes. The maternal grandmother of former British Conservative Prime Minister Edward Heath was the wife of an illiterate farm worker in Kent. She had a very beautiful daughter who, on leaving school at fourteen, went into domestic service with a well-off family from Hampstead, who spent their summers at Broadstairs in Kent. Here she had a great opportunity for learning upper-middle-class ways. Yet she took up with, and married, a local carpenter, Will Heath, much to the displeasure of her mother who, in classic allusion to the association between female beauty and social mobility, lamented that 'with her looks she could do a lot better'.[33] In fact beauty, enhanced by domestic training, was wiser than the mother knew, for Will Heath was himself an upwardly mobile type (though almost certainly the girl *could* have done 'better', that is, had more choice than offered itself to most young women).

Throughout the century beautiful young women continued to use the fashion shop and the stage as platforms from which to move into more lucrative positions whose essence was sexual. But opportunities for girls who wished to remain 'respectable' greatly increased as openings occurred in shops which once had employed only men.[34] No doubt girls of all shades of looks gained such employment (again nothing spectacular on the social and economic scale) but the reactions of such commentators as Mayhew (like Pepys before him) to encounters with beautiful sales-girls,[35] as well as the comments about the business value quoted in the previous chapter, indicate the advantages of beauty in this humble (and generally non-sexual) career. So too with the posts of 'office girl' and stenographer which appear towards the end of the century as a part both of the general expansion in clerical and service trades, and of the beginnings of the very slow decline of the male clerk. There remained many traditional occupations which expanded as cities, and middle-class consumer demand, expanded. Certainly the aged and worthy could attract sympathy, but a beautiful flower girl was more likely to be irresistible (and thus commerically viable). Even the young women whose menial tasks were to clean the front steps of elegant houses, the 'step girls' of late-Victorian and Edwardian London, themselves clearly gave a high rating to personal appearance.

Popular theatre of various kinds developed greatly from the middle of the nineteenth century onwards. Many qualities went to make up the popular music hall star, but without doubt employment opportunities multiplied for chorus girls and dancers, whose prime qualifications had to be a good figure and attractive features. A main function of such French theatres as the Vaudeville or Théâtre de la Porte Saint Martin was the display of beautiful women. The ultimate enshrinement of the display of enticing womanhood came with the founding of the Folies Bergère on 2 May 1869. Writing of the 1870s and 1880s in the USA, Lois Banner quotes a contemporary as remarking that 'it became a question of actresses seeking a situation not whether they were good actresses, but whether they were pretty and were willing to exhibit their persons', and herself comments that 'actresses won their roles not for talent, but because of their physical appearance and their willingness to wear scanty attire'.[36] To the worthy middle class the term 'actress' continued to be synonymous with that of 'prostitute'. Many actresses, singers, chorus

63 'Step girls', photograph from George Sims, *Living London. Its Work and Its Play. Its Humour and Its Pathos. Its Sights and its Scenes*, Vol. II, 1903

girls and dancers undoubtedly were prostitutes; some were celebrated courtesans (as we shall see in the final section of this chapter). Theatres of all types served as meeting points for prostitutes and their clients, the promenades at the Folies Bergère and at the Empire, Leicester Square, London, being but two of the more infamous and conspicuous examples. The woman who sought to exploit her beauty by going on the stage sometimes also decided to exploit her sexuality in the traditional way for high potential profits, or was sometimes forced to grant sexual favours through necessity, the need, perhaps, to gain the favour of her employer. The famous courtesan Léonide Leblanc, whose first employment was at the Belleville Theatre in working-class Paris, later wrote of how an actress was forced to make her way by earning the good graces of author and director, actor and critic.[37] The problem is to determine how far a woman's earning power derived from granting sexual favours and how far from her appeal to, comparatively speaking, large and, again comparatively speaking, *impersonal* audiences. The point is simply that the opportunities were increasing for a beautiful woman to profit from the deployment and display of her beauty, without this profit being entirely tied to actual sexual activity. The market value of autonomous beauty was going up.

Women had for centuries served as artists' models: here the emphasis is on display of beauty, and, eventually, more or less public display, though the exact balance between that and sexual exchange would vary with individual circumstance. What is certain is that a woman without beauty would be unlikely to succeed as a model, although it is also true that the many life classes in the arts schools, which grew in numbers in the nineteenth century, could not always afford to be too choosy. There were, as a result, shillings to be earned by a poor and not necessarily pretty woman willing to stand motionless and naked in the draught (the difficulty of securing models with the desired attributes is illustrated by the failure of Alexander Walker to illustrate properly his different 'types' of female beauty, most of his photographs appearing to be of the same not very striking model – though purchasers were no doubt pleased by her nudity.)[38]

Before examining the particular case of the Pre-Raphaelite models, which raises a number of important issues relating to the main arguments of this book, let us consider 'models' in the contemporary (or 'modern') sense of the term, the precursors of Twiggy, Shrimpton and Grace Jones. The historical evolution was a slow one. By the middle of the century shops were using girl apprentices, whose apprenticeship was paid for by their parents, to show off shawls, mantles and cloaks to customers. In the later nineteenth century the more beautiful salesgirls (often recruited in the first instance, as we have seen, for their beauty) began to double as 'mannequins', parading particular fashions for the benefit of a customer; sometimes young women were specially recruited to fulfil this particular function. Mannequins made more than the mere salesgirl (the crucial change is from apprentices whose parents do the paying to mannequins who are so attractive that they are specially paid), but they did not become household faces or household figures, only customers knew them, and then only by their first names (as a lady would know her chambermaid). The first photographs of mannequins did not appear till 1910, and they remained anonymous. The faces that are photographed and circulated are those of the 'beauties' discussed in the final section of this chapter. For the first half of the twentieth century the faces and figures seen in the fashion magazines were those of society ladies and successful actresses; the model as we know her today was a product of the cultural revolution of the 1960s which is the subject of chapter eight.

The actual creation of the mannequin in the mid-nineteenth century has its own particular relevance to certain themes of this book. Charles Worth, an Englishman born in 1825, was in many ways the epitome of the good-looking salesman of ladies' fashions, beginning his career at the Piccadilly store of Swan and Edgar. But he was also an architect manqué, family circumstances being too straitened to permit him to follow that career, and a man of more than usual initiative and energy. He had only the most exiguous savings when he made his move to Paris, where, I would suspect, his looks played a bigger part than his latent design talents in securing him employment at the fashionable shop of Gagelin et Opigez, which sold shawls and dress materials at 93 rue de Richelieu. Within months he had married a fellow sales assistant, the also very good-looking (photographs exist of both) Marie Vernet. Worth did the sales talk, while elegantly draping the Maison Gagelin shawls around Marie.[39] He also began designing clothes for her, which Gagelin et Opigez were only too delighted to sell. Hence Marie Vernet's claim to be considered the first mannequin in history. With his wife very much a partner, in 1858 Worth established his own business. It was an easy step from his use of Marie as a mannequin to the recruitment of attractive young women, several of them English, to perform the task of putting on one of his new dresses whenever this was requested by a customer. Normal attire for the mannequins was fashionable, but always black, to ensure that they kept in their humble place.

If we wish to encapsulate the role and function of the beautiful artist's model across the century we need scarcely do more than glance from the works of William Etty in the 1840s to those of J. W. Waterhouse in the 1890s, noting that nudes, including male ones, were appreciated by no less a personage than Queen Victoria herself.[40] The most thorough and scholarly analysis we have of any one group of artists' models is Dr Jan Marsh's brilliant and original *The Pre-Raphaelite Sisterhood*. The next few paragraphs draw heavily on that book; like all truly scholarly works, it offers sufficient evidence to enable one sometimes to disagree with the conclusions drawn by the author. The most important members of the original Pre-Raphaelite Brotherhood, founded in 1848–49, were John

64, 65

64 *Venus and Cupid*, William Etty, *c.* 1840

65 *Hylas and the Nymphs*, John William Waterhouse, 1896

Everett Millais, Dante Gabriel Rossetti and William Holman Hunt; later associates were Edward Burne-Jones and William Morris. The term 'Pre-Raphaelite', when applied to a woman, quickly came to connote a particular type of female beauty, as surely as 'Byronic' connoted a particular type of male beauty; furthermore, the Pre-Raphaelites were often associated with Botticelli as presenters of a particularly disturbing type of sexual beauty.

There are two central questions. The first, in two interlinked parts, is: were the models chosen by the Pre-Raphaelites truly beautiful, and were they chosen because of their beauty? Secondly: did they derive a positive advantage through being chosen as models? The second question seems to be easy to answer. All of the models came from very humble backgrounds. Emma Hill was the daughter of a bricklayer; Jane Burden was the daughter of a stableman; Annie Miller was brought up in a Chelsea slum by her uncle and aunt, the former a cobbler, the latter a washerwoman; Fanny Cornforth came from a poor rural background, her father having possibly been a blacksmith, and her employment in London was as a prostitute; Lizzie Siddall was the daughter of an ironmonger, who kept a small shop in the Old Kent Road. Only Georgie Macdonald was truly born into the respectable lower middle class, her father being a Methodist minister. The Pre-Raphaelite painters range from the solid, if not particularly well-off, professional middle class to the fairly affluent, with claims to gentry status.[41] There can be no question but that through their association with the artists these women were lifted into a new social status, either marrying one of the artists (Emma Hill married Ford Madox Brown; Jane Burden married William

Morris; Georgie Macdonald married Burne-Jones; and Lizzie Siddall married Gabriel Rossetti) or making an advantageous marriage elsewhere (as did Fanny Cornforth, who also later became Gabriel Rossetti's mistress; there was, as is well known, a good deal of swopping around). Nor can it be doubted that these liaisons brought a level of intellectual and artistic fulfilment which would never have been attained otherwise.

As to the question of the women's beauty, we have, of course, the Pre-Raphaelite paintings themselves to go by: Annie Miller in *The Awakening Conscience*; Fanny Cornforth in *Fazio's Mistress*; Jane Morris in *La Belle Iseult*, and many of the really sexy later paintings by Gabriel Rossetti, including *The Bower Fields*; Emma Hill in *The Last of England*; Lizzie in *Regina Cordium*, or the Millais *Ophelia*. However, painters can idealize or, put more simply, beautify, their models. In fact, guided by Dr Marsh's indispensable researches, we can limit the area of uncertainty to two of the models. All but Lizzie Siddall and Jane Burden, as the written and visual evidence makes abundantly clear, were what the Pre-Raphaelites themselves termed 'stunners', and what that age, our age and all ages before and in between would have perceived as extremely beautiful women. Jan Marsh meticulously examines all the accounts of how Lizzie Siddall was 'discovered'. It is her contention that Lizzie was in reality a rather plain girl (by the standards of the time, at least, for, Dr Marsh is of the persuasion that 'the concept of female beauty is entirely a social construct'), and that the Pre-Raphaelites reconstructed her into a beauty in their paintings, retrospectively decreeing that she had always been one.[42] In 1849, Lizzie, then aged twenty, was working in a milliner's shop off Leicester Square when Walter Deverell, at that time studying art with Gabriel Rossetti and Holman Hunt, was looking for a model to play Viola dressed in the male part of Cesario for his large oil painting *Twelfth Night*. Important considerations would be that the model could readily be dressed up as a boy and should have red hair (despite the contemporary prejudice against red hair in women).

At any rate Deverell secured his model – the fee of one shilling an hour was a considerable attraction set against the erratic seasonal nature of millinery work – and Lizzie Siddall makes her first appearances in the sketches for, and the finished oil painting of, Deverell's *Twelfth Night*. On the basis of this work it is impossible to judge her either plain or beautiful, though we can appreciate the fine legs, which shocked many Victorian viewers.[43]

Entirely properly, Marsh is highly sceptical of accounts written many years later by William Michael Rossetti and Holman Hunt declaring that from the first Deverell was struck by Lizzie's stunning beauty. Hunt has Deverell announcing triumphantly to Gabriel Rossetti: 'what a stupendously beautiful creature I have found, by Jove! She's like a queen, magnificently tall, with a lovely figure, a stately neck, and a face full of delicate and finished modelling . . . ' Marsh believes that Lizzie was chosen simply because she fitted Deverell's immediate requirements, and that for some time she continued to be 'known only as a "plain" model'.

With red hair, she had prominent eyelids, pale eyes fringed with gingery lashes and a long top lip which may have covered protruding teeth. It is not intended to endorse this description as ugly, since I believe such judgments to be part of the continuing oppression of women, but there is no doubt that in the Victorian period, women's looks were important, and by the criteria of the time Lizzie's appearance would not have been highly rated.[44]

In support, Marsh cites the poet and womanizer William Allingham, who was apparently not greatly attracted to Lizzie: after her death, but before her posthumous reconstruction as a beauty, he wrote: 'Her pale face, abundant red hair and long thin limbs were strange and affecting – never beautiful in my eyes.'

This is an interesting statement which bears further examination, and should be taken in conjunction with the other visual evidence. Dr Marsh reproduces a self-portrait by Lizzie, dating from 1853–54, and a photograph probably taken in the mid-1850s. In an earlier and perhaps deliberately popularized and exaggerated article, Dr Marsh had written: 'Lizzie, as her honest self-portrait shows, had a plain round face with pointed features, hooded eyes and an unfortunately long upper lip.'[45] The photographic portrait does bring out the upper lip, yet at the same time has a distinct quality of sex appeal about it. How damning is a slightly prominent upper lip? This feature is apparent in an 1854 drawing

66
67

*66 Self-Portrait*, Lizzie Siddall, *c.* 1853–54     67 Lizzie Siddall, photograph, mid-1850s

*68 Drawing of Lizzie Siddall*, Gabriel Rossetti, 1854

of Lizzie by Gabriel Rossetti, but in this she is ravishingly beautiful, lip    68
and all. By this time Lizzie was married to Rossetti and it may well be
that his love for her contributed to his 'glamorization' of her portraits.
There is, however, another Rossetti drawing (not reproduced by Marsh),    69
unglamorized, straightforward, very appealing, which, I would surmise,
is as accurate a representation of Lizzie Siddall as we are likely to find. To
return to the self-portrait, to me it too, in its very austerity, contains
clear elements of sex appeal. Taking these, and the other appealing
elements already noted, together with Allingham's phrase about Lizzie's
appearance being 'strange and affecting', I would produce an interpretation rather as follows. The mid-Victorian era was one in which conventions and confusions about the nature of beauty were still strong; Lizzie
Siddall, it is clear, was not as manifestly beautiful as Annie Miller or
Fanny Cornforth, yet she had sufficient personal beauty to make her
highly personable and certainly far from plain or ugly. Allingham, the
poet, though aware of her appeal, could not fully break through
contemporary conventions about thinness and red hair, while Millais and
Rossetti, the painters, could. Undoubtedly, there was a process of
glamorization in the rendering of her in paint, which turned her from an

69 *Drawing of Lizzie Siddall*, Gabriel Rossetti, 1855

70 (right) Jane Burden (or Morris), photograph, one of a series taken in the garden of Gabriel Rossetti's house in Cheyne Walk, 1865

attractive, personable woman into a Pre-Raphaelite beauty. It is a nice fairy-tale idea that plain Lizzie Siddall was transformed into an ideal of beauty, as it is a nice political fable that ugliness is part of a socially constructed oppression. Lizzie Siddall was not ugly, nor even plain; if she had been, she would not have enjoyed such success and esteem as she attained. (As with so many of the women in this book, the notion of her 'success' has to be carefully considered: Lizzie Siddall, sadly neglected by Rossetti, became addicted to drugs and died in her early thirties.)

Broadly the same considerations, I believe, apply to Jane Burden, also described by Marsh as 'plain'. In 1857 Gabriel Rossetti and some of his younger disciples were engaged in painting murals for the Oxford University Union Society (i.e. students' union). They were in constant need of female models, and as constantly preoccupied with thoughts of 'stunners'. One evening at the theatre, Rossetti spotted two girls, Jane and Bessie Burden, sitting in the cheap seats in the gallery. He accosted them immediately after the performance and invited Jane to come next day to model for the Union murals. To Marsh it was 'somewhat perverse to pick Jane as a representative of female beauty'. Undoubtedly, 70    photographs of Jane taken in 1860 do not show her in a terribly appealing light. Yet it would seem reasonable to believe that Rossetti accosted her in the first place because he saw something striking in her physical appearance, not simply because he thought her notably plain. She certainly emerges as ravishing in some of the most famous of all of the later Pre-Raphaelite paintings, including *Queen Guinevere* (or more 71    correctly, *La Belle Iseult*) by William Morris (whom she married, and

71 (right) *La Belle Iseult* (wrongly described as *Queen Guinevere*), William Morris, 1858. Iseult is the pre-Arthurian Irish princess loved by Tristram of Brittany (Tristan and Isolde in Wagner's opera)

from whom she derived wealth and status), and *La Pia de' Tolomei* and *Proserpine* by Rossetti (whose long-term lover she became after she tired of Morris). It should also be noted that a portrait photograph of around 1865 presents Jane as a very beautiful woman, strikingly like the rendering of her in the Morris painting. Jan Marsh has declared it a part of Rossetti's 'genius' that he was able to persuade others to accept his prescription as to what should be accounted beautiful. She continues: 'Since the concept of female beauty is entirely a social construct, it isn't quite true to say that he made us believe an ugly girl was pretty, but almost single-handed he enlarged the definition, so that Jane Burden's looks became a standard of feminine appeal . . .'[46] There are problems with this statement. We have to be clear whether we are talking about Jane as she appeared in the paintings or Jane as Marsh alleges she was in real life. As she appears in the paintings, she would, I am sure, have appealed strongly to most men in the seventeenth and eighteenth centuries, as well as in the nineteenth and twentieth. Rossetti's 'genius' lay, as it were, in spotting talent of which others, more bound by convention, were less perceptive. If 'enlarging the definition' means showing, as I have insisted throughout this book, that beauty, as an autonomous and universal quality, comes in many styles, then I agree

72

73

that Rossetti did so. The real Jane Burden was not ugly, though probably she was not as lovely as her representations in *La Belle Iseult* or *Proserpine*. Her looks, till the Pre-Raphaelites created a new, or perhaps restored an old, fashion, were not fashionable, but I have already suggested that in the real world fashion was less omnipotent than is often maintained. To answer my opening question: most of the Pre-Raphaelite models were indisputably beautiful, and none were less than personable; they were indeed chosen on account of their good looks.

Whatever differences of interpretation there may be, I am entirely in agreement with Marsh's notion of the 'career prostitute' and the idea that prostitution could be a planned and practical choice for a woman which could lead to considerable material and social advancement.[47] Fanny Cornforth did well from the profession, in which her outstanding good looks gave her enormous confidence. Her meeting with Rossetti, which brought her into the Pre-Raphaelite circle, took place in the street; and *she* accosted him. Jan Marsh also refers to the successful career of Sarah Tanner, whose progress is charted in full in the diary of A. J. Munby, that remarkable observer of Victorian womankind:

Saturday, 30 July . . . Going to the Opera, I met in the Strand one Sarah Tanner,

72 (left) *La Pia de' Tolomei,* Gabriel Rossetti, 1880. La Pia is a character from Dante's Purgatory, tragically imprisoned by her cruel husband

73 (right) Jane Burden (or Morris), studio photograph, 1860

who in 1854 or 5 was a maid of all work to a tradesman in Oxford Street: a lively honest rosyfaced girl, virtuous & self possessed. A year or so after, I met her in Regent St. arrayed in gorgeous apparel. How is this? said I. Why, she had got tired of service, wanted to see life and be independent; & so she had become a prostitute, of her own accord & without being seduced. She saw no harm in it: enjoyed it very much, thought it might raise her & perhaps be profitable . . . During the next two or three years I saw her twice or thrice at intervals on duty, and generally stopped to talk. She was always well but not gaudily dressed; always frank and rosy and pleasant, and never importunate: nor did I ever hear her say a vicious word. Yes, she continued to like it – she had some good friends, & was getting on nicely. After this I never saw her till tonight, when I met her in the Strand, walking with another young woman. She was stouter & healthier than ever, and was dressed, not professionally as a 'lady', but quietly & well, like a respectable upper servant. She stopped with a frank smile, & shook hands; and How is this? said I again. 'Well, I've left the streets & settled down,' she said quietly. 'Married?' I asked. 'Oh no! But I'd been on the streets three years, and saved up – I told you I should get on, you know – and so I thought I'd leave, and I've taken a coffeehouse with my earnings – the Hampshire Coffeehouse, over Waterloo Bridge.' . . . Now here is a handsome young woman of twentysix, who, having begun life as a servant of all work, and then spent three years in

voluntary prostitution amongst men of a class much above her own, retires with
a little competence, and invests the earnings of her infamous trade in a respectable coffee-house, where she settles down in homely usefulness and virtuous
comfort! . . . [48]

We are back firmly in the world where a woman's beauty was of no
real value unless directly associated with the selling of sexual favours.
The considerations affecting the different remuneration and the different
social success of prostitutes in the later nineteenth century were little
different from what they had been in the eighteenth. From 1804, there
was in France a system of registration and of legally recognized brothels
(made more rigorous in the 1840s), and it became difficult for women to
avoid becoming hopelessly in debt to the brothel keepers, so that upward
social mobility, even for the beautiful, may well have been less of a
possibility than it had been in the eighteenth century. Céleste Vénard
(later famous as the actress and courtesan Mogador) was, at sixteen, a
registered prostitute:

What tortures we suffered! To have to laugh when you want to weep, to be
dependent and humiliated when you pay so dearly for the little you possess! If
someone killed the wretched creatures who expose themselves to this, they
would do them a service . . . Love takes a cruel revenge on the women who
profane its image. [49]

She explained how she had hoped, through prostitution, to transmute
looks into wealth: 'I saw myself rich, and covered with lace and jewels. I
looked at myself in my little bit of mirror; I was really pretty . . . ' [50]
Only because of her beauty did she escape, one of her clients – apparently
also impressed by her desire to become an actress – buying out her debts
to the brothel. [51]

For the fortunate, Paris offered the highest prizes (see section six), but
at the middle level a beautiful girl probably did better in London.
Journalist Henry Mayhew found one twenty-seven-year-old earning
four, five, sometimes eight and ten pounds a week, [52] when a successful
artisan might be earning only two. William Booth, founder of the
Salvation Army, lamented that 'there is no industrial career in which for
a short time a beautiful girl can make so much money with so little
trouble as the profession of courtesan'. [53] B. Pierce Egan's *Life in London*,
published at the end of the 1860s, makes it clear that in the higher-class
brothels the women did rather well, but they had to be beautiful. [54]
William Acton, in his classic study of prostitution dating from the same
period, described the life of the elegant prostitutes of the Argyll Rooms
in London's West End, who would expect food, drink and an evening's
entertainment, plus a fee of two or three pounds: quietly, though
expensively dressed, they were also 'pretty'. [55]

## 4 *The Two Georges: The Personable and the Plain*

The careers of two of the nineteenth century's most famous and successful women, George Sand and George Eliot, were built on intellectual and literary talent. It did not happen very often, but it was possible for the occasional woman to make a name irrespective of looks, provided, however, that she was born into a good position in the social hierarchy. Plain women did not usually cross any class barriers (many of the great hostesses of the nineteenth century were no more beautiful than the majority of their predecessors in the eighteenth, but, to take two instances, the fat and plain Mme Auberon came from a good family, her mother, Mme de Nerville, having had a salon before her, while the no more than personable Mme Arman de Caillavet came from the wealthy Jewish aristocracy). My concern here is with the private sphere. Neither of the Georges was beautiful: George Sand could be termed personable; George Eliot was very definitely plain, perhaps even ugly. Were their private lives, accordingly, very different? How, anyway, does one rate success or estimate happiness in a person's private life?

With respect to these two individuals, for whom there is no shortage of biographical information,[56] it could well be true that what constituted happiness and success for the one would not necessarily do so for the other. How much depended on opportunity, and how much on choice? George Sand lived a high-profile, 'romantic' life, a life of many loves and many liaisons. George Eliot defied Victorian respectability by living, from her mid-thirties, with a married man; she believed deeply in monogamy. The two Georges belonged, of course, to different eras (though there was only fifteen years difference in age) and to different countries: the London of the 1850s and 1860s had no equivalent in the Bohemian milieu of Paris in the 1830s and 1840s.

Yet assessing personal happiness, and relating it to wealth or status or, as is my intention here, to looks, is perhaps not an utterly impossible task. It is fairly easy to pin down the conditions which for most people would constitute absence of happiness: material deprivation; lack of food, shelter and sex; the contempt of others; loneliness. It is fairly easy, too, to see what those with opportunity, wealth and power go after in the name of happiness: material comforts, prestige, the esteem of others, sex – whether with one beloved partner for life, or with a large number of highly desirable partners, the point being that the successful and happily fulfilled do realize their choices and are not forced to take only what their situation will allow. Whether renown and tranquillity in old age compensate for unfulfilled youth, or a despairing old age cancels out a mainly prospering life or an idyllic twenty years of youth and early middle age are, however, questions easier raised than answered; happy years, I would think, can never be cancelled, but years lost never compensated for.

Neither George Sand nor George Eliot ever suffered material deprivation, and both eventually made considerable sums from their writings.
Success came much earlier to George Sand, whose first novel, *Indiana*
(1832), published when she was twenty-eight, was a bestseller. Other
highly popular works quickly followed, and she in fact amassed such a
fortune as to free her from any inhibition in following her every whim
and fancy. She was a celebrity, a 'character', who wore men's clothes and
smoked cigars; she was the mistress of famous and distinguished men,
including one special idol of French society, the musician Chopin, as well
as the romantic writer and dramatist Prosper Mérimée and the respected
poet Alfred de Musset; she had scores of admirers, all ready to speak of
her beauty and graciousness; and she was a public figure of note,
devoting her literary talents to the Republican cause in 1848. George
Sand had two children, and was involved in an agonizing tug-of-love
over the possession of her daughter.

George Eliot's first novel (*Adam Bede*) was published, to great acclaim,
in 1859, when she was forty; within ten years or so she was fully
recognized as the greatest living English novelist. She suffered several
emotional involvements which were not reciprocated; she knew herself
to be plain, and that, clearly, was what the men she became attached to
thought. The man she lived with, George Henry Lewes, provided
immense mental and moral support, and it was from the time of her
liaison with him in the late 1850s that her novel writing began; but she
was always very conscious of the irregularity of the liaison. George Eliot
had no children. While readers begin to draw their own conclusions, let
me add a little more detail.

George Sand, born Aurore Dupin de Francueil in 1804, was the
daughter of an impoverished landowner in Berry, just south of Paris; she
was brought up, and given a fine all-round education, by her father's
mother, in the tiny Château of Nolant. In 1822, at the age of eighteen,
more because it was the thing to do than from any deep personal feeling,
she married Casimir, son of the Baron Dudevant, so that she later
inherited the title Baronne Dudevant. Within a year she had her first
child, a son, Maurice. But as a young woman of spirit and creative
energy, she was unsuited to the routine duties of a provincial wife among
the minor nobility, which were all her husband required of her. Her
daughter Solange was born in 1827, though it is generally thought the
father was not Dudevant, but probably the naturalist Stéphan Agusson
de Grandsagne. Four years later, aged twenty-seven, she parted from
Dudevant, taking her two children to join her handsome, if indolent,
nineteen-year-old lover, Jules Sandeau. She had a sufficient allowance
from her husband to support a Bohemian life amid the students of Paris.
There is no reason to doubt that the watercolour by Candide Blaize is a
good likeness of her at this time: the pendulous lower lip, the slight
double chin, the over-large nose, on which others commented, are all

74

74 *Portrait of George Sand,*
watercolour, Candide
Blaize, *c.* 1830

apparent.[57] Yet this is still a sexy face, and one appreciates how she could look specially appealing clad in male attire; she did in fact frequently dress as a male student.

With Sandeau she produced a number of short stories which they jointly signed 'J. Sand'. Then in May 1832 came her own novel, *Indiana*, published under the name 'G. Sand'. At this time she spelled her new name in the French fashion, 'Georges', the English 'George' coming later as part of her highly contrived self-presentation. *Indiana*, a romantic story stressing a woman's struggle against social restrictions, particularly those of marriage, was an enormous success, as were the not dissimilar *Célia* (1833) and *Jacques* (1834). It is always easy to say afterwards of a bestselling author that conditions were absolutely right for her success, and Sand's novels are certainly so clearly of their time that they have not lasted well; yet there was a new boldness about them, and Indiana's words to her husband, 'You have the right of the stronger and society confirms it; but with my will, sir, you can do nothing', are deservedly preserved in the feminist canon.[58]

Sand was famous and rich, and she embarked on the first of her highly publicized romances, with the tall, blond and beautiful viscount Alfred de Musset, who was six years her junior. Travel, I noted in the previous chapter, was a spreading fashion. Together they went to Italy; but he chased after other women, she got a bad head cold, he caught typhoid fever – a fine mélange of romantic incident, improved upon when, in response to his infidelities, she took up with the handsome young Italian doctor ministering to the typhoid, Pietro Pagello. She and de Musset parted, reunited, parted finally, and meantime created an enormous correspondence. Her six weeks of anguish over the loss of de Musset are recorded in the *Journal intime*, not published till 1926: 'Oh, God, you know you have invented no greater torment for the guilty. It is their hell in this world.'[59] She bounced back quickly and was soon energetically promoting again her cigar-smoking, betrousered, and in many ways bewitching image, while launching into other romantic liaisons. She was just good looking enough to be able to do both (given my comments in chapter two, I should in fairness mention that the one characteristic all of her lovers singled out was her eyes, which undoubtedly added to her striking appearance, though did not, I think, make her beautiful). There followed the still more glamorous and long-lasting relationship with Chopin, one episode from which formed the basis of the novel, in essence a travel book, *A Winter in Majorca* (1842). The affair with de Musset was subsequently written up in the more revelatory *Elle et lui* (1859), prior to which she had already produced *Story of my Life*, serialized in *La Presse*, then published in book form in 1854. But in the autumn of 1837 she was rehearsing the reasons which made life scarcely worth living – principally that her daughter had been stolen from her by Dudevant.[60] Sand perhaps reached the height of her prestige in the late 1840s when her literary talents were used in support of the Republic of 1848, but up to her death in 1876 she was lauded as a *grande dame* of French letters. That success was fundamentally based on creative energy and literary skill, but it may be doubted whether the particular self-fuelling life style and career could have been pursued without the basis of a presentable appearance on which to create the exotic image.

With Mary Anne Evans (later Marian Evans, and later still, in conscious tribute to the French novelist, George Eliot) the physical attributes were different, not excessively different, just sufficiently different. She had a long, prominent nose, heavy under-jaw, and the dark lugubrious look of one who had never really been touched by youthful charm; contemporaries described her as 'horse-faced'.[61] She had a prodigious intellect, and by her twenties was thoroughly knowledgeable on contemporary, and particularly German, philosophy, and the recent advances in the sciences; she was a witty observer of the human scene, and a lively conversationalist. Thus, while it is important to get the matter of looks correct, it is important also to note her many other attractive qualities. While her private writings are full of yearnings to find a life's partner, she did in 1845, when she was twenty-four, reject a proposal from a perfectly personable young man. Her first real involvement was with the publisher John Chapman, a notorious philanderer, very conscious of the 'mystery and witchery of beauty', but not always over particular in that connection. His wife, fourteen years older than himself, was reckoned plain, but as the daughter of a Nottingham lace manufacturer she brought a substantial fortune with her. Installed in

Chapman's house along with his wife was a good-looking governess, Elizabeth Tilley, in fact Chapman's mistress. Marian, already known for her studies in German philosophy, joined this ménage for a time, quickly arousing the jealous hostility of the other two women. We cannot know for certain whether she had a sexual liaison with Chapman, though George Eliot's biographer, Gordon S. Haight, thinks she probably did; at any rate Marian was clearly very much in the power of Chapman's physical appeal. Together in May 1851 they visited the ruined castle at Kenilworth. Chapman made this poignant record in his diary:

As we rested on the grass, I remarked on the wonderful and mysterious embodiment of all the elements, characteristics and beauties of nature which man and woman jointly present. I dwelt also on the incomprehensible mystery and witchery of beauty. My words jarred upon her and put an end to her enjoyment. Was it from a consciousness of her own want of beauty? She wept bitterly.[62]

The relationship with Chapman continued as a professional one when he bought the *Westminster Review* and she edited it. The next important relationship was with the pioneer sociologist Herbert Spencer. In looks and virility Spencer was no Chapman, but he and Marian shared intellectual and cultural interests. When Spencer took her to the opera she wrote to friends: 'see what a fine thing it is to pick up people who are short-sighted enough to like one'.[63] But Spencer, in fact, was very conscious of physical beauty, and indeed was one of the leading latter-day physiognomists convinced that beauty was linked to personal, cultural and intellectual qualities (though Marian Evans provided a most

75 *George Eliot*, watercolour, Caroline Bray, 1842

palpable demonstration of the contrary). In 1854 he published two essays to this effect, concluding with one of the least fetching of all the aphorisms to which this complex subject has given rise: 'the saying "that beauty is but skin-deep" is but a skin-deep saying', and, most ungallantly, illustrating ugliness with features which could very readily be identified with Marian Evans.[64] In her letters of this period she frequently laments her own ugliness: 'I am a hideous hag now, sad and wizened', 'haggard as an old witch'.[65] Late in life Spencer blamed on Marian's lack of beauty the fact that he took his relationship with her no further;[66] but in truth he was a somewhat feeble creature and probably a dedicated celibate at heart.

When Marian first met George Henry Lewes, scholar and journalist, and joint founder of the intellectual magazine *Leader*, she was not taken by him. His friends reckoned him one of the ugliest men in London; Jane Carlyle spoke of 'an immense ugliness' and she and others sometimes referred to him as 'Ape'. His jaw was very narrow, but he had wide cheekbones and brow; his nostrils were large and his face was pale and deeply pockmarked; he was small and slightly built: 'a sort of miniature Mirabeau in appearance', wrote Marian.[67] But Lewes had quite potent charms: he had married the beautiful nineteen-year-old niece of the Earl of St Vincent, a young woman of considerable intellectual interests and linguistic talent. Lewes was lively, witty, and a great mimic: he could always attract a fascinated circle around him. His marriage began well, but as he went travelling more and more, his wife took at least one lover; her fifth son was fathered by Thornton Hunt, Lewes's partner on the *Leader*. By the time Marian Evans, now aged thirty-four, came to know him, his marriage had effectively ended, though divorce was not a possibility. She made the bold decision to live with him as his wife, a most fruitful partnership which encouraged her to embark on her career as George Eliot the novelist, though also caused her much anxiety because of its 'irregularity'.[68] While one correspondent in 1869 remarked 'one rarely sees a plainer woman; dull complexion, dull eye, heavy features', she did in fact assume a statuesque, commanding appearance as she grew older: indeed the young Brett Harte remarked in January 1880: 'I spent a delightful hour with George Eliot (Mrs Lewes) on Sunday last at her house. I was very pleasantly disappointed in her appearance, having heard so much of the plainness of her features. And I found them only strong, intellectual, and *noble* – indeed, I have seldom seen a grander face!'[69] The death of Lewes in 1878 was a blow. But on 6 May 1880, when George Eliot was sixty, she married the tall, handsome John Walter Cross, who was forty; she died seven months later.

Both George Eliot and George Sand had used to the fullest the talents and endowments with which they were born. Indeed, though neither had suffered discomfort on that account, they had both nobly criticized some of the conventions of their time, and generally identified themselves with liberal–progressive causes. George Sand was no Marie Duplessis, no Lola Montez (see section six), and could never have built a career on personal appearance alone, nor, I believe, could she ever have broken out of the desperately humble circumstances of a Duplessis (daughter of a pedlar) or a Mogador; instead (coming from a comfortable background) she was able to live a life of high sexual adventure *with men of her own choosing*. It would seem that distinction in other fields, allied with a sufficiency of personal appeal, served her well. In outline the features of George Eliot bore some resemblance to those of George Sand; but she remains one of the most famous examples of someone for whom no amount of advice from *The Ugly Girl Papers* or *How to be Pretty though Plain*, no amount of assertion that external beauty is but the outward projection of internal qualities (which she possessed aplenty), could have enabled to project the allure George Sand achieved. Her twenties and early thirties were immensely productive, and so in one sense very fulfilling; but happy? – I don't think so. Both, of course, as deeply thinking women, experienced the angst of the human condition, but George Eliot could not truly write, as George Sand could (with perhaps some omission of the joys of youthful passion): 'I have had times of happiness [des *bonheurs*, plural and italicized, not, of course, 'happiness', constant, universal and in the singular], that is to say joys in maternal love, in friendship, in reflection and in reverie . . . I have tasted only those pleasures, for which I could ever have thirsted.'[70] George Sand claimed that she had a 'contempt for the conditions of normal happiness'.[71] 'Normal happiness' was what George Eliot wanted, but even that came late and was still not quite normal enough.

## 5 *Private Lives*

We know, in very general terms, that across the nineteenth century the ability of young people to make their own personal choices in marriage increased and that there was a decline in the institution of the arranged marriage, though for families, and indeed often for individuals contemplating matrimony, wealth and status continued to be important concerns. Personal choice does not necessarily simply imply good looks; as in any age, individuals have to accommodate to their circumstances and opportunities, and to the implacable fact that, although the beautiful are always with us, there are always far too few of them to go round. Beauty, and the lack of it, is noticed, commented upon, and is sometimes a preoccupation, with men as well as women. Edmond Got, aged eighteen in December 1840, struggling to begin a theatrical career in Paris, asks, in the second entry of his journal, 'What is it that I am?' His answer: 'Nothing.' What is it that he desires?: 'Everything.' But then the real lament: 'But poor, not at all good-looking, – and thus miserably timid. '[72] (In fact it is clear that he was quite comfortably off and, possibly more important, had many contacts, so that he was quickly embarked on a career at the Comédie Française.)

Preoccupation with beautiful celebrities had intensified by the end of the century; Max Beerbohm's *Zuleika Dobson* (1911) was, in part, a satire on the cult of the international beauty (the young men of Oxford all drown themselves for the sake of the beautiful Zuleika, a stage star, whose photograph is known to all). However, the sources for truly private lives remain very fragmentary. We learn much about happiness and unhappiness in love, but not much about the role of beauty, particularly since visual evidence is usually lacking. The pain of ugliness is apparent, but overall one is struck by the way in which the nineteenth century in general is indeed an age of restraint; it is also clear that for the majority of real lives, whatever miraculous visions may be glimpsed at a distance, in etchings, or in photographs, encounters offering genuine opportunities to get to know members of the opposite sex are not frequent.

From the beginning of the century we have an account by a journeyman printer of his two courtships, one resulting in rejection, the other in marriage. In his journal, dated January 1809, he is looking back after nearly four years of a marriage in which he has allied himself to a deeply religious family and during which he has risen to become a partner in a printing firm. Evidently, within a very limited circle, he has acted from personal choice, but what he sees as really governing his actions is 'wise providence'. Beauty is not mentioned:

About this time I fell in love, made an offer of marriage, but was rejected. This I have no doubt was overruled by a wise incalculable advantage, as had this match taken place, in all probability the person who had been more immediately the instrument in God's hand of awakening my drousy & languid conscience and consideration about eternity would have perhaps never been brought within the circle of my acquaintance. When Ann Collie, with whom I had been long acquainted, & who had been the object of my choice in my younger years, though the thought of my own youth, and the danger of my affections leading to precipitancy, made me resolve, however reluctantly to check myself in time, & break off all intercourse at least for a time. This was done, – and after the interval of many months, if not years, it was again commenced and for the same reasons abandoned. – It was a considerable time after this second break off, that my affections were engaged to the other, & to whom I proposed marriage. – But my suit being rejected, in a few months, I resolved to attach myself to my first love which I did, & on the 25th day of October, 1805, we were married in her father's by the Rev Mr James Struthers.[73]

A description of her engagement, seventy years later, by an upper-middle-class young lady is even more phlegmatic. In the spring of 1875 Elizabeth Hardcastle was in Rome, seeing the sights. Her diary consists of brief, almost laconic entries, reminiscent of the formal minutes of a business meeting. Mostly they refer to the other Britons in Rome at that time. Miss Hardcastle is sensitive to human beauty: of one couple in the circle she notes, 'they are both so handsome'.[74] A trip to Ostia and Castel Fusano was aborted because of rain: 'Graham was to have gone in our carriage so after breakfast he turned up and we sang a duet and then went to the Borghese Gallery where Mr Freeman joined us.' Four days later (Sunday, 11 April 1875) these two characters are mentioned again: 'church twice. Walked with Mr Freeman and Horace Thornton to S. Peters to hear Vespers. Graham came to tea.' The entry for the next day consists of three sentences:

Rode with the Miss Colville's, Captain and Mr Bland, Horace Thornton and Graham to the Cook Valleys. Robert Graham asked me to be his wife which after much consideration I consented to. Mr Freeman went away this morning.

The day following the proposal and acceptance merits two sentences, and the bridegroom-to-be only his surname: 'Graham brought me over the sweetest letter from his mother. Afternoon we went to see the Vatican pictures together.' There is no other sign of family considerations or interest; this is an authentic nineteenth-century individualistic, romantic engagement. Pasted in beside the crucial entry there is a photograph of the intended, an agreeable, if not particularly striking, member of the gentry class. Nowhere has there been any comment on his looks, nor, indeed, on any of his other attributes. Yet Miss Hardcastle was a witty and highly literate young woman. The diary opens with a sparkling description of her sister's wedding, in which the members of the bridal procession are termed 'the mourners'. The 'Cook Valleys' in the quotation above derive their name from the tourists ('Cookies ' or 'Cookisti') delivered there by the travel firm Thomas Cook. The making public of the engagement nine days later is rendered thus: 'We divulged the awful secret to the Roman world causing thereby a great sensation.' The wedding is not described, nor the honeymoon, though there is a full description of the arrival at Skipness, the Graham home, the welcome by local farmers, the settling in, the rounds of visits, but there is nothing at all which hints at physical attractiveness, let alone sexual feeling.[75]

The Anderson family papers at Stanford University provide us with quite a full account of the courtship, and first years of marriage, of Melville Anderson and Charlena Van Vleeck, educated Americans in the 1870s; marvellously, they also contain photographs, so that we can see    76, 77 that both Melville and Charlena were agreeable enough, but not strikingly good looking. They were thrown together because Melville was a student in lodgings, and Charlena was the landlady's daughter. Their courtship was an undemonstrative one, and in the early stages of marriage they happily accepted long separations in the interest of Melville's career as an academic. In the copious letters from both partners

76 Melville Anderson, personal photograph in Anderson Family Papers, 1876

77 Charlena Anderson, personal photograph in Anderson Family Papers, 1876

there is never any reference to the physical appearance of the other.[76] It is, naturally, impossible to be certain, but this seems to be one of those placid relationships in which neither looks nor great sexual activity had major importance.

In the previous chapter I cited the various comments Mary Hallock made on the personal appearance of people encountered on her travels within the United States, yet in all her references to her husband, whom she clearly loved, she never once says anything of his looks. Very different, as we have learned from Professor Peter Gay, were the sentiments of an exact contemporary, Mabel Loomis Todd, to whom it was most important that her husband to be was 'very good-looking'; her subsequent lover, Austin Dickinson, twice her age, had many personal qualities, and high social status, but he was also 'the finest looking man I ever saw'.[77]

What all the evidence makes clear is that, while often not a critical factor in marital choice, in one way or another, looks are frequently (though, of course, not invariably) noted and remarked upon. To women of secure social status and independence like George Sand good looks in a man were a highly esteemed quality; for most women, anxious for a successful and enduring marriage, other qualities would be placed first. Women, whether beautiful or not themselves, recognized beauty in other women, and often responded warmly to it. Mary, Lady Monkswell, was aware of her own lack of looks (which we can judge for ourselves from the photograph of her, published with her *Journal*)[78] and was pleased to have a flattering likeness made of her: 'I look so mild, sensible & pleasant I really do not know myself.' She appreciated beauty in others, in its various types, including the Pre-Raphaelite:

I like Mrs Freshfield particularly & she is really beautiful. She is tall & graceful & her face is like a pre-Raphaelite picture, large drooping eyes, a lovely mouth, a pointed chin & a little dimple in it . . .
Beautiful Mrs Julian Goldsmid with whom I fell in love . . . Mrs Julian G. is a fair Italian about 26, with lovely blue eyes, a sweet smile & sweet voice . . .
[Referring to '200 young women' skating] . . . The beauty of the girls was something to make one scream with delight. The older I grow the more slave I am to beauty . . .[79]

Very many men were slaves to female beauty. For the ugly men (who were not princes of the royal blood, or emperors, or, at any rate, wealthy bankers) this could be a cruel servitude. Stocky, plain William Morris painted wonderful visions of gorgeous women, and imagined them filling the streets of his utopian Nowhere; but he lost Jane to Gabriel Rossetti, everyone's model of the dashing, sexually successful bohemian. Earlier in the century William Etty had made his name and fortune almost exclusively through the painting of beautiful nudes. His success is unchallengeable testimony, if any were needed, to the ability of his contemporaries to appreciate beauty which was nakedly and unambivalently physical. Etty himself admitted that 'the female form, in its fullness, beauty of colour, exquisite rotundity, may, by being portrayed in its nudity, awake the nature in some degree an approach to passion' and that he might have (unintentionally, he claimed) tended at times to 'voluptuousness'.[80] But voluptuous or not, Etty, lifelong bachelor, had no outlet for his 'passion', for his 'personal appearance said as little in his behalf as his tongue. Slovenly in attire, short and awkward in body; large head, large hands, large feet, a face marked with smallpox, a quantity of sandy hair, long and wild.'[81]

The ugly painter with the beautiful models is a real-life variant on the Beauty and the Beast theme (though the real-life 'beasts' did not always have the luck of the fairy-tale one). Best known, probably, in this respect is the dwarfishly deformed Toulouse-Lautrec of the 1890s (though his raddled prostitutes and chorus girls neither were, nor were painted as, beauties). The specialist in the painting of beautiful women was Toulouse-Lautrec's contemporary, Boldini, an entirely conventional portrait painter with enormous facility, and the special gift of bringing out the sexual allure of his sitters (one of Beerbohm's nicest touches is to have had Zuleika Dobson painted by Boldini).[82] Though he was immensely wealthy (from painting so many famous beauties), Boldini was not greatly appealing to women: on one social occasion, as he approached a group of young ladies, a loud voice declared, 'the toad is approaching the strawberry patch'.[83] Boldini certainly did have affairs with his first Paris model, Berthe, and, later, with the Contessa Gabriella de Rasty; he finally married when he was seventy-nine. One could argue that he didn't do badly for an ugly little man, and that a woman with his looks would have stood no chance whatsoever.[84]

Etty and Boldini were mediocre painters who painted for a market, and cannot be compared with the giants of Romanticism or of Impressionism and Post-Impressionism. That they painted as they did was no doubt basically determined by the level and nature of their talents; but it may be, too, that insecurity founded in unappealing personal appearance pushed them towards seeking popularity and social acceptance.

## 6 *Grand Horizontals and the Rise of the International Beauty*

The first and second themes of this book are concerned with changes in the evaluation of beauty. My general premise has been that the life chances of the beautiful will be affected by the evaluation of beauty prevailing at the time. However, it is also true that the actual experiences of some beautiful people can, in turn, bring about further changes in the way in which beauty is evaluated. That is a point I hope to bring out in this section, while primarily trying to establish the precise importance of personal appearance in the successes (and tragedies) of certain rather famous women. These women, once more, are a tiny minority of a tiny minority; but a remarkable number of them indisputably enjoyed a quite startling social promotion. While many of the clichés about expanding opportunities and dramatic reversals in class position in the nineteenth century contain little truth, there can be no doubt that for beautiful women, however humbly born, the *possibilities* of leaping social barriers were greater than ever before.

However, one portentous paradox must be registered immediately. Publicly the societies which developed throughout the century put a high premium on the standards of familial and sexual morality inculcated by the Christian churches. Thus, though by the end of the period the notion of the international beauty – her likeness widely known from photographs – was fully established, in order to achieve considerable material and social success, most of the women discussed here had to forfeit their social respectability. We are only in the 'modern' age when women (or men for that matter) can derive the maximum advantage from their beauty without in any way forfeiting their respectability.

Some distinctions must again be made between what happened, and could happen, in the USA, Britain and France (or perhaps, more accurately, Paris). In the later nineteenth-century USA certain beautiful women, both American and foreign, enjoyed the same sort of renown, circulation of photographs, and so on, as such women enjoyed elsewhere; but whatever the intimate detail of their private lives, their fame rested on their beauty itself, and on their achievements as actresses or singers: they were not courtesans. American society was both the most moralistic, and, with respect to beauty, the most 'modern'. Among British beauties of the period, part of their fame might be known liaisons with such prestigious persons as the Prince of Wales, but such liaisons were not essential to success as a beauty, as the example of the actress Ellen Terry (whose life was 'unconventional', but in no way promiscuous) shows. Paris, both before and during the Second Empire, and during *la belle époque*, was the setting for an established class of courtesans, at least as celebrated as genuine members of high society ('*le monde*'), but who constituted the not respectable '*demi-monde*', in the useful, and much-used, phrase of Alexandre Dumas *fils*; they were, in an even more expressive coinage of the Second Empire, *les grandes horizontales*. In origins, though not necessarily always in fame, these women were international. Of twenty of the most celebrated (La Paiva, Ozy, Savatier, Mogador, Montez, Duplessis, Schneider, Castiglione, Pearl, Letessier, Barucci, Skittles, d'Antigny, Bellanger, Leblanc, Otero, de Pougy, d'Alençon, Cavalieri and de Mérode), three were Italian, three were British, one was Spanish, one Russian and one Austrian.

The salons of nineteenth-century Paris do not have quite the celebrity of those of the Enlightenment, though running a successful salon continued to be a means by which a woman could cut an important figure. As already briefly noted, the major *salonières* of the period owed more to birth and wealth than to personal beauty. However, the case of

78 *Jeanne Detourbey*,
Eugène-Emmanuel
Amaury-Duval, 1862

Jeanne Detourbey suggests that for a woman of lowly origins to become a great society hostess the passport of beauty was required. Born to a poor family in Reims, Jeanne Detourbey worked first as a wool picker in a factory, then as a bottle washer in a Reims champagne house. That she was genuinely beautiful is attested by verbal accounts, by the reactions she aroused,[85] and by the 1862 portrait by Amaury-Duval in the Louvre. Her early rise from her proletarian origins was that of any other fledgling courtesan, attributable, in the words of Cornelia Otis Skinner, to 'an inborn intelligence and a calculating evaluation of her own beauty and God-given charm'.[86] She came, of course, to Paris, where one of her first noteworthy lovers was Marc Fournier, director of the Théâtre de la Porte Saint Martin. That an acting career sometimes required talent as well as beauty is suggested by the fact that Detourbey did not persevere with a career on the stage. She moved on to a more prestigious figure, celebrated in both *monde* and *demi-monde*, Emile de Girardin, owner of *La Presse*, founder of *La Liberté*, and practising politician, through whom she encountered, and had a brief liaison with, 'Plon-Plon', Prince Napoleon. After an affair with the inevitable Alexandre Dumas *fils* she succeeded in marrying the Comte de Loynes: though the outraged family were able to secure the annulment of the marriage, Jeanne clung on to the title and a substantial inheritance, tangible means on which to support the celebrated salon she ran from 1870 to 1908.

Let us add the Comtesse de Loynes to the list of twenty well-known courtesans. Let us then take some measure of the potential for social mobility by doing a quick breakdown of the social origins of the twenty-one. (We must also, of course, try to establish whether all of them were in fact beautiful.) Three were from the nobility, four from the respectable middle classes, fourteen from 'the popular classes'. The best way of giving meaning to that term, which, broadly, comprises the lower middle class, the urban and rural working class, and the yet lower class of itinerants and casual workers, the 'residuum' as it was called in Victorian Britain, is to look individually at the fourteen.[87] Thérèse Jachmann (known as La Paiva), born in 1819, was the daughter of a tailor in the Moscow ghetto. Rose Alphonsine Plessis (Marie Duplessis, 'La Dame aux camélias'), born in 1824, was the daughter of a pedlar in Normandy. Elisabeth-Céleste Vénard (Mogador), also born in 1824, was illegitimate and brought up erratically by her mother, who for a time worked as a cashier in a hatter's; she spent part of her teens confined 'for her own safety' to the women's prison of St Lazare. Eliza Emma Couch (Cora Pearl) was born around 1835 in Plymouth, the daughter of a music teacher of Irish origins, who shortly deserted her mother. The origins of both Caroline Letessier and Giulia Beneni ('La Barucci') are, literally, obscure, though it is possible that Letessier's foster father was a butcher, while it is known that La Barucci was born in Rome. Catherine Walters ('Skittles') was born in 1839, daughter of a minor customs officer in

Liverpool. Blanche d'Antigny (she simply adopted the title), born in 1840, was the daughter of a carpenter in Martizay, near Bourges. Julie Leboeuf ('Marguerite Bellanger'), also born in 1840, came from an agricultural worker's family near Saumur. Léonide Leblanc, born in 1842, was the daughter of a stone breaker. All of these were courtesans of note under Louis Philippe or during the Empire of Louis Napoleon. From among the famous courtesans of *la belle époque*, Caroline Otero came from a Spanish gypsy family, Lina Cavalieri (born in Rome, 25 December 1874) from an unknown Italian one.

These bare details of birth and origins say no more than that it was *possible* for a woman of the humblest background to achieve the wealth and celebrity of the *demi-monde*, to a degree which had not been true of previous centuries. The same elements of ambition, determination, strategy and luck were required, as we shall see from looking further at some individual cases. Was beauty the central prerequisite? Yes, even more so than before – in that beauty of different types, as against conforming to a conventional image, could bring success. La Paiva was said not to be beautiful,[88] but in the absence of portraits I simply do not know whether this was so or not; it is *possible* that the adverse comments mean that her Russian Jewish looks did not match the conventions of the day, and that her considerable social success (she became first Marquise de Paiva, then Countess Henschel von Donnersmarch) was due to a sufficient number of influential men appreciating her particular type of beauty, but that must remain an open question. The looks of Cora Pearl – as well as her manners and speech – were also much criticized. Commenting directly on her appearance, Alphonse Daudet (author of *Lettres de mon moulin*) wrote of her 'hideous head', which he also described as 'a clown's head'; and he clearly regarded the 'lithe young body', grudgingly admitted in passing, as no compensation for the 'sewer of a mouth' and 'comic English accent'.[89] The Comte de Maugny, in his *Demi-Monde under the Second Empire* (published under the pseudonym of Zed), recalled of her:

English by birth, character and allure, she had the head of a factory worker, neither good nor bad, violent blond, almost red, hair, an unbearably vulgar accent, a raucous voice, excessively coarse manners, and the behaviour of a stable-boy.[90]

Her outstanding success, de Maugny complained, was beyond his comprehension. In short, while her looks and style were condemned by aesthetes, Cora Pearl was bedded by every rich and powerful Frenchman who could lay hands on her. Portraits show why: her face was perfectly proportioned, slightly boyish, as is sometimes the way with the Irish, and in fact, enticingly beautiful. 'Zed' greatly praised the Liverpool girl, Skittles (Catherine Walters):

79

79 Cora Pearl, engraving, Leopold Flameng, *c.* 1860

80 'Skittles' (Catherine Walters), photograph, *c.* 1860

English like Cora Pearl, but as beautiful, elegant, distinguished, and graceful, as Cora Pearl was lacking in these qualities.

She had blond hair, a natural blond, deep blue eyes, striking complexion, perfectly proportioned features, slim build, aristocratic curves: a real treasure ['un vrai keepsake'].[91]

80    Enough portraits exist to endorse thoroughly this description, as indeed they exist to demonstrate that beauty *was* an immediately recognizable characteristic of almost all of the other courtesans considered in this section. For Mogador and Letessier one has to rely on written accounts as (late) photographs or portraits are inconclusive.[92]

Throughout this book I have spoken of beauty as a *relative* universal, which is to say I do not deny that changes take place in conventions as to what constitutes the most admired type of beauty in any particular age. Generally, but not exclusively, beauties of the middle and later nineteenth century are plumper than those of the late twentieth century. It

81    may be that the thin, pale Alphonsine Plessis appealed specially to the sensibilities of high society in the 1840s, though her contemporaries

82    Alice Ozy and Lola Montez have those proportions which (to me at least) speak of universality. In general, questions of hairstyle and costume (that is to say, self-presentation) apart, there does not appear to be a style of beauty peculiar, respectively, to the earlier nineteenth century, the

81 *Marie Duplessis*, Edouard Vienot, *c.* 1845      82 *Lola Montez*, Joseph Carl Stieler, *c.* 1840s

Second Empire and *la belle époque*. La Barucci (Second Empire) was dark
with strong, striking Italian features; Cavalieri (*belle époque*), under dark      83
hair, had delicate, soulful features; but then La Belle Otero (also *belle*      84
*époque*) had the heavy looks of the Spanish gypsy that she was. Caroline
Letessier (Second Empire) was slim, as were Cléo de Mérode and
Emilienne d'Alençon (*belle époque*), while Blanche d'Antigny (Second
Empire) matched convention exactly with her sweet, slightly chubby
face, dimpled chin and plump figure. Léonide Leblanc (Second Empire)
was a blonde with a plump face and turned up nose; Ozy was dark with
an oval face whose features were perfectly proportioned; Liane de Pougy      85
(*belle époque*) was dark, with a strong aquiline nose; Cléo de Mérode was      86
dark, but in looks a fragile gamine.

The careers of these women involved an intelligent, often calculating,
exploitation of their looks, sometimes bringing in ancillary talents, such
as ability to sing, or dance, or ride. The exploiter might be solely the
woman herself, or, initially at least, an 'agent' (male usually or, possibly;
female). In conversation with the actress Judith Bernat, Marie Duplessis
appeared to be assuming total responsibility for her own destiny:

Why did I sell myself ? Because honest work would never have brought me the
luxury I craved for, irresistibly . . . I wanted to know the refinements and
pleasures of artistic trade, the joy of living in elegant and cultivated society.[93]

83 Lina Cavalieri, photograph, *c.* 1895      84 La Belle Otero, photograph, *c.* 1890

In fact the first to perceive the commercial value of her beauty had been her own father, who, in effect, sold her for a year to a wealthy septuagenarian in Normandy.[94] Rose Alphonsine (as she still was) then took herself off to Paris, her looks securing her the relatively menial jobs which at least kept her clear of the registered brothels while she also worked on her own account as a prostitute. A widower named Nollet, also spotting her dazzling potential, encouraged her to change her name to the more aristocratic-sounding Marie Duplessis. Her launch into the society to which she aspired was achieved when she became the mistress of the Duc de Guiche-Gramont. Thereafter she had merely to *appear*, at the theatre, at a dance, in a salon, to attract the attention of the rich, or the celebrated, such as Alexandre Dumas *fils*, who based his *La Dame aux camélias* on the Duplessis who had set herself up in a lavish suite on the Boulevard de la Madeleine, and with whom he had a passionate and ill-starred affair. The real Rose Alphonsine Plessis was only twenty-three when, on 3 February 1847, she, like La Dame aux camélias, died of consumption: beauty had taken her out of a squalid social background, but it could not overcome the disease which was probably also the legacy of that background.

Mogador has already been quoted on the motivation that took her into prostitution; of her career, she wrote, 'Fortunately for me, I had understood from the first that a love-affair is like a war, and that tactics

85 Liane de Pougy, photograph, *c.* 1890    86 Cléo de Mérode, photograph, *c.* 1890

help you to win it.'[95] After her release from the brothel, modest success came, not in acting, but as a dancer, first at the Bal Mabille on the Champs Elysées, where it was her partner Brididi who gave her the compelling name of Mogador, after the fortress just captured by French troops in Morocco, and then at the Théâtre Beaumarchais. An affair with the leading circus impresario Laurent Franconi led to an engagement (brief, as it transpired) as an equestrienne; a further one with the Duke of Ossuna established her as a courtesan. Dancing and horse-womanship were two obvious ways to display a beautiful figure.

Like many another comely woman in poor circumstances, Blanche d'Antigny had begun as a shopgirl, attracting the attention of a visiting gentleman who took her with him to his native Bucharest, where the single compensating circumstance was that she learned to ride.[96] Quickly back in Paris she got a job as a rider at the Cirque d'Hiver which led, within a couple of years, to an engagement as the 'living statue' of La Belle Hélène in *Faust* at the Théâtre de la Porte Saint Martin. Within a couple of weeks she was launched as a courtesan.

An important, and perhaps critical, factor in the rise of Catherine Walters to eminence as the courtesan Skittles was the skill in horseriding which she somehow acquired when her family moved out from Liverpool to the nearby Wirral peninsula.[97] Her first important employment when she went to London in search of fame and fortune was in showing off horses (and, concomitantly, herself). Her first really important lover in London was Lord Hartington; but prospects were more consistent in the Paris of Louis Napoleon, whither she betook herself. Marie Dolores Eliza Rosanna Gilbert ('Lola Montez'), born in Limerick, Ireland, in 1818, reared in India, educated at Montrose in Scotland and at Bath, in England, came of a respectable middle-class English family. To escape an arranged marriage with an elderly, though very rich Supreme Court Judge in India, she eloped with, and married, a young officer, who subsequently deserted her.[98] She was beautiful; she had to earn a living: so she took lessons in Spanish dancing. Though she had no great talent for it, it was upon dancing that, as Lola Montez, she founded her career as European lover (she had a much-publicized affair with the great romantic composer and pianist Franz Liszt), courtesan (she was a celebrity in the Paris of the 1840s, and was left considerable wealth by the newspaper proprietor Henri Dujarier), and adventuress (supremely confident in her looks, she simply forced herself on King Ludwig I of Bavaria – nicknamed 'the new Du Barry', she was, till the Revolution of 1848, effectively uncrowned Queen of Bavaria).

Dance was the first career of Cléo de Mérode, and dance or mime the main second string and means of self-display for such contemporaries as Caroline Otero and Liane de Pougy (to whom Sarah Bernhardt gave the advice: 'Display your beauty, but once on the stage you had better keep your pretty mouth shut').[99] A nice variation was practised by Emilienne d'Alençon, who began attracting attention, and rich lovers, by performing an act with trained rabbits at the Cirque d'Eté (and so may have been an inspiration for the fictional Zuleika Dobson, whose forte was performing conjuring tricks on stage); later d'Alençon kept herself on display by doing her act at the Folies Bergère. Lina Cavalieri had more orthodox talents as actress and opera singer.

Have I taken it too much for granted that these women were well rewarded for their skilful deployment of their most potent weapon, their looks? Duplessis died at twenty-three, La Barucci, risen also from poverty, at around thirty-three, and also from consumption. From her late thirties till her death in her fifties Cora Pearl led a rather sad, neglected existence. Blanche d'Antigny died at thirty-four. For those who lived out the allotted span there was, of course, no avoiding the ravages and the pains of age. But most amassed considerable fortunes, and some acquired genuine titles. Alice Ozy, whose foster mother had exploited her charms by having her serve in the family jeweller's shop, accumulated enough lovers as an actress to be able to retire early from the stage, and made so much out of them that, even when all looks had gone, she could afford a succession of young lovers.[100] Lola Montez, back in England, married a rich officer ten years her junior, but, accused of bigamy, had to flee to the USA: here she had a prosperous career as a lecturer and writer on women's rights, and on 'beauty'.[101]

Enduring success (as far as that can be measured) does seem to have been slightly more certain for the courtesans of *la belle époque*, but this is related to particular developments in the evaluation of beauty itself, to be discussed at the end of this section. Here it may be noted that Anne-Marie Chassaigne came from a respectable middle-class family, making a perfectly sound marriage to a naval officer. She, however, made the decision to leave him and their child, believing, rightly, that her great beauty could be turned to good account in the Parisian *demi-monde*. Colleagues gave her the name of Liane, and from her first important lover she borrowed the name de Pougy. After a long career as reputedly 'the most beautiful courtesan of the century' (not really a statement of any absolute value – Cavalieri was reputedly 'the most beautiful woman in the world')[102] she married the Roumanian Prince Georges Ghika, many years younger than herself, and lived out the rest of her life as part of the international set.[103]

One famous figure from *la belle époque* I have not yet mentioned. Margarethe Zelle ('Mata Hari') just escaped being plain, and was scarcely more than personable.[104] She came from a solid Dutch family, but her father went bankrupt. She answered a Dutch army captain's advertisement for a wife, and went to Java with him. Then in 1902, aged twenty-six, she turned up in Paris. She never had the easy success of an Otero or

87

87 Mata Hari, dressed for one of her exotic dances, photograph, *c.* 1907

a Cavalieri, and made her way by doing exotic, nearly nude, oriental dances as 'Mata Hari'. She formed German connections, lacked the looks to re-establish a position in Paris, and short of status, short of cash, scarcely understanding the gravity of what she was doing, became a German agent. Her sad and, it should be said, dignified end, during the First World War, is well known.

Some courtesans actually started out from quite elevated social circles. Apollonie Savatier, nicknamed La Présidente, and consort of intellectuals rather than rich men, was daughter of a viscount and prefect of the Ardennes; Cléo de Mérode had a real entitlement to her *particule* (she came from the Austrian branch of the family) and was certainly born into quite a substantial life style. The Countess of Castiglione, included in my count of three Italians, was perhaps a courtesan more in the original sense of the word (lady of the court) than in the nineteenth-century one. Having been the mistress of the brilliant Piedmontese politician (and architect of Italian unification) Count Cavour, she was sent by him to the court of Louis Napoleon to influence the Emperor in favour of Pied-mont. Castiglione was scarely successful in her mission, but she clearly enjoyed her status as imperial mistress and much-desired lady of the court.[105]

Such ambitions and intrigues were alien to the puritan, republican culture of the United States, where, however, the printing presses had got moving early in the reproduction of images of beautiful women. In her authoritative and scholarly study *American Beauty*, Lois W. Banner argues that in the United States what was considered beautiful in women changed every twenty years or so: before the Civil War the frail, willowy woman, described by Lois Banner as the 'steel-engraving lady', domin-ated the fashion magazines; in the decades after the Civil War favour switched to the heavy, buxom model of beauty, termed by Dr Banner the 'voluptuous woman'; in the 1890s the vogue was for tall, athletic, 'natural' women, this image crystallizing in the 'Gibson Girl' of the satirical drawings by Charles Gibson.[106] The notion of changing fashions in beauty is, of course, central to all standard histories of the subject; given the meticulous documentation which supports Banner's impres-sive monograph, it is impossible to doubt that she produces an accurate representation of changing emphasis in the fashion magazines, and perhaps even in types of actresses and chorus girls involved in popular entertainments. In any case, Banner does acknowledge that:

Despite the importance of the voluptuous woman as a measure of beauty among American women, she never completely carried the day. Both the steel-engraving lady and the natural woman were also popular in the late nineteenth century.[107]

In fact what made a beautiful woman successful in the USA, as every-where else, was not so much conformity to a particular fashion, as her

inherent beauty, whatever its type. The two best-known American
beauties of the late nineteenth century were the actresses Lillian Russell     88
and Marie Doro: they are very different, Russell the blonde doll,     89
appealingly innocent looking, Doro brunette with a cheeky up-turned
nose.

Banner identifies Lillian Russell, leading star of the popular musical
stage from the late 1870s onwards, as personifying the 'voluptuous
woman'. Yet, Banner's own scrupulous account of Lillian Russell's
appeal scarcely supports this generalization: she had a 'lithe figure' and
was known as 'airy fairy Lillian'.[108] Slightly oddly, in my view, Banner
then continues: 'As Russell grew older, her originally lithe figure grew
heavier, as though she felt herself obliged to modify her appearance to
conform to a standard that the British Blondes, among others, had
originally established. More than this, she loved to eat . . . '[109] Now the
British Blondes, a troupe of, for the time, shockingly sexy dancers, had
first hit New York in 1868, and had had their 'triumphant march'
through the United States in 1869 and again in 1872. If the voluptuous

88 Lillian Russell,
photograph, 1889

89 Marie Doro,
photograph, *c.* 1905

model which they allegedly established was so important, why was Lillian Russell, with her lithe figure and 'airy, fairy' appearance, so successful in the late 1870s and early 1880s? Perhaps she grew heavier as she grew older because, in the normal regrettable course of events, people do tend to grow heavier, unless they exercise special care with regard to diet; evidently Lillian did not do this. That she became a byword for beauty through to 1890 is not to be doubted: 'For two decades she was the most photographed woman in America, and people went to her plays to see more than the productions.'[110] Nor can there be any doubting the testimony of the late 1880s: 'She was a voluptuous beauty, and there was plenty of her to see. We liked that. Our tastes were not thin or ethereal.'[111] Yet the photograph dating from 1889 shows, not so much the 'avoirdupois' identified by Banner in commenting on this portrait,[112] as a beautiful fresh face and elegant figure. Of Banner's conclusion that 'she incarnated the voluptuous woman and brought elegance to the ideal',[113] the latter part seems to me more to the point than the former. Russell had established her popularity before filling out to voluptuous contours; once established, her enormous celebrity was

88

not affected by the scarcely abnormal or contrived fact that she subsequently put on weight. In any one decade or generation different tastes and proclivities coexist; women of different ages will all be competing for the limelight, older ones with the advantage of popularity, triumphs, and status already achieved, younger ones with the advantage of youth, and perhaps novelty – a shape acceptable in the one may not be so in the other.

The most important development in the United States, with respect to the growth of a 'modern' evaluation of beauty, and enhanced life chances for the beautiful, was the invention of the *commercial* beauty contest. The 'commercial' must be stressed, because forms of beauty contest go far back into the past, with the crowning of a queen at May Day or other local festivals, and are part of the traditional vision of women as inherently the beautiful sex. The 'modern', American element is the attempt to capitalize commercially on the appeal of beauty. The great pioneer entertainments entrepreneur Phineas T. Barnum had attempted to organize a live beauty competition in the 1850s, but had fallen foul of respectable opposition to the notion of women displaying themselves. Such objections were eventually circumvented with the help of the technology (the half-tone plate) which from the late 1880s permitted the reproduction of photographs in newspapers and periodicals. The first properly organized nationwide beauty competition (conducted on the basis of photographs) was set up by another great entrepreneur of the circus, Adam Forepaugh, in 1888: 11,000 women submitted photographs for a prize of $10,000 and a starring role in one of Forepaugh's productions; the winner was an actress, Louise Montagne.[114] In working-class areas it was possible to ignore respectable convention and hold parades of beautiful women in what were known as dime museums. Lois Banner claims that such 'beauty contests were significant means of transmitting to immigrant men and women American standards of physical appearance'.[115] More probably, they were a significant means of turning the universal appeal of female beauty into quick dollars for the owners of the museums. Above all, beauty competitions, and the display of photographs in the press, made personal beauty a matter of consuming interest.

According to Banner, when in 1882 Lillie Langtry (then in her late twenties) first toured the United States as an actress, 'many Americans did not find her attractive'.[116] Lillie was athletic and English in appearance, rather than rounded and voluptuous. There were reservations too about her strongly marked mouth and nose, though received wisdom on the latter seems to have been, as one might expect, somewhat confused. Banner's argument is that eventually there was a swing in favour of Lillie's type of looks:

The change from the small to the long nose, for example, can be seen to occur abruptly in *Godey's Lady's Book* in 1887, although the newer feature is apparent earlier in *Harper's Bazaar*. In 1877 Robert Tomes, *Harper's Bazaar* editor, wrote that the Grecian nose was generally accepted as the most beautiful, but that some people still preferred the retroussé.[117]

Whether the arguments were those of high fashion, or more vulgarly jingoistic – a Chicago newspaper declared that Lillie 'could not compare with scores of American ladies in every city where she is on exhibition'[118] – the critical fact is the emergence of beauty as a subject for debate (and no one pretended that the debate was about beauty as truth or the reflection of interior goodness).

Whether American perceptions of Lillie really did change is not a central point. What is important is the strategy by which Lillie Langtry had, well before coming to the United States, established herself in England as a renowned beauty. With Langtry it was not a question of having had any kind of success on the stage; quite simply she set out from a very early age to exploit in a most single-minded way her personal appearance, which, as a plentiful choice of portraits and photographs demonstrate, was so devastating as to make any discussion of conventions of beauty practically irrelevant. She came from a well-connected family in Jersey, where her father was an Anglican rector. In order to reach the fringes of London society, her major target, she made a reasonably good marriage to an undistinguished member of the gentry class. In London artists were keen to paint her, and she saw clearly the advantage of encouraging them. *Jersey Lily* by Millais became one of the most famous ever renderings of female beauty; a lesser artist, Frank Miles, did sketches of her which were sold as originals and reproduced as postcards.[119] Lillie could not afford to dress other than plainly, but she made an impact at all the social occasions she attended, displaying boldness and independence of spirit (her husband was a man without grace or style) which attracted still further attention. Lillie sought no other career than to promote herself as a society beauty, and as such she came to the attention of the Prince of Wales. Their first assignation was arranged by an intermediary, much practised in such matters; it took place in 1877 when Lillie was twenty-three, the Prince of Wales thirty-six. Public recognition as a mistress of the Prince of Wales brought to a climax the career of Lillie Langtry as a professional beauty, whose likeness circulated in Britain, across the Atlantic, and even across the Channel.

Unlike the mistresses of Charles II she gained no direct material reward from her liaison with royalty. With or without the embraces of 'Bertie', she was an acknowledged beauty, that beauty underwritten by Sir John Everett Millais, James McNeill Whistler and Oscar Wilde; but the royal association was a final seal of approval which accelerated still further the circulation of reproductions and postcards. Lillie preferred the

90 *Jersey Lily*, John Everett Millais, 1878

handsome and dashing young Prince Louis of Battenberg, and became pregnant by him. As was no more than to be expected, she was discarded by the Prince of Wales. Needing to find a more active means of cashing in on her assets, she now took to the stage. Opinion is divided as to whether she actually had any real talent for acting. My guess is that she was far from incompetent; as a beauty and a celebrity she was able to do reasonably well in her new career. But the important extrapolation is the sequence of events: status as a beauty first, career as an actress subsequently.

The actual existence of an internationally known, publicly acknowledged beauty was something new. In the seventies and eighties Lillie

Langtry had only two rivals, Ellen Terry and Sarah Bernhardt. Compared with Lillie, Ellen Terry was a different kind of beauty and from a different social background.[120] Indeed, for a considerable time her career seemed to demonstrate the hazards, rather than the advantages, of beauty. That she ultimately became a celebrity owed most to her acting talent and to her determination to rebuild her own life and find a means of supporting her children; but, of course, it depended also on her beauty. Ellen Terry came from an acting family; her direct physical appeal is apparent in the famous painting of her, aged sixteen, by G. F. Watts. In that very year Ellen was married to the ageing artist. Watts's

91

91 *Ellen Terry*, George Frederick Watts, c. 1864

claim, rather like that of some of the Pre-Raphaelite painters at the same time, was that he wished to educate and elevate Ellen; he may possibly have been impotent. Anyway, life with him was grim and gloomy, and Ellen shortly fled to live in poverty with an architect, by whom she had two children. Although, before her marriage, she had shown outstanding talent on the stage, she had cheerfully put all theatrical ambitions behind her. Desperate to find a means of supporting herself and her children, she returned to the stage and was fortunate to the extent that the greatest male actor, and theatrical figure, of the later nineteenth century was still looking for an ideal leading lady.

John Henry Brodribb, nine years older than Ellen Terry, was born in 1838 into a poor Cornish family; however, he did inherit £100 from an uncle. He was not particularly good looking, was, as an adolescent, called 'spindle-shanks', and he had a stutter; nevertheless, he was determined to become an actor, and the £100 helped.[121] Under his stage name of Henry Irving he was already enjoying considerable success when Ellen Terry teamed up with him. His appearance did seem to improve slightly as he matured and Ellen herself recorded later, 'I doted on his looks.' As a highly popular actress Ellen, in common with other actresses, had her likeness featured on the postcards of the 1870s and onwards; but sheer looks alone ensured that she was rated in addition as a fashionable beauty.

Sarah Bernhardt (born Henriette Rosine Bernard) did not conform to the convention of the voluptuous woman. She was thin, with a profoundly appealing, unorthodox Jewish beauty, and the faintest suspicion of a too-long (though highly enticing) nose. Fortunately her looks at the time of her debut at the Comédie Française in 1862, when she was eighteen, have been recorded by the great pioneer photographer Félix Nadar. In career terms, and in exploitation of her sexuality, Bernhardt is nearer to Langtry than Terry, and nearest of all to the courtesans discussed earlier. Although both she and her mother (a Dutch Jew) were illegitimate, they lived in fairly comfortable circumstances, since her father settled money on her, and their circle included such luminaries as Alexandre Dumas *père*, the composer Rossini and the Duc de Morny. She got an early start at the Comédie Française, but had to leave after insulting the leading lady there. For a time she lived quite openly, and apparently happily, as a kept woman; she had a son, probably by the Prince de Ligne, though later she was reported as saying, with deliberately mischievous humour, that she never could remember whether the father was 'Victor Hugo, Gambetta, or General Boulanger'.[122]

92

She resumed her acting career at the Odéon in 1866. While there can be absolutely no gainsaying her supreme talent in voice, expression and sheer daring and originality, it is true that, uniquely in Paris, the Odéon, the left-bank theatre of the radical young, provided the right ambience for Bernhardt's particular abilities. A true actress, and not simply a star,

92 Sarah Bernhardt, photograph, Félix Nadar, 1862

she took on an enormous range of parts, including several that called for concealment, not projection, of her looks. By 1869 she was being lauded as a great, if not the greatest, actress of the day. The personal bravery, which was a marked characteristic to the very end of her long life, showed itself in her refusal to leave Paris during the events of 1870 (Franco-Prussian war, Prussian siege and the Commune). In 1872 she returned to the Comédie Française. But she was not a woman to be fitted into any compartment, however elevated, and in 1880 (at the age of thirty-six) she again broke with France's premier theatre and set out on a series of foreign tours which established the basis of her international reputation – as both actress and beauty. A grandmother in 1889, she now had the statuesque looks which are familiar from the photographs of her in various dramatic roles, taken by Nadar's less gifted son, Paul; yet the air of youthful appeal was remarkably well preserved. From 1893 she directed her own company at La Renaissance and in 1899 the Théâtre Sarah Bernhardt was established at Châtelet. Along the way she had contracted one not very successful marriage, and had had many lovers: as well as directing, and playing an incredible range of parts (including male ones), she channelled her formidable creative energies into painting and sculpture. All that, and beauty too! Given such talents, would she not have made her mark in the world even without great beauty? Almost certainly, yes (in this book of few heroines, and fewer heroes, Sarah Bernhardt, along with Ninon de Lenclos, stands out as one of the great women of the past): yes, with the proviso that she were at least as presentable as Mata Hari; a really plain woman could not have succeeded on the stage, though perhaps (recalling George Eliot) a career as an artist and writer might have been possible. But for the life of Sarah Bernhardt as it actually unfolded, her beauty was crucial at five stages. Without it she would not have got started at all in 1862. It enabled her to live comfortably as an *entretenue* (or, in effect, courtesan) when ejected from the Comédie Française, and while subsequently establishing herself at the Odéon. It was vital in getting her a fresh start at that theatre. Along with her dramatic talents it was instrumental in winning the acclaim and devotion which swept her back to the Comédie Française and on to international fame. And, finally, her acknowledged position as a great international beauty in the last decades of the century (as well as her supreme dramatic artistry) depended on the remarkable, unfading quality of her striking looks.

In 1896 the Director of *L'Illustration* put on a form of beauty competition. Like those already being organized in the United States, it depended on photographs of the competitors, but unlike them it was not open to the general public, being confined to actresses. Sarah Bernhardt, her great theatrical rival Réjane, and even Otero, were only runners up. The winner was the youthful Cléo de Mérode, still in her teens.[123] In the end, there is no denying the power of youthful beauty. However, the major point here is that the French competition marked a further stage in the march of female beauty out of the boudoir, and the world of the personal and purely sexual exchange, into the wide public world where it is gaped at, and *paid for*, not by princes and bankers, but by the masses. And for this particular epoch I shall not overstate the value of youthfulness. Women who had established themselves many years before (Bernhardt, Russell, Terry) maintained their appeal, their following – and the *value* of their personal appearance. In 1897, for example, a photograph of Ellen Terry in one of her last great roles, as the laundress Madame Sans-Gêne in Sardou's play of that title, was used in an advertisement for 'Nixey's

93 Blue'. A famous beautiful face, in a relevant context, was a great advertising *coup*; but advertisers were now appreciating the value of associating even an unknown face with their products – provided, of course, it was a beautiful face.

Thus the way in which the beauty of actual people (famous or unknown) was publicized and, in diverse ways, turned in for a cash price

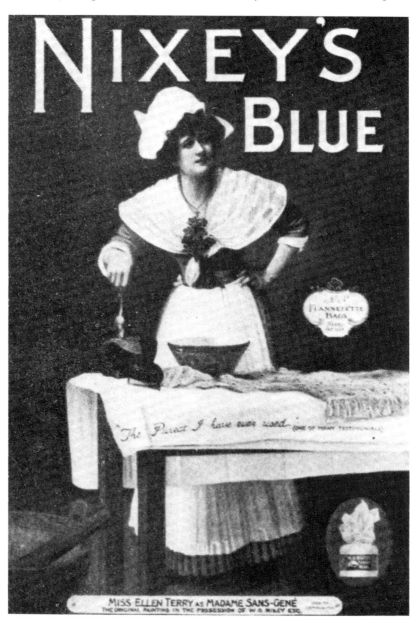

93 (left) Advertisement for 'Nixey's Blue' using photograph of Ellen Terry as Madame Sans-Gêne in Sardou's play of that title, 1897

94 (right) *La Rose de Grenade*, poster for French film, featuring Lina Cavalieri, 1919

was going to have its effect, as the twentieth century advanced, on the general evaluation of beauty. Human beings would continue to want to believe in beauty as connoting moral excellence; but the evidence was multiplying that it possessed an entirely autonomous value. That evidence, certainly, related almost exclusively to women; but already in 1900 the first movie cameras were rolling – commercial fiction film would bring the evaluation of male beauty also into the centre of contention. The large, but logical, stride from *belle époque* to the era of film was personified by the fascinating Cavalieri (whose life would make an excellent subject for serious research). At the age of thirty-nine she entered the world of American movies, playing opposite her husband Lucien Muratore in *Manon Lescaut* (1914). She returned to make films in France and Italy; but *La Rose de Grenade* (1919) was no great success and really marked the end of this brief career.[124] Cavalieri had done well in her day, but for this lovely courtesan the cinematograph had arrived just too late.

94

# 7 The Twentieth Century to 1960

## 1 *Movies, War and the Fashion Revolution 1905–25*

Changes in fashion are relevant to this study only when related to the changing significance of beauty. The relationship is not a simple one. As I have already suggested, fashion has a logic of its own, operating in a process of innovation, leading to exaggeration, leading to reaction. However, the series of changes which took place in women's dress between the beginning of the twentieth century and the 1920s placed a higher premium than ever before upon natural endowment of form and feature. Heavy use of cosmetics, while, in one sense, concealing the natural attributes of the face, at the same time has the effect of drawing attention to the face as seldom before. Although it has its own logic and its own *raison d'être*, fashion is never totally independent of the social and political context. For the period we are now concerned with, the contextual factors are complex and of many types.

'Emancipation' is a sweeping, and in many ways suspect, term; but certainly over a generation or so there were striking developments in the role, status and activities of women, from participation in such outdoor pursuits as cycling, tennis and hiking, through political activism, and the winning of the vote (in Britain and the United States), to some expansion in job opportunities. Estimates differ as to the direct influence of the First World War on these and other aspects of the general question of the changing position of women. For myself, I believe that the unprecedented demand for women's labour in time of war was critical in concentrating change into a short period of time; and that the new activities undertaken by women, their frequent and unaccustomed appearance in public places, and the shortage of material brought about by war, all did have a direct effect on dress and self-presentation. At the same time I recognize that in the world of high fashion the first portentous innovations were those of the radical Parisian dress designer Paul Poiret in the first decade of the new century. Clearly, within the world of fashion, there was a deliberate attempt to echo, a century later, the less trammelled, more 'natural' styles of the First Empire. Yet, the unique influence of war is neatly encapsulated in the twofold circumstance that it was the compulsory enlistment of Poiret in the French army (where he secured invaluable economies in the making of military uniforms) which made it possible for 'Coco' Chanel to establish her ascendancy, while at the same time her natural instinct for simple 'peasant' clothing was reinforced by the need, in a time of shortages, to make use of the hitherto despised material jersey knit.[1]

I have described fully elsewhere the varied processes of change which come into play when society is at war.[2] Of particular relevance here is what I have termed the psychological dimension of the interrelationship between war and society, involving a profound feeling that such a horrific war *ought* to be accompanied by substantial change, in the role of women as in many other spheres, a powerful reaction against the generation which had previously set the standards and, it could be argued, had been responsible for the catastrophe of war, and a belief that the future, if there was any future, lay in the hands of youth. The new styles of the twenties were better suited to youth than to age; most critically for our study, they exposed more of the body and the face than ever before.

The war was an enormous upheaval, disrupting traditional patterns of life, making possible new ways of doing things, and new ways of looking at the world. In face of the carnage and horror of war many found it impossible to maintain their Christian beliefs. The rise of secularism is, of course, a long-term phenomenon. But it is certainly true for the period we are now about to study that Christianity was no longer the all-pervasive force within which attitudes to beauty were determined: true, at any rate, for large numbers in urbanized, highly integrated Britain, and in the urban areas of the United States and France, if not for the Middle West and Southern United States, where certain Protestant denominations still held sway, and rural France, where the Catholic church remained the major social and ideological institution. Even so, during the war, from remote rural areas throughout the Western world, from the mountains of Wales and Scotland, as well as the provinces of France and backwoods states of the USA, men went out to fight, and to encounter the values and experiences of urban civilization. Everywhere more people than ever before had more chance glimpses of the truly beautiful and were in a better position to perceive and compare the varieties of beauty possessed by that fateful minority, whose acknowledged value, as we saw at the end of the previous chapter, was already sharply rising.

The new industry of film making was, by the time it had become fully organized and capitalized in the 1920s, the greatest single source for the employment of beautiful people so far created. As it happened, the war period formed, in Europe, the great divide between film as a thoroughly working-class entertainment, usually presented in small halls, often in association with music hall items, an entertainment whose primary appeal was its 'magical' quality, and film as a cultural form, with its own massive, custom-built 'picture palaces', appealing to middle- as well as working-class audiences. This condition had already arrived in the USA by 1914; hence American cinema's ability to attract such 'stars' as Lina Cavalieri. The war was irrelevant to the circumstance that it was actually during it that the epoch-making *Birth of a Nation* by D. W. Griffith was released, together with some of the best early Chaplin films. Chaplin, we know, appealed greatly to soldiers slogging it out against the squalor and appalling odds of the Western Front, while patriotic middle-class audiences at home flocked to propaganda documentaries, a key event being the showing in 1916 of *The Battle of the Somme* at the Empire, Leicester Square.[3] The first decade which followed the war was the first true movie age, and with the movies came a whole new literature, preserving images of the stars in a form which could be pored over and pinned to bedroom walls. A French firm published guides to both female and male stars: commercial cinema had made personal beauty more of a public matter than ever before, and, the latter guide claimed (with fair accuracy, I believe), 'overturned all the old conventions about the unimportance of male appearance, imposing a general and absolute rule that heroes must be beautiful'.[4]

## 2 *From Surely a Duty to Nearly a Joy*

The insistence that it is a woman's *duty* to make herself as beautiful as possible, so firmly enunciated in the Victorian era, certainly does not disappear from the beauty manuals, but is softened with suggestions that, in making up and dressing up, a woman will be giving expression to her own personality, giving pleasure to herself, and indeed will perhaps be indulging in activity that she really rather enjoys. There is a greater emphasis than ever before on health and naturalness, and, for the first time, though in a very discreet way, a few hints point to the connections between looking good and arousing sexual desire. A standard French beauty guide, first published in the 1920s, declared that, whatever her condition in life, a woman 'must never neglect the cultivation of her beauty'. But it continued:

It is not only to be happy in love that you must, dear readers, offer to the sight of your fellow creatures an agreeable appearance, it is also for you yourself, for your moral health, so that you do not become more and more sad behind your despondent face.[5]

Though the preface to this work contains a token inclusion of male readers as well as female ones, it is clear that the book is intended entirely for the latter. Indeed, despite the new interest in male looks brought about largely by films, there is no suggestion anywhere that men should ever dream of going beyond shaving, having regular haircuts, and taking some care over their dress, to the actual use of cosmetics. In an auto-biography primarily concerned with the achievement of business and social success, Mrs Hortense Odlum, the prospering owner of a women's fashion shop in New York, set out what were widely seen to be the essential differences between men and women in this respect. A woman is

used to experiencing change in fashion. She knows that each season will shorten or lower skirts and waistlines, that certain colors will be in prominence, that a particular kind of influence is at work on the kind of clothes she'll wear a few months hence. She's ready for the change when it comes. She's already thought of the new styles in connection with herself and she's prepared to adapt them to her own needs and requirements.

Her husband on the other hand is never subjected to violent change in the fashion of his clothes. His trousers become fuller over a long period of years; he discards his stiff dinner shirt for a soft one only after soft dinner shirts are no longer news. The fundamentals of his wardrobe remain but little changed. In fact he clings with dogged determination to certain convictions that seem as silly to women as our hats do to men! . . .

. . . While it is true that women demand comfort today in their clothes – we've come to look upon corsets that bind our bodies and shoes that cramp our feet as expressions of decadence – there is an additional requirement in clothes of women. We use them as a means of expressing our personalities and as a way of enhancing our attractiveness. Masculine attractiveness stems much less from physical beauty than feminine. A fine and honest mind, a kind and sensitive heart and spirit are the first essentials to true beauty for either man or woman, but physical beauty in women is much more emphasized. When we catalogue a man's good points we are apt to comment on his physical attributes last of all. But the first thing we usually say about a woman is that either she is or she is not attractive looking. The important requirements for a man's physical attractive-ness is that he be neat and well groomed, but for a woman in addition to those, we expect her to be decoratively dressed.

Makeup, over which the War Between the Sexes is constantly waged, is part of this decorative element. It is unnatural, men rage, and therefore ugly. Women paint their finger nails garnet, their lips flaming red and their eyelids blue, green or brown, not in an attempt to simulate nature, not even to improve upon nature, but to add a quality which otherwise is lacking. It's a kind of extension to their physical bodies of the gaiety and picturesqueness of their clothes.

Masculine beauty and charm have today come to mean a pleasant naturalness (though a shaved face, I suppose, is not completely natural). There was a time when men, too, painted and powdered and their physical appearance was judged by a different standard from the one we use today. Feminine beauty cannot be judged by the standard which men apply to themselves. If men would realize that what would appear as unnatural and artificial applied to them is not necessarily so for women, I think there would be less criticism. Makeup to women does not mean artificiality as it does to men. A frivolous hat does not mean a frivolous heart, nor fragile high heeled slippers an addled mind! Because men are more conservative by nature than women they must try to remember that what may look strange and even shockingly daring to them creates no excitment or comment among women . . .[6]

No sign of the influence of male movie stars in this upper-class document, certainly. But in its very defensiveness there is rich unwitting testimony to the heightened preoccupation with female self-presentation in the twenties, as compared with the pre-war years.

Such preoccupation called for more outside assistance than ever before. As a later American War Department manual on the setting up of a 'beauty' business pointed out, 'women couldn't cut their own hair and they soon discovered that, once cut, it required special care to look well'. At first, as bobbed hair gained in popularity, many women went into men's barber shops for cutting and trimming. But 'they soon wanted additional services not offered by barbers. They turned to available beauty shops and the increasing demand for service brought new shops.' [7] The most important service offered by the beautician at this time was permanent waving. The first machine had appeared in 1910, but permanent waving only became widely practicable and popular in the 1920s. In that decade American women spent $250,000,000 for permanent waving alone. The manual summed up the situation at the end of the inter-war period:

Certainly a tremendous aid to the growth of cosmetology has been the attention given to hair and skin care, make-up, and good grooming in general by magazines, newspapers, and the radio. Advertisers of the many beautifying and cleansing products also have played a big part in sending more and more women to beauty shops. And possibly the greatest influence of all has been the motion picture, setting fashions in hair arrangement and make-up.[8]

A French publication, *The Beauty Industry*, published in 1930, celebrated the achievements made by institutes of beauty since the first one had been founded in 1895. The book pointed out that the success of feminism had increased, rather than destroyed, demand: women competing for jobs with men had to look their best.[9] The great expansion, in the late nineteenth century, of the advertising of beauty lotions and beauty aids continued, almost exponentially, in the twentieth. More critically, an increasing number of advertisements aimed at men began to appear, advertisements for hair creams, after-shave lotions and treatments for pimples, baldness and greying hair, suggesting that Mrs Odlum's view that men were still required only to be neat and well groomed was not universally valid.[10] With such evidence it is difficult to determine how far there was genuine demand – whether stimulated by a desire to emulate male movie stars, an ambition to cut a dash at the local palais de danse, a belief that somewhere there was a world of open sexuality open to the beautiful and youthful looking, or fear of unemployment – and how far skilled entrepreneurs aware of the power of carefully conceived advertising themselves created such demand as there was. Most striking is the fact that a new form of the nose machine which became available in the twenties was quite manifestly directed at least as much at men as at women. 'M. Trilety's Newest Nose Shaper' was a vicious-looking metal object, held over the nose by straps buckled round the head, and fitted with an array of screws which could be tightened to apply pressure to the offending width, length, bump or crookedness. A ghastly little gadget of this sort existed, not to create a particular fashionable image, as perhaps hair cream did, but to mitigate ugliness – 'the Successful Correction of Ill-Shaped Noses', in the words of 'M. Trilety's' advertisement.[11]

Nineteenth-century manuals, implicitly or explicitly, had advocated a principle (for women) of growing old gracefully; their usual position was that cosmetics were needed only by those over thirty. Unwittingly perhaps, rather than deliberately, the manuals (and advertisements) of the twenties bring out the importance of being, or of appearing to be, young. This comes out slightly obliquely in a French work which ostensibly aims to demonstrate *How to be Beautiful at Every Age*. The witting argument is that love is more important to a woman than admiration and that it is better to be pretty than beautiful:

Without being truly beautiful, a woman will please enormously if along with a pleasant face she has a good heart, good humour, a fine spirit, animated expression, gracious gestures, elegant walk and, in addition to all that, a smile. It is the *pretty woman*, the one of whom one says that she has the *beauty of the devil*, who attracts us most, for from her whole being there escapes a bewitching charm, undeniable, which touches our spirit, dominates us, while the *beautiful woman*, too majestic, only leaves in our spirit the charming memory of a very beautiful object, rare and curious which we have viewed with pleasure without dreaming of possessing it. Relations are easier with the pretty woman because she *attracts*, while the beautiful woman *imposes*, which is very different. But, alas! a woman does not for ever remain at the stage of puberty; quickly she sees disappear the rose from her cheeks, the sparkle from her eyes, for that beauty – even the most pure – has only a limited time, being scarcely more than an illusion.

With the standard optimism, the text, having come very close to identifying prettiness (attractive) with youth, while perhaps dismissing more enduring beauty as 'imposing', goes on to remark that, happily, there are methods, which it is the purpose of the book to describe, for slowing down its disappearance.[12] *How to Please and to Remain Young* (also French) remarks that women of forty, considered out of things a quarter of a century previously, now dress like youth. *Beauty for Every Woman* (British) is straightforward about the mood of the time: 'The

beauty which comes from discomfort is not what we seek today. No
modern girl would dream of shutting up her body in corsets so tight that
she might faint at any time, whereas girls of fifty years ago would have
been horrified at the thought of using powder, rouge, and lipstick.' [13]
*Beauty for All* (French) is clear also that make-up is now perfectly
acceptable; the only thing wrong is applying it badly. [14] As in previous
eras, beauty guides have to be optimistic in one way or another. In
general the tone in the inter-war years is to admit that perfect natural
beauty is a very rare gift. While the heavy use of cosmetics is acceptable,
the real answer is seen to lie in health and vitality.

Today we can all have our share of beauty even if, at our own christening, our
fairy godmothers forgot to bring us perfect features. We cannot change our
features but each of us can have the attraction of a clear skin, bright eyes, and
pretty hair. Our figures can be as we wish them to be. There is no need to have
round shoulders, over-fat legs and hips, or an ugly walk. Simple exercises will
give you a graceful carriage, and keep your figure trim and neat. [15]

Everywhere there is emphasis on exercise and physical culture. Much
more explicit attention is now paid to breasts, rump and thighs: 'a breast
is beautiful if it is firm and of medium size'; 'a fine leg gives elegance and
sets desire on fire'. In general, we are told, 'it is beauty which gives so
much spice to love, for a man never forgets the delicious minutes he has
passed in the arms of a beautiful woman swooning and palpitating'. [16]
What the books are saying is matched by what the younger women are
wearing:

The sexual provocation of shortened skirts was further increased by wearing
open lace work stockings and rolled hose that often bared flesh as well as
contour. Silk stockings had become a necessity for the new-fashioned women
and an object of gift-giving and male attention, and sheerer models were
overwhelmingly favoured by the young whatever the increased expense. Surely
mere utility would not have dictated silk rather than lisle nor made the sheerer
models more desirable. An enormous variety of colors, patterns, and degrees of
opacity were displayed for the young woman's market – all helped to draw
attention to the leg. [17]

It would be quite wrong to suggest that the beauty manuals consistently
present what I have called a 'modern' view of beauty. Much of the old
contradiction and confusion remained, as seen in this French account,
which while trying to assert the value of spiritual and moral beauty as
against purely physical beauty, is in fact as lucid as Federigo Fregoso in
admitting the autonomous power of beauty:

Unfortunately, beauty leads to vanity. A girl who is incessantly told that she is
beautiful, becomes an absolute demon whose good and bad humours have to be
endured and whose every caprice must be satisfied. Incessantly petted, adulated,

caressed, she believes that everything is permissible for her. The older she gets, the more she becomes capricious, authoritarian, abusing the power given to her by her beauty. The power of beauty is so great that all discussion is futile: all one can do is bow before that powerful and invincible sovereign.[18]

As always we are in the realm of shifting emphases, of eddies and counterflows, not of one conclusive sea change; but the emphasis on rumps and legs and breasts clearly signals a more open recognition of the sexual associations of beauty. There were many who denounced the blatant sensuality of twenties fashions.[19] More to the point, there were still millions who could not aspire to the physical image. Poverty, more than bourgeois respectability or dynastic ambition, remained an obstacle to the full emergence of a modern appraisal of beauty. Thus a series of articles on 'beauty' published in *Le Petit Parisien* produced this angry and rather bitter response from 'a woman of the people':

For a woman to be beautiful, sir, be certain that it is necessary above all that she be good and simple; among the people, one is almost always both. Is it necessary to have a complexion of porcelain to be beautiful? What a strange beauty is that which dares not laugh, nor cry, for fear of cracking its cheeks! And then, why run so hard after the impossible simply to arrive with the same nothingness? If women of forty have wrinkles, it is usually grief which has brought them about and there is nothing more respectable than grief. We, those who set out every day for the office or the workshop, we don't have the time (or the money) to go to the institute of beauty; but the spouse, and the children who see us return in the evening, most certainly find in us the greatest beauty. Tell me, sir, what little child would swop his mother for a lady with well tended cheeks, but without a smile, without caresses (that would destroy her make-up!)

To disperse the cares which preoccupy the flighty, they would only need other cares, those of the household, those of bringing up children; it would be enough for them to find ways of making their husband happy, of raising in a healthy and decent fashion the children given to them by the Good God. Sure, that gives one wrinkles, as crying in front of a cradle suddenly empty dulls the sparkle of the eyes; these wrinkles are the wrinkles of faithful grandmothers, who, when they arrive in front of the Judge, will not notice that they are no longer beautiful.[20]

A universal cry, one might say, and one which was to be repeated many times in different forms; yet in its very intensity it could be seen to be arguing for a moral view of beauty which was falling out of favour.

Such sentiments belonged to passing public mores and can be set against some striking portents of the coming mores. The most brash and unsubtle of these was the Miss America competition, launched in Atlantic City in 1921, and based on the simple premise of the autonomous value of beauty – specifically that beautiful girls parading in bathing costumes would pull in the tourists. Despite the best efforts of the organizers to stress the wholesomeness of the contest and to play

down its sexuality, the unambiguous significance of the latter was strong
enough for the promoters to be pressured in 1928 into abandoning the
contest – not because it was held to be degrading for women but because
it was immodest. The relative potency of the different forces can,
however, be gauged from the way in which uninterrupted presentation
of the contest was resumed in 1935. What ideal of beauty did the contest
attempt to ratify? No one ideal, just beauty. Lois Banner finds it 'curious'
that the second winner in 1922 'differed considerably in face and figure'
from the first winner, Margaret Gorman.[21] We need not feel that there
was anything curious about it at all, though we should remind ourselves
that at this level any decision as to one contestant being more beautiful
than another was quite unreal; the firm line, as I have already said, is
between those who, without manifest absurdity, can enter a beauty
contest and those who cannot.

It is frequently pointed out that after the extremes of the 'flapper' style
in the 1920s, fashions changed greatly, ushering in, it is sometimes said, a
new kind of sexuality. Actually, there is only one kind of sexuality:
sexuality (the argument is with respect to majority sexuality; there are of
course various minority forms, but these are not at issue here). Whether
thighs and knees were concealed or not, whether breasts were flattened
or uplifted, whether hair was worn short or long, a basic concept of
physical beauty, always known, but always subject to ambivalences and
confusions, had been exposed in the 1920s as never before; there would
be no cover-up. Robert Roberts, in his account of young manhood in
working-class Salford, firmly knocks on the head any nonsense about
twenties fashions being 'sexless' or 'androgynous':

What undoubtedly attracted young men of the period was legs! Far from looking
male, girls, with that daring length of limbs on show, appeared not less but more
delightfully feminine than ever. Young men in dance halls, talked 'legs' – ankles,
calves, shapes.[22]

What had been shocking for many, became almost commonplace. In
1939, the popular London publishers Odham's Press published a ten-part
series, *Success and Happiness through Charm*. The tone is very much that
of the beauty guides of the 1920s, the usual wild optimism, of course,
but otherwise calm and sensible. Sex within marriage is highly rated,
though any suggestion of extra-marital sex is totally repudiated.[23] The
pamphlets are illustrated throughout with clever drawings and well-
taken photographs. One photographic close-up, head and shoulders, of a
young man and a young woman, with lips set in seductive Hollywood
fashion, has the caption: 'a lovely mouth can be so tempting and
expressive'.[24] The very first pamphlet has a nude photo of the young
woman taken from the back, and two photos showing her face and bust.
The second pamphlet has another bosom shot, and a nude just concealed
by the water in her bath. But most striking of all, the frontispiece to this

pamphlet consists of what is effectively a full-frontal nude – whose pubic hair has either been shaved or touched out in the photograph.[25] Such a photograph was relatively rare even in the men's magazines of the time. Its appearance in a serious work clearly aimed at women is an indication of a gathering recognition that beauty is to be found in the natural unadorned body, rather than in the fantasies of fashion.

## 3 *Beauty in Public Life*

We are not in an age when it is thought proper to give much serious attention to the personal appearance of male politicians. We are still a long way from mass exposure before the democratic electorate, still further from exposure within the intimacy of the home; in fact, for the next thirty years sound radio was probably as potent a medium in politics as film, putting a premium on qualities of voice rather than physical appearance. None the less, an important hint of what a visual medium of mass communication might achieve does appear in the very last year of the war, when Screen Advertising Inc. ('your product shown in miniature photoplays to six million people') began writing to Congressmen with the following proposition:

At a trifling cost to you, we will take a few hundred feet of motion pictures, showing you in your Committee Room, at your desk or anywhere else that you may select and, with appropriate titles, drive home to the voters the excellent work which you are accomplishing. From the original negative can be made a sufficient number of positive prints to serve the motion picture theatres in your District. If you wish us to, we will also arrange for the exhibition of these films. Why not count on every possible vote in your District?[26]

The shape of things to come indeed! Two caveats, however: first, not a great deal came of this particular scheme; second, displaying a politician at work, making speeches, etc., does not automatically and immediately mean an emphasis on his physical appearance – after all politicans had for generations happily shown off their (often) ugly mugs on election literature. Nevertheless, in the United States of the inter-war years *some* attention to the beauty or otherwise of politicians is discernible.

Perhaps there is as much traditionalism as modernism in the way the distinguished journalist Mark Sullivan described the first session of Congress which met to hear President Coolidge's address in December 1923, traditionalism in the song of praise for the ladies, modernism in the belief that the dowdiness of the politicians was even worth commenting on:

The House galleries filled up first and remained throughout the one part of the picture that was most pleasing to the eye during the joint session of Congress which heard the President's message to-day. The galleries were mainly filled by women who in their bearing, their choice of colors for their dresses and the alert intelligence of their countenances seemed rather the superiors and certainly more distinguished looking than the men of the two chambers who filled the floor.

As you looked at the Representatives and Senators you were convinced that for such achievement as comes out of them we must rely on the capacities inherent in average men. In clothes and in countenance they were conspicuous, so to speak, in their averageness. There was hardly an outstanding head or face among them. As to clothes, the ordinary sack suit was universal. There were not five examples of the 'frock coat' that was almost the indispensable uniform of the Senate of twenty years ago. To the eye it was like a meeting of the Farmers' Co-operative Association of Des Moines, Iowa, or a session of the male members of any small-town church.[27]

Woodrow Wilson, United States President at the end of the war, was a distinguished enough – if unexciting – looking man. The Republicans had no very brilliant figure to put up against him, nor did they have any very positive policies on which to fight the 1920 election. It is in such circumstances, I have already suggested, that the factor of personal physical appeal may come into play. At any rate, Professor Edward Pessen has observed that the undoubtedly good-looking Warren Harding won the Republican Presidential nomination in some degree because of his looks, at a time when calm reassurance was required rather than vigorous policy making,[28] going on to take the Presidency in the 1920 election. Professor W. E. Leuchtenberg has developed the point in declaring that Harding 'had no qualification for being President except that he looked like one'.[29] Harding died in office – because, according to one insider, he felt that as President of a Prohibitionist nation, he ought perhaps to give up alcohol himself; within a fortnight of this grave decision he was dead.[30] Harding's Vice-President, Calvin Coolidge, scarcely looked like a President; indeed the phrase 'funny looking' might have been coined for him, yet Sullivan made quite an issue of the 'ingratiating appeal' of Coolidge's 'boyish features', 'blue eyes' and 'very blond head'. His appearance, Sullivan maintained, 'seems to say: "I am only a young fellow here, and I am new on this job, and I hope you will give me a kindly hand."'[31] Having succeeded, as Vice-President, to the Presidency, Coolidge retained it in his successful campaign of 1924 on the slogan 'Keeping Cool With Coolidge'. Coolidge did not stand for re-election in 1928, the Republican mantle being inherited by the highly energetic and, in many respects, public-spirited Herbert Hoover, who had behind him a distinguished record as organizer of American relief operations at the end of the First World War: there was no call for distinction of appearance, and Hoover did not provide it.

There is no real evidence in all this of looks being a matter of any great interest to the electorate, or even of looks being thought by political commentators to be a matter of significance. The sharpest illumination

95

95 Warren Harding,
photograph, 1923

of the differences in this respect between the era of Franklin D. Roosevelt
and that of John F. Kennedy, Mayor John Lindsay and Governor Ronald
Reagan is provided by Roosevelt's first campaign for the Presidency, that
of 1932 against the incumbent Herbert Hoover. One undisputed quality
possessed by Roosevelt was that of extreme good looks; one undisputed        96
feature of this campaign was that Roosevelt was 'on display' (in the
words of the *Kansas City Journal Post*)[32] as perhaps no candidate had ever
previously been – he undertook a daunting cross-nation campaign
addressing vast open-air meetings. Roosevelt, member of an upper-class
New York family, and relative of the former President Theodore
Roosevelt, was undoubtedly one of those whose birth was deeply blessed
by that good fairy of whom the beauty guides often liked to speak.
Family connections and good looks had given him an early and successful start in politics: he was Assistant Secretary of the Navy during the
First World War, and Democratic Vice-Presidential candidate in 1920.
Then, at the age of thirty-nine, he was struck down by polio. Ambition
and courage united in a fight-back which brought him the governership
of New York. There was much opposition to him within the Democratic
Party, and his eventual nomination as Presidential candidate was no soft,
or compromise, choice.

But the choice made, the question remained: was the Democratic candidate physically fit for office? – was he not still a hopeless cripple? One reason for the exhausting whistle-stop tour, 'tacit rather than expressed', as the *New York Times* put it, was 'to demonstrate to the people' that Roosevelt was indeed 'a man of fine physical stamina and rude health'.[33] Comments there were on this issue in plenty; but very, very little directly on Roosevelt's personal appearance, a matter still obviously considered to be irrelevant or ruled out by good taste. Roosevelt did, in fact, dress in a manner calculated to draw attention to his looks, and his campaign photos showed him without his spectacles, eyes brightly shining, features highly lit to give a clean-cut appearance, the thickening jaw subtly lightened. Journalists used a surrogate language in referring to his looks (rather as good taste sometimes decreed that a man congratulate a woman on her hat rather than on her actual physical looks). He is 'dapper in a dark suit and dark overcoat'; he gives 'his white dotted blue necktie a final tug'; 'his features' widen 'into a warm smile which is positively infectious'. Photographs show 'Roosevelt in Three Characteristic Poses'. A woman journalist recalls that when she first saw him in 1920 'he was a handsome and radiant figure', but in respect of the 48-year-old Roosevelt of 1932 contents herself with

96 Franklin Roosevelt greeting governor Cox, photograph, November 1920

referring to 'a physical disaster so valorously surmounted and lightly borne that it has become almost an asset'. Otherwise, she adds, 'his luck has held, the luck of being a well-born and comfortably circumstanced American, happily following a chosen career'.[34] In an interesting twist, in fact highly typical of attitudes which last till the sixties, the Democrats insist that it is the Republican enemies who 'love to emphasize his good looks and "personal charm", subtly suggesting that nothing lies behind it'.[35] This was not wholly accurate: what the Republicans paraded was Roosevelt's image as a slightly effete aristocrat, out of touch with the ordinary American.

Undoubtedly Roosevelt's striking appearance did generate excitement at the meetings he addressed, but, of course, beautiful clean-cut features cannot mean much to vast audiences of thirty to fifty thousand. A writer in *World Telegram* pinned down how the state of the technology determined which personal quality was really Roosevelt's winner:

Governor Franklin D. Roosevelt may not win the election, but he has already won a championship. He is the best radio broadcaster among all recent Presidential candidates. Nor is this an unimportant title. Within eight years political parties may hold auditions rather than conventions [that didn't happen but they would, *eventually*, hold televised conventions] . . . The voice of the democratic nominee falls with such a pleasant cadence on the ear that on certain occasions the soothing sound of the man dims any sharp criticism of the sense.[36]

In a vast stadium the voice was again the major asset, even if 'there were whispers of admiration from those near the speakers' stand' (' "He looks like an athlete," remarked an eager woman'):[37]

The stadium had been wired for loud speakers and the Governor's deep resonant voice floated through every nook and corner of the big green field.[38]

Roosevelt did win the election, and he won it because, at a time when the country was devastated by economic depression, he offered the Americans hope. Through his formidable political talents and powerful personality he secured three further terms of office, up to his death in 1945. But he certainly contributed to an image: without doubt he acted like a President, but he also 'looked like one'. That is not to say that any fashion was set. Roosevelt was succeeded by the incumbent Vice-President Harry Truman, whose appearance recalls Mark Sullivan's scornful description of the 1923 Congress.

There is little evidence of looks playing any part in political choices in early twentieth-century Britain or France. Of characteristics apart from political talent, social background was by far the most important, to the extent, indeed, that it really outweighed talent, except in so far as 'talent' was in any case equated with having the correct manners, assumptions and prejudices. In the Labour Party, struggling to eclipse the Liberals in the 1920s, one way of securing a parliamentary nomination, and thus the possibility of a launch into a political career, was to have sufficient private funding to spare impecunious constituency parties the burden of meeting electoral expenses. It is true that Labour's leader till 1931, Ramsay MacDonald, was strikingly handsome[39] and remained so throughout his later years. Contrary to what has often been written of him, he did distinguish himself from his colleagues by qualities of industry, intellect and political sensitivity. He had emerged as leader before the First World War, and really there was no viable alternative when he was re-elected leader in 1922.[40] The image he presented was a complex one, yet it is clear that in giving him 'charm and personal magnetism', good looks did play a part in the favourable impact he made.[41]

97

Behind success in the higher echelons of the French Civil Service lay the interlinked factors of wealth, social status and education. In the United States the permanent government service was not nearly as highly rated as in Europe and was expected to be, and largely was, staffed by the relatively mediocre in talent, and often also in deportment and appearance.[42] In Britain, while there was recruitment from the middle class as well as from the upper class, the qualities sought, and certainly admired, were those of poise, breeding, manners and good appearance (which is not necessarily the same thing as striking beauty). The head of the British Civil Service throughout the inter-war

97 Ramsay MacDonald,
photograph, *c.* 1910

years, Sir Warren Fisher, was noted for his handsome good looks. That supreme upper-class standard setter of the inter-war years, Sir Francis Newbolt, advised in his *Handbook* for appointments to the colonial service: the candidate's 'physical appearance will, of course, have been noted at once, the cut of his face and the extent, if any, to which he has the indefinable quality of "presence". Colouring, build, movement, poise will have come under review, and even such superficialities as style of dress and hair, health of skin and fingers.'[43] For the upper Civil Service as a whole, as the 1931 Royal Commission on the Civil Service freely admitted, indeed boasted, great weight was placed on the 'interview test', it being denied, utterly unconvincingly, that this interview 'offered scope for the display of class prejudice';[44] it did obviously offer scope for the assessment of personal demeanour, if not simply good looks. Within the British upper class and governing circles (practically coterminous at this time, as I have argued elsewhere), imbued with the ideals and inclinations of ancient Athens, there was already a disposition towards giving a high evaluation to male good looks. This can be seen very clearly in the ascendancy which Rupert Brooke established over his immediate associates at Cambridge just before the First World War, or in a rather similar ascendancy established a little earlier by the novelist and barrister John Galsworthy, who was:

Born among the wealthy classes, supplied from boyhood with every comfort and advantage, at a Public School and Oxford, intimately acquainted with horses and dogs, an experienced traveller for sport and pleasure, a welcome guest in Society, *handsome*, strong, a good athlete, married to a lady of remarkable *beauty*, charm and intelligence. (my italics)[45]

As Ben Pimlott, biographer of Hugh Dalton, has recorded, on his very first day at Cambridge, 'Dalton met Rupert Brooke, and immediately fell under his spell.' Almost forty years later Dalton recorded that, 'no Cambridge friendship of mine meant more to me than this, and the radiance of his memory still lights my path'.[46] Dalton himself was nearly always something of an outsider in his political career (he was one of those whose money came in useful in securing a Labour seat in the 1920s):[47] he was a difficult man by nature, but in that, and in his lack of popularity with persons of his own class, his ungainly appearance undoubtedly played a part.[48] From all this I conclude that in the masculine power game in Britain in the early twentieth century beauty was certainly not particularly important, especially when compared with class position, but that it was nevertheless useful to be personable, and that there was the possibility of discrimination against men who were not at least that. The prodigy at the end of the thirties, who became personal secretary to Churchill during the Second World War, John Colville, had the special good looks which could serve so nicely to underwrite precocity.[49]

The admiration denied to government servants in the United States was directed with full flourish towards entrepreneurs and business executives. Admiration for the truly self-made man was completely genuine; and it was certainly possible to have an ugly face and yet make a fortune. But recruitment into positions with high prospects within established businesses very largely came from the well-educated upper sectors of American society. At Yale two or three outsiders might be invited to join the exclusive Skull and Bones club, an excellent moving staircase to high status in American business; looks might help, but the selected students would need to have shown concrete achievement, say as football captain, editor of the *Yale Daily News*, brilliant scholar, or, perhaps, charismatic student politician. At Princeton looks were one of a dozen or so headings on which students rated their classmates.[50] Dr Paula Fass, who has studied the whole issue very thoroughly for the 1920s, has shown that in rating among classmates and, therefore, in election to the influential fraternities, involving in turn the high road to good jobs, looks did count; but what mattered above looks was the right social background or, at the very least, complete conformity to the attitudes and manners associated with that background.[51] Again, I draw the conclusion that beauty was far from a necessity, but that not being at least personable could be a disadvantage.

## 4  *Servants, Shops and Movie Stars*

From those moving in the powerful circles of society, let us turn to those who served them. In general, the trends continued, and probably accelerated, whereby high-status servants were usually good-looking servants, and whereby shop assistants in high-class shops usually had a good appearance. Some detail may be gleaned from the recollections of Gordon Grimmet, who from being a coachboy (or 'tiger', as they were called) during the First World War rose to being a footman to Lady Astor. 'Tigers', who sat on the box of the carriage, were, Grimmet noted, 'preferably small and sweet faced'.[52] Grimmet moved to a job as lampboy to the Marquis of Bath at Longleat, then, while the war was still on, to the post of third footman.

We were chiefly there as ornaments, for after we had dinner we lined up in the beautifully dim-lit corridor and just stood there for the rest of the evening. It wasn't easy because we weren't expected to move, and powder as it hardens on the head seems to drag the hair by the roots and this caused the scalp to itch!! Nevertheless there's something artistically satisfying in wearing full livery and carrying it well. It encourages graceful movement and gesture and adds a bit of theatre and glamour to the occasion.[53]

Grimmet also served at Bath's London house in Grosvenor Square. He 'enjoyed walking in the nearby Hyde Park'.

I'd parade there in my waistcoat, with my starched shirt, white bow and livery trousers and the girls would all turn their heads and say, 'There's a footman' and I'd feel no end of a dog. I was a gayer bird than the soldiers in their khaki and a rarer one.[54]

Appearance seems to have counted for much in his appointment by Lady Astor: 'He looks a big strong boy, Lee', she commented to the butler. As an attractive male and good dancer, Grimmet also made a good marriage: though only a second footman, he married the head gardener's daughter, who enjoyed some status as a floral arranger inside the Astor household.[55] The butler, Lee, was reared in poverty from the age of four and when his father died and the family farm was sold up he seems to have gained his early appointment in domestic service almost entirely on the basis of appearance alone. He was appointed first footman to the Astors in 1912, the appointment being made by Parr the Steward who commented, 'her Ladyship doesn't like pigmies'. At his first meeting with Lady Astor she remarked: 'I hope you stay. Look after him Parr, he seems a nice boy.'[56]

Although by this time good looks in female servants were often highly prized, the story could still be rather different for them. While the association between beauty and sexuality was more openly recognized than ever before, and fashion was more directly sexual – or perhaps because of these developments – sexuality in servants was very much not encouraged. Speaking of himself and a female servant at Longleat, Grimmet recounted that: 'It was a rule of the house of course that we should never be in a bedroom together. For a man and a woman to see a bed in company would, in the eyes of our employers, only excite evil thoughts.' He further remarks that: 'There were some establishments that, as the sons reached adolescence, made a sort of tally of their maids' attractions. Those girls that came high on the list were gradually phased out and replaced by plain ones.'[57]

In earlier ages the social promotion of a beautiful woman, usually achieved by a stage-by-stage process of careful exploitation of her advantages, almost invariably involved the conceding of sexual favours, though, as we saw, the professional beauty, admired by the masses, was emerging at the end of the nineteenth century. The paradox of the 'modern' evaluation of beauty as an autonomous status characteristic is that, although the value is intimately associated with sex appeal, it is not dependent on the actual occurrence of sexual transactions. In the earlier twentieth century one set of norms was being replaced by another, although the process was far from uniform or linear. If I try to establish the point from the careers of two of the most famous of all twentieth-century women, I do so from the early part of their careers which were far from untypical, rather than from their later elevation to the very pinnacles of success.

Gabrielle Chanel was born in Saumur in south central France (*not* Saumur on the Loire) in 1882. Her father was a travelling salesman and, although Gabrielle already had an elder sister, he was not then married to her mother, though the parents did marry the next year. The mother died young, and Gabrielle was placed in the grim and austere environment of a local orphanage. At seventeen, 'just a young peasant girl brought up by charity',[58] she moved on to the Notre Dame boarding school in the small town of Moulins. Such were the complexities of her family background that she had an aunt, Adrienne, who was actually the same age as herself. They were beautiful and they were close friends. It was natural both that they should get employment as shop assistants in an enterprise specializing in trousseaux and layettes and that together they should live in at the shop. Natural also that, in a garrison town which at that time housed one of France's classiest regiments, the 10th Light Horse, containing 'both the scions of the Faubourg St Germain and the fine flower of the landed gentry',[59] they should attract the attention of the young bloods, particularly since during the racing season the girls did some occasional work at a tailor's shop specializing in equestrian outfits. Gabrielle and Adrienne both made clothes themselves, and in 1903, shortly before her twenty-first birthday, Gabrielle took a room of her own where she saw clients privately. She also had ambitions towards singing: her voice was not brilliant, but her sexy appearance helped her to get a job in a song and dance routine in a local café. (Unfortunately, because of copyright difficulties, I have been unable to reproduce any early photographs of Chanel – readers are referred to *Chanel* by E. Charles-Roux, Paris, 1976.) As she already had a large following of cavalry officers, she was extremely good for business. Her two songs were 'Qui Qu'a vu Coco dans l'Trocadero' and 'KoKo Ri Ko': henceforth she was 'Coco' Chanel.

She was ambitious, and though such talent as had so far revealed itself lay rather in dress making than in singing, she sought an audition in a café in the important town of Vichy. However, much more important to her career was the fact that she had established a relationship with a wealthy infantry officer, Etienne Balsan. She went to live on his estate at Royallieu where, apart from working with the horses, she led a generally idle life. For an orphan peasant girl she was not doing badly; but, though she proved herself an excellent horsewoman, no definite career was developing. Then she set herself up in Balsan's Paris flat, making hats. Through her horsey connections she met the Englishman Arthur 'Boy' Capel. The mainspring of her social success was still her sexual attractiveness to men, and Capel put up the money for a shop for her on rue Cambon. But the shop seemed a hobby rather than a vocation: Gabrielle tried to become a dancer, but showed little real talent here either. The money again came from Capel when she decided to open a shop in the fashionable resort of Deauville.

The orphanage-educated peasant girl had come a long way. The single
consistent factor behind this success had been the admiration and support
of men, evoked by her beauty and continuing youthfulness (at twenty-
eight she looked no more than eighteen). She was not a courtesan, still
less a 'grand horizontal'. She was a new woman in a new age,
emancipated, happy in the company of men, but anxious to establish a
career independent of male subsidy. Her subsequent staggering success,
partly due, as I have already indicated, to the way in which she was able
to exploit the special circumstances of war, I leave out of the reckoning
for the moment, as I turn to Greta Gustafsson, born a full generation
later, whose beauty took her rapidly upwards without any sexual favours
being involved.

Greta Gustafsson was born in Stockholm in 1905. Her father was a
street sweeper. When he died she, at the age of fourteen, had to seek
work. Her first job was lathering faces in a local barber's shop. Her
beauty was already striking, and here she was spotted by the son of the
founder of Sweden's largest department store, PUB, where, like so
many other beautiful girls, she got a job as shop assistant. However,
there was a special quality to her looks: while Chanel at twenty-eight had
looked eighteen, Greta Gustafsson at fifteen looked twenty. She was
asked to model hats for the store, and in 1920 (when she was fifteen) the
PUB spring catalogue, distributed in 50,000 copies, had pictures of her        98
modelling hats. Not surprisingly, she then got some work as a fashion
model, a role in which a little dramatic talent is useful. At the same time
she deliberately sought roles as an extra in the Stockholm film studios.
The following year she did appear in a film, though a rather modest one,
promoting PUB. In the same year she got a part in *Luffar-Petter* (*Peter the
Tramp*). The director said: 'Her voice did not impress me, but her
appearance did . . .'[60] The cinema, of course, was just at the beginning
of its worldwide dominion. PUB would not give her leave to take larger
roles, so she made the calculated, but courageous, decision to break from
her career as shop assistant and part-time fashion model. Even if we had
heard no more of her, she had still done very well for a daughter of a
street sweeper. However, as with other beautiful women who got right
to the top, she clearly did have talent, for she won a scholarship to the
Academy of Dramatic Theatre in Stockholm. With an international film
career now firmly in her sights (silent film was *the* international medium)
she changed her surname to one that could be easily pronounced in any
language: Garbo. She was all of eighteen. At nineteen she went to
Hollywood; the rest is legend. She had not, it seems clear, had to grant
any sexual favours. Her Swedish director, who went with her to
Hollywood, was, in fact, a homosexual. Garbo never married, though
she had celebrated affairs with the great musician Stokowsky (who was
twenty-three years older than she was), film actor John Gilbert, Gayelord
Hauser, George Schlee and Cecil Beaton.

⊞ PAUL U. BERGSTRÖMS AKTIEBOLAG. STOCKHOLM

# DAM-HATTAR

från de enklaste till de mest eleganta

Mod. ›CLARY›
Damhatt av filt i
beige, marin, svart,
brunt, fraise el. röd=
brunt        Kr. 28.—

Mod. ›ETHEL›
Damhatt av sammet
i cerise, ljusblått,
mörkblått,    brunt,
mullvad, lilas eller
beige        Kr. 25.—

Mod. ›JANE›
Damhatt    av
sammet i grönt,
marin, brunt el.
mörk lilas
Kr. 48.—

Mod. ›HELNY›
Damhatt av filt i beige, mullvad, brunt,
neger, jade, vinrött el. marin Kr. 28.—

Mod. ›SOLVEIG›
Damhatt av filt i brunt, svart, grönt,
marin el. mullvad              Kr. 35.—

98 Illustration from PUB department store catalogue, Stockholm, 1920, showing
photographs of Greta Gustafsson modelling hats

Chanel meantime (just to round that story off) had paid Capel back all
he had advanced her, and had registered herself as a couturière. In dress,
simplicity was the key note; and Chanel was the top couturière at the
heart of that transformation. But with simplicity in dress went sophisti-
cation in cosmetics and exoticism in perfume. In the fashion world of the
1920s the three were linked more closely together than ever before.
Chanel had the chemist Ernest Beaux experiment with a number of
complex perfumes and she selected the one which she marketed as

Chanel No. 5, in its strikingly simple and 'modernistic' crystal cubes with simple lettering. On the sales of Chanel No. 5 Gabrielle became a millionairess several times over.

Other stars had already made the Hollywood which welcomed, though never knew quite how to treat, Garbo. Gladys Smith was born into a lower middle-class Toronto family in 1893. Her father died when she was not yet five; she went onto the stage when she was five and a half. By the age of eight she was well known upon the Toronto theatrical scene. At ten she made her New York debut and was now supporting the family. Even at this tender age she set out seriously to study other actors. Seriousness and talent, clearly these are the vital factors. She was a good-looking little girl, but should one be speaking of looks with respect to a pre-pubescent child? Probably yes, in fact, since had she been a plain little girl it is highly unlikely that she would have been accepted on the stage in the way that she was. She was also a determined little girl, and she quite deliberately forced herself on the leading Broadway impresario, David Belasco. He it was who gave her the name of Mary Pickford. She did well, but found herself without a part at the end of the season. Reluctantly, therefore, she took herself to the film company Biograph on 14th Street. There was only one film director at Biograph, D. W. Griffith; he cast Mary, now actually sixteen, as a ten-year-old with a very brief appearance in *Her First Biscuits*.

. . . inexplicably, the camera portrays some people as looking better than they really do, others worse. In some rare individuals it highlights and transmits a striking quality. It takes nothing away from Mary Pickford to say that she could not have been as beautiful as that glowing on the screen. Rather, whatever it is that makes one person in a million so photogenic that the rest of us look at her with fascination, reflecting emotions from love to hate – whatever that is, Mary Pickford had it. You can see it there on the screen, just the way the camera recorded it on April 20, 1909.[61]

In the harsh film light a youthful complexion, such as Mary possessed, was also a great advantage. She took a serious interest in editing, make-up and film acting. Mary had a special photogenic quality, she had talent, she had dedication; she also had natural beauty. It was not customary at the time for film actresses to be known by their own names, but Mary Pickford did become something of a name as 'Little Mary'. She worked for various directors, and then for Adolph Zukor, who decided to forsake the shorter film for four-reelers: *Tess of the Storm Country*, released on 30 March 1914, was a great success. Soon Mary Pickford was making $100,000 a year. In the middle of the European war, and a few weeks after American entry into it, the announcement was made of the establishment of the Mary Pickford Motion Picture Company: she was twenty-three and earning $10,000 a week. Five years earlier, in January 1911, she had married a fellow actor, Owen Moore, a very beautiful

99

99 Mary Pickford,
studio photograph for
advertising purposes,
*c.* 1920

man, but with little talent and no great strength of character. Moore might perhaps have had a great career as a footman or a gigolo; as it was, he is yet another beautiful man to end up in the dustbin of history.

The film which brought to the cinema serious recognition by the middle and upper classes was Griffith's *The Birth of a Nation*, released in June 1915. This was seen by a successful actor, then thirty, who had previously been contemptuous of the medium. He now signed a contract stipulating that he must be directed by Griffith himself. This actor had been born in Denver, Colorado, in May 1885, the illegitimate son of Ella Fairbanks and Charles Ulman, who was Jewish. It was from his father that Douglas Fairbanks inherited his dark skin, which was much resented by his mother. Fairbanks as a youth was energetic and good looking, and had the assurance which often goes with these characteristics: it was his 'assurance' which impressed the English actor Frederick Warde, who met Fairbanks when he was fifteen. Fairbanks undertook various jobs, cashing in on his looks and charm. In January 1905 he was in the chorus in a Japanese operetta. He made a strong impact on the Broadway star Grace George, who recommended him to her husband, the producer William Brady. More than mere looks, perhaps, what impressed about
100     Fairbanks was his virility, personality and energy. But as with any

beautiful woman, there were winnings to be made in the sexual stakes. In June 1907 he married Beth Sully, daughter of an upper-class cotton trader. To gain acceptance, Fairbanks had to promise to forsake the theatre for business. But soon he was back in the theatre, the marriage being (for the time being) a secure and happy one.

As a film actor, Fairbanks starred in *The Lamb*, which showed that, in addition to all his other qualities, he had that special photogenic element. His fame was secure with the success of *His Picture in the Papers*. Mary Pickford had seen, and admired, Douglas Fairbanks on the stage. In November 1915 they met in person for the first time. In the post-war years they were to be, respectively, 'America's sweetheart' and 'the most popular man in the world';[62] they also married each other. The third star who created part of a kind of triumvirate in these years was Charles Chaplin: Chaplin was certainly a personable enough fellow, but in the case of his successes one could not escape the conclusion that talent rather than looks was the important ingredient.

Before ever he became a star, Fairbanks was at least making a living from his wits and his looks: before she became a star Greta Garbo had risen considerably above her origins. No doubt Clara Bow, born into a desperately poor Brooklyn family, her father being a waiter and odd-job carpenter, would, in any age, have made something of her exceptional looks. Or would she perhaps have been seduced and betrayed? Or

101

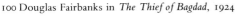

100 Douglas Fairbanks in *The Thief of Bagdad*, 1924

perhaps, as a red-head, she would have been ignored unless, that is, she happened to encounter a Pre-Raphaelite painter. But the times seemed to be especially right for her. In 1921 there was a movie magazine competition for the 'Most Beautiful Girl in the World'; competitors simply had to send in photographs of themselves. Clara sent in two taken by the nearest photographer. She won. Largely on the strength of this she got a part in *Down to the Sea in Ships*. She rapidly came to be one of the best-known handful of sexy stars of the twenties. She cracked up, and at forty-seven was in a sanitorium.[63] She was not psychologically well suited to take the stresses and temptations of Hollywood life; on the other hand, remaining poor and unknown she might have cracked up anyway. Her final stardom aside, what Clara Bow exemplifies is the opportunity to dream, if no more, which movies, and movie magazines, and photographic beauty competitions offered to young women whose humble origins were in some way compensated for by good looks.

Rodolpho Guglielmi, born in May 1895, came from a solidly prosperous middle-class family in Castellaneta in Italy. There was no pressing need for him to come to the United States at the end of the war. But when he did, he found himself facing starvation. As with a Jeanne Bécu or a Lillie Langtry, a calm assessment of his assets and their potential was called for. Principally, his assets were: romantic good looks and Italian

101 Clara Bow,
photograph, *c.* 1923

102 Rudolph Valentino,
photograph, *c.* 1923

102

grace. He became a professional dancing partner, a 'taxi-dancer', or
gigolo. As his first boss put it: 'With your looks and manner, you're
going to spend a lot more time in bed with your partners than on the
dance floor. Make sure you do it in your own time and not in mine.'[64]
Guglielmi, in fact, habitually took what he called his love break between
the tea dance and the evening dancing session. He deliberately worked on
his dancing so that he could win a star position at the elegant Maxim's,
for which post he delved back deep into family history in renaming
himself di Valentina.

He was doing well, drawing heavy financial support from his rich
mistress, when he fell foul of the sort of risk almost all those who live by
their looks and sexuality must run: his mistress shot her husband.
Guglielmi, therefore, fled to San Francisco. Here he fell in with film
people who had travelled up from Hollywood. His striking appearance
made a considerable impression, but in fact he had no immediate success
in film and was forced to seek employment exploiting his skill as a
dancer. It might have ended there: the varied life experiences of a
beautiful male. However, he caught the eye of the established May
Murray, who insisted on having him as her leading man. On the strength
of this, Guglielmi (or di Valentina), who certainly had no shortage of
sexual partners, got married, unfortunately to the frigid Jean Acker; on
marrying he stabilized his name as Rudolph Valentino. It was the top-

ranking script writer June Mathis who picked out Valentino for *The Four Horsemen of the Apocalypse*. The rest, if I may dare to repeat the phrase, is legend. His life was stormy, and very short: we are all familiar with the massive crowd scenes after Valentino's death, which cannot, of course, have been any consolation to Valentino. But to see in his death some inevitable retribution for living by sex appeal alone is to underestimate the force of contingency in history and the unexpected lethality of the most harmless-seeming attack of appendicitis.

In the past, it had not been terribly important for male actors to be beautiful, if they had some talent. Generally, film made it the rule that film actors must be beautiful, as most stage actresses had always had to be – we've noted some exceptions, but no famous actress was actually plain. There were to be male stars who did not fulfil any plausible standards of beauty, usually taking specialized roles, as character actors or as tough-guys: Wallace Beery, James Cagney and Humphrey Bogart are examples (Bogart, in his earlier years, had played juvenile leads on stage). There are no exact analogues, perhaps, among female stars, but one or two, who did occupy traditional glamorous roles, in fact fell well short of the standards of beauty set by the likes of Clara Bow, Gloria Swanson, Greta Garbo or, at the end of the thirties, Vivien Leigh. Even without a horrible accident at the age of eleven, when the Christmas tree candles burned all the skin off her face, Bette Davis was never going to be a beauty. However, that accident certainly didn't help. Her sympathetic and highly professional biographer, Charles Higham, in effect makes the point by omission: 'She never thought of herself as attractive, yet she was: her infectious laugh, her stylish swinging walk, her trick of balancing herself on her heels and turning unexpectedly, her quick wit, and her wide blue eyes started to draw the attention of young bloods.'[65] She had a date with Henry Fonda: 'She was very attracted to him, but he says he was not attracted to her.'[66] What she did have was a driving will, backed up by that of her mother, to become a successful actress.

About the burning theatrical talent there can be no doubt and already by the age of twenty she was on the edge of a great stage career. Again, I should let Higham speak, leaving the reader to draw his or her own conclusions:

103     Physically, she still has an odd, unfinished look. The mousey hair, the bald, burned-through face, the pale blue eyes that widen constantly to emphasize a point, the small mouth, long neck, and gawky figure do not add up to a picture of conventional prettiness. But she is nevertheless immensely attractive. She exudes vitality, energy, wit, and style. Instinctively, without forcing it, she projects an ice-cold sexuality, intelligence combined with passion, sheer nerves coupled with passive reason. She is a picture of furious aggression, with her vulnerability and terror of life, her obvious virginity, making her irresistible. Her movements, crucial to an actress's individual I, are already those of an original.

103 Bette Davis, photograph, early 1930s

She walks very quickly, very impatiently, with an odd combination of the feminine in the looseness of the hips, the thrust of the large breasts, and the masculine, in the firmness of step, the athletic resolution in the well-shaped legs . . . The theater is a means of escape for her great inner tensions and strains and from the harsh realization that (a disaster for some girls) she isn't a beauty.[67]

Although her true passion was the stage (and indeed she thought Hollywood vulgar), none the less it was through Hollywood that success ultimately lay. Her first screen test resulted in rejection. However, it was in the 1930s that Warner Brothers began their great series of films characterized by powerful social realism: for such films Bette Davis was ideally suited. Though still a virgin, she performed with great conviction in the sex scene in *Cabin in the Cotton*. While other actresses shrank from the part, she actually coveted the role of Mildred in MGM's projected film *Of Human Bondage*, based on Somerset Maugham's novel about the destructive powers of a loose and sluttish woman. 'No other actress in Hollywood would have dared face a camera with her hair untidy and badly rinsed, her clothes cheap and tawdry, her manner vicious and ugly. She worked like a dog on her cockney accent . . .'[68] It may well be true that, once established ( she won an Oscar for *Dangerous*), her very lack of manifest beauty gave her a reassuring appeal to audiences.[69]

Another actress who became a great star, though not possessed of *all* the attributes of true beauty, was Katharine Hepburn. A schoolmate is reported to have said to her: 'You! An Actress? You're too skinny and funny-looking!'[70] Helen Lawrenson, in March 1981, recalled that when, as an editor of *Vanity Fair*, she met Katharine Hepburn in February 1933:

She had small, deep-set eyes, a mouth that seemed to have too many teeth, a prominent jaw, and a face absolutely covered with freckles. I would never have recognised her, had it not been for that hideous aristocratic voice . . . She had a phobia about her long scrawny neck and always tried to hide it.

When she met *Vanity Fair*'s urbane editor 'her plain face seemed to glow'.[71] There is a touch of cattiness in this. Hepburn certainly came much nearer to beauty than did Bette Davis; and such is the magic of the camera in regard to certain people, and such the power of make-up and lighting, that in most of her movies Hepburn appeared as a beauty in a way that, whatever the tricks of the trade, Davis never could. Unlike most film stars, Hepburn came from an educated upper-class back-ground and, of course, she always managed to project a good deal of that into her roles. Hepburn was not quite beautiful, Davis not quite plain: together they are exceptions who point up the rule that beauty was the first letter of recommendation necessary for the successful star. More positively, comparison with Clara Bow and Greta Garbo is instructive. Davis had the advantage of a middle-class background, Hepburn of an upper-class one; for escape from the slums of Brooklyn or Stockholm, beauty had, as in the past, been the vital passport. And for certain universally coveted parts it would always be the vital passport. When it came to casting the film of Margaret Mitchell's highly successful novel *Gone with the Wind*, Bette Davis was clearly the best-qualified actress for the role of Scarlett O'Hara; her looks, alas, simply did not match up to Margaret Mitchell's luscious description.

The part was won, against such candidates as Paulette Goddard, Jean Arthur and Joan Crawford, by an actress whose looks in real life were every bit as stunning as those set down, in fiction, by Margaret Mitchell; looks assisted, it should be added, by mastery of the difficult southern accent, and a piece of luck. The young English actor Laurence Olivier was just beginning to make his career in Hollywood; his agent happened to be the brother of *Gone with the Wind* producer, David O. Selznick, and through this contact Olivier was able to recommend his own wife, Vivien Leigh. Olivier recorded: 'I looked back at Vivien, her hair giving the perfect impression of Scarlett's, her cheeks prettily flushed, her lips adorably parted, her green eyes dancing and shining with excitement in the firelight; I said to myself, "David won't be able to resist that."'[72]

## 5 *Celebrities and Private People*

Film stars were one new type of celebrity; sports stars were another. To be a sports star you had, obviously, to have sporting talent; no amount of beauty would create an ace serve. The characteristic binary development of the modern world was both for beauty in itself (in men as well as women) to be more highly esteemed and more highly rewarded, and for women to have new opportunities which did not depend exclusively or mainly on personal appearance. Suzanne Lenglen became an international tennis champion at the age of fifteen. Her victory at Wimbledon in 1919 over Mrs Lambert-Chambers, who was thirty-five, made her an international celebrity.[73] Health, fitness, youth, and the concept of the emancipated young woman (those younger women in Britain who had not been enfranchised in 1918 gained the vote without fuss in 1928) were preoccupations of the twenties. Lenglen was an almost perfect symbol; but while film played an important part in publicizing her achievements, there was real drama in her subsequent struggles for supremacy with the young American tennis player Helen Wills. Suzanne Lenglen was not a fully 'modern' phenomenon (in the particular technical sense employed in this book): commentators still felt it necessary at times to pretend that she was pretty, when, in fact, though slim and lithe, she was rather plain. Her historical importance is that, at a time when the autonomous value of beauty was, openly and publicly, going up through the roof, she attained fame and fortune through a type of talent which had, in previous eras, been little esteemed in women.

Amy Johnson became a media star in the early thirties. Her qualifications were serious ones: she was a graduate of Sheffield University who, learning to fly in her spare time, became an outstandingly good pilot and mechanic. She was sponsored by the *Daily Mail*, from whom she won a £10,000 prize for her solo flight to Australia in 1930. She had prepared herself 'by careful meteorological study and by learning Ju-Jitsu and other defensive arts lest she fall among Arab Sheiks or Dyak head-hunters'.[74] Her subsequent marriage, unhappy as it proved, to the ex-RAF pilot J. A. Mollison was also the subject of great newspaper attention. Amy Johnson was neither beautiful nor sophisticated; gifted with real talents but not the surface ones, she fell a victim to the culture which had projected her to fame in the first place.

104        With her one may contrast Lady Grace Drummond-Hay, who had
poise, modest literary talent, and a title; and who is, furthermore, a
classic example of a woman adequately personable in face and form to be
able to project herself as a beauty. Underpinning her success was her
long and happy relationship with the distinguished German journalist
Karl H. von Wiegand, who provided her with many of her contacts in
the world of journalism. Strongly supporting it was her photogenic
quality: her weekly reviews of world affairs in *The Sphere* were always
accompanied by a photograph of her, either on location (wearing a veil in
Egypt, or chatting to a local pasha, for instance), or in the form of a
carefully, and sexually, posed portrait bust. On 28 May 1928 the main
front page story in the London *Evening Standard* was that Lady
Drummond-Hay was to be the first woman to cross the Atlantic in the
commercial airship *The Graf Zeppelin*; a sub-story on the same page
announced that, 'Lady Drummond-Hay is perhaps the youngest grandmother alive. Her step-grandson, who is 21, is only a few years younger
than herself.'[75] She certainly looks very young in the accompanying
photo, although she was now actually thirty-two. The story, and the
photograph, appeared in most of the morning papers next day.
        The flight did not actually take place till October when both von
Wiegand and Lady Grace had commissions to provide accounts of the

104 Lady Grace
Drummond-Hay,
international news agency
photograph, 1928

flight for syndication throughout the world's press. Usually a short report by him appeared on the front pages, with a much longer report by her, accompanied by a photograph, inside. Some newspapers simply printed her photograph with a brief caption: for example, 'This is an especially posed and personally selected portrait of Lady Drummond-Hay, beautiful English noblewoman, the first woman to cross the Atlantic in a commercial airship, the Graf Zeppelin.'[76] One photograph of her taking breakfast on the airship brings out that though attractive enough, she was no authentic beauty. However, the impression she created was summed up thus in a radio broadcast after her death:

First of all she was very beautiful. To those familiar with their Arabian Nights Lady Grace Drummond-Hay was remindful of Scheherezade. She was a flower-like woman, gracefully petite. Her hair was darkly beautiful, a fitting frame for her rose petal complexion. There was an enormous doll-like perfection to her nose and lips. But her large brown eyes, kindly but mysterious, gave her an Oriental quality, emphasised by her long dark lashes which made her look like a beauty strayed from some cherished Eastern bower.[77]

No such description could ever have been applied to another high-born lady, an American, who was to become one of the most famous of all women on the twentieth-century world scene. As her earliest writings make clear, Eleanor Roosevelt was very conscious from childhood of her own lack of good looks.[78] As a sufficiency of photographs demonstrate, she was in that category which most would term plain, and some would even call ugly; she did, however, have a good slim figure. As a young woman of character and compassion, she worked at the Rivington Street Settlement in the slums to the south of Houston Street in New York City. She was admired by even the more frivolous of her debutante friends, and gained many admirers among serious and eligible young men. One of these was her cousin Franklin D. Roosevelt, on whose looks I have already commented.

Franklin Roosevelt's most fateful action as a gay, charming, princely young man of twenty-one was to pick shy, somewhat plain Eleanor Roosevelt to be his wife. It showed remarkable perspicacity. We can only guess at his reasons; his courtship letters were burned – by Eleanor Roosevelt, probably in 1937 when she was writing the first volume of her autobiography and his youthful avowals of constancy until death perhaps were too painful to read. She said she burned them because they were too private. He preserved hers.[79]

The marriage took place in 1904 and for ten years it was highly successful. In the winter season of 1913–14 Eleanor employed Lucy Page Mercer, then twenty-two, as a part-time social secretary. Lucy was a beauty, in looks a perfect match to Franklin Roosevelt himself. The two beautiful people became lovers; for plain Eleanor the blow, when in 1918 she finally became aware of the truth, was a heavy one: 'the bottom dropped out of my own particular world and I faced myself, my surroundings, my world, honestly for the first time. I really grew up that year.'[80] Lucy was a Catholic; marriage to a divorced man with five children would run counter to her religion. Roosevelt was a politician; divorce would spell ruin to his political career. He gave an agreement never to see Lucy again (which he, in fact, broke), and the marriage with Eleanor survived. For Eleanor the personal unhappiness was immense; but she became a more and more commanding political figure in her own right, always more committed, always more compassionate than her husband, and after his death at the end of the Second World War she emerged unchallengeably as First Lady of worldwide internationalism. We are back to perennial themes here. Consciousness of one's own plainness is always painful. How far, as I have asked before, can achievement and fulfilment at any stage of life compensate for profound unhappiness at another?

The diaries, letters and personal reminiscences of less famous people offer no clear guidance as to the influence in their lives of personal beauty, save to suggest that, as always, it is a disturbing influence. Mother and daughter relationships can be especially intense (it was Eleanor Roosevelt's mother who made her particularly conscious as a little girl of her ill looks). One of the most illuminating personal documents of the home front in Britain during the Second World War is the War Diary of Ann Meader, a successful writer, aged forty when the war broke out, living alone with her daughter, then aged sixteen. Almost the first entry reads: 'Went out with Helen. Without make-up she is the mischievous child of convent days; with it, an up-to-the-minute young lady surveys a world far beneath her aspiring feet. She is beautiful!'[81] Two nurses, 'Bish' and 'Stew', are billeted on the lavish Birmingham family house: 'How young – how pretty – Bish looks. "Stew" is older and less ornamental, but equally charming.' Frequently Bish 'is in trouble with young men, who make her acquaintance and thereafter dog her footsteps, and wait to bring her home'.[82] Among other things, the diary is remarkable for Mrs Meader's full expression of her own longings and desires. At one point she notes that 'some men desire only the outward show, the meticulous fastidiousness of appearance that takes the place of achievement in better pursuits'. Where, she asks, 'is the love that sees beneath the surface?'[83]

105        The power of Helen's beauty is manifest (and a photograph accompanies the diary). Of one aspiring boyfriend it is remarked: 'Les has matured but he will never cope with so masterful a "blossom" as Helen who is seventeen this week.'[84] Helen gets a part in a mannequin show; frequently it is suggested that she should go into films (Mrs Meader had several contacts in the world of the arts and entertainment, including Walter Greenwood, author of the novel which became the successful wartime film *Love on the Dole*). The upheavals of wartime created many

105 Helen Meader, private photograph accompanying her mother's wartime diary, 1940

incidents of sexual harassment for Helen, many opportunities for casual encounters with men, usually officers, for her mother. The diary meticulously notes male appearance – the eyes of a stranger in the mess had given her 'an indescribable thrill', though he was 'nothing spectacular to look at . . .'[85] Some comments on her own sex are contemptuous, or perhaps pitying: 'Saw prostitutes out in the rain at 7 o'clock off Piccadilly. Poor specimens.'[86]

'Poor specimens' still abounded among the undernourished British working class. In *English Journey*, based on a journey he undertook in the early thirties, the novelist J. B. Priestley observed the poor appearance of older working-class males in, for example, Newcastle: 'I noticed nothing but a lot of miserable fellows hanging about, probably looking for the chance of a job . . . Slatternly women stood at the doors of wretched little houses, gossiping with other slatterns or screeching for their small children, who were playing among the filth of the road side . . .' The men of the North East he sees as 'stocky toothless fellows'.[87]

One particularly harrowing and moving reminiscence of life during the Depression is Helen Forrester's account of a middle-class family fallen upon desperately hard times in Liverpool.[88] Dressed in tatters, she is constantly picked upon because she wears glasses. In cruel defiance of the law, which did little enough for the helpless child, she has been taken away from school by her parents so that she can look after the younger children. Her younger brother tries to be comforting:

'Perhaps you will marry a Prince', he suggested hopefully. 'Perhaps', I agreed, though I knew that girls as ugly as I who also wore spectacles did not stand a chance of matrimony; my mother had always indicated that such was the case and I think I had already been written off as a future maiden aunt. This did not stop me, however, from dreaming for the rest of the afternoon that I married the beautiful, humane and exciting Edward, Prince of Wales.[89]

'Without an education', she records later in the book, 'I saw myself being kept at home until my parents died and then becoming some bad-tempered old lady's companion-help, subject always to the whims and fancies of others. I knew I was far too plain ever to hope for marriage.'[90]

This consciousness of her looks undoubtedly cast a further blight over a young life already sufficiently blighted. In face of the most unpromising circumstances, Helen Forrester succeeded in educating herself through night classes, eventually married, and became a successful writer; possibly eventual escape compensated for the childhood despair. The main escape route for the good-looking working-class girl is suggested in Walter Greenwood's fictional *Love on the Dole*: Sally Hardcastle becomes the mistress of the local bookmaker Sam Grundy, and is thus able to provide some funds for her pitifully impotent father and secure a job for her brother.[91]

Beautiful women could now be celebrities, and cash in on their beauty, without necessarily granting sexual favours. But beauty could cause problems for young males (even if subsequently contributing towards career success). At his first prep school, the young Laurence Olivier 'reportedly sang like an angel and was as pretty as was needed to attract the worst in certain males'. He suffered much brutality; then the attentions paid to him at his next school, 'no matter how unwelcome', gained him the title of 'school tart'.[92]

## 6 *The 1950s*

This chapter has been primarily concerned with the manner in which social and technological changes in the first half of the twentieth century encouraged a greater appreciation, among greater numbers of people than ever before, of human physical beauty. However, the power of tradition remained strong, the weight of convention heavy, and it is my main purpose now to show how far the United States, Britain and France in the late 1940s and the 1950s still were from a 'modern' appreciation of beauty.

It is often claimed that the cultural norms of Western society were by 1950 thoroughly American. In fact, far from being the centre of an all-pervasive international culture, the United States in the 1950s was an inward looking, self-regarding, parochial society, while at the same time it was affluent, colourful and, in some respects, 'modern' in ways in which European countries simply were not. Far from being part of an American-dominated international culture, these countries were still very much dominated by their own traditions, and very 'backward' in comparison with the United States. That full international cultural exchange which is an essential prerequisite of a completely modern conception of beauty had yet to come.

*Reader's Digest* in February 1954 carried an article entitled 'Meet the Typical American – Male and Female'. The typical male was said to be five foot nine inches tall, weighing 158 pounds; the typical female five foot four inches, weighing 132 pounds; it was said of the latter that she 'can't stand an unshaven face'. Two social historians of the period comment:

As the average weights of men and women might suggest, many Americans were on the heavy side. The relevant styles encouraged this. Women in pleated skirts falling a few inches below the knees were expected to be shapely in a plump sort of way. Bikinis were largely limited to the girlie magazines. But big breasts, symbols of motherhood, were definitely in vogue. For men, excess flab was easily concealed beneath baggy pleated pants, suits and shirts that did not follow body lines, boxer shorts and bathing trunks, Bermudas with knee-length socks. So in this decade of suburban prosperity, many people carried paunches as if they were symbols of success.[93]

Public discourse on matters of beauty and sex appeal was marked by a combination of vulgarity and prudishness; comments on personal appearance tended to be highly ritualized, unsubtle, and lacking in any real aesthetic sensibility. Once the phrase 'vital statistics' had applied to government compilations on fertility and mortality: now the phrase, used to signify bust, waist and hip measurements in women, became something of a fetish. As social historians Miller and Nowak put it

a standardised image of sensuality grew in importance. That image stressed the secondary sexual characteristics of both sexes. Mannerisms seemed ever more significant: walk, gestures, voice, dress, size of tits and hips. External appearance was a woman's proof of her sensuality. Men were expected to conform to a physical role, but women had to comply in that respect far more . . . women inevitably turned to elaborate artifice . . .

The conventional image of what constituted male sex appeal was summed up in the expression 'beefcake': men were not supposed to be pretty or beautiful, or if they were, this was not supposed to be remarked upon.[94]

In the era of McCarthyism and Cold War American governments and large sections of the American people were mistrustful of a Europe of welfare states and large socialist and communist parties. The emphasis was on the perfection of American married life. Sex was a matter for silence, for sniggering, or for monumental pomposity, as in the Kinsey reports on human sexual behaviour.[95] Yet American economic and technological development advanced at phenomenal speed. In 1946 there had been only seven thousand TV sets in America; by 1960 there were over fifty million. From 1956 onwards Americans were spending more time watching these sets than working to earn a living. Between 1950 and 1960 home ownership increased by over nine million, and car ownership by over twenty-one million; a comprehensive 40,000-mile interstate highway system had come into existence.[96] Fundamentalist Christianity, small-town notions of social values, and barbaric attitudes towards race relations persisted; but in so many other aspects the United States seemed the multicoloured world of the future.

By comparison the European countries were grey and poverty stricken. Economic expansion, the achievement of levels of purchasing power upon which alone genuine cultural exchange could be based, came only slowly during the 1950s. Britain's rulers believed that Britain was still a great imperial power, and acted accordingly; traditional class attitudes still pervaded society. What was supposed to be a pungent critique of British society by a left-wing film maker showed just how persistent was the cosy, unreal world inhabited by the upper class:

Let's face it; coming back to Britain is always something of an ordeal. It ought not to be, but it is. And you don't have to be a snob to feel it. It isn't just the food, the sauce bottles on the café tables, and the chips with everything. It isn't just saying goodbye to wine, goodbye to sunshine. After all, there are things that matter even more than these; and returning from the Continent, today in 1957, we feel these strongly too. A certain, civilised (as opposed to cultured) quality in everyday life: a certain humour: an atmosphere of tolerance, decency and relaxation. A solidity, even a warmth. We are home. But the price we pay is high.

For coming back to Britain is also in many respects like going back to the nursery. The outside world, the dangerous world, is shut out: its sounds are muffled . . . Nanny lights the fire, and sits herself down with a nice cup of tea and yesterday's *Daily Express*; but she keeps half an eye on us too . . .[97]

In September 1962 an article in *Paris Match* invited readers to remember the France of the early 1950s.

At that time the traveller who, after a long stay in the United States, found himself back in Paris would be struck with a blow to the heart. Still completely enveloped by the intense life of American cities with their unheard of prosperity, his eyes still full of pure white sky scrapers and the bright play of colours, he is back in a leaden world with, in the grey streets, only a handful of cars, all uniformly black. The women are pretty badly dressed, the men often in overalls. Passing the stunningly old fashioned shops, our traveller can scarcely avoid reflecting bitterly: 'the future today belongs to the new nations. Europe can only weep amid her ruins.'[98]

True, there were dissenting groups in all three countries, but, far from forming one international movement, each took its own distinctive form: Beatniks in the USA; teddy boys, angry young men, and the Campaign for Nuclear Disarmament in Britain; 'existentialist' youths, congregating first in jazz cellars, then in discos, in France.

In such a climate of parochialism, it is not surprising that the beauty guides of the forties and fifties do not differ significantly from those of earlier in the century. The more open emphasis on physical attributes such as breasts and legs continues. The key word in most American beauty guides is 'grooming': sensible enough in their way, they are at the same time hymns to conformity and deception.

Perfect grooming is to every woman's appearance what wheat is to the diet, what steel is to industry. It is basic! . . .

Do not hesitate to wear 'gay deceivers' if you need them. Many prominent actresses and models do![99]

For black Americans, male and female, the advice, without exception, is to use every device to look as much like a white as possible. A guide to grooming for 'Negro girls', published in 1959, demonstrating the humanity and understanding which is so often the mark of such guides, insists that 'the color of your skin is not important'.[100] The change comes in chapter five:

Up to this chapter your personal problems are not too different from any other girl your age. You are exactly like any other girl, in fact you might even be prettier and smarter than some; your skin may so easily be the same color as hers but you think there is a difference and the difference shows. When we come to the discussion of hair, you feel pretty sure that this is where the difference begins. Hold on there! this is not exactly true.

There is a large percentage of girls with skin either the same color as yours, or a little darker or lighter that are not faced with a difference in the grade of their hair at all. But if you're on the other side of the fence, there is a difference and you're anxious to do something about it. Sure, it has made you wonder many times . . . why did I have to have this kind of hair? You're not alone with such thoughts and the color of your skin doesn't enter into it. Girls of other races worry and complain about their hair, too. Many of these girls have hair that is so tightly curled that they too must resort to hair straightening methods . . . the burden may be easier when you know you don't carry it alone.

Instead of wishing for the 'fairy godmother' to come down and touch you with her magic wand that will give you a new kind of hair . . . work for a head of hair that you'll be proud of.[101]

The affluent teenager was already a distinctive and much remarked upon phenomenon of post-Second World War American society. Special guides for teenagers appear also in Britain in the 1950s. The very title *Glamour: Film Fashion and Beauty* establishes the perceived importance of one of the major forces highlighted in this chapter, the cinema. While male readers are invited to send in photographs of themselves, all the tips on glamour and fashion are quite clearly aimed at girls. Most of the photographs are of female film stars, British and American, but there is also a double spread of male stars, captioned 'What is this thing called "beefcake"?', together with fullpage photographs of Richard Burton and other specially favoured male stars. 'What's your type?', female readers are asked.[102]

In France the distinguishing feature is a stronger emphasis on the uses of cosmetic medicine. In general the muddle and hypocrisy, the fiction that beauty is self-created, are as strong as ever. One writer insisted that in a pretty woman there is really no more than twenty-five per cent of natural beauty, a further twenty-five per cent being 'radiant beauty' (that is to say, 'that beauty that comes from a noble spirit and a contented heart'), while the remaining fifty per cent is the result of careful grooming.[103] There is a straight throwback to the late nineteenth century, and indeed to theological notions of beauty, in the categorical statements that 'it is ugliness which is immoral', and 'what is ugly must be destroyed'.[104] *Medicine in the Service of Beauty*, published in Paris in 1955 by Dr Charles Mayer, is at times distinctly unscientific:

To create, or to give full value to one's beauty, it is first of all necessary to learn to triumph over one's own enemy: one's self. The body given to each of us by nature is not always perfect. Often one aggravates the imperfections. The first rule therefore is negative: do not deliberately create ugliness. It will then be possible to improve one's appearance by the various procedures given in this book. Their effectiveness is far from being negligible. Another imperative, too readily forgotten, consists in taking care of the expression on one's face, which reflects the image of one's interior being. One must strive to eliminate from one's self all moral ugliness. A perfect beauty can be diminished by lack of gentleness in one's expression. In contrast to that, there are ugly individuals whose expression of profound goodness overcomes the lack of balance in their features. By the same token, it is not always the cold beauties who succeed, and if they do their beauty is soon over.[105]

The concluding hope is that this thought will serve as consolation for both men and the women 'whom nature has disinherited', together with the thought that 'in the domain of beauty there is no blemish without remedies'. Where this French work does distinguish itself from almost everything published in Britain and the United States is that it does devote several pages to the question of masculine beauty, remarking that men too are troubled by being ugly. The recommended remedies are exercise (rather than sport) and, if necessary, cosmetic surgery.[106]

To drive home the point that traditional attitudes were still very strong in the post-war years and in the 1950s, I want to examine three documents of very different types: a widely circulated work of popular art history by a well-known art critic, a very private piece of fan male written to the film star Ingrid Bergman, and an award-winning Hollywood film. Clifford Bax's *The Beauty of Women*, published in London in 1946 in the war economy format of the time, is essentially a study based on the representations of women by painters throughout Western civilization. Its final conclusion that 'a true sense of beauty may, in fact, proclaim the nobility and the immortality of the almost forgotten "soul"' is testimony to that obviously deeply felt need in many human beings to give external beauty deeper meaning. What he says on a more troubled topic exactly represents the new state of confusion about beauty reached in the aftermath of Freud: 'when a man looks upon the beauty of a woman his aesthetic delight is dangerously confused with his sexual interest'; 'it is, in fact, part of the human tragedy that man's appreciation of woman's beauty must inevitably, for the fierce purpose of life force, be mixed up with sexual desire'.[107]

The regret over the nature of sexuality is more discreet, the association of beauty with other qualities more pronounced, in a fan letter written to Ingrid Bergman by an American ex-serviceman from North Carolina in February 1947 (and preserved among the papers of her public relations representative). The writer has just seen Bergman on stage in the role of St Joan; he refers obliquely to the fact that in her screen roles she has played women whose standards of morality were less than perfect, but still feels that her own personal beauty must represent some deeper moral uplift:

> It may surprise you to learn that in spite of the nature of some of your roles, I have gained a similar uplift from seeing your portrayal of your varying roles, the personality of Ingrid Bergman is too dominant, ever to be subordinated to the more careless aspects of any character you may play. I think that anyone who follows you on the screen, loves you not so much for your inspired acting, as for the physical and spiritual beauty which are as natural to you as the air you breathe. This holding of the mirror to the better side of nature, I shall always contend, is the chief reason for your continuing and growing popularity.[108]

He then refers to the fact that during his service overseas he 'saw several top entertainers put on shows that were insulting in their vulgarity', even though the greatest cheers came for Jack Benny when (restoring the prim moral tone) he declared that he had been married to the same woman for

106 Ingrid Bergman, photograph, *c.* 1946

seventeen years. 'All of which seems to bear out my convictions that our inherent preference for beauty rather than sensationalism, is the real secret of your popularity. To us, the audience, you represent that high degree of beauty and virtue to which we all aspire, however failingly.' Now he alludes, very indirectly, to rumours he has heard about Bergman's private life and the possibility that she may be involved in a divorce: 'Whatever your choice of course, I know that Ingrid Bergman can never be false in word or gesture, nor less beautiful in form and spirit. May God bless you.'[109]

My third source for pointing up the confusions and conventions which overlaid attempts to engage with problems of physical appearance is the 1955 independently made Academy Award-winning film *Marty*, distri-

buted by United Artists.[110] This honourable film offers a penetrating
insight into the manners and morals of sections of working-class and
lower-middle-class New York. Young males seek their marriage partners at the Stardust Ballroom which, we learn, is 'loaded with tomatoes'.
An even more vulgar word is used to describe the accessible young
women (nurses as it happens) some of the younger men are fortunate
enough to date: 'squirrels'. Marty, however, misses out on all this. As he
cries out when his mother once again raises the question of marriage (he
is thirty-four): 'I am just a fat little man. Fat ugly man. I'm ugly. I'm
ugly.' Ernest Borgnine, already an established star in tough masculine
character parts, no handsome pin-up for sure, carries conviction in this      107
part, letting his stomach sag and exuding a general air of defeat.
Persuaded to go to the Stardust Ballroom, he meets a young woman,
brought on a blind date by a young doctor and then rather callously
dropped. She describes how on her last visit to the ballroom she'd sat for
an hour and a half: guys who approached her for a dance would suddenly
have a change of mind at the last minute. Dancing with her, Marty
consoles her in her self-doubt and loneliness with words of consummate
charm: 'You see you're not such a dog as you think you are', followed
by, 'guess I'm not such a dog as I think I am'.

107 Ernest Borgnine as
Marty, in the film *Marty*,
1955

108 Betsy Blair as Clara, in
*Marty*, 1955

Clara, 'the dog', is twenty-nine. Marty and Clara, of course, get on
very well together, but Marty's friend Angie, his peer group of male
chauvinist young bachelors, and even his mother, are utterly contemptuous: Clara is 'scrawny', 'a dog', and looks at least fifty years old. The
truly revealing irony about all this is that the actress, Betsy Blair, who
plays Clara is in fact strikingly beautiful and no attempt had been made
by the make-up department to render her otherwise. Her unattractiveness is simply symbolized by her dress, which is very formal, by the fact
that she is a successful teacher of chemistry, that she is quiet and shy, and
above all by contrast with the 'squirrels': thus the entirely false equation
is made that plainness equals failure to project immediate availability.
Any normally functioning male meeting Betsy Blair would, in the
lapidary words of Clifford Bax, find 'his aesthetic delight . . . dangerously confused with his sexual interest'. The simple fact is that it was
quite impossible for Hollywood in the 1950s to put a genuinely plain
woman on screen, at least in a contemporary drama with which
audiences were expected to identify: the trick to reassure, and of course
fool, mass audiences was to assert someone's unattractiveness and then
show that (by a hundred miles!) she was not so unattractive after all, and
indeed could find love and marriage. Verbally the old comforting
convention that beauty is more than skin deep was being restated,

108

though the visuals, actually, were saying the opposite. (I don't think the point is invalidated by William Wyler's *The Heiress* (1948), a classic costume drama, based on the nineteenth-century Henry James novel *Washington Square*, mentioned in chapter six, in which Olivia de Havilland is made to look fairly plain; it is intriguing that Betsy Blair had similar roles in two European art movies, the Spanish *Calle Major* and the Italian *Il Grido*, but scarcely relevant to a discussion of mainstream ideas in the United States of the 1950s.)

No discussion of beauty in the forties and fifties could fail to refer to the career of Marilyn Monroe, a career which epitomizes both the power and the tragic fragility of beauty, which points up the stultifying hypocrisies of the time in the matter of sex and sex appeal, and yet also points the way to the sexual liberation which was a central part of the cultural revolution of the sixties. Marilyn Monroe was the supreme 'sex symbol' of her time, the very phrase being a phrase of her time, the last era before the 1960s. There was only one Marilyn Monroe and her best films show the fruits both of her own immense efforts to become a true actress and of a fascinating inborn talent. Once more, however, if we look to the very early career we can see the kinds of opportunities which were also open to thousands of other girls whose names will never become known to history.

Norma Jeane Monroe (her mother's maiden name, though she was sometimes also known as Norma Jeane Baker) was, for a white American of her generation, born in low (if not abysmally so) circumstances on 1 June 1926 in Los Angeles general hospital. Her mother worked as a film cutter; she never knew who her father was. There was a record of insanity on the maternal side and Norma Jeane, as a child, was brought up by a series of foster mothers. The last of these, when Norma Jeane was fifteen, offered her the alternatives of marrying a local aircraft fitter, Jim Dougherty, or returning to an orphanage. Just turned sixteen, Norma Jeane was married in June 1942. The marriage seems to have established itself reasonably well by the point when Dougherty was sent overseas, with Marilyn herself taking a job in an aircraft factory. She later commented:

I wore overalls in the factory. I was surprised that they insisted on this. Putting a girl in overalls is like having her work in tights, particularly if a girl knows how to wear them. The men bussed around me just as the high-school boys had done. Maybe it was my fault that the men in the factory tried to date and buy me drinks. I didn't feel like a married woman.[111]

There was no sign of a break in the essentially working-class career pattern till the appearance at the factory in late 1944 of an army photographer charged with taking morale boosting shots of attractive women doing war work. He spotted Norma Jeane at once and was

109 Marilyn Monroe aged nineteen, photograph, 1945

responsible for launching her on a career, the quintessential one for the
dumb beauty, as photographic pin-up.

Norma Jeane was not in fact dumb, but she was certainly quite
strikingly beautiful. The point has to be made since it is sometimes
suggested that her beauty was in some way constructed, through the use
not just of cosmetics, but also of cosmetic surgery. It is true that from a
very early age she was an expert in the application of make-up in the
heavy style then in fashion. Her hair was naturally blonde, but, of
course, was bleached. She was to be well ahead of her time in going

jogging in order to preserve a slim, though buxom, figure. The first cosmetic surgery she had, also a few years later, was of a very minor kind: first to straighten her teeth, then to remove two tiny moles from her chin. Her appeal was in astonishing natural beauty, perfectly combined in face and figure; her figure was in keeping with the admired 'vital statistics' of the time, but needed neither support nor constraint. The visual evidence is overwhelming; it can be corroborated with some verbal statements. Ben Lyon, casting director at Twentieth Century-Fox, said: 'She had a good face. You can tell with some faces – the way the flesh sits on the bones, the planes and angles – that they'll photograph well . . . In addition, there was the way she moved.' Hollywood gossip columnist James Bacon says that his first thoughts on meeting Marilyn Monroe in 1948 were: 'Holy God! She's so exciting . . .' He added 'There was something about this girl. The moment you met her you knew she was going to make it.' Billy Wilder, Hollywood director, presuming that Monroe was wearing a bra, and discovering that she was not, commented: 'Her bosom was a miracle of shape, density, and an apparent lack of gravity.'[112] Women observers sometimes confuse a non-existent platonic notion of beauty with the only true (sexual) quality, but what they say can clinch the issue. Here is Marion Marshall, later Marion Wagner, actress wife of Robert Wagner:

> Marilyn was the most spectacular girl I ever met, not particularly beautiful, but she radiated a special dynamism. I remember, when I first saw her, she arrived late as usual, after all the other girls. I'm sitting with all these very sophisticated models, dressed in silks, with the gloves and hat and all that, and Marilyn came in a little scoop-necked gingham sun dress, her hair unbleached and unstraightened. When she walked in, it was like the room stopped, and everyone in the room knew she was going to get the job, and she did.

Finally journalist Robert Cahn:

> At the bar a weary press agent was asking for his fifth high ball when he glanced toward the doorway where Marilyn Monroe, recently acquired studio starlet, had just arrived. And mid a slowly gathering hush, she stood there, a blonde apparition in a strapless black cocktail gown, a little breathless as if she were Cinderella just stepped from the pumpkin coach. While the long-established female stars silently measured her, young Marilyn Monroe, who has logged less than fifty minutes' screen time, stole the show . . . Finally, as the guests sat down for dinner the blonde was installed at the head of No. 1 table, at the right hand of company president, Spyros Skouras.

These quotations have taken me a little ahead in time. The next stage in the Norma Jeane story was her meeting with André de Dienes, a photographer of rather more ambitious cast than the man from the army. She now very definitely saw her future career as being in film, and in 1946 she both secured a contract as a stock player at Twentieth Century-Fox (who

109

gave her the name Marilyn Monroe) and divorced Dougherty. For the time being there were two more significant sources of income: posing for nude photographs, and working as a call girl (the kind a rich and fastidious man would be happy to spend a whole evening with as well as the best part of the night). 'Modern' in so many ways, Marilyn's career also had something in common with that of a nineteenth-century 'horizontal'. She clearly did use her great sexual attractiveness to win the favour of men powerful in the film industry. It would not be unfair to say that she slept her way to the point at which her film career could take off. At first her screen roles were tiny, but they brought in masses of fan mail. She was at the same time appearing in pulp magazines across the country and abroad. She had become a national pin-up, and to the troops in Germany she was 'Miss Cheesecake of 1951'. With *The Asphalt Jungle*, released in June 1950, came her first substantial role; as she was already a kind of celebrity, this led quickly to a role in the more prestigious *Clash by Night* from a play by Clifford Odets. It was after the release of this film that it became widely known that the delicious nude in an immensely popular calendar series was Marilyn Monroe, in a pose taken in 1949. In the pinched and prissy morality of the time this revelation might have destroyed Monroe's film career, but she was able to turn it to her immense advantage, having the story put out that she had only posed out of dire need for money for the rent. Added to the image she was already establishing, this set her hurtling into orbit as the greatest sex symbol of all time. She received massive publicity, including the high-status accolade of a feature in *Life*, which declared: 'the genuine article is here at last – a sensational glamor girl, guaranteed to entice people from all lands to the box office'.[13] In December 1953 one of the nude calendar shots appeared in the pages of the first edition of a new magazine, *Playboy*; clothed, she also appeared on the cover. While all this was going on, it must be stressed, Marilyn was devoting prodigious efforts to being taught how to develop to the fullest her original, though wayward, talents as an actress.

*Monkey Business*, with Cary Grant, was followed by *Niagara*, and *Gentlemen Prefer Blondes*, with Jane Russell. The first film to do full justice to her truly remarkable talents, as the serious critics recognized, was *How to Marry a Millionaire*. Now a top Hollywood star, she married one of the country's great sporting heroes, Joe DiMaggio, a recently retired baseball star. *River of No Return* and *There's No Business Like Show Business* were followed by two truly distinguished performances in *The Seven Year Itch* and *Bus Stop*. Divorce from Joe DiMaggio was followed by marriage to Arthur Miller, the playwright whom she had long both admired and fancied: it must also be stressed that Marilyn had genuine intellectual ambitions, a passion for reading and for learning and for serious discussion. She made *The Prince and the Showgirl* with Laurence Olivier, widely rated as the greatest classical actor of his time, and *Let's*

*Make Love*, with Yves Montand, whom she had also long fancied, and with whom she had a very serious affair. Then came *Some Like It Hot*, the timeless film in which she gave an immortal performance.

Marilyn always feared being struck down herself by inherited insanity. She had a very disturbed childhood (about whether she was actually sexually assaulted as a child, as she sometimes claimed, it is impossible to be absolutely certain). She was constantly preoccupied with the question of who her father might have been. She suffered seriously from congenital gynaecological problems. She may or may not have had one, or many, abortions. All of her marriages broke down. From quite early in her career she drank too much, and increasingly took large doses of a variety of drugs supplied to her by various doctors. She became more and more difficult to work with. She tried Olivier's patience to the limit, and, though nothing of this can be seen in the film, she drove her co-stars on *Some Like It Hot*, Tony Curtis and Jack Lemmon, to distraction: Curtis was impelled to the cruelly graceless remark that kissing Marilyn was 'like kissing Hitler'.[114] She was involved sexually with some of the era's most famous and desirable men, including both John F. Kennedy and his brother Robert. Kennedy will feature in the next chapter, but it is worth noting here her remark on how fine it would be to have a President 'who was so young and good-looking'; and that he was better than old uglies who had neither brains *nor* beauty.[115]

Marilyn Monroe died from an over-dose of drugs. As is well known, her death was surrounded by some strange circumstances. It does seem clear that the announcement was held up for several hours (and there may even have been an attempt to resuscitate her), probably in order to cover up the association with Robert Kennedy. That she was actually murdered seems highly improbable; it is, however, quite likely that she did not consciously intend suicide.[116] Here these are not central matters: the point is that the great screen goddess, with an unprecedented reputation, had met a tragic death.

Let me repeat that the ascent from poor background, to early marriage, to factory work, to pin-up and call girl, and even to starlet, suggests the kind of career that was potentially open to poor, but beautiful, girls everywhere. Marilyn Monroe got her first breaks, such as they were, essentially because of her looks. She had ambition, dedication, special and appealing quirks of personality, and real talent: through these she achieved her exceptional position. But she also carried with her a terrible load of personality problems. No doubt the world in which she worked was a cruel and exploitive one. Much of her early progress, as with many other women, was due to granting sexual favours to powerful men, though this does not seem to have bothered her very much. Her time was one of continuing repression and hypocrisy and therefore, no doubt, a time of unnecessary stresses. Yet she did have many loyal and loving friends. We should ask here, how would Norma

Jeane have fared had she been plain? We don't know, of course, but to have had plainness added to everything else could well have meant an even unhappier life and perhaps an earlier tragedy. As to happiness, that is always hard to calculate. Marilyn Monroe did enjoy the fulfilment of relationships which, for short periods at least, went well, as with Miller and DiMaggio; she enjoyed beautiful men in her earlier life and famous ones in her later; above all, she had the fulfilment of resounding and acknowledged success in her chosen career as superstar. Personal beauty was the essential ingredient.

# 8 The International Cultural Revolution of the 1960s

## 1 *The Detonators of Change*

The first theme of this book is that at all times beauty has been recognized as having a special potency of its own, but that the implications of this, never entirely straightforward in any case, have usually been severely limited by the persistence of traditional conventions and myths. The various developments which, in shorthand fashion, can be subsumed under the term 'modernization' have led to some of these conventions and myths being challenged, but the traditional approach to beauty has proved extremely resilient: many today still hold to the older conventions and many more, perhaps, would dispute the very term 'myth'. Nevertheless, the coming together from the late 1950s onwards of certain economic, technological, social, cultural and political changes created that special phase of modernization best defined, for the purposes of this study, as the International Cultural Revolution of the 1960s. Entailed in this 'revolution' was the triumph of the 'modern' view of beauty, of beauty as an autonomous status characteristic – not, of course, in the hearts and minds of every single individual, but in society at large, in its public mores, its newspapers, its advertisements, its television programmes, its social, cultural and political behaviour. More and more people than ever before did in fact behave as if they recognized that 'mere' beauty had a particular value of its own. In the traditional view – and elements of the traditional view persisted well into the twentieth century – the major status characteristics were wealth and social position; beauty, apart from being an enticement to the sin of lust, was seen as a menace to both of these. In the 1960s beauty was universally praised and sought after; it had achieved a kind of parity with wealth and status, and certainly was no enemy to either.

Throughout this book, I have also stressed that, while the response to beauty is a deep sexual instinct, reasonable living standards and real opportunities for comparison, contrast and choice, as realized, for example, through living in a major urban centre, or through travel, or through cultural exchange, or through all three, are necessary for a full appreciation of beauty in its many varieties. Hence the primacy I give to the point that the cultural transformations of the 1960s were *international*. I have already drawn attention to the way in which, despite the many facile myths about a universal Americanization, Western Europe for most of the fifties was still very different from the United States, and the United States itself was in so many ways inward looking and parochial. But in the 1960s, European life styles and fashion penetrated even to the American Mid-West. International pop culture, with important components from black America and working-class Britain, became all pervasive. The United States and the world became aware as never before of the breathtakingly various types of beauty particular to America's very different ethnic groups or to certain types of intermarriage. On the screens of cinemas and of domestic television sets, in the European countries as in the United States, there appeared film stars and models drawn from a great array of geographical and national backgrounds.

The imperatives behind the International Cultural Revolution were, no doubt, primarily economic and technological though not, I think, exclusively so. Prior to 1955 very few multinational companies existed; by 1967, 187 of the US's five hundred largest firms were multinational, and between 1960 and 1970 their sales almost tripled.[1] However, many of the first initiatives towards the international culture – French discos in New York, or British pubs in San Francisco, say – were carried out by small entrepreneurs. Of the three countries which I have chosen for close study, the one demonstrating the most startling economic change is France. In the decade after 1954 France not only showed complete recovery from the depredations of war, but moved towards a new, highly efficient, highly co-ordinated, high-spending economy, in which the agricultural sector was both drastically reduced compared with pre-war times, and was itself highly mechanized. Changes in Britain were less profound, but Britain, though with lower growth rates than those of France and other industrialized countries, also moved towards what could not inaccurately be termed 'affluence'.[2] Britain, France and other European countries were no longer relatively passive victims upon which any old cultural rubbish from the United States could be dumped. They could buy, but they could now also produce and sell. Since the First World War the European countries had, in large quantities, taken the products of the Hollywood movie industry, themselves, as I have said, a factor in the widespread diffusion of standards of beauty. American dance music was also a considerable influence, but the main identifiably American products actually purchased by large numbers of families were those of the pre-packed food industry, soups and cereals in particular. One of the prime characteristics of Western society as it developed in the years after the Second World War, and particularly in the fifties and sixties, was that money became available, not just for the purchase of slightly fancy food stuffs, but for products associated with leisure hours, gramophone records, television sets, etc. Thus the pressures generated from within capitalism towards the international marketing of, say, Heinz soups, or Kelloggs Cornflakes, now turned more and more towards the international marketing of the sorts of products which are consumed in leisure time.

I don't wish to speak here of 'typical' individuals: the beauty of internationalism is that it throws up celebrities, who are 'different'. One was the Scottish actor Sean Connery, whose slow, deliberate Edinburgh accent had the perfect mid-Atlantic nuances and comprehensibility for the new international culture: he, as *Paris Match* pointed out in April 1963, exuded sex appeal, as did the actresses from many countries who appeared with him.[3] The same journal, towards the end of the same year, summed up the miscellaneous and cosmopolitan characteristics of the fashion designer who also achieved an international hegemony: Mary Quant's style was 'a little "beatnik", a little "cookie", a little "dandy"'.[4] An American fashion writer, remarking that 'all the girls copy one another', admitted that 'the trend-setters among them copy French and Italian film actresses as Hollywood stars seem rather behindhand nowadays'.[5]

In an international culture it was appropriate that there should be international love affairs, and sometimes international weddings, all publicized by the press, and thus again, of course, drawing attention to beauty in all its international glamour and variety. Triangular, quadrilateral, and still more complicated entanglements were for long an expected feature in Hollywood, but there was a European, indeed genuinely international, dimension to the thunderstorms in the *dolce vita* of world cinema, bringing together the names of the French film director Roger Vadim, his first great protégée, Brigitte Bardot, Annette Stroyberg, Sacha Distel, Yves Montand, Marilyn Monroe, and Montand's wife, Simone Signoret. The slightly parochial affair between British photographer David Bailey and British model Jean Shrimpton, both top international celebrities, was followed by the former's marriage to Catherine Deneuve, French film star of international eminence. A soppy little story carried by *Paris Match* in September 1965 about a couple of slightly less well-known individuals drives home my contentions about both the growth of the international dimension, and the enthusiastic participation of the press. The item is entitled 'The One Who Has Conquered the Most Beautiful Girl in the World: A French Student':

Ingrid, the beautiful fiancée from Nuremberg, cries out in French: 'How suntanned you are!' Roland, the French student, replies to her in German: 'Ich wusste dass du die Schönste warst!' [I knew very well that you were the most beautiful!] And Roland takes in his arms the girl whom he will marry in two years time, Ingrid Finger, twenty years old, whom a jury in Palm Beach has just consecrated 'Miss International Beauty 1965'. Their story is but one of the happy results of the extensive interchange between young people of the two countries: this year 150,000 young people aged twenty visited Germany. Three years ago Roland Cottrey, who had just passed his final school examinations, was on holiday near Sète. The Finger family happened to be passing through: Ingrid and her parents, citizens of Furth, a town near Nuremberg, were looking for a camping ground for the duration of their holiday.

And, beneath the sun of Hérault, the lightening struck. Ingrid and Roland together spent four weeks of bliss: swimming, volley ball, water skiing. When the holiday ended, Roland was already calling Ingrid by her family pet name, Ingelé [in French, little hedgehog]. He spent the Christmas vacation at Furth. She met his parents in Paris. In the meantime, Ingrid entered the Studio Suzanne, the school for models in Nuremberg. Her file contains her measurements: height 1 metre 70, weight 55 kilogrammes, bust 91 centimetres, waist 58 centimetres, hips 91 centimetres. And these perfect proportions contributed to her successive elections in 1965 as Miss Munich, Miss Bavaria and, on 14 May last, Miss Germany. Invited to Palm Beach, she walked off finally with the supreme accolade: the title of Miss International Beauty. Ingrid received a prize of ten thousand dollars, a gown of white silk, bracelets, a necklace and earrings. She wears that gown every evening and sleeps in her jewels. But she has deposited her ten thousand dollars in the bank: in two years time, she will marry Roland, who is finishing his studies at L'Ecole Nationale Supérieure de Chimie in Paris. These ten thousand dollars, they will be the dowry which Miss Beauty offers to the little Ingrid.

Whatever the defects of the literary and narrative style, the accompanying photographs show both Ingrid and Roland to be beautiful young people indeed.[6]

Female Hollywood stars of the fifties were beautiful alright, but, with the explosive exception of Marilyn Monroe, they tended to conform to a rather limited range of types consonant with the all-American ideals of domesticity discussed in the last chapter: big breasts were highly respected, but preferably allied to an air of innocent wholesomeness. The only challenge to Marilyn Monroe as the great sex goddess came from European stars appearing, initially, in European films: first Gina Lollobrigida, and then Vadim's 'discovery', Brigitte Bardot. The sexuality of these two actresses was as directly evident as that of Marilyn Monroe herself. A more interesting case for our present purposes is that of Monica Vitti, star of Antonioni's film of 1959, *L'Avventura*. Monica Vitti had a long, Roman nose, a lean, intensely sensitive look, and struck audiences at the time as being 'different'; different types of beauty were now acceptable as never before. Along with Monica Vitti there appeared for international audiences a rather special type of mature Italian male beauty, in the person of Marcello Mastroianni.

As new types of beauty, both male and female, forced their way onto the screens of some commercial cinemas, Hollywood itself began to see the virtues of international film making, where the low costs and high

110 Monica Vitti in *L'Avventura*, directed by Michelangelo Antonioni, 1960

talents of European countries could be exploited. Paramount's 1960 film about alleged female collaborators in the Second World War, *Five Branded Women*, was a classic in the genre of exploitation movies – films which, often behind the façade of an apparently serious topic, pandered to the audience's appetite for sex or violence or both – then coming into vogue. It called for five actresses who, appearing with their hair shorn, required a very high level of natural beauty. 'Paramount's latest wartime picture is a good example of the new international look in moviemaking. It was produced by Italy's Dino DeLaurentiis, directed by America's Martin Pit, and photographed in Italy and Austria. Its five shorn actresses were recruited from three countries – two each from the US and Italy, one from France.'[7] In January 1966 the cover story for *Life*, accompanying a photograph of Catherine Spaak, was simply 'The New Beauties'. In the table of contents the story was given as: 'Film Beauties of Europe: The Common Market has a Full Stock of Glamor'. Most revealing of all was the title at the head of the actual story inside: 'The New Freewheeling Film Beauties of Europe'. In the comments attributed to, or made about, these actresses, uninhibited expression is given to the notion of the autonomous value of beauty; the talent of these strikingly different women, it is made clear, lies almost exclusively in their personal appearance. Italy's Marilou Tolo, twenty-two, whose 'tawny good looks made her a fashion model at fifteen, a TV page girl at sixteen and a starlet at seventeen, has never had a camera problem'. Austria's Marisa Mell recognizes where she is, and why, at the age of twenty-four, in protesting: 'I can be more than my eyes and legs.' Most direct is Catherine Deneuve: 'I owe my start in movies entirely to my face and body.'[8]

British stars, each with particular qualities of beauty of their own, gained international renown as well: among women, Julie Christie and Vanessa Redgrave; among men, Peter O'Toole, Terence Stamp, Michael York and, as already mentioned, Sean Connery. If ever there was a time when one particular convention of beauty reigned above all others (and I have suggested that in real life as practised by flesh-and-blood people the writ of such conventions has always been limited anyway), that time was utterly destroyed in the 1960s with films, and, of course, television, presenting beauty in its many varieties (I shall come to non-Caucasian types shortly). With a pleasingly vulgar directness, the Italian actress Claudia Cardinale expressed to an American audience one of the possible consequences: 'You used to look only at the bosom. Now you look at the legs, the body, the whole girl.'[9] Many of the themes informing this

111

111 Terence Stamp, photograph, *c.* 1964

112 David Hemmings, photograph, 1967

chapter were clearly expressed in the English-language film which Antonioni made in London in 1967. Set in 'swinging London',[10] *Blow Up* features a successful photographer, Thomas, who has a corps of lovely cavorting dolly girls at his disposal, as well as encountering a rather classier young woman played by Vanessa Redgrave. Antonioni had in mind one of the famous real-life photographers, such as David Bailey or Lord Snowdon, and originally intended Terence Stamp for the part of Thomas. Stamp, however, being totally preoccupied with his current love affair (sign of the times), was not available, and the part went to the equally beautiful David Hemmings. Of these British male figures    112 Antonioni said: 'They are the heroes of the age, they have invented the new canons of beauty.'[11] Actually, they had not, in my view, invented new canons of beauty, but had revealed, what many had known previously, though were prevented by prevailing ideologies from saying: that beauty comes in different types and is to be found in males as well as females.

For reasons already explained I have deliberately stressed the international dimension. However, there were other forces more directly at work in changing sensibilities about the nature of beauty. Economic growth brought new spending power to certain important groups, most critically, young people in general, racial and ethnic minorities, the provinces as against the metropolis, and, to a perhaps less significant degree at this stage, women. Everywhere, throughout the sixties, youth, racial and ethnic communities, the provinces, and, eventually, feminists, were in revolt against old authorities and old conventions, and this could include, as we shall see, conventions about beauty. New sorts of women's magazines are an important phenomenon, and an important source for changing appraisals of beauty. So also is the American magazine *Ebony*, founded at the end of the Second World War in response to the emancipating effects that war had had (albeit in imperfect and ambiguous degree) on the 'Negroes' at whom the magazine was aimed:[12] in the sixties *Ebony* enjoyed a striking expansion in sales and in page upon page of up-market advertising.

A survey conducted over a fifteen-year period, and published just at the very end of the fifties, pinned down the essential features of the new status of the American teenager: 'the gap between generations is widening . . . and . . . both juveniles and parents are often baffled by the other's behaviour.'[13] The root of this disturbing phenomenon was the new spending power of the teenage consumer. Highschool boys and girls in America now had four times as much money to spend as their counterparts had had in 1945, two-thirds of this coming from their parents, one third from their own earnings. Children were now often making their own decisions, leaving their parents with little authority. 'Our salient discovery is that within the past decade the teenagers have become a separate and distinct group in our society.'[14] 'Your Teenager', said *American Mercury* in September 1958, 'is Big Business': about 800,000 teenagers had full-time jobs, with nearly 4,700,000 working part time; in the summer vacation the number of teenage earners rose to about 9,500,000. Government census bureau statistics showed that there were more highschool students working after school than at any time since the Second World War. The article then reported the discoveries of a businessman curious about teenage spending within his own household. He found that whereas his wife was buying three pairs of shoes a year, his fifteen-year-old daughter was buying six. He discovered further that his son was purchasing more socks, T-shirts and ties than he was. Finally, to keep his 1944 car running, his teenage son spent three times as much as the father on car maintenance.[15]

'They Will Be Our Rulers Tomorrow', declared a French account of April 1964, pointing out that in France there were five million young people between the ages of sixteen and twenty-four, born and living in a world full of change: the young person was a voter, but above all a purchaser.[16] The same article claimed that young people had none of the traditional respect for marriage as a means towards consolidating and perpetuating the family; as all surveys agreed, young people were more sexually active than the young of any previous generation. Conscious of the potency of their youthfulness, young people saw no need for fashions designed to conceal the imperfections of age, and little for the polite conventions which avoided the real facts of beauty and ugliness. The rise of youth was a universal phenomenon but, perhaps because Britain was in other respects so conservative and conformist, it was from that country that the impetus to the international youth style came. As Rudi Gernreich, Californian designer in 1964 of the topless bathing suit, put it: 'It really started, I would say, in the late Fifties in London. The young London people began to instinctively change their attitude in the way they dressed to symbolize what they stood for. Then all the young people from all over the world started to identify with what the British started.' You could almost say, he concluded, that 'the old adage "clothes make the man" just didn't apply any more'.[17]

It is not here argued that young people consciously adopted what I have called the 'modern' evaluation of beauty, nor that in the way they dressed they were issuing a conscious manifesto on behalf of that approach. Young people were very aware of image and identity, which was often a very different thing from showing off natural beauty, or the lack of it. But I do argue that the attitudes and behaviour of youth cut across some of the conventions which had continued to bolster the 'traditional' evaluation of beauty. The more thoughtful, and the more intellectual, among the young, principally those at universitites, did argue for a new kind of openness, a new honesty. A recent female graduate of Yale explained in October 1967:

I deeply feel the inadequacy of the values I learned while growing up. Categories of social worth; drive for possession of things and people; the academic definitions of what is worth knowing and doing; the myth of America's good intentions around the world – all of these break down in the search for what is really important, and for a style of life that has dignity.[18]

Such an outlook, obviously, could lead directly away from any preoccupation with personal appearance; yet the tone is that of openness, an openness which, as we shall see, reached an exaggerated form in those adopting an explicitly hippy life style. Openness in itself was part of the important revolution in sexual attitudes which we must now discuss.

Youth rose to unprecedented power just at a time when, in reaction to the generally narrow conformity still prevalent in the early fifties, a new uninhibitedness, a new openness, a new explicitness, a new 'permissiveness' (to use the word popularized in the sixties), was being engendered. There is a direct interrelationship: it had always been a function of age to try to control sexuality in the young; now the young were going their own way. However, the main origins of the transformation in sexual attitudes came from the adult world. The key points, in what might be termed the modernization of sex,[19] are sexual relations without risk of procreation (achieved, though insecurely, in the nineteenth century, consolidated somewhat in the twentieth) and then sexual relations without the necessity for marriage, a phenomenon of all eras, of course, but most widely evident and publicized from the 1960s onwards; the latest twist in the post-sixties period was to be the advent of conscious procreation without necessity for or intention of marriage. (The Aids scare may have re-emphasized the virtues of fidelity, but not necessarily those of marriage.) Apart, of course, from their relevance to this present study, these were developments of immense importance for many aspects of human history. Earlier, I made a threefold distinction between public mores, people's actual behaviour, and their private inclinations. In general, it was a result of the transformations of the sixties that the three came into closer congruence with each other than ever before. Nonetheless, the relationship between the different types of evidence and these three modes of attitude and behaviour remains problematic. Novels and films and the many artifacts of popular culture, together with the attitudes of the agencies of official and unofficial censorship, will tell us something about public mores; social investigations and surveys, of which there were many in the sixties, will tell us about all three modes, but may not always be altogether accurate on actual behaviour.

What is absolutely beyond dispute is that there was *change* and that, as far as such a chronological point can ever be established, the critical time was around 1959–60. It was in 1959 that the moves were concerted which led to the publication, prosecution for obscenity, and acquittal of the long-banned D. H. Lawrence novel (obtainable however in Paris) *Lady Chatterley's Lover*. Already in July 1959, in the United States, Judge Bryan had ruled that the book could legally be sent through the American mails, remarking that: 'the record . . . indicates general acceptance of the book' and adding that: 'in one best-selling novel after another frank descriptions . . . and "four letter" words appear with frequency'. His general conclusion was that: 'These trends appear in all media of public expression, in the kind of language used and the subjects discussed in polite society, in pictures, advertisements and dress, and in other ways familiar to see. Today such things are generally tolerated whether we approve or not.'[20] Again, the issue was international. *American Mercury*'s first article for 1960 was on 'The "Lady Chatterley's Lover" Case', while *Paris Match* took up the same matter in November, remarking that publication had essentially been authorized by 'a revolution in British morals', adding the explanation that, 'the war, the aeroplane, and cultural exchange with the continent had liberated the British from their ancient Victorian complex'.[21]

Far more important, however, were the changes in what was being shown in the cinemas of practically every town and village (the English town of Wakefield imposed a local ban on *Room at the Top*) in the West. The British film censors, with deliberate self-awareness, referred to the way in which they were now permitting love scenes in British films which not long before they would only have accepted in imported French films for adult audiences.[22] *Life*, in its issue for 29 February 1960, cited such recent Hollywood films as *Suddenly Last Summer, Anatomy of a Murder, The Best of Everything, A Summer Place, Blue Denim, It Started with a Kiss* and *North by North West* in support of its contention that there was 'a general awareness that American movies have suddenly become more "frank," "adult" or "dirty"'.[23] The Hollywood 'sexual revolution' of this time was a highly circumspect and controlled one – director Billy Wilder put it nicely in commenting that the times were 'almost right for a movie about a young man who has a passionate love affair with his mother. At the end he learns that she is not his mother and he commits suicide.'[24] But change there definitely was and, in many ways more important, the *belief* that there was change was widely diffused.

The point to be made about the sixties is not that vast numbers of people suddenly adopted promiscuity or permissiveness as a way of life – the evidence is overwhelmingly to the contrary – but that more and more people were making personal choices rather than choices decreed by convention or authority (these choices could often be in favour of the most conventional religious-based morality), and that the significance of sexuality and personal attractiveness was recognized more fully than ever before. In an interview given in New York, Alexander Plunket Greene, husband of Mary Quant, was quoted as saying: 'It used to be that a girl was attractive until she caught her husband. Then she let go. In England now, girls choose husbands because they like them. And they don't give up so soon.'[25] Ultimately, the advent and wide use of the female contraceptive pill was to have considerable impact; but although the 'era of the Pill' has been dated from the World Medical Conference held in Tokyo in 1955, its wide usage dates from the early seventies rather than from the 1960s. Still, an important point is that contraception was now widely talked about (in France, as well as in Britain and the United States) and so the notion of sexual permissiveness was widespread, even though, as was frequently shown, those practising it were usually not using the Pill and quite often were not using any contraceptive method at all. These varied, but highly significant, points emerge if we consider a survey conducted in England by Geoffrey Gorer in April and May 1969 (which can be compared with the earlier survey he carried out in January 1951).[26] In the 1951 survey only fifty-one per cent of women had declared sex to be very important in marriage; now sixty-seven per cent of women thought sexual love to be very important. Twenty-six per cent of men and sixty three per cent of women (in the 1969 survey) were virgins at the time of marriage; a further twenty per cent of men and twenty-six per cent of women had married the person with whom they had first had sexual relations. Two-fifths of all couples were not using any form of birth control; of the nineteen per cent of married women on the Pill there was a marked concentration in the younger and also in the wealthier groups. Gorer quoted the views on the Pill of a twenty-four-year-old wife of a schoolteacher, a highly religious Non-Conformist: 'Good. I was very biased against it medically when I first heard about it – but nothing based on real scientific knowledge. In all other respects it makes the love side of marriage so much freer, it can only be a good thing.' Gorer's findings did not suggest that the Pill was leading to infidelity among the married. To the question, 'Now that the pill provides absolute safety, do you think faithfulness is or is not as important as ever in marriage?', ninety-two per cent replied in the affirmative.

Of the unmarried people interviewed by Gorer, forty-four per cent said that they had a special girlfriend or boyfriend. But sexual permissiveness was very far from rampant in the Britain of the late sixties. What he really found was nothing too surprising: the immense variousness of human behaviour. However, the signs clearly are of a definite trend towards personal decision making and away from older social controls. Half of those with a regular boyfriend or girlfriend spoke of being on terms of 'real physical intimacy', but for a quarter of these, apparently, this did not include full sexual intercourse. On the one hand there was the twenty-one-year-old daughter of a railway worker who said: 'I have been brought up to believe that you should wait until you are married; and I think if you love someone enough you can be prepared to wait until marriage.' On the other hand was the nineteen-year-old lorry driver who had been sexually active from the age of fifteen and who remarked: 'If it comes along you don't turn it down'; and the eighteen-year-old daughter of a skilled worker, hoping to go to university, who had been sexually active at sixteen and replied: 'Twice a week if I like the boy. It depends on exams!' Gorer's findings can be amplified by the more detailed study of 1,873 young people aged fifteen to nineteen carried out by Schofield. Of these, only twelve per cent of the girls had had sexual intercourse, but of the engaged ones thirty-seven per cent were sleeping with their boyfriends. Another study, this time of third-year university students at Durham carried out in 1970, revealed that ninety-three per cent of the girls had been virgins when they came to university, but that by the third year the percentage had dropped to forty-nine.[27]

Use of contraceptives, or perhaps one should say effective use of them, had not kept pace with changes in moral attitudes. Gorer found that the majority of sexually active unmarried people were not regularly using any form of birth control. The consequences can be found in the official statistics: the number of illegitimate births had been five per cent of the total at the beginning of the fifties, was 5.8 per cent at the beginning of the sixties, and had risen to 8.2 per cent at the beginning of the seventies;[28] this was an indication, of course, not merely of promiscuity, but of the way in which illegitimacy was losing its Victorian stigma. In sexual behaviour, as in many other things, Britain was a more homogeneous country than either the United States or France. The US had its high-living university and higher professional communities, and also, in the later sixties, its growing hippy culture: the two rather came together in what was often recognized as a distinctive Californian culture. Elsewhere, the bible-belt ethics of traditional America still held sway. In France, while the sexual climate of intellectual Paris had always been freer than anywhere else in the West, there remained pockets of rural Catholic puritanism. Nevertheless, the fact of a general transformation in all three countries is undeniable. The articles of Françoise Giroud in *L'Express* are a sensitive chart to changing sensibilities in France,[29] and suggest that by November 1966 the mutation in sexual morality was widely spread: such popular women's journals as *Elle* and *Marie-Claire* were now openly discussing questions of sexual fulfilment.[30]

American academia in the late 1940s and early 1950s had produced the lumbering, circumlocutory Kinsey reports, *Sexual Behavior in the Human Male* (1948) and *Sexual Behavior in the Human Female* (1954). Probably only the American academic community could have produced the immensely detailed experiments and surveys which resulted in the publication in Boston in 1966 of *Human Sexual Response* by William Masters and Virginia Johnson. Masters and Johnson had no difficulty in recruiting volunteers for their many fascinating experiments: their book rather echoed changes already taking place than sponsored them. Two features of the Masters and Johnson report are of particular significance for my own study. First of all, that their very frank and nakedly physical findings could be openly published in all their explicit detail, and then fully and publicly discussed, helps make my point about a completely new openness in the discussion of all matters relating to sexuality and physical attractiveness. Secondly, Masters and Johnson were at great pains to suggest the essential similarities in male and female sexual responses and behaviour. It may (or may not, I am not qualified to speak) be true that they allowed an ideological commitment to the notion of complete equality and parity between men and women to colour what the actual empirical evidence proved: what is important is that here was weighty support for the argument that women should choose their men in the way that men, given complete freedom, had tended in the past to choose their women.

The sixties could well be termed 'the era of the explicit': explicitness almost always meant explicitness in sexual matters, but this necessarily involved explicitness about the facts of sexual appeal and therefore of personal appearance. Now, I must repeat that I do not ignore the factors, entirely apart from physical beauty, which can lead to sexual attraction and love; sixties freedom meant the freedom of personal choice, and personal choice is based on many factors. But it did also entail the freedom to remark on the blunt facts of personal appearance in a manner which broke the long-held conventions of polite society, where a woman was pretty by virtue of being a woman, and a man was measured by his achievements, not his looks. In discussing 'the beautiful people' (and some of the ugly ones) in the next section, I will report more fully on the comments about the personal appearance of real people made during the sixties. Here I just want to comment briefly on the development of an environment in which it became more common for blunt judgments on personal appearance to be uttered. The overwhelming number of private conversations are never recorded, of course, so we do not really know the sorts of things people actually said to each other about their looks. My evidence must largely come from popular periodicals, newspapers, films, and from the new school of naturalistic novels, featuring such writers as Kingsley Amis (in the UK), Bernard Malamud, Norman Mailer and Philip Roth (in the USA) and Françoise Sagan (in France), launched in the early fifties but becoming in the late fifties and in the sixties more pervasive and more representative of life as widely lived.

One of the great strengths of Amis as a novelist is his ability to record accurately the things people actually think and indeed say, rather than what, by polite convention, they ought to think and say. There is a fair amount about personal appearance in Amis's first novel, *Lucky Jim* (1953). The matter becomes almost a major sub-theme in *Take a Girl Like You* of 1960, where Graham McClintock is clearly identified as a funny-looking character whose consistent run of misfortunes springs from the fact that women find him deeply unattractive and very easy to exploit. Amis describes him as 'a chap so clearly constructed for the Glasgow music-halls, a chap whose whole frame cried out so audibly for a glengarry, a kilt and a curly walking-stick'. McClintock himself at one point cries out that people too readily assume that ugly men are quite happy to pair off with ugly women when in fact they want beautiful women just as much as other men do.[31] Possibly the clearest expression of beauty as an autonomous status characteristic is to be found in John Braine's novel of 1957, *Room at the Top*: Charles, boyhood friend of the hero, Joe Lampton, had evolved a system of grading women from one to ten, the women in the top grades being those with the greatest physical beauty, and the implication being that rich and successful men got their women from the top grade, others having to make do with lesser grades.[32] The film of this novel (released in 1959), which was of course aimed at mass audiences, actually slips back towards the more traditional position in which the grading, devised by Joe Lampton himself, is linked to social class rather than mere beauty. Thus the immensely wealthy Susan Brown, only rated grade two in the book, is unambiguously rated grade one by Joe, stressing her upper-class position rather than her sex appeal; a good-looking working-class girl, beautiful but dressed very tartishly, is rated grade ten. So the matter is far from clear cut; but what is happening is that personal beauty is being openly discussed in relation to the other more traditional status attributes of class and wealth. In certain circles, mainly those dominated by young people, there was a fetish for openness and honesty in personal relationships, most strongly asserted in the Californian subculture; this did not necessarily mean complete explicitness about personal appearance, but it could be a precondition for such explicitness. A hostile reporter recorded that 'openness in speech is more than an occasional matter, even more than a habit: it is a code. The code not only prohibits indirection, but frowns on the use of the conventional language of social deceit.'[33] Social deceit, and of course all the little polite conventions which make civilized life possible, necessarily continued: but it was becoming possible to say in the sixties, not that the emperor had no clothes, but that what he had under his clothes was scarcely worth looking at.

In this section I have talked of the internationalization of culture, the new imperatives of youth and other hitherto underprivileged groups, and the growth of new sensibilities in regard to matters of sexuality and physical attractiveness. Lastly, in setting the context for the study of more specific developments, I must mention the explosion in mass communications, with particular reference to television, and to the new style of advertising usually associated with Madison Avenue, but also developing semi-independently in Paris and in London. Advertising may well be thought the very soul of deceit, the sworn enemy of the frankness and openness of which I have just been speaking. But the new advertising of the sixties was also bold, uninhibited, witty, naturalistic rather in the way of an Amis novel, explicit, and, of course, fully exploitive of the appeal of a beautiful face and figure, whether female or male.[34] The beauty was that of anonymous models rather than of people of established status (though modelling quickly became a means of achieving status). The new advertising was involving, rather than distant and authoritarian; it advertised the artifacts of the consumer society, rather than the quack medicines of the past. The fifties had been the great age of the expansion of television in the United States; it was in the sixties that television also became the basic visual medium in France and Britain. International beauties continued to be recruited into everyone's consciousness through film, but television, situated in the family sitting room, is far more intimate and involving than film: in that process of comparison, contrast and choice to which I have already several times referred, the beautiful person on the small screen in the sitting room is an even more disturbing phenomenon than the beautiful person at some distance on the large screen.

## 2 *Miniskirts, Blacks and Beautiful People*

Because of rising living standards and better medical care, young people growing up in the later fifties and early sixties were stronger and healthier than ever before. Phrases like 'people were more beautiful than ever before' (or 'the Italians are lovelier than the French') are imprecise and unsatisfactory. What happened was that those born with a good bone structure and balanced features were less likely now to fall victim along the way to some wasting or deforming disease, or even to bad teeth. Thus the proportion of beautiful people in the population did go up. More important, the proportion of the personable in the population, those whose attractiveness lay in their healthy youthfulness and general vivacity, rather than any rare distinction of beauty, also went up. Of course, physical handicaps of many sorts persisted, but the toll of deficiency diseases and congenital deformities declined.

If there were more beautiful young people around, and very many more lively and personable ones, can one also argue that the youthful fashions of the sixties were simply designed to enable these young people to show off their natural attributes in the most direct way? Such an argument would not be incorrect, but, given the complex processes which always lie behind fashion changes, it would be incomplete. However, for our present purposes the crucial point is that the distinctive styles of the early and mid-sixties definitely did not conceal imperfections, nor did they establish a model silhouette which could then be widely imitated; what they did do was to expose natural endowments. Tight, unpleated, hip-slung trousers, based on the traditional American blue jean, but developed from a shop established in Carnaby Street, near Oxford Circus in London, by the young Scottish dress designer John Stephen, admirably suited shapely young men, but did nothing to hide scrawny legs or protuberant stomachs. The attention to male fashion, and therefore to male personal appearance, is of great significance. However, it may be noted that, although the general shape of the male leg was now shown off, the leg itself remained concealed. There was almost no concealment in the miniskirt, invented for female wear by the British designer Mary Quant in 1964.

It is probably true that all fashion in some way or another serves an erotic purpose, but miniskirts were quite explicitly and directly sexual, drawing the eye as they did high up the thigh; on a young woman with shapely legs they were absolutely ravishing. Their spread from avant-garde circles in London was relatively slow, but over the next two to three years they asserted increasing sway, even over those to whom they were very little suited. They were succeeded by the equally revealing, though, despite the name, not so erotically enticing, hot pants. Then, having gone through the process of exaggeration, fashion now went through that of reaction, and dress lengths were shortly back where they had been in Edwardian times. But the internal logic of fashion is distinct from the main point being made here that it had been stated more definitively than ever before that if a young woman had the natural endowments of beauty she had no need of the concealments of fashion as traditionally understood.

Of course, there were many reasons for girls to wear what they did:

they might desire to shock, they might desire to allure, or they might simply desire to be informal and comfortable, as when wearing a male football jersey as a miniskirt, or a pair of jeans. A prime example of fashion's natural tendency towards exaggeration, and the stress of the times on natural sexuality, was the invention by Rudi Gernreich of the topless bathing suit. It was a few more years before common sense and convenience, and a rejection of the pointless taboos of conventional society, led many women at bathing beaches simply to leave off the tops of their bikinis. For some women who in the later sixties and early seventies gave up wearing brassieres, it was a matter of political protest (brassieres, somewhat illogically, being equated with male oppression of women), for others it was a matter of comfort and convenience, and for still others again part of a realization that (something feminists ignored) there were few more enticing sights than the outline of breasts unconstrained by a brassiere.

Fashion was not fixed forever in the sixties, but continued to evolve, change, go backwards. But no one fashion ever again set one universal convention as it had previously done; women and men could pick and choose as to what they thought suited them personally, and it was now open to a woman to choose the style which quite nakedly showed off her best features. Whatever the motivations and intentions, this did in fact involve a recognition of the intense power of beautiful natural endowments, as distinct from the artificialities of fashion and costume. I do not wish to overstate the case for 'naturalness' because, with all the concentration on personal appearance, there was also a vogue for one particular device which can scarcely be described as natural, that is the wig. But the fundamental consideration remains, and was well summed up by the *New York Times* fashion reporter Marilyn Bender in 1967: 'The purpose of fashion used to be dissimulation, the pretence that women were pretty, had perfect bodies, romantic spirits and that they were essentially helpless. Pop fashion, like pop art, lays the subject on the line. Fatty knees, wrinkled elbows, ruthless natures are exposed for all to see.'[35] Or, as *Life* put it at the end of the decade: 'Fashions came and went – instantly – but the basics were dependably conspicuous.'[36]

The new fashions showed off the natural endowments of youth, just as the new internationalism showed off the varieties of beauty from many different countries. This book is deliberately confined to Western civilization, partly because, as a matter of objective fact, it is Western civilization which still dominates the world, but mainly because I simply have no qualifications to write on any other civilizations. Yet, what of that minority community within the United States, that of the Afro-Americans, blacks, or, in the language both of white Americans and of themselves at the beginning of the 1960s, 'negroes'? (It is one obvious sign of the growing influence of this underprivileged minority that by the end of the decade 'negro' has given place to 'black' or 'Afro-American'.) My main source is *Ebony*, by the end of the fifties a large and lavishly produced monthly colour magazine, owned by a black family and produced by a mixed staff on which blacks were in a majority, selling three quarters of a million copies, and probably reaching a total of five million readers. The quality of the writing and of the photojournalism in *Ebony* is very high indeed; the tone is liberal, common sense, strongly in favour of black civil rights, and deeply proud of black achievements within the framework of American society. (To see *Ebony*, or any other journal for that matter, as the voice of all blacks would, of course, be absurd.) Consistently, there is throughout a very heavy emphasis on questions of personal appearance, discussed at two quite different levels. Most of the items are relatively trivial in nature, though, even so, informed with a sharp practicality and wit, apparently being mainly aimed at black women exercised by the problems of securing a husband; but some articles firmly tie in the question of personal appearance with that of civil rights – as blacks become more assertive and more powerful, they must present an appearance of which all blacks can be proud.

Before looking at these matters, and then going on to the quite cataclysmic changes in black attitudes towards beauty which take place in the middle of the decade, I want to establish a little more firmly the background and aims of *Ebony*. A photo editorial in the issue for July 1956, referring in particular to the Montgomery boycott organized by the Reverend Ralph D. Abernathy, talked of the emergence of 'a new kind of Negro', adding 'see photo on opposite page'. The photo shows a very dapper black man, in soft hat, short overcoat, carrying gloves and briefcase, and about to board an Eastern Airlines plane: the emphasis is firmly on the importance of self-presentation. Almost ten years later, in November 1965, in an article on what it called its 'nativity', *Ebony*, as it were, set out its stall within the context of the changing economic position of the black American.

To 'accent the positive' as EBONY has done, is to give Negro America a sorely needed psychic lift. Nowhere is this lift more in evidence today than in the advertisements of high caliber which it has attracted to its pages within the last decade. When EBONY first began publication, it had never occurred to most national manufacturers of commodities which millions of Negroes as well as whites buy, to place advertisements in Negro publications. When major firms did advertise in the Negro press, which was very seldom, it never crossed their minds to use Negro faces in the ads, or to picture black youngsters eating national brand cereals, or colored people riding in an automobile, be it Ford or Lincoln, or buying a soft drink for their children. Now in EBONY there are strikingly beautiful ads of Negroes doing all these things.

Look at the handsome young brownskin couple extolling the delights of Coca Cola in fullpage color, or the good-looking young Negro in the 'Camel Time' ad, the stunning brown girl smoking a Newport, and those wholesome Negro families now pictured getting into sleek and shining cars. Twenty years ago, to expect to see such advertisements in a colored magazine would have been unthinkable. In the field of the American commercial, EBONY had been as much of a pioneer as was brownskin Matt Henson when he became the first man to set foot on the North Pole. That EBONY can now afford not only to have color covers, but feature articles *in color* inside the magazine is due to its determined and dogged assault on the white battlements of Madison Avenue advertising. It was not easy to make 'the walls come tumbling down.' But they did. Result: now even the New York Times, Life and The New Yorker picture Negro models in ads – not of the once popular 'ham what am' variety, either.

Five years after the birth of EBONY, its publisher presented a series of authenticated facts to the advertising agencies that helped open their eyes to the dollar value of the Negro market. Nine out of ten EBONY readers carried life insurance. Four out of ten EBONY readers owned cars. Two out of ten in 1950 possessed television sets, and the same percentage bought pianos. One out of four had graduated from college and were potential culture buyers. EBONY had its circulation authenticated by the Audit Bureau of Circulations, and its contents indexed in the Readers' Guide to Periodical Literature. The result is that today EBONY'S advertising is voluminous, the format of the ads most attractive and, if they were to be one hundred per cent visually believed, *all* Negro Americans are good looking. (Typical example, the charming *café au lait* couple at their lovely dining table advertising Simplicity patterns.) To see ourselves presented so handsomely in commercial advertising (which now has spread to other national publications) is a great positive achievement due to EBONY.[37]

*Ebony* did indeed carry a large number of advertisements featuring black models; it also carried a very large number of advertisements for hair straighteners, skin whiteners, and many other beauty aids designed to help blacks look as much like whites as possible. It was, as we have already seen, the orthodoxy of the late fifties that black women, if not black men, should always straighten their hair. As well as regular articles on grooming and make-up, and on fashion, there were frequent articles on beauty competitions, on the personal appearance of famous black women, on 'best-dressed Negro women', on such questions as 'what is the best age for beauty?' (treated in a rather typical double-edged, witty way – 'beauty experts say women, like wines, improve with age', but 'science, skin specialists, even Doctor Kinsey, have not succeeded in dousing the average male's enthusiasm for a young bustling companion'),[38] and each year, in June, an article on 'eligible bachelors'. These last features do not in any way, as one might at first imagine, take the line that men should be assessed on their looks – in fact most of those selected were earnest, bespectacled, and distinctly unglamorous, what they stood for being primarily economic success; the cutting edge of every article was what these men were looking for in a woman. Yet even in this exercise *Ebony* manages some of its usual double-edged wit:

'baseball player Willy McCobey, 24', one of the 1962 eligible bachelors, 'of the San Francisco Giants describes his ideal woman as sports minded, honest and understanding, with charm and beauty. Being a realist he says he'll sacrifice a little beauty if the woman has all the other qualities.' The summing up for 1964 was: 'As with last year's round-up, the bachelors placed a premium on brains and personality but admitted that beauty still rates as a strong consideration.' The summary for the following year gives the same emphasis to intellectual and other sterling qualities, but then adds with significant use of block capitals, 'NOT ONE OBJECTS TO BEAUTY'.[39]

At the core of all this lies the assumption (never in any way stated explicitly) that a black woman will have a struggle to attain even a plain, though economically successful and upwardly mobile, black man and that indeed (though this is never even suggested explicitly) she will be lucky to do so. Her energy should be directed to making herself look as much like a white woman as possible. It is recognized that a black man may occasionally marry a white woman; this will happen when the black man is economically very successful so that the marriage will actually represent an economic and social advancement for the white woman concerned. The question is not broached of whether it is a sign of status for a black man to manage to marry a white woman; nor is there any hint of the even more distressing possibility that black men actually find most white women more beautiful than most black women. However, in December 1965 there was a sad letter from a black girl ('I'm considered pretty') lamenting that black men were going after white women and ignoring black ones, while white men were not going after black girls.[40] When, at the end of the decade, Hollywood did get round to treating this issue in *Guess Who's Coming to Dinner* (a very honourable and very witty film, though reviewed by one black critic as 'warmed over white shit') the relationship was black man–white woman, and the man was mature and very successful, the woman very young. The black man's father, not knowing at the time that the son's intended was white, actually unloaded the remark that it was entirely proper for a husband to be fifteen years or so older than his wife.

The successful black women featured by *Ebony* all had the whitified look; this is particularly evident in the cover and illustrating article of October 1961 on – and the pun may have been intended – 'Ebony Fashion Fair Beauties'.[41] Wherever black girls did well in beauty competitions open to both blacks and whites *Ebony* was there reporting enthusiastically; invariably what the black girls won was never more than a consolation prize, but then, as seen in *Ebony*'s highly professional photography, they were never particularly beautiful (in the sense in which I use the word throughout this book). The puzzle is explained when it is appreciated that these competitions featured 'talent': usually singing ability, as well as mere physical beauty. The heading in the issue of September 1958 was

'SAN FRANCISCO BEAUTY "FIRST"': Negro Girl makes way to city finals'. The actual story is not so up-beat:

When beauties representing all the states and several territories of the US gather in Atlantic City to compete for the Miss America title this month, there will not be a Negro girl among them – but the hand-writing is on the wall. It was put there by diminutive Carolyn Smith, a San Francisco State College student, whose showing in the Frisco contest served notice that Negro-American beauties can hold their own with the best.

Carolyn, 18, breezed through the preliminaries, survived the semi-final round and walked off with the crown as "Miss Grand Talent" and "Miss Congeniality" and one of the city's nine finalists.

The Queen's tiara went to hazel-eyed, bronze-tressed Judy Wilson, 20, a class mate of Carolyn's at San Francisco State.[42]

In the summer of 1965 a 'Negro girl' did win a victory of sorts, but again the story, under the heading of 'NEGRO GIRL IN "MISS AMERICA" RACE: Voice student wins "Miss Rochester" title', was more revealing than the editors seemed to realize:

Sarah says she didn't know measurements were 36, 24, 35 until judges told her, adds: 'I guess they are right.' Class mate Carol Game was Sarah's runner-up for title. Second balloting gave title to Sarah after a tie between the two. Girls were judged on five qualities: bathing suit appearance, talent (50%), formal gown appearance, charm and poise. Said one judge: 'It was close between Carol and Sarah. But Sarah placed very high on talent.'[43]

My deduction from all this would be that black women were not really expected to look beautiful, though they were expected to be able to sing. Some black women, of course, *were* very beautiful, and in the less prejudiced international scene at the Cannes Film Festival black models won titles as International Queen of the Cannes Film Festival in 1959, and again in 1960.

It is 1966 which emerges as the fulcrum year of change, and I can set this up nicely with reference again to the *Ebony* issue of November 1965. As well as the article about 'Ebony's nativity', this issue also contained an article on men's fashions, referring to 'the shaped, tight-fitting line which highlights the body'; more germane to my present purpose, it contained an article entitled 'Instant Hair'. This, significantly enough, was a witty and light-hearted article on a topic which had always been of deathly seriousness for black women. Referring to her own 'clowning glory' the author notes that, in imitation of 'the Beatle Baez look', whites are now straightening out their curly hair: 'the finest human hair is European . . . American hair, they say, is too brittle for wig-making. And Negro hair? We are basically consumers, remember? Not pro-ducers.' The article is essentially in celebration of the many varieties of wig now available. What is most significant is that this article provoked a pointed, and even angry, reader's letter, published in the January 1966 issue:

It seems to me there is an on-going need for practical fashion and beauty information for women of color. I am sick of seeing negro women 'lift' make-ups intended for the 'natural' look on white skin, transformed to the 'unnatural' look on us. Isn't it possible to assemble and present shades, tones, colors, hues, etc., that are appropriate to our color ranges, and face types? I have seen enough bleached blondes to make me everlastingly determined not to lead this one life in such a horrifying, stupefying and shocking manner. Nor will white lipstick ever enhance the natural beauty of my lips. I have looked at white fashion and glamor magazines that give instructions for improving everything from tired hair to tired feet and go through mental gymnastics trying to figure what and how much can be appropriated – not to mention the dollars invested on experimentation. With a daughter approaching her teens, I become very conscious of this especially when she asks, 'Is it true, blondes have more fun?' Maybe – but who the devil wants to be the object of it, especially behind one's back? I am sure there are many others who feel the same way.[44]

In the very next issue (no doubt planned several months in advance) *Ebony*, nevertheless, plunged straight on with a full-colour cover entitled ARE NEGRO GIRLS GETTING PRETTIER? The six models on the cover and most of the women photographed inside were of the usual *Ebony* type. The verbal message inside was basically: 'experts say better nutrition, grooming know-how have brought improvement'. Gone, claimed the article, 'are the spindly legs, sagging bosoms, unruly rumps and ungroomed heads that marred many a potential lovely of yesteryear. Such common flaws have been displaced by a feminine refinement, both facial and physical, that has elevated today's young lady of hue to a place of prominence among the most pulchritudinous.'[45]

The article provoked some stinging letters, four of which demand quotation in all their pungent fullness.[46] The first is essentially traditional in attitude, but the other three are bombshells:

How dare you? We Negro women are the only women in the world who don't get any praise for our beauty. Now you decide to write an article called, 'Are Negro Girls Getting Prettier?' We have been pretty all along. Just up until a few years ago we had no access to cosmetics, wigs, etc. White women have been using these things for years, and could afford them I might add. I suggest you rephrase your article to: 'Are Negro People (male or female) Getting Smarter?' According to that article you published, no – dumber.

Now the three bombshells:

Your February, 1966 issue of the magazine asks the question: 'Are Negro Girls Getting Prettier?' Why don't you put some Negro girls so we can see (instead of the half white)? Are you ashamed of the Negro girl? Or do you go along with the white man's premise that a Negro can only be good-looking when he/she is mixed with the white race?

The cover of your (Feb) issue delivered today made me (and a lot of other people I'll wager) wince. It should be titled 'Are Negro Girls Getting Whiter?'

Come to my high school and I'll show you some girls to photograph who will illustrate, I believe, that Negro girls have always been pretty.

Yes, Negro girls are getting prettier! But your cover is a refutation of the statement. The majority of us are dark brown with bold features. The girls on your cover do illustrate various types of beauty. You have, however, omitted several other beautiful types which are much more typical of our people.

In June 1966 *Ebony*, itself, editorially made the break. The cover heading was: 'THE NATURAL LOOK: New Mode For Negro Women'. The cover photograph was of the most beautiful black woman I personally have ever seen, an absolutely beautifully proportioned and intensely appealing face, surmounted by close-cropped fuzzy hair. (To my regret, because of invasion of privacy legislation, I have been unable to obtain a print of this photograph.) For once this was no model or blues singer, it was Diana Smith, a twenty-year-old Chicago civil rights worker. The main article inside, 'The Natural Look: Many Negro women reject white standards of beauty', is of such seminal significance that I have to quote extensively from it.

A Frenchman who had been in this country but a short time was astonished to encounter on the street one day a shapely, brown-skinned woman whose close-cropped, rough textured hair was in marked contrast to that of Brigitte Bardot – or any other woman he'd ever seen. Intrigued by her extraordinarily curly locks, he rushed up to her and blurted in Gallic impulsiveness: 'But I thought only Negro *men* had kinky hair!'

His prior observation had not been entirely incorrect, for, throughout the ages, American women of color have conspired to conceal the fact that their hair is not quite like any other. This key element in the black female's mystique was, until recently, challenged only by a few bold bohemians, a handful of entertainers and dancing ethnologists like Pearl Primus, whose identification with the exotic placed them beyond the pale of convention. But for the girl in the street – the coed, the career woman, the housewife, the matron and even the maid who had been born with 'bad' or kinky hair, the straightening comb and chemical processes seemingly offered the only true paths to social salvation.

Not so today, for an increasing number of Negro women are turning their backs on traditional concepts of style and beauty by wearing their hair in its naturally kinky state. Though they remain a relatively small group, confined primarily to the trend-making cities of New York and Chicago, they are frequently outspoken, and always aware of definite reasons why they decided to 'go natural'.

'We, as black women, must realize that there is beauty in what we are, without having to make ourselves into something we aren't,' contends Suzi Hill, 23-year-old staff field worker with the Southern Christian Leadership Conference. A veteran of the Dixie civil rights fight currently involved in Dr Martin Luther King's crusade against Chicago slums, she is quick to add, 'It's practical. It rids us of those frustrations Negro women knew so well, the fears that begin when you're little. So many little Negro girls feel frustrated because their hair won't grow, or because they have what is called "bad" hair. They aren't made to realize that they have nothing to be ashamed of and go through a life-time of hiding from themselves – avoiding swimming, being uneasy at dances when they start to perspire, because their hair will "go back," running from the rain. By the time they're adults, this feeling has become so much a part of them they're even afraid to answer the telephone if their hair hasn't been done. Negro women are still slaves, in a way.'

'Economics is a part of it too,' notes Diana Smith, 20, another stalwart at King's urban headquarters where natural hair has become a badge of honor. 'It's a shame, but many poor Negro housewives take money that should be grocery money and use it to get their hair done. Now that wigs have come along, I see kids whose families are on welfare, wearing them to high school – wigs and raggedy coats. Society has forced the standard of straight hair on them to the extent where they feel it's something for which they should sacrifice.'

Though a note of protest underscores the commentary of most in the natural hair coterie, others present varied reasons for having made the big change. Singer Abbey Lincoln, who has been extolling natural styles and 'the beauty of the American black woman' for more than five years, asserts, 'Mother Nature is always right and we should concentrate on enhancing what has been given to us. Our women have always had a thing about their hair in this country, but that day is on its way out.' A young art student who hasn't straightened her hair for two years, remarks, 'I never liked elaborate curls. I just feel more black and realistic this way.' An interior designer who alternates between periods of naturals and processes says, 'I believe in choosing whatever goes best with my features and the feeling I want to express. That long, straight Caucasian look just doesn't go with me.' A part-time model states, 'It was the natural thing to do. After all, I wasn't born with a straightening comb in my head.' And a New York clerical worker simply states, 'I just got tired of getting up every morning and trying to touch up those edges before I went to work.'

While some are willing to concede that 'A woman shouldn't wear a natural if she doesn't feel comfortable with it, but she should have the right to make a choice,' others preach the gospel of kinkiness, viewing the trend not as a fad, or style, but more a religious crusade from which no potential convert should escape . . .

Though hair has become the focal point in this muted rebellion against prevailing beauty standards, it cannot be separated from other changes taking place in the psyche of the American Negro. 'Black people have been taught to be ashamed of themselves and their blackness for so long that it has been difficult for them to accept each other,' comments a New York clothing designer. 'Lips are only right if they're thin, and so are noses. You'd be surprised at the number of people who wear only clothing that is black, brown, or of other dark shades – especially if they happen to be dark-skinned. They must be taught to be proud of themselves as belonging to a beautiful people, a proud people.'[47]

Of the letters printed in reaction to this article, eight expressed strong hostility to the idea of the natural look, seven strong support, though one of these noted that opinion among those with whom she had discussed the matter was overwhelmingly against; two further letters did not express an opinion either way.[48] The arguments against tended to take the line that since white women spent hours beautifying themselves, and usually started out with hair whose 'natural state is stringy and straggly', why shouldn't black women do the same?, or suggested with heavy sarcasm that the next stage would be grass huts and 'rings through our noses'. The most positive response with respect to the natural look actually being appealing, as distinct from racially correct, came from a white, and male, reader:

To me the women photographed to illustrate it were among the most beautiful I had ever seen. The 'white standards of beauty' they reject are the same standards that choke our cities and suburbs with garish ugliness.
    May we all become more natural . . . in every way!

The most pungent female expression of hostility was:

It may not be a secret that our hair is the so-called 'bad' type and gives us trouble sometimes, but let's assure this: 'We don't have to go around PROVING it!'

Over a year later, *Ebony* returned to the topic, with the cover featuring 'Natural Hair – New Symbol of Race Pride', but this time showing leading male singers and actors. For the first time reference is made to the new slogan of the black liberation movement, 'Black is Beautiful'. In the analytical terms of this book, black is no more beautiful than white is beautiful. The relevance for our study of the upheavals of the sixties is that they helped to bring about an appreciation that to attain some kind of acceptability it was not necessary for black women to pass themselves off as imitation white women, and that, indeed, some black women were extremely beautiful in their own right and in their own style. Inevitably, many blacks, men and women, like many whites, remained plain or ugly; the sad fact was probably that, on the standard of beauty as a 'relative universal' (within the evolution of Western society), a higher proportion of the ill favoured were to be found among blacks. And just as the miniskirts and hot pants of the sixties gave way to other fashions, so very many black women continued to opt for Caucasian hairstyles. (It should be noted that many blacks have a considerable admixture of white genes, with the result that their hair is often naturally straight anyway.) The enduring point is that new choices had been opened up, and beauty was being recognized as a natural physical quality, not something related to the slavish imitation of convention.

It was a part of the new sensibility, tied also to further reforms in favour of greater equality for women, and to the activities, particularly in the United States, of the Women's Liberation Movement, that the actual personal appearance of men, as well as their clothing styles, was receiving more and more attention. In March 1964 a top male film actor had this written about him:

While most people who have seen him agree that his boyish face belies his 37 years, they would disagree with his self appraisal of 'averageness'. At six-foot-two, he is four inches taller than the average American male and there is nothing average about the feline grace of contained power with which he moves his lean frame across the stage or screen.

Undoubtedly one of Poitier's biggest assets in today's climate of changing racial values is the dark complexion of his handsome, clean-cut face.

Sidney Poitier had himself modestly said: 'I am blest with a kind of physical averageness that fits Negroes between 18 and 40. I look like what producers are looking for.'[49] The real point was that Poitier's colour was no longer an obstacle to the perception on all sides that he was

113 Sidney Poitier, photograph, *c.* 1967

a very handsome man. And whatever the confusion still attending black 113
women in America, one, a model from Detroit, had established herself
on the European scene by mid-1966 as one of the most photographed
models of the time: Donyale Luna.

This really does drive home the point that the many varieties of beauty
were now being recognized. It is simply not a matter of Jean Shrimpton's
type of beauty being 'in' one year, and that of Twiggy the next. Such
being the way of the fashion industry, and such the way of the mass
media, it is true that one type would be very strongly featured at one
point in time, and another at another; but for ordinary people with
ordinary reactions, both Twiggy and Jean Shrimpton, and many, many
others in all sorts of different types, were beautiful. The achievement of
the sixties was that there was less pressure than ever before to conform to
dictates and conventions in this matter.

I concentrate for a moment on Jean Shrimpton ('The Shrimp') and
Twiggy (born Lesley Hornby) partly because, in respect of recognition
in the annals of history, they will stand with Ninon de Lenclos, Nell
Gwyn, Lola Montez, Lillie Langtry and Marilyn Monroe (that they
should do so is in itself an historical phenomenon of the greatest
significance), but also because, though they were exceptionally gifted,
and exceptionally fortunate, their careers do give an insight into the way
in which opportunities for the beautiful had again broadened and
changed.

First there is the great, and I think insufficiently recognized, paradox,
which I have already alluded to once or twice. In the climate of
explicitness the relationship between beauty and sexuality was more
openly paraded than ever before; among the highest of compliments was
to call someone 'sexy' (in a subsequent decade the phrase 'sex appeal'
came, repetitiously and tediously, to be used metaphorically, as in
'subsidized bus services have political sex appeal') and sexual attractiveness and sexual success were among the most greatly envied and most
highly prized attributes. Yet, whereas the fame and fortune of Ninon de
Lenclos, Nell Gwyn, Lillie Langtry and, in some degree at least, Marilyn
Monroe, had depended on the granting of sexual favours to men, the
sheer economic demand now for beautiful faces meant that women,
while in a sense exposing their sexuality (as of course did men in similar
roles), were not required to grant actual sexual favours. This had been a
long, steady process: many actresses (Sarah Siddons for instance) had
made it on looks and talent alone, as subsequently did many film stars,
including, for example, Greta Garbo.

The late fifties and early sixties mark a culmination and a multiplica-
tion of certain cultural aspects of those developments which, with my
usual hesitation, I designate 'modernization'. The particular development I am concerned with here is that of the rise in importance and
prestige of the photographic model, a rise intimately connected with the

developments in advertising mentioned earlier. Of similar importance in creating job opportunities for the good looking were the growth of television commercials, of television soap operas and situation comedies, the growth of public relations, the advent of boutiques, the advent of mass eating places aimed at young customers, the boom in pop music. The sense of the marketability of beauty is revealed in the sudden development in the late fifties of agencies of various sorts, and especially modelling agencies, for example that of Catherine Harlé in Paris, or of Lucie Clayton in London. When I speak of opportunities here, I am speaking of opportunities for men as well as women. If a woman is selling herself essentially on her beauty, then, in the last analysis, it is men she will have to please: but, if it is clothes she is modelling, it is women who will be buying the clothes. Modelling agencies and model-ling schools were often run by women. Such is the background to the striking fact that Jean Shrimpton and Twiggy (and also, for that matter, the dress designer Mary Quant) owed a great deal to the perceptiveness and support of the particular men with whom they were closely associated.

Jean Shrimpton was born in November 1942, her father at that time being in the RAF. He was a businessman in the building trade, but with his wife owned a seventy-five-acre farm in Buckinghamshire. Jean Shrimpton, therefore, came from the lower fringes of what I have elsewhere termed 'the extended upper class';[50] she went to a convent school and was brought up with horses – in David Bailey's words, 'a county chick, all M.G.s, daddy, and chinless wonders'.[51] A social phenomenon of the post-war world had been the way in which the upper class had moved into the various branches of the media and advertising (as well as more traditional pursuits such as banking, accountancy and the higher levels of the law). The term 'model' was also widely used to connote expensive prostitute (in a famous letter to the *Times*, at the height of the Profumo affair, whose central protagonist was the high-class prostitute Christine Keeler, always referred to in the press as a 'model', Lucie Clayton wrote that she presumed it would be only fair if the models in her agency in fact referred to Christine Keeler as 'the well-known journalist'), [52] but modelling was already recognized as a proper career for a respectable upper-class English girl, and the rewards of photographic modelling were already much higher than those of the more traditional mannequin. However, like so many others, in 1960, at eighteen, Jean Shrimpton enrolled for a course in shorthand and typing.

Now there are plenty of family snaps of Jean Shrimpton from a very early age. She was very much in the upper-class English style, long legged and slim, with a lovely innocently sexy face. She was also well brought up, and shy; possibly, belonging to an affluent environment in which most of the girls were personable and well groomed, she was not fully aware of her own beauty. Others were. While sitting in the

114 Jean Shrimpton, photograph, 1966

lunchtime sun in Hyde Park she was spotted and approached by film director Cy Endfield and persuaded to meet his producer; however, the latter turned her down. She was then approached by a photographer: taking the cue, and being both fed up with shorthand and typing and under no pressing necessity to earn her own living, she enrolled at a model school.

It is customary in guides to modelling, in fact it has become a cliché, to say that models do not have to be stunning beauties – indeed Jean Shrimpton says this herself in *The Truth about Modelling*.[53] It is also always pointed out that photographic models have to be on the slim side since it is one of the quirks of the camera that it represents a person as if with an additional fine layer of flesh, making them look heavier than they really are, by as much as ten pounds.[54] But this scarcely adds up to a case that models are socially constructed, or manufactured by the media, or whatever: they sell on what they look like in their photographs, that is to say, with this 'extra layer of flesh', so it is absurd to argue that a new style of scrawniness is being created. Anyway, as I have argued throughout this book, slimness has always been highly regarded, fatness never praised. The notion that almost anyone, given the right circumstances, can be constructed into a model is perhaps best met by Jean Shrimpton's own fairly gentle words: 'A heavy jaw-line, or squashy or bumpy nose is not helpful', and the eyes 'mustn't squint or disappear when you laugh'.[55] Certainly there is a quality of being photogenic which, it seems, some people have and some people do not; but, principally, being photogenic means being able to be natural in front of the camera, not freezing, a matter essentially of character and training.

Shrimpton went to a good modelling school, she signed up with a top agent, Lucie Clayton, she had contacts, she was beautiful, she was photogenic. Of course, the competition was fierce, but I personally do not find it terribly surprising that she was quickly in great demand. The way she put it herself in 1964 is very fair, provided one recognizes 'gawky' as a highly relative term: 'one of the reasons for my success was that my gawky looks just happened to fit the fashion trend three years ago. Now the casual clothes and fashions I helped to publicise are in every shop.'[56] Without her association with David Bailey, Jean Shrimpton would probably have led at least a moderately successful career as a photographic model. They moved in the same circles, of course, and Bailey was not immediately struck by her potential; she seemed too inexperienced. But when they did team up, he exerted an enormous influence over her and it seems reasonable to accept her own estimate that he played a crucial part in her rise to a position of being for several years the world's top model.[57]

Would she, in another age, have had the equivalent success? Almost certainly not. Given the same looks and the equivalent family background, she would probably in any age have led a quietly successful and fulfilling life. Men in all ages would have found her beautiful, but only the early 1960s offered the peculiar opportunities that she had the looks to exploit. I have raised the question of how natural was the natural look of the sixties. From the start Jean Shrimpton paid the greatest attention to making her already large eyes look as large and striking as possible. To prepare for the cameras, her make-up took her forty minutes; she describes this in some detail and then, interestingly, continues: 'I hope all this hasn't given the wrong impression. Because the aim of going to so much time and trouble is to look as natural as possible. To look as if you have no make-up on at all. These artifices merely cover up your blemishes.'[58]

Lesley Hornby was born (in 1949) into an entirely different family background, not working class, as was often said, but essentially surburban lower middle class. Her father's job (he was a master craftsman from Bolton) was no doubt in essence upper working class, but his post-war employment at the MGM studios in Boreham Wood gave him a rather higher status and income. The family owned their own house in the quintessentially lower-middle-class London suburb of Neasden, and they had their own car. Lesley's mother had come from a poor background, and had worked as a shop assistant in Woolworths; she'd been a most attractive woman (she got engaged four times), and, not being able to afford make-up, used to put soot from the fireplace round her eyes, and always pinched her cheeks before entering a room. Twiggy – she was not called this in her childhood but, contrary to what is often said, she had acquired this nickname before being launched as a model – was much more involved in the real youth revolution of the time than Shrimpton, making her own dresses in order to conform to the uniform style of her own particular group. She claims that she 'really hated what I looked like as a teenager . . . In all these pictures of me at around twelve I am wearing a brassiere with Kleenex stuffed in.'[59] Nonetheless, such were her neat figure and stunning looks that several people already thought that she was, or ought to be, a model.

In March 1965, when she was fifteen and a half, and still at school, she met Nigel John Davies, or Justin de Villeneuve, as he was already calling himself. He was twenty-five and came from an incontrovertibly working-class family. Britain remained very much a society divided up by social class, but it was a consequence of the social reforms of the 1940s that a kind of classless group did grow up of tough, independent-minded individuals, taking jobs on the fringes, or in the interstices of the class structure – general building and decorating, antique dealing, hair-dressing, bouncing at clubs, etc., etc., and often on the edges of the law. Justin de Villeneuve had led a tough, colourful and sometimes semi-villanous life. At the time of his meeting with Twiggy he was working on an antique stall with Graham Morris-Jones, with whom he also had a partnership in interior decoration. Justin de Villeneuve's rise obviously owed much to personality, intelligence and guts; but, arguably, the particular roles he fulfilled were dependent on the fact that he was extremely good looking. In his own description of his partnership with Morris-Jones he says: 'He was an architect, he did the jobs, and I was the front man, I would talk the deal and wear the nice clothes. I always looked smart. First impressions are important.'[60] Twiggy met Justin at the hairdressers where his brother Tony was working. Twiggy's reaction was: 'I thought he was lovely. Everyone liked him – everyone always does.' Justin's reactions: 'There was this lovely little girl, so tiny and so beautiful. She was breathtaking.' From time to time during this book I have mentioned the significance of voice, and have insisted always on separating voice as a personal characteristic from that of beauty properly defined. It is interesting therefore that Justin should add that Twiggy had an absolutely awful voice; he continues, however, that people were always charmed by it – the overwhelming good looks simply made the voice seem charming.[61]

The immediate development does show the force of contingency in history. It happened that Tony had a friend who dabbled in photography, and Twiggy was taken down to Wimbledon Common to pose for a few shots. Justin claimed (admittedly later, but there seems no reason to doubt the testimony): 'When I saw her being photographed on Wimbledon Common that day, that was the moment I knew I would crack it. I knew a few models and I had seen them work before, and Twiggy just had something about her that was absolutely right. And she was just a kid of fifteen.'[62] It may be noted that Justin's reactions were entirely self-centred and oriented towards his own success, just like the reactions of the roué Du Barry in seventeenth-century Paris. He was not looking at Twiggy as a sex object for his personal gratification, but as someone with a marketable value which could bring recognition to him. Twiggy continued to live at home while Justin adopted a paternalistic managerial role towards her, taking her first of all to one of the great progenitors of sixties fashion, Biba. As Twiggy explained, 'Justin has a lot of charm and he charmed my mum and proved he wasn't going to do anything dreadful.'

It was Tony, before there was any hint of actual public success, who invented the name Twiggy, though Justin generally referred to her as Princess. And it was actually quite independently of Justin that, while Twiggy was buying herself an old fur, a photographer – seeing her as she looked before there was ever any question of her being constructed into a public figure – took a photo of her for an article in *London Look* about young girls wearing old clothes. Twiggy had a natural affinity for clothes and a natural talent for making them; Justin wasn't the only person to think that she had a great future as a model. But modelling schools would not accept anyone less than five foot seven tall or with less than a thirty-three-inch hip.

In shape I wasn't much different then from what I am today. My legs – well, you know my legs, I hate them. They're so thin. I was six and a half stone in weight, which I stayed for a long time. I have been up as far as seven and a half, but I'm down to seven again now. I am five foot six. In shoes I'm three and a half or four, in dresses size six. At that time I had a thirty and a half bust and thirty-two hips. I did wear a bra, amazingly. I was desperate for a big bust, although flat-chested was getting to be the look – little vests and shetland jumpers and shorts were just starting to be around . . . for most people before this time, the thing was to look older and sophisticated. Fashions were for the twenty-fives and over.[63]

But there was no quick road to success. Photographer Michel Moly-neux, to whom she was introduced by Justin, agreed 'She's got a lovely face, she could have a chance', and advised them to go to *Queen*; but she was not warmly received there. Justin's male friends appreciated the trousers which Twiggy was able to run up quickly, and it was decided that together they would open a boutique. Twiggy was taken up by Susan Robins of *Woman's Mirror*, one of the new magazines featuring youthful fashion, but the fashion editor Prudence Glynn thought Twiggy was too small, though she took her on for head shots featuring the beautiful face. At this stage, then, the position was that Twiggy's extraordinary beauty was very widely recognized, but she was running up against a prejudice or convention about the appropriate size for a model; on the other hand, youth was very much the rage, and the trend in fashion was towards the sort of things that would suit Twiggy very well. Maybe an element of artifice and grooming did help to resolve the impasse. Twiggy had an eight-hour session at exclusive hairdresser's Leonard's, the time being largely taken up with repeated drying out, to see if the very, very short style being designed for her was exactly right. As Justin said:

She really looked extraordinary when she emerged at the end of that day. I had always thought her head was the most wonderful shape, but now her hair was cut so cleverly to show the shape – she was an amazing sight. All the clients at Leonard just turned and gasped. There was this little cockney girl in a little white gown, with her long neck and her huge, huge eyes – she looked like a fawn. She looked like Bambi: I knew then that she really was going to make it.[64]

115 Twiggy, photograph, 1967

She definitely was photogenic. She was photographed in her new style by Barry Lategan, who was already booking her for modelling jobs, when Deirdre McSharry, fashion editor of the *Daily Express*, saw the Lategan pictures – contingency perhaps played a part here, for McSharry was herself a client of Leonard. Two pictures were taken at the *Express*, which then devoted a whole page to this message: 'This is the face of '66 – Twiggy, the Cockney kid with the face to launch a thousand shops and she's only sixteen.' This might not have meant too much since only a short time before Deirdre McSharry had written of Donyale Luna as *the* look of 1966. But since Twiggy really was both beautiful and different, that article did launch her career: a visit to Paris, the launching of the Twiggy line, the stupendous visit to the United States. It was mainly American commentators who insisted on seeing Twiggy as some kind of commercial or media fabrication – some seemed to think, Justin complained, that he had deliberately starved her to this shape.[65] Of course, the whole set up of fashion and exaggerated media coverage existed to be exploited; but as far as anything ever is, the Twiggy–Justin act was a genuine one founded, to repeat, on the fact that both were genuinely physically very attractive people.

The American television company ABC made three Twiggy films: *Twiggy in New York*, *Twiggy in California* and *Twiggy Who?* Generally great emphasis was laid on her skinniness and alleged absence of breasts, with such charming statements as: 'From the neck down, forget it.' (The English version was wittier, though not necessarily in the broad perspective more tasteful: car stickers read 'Forget Oxfam. Feed Twiggy.') Twiggy herself was given to responding to questions about what she thought of her figure with the line that she didn't think she had one. This has been taken up by feminists and other historians to argue that somehow, by commercial chicanery and deliberate contrivance, people were led to switch from loving big breasts to loving none at all. But the fact is that Twiggy, with her thirty-one-inch bust, had beautiful, small, but perfectly proportioned breasts, as can be seen quite clearly from the photograph of her in a bikini reproduced as Ill.116. And, as I have shown from time to time, girlish breasts have always been very highly rated. Twiggy has remained a celebrity in a way that Shrimpton did not – Twiggy of course started younger. From photographic modelling, she moved to television commercials, and then to films, starting with *The Boyfriend*, directed by Ken Russell. Twiggy was immensely sexy, but like Jean Shrimpton she seems, in a permissive age, to have lived a life of fairly traditional sexual morality. These women, as I have said, sold their looks, which were equated with sex, but they certainly did not sell sex.

Without their looks, Shrimpton and Twiggy would have been nowhere. This was essentially true of the many new film stars of the period, some of whom I have referred to already. With the famous male beauties of the period the processes leading to success were slightly different. The

116

116 Twiggy posing in a bikini, photograph, 1971

photographers Terence Donovan and David Bailey undoubtedly had talent, as had such actors as Terence Stamp, David Hemmings, Michael Caine and Sean Connery. In a wider historical perspective the most important characteristic of all of them is that they came from solidly working-class backgrounds. Two considerations emerge. First, with regard to these uniquely successful working-class products, it seems reasonable to argue that, while, of course, the basic ingredients of success were talent and the opportunity offered by the current cultural context, personal beauty operated as a characteristic which could out-trump, as it were, the old imperatives of class. Secondly, and what I am most keen to establish here, because most of these highly socially mobile and successful males were in fact personally beautiful, beauty did in fact become associated with success, as a necessary, or at least likely, component of it.

As with Monroe, Shrimpton and Twiggy, special attention must be given to the pop group the Beatles. From the time of their amazingly successful American tour in 1964, the Beatles were international figures of the first order. An American female student who saw them on tour commented: 'It was really fun to watch them. At first I couldn't tell them apart . . . They were cute; they were charming; they were clever; they were talented . . . They had different characters. Like John, the strong, sort of satirical, and then, of course, Paul, the cutest one.'[66] In one of its uses in American English, 'cute' is very similar to the French *joli*, and can almost be rendered as 'beautiful'. The girl was right: Paul McCartney was beautiful, George Harrison was good looking in a rather conventional way, John Lennon was personable and sensitive looking, Ringo Starr, who had been specially recruited into the original group as a brilliant drummer, was less well favoured. But, as drummer, Ringo Starr sat at the back, and collectively the Beatles presented an appearance of youthful good looks and charm in which the sexuality was not too stridently stressed. The Beatle haircut, not short back and sides, and not long and Italianate, but a clean-looking mop which linked them together in the collective image, was a real innovation. As the decade advanced, the Beatles switched to the hippy, long-haired image. The essence here is that a great deal of attention was concentrated on their appearance. Particular 'looks' taken after some famous and beautiful female had long been known; but the idea of a male, Beatle look was relatively new, and testifies to the way in which masculine appearance was now becoming almost as relevant a consideration as feminine appearance. In fact, the two great points of reference in this respect in the 1960s were the Beatle look and the John F. Kennedy look, to which I shall return in the third section of this chapter. More generally, pop groups of all types, travelling around the country, often attracting enormous audiences, offered standards of male appearance with which the large numbers of young females in the audience could compare the boys known to them.

It was actually in Portugal that the footballer George Best was christened the Footballing Beatle. But many of the assessments of him in England essentially saw him in these terms: as a handsome, sexy mass entertainer, with a particular appeal for youth, and above all female youth. In a reference to Pelé, the utterly brilliant, but rather ugly Brazilian star who dominated the footballing scene in these years, Best remarked: 'If I'd been born ugly you would never have heard of Pelé. I don't mean

117 George Best,
photograph, 1971

that women weakened me or anything like that, I simply mean that
without them I might have concentrated more on the game and therefore
lasted longer in the game.'[67] Here Best is, as it were, presenting himself
as the Lloyd George of football, so attractive to women as to be running
the risk of being distracted from the main task in hand. Shortly he was
to become the Duke of Monmouth or Marquis de Cinq-Mars of his
profession: his career collapsed into disgrace and ignominy as he succumbed to drink, womanizing, and illusions as to his invincibility.
(However, though he ceased to be a footballer, he remained something
of a celebrity.)

George Best was born and brought up in working-class Belfast.
Although the contemporary phase of the Ulster troubles had not yet
begun, Belfast was none the less one of the least joyful places in the
United Kingdom in which to be reared. Best was an incredibly gifted
natural footballer, never at any time able to explain how he did the
brilliant things he did do – he operated instinctively. As a kid he was not
good looking: 'I was very unattractive and I remember the birds teasing
me. They used to shout "look at the skinny, ugly sod" when I walked
past them.'[68] This may or may not have been factually accurate, but in
any event the childhood ugliness matured into highly dramatic, very

117    unconventional good looks. As a youngster he was spotted by one of the Manchester United scouts and brought over to play for a Manchester United youth team. It was easy enough for wealthy clubs to recruit lads from poor backgrounds in this way; most of the youngsters never got anywhere. But Best was exceptional, and he made his league debut in 1963. It would be over-romantic and inaccurate to suggest that he enjoyed a run-away schoolboy hero success, but he certainly began quickly to draw attention to himself. He had phenomenal control over the ball, a wondrous range of tricks with which to take the ball past opposing players, and an ability to score goals from all positions. He was one of those players who brings excitement to a game the moment he touches the ball.

Most footballers were working class in origin and generally very conscious of the need for discipline, and for keeping in strict training, in order to maintain their position; the age of football as a mass entertainment provided by glamour boys was just beginning. Best was a showman. He grew his hair much longer than was usual, then he grew a moustache, and then a beard. He projected an image of animal potency, and indeed, if not highly sexed, he was certainly always ready to avail himself of every opportunity that came along; as he said, he made up for all that contempt girls had shown him in his childhood. Michael Parkinson has put it this way: 'There never was a boy more ideally equipped for his place in time. In the early sixties the Beatles created the first post-war generation with its own culture and real individual identity. Looking at Best's career in those first few years it is impossible not to regard him as the fifth Beatle.'[69] Whenever Best touched the ball on the football field, the girls screamed, as they screamed also in response to the Beatles. Much of his appeal, of course, as with that of Lord Byron, lay in his reputation as a stud; but then, as I have said over and over again, looks and sexuality are intimately interrelated. Now, I am not arguing for one moment that George Best became a star footballer, an international with the Northern Ireland side (which he described as 'a joke') and Footballer of the Year in 1966–67, because of his looks. If he had been as ugly as Pelé or Stanley Matthews, he'd have been as great a footballer, and indeed, as he himself suggested, perhaps an even greater one since he wouldn't have been subjected to the same temptations.

But the point again is the association between success, or, more accurately in this case, the combination of celebrity and notoriety, and good looks. Other footballers have opened boutiques, put their names to lines of clothing and sports equipment, acquired agents; but Best was the only true footballing super pop star – he could not have been that without his looks and sexuality. A cool, sophisticated married woman described to Michael Parkinson how at a party she was struck by Best who 'had the most marvellous eyes and a shy boyish charm', and how she was still working out how she should go about seducing him when a young blonde came up saying, 'Hi, I'm Julie, would you like a quick fuck?', and took Best off with her.[70] That's a story which well encapsulates one aspect of the sixties, and Best's place in it.

There is space here to refer to just one other sportsman, who brings together some of the other themes of this chapter. The black American Cassius Clay was one of the greatest heavyweight boxers of all time, remarkably lithe and agile. He was also witty and voluble. He became an activist on behalf of the black Muslim movement and took the name Muhammad Ali. It would again be absurd to say that the media created Muhammad Ali; he created himself, but of course exploited the media to the full. He was also a great athlete and brilliant boxer. He said of himself that he was 'the greatest', and proved it over and over again; he also said, and this is the critical issue here, that he was 'the prettiest'.[71] This was also true. Muhammad Ali was yet another example of much publicized male celebrity becoming equated with male beauty. The consequence of all this was to put a premium on male good looks. Most men did not have the looks of Terence Stamp, or David Bailey, or George Best, or Muhammad Ali, and almost none had their talent; but as opportunities expanded in all the ramifications of advertising, public relations, popular culture, discos, British-style pubs, and so on, those who did have the appearance of a Poitier or a Connery stood in line for at least modest advancement.

118 Cassius Clay (later Muhammad Ali), preparing for the fight with Brian London, photograph, 1966

But what I am talking of is opportunities for the beautiful, not of embargoes against the plain or ugly; vibrant, febrile societies gobbled up talent in whatever physical shape it came. But, crucially, the old dishonesties, the old confusions between talent, or other qualities, and mere physical appearance, were disappearing. If someone was actually ugly, it was now more acceptable simply to say so. Already in the early 1960s Barbra Streisand was on the way to becoming 'America's biggest female box-office personality'.[72] She'd had a hard time of it in acting school, where her prominent Jewish nose made her an unlikely candidate for the conventional juvenile lead; she therefore turned to singing and she had, without doubt, a remarkable singing voice. In her first Broadway roles she was deliberately cast as the plain girl, beginning the show with lamentations as to her lot. Her first outstanding success, *Funny Girl* (which became an Academy Award-winning film), opened with the chorus singing 'If a Girl Isn't Pretty'; in one of her song hits she lamented 'Nobody Makes a Pass at Me'. In interviews Streisand repeatedly harped upon her own perception of her lack of good looks. This may possibly have been a publicity gimmick, but on the whole it seems to have betokened a deep insecurity:

She genuinely fears that her looks are too great a handicap for her talent to overcome. 'I'd like to be beautiful but sometimes I think I am strangely put together.' When someone talking to her avoids her eyes, she gets upset . . . 'I think he can't bear to look at me. They always write about me as the girl with the Fu Manchu finger nails and the nose as long as an ant-eater's. This hurts far more than if they wrote that I was a terrible singer – which they never did.'[73]

That was from an interview in 1966 when Streisand was already becoming well established. Four years later she made this sad comment: 'There is this joke about a girl who went to the hairdresser and said, "Give me a Barbra Streisand look." So he took the hairbrush and broke her nose. I guess I do have a strange face.'[74] This is not to deny for one moment that Streisand's vitality and talent and, no doubt, her acceptable figure, rendered her attractive to many men; there are many articles praising her appearance – for instance *Le Figaro* in December 1965 spoke of her 'slightly clownish, yet seductive face'[75] – and she has had many highly publicized affairs with some of the world's most eligible men. The point is the openness and, in a sense, honesty: *Marty*, in the end, had been dishonest in its portrayal of an allegedly plain girl; *Funny Girl* did not have that basic dishonesty. Beyond that, it was possible openly to distinguish between Streisand's immense and indisputable talent and her looks. No longer was it an essential convention that a successful star must also be supremely beautiful.

## 3 *Beauty: An Autonomous Status Characteristic*

The sixties were a time of much turbulence and of active protests by the various groups I identified in section one. The year 1968 marked the great climacteric, when many different grievances merged together with the strong hostility felt by liberals and progessives everywhere against the US's involvement in, and conduct of, the war in Vietnam. Inevitably a book like this, concentrating on the very limited topic of beauty, misses much of the drama and significance of these years; however, it is my purpose to relate the changing evaluation of beauty to the changing historical context. It is often said that after all the excitement of 1968, the seventies were years of conservative reaction. This is not at all true. On the whole, for all the inequalities that still exist, the black civil rights movement did make permanent gains, and the movement for women's rights became stronger and stronger; the attitudes and aspirations of youth may have changed, but the place of youth in society was recognized as never before. The political revolution, the irreversible change in economic structures, which many protesters were looking for in 1968, certainly never came. But, despite everything that has been written since about the emptiness and phonyness of the aspirations expressed in the sixties (there, as always, being of course much truth in that), the evidence of significant cultural change seems to me irrefutable.

In particular, naturally, I refer to the critical change in the way in which personal appearance was evaluated, seeking concrete evidence in three areas: the empirical studies carried out by university psychology departments during the period; the guides to grooming which flourished still more than ever before; and the worlds of business and political life. Academic research into new areas may profoundly change the way research, and perhaps teaching, are conducted, and may eventually affect society, through, say, technological innovation, or new theories of social policy. But very often academic research follows, rather than leads, the social fashion. An important article in the *American Journal of Sociology* in 1983, 'Beauty as status', by Murray Webster, Jr and James E. Driskell, Jr, basically a survey of the previous literature, offers a useful bibliography which, excluding a few general items and those after 1980, contains forty-six directly relevant articles.[76] Adding noteworthy omissions from 1952, 1966, 1971, 1972, 1975 and 1978, we have fifty-seven articles published between the 1920s and 1980. Classified by date of publication, they break down as follows: 1920s:1; 1930s:1; 1940s:0; 1950s:2; 1960–64:1; 1965–69:5; 1970–74:22; 1975–79:26.[77] This indicates that the critical breakthrough in this area of research came in the early 1970s, with continued development into the second half of the 1970s. The changes of the 1960s, I would argue, had drawn attention to beauty as a characteristic of high value and had brought it to the attention of academics as a suitable subject for investigation.

Now the sorts of experiments conducted by psychologists, social psychologists and sociologists, since essentially they take the form, in one way or another, of students being asked to give their reactions to other students of various degrees of personal beauty, deal with what I have already defined as inclination, rather than behaviour, or, of course, public mores. Since it has been part of my argument that personal inclination has remained relatively unchanged, while public mores, and to a degree actual behaviour, have changed quite considerably, I would not expect anything startlingly new to emerge from these experiments: they perhaps tell us, rather, about some of the timeless features of human response and character. Their significance, however, is threefold: first, as already noted, the fact that so many experiments of this sort are being carried out, and the historical period in which they are being carried out; second, the assumptions which the researchers bring to bear in their experiments; and, thirdly, the fact that these experiments make public facts about the nature of beauty which many in the past may have surmised, but which were not part of public orthodoxy, and thus reinforce the 'modern' evaluation of beauty. If one compares the very few studies up to and including (publication in) 1960 with the studies published from 1968 onwards, there is an assurance, and even a ruthlessness in the latter about what can be defined as physically attractive or not physically attractive, whereas there is a hesitancy, or perhaps rather benign naivety, about the earlier studies.

The 1921 article by F. A. C. Perrin, 'Physical attractiveness and repulsiveness', used four groups, attractive boys and attractive girls, unattractive boys and unattractive girls. It started from the sensible, but not very precise premise that 'the physical characteristics of an individual constitute a large group of the total series of effects produced by that individual on others'.[78] The tentativeness, or perhaps gentlemanly discretion, comes out in the admission that it was considered 'inadvisable to permit a discussion of physically unattractive people'. The conclusion that physically attractive people are more likely to mingle more, to learn more, and so on, is not of the sort to bowl us over with the power of experimental psychology.[79] The 1937 article is the (among those professionally interested in the subject) well-known article by Wilfred Waller on the 'rating and dating complex', which now seems a rather simplistic, impressionistic and uninformative statement of the obvious, that is that students who for various reasons rate more highly date more often.[80] The 1960 article, a British study conducted with the help of a British newspaper, claimed to have revealed countrywide and agewide agreement on what constituted 'pretty', on the basis of the rating by readers of twelve photographs. The thoroughly unhelpful conclusion was that the faces regarded as pretty 'included none which could be called (at least as far as the experimenter could surmise) either "very beautiful" or "plain"'. We are still in the comfortable world of the grooming guides.[81]

Waller had argued, sensibly enough as far as it went, that there was a great deal of prestige value to be gained from being seen with an attractive person. As I have already suggested, the question of the significance of personal appearance impinges on three spheres: public life, life chances, and personal life (marriage, etc.). Sociological and psychological investigators have, on the whole, ignored the first sphere. Before the 1960s, only fairly obvious generalizations existed in regard to the second. With regard to the third sphere the orthodoxy was that propagated in an article in 1952 by Erving Goffman. This orthodoxy, the 'matching hypothesis', very much matched the orthodoxy of 1950s society as a whole, the orthodoxy attacked by Kingsley Amis's Graham McClintock. In Goffman's summary: 'A proposal of marriage in our society tends to be a way in which a man sums up his social attributes and suggests to a woman that hers are not so much better as to preclude a merger or a partnership in these matters.'[82] It also involved the premise that a plain person will choose another plain person, a slightly more attractive person a slightly more attractive person, and so on; in other words, that levels of attractiveness will match each other in marriage choices.

The work of crucial significance in the mid-1960s (not so much in the sense of being 'true', but in the sense of reinforcing the modern evaluation of beauty) was that which suggested that, on the contrary, what both men and women really wanted was a partner of high physical attractiveness, whatever their own level of attractiveness. This in turn led to a dispute over whether in fact men and women really react in the same way over this particular issue. In the sphere of life chances, the research of the early 1970s suggested that it was generally thought that people of high physical attractiveness would be more successful in life and that indeed in an empirical situation good-looking female students would be graded more favourably than less attractive ones. Let us now look at some of the detail in regard to these contentions and debates.

The experiment which seemed to refute the 'matching hypothesis' was conducted by Walster, Aronson, Abrahams and Rottman, and reported on in 1966.[83] The experiment sounds fun for those who organized it; it was obviously fun for some of the subjects and presumably quite painful for others. College freshmen were invited to buy tickets for what was billed as a 'computer dance', that is a dance where they would be paired with an ideal partner selected by computer. In fact the students were secretly rated in advance on personality, intelligence and social skill, and then also, as they purchased their tickets, on physical attractiveness. The students were then paired on a random basis, save that great pains were taken to avoid the solecism of having a short man dancing with a tall woman. According to the Goffman hypothesis, students who obtained, by chance, partners whose social desirability level was the same as their own would like each other more than those who were fixed up with partners whose social desirability levels were inferior or superior to their own. Halfway through the dance the students filled in questionnaires containing questions relating to how much the subject liked his or her partner and whether he or she would like to continue the relationship. Follow-up interviews four to six months later established whether or not the relationships had indeed been continued. The conclusion was clear: the only apparent determinant of how much each student liked his or her partner, how much he or she wanted to see the partner again, and how often they did in fact see each other again, was how physically attractive the partner was. The more physically attractive the partner, the more he or she was liked.[84]

Attempts to find additional factors which might possibly predict attraction were not successful; for example, students with exceptional social skills and intelligence levels were not liked any better than those with lower levels. Nevertheless, the correlation between physical attractiveness and liking was not perfect: a perfect correlation would be represented by the figure 1; in fact it came at .78 for the men, and .69 for the women.[85] A further group of researchers, Stroebe, Insko, Thompson and Layton, seized on this discrepancy to argue that in fact this showed that women are significantly less affected by physical attractiveness in men than men are by physical attractiveness in women.[86] The variation is in fact of the order of exactly nine per cent and I suppose whether one regards that as significant or not is to some extent a matter of opinion. The most judicious summing up would probably be that, in the particular conditions of this experiment, physical attractiveness quite clearly was the key element for both men and women, but in slightly lesser degree for women than for men. Stroebe and his associates then conducted an experiment of their own using photographs divided into three levels of attractiveness, particular care being taken 'to include extremely attractive and extremely unattractive pictures in the sample'.[87] As well as being given the photographs of potential partners, subjects (again students – being involved in experiments of this sort was clearly an occupational risk at certain American universities) were given (invented) descriptions of their attitudes, the experiment being designed to assess the weighting of physical attractiveness as against attitude similarity. To their own satisfaction at least, the experimenters came to the conclusion that 'physical attractiveness is a more important determinant of opposite-sex attraction for males than for females'.[88] This may well be so, for, as I observed in chapter two, we really don't fully know the answer on this one; personally I would give greater credence to an experiment based on actual meetings than one based on photographs, and I would suspect that students in this experiment were likely to give the answers they felt they ought to give rather than responding in a deep and genuine way. Nevertheless, it is true that even the computer dance experiment did show some differential between male and female reactions.

Stroebe *et al.* also made the case, a rather obvious one, that the subjects in the computer dance experiment were not constrained by the pressures and inhibitions of real life (that however, presumably, was the point of the experiment and it is in that that its principal value lies). The same point was made, perhaps more effectively, by Berscheid, Dion, Walster and Walster, also reporting in 1971.[89] The point stressed by both groups of researchers was that the computer dance situation minimized, or indeed practically obliterated, the risks of rejection. As Berscheid and company nicely put it, those who by chance secured partners more attractive than themselves were 'assured not only of social contact, but of the fruits of social courtesy norms for the duration of the dance'.[90] In addition, 'those who had achieved their ideal goal of a physically attractive partner may have shown more interest in *retaining* it than they might have shown in trying to *attain* it initially'.[91] Berscheid *et al.* conducted two experiments to see whether the matching principle might reassert itself if the individual were required actively to *choose* a partner, rather than simply evaluate one already provided, and to discover what the effects would be if the possibility of rejection by a desirable partner was emphasized. Their conclusion was still that physically attractive partners were markedly preferred by everyone, women as well as men, but that *within* this general trend it was apparent that men and women of lesser attractiveness did tend to choose less attractive partners than did the highly attractive students.[92]

A number of other experiments in the early seventies examined these aspects further. Huston (1973) again found the ubiquitous effect that, overall, men generally preferred to date the most physically attractive women, but that this was most pronounced when they were assured of acceptance; subjects who were not guaranteed acceptance believed that the highly physically attractive women would be significantly less likely to want them as a date than would either the moderately attractive or the unattractive women.[93] Or, as Stroebe and his associates put it, in the cold calculating prose of this type of discourse: 'As in any bargaining situation the participants in the dating game have to learn the range of outcomes available to them. Being turned down or never asked for a date is embarrassing and frustrating, and the less attractive individuals, in order to avoid further frustration, possibly learn to stop trying for the most desirable and unavailable dates.'[94]

Here, then, we have two types of experiment. The first, the computer dance, probing people's private inclinations: what they would do if there were no constraints, including their own unattractiveness, upon them. The second type of experiment brings in the effects of that sort of personal constraint. A third sort of experiment examines people who are already committed to genuine real-life relationships, either engaged or going steady. Here it was found, not surprisingly, that people of relatively similar levels of attractiveness tend overwhelmingly to associate with each other, and that other such factors as attitude similarity and role compatibility came into play. In the cold jargon:

The results indicate that physical attractiveness, both as subjectively experienced and objectively measured, operates in accordance with exchange-market rules. Individuals with equal market value for physical attractiveness are more likely to associate in an intimate relationship such as premarital engagement than individuals with disparate values.[95]

Let us now turn to the experiments which cast light on the relationship between a beautiful appearance and a person's life chances. Dion, Berscheid and Walster conducted an experiment (reported in 1972) in which sixty students, thirty males and thirty females, were asked to predict the personality and life chances of persons represented to them in photographs. The researchers had prepared twelve sets of three pictures, half of women of different levels of physical attractiveness, half of men of different levels of physical attractiveness. Half of the mixed group were given female photographs to respond to, half male photographs, that is to say, some of the subjects were rating people of the opposite sex, some people of their own sex. The subjects were told that the purpose of the study was to compare their ability, as untrained college students, to make accurate predictions, compared with that of trained graduates. The experiment unambiguously showed that both male and female students, regardless of whether they were responding to male or female photographs, assumed that physically attractive persons possessed more socially desirable personalities than unattractive ones, and predicted that their lives would be happier and more successful, in both the social and professional sphere. Dion, Berscheid and Walster entitled their report 'What is beautiful is good',[96] which could, of course, be seen as taking us right back to Plato and the most thoroughgoing traditionalism. However, in my view, they should rather have entitled the article 'What is beautiful is successful', the qualifications for and attributes of success discussed by them being in fact highly secular and very far removed from traditional ideas about godliness and truth.

Although most studies confirmed the very positive advantages of being good looking, it is relevant here to bring in some of the areas where being good looking could seem to have adverse affects. For instance Krebs and Adinolfi showed that being too pretty could activate envy and so operate as a liability for both males and females looking for a college room mate. Accused swindlers could be seen as more dangerous and given longer sentences when they were attractive, as compared with those who were unattractive, though for most crimes where attractiveness is not an obvious asset in commissioning the crime, attractive defendants were treated more leniently. Dermer and Thiel showed that when rated by unattractive raters, attractive people may be perceived as vain and egotistical, as likely to have extramarital affairs and seek divorce, and as unsympathetic to the oppressed of the world.[97] Clearly what is being said here is not that what is beautiful is good, but simply that in evil-doing beautiful people are once again likely to be more successful than unattractive ones: they are seen as more accomplished swindlers, who are more successful in sexual adventures.

Some studies simply concentrated on the long-held suspicion that, in an essentially male-dominated world, beautiful female students were likely to have advantages over less beautiful ones. A study of the sixties suggested that even in large classes where it was very difficult for the instructor to know students individually, beautiful girls tended to get the benefit of the doubt in the grading of papers, and suggested that this was because their faces and names did stick in the minds of instructors. A more systematic experiment, reported in 1974, was conducted by Landy and Sigall at the University of Rochester. A group of male college students were asked to evaluate one well-written essay and one badly written essay, both supposedly written by female students: one third of the essays of both types had a photo of an attractive girl attached to it (as the alleged author of the essay), one third had no photo, and one third had the photograph of an unattractive girl attached.

The subjects who read the good essay evaluated the writer and her work more favourably than the subjects who read the poor essay. The subjects also evaluated the writer and her work most favourably when she was attractive, least when she was unattractive and intermediately when her appearance was unknown. The impact of the writer's attractiveness on the evaluation of her and her work was most pronounced when the 'objective' quality of her work was relatively poor.[98]

What is being said here, and this confirms the earlier experiment, is that on the whole real academic ability, irrespective of looks, will be recognized, but that down at the bottom of the scale where the essay is in fact quite bad, beautiful girls will get some compensation, while others will not.

From the foregoing brief survey of academic research I wish to stress two facets. First that the concerted study of the subject of personal appearance essentially begins in the 1960s, and that it accelerates into the 1970s as the transformations of the sixties begin to impinge upon academia. Secondly, whatever the precise language used by researchers in reporting on their findings, beauty is now, in a cool and dispassionate way, far removed from the excitements and confusions of the traditional view, and is clearly recognized as a characteristic of high value in the lives people lead in the late twentieth century.

I want now to turn again to one of my staple source materials, 'beauty' or, rather, grooming guides, to see whether their nature and tone has changed in a way which can be taken as consonant with the other changes I have been discussing. In chapter five I suggested that in the later nineteenth century a clear sign that a modern evaluation of beauty was gaining at the expense of the traditional one was the replacement in grooming guides of any suggestion that attention to personal appearance was a frailty which needed to be apologized for, by the categorical insistence that making the most of her physical appearance was a woman's absolute duty. Elements of joyfulness had appeared from the twenties on, but the great change of the sixties is that all the agonizing and the moralizing disappears. While one French *Encyclopedia of Beauty and Wellbeing* boasted on its first page about cutting the 'pseudo-philosophical verbiage',[99] most guides in fact simply plunged straight in, taking it for granted that for women (to stick with them for the moment) nothing is more natural and sensible than having an interest in their personal appearance. Some go as far as to insist – rightly, in the light of the other developments we have been discussing – that a good personal appearance is essential for social and business success; others lay as much emphasis on the notion that making up or dressing up is fun, the sort of fun every woman will instinctively wish to indulge in. There is no suggestion either that this is a stern duty, or that it is an indulgence which needs to be excused. That is one important aspect of the modern evaluation of beauty as it emerged from the International Cultural Revolution. What, however, is also often stressed is the relationship between a good appearance and sexiness. No longer is there any suggestion that to be too beautiful is to be suspect because too sexy: sex is in itself a good thing, fun, like making up, and the relationship between sex and personal appearance is openly acknowledged.[100]

It would be wrong to expect beauty guides to be totally 'realistic', after the style of the academic articles reporting on psychological research that we have just been considering; a beauty guide which says that all it is offering is a little self-amusement, which won't in reality make a woman look terribly different, won't sell many copies. That said, there *is* a much greater realism: there is greater restraint and accuracy in the description of cosmetics and what they can actually do. Nowadays, said one guide, women asked only the believable from cosmetics and, for that reason, advertisers tended to give scientific information in their advertisements (no doubt government regulation has played a part also). The same guide pointed out that 'modern woman's chief difficulty could well be to discern how to pick her way sensibly through the barrage of advice which is openly showered upon her by magazines, newspapers, beauty consultants of all kinds'.[101] In general, therefore, grooming advice sought to be as direct and factual as possible.

It would be absurd to claim that the word 'beauty' is now used exclusively in the way in which I have used it in this book, in the 'modern' sense, as an autonomous physical characteristic with a very high value of its own. 'Beauty' is used very much to mean self-presentation, involving grooming, make-up and fashion; it is still also often used to mean the entire personality, as in 'beauty is an attitude of mind'. However, it is noticeable that some books do speak of, for example, 'poise', 'personality', 'charm', or 'good grooming', recognizing that these are the qualities that can be achieved by skill and effort, while natural beauty really is something rather different.[102] I wouldn't wish to make too much of this point, though I would stress the way in which, in consolidation of a trend we have noted throughout the twentieth century, overwhelming emphasis is given to the notion of 'naturalness', in contrast, in particular, to slavishly adhering to any one convention.

Now, of course, there were the styles already mentioned, associated with, for example, Jean Shrimpton or Twiggy, and a strong emphasis on the youthful, girlish look. Women who felt the need to follow the particular fashion of the hour were helped to do this by the fashion and grooming pages appearing in the many available magazines and periodicals. But in the less ephemeral publications, the overwhelming stress is on health and fitness, dieting and slimming, not in order to achieve an artificial appearance, but in order to give natural qualities the best opportunity of shining through.[103] Injunctions about the need to keep strictly in fashion are, on the whole, replaced by the line that each individual person has a style of their own. 'Natural', in this context, is, inevitably, a relative term. Some may argue that slimming is not really natural. All guides recognized, with Jean Shrimpton, that the achievement of an appearance of the natural might in fact depend quite strongly on artifice. All guides took pride in the democratic fact that such artifices were now more widely available to all social classes than ever before.[104] And I would seriously distort the facts if I did not mention the great attention, especially, as it happened, in France, now being given to cosmetic medicine and cosmetic surgery.[105] As I have already made clear, I believe that slim legs have always been thought beautiful, save that, since for most centuries legs were scarcely on view at all, not a great deal of attention was given to the issue. Sixties styles did focus attention on beautiful legs, and therefore, of course, on their opposite: hence, in particular, the discussions of treatment for the condition which French medical cosmeticians defined as 'cellulite', though other medical men denied its existence.[106]

A feature of the modern evaluation of beauty, as I have described it, is an attention to male beauty as well as female: the actual living examples of, among others, Sydney Poitier, Paul McCartney, Muhammad Ali and George Best have already been cited. In the 1960s and afterwards, the tonnage of material aimed at women continued to outweigh by far that aimed at men, but none the less the sixties were marked by significant changes, most obvious in the grooming and fashion articles specifically aimed at men in a number of magazines, but also apparent in guides exclusively concerned with masculine appearance, and also in special sections in guides primarily aimed at women. How much attention most men actually paid to the advice directed at them, or, indeed, how aware of it many of them were (women, no doubt, had always taken the advice directed at *them* with a certain reserve) is not an issue here; the point is, the stuff existed, as never before. Two major aspects of a man's life, it is argued, now require him to pay great attention to his personal appearance: his sexual activities, and his business and professional life.[107] A man's appeal, according to one French manual, no longer depends solely upon his intellectual, financial and social attributes (the ones traditionally recognized). A man conscious that he has made the most of his appearance, it continues, who is relaxed and lively, in good health and attractive, will easily win over one who is tired, fat, or who has obvious physical flaws.[108] The man who exploits, says another French guide, all that fashion, industry and medicine have to offer will do best in both his professional and his private life; if he is confident in his own appearance he will open many doors and many hearts.[109]

One might surmise that the man who had to go to great lengths in the attempt to alter his personal appearance might not be at all confident; the all-important unwitting testimony is that the man who is already good looking will be at an advantage. In earlier chapters I indicated occupations where beauty could stand a male in particularly good stead. By the sixties, service itself was no longer a major source of employment (though servants with the right style and appearance were more highly prized than ever by those who could afford them), but service trades were expanding in all directions. The most obvious new occupation was that of male model – Catherine Harlé's agency in Paris started taking on male models in 1957[110] – but the whole pop, fashion, media, public relations world was pervaded by an atmosphere which put a premium on good appearance. Formerly the Chief of Protocol at the White House had tended to be a venerable type, strong on stuffiness, skilled in diplomacy: the new thirty-six-year-old incumbent of 1965, together with his good-looking wife, formed an attractive team, looking 'like the former college prom queen and football captain at a five-year class reunion'.[111] Even in the orthodox business world appearance was counting for more and more, a summary of the situation as it existed at the end of the decade being set out in an elaborate French textbook entitled *Professional Success*, which drew mainly on American experience:

For very many years, in business, little value was accorded to self-presentation, demeanour, and appearance in general. However, modern companies have completely revised their outlook on this point and they attach growing importance to the physical appearance of their executives.[112]

No doubt being personable was more crucial than being truly beautiful; but at the same time opportunities for the beautiful were greatly expanding.

Of course there were very many jobs where many other qualities were far more vital than good looks, and very many ill-favoured men continued to hold positions of power and responsibility. Job opportunities – not all of which were specially dependent on a beautiful appearance – were continuing to expand for women (though some of the more important developments did not come till the seventies). But it was very clear that, even more exclusively than with men, the service, media and public relations posts required beauty: two areas of employment which later drew unfavourable attention for their evident assumption that only beautiful women were suitable were those of television presenters – Barbara Walters, the USA's most famous female presenter, had briefly been a model – and 'air hostesses' (as the term was in the sixties). For a woman to achieve a senior position anywhere outside of traditional female professions (such as hospital care), and a position of real power anywhere, was still most unusual. What part looks played in the careers of the few who did single themselves out is a subject, manageable, I believe, if attacked with rigour rather than passion, which awaits its PhD researcher. I simply note that the two leading women in the British Labour government, 1964–70, Jennie Lee and Barbara Castle, and the first woman University Dean (at Brest, 1968) in France (subsequently, 1976, Minister for Universities), Alice Saunier-Seïté, were all considerable beauties in their day.[113]

But it is to the world of male politics I now wish to turn. Events in the United States partly reflected the trends I have been discussing, partly accelerated them, and, in addition, threw up a potent metaphor for the political desirability of youthful good looks in the 'Kennedy image'. These events also, however, demonstrate that even in a subject as broadly thematic and anthropological as this one, the weight of contingency cannot be ignored. When, in the late summer of 1959, it appeared that John F. Kennedy might beat Hubert Humphrey for the Democratic Presidential nomination, the attention of the media, in the traditional way, was focused entirely on Kennedy's beautiful wife, Jackie.[114] As it happened, Kennedy's rival, like many politicians before him, was no impressive example of male pulchritude. As W. L. O'Neill wrote of Humphrey a decade later, when the days of discreet silence about the harsh facts of personal appearance were truly over: 'He was overweight, and with his big balding dome, square little chin, and rat-trap mouth offered a rather comic appearance.'[115] Kennedy's youthful good looks were at the time thought by the professionals to be a disadvantage, signifying nothing other than inexperience.[116] Only with the first televised encounter between Kennedy and Nixon did the notion of the special appeal of good looks begin to be canvassed.[117] Yet, even at the time of the new President's first visit to Canada most of the attention remained on the beauty of the Presidential consort; however, a Canadian (female presumably, though this is not made clear) was reported as saying of Kennedy 'He's just a living doll!'[118] Kennedy's victory and the

119 John F. Kennedy making his inauguration speech, 20 January 1961. Kennedy's looks may be compared with those of Eisenhower (front left), Johnson and Nixon (front right)

fact that as President he was much in the public eye helped to ratify the association, to which the other trends we have noted were favourable, between beauty and success, and Kennedy himself, more particularly after his assassination, became a metaphor for that success.

In May 1965 *Life* put on its cover John Lindsay, the Republican aspirant to the Mayorship of New York. The article inside declared:

> With youthful verve and the long-legged grace of a heron, John Vliet Lindsay, six feet three inches tall, strode into the race for Mayor of New York and Republicans all over the country broke into ear-to-ear smiles . . .
>
> Lindsay is 43 years old and possesses enormous personal charm . . .
>
> Women surround him quickly. Their eyes light up and they try to prolong his handshake, a reaction that inevitably reminds many of Jack Kennedy's campaign days.[119]

Within less than a year, the spotlight was on a candidate, also Republican, for the Governorship of California:

> The speaker stands tall on the rostrum, gazing across a thicket of scarlet carnations in the ballroom of San Diego's El Cortes Hotel. Every seat at every table is taken; every eye is eagerly fixed on him. Across the twenty feet that

separate the dais from the first row of tables he looks almost twenty years younger than the fifty four he is. The sober brown suit, the tapered white collar, the discreet tie are impeccable. His face is tanned, his smile dazzling. Not a hair is out of place (and not a gray strand is visible). He looks strong and youthful and vigorous. He has that new, clean, young look in American politics – the charisma of a John F. Kennedy, a John Lindsay, a Mark Hatfield.[120]

The candidate was the former actor and television presenter, Ronald Reagan.

Reagan was shortly to win the Governorship against the Democratic incumbent Edmund G. Brown, leaving Brown to complain bitterly about 'two-dimensional politics', 'packaged politics', and the evil influence of television: in doing so he pinned down that in his appearance (though also, to be fully accurate, in his voice) Reagan had an asset of great value:

> For two-dimensional politics, Reagan is also blessed with surface features that are immediately appealing: a resonant voice with a tone of natural sincerity and just the right touch of boyishness, a hairline as unmoving as the Maginot Line, and a ruggedly handsome face that is neither unusual enough to jar the viewer nor so deeply wrinkled that it can't be smoothed out with make-up. He will be sixty – the same age as Humphrey – but most Californians would probably guess, on the basis of *appearance*, that he is ten to fifteen years younger than the former Vice-President.[121]

Two-dimensional or not, the trend was set. *Harper's* said of an aspirant (unsuccessful as it happened) for the Republican Presidential nomination in 1968: 'No longer is he *a* young man on the rise: he is *the* young man on the rise . . . He has the golden good looks and the deliberately modulated baritone of a candidate in the telegenic age.'[122]

The association of Reagan with Kennedy may seem odd, perhaps even offensive. But the matter is a non-ideological one. Kennedy is simply a metaphor for beauty as an autonomous characteristic which, independent of political programmes or ideas, has political value (which is not to say that it is an *essential* ingredient of success – a quick roll call of presidents and prime ministers since Kennedy will immediately establish that; the argument is not that Kennedy made beauty indispensable, but that he ratified the association between beauty and success). It may be undesirable that looks should have this value; or it may in fact be an advantage that looks should be openly considered, as a prelude to separating them out from more worthwhile qualities such as integrity or wisdom. Commercialism, misrepresentation, two-dimensional politics and the meretricious packaging of just about everything were inescapable facets of sixties society. Yet there was an admirable honesty, too, in facing up more squarely than ever before to the facts of human physical endowment. To medieval man deformity or disability was a sign of evil;

in more recent centuries they were matters to be politely ignored. It was, in fact, at the very end of the sixties that governments instituted the policies that have resulted in special, and quite explicitly advertised, facilities for the disabled.[123]

# 9 Conclusion: Beauty and Society Today

'The Beautiful People' was a phrase coined during the sixties. It serves well to pin down the significance beauty had now achieved, its use indicating that beauty was something to be singled out and remarked upon. 'The Beautiful People', as well as being beautiful, were also prosperous, and greatly envied for their conspicuously lavish life style. They were not godly people, they were not chivalrous people, they were not illuminated by an intense inner light; the phrase fairly and squarely linked beauty and material success. Many of them, both male and female, came from working-class or other disadvantaged backgrounds. More than ever before, and more unambiguously than before, beauty was a factor in social promotion. Many other forces were at work in dislocating class and age barriers, in offering fame and fortune to individuals with what, not many years before, would have been the wrong colour of face or an unacceptable manner of speech; but among those best placed to exploit the new opportunities were the well favoured in body and features. The selling power of beauty was seized on as never before. The youthful, healthy, sexy appearance was everywhere extolled. In a television age, it quickly came to be perceived, good looks would give a political candidate an immediate and uncovenanted benefit. When the good looking were clearly advantaged, and the ill looking as clearly disadvantaged, the older demand of good taste that one did not explicitly refer to a person's looks, whatever category they fell into, fell out of fashion. In 1969 a new modelling agency in London boldly called itself 'Ugly'.[1] It was recognized that, as always, those who were not beautiful could be striking and even attractive. But the pretence was much less likely to be made that they were actually beautiful. True beauty was too clearly recognized, too highly prized, to be confused with other physical (or mental, or moral) qualities, however valuable these might also be. In all this there was much cruelty, but also a certain honesty. As the special value of beauty was openly recognized, so also were the special needs of the handicapped.

Almost two decades on from the end of the sixties, it appears that the new appraisal of beauty will be with us for some time, despite the gathering strength of feminism, which was hotly opposed to it, many changes in fashion, and various reactions, or alleged reactions, against what were represented as the excesses, or the empty contrivances, of the sixties. One symbol of the triumph of the new attitudes was the 1974 Hollywood film *The Way We Were*. Robert Redford, a top box-office attraction, universally recognized as the epitome of one type of male beauty (there is a cross-reference to him as the ultimate in masculine desirability in another film, *Alice Doesn't Live Here Any More*) was teamed with Barbra Streisand, whose successes, and looks, were discussed in the previous chapter.[2] Comparison with *Marty* is instructive in showing how attitudes and conventions about personal appearance, within the medium which was itself a great force in generalizing evaluations of beauty, had changed over the period of the cultural revolution: while *Marty* was fundamentally – in intention, if not exactly in realization – a film about two ugly people, *The Way We Were* was far more than a film about a beautiful man and a not-quite-so-beautiful young woman. Hubble Gardner (Redford) is a smooth, conservative, all-American college boy; Katie Morasky (Streisand) is, at the same college in the 1930s, President of the Young Communist League, a pacifist, and anti-Fascist activist. Hubble is an oarsman and athlete, and always has a gorgeous co-ed on his arm; Katie persuades a large gathering of students to take the Peace Pledge. She tells him that he is 'decadent and disgusting', yet the film pointedly shows us that she finds it difficult to take her eyes off him. He is the model of the White Anglo-Saxon Protestant, always smiling, to whom things come too easily (at college he sells a short story, and shortly afterwards a novel; he is invited to Hollywood); she is Jewish, intense and serious, ill at ease in the social world of the conservative rich. But, unlike Clara in *Marty*, she is no passive wallflower.

120

She gets a job as an assistant radio producer (the opening sequence of the film), goes to a nightclub, and sees him there, now a Second World War sailor, drunkenly asleep. A flashback establishes the background points about their college days, then in the next sequence, she takes him home and, as the phrase might be, were the sexes reversed, 'takes advantage of him'. An edgy, difficult, though obviously deeply felt relationship begins. On one occasion when they are apart she phones him at night and begs him to come over to her, promising in a characteristic sixties-and-after role reversal, 'not to touch him'. There follows a very central passage of dialogue. 'It's because I'm not attractive enough, isn't it?' He does not reply to this, and after a pause she continues: 'I'm not fishing . . . I know I'm attractive . . . sort of . . .' There's a further pause. 'I'm not attractive . . . I'm not attractive in the right way . . . am I?' He still makes no response. 'I don't have the right style for you . . . do I?' Still no response and she adds: 'You're my friend.' Now he comes in. 'No . . . you don't have the right style.' 'I'll change', she responds.

120 Barbra Streisand and Robert Redford in *The Way We Were*, 1972

Then, moments later: 'Why can't I have you?' He says nothing about looks, but responds: 'Because you push too hard.' He adds, 'You expect so much.' To this she responds, 'But look what I've got', and it is clear that by this she means such a beautiful sex object as him. They marry and live together for a time in the Hollywood of the McCarthy era. They separate, and then, in the final sequence of the film, bump into each other again some years later in New York, where she is now a Ban the Bomb activist. He is with a beautiful woman; she is no longer straightening her hair.

In the real world, two trends continued and accelerated: the growth of the communications and service industries, and the entry of greater numbers of women into areas hitherto dominated by men. The evidence is overwhelming that women competing in the job market felt even greater pressure than ever before to pay the most meticulous attention to their personal appearance.[3] How far natural good looks, as distinct from good grooming, were important, is less easy to establish. It was clear that in the communications industries, where it was important for a man to be at least personable, it was imperative for a woman to be beautiful. Thus, although the main trend since the 1960s had been to stress more than ever before the significance of male good looks, there can be no denying that questions both of looks and of grooming continued to pervade all aspects of the lives of women to an extent that they did not for men; this reflected continuing (despite very many real changes) economic, social and political inequalities between the sexes, but perhaps also deeper psychological differences, as suggested in chapter two. There are a number of points here which will receive further attention shortly, but first it is important to take the measure of the evidence that with regard to career prospects in general, for both men and women, looks had become an important factor.

Most of the experiments conducted in ever increasing numbers in psychology departments across the United States were concerned, very properly, with other issues in addition to that of the significance of 'physical attractiveness' (since this quality was always represented by a head–and–shoulders photograph, it comes as near to what I have been calling 'beauty' as makes no difference). Researchers were concerned about discrimination against women, about the way in which certain jobs were typecast as being inherently and exclusively suited either to men or to women, and with the question of what particular qualities defined either as 'masculine' or 'feminine' were suited to different types of jobs. To understand this body of research, therefore, it is important to consider the concept of 'psychological androgyny' which was much used in it. The notion that all males, genetically, possess some female characteristics, and vice versa, is an old, unsurprising and eminently sound one. The term 'androgynous', correctly used, means being possessed of *all* of the *physical* attributes of both male and female. During the seventies the concept came into wide use in certain branches of knowledge, notably in art history, where the physical emphasis was maintained, and in psychology. In a sense, the usage was both tautological and exaggerated to an absurd degree (we *all* do have masculine and feminine traits anyway); and the painted representations of male bodies deemed 'androgynous' in fact quite clearly had male, and only male, sex organs, and male, not female, breasts. However, as long as the term was clearly seen as a metaphorical and technical one, it could be useful (problems could arise when polemicists took the condition to have a real existence, apart from that mixture of genetic inheritance which had long been known about). Psychological androgyny was defined first by Sandra L. Bem in the article 'The measurement of psychological androgyny', published in 1974; subsequent researchers usually dropped the important qualifier 'psychological', which was, after all, implied by the context of their researches – but it is important to note that none of the items which went into the Bem measurement betokened personal appearance. Here is the full list of these items.[4]

| Masculine Items | Feminine Items | Neutral Items |
| --- | --- | --- |
| Acts as leader | Affectionate | Adaptable |
| Aggressive | Cheerful | Conceited |
| Ambitious | Childlike | Conscientious |
| Analytical | Compassionate | Conventional |
| Assertive | Does not use | Friendly |
| Athletic | bad language | Happy |
| Competitive | Eager to soothe | Helpful |
| Defends own | hurt feelings | Inefficient |
| beliefs | Feminine | Jealous |
| Dominant | Flatterable | Likeable |
| Forceful | Gentle | Moody |
| Has leadership | Gullible | Reliable |
| qualities | Loves children | Secretive |
| Independent | Sensitive to needs | Sincere |
| Makes decisions | of others | Solemn |
| easily | Shy | Tactful |
| Masculine | Soft spoken | Theatrical |
| Self-reliant | Sympathetic | Truthful |
| Strong personality | Tender | Unpredictable |
| Willing to take a | Understanding | Unsystematic |
| stand | Warm | |
| Willing to take | Yielding | |
| risks | | |

Without dwelling on the assumptions behind this classification, one could just note that no sane individual would be likely to come out as entirely 'masculine' or entirely 'feminine'. In experiments which made use of what became canonized as the Bem Scale, subjects rated themselves on their possession of these various items: males who had a predominance of masculine items, and females who had a predominance of feminine items were then rated, respectively, as male and female; males who had a predominance of feminine items and females who had a predominance of masculine items were together rated as 'androgynous'.

That matter of definition out of the way, we can now look at some of the points made by the research of the past decade or so. From the fundamental, and indisputable, point that women were discriminated against in all sorts of employment, researchers went on to examine jobs which were thought to be essentially masculine, essentially feminine, or 'sex-neutral'. Other research, located more specifically on physical attractiveness, meantime, suggested that the most physically attractive ('beautiful') men were thought to be the most masculine and the most physically attractive women to be the most feminine.[5] Thus, apart from any more general implications of beauty, beautiful men seemed to have an advantage in masculine jobs (the research dealt with white-collar, not manual, occupations) and beautiful women an advantage in feminine jobs. Further research suggested that, despite the undoubted general advantages clearly demonstrated in other work (much of it discussed in the previous chapter), outstanding beauty was actually a disadvantage to a woman wishing to enter the masculine domain of management: one pair of researchers concluded that a woman who wished to compete successfully here should make herself 'as unattractive and masculine as possible'.[6] These experiments referred to point of entry into a profession, to the decisions likely to be taken by personnel managers or others conducting initial interviews. Studies of the behaviour of interviewers or 'raters' indicated that the more purely masculine, or the more purely feminine, the interviewer, the more highly physical attractiveness was rated; the 'androgynous' apparently did not put so much weight on mere physical attractiveness.[7]

   Against this background of knowledge, Linda A. Jackson, reporting in 1983, conducted an experiment which involved mailing a questionnaire to genuine real-life personnel consultants. The consultants were to rate candidates in respect of six occupations, two 'male' (Computer Systems Analyst and Operations Researcher), two 'female' (Dietician and Bank Teller), and two 'sex-neutral' (Vocational/Educational Counsellor and Health Practitioner). To assist them, they had photographs (eight were used, two of attractive males, two of unattractive males, two of attractive females, and two of unattractive females), a summary of the applicant's academic record, and a 'self-impression questionnaire', in which the candidate gave his or her own assessment of the Bem qualities: the consultant thus had a statement of relevant personal qualities, while the researcher had the basis for allocating applicants as masculine, feminine, or androgynous.[8] Dr Jackson concluded that the spelling out of personal qualities helped to mitigate sheer sexual prejudice, consultants rating candidates as suitable on the basis of their possessing the 'correct' qualities, rather than the 'correct' sex. In the sex-neutral occupations, physical attractiveness was particularly important. These were the aspects which the author herself chose to highlight in the summary of her research published in *Psychological Abstracts*.[9] But for all the intriguing refinements, what comes through strongly in the article itself is the all-pervasiveness of the influence of beauty, there being no question of beautiful women being handicapped for any of the occupations:

Physical attractiveness influenced ratings as to the sex-linked occupations, as predicted, but also influenced ratings in the sex-neutral occupations. Physical attractiveness influenced starting salary recommendations across all occupations, suggesting that attractiveness may have not only social value but also monetary value.

As an explanation of the phenomenon of higher salaries for the beautiful, Dr Jackson suggested that attractive applicants may have been seen as having 'more occupational alternatives (as well as social alternatives)' so that a higher starting salary would be necessary to attract them to employment.[10]

But perhaps if appointment panels were chosen in a different and more careful way, then the prejudice in favour of beauty might disappear? In an experiment concerning the rating of applicants for a post as head of a furniture department in a large department store, T. F. Cash and R. N. Kilcullen used as raters, not actual personnel consultants, but, in the traditional way, a group of college students, divided into 'male', 'female' and 'androgynous'. 'Applicants' were represented in the usual way by eight photographs. From both male and female evaluators, the highest ratings for the job went to, first, the attractive women, and then the attractive men. The results from androgynous raters were similar, though less pronounced.[11] The job had been deliberately chosen as one requiring interpersonal skills; earlier research had suggested that physical attractiveness was thought to be very important in such jobs, though not necessarily so in other jobs.[12]

If the possibilities of manipulating interview boards were limited, could candidates usefully present themselves in such a way as to enhance their own physical attractiveness, and thus diminish the advantages of the naturally beautiful? An experiment, involving only female interviewees, though male and female interviewers, was summed up by its author, Robert Baron, as 'Self-presentation in job interviews: when there can be "too much of a good thing"'. Female interviewers reacted favourably to the attempts at projecting physical attractiveness, males unfavourably. Baron explained the unfavourable male reaction (which, of course, would be critical in the actual job market) as being because males know that they are already predisposed to make decisions on the basis of appearance, and thus in this case deliberately and self-consciously reacted against this tendency (female interviewers, on the other hand, had admiration for, and probably empathy with, the attempts of fellow women to make the best of themselves).[13] Baron's explanation with respect to male reactions is unconvincing. It may be, as I have suggested once or twice throughout this book, that what males go for is natural beauty, and that there is some resentment at artificial attempts to construct it.

The overall conclusions are clear, though not dramatic. We run little risk of aristocracy, or plutocracy, being succeeded by calocracy (rule by the beautiful). Definitely, the beautiful of both sexes are advantaged; any taboo against beautiful women in 'masculine' executive positions would

almost certainly seem to have disappeared by the early eighties –
television, where the successful female executives in soap operas are
invariably beautiful, may have played a part here. Beautiful people
seemed likely to command higher starting salaries, but the emphasis on
beauty was most marked in respect of the sort of employment where it
would be a tangible asset, employment involving communication and
interpersonal relationships (but then, of course, the general trend anyway
was towards emphasizing both of these). It might well be possible to
construct the kind of interviewing committee which would not place
weight on personal appearance, but as selection procedures actually
existed it was clear that such weight would be placed. The assumption,
anyway, that beautiful interviewees were passive (as photographs are
passive), while significance attaches exclusively to the reactions of
interviewers, should not rest unchallenged. Beautiful men, as at least one
survey confirmed, consciously and confidently exploited their good
looks.[14] All historical experience suggests that this would also be true for
beautiful women.

During my long dive into the turbulent waters of early modern
Europe I suggested that the professions, especially as they emerged in the
eighteenth century, in which beauty was an asset were those related to
personal service (mainly men), sexual service (women) and selling (men
and women). Expand the boundaries to take in the gathering and
dissemination of information of all sorts, include the communications
revolution and the other transformations of modernization, particularly
in its intense 1960s phase, and the same is broadly true today. Projection
of, and profit from, sexuality by beautiful women need no longer
involve sexual services, though, of course, prostitutes and call girls still
exist, as well as a whole recent variety of strippers, massage-parlour and
peep-show girls – here the old hierarchy of beauty is more firmly articulated than ever.[15] The existence of women with money, independence
and few inhibitions created the market for the male prostitute and the
male stripper, and such clubs as Chippendales in New York, where the
audiences were exclusively female and the strippers exclusively male.
Beauty was not necessarily absolutely essential in either profession, but
certainly neither was a job for the man who was less than personable.
Males were being scrutinized as sex objects in the way in which women
always had been, as is suggested by an item in one of Britain's tabloids
(whose accuracy, no doubt, is symbolic rather than literal):

Stripping policeman Mike Marcus was a big flop when he took down his
particulars at a hen party. As soon as the all-girl audience copped an eyeful of the
bawdy bogus bobby, they burst out laughing and demanded their money back.
Disappointed reveller Kerry Baker said: 'I wanted to take a close-up with my
camera – but I'd have needed a zoom lens!' . . . when he came to the big finale the
girls decided macho Mike didn't have mucho to write home about.[16]

The serious cry to women to assess their men as their men had assessed them had come in Germaine Greer's *The Female Eunuch*, first published in 1970. A woman should not continue:

to apologise and disguise herself, while accepting her male's pot-belly, wattles, bad breath, farting, stubble, baldness and other ugliness without complaint. Is it too much to ask that women be spared the daily struggle for super human beauty in order to offer it to the caresses of a sub-humanly ugly mate?[17]

Less frivolous than the *Sun*, less baleful than Germaine Greer, and more joyful than both is the photographer Roberta Juzefa:

I have always believed the male form is equally as beautiful than the female but in photographing the male body, you must approach it leaving all preconceived thoughts behind, using intuition as a guide. Many photographs of men destroy the male mystique. Posing and looking directly into the camera's eye immediately loses the picture's erotic appeal. Most male models take up female gestures posing through conditioning which also makes the photograph look ridiculously wrong.[18]

*The* professions, established in the sixties, which continued to offer expanding opportunities for the beautiful, were those of model and TV presenter. The Ford Modeling Agency of New York, built up by Eileen Ford, is today a multi-million-dollar corporation. The commercial value of beauty is succinctly summed up by Eileen Ford herself:

I can justify my models' fee, if I have to, in fifteen seconds. Cheryl Tiegs's endorsement of Seers Roebuck's Sportswear increased sales by 20%, Christie Brinkley's line of bathing suits boosted the manufacturer's profits by $6,000,000 a year. Lauren Hutton sold God knows how many million dollars worth of extra Revlon cosmetics – what my girls got *wasn't enough!*[19]

Rewards for male models were not so high, but the use of male models to advertise practically everything was inescapable. The more rewarding field for men was that of performance in television commercials (though still attracting nothing like the prestige of the top female photographic model). Both male and female were featured in a British commercial for an electric razor, with which she shaved him. As a woman journalist commented: 'He smiled at her through his designer stubble (a smile to weaken your knees).'[20] But one enduring difference between male and female opportunities pervaded this world as well:

The Eileen Ford Agency is not interested in anyone over 22 . . . For men, in some instances, older is better. The wrinkles that bring an end to a woman's career can be an asset to a man's face. Those lines of character and maturity and those little gray hairs can add years to a man's modeling career . . . While the majority of modeling work is done by men in their late 20s, a man can work well into his 40s if he chooses.[21]

Though scarcely needed, research showed that physically attractive communicators were effective communicators.[22] In the sixties, television news presentation in all countries had tended to be dominated by older men, several with genuine reputations in the world of journalism, all conveying by their appearance authority, wisdom and reliability. As women began to make their appearance in this highly visible profession, it was widely noted that they were much younger, and much prettier. However, by the eighties, although the old-style male figure was still much in evidence, two other developments had become apparent: specialist women television reporters of proven expertise were not necessarily very beautiful, while younger male presenters often quite notably were. Television presentation in many ways forms a test case for the ideas put forward in this book. Reading the news is not as easy as it seems. It certainly calls for a number of capabilities though it does not, I think, call for any very deep intellectual or creative talent. But, by the very nature of the job, it is essential that a television presenter should be presentable. Undoubtedly there still is a differential as to demands made of men and demands made of women: on the whole, we accept presentable men but demand beautiful women. At all events, it would simply be counter-productive and deeply embarrassing if, in the name of some new kind of equality of opportunity, we pushed ugly women, or

121 Grace Jones, model and actress, in *View to a Kill*, 1985

122 Nastassia Kinski in *Tess*, 1980

ugly men, into the role of newsreaders (for more active, more involving, more creative roles it may be different). We again come up against the fact that distinctions of personal appearance do definitely exist: it does not to me seem any more unfair that a good appearance should be required of a television newscaster than that an ability to sing should be required of a choirboy.

But while the fact of beauty remains unchanged, that modern tendency, so greatly accelerated in the sixties, the ability to appeciate the many different varieties of beauty, continued. Models, film and TV stars, television presenters and newsreaders come from all the ethnic groups represented in Western society (and, for example, are featured in the illustrations to the guide already cited, *How to Get Work and Make Money in Commercials and Modeling*). To be sure, the chosen few fit within the parameters of universal beauty as developed in Western society, and as described in this book; but, however much criticized for not resembling the ordinary members of their group (what model or star does resemble the ordinary members of their group?), they are manifestly not simply imitation Caucasians; a British example is the model Grace Jones.    121
Among the most highly regarded Caucasian beauties, no one style or convention predominated, as can be seen from photographs of film

122–24    actresses Nastassia Kinski and Isabelle Huppert, film actor Richard Gere
          (star – sign of the times – of *American Gigolo*), or models Cheryl Tiegs
          and Christie Brinkley. The best tale of the times was that surrounding
          Vanessa Williams, the first black girl to win, in 1983, the Miss America
          Competition. She was no plain girl winning runner-up prizes for
          singing, as happened in the fifties and early sixties: her appeal and
          achievement were transparently sexual. Within days, Miss Williams had
          been forced to resign her title because *Penthouse*, an American magazine
          specializing in explicit full-frontal nude photographs of women, announ-
          ced that it had just such photographs of Vanessa Williams, which,
          furthermore, featured lesbian caresses with a nude white girl and
          bondage scenes.[23] However, that is not the note on which I wish to end.
          The key note is the arrival in the manifestly non-sexual role of TV
          announcer, of beautiful people of both sexes, and of all varieties of
          beauty.

             I am speaking, as ever, of beauty, not grooming. But as the rewards of
          beauty increased, so also did pressure to put forward as good an
          appearance as possible, and the resources, in the way of cosmetics, beauty
          farms, health cures, etc., etc., were greater than ever before. Of course,
          some groups, most notably the punks, used artifice for purposes far

123 (left) Isabelle Huppert, photograph, 1978

124 (right) Richard Gere in *American Gigolo*, 1979

other than appearing desirable. After the shake-ups of the sixties, fashion very much settled into older routines. But the self-presentation of the 1980s was worlds away from that of the seventeenth and eighteenth centuries, when a broadly conventionalized image was essentially what was aimed at. Now, a much more personal, individualized image was the objective, which could be liberating and joyful (as on the whole the transformations of the sixties had been), or could impose upon a person (I am mainly, but not exclusively, speaking of women here) a deep feeling of dissatisfaction and distress that true beauty, so widely exemplified and lauded at every turn, was almost as far away as ever. Writing in *The Beauty Trap* (ensnaring women not men), Nancy C. Baker noted that in the decade up to the end of 1984, cosmetic purchases in the United States had increased by ten per cent per year, and the diet industry had grown into a fourteen-billion-dollar business.[24] Dissatisfaction with individual aspects of personal appearance was recorded by Lakoff and Scherr as a widespread phenomenon.[25] Perhaps the most significant phenomenon was the enormous increase in the amount of cosmetic surgery being carried out. Partly, of course, this was because the facilities and techniques existed, and partly because a sufficient number of individuals had the money to spend on the treatment. However, the commissioning of plastic surgery does seem to me a very real and direct recognition of the autonomous (that is to say, purely physical) character of beauty. The older idea had been that through charm, cheerfulness, character and personality, assisted first by wigs, and curls, and powders, and patches, then by the judicious and discreet application of a few natural cosmetics, then by sheer hard work and devotion to good grooming, a woman could achieve all that was required. The use of surgery recognizes that when the structure of the face, or of the body, is wrong, none of these is enough; actual *physical* alteration is required.

One must be careful in using the testimony of beauty specialists and cosmetic surgeons, who, after all, have a commercial interest in persuading people of the need to make use of their skills. However, Dr Norman Martin, Beverly Hills cosmetic surgeon, may not have been totally wide of the mark when he said in 1985: 'It became important now to be competitive in looks as well as skills.'[26]

The counterblast to the money lavished on, and the huge profits made out of, cosmetic products and devices, was the feminist attack on the whole obsession with beauty and grooming. Wittingly, the writings and attitudes of the feminist critics form a profound opposition to the trends developing out of the cultural revolution of the sixties, though they are themselves a part of that revolution. Unwittingly, the very existence of the critique offers a recognition that the prevailing evaluation of beauty was exactly as I have stated it. And the feminist critique is related to the wider cultural transformations in that it is highly explicit about the issue of beauty; it shows that there is indeed an issue. Feminists argue that the current preoccupation with beauty forces women to try to conform to stereotyped ideals of beauty, instead of giving unrestrained expression to their natural selves. They argue that it produces anxiety, and indeed illness, in particular anorexia nervosa and bulimia. It entails women spending excessive amounts of time and money on the products of a beauty industry which, simply in pursuit of profit, deliberately creates false needs. This judgment may actually be a little contemptuous of women themselves and does ignore the apparent gratification which women derive from the various aspects of self-presentation. Feminists argue that it is demeaning to judge women by their looks when any human being should be judged by qualities of much greater worth, such as kindness or intelligence; they find the terms used to describe women – 'lovely face', 'nice legs', 'good body', 'stunning looks', etc. – insulting. Whether the individual women concerned, or women as a whole, really feel, or should feel, insulted, is a moot point. It may be remembered that one of Bem's items defining the feminine was 'flatterable'. It is true that Paul Newman is not alone among beautiful males in complaining that constant reference to his blue eyes distracts attention from his achievements as a highly intelligent actor and director. But I am dubious whether such compliments to man or woman are really a great burden.

However, the feminists' case is that there is an emphasis on what they regard as the trivial, and that this emphasis on looks separates women from men. While women's lives are actually affected by a constant preoccupation with their looks, men's lives are not so affected; in particular, while men continue to attract admiration as they age, admiration is sharply and cruelly withdrawn from older women. Some feminists, though not all, see the whole process as one imposed by men on women, designed to hold women in a position of political inferiority. It is true that men, all other things being equal (which they very seldom are), prefer beautiful women to plain ones. But men also esteem many other qualities in women. With regard to the question of grooming and fashion, men, as I have shown, have frequently protested against what they see as the creation of false images. In common with many non-feminist commentators, feminists believe that beauty is socially constructed, and that standards of beauty vary greatly from age to age. Create a different kind of society, and there would be no cruel, unfair distinctions of beauty; in the right society, everybody would be seen as beautiful. This may be a comforting myth, helpful for energizing the activists, and for distracting attention from current reality; but I cannot believe that it is anything other than harmful in dealing with the very real problems which the feminists themselves have identified.

I find myself greatly in sympathy with much of what is said by Nancy C. Baker in her *The Beauty Trap: How Every Woman Can Free Herself From It*. She recognizes the power and value which true natural beauty, as I have defined it, actually has. Her answer to the stresses and misery of trying fruitlessly to emulate that beauty is redefinition (as, broadly, it is with most feminists):

Isn't it time that we redefined beauty for ourselves so that it includes far more than perfect features, artfully enhanced by makeup, hairstyling, and clothing? My own new definition, for instance, is that a truly beautiful woman makes the best of her physical assets but, more important, she also *radiates a personal quality which is attractive*. Unlike the woman with a gorgeous face and body who is obsessed with herself, my ideally beautiful woman exudes concern for others, as well as intelligence, enthusiasm, humor, and self-confidence. These are all qualities we can cultivate in ourselves, and they're qualities that will last us a lifetime.[27]

Personally, I am not sure that definitions can be altered that easily (although I recognize that many people already do use the word 'beautiful' in this way, though usually, I believe, not consistently); what happens if women change the definition but men don't? More important, don't we need a word to describe 'the woman with the gorgeous face and body', who need not necessarily (this is the sort of silly slander which weakens feminist arguments) be 'obsessed with herself'? I prefer to reserve the word 'beautiful' for a manifest and important phenomenon which will not go away through any amount of juggling with words. In any case this attempted 'redefinition' of beauty really differs very little from the encouraging noises made down the ages by the more optimistic beauty guides – much good they have done!

However, I do understand very well what Ms Baker means by the 'beauty trap' and support the 'steps for escaping' which she reserves for her final chapter:

*The first step in escaping* from the beauty trap is simply to realise that it exists and to admit to ourselves that we have become trapped. We must acknowledge that we have overblown expectations of physical attractiveness, and we must admit that chasing elusive and transient feminine beauty is a loser's game.

Another important step is to '*recognise that a woman's looks do not determine her worth*'. A third step which may be picked out from the complete list is:

*Discuss the importance of physical beauty with your man.* Ask your husband or lover or friend which qualities he most values in you, and chances are, your appearance will be far down on the list. For many men, intelligence, compassion, wit, and other assets outshine the importance of physical attractiveness.[28]

I would, however, add one step of my own: recognize that among a lucky minority true physical beauty does exist (those with 'perfect features', or 'gorgeous face and body') and has a special value and power of its own which it is simply useless to deny. It is certainly futile and offensive to accuse such women of being inevitably self-obsessed, or cold, or callous, or whatever – many beautiful women, quite evidently, have possessed numerous other fine qualities as well.

However, feminist ideas have, without doubt, inspired many very desirable developments. Feminist groups have taught women not to crucify themselves over the image society has, or they think society has, of them. The most obvious success, in the United States, has been with respect to those seen by others, and so described by themselves, as 'fat'. The magazines *BBW* ('Big Beautiful Woman') and *Radiance* persuade fat women to be what they are, to aim at fitness, but not slimness. Fat women are unlikely to be top fashion models, or leading film actresses, or television presenters; but then most women, and men, of all shapes and sizes are unlikely to be top concert pianists. Whether knowingly or not, the fat woman's movement is a part of that explicitness which forms an important aspect of the modern evaluation of beauty.

Questions of personal appearance are not simply trivial matters fit only for the pages of the fashion magazines. The feminist critique has shown that, as have the topics examined in the psychological journals. In the mid-seventies, the BBC ran a documentary about the Suffragettes entitled *Shoulder to Shoulder*. A number of people, male and female, including myself, felt that it was fair neither to the Suffragettes nor to contemporary women, that all of the great heroines of the women's struggle were portrayed as extraordinarily beautiful TV actresses. A rumbling issue in the Britain of today concerns the publication in the tabloid newspapers, each morning, of a photograph of a topless young woman (popularly known as a 'page three girl'). Do such photographs give innocent pleasure to millions, or do they incite sexual violence? Do they demean women? Some women? All women? Much emphasis is placed on the bare breasts, but the simple, though often ignored fact is that no woman could be a page three girl without having a beautiful face. The issues are not simple (personally, I favour censorship for violent pornography); but the facts and their implications have to be sorted out before they can be properly addressed. Jumping out of the present, and going back through some of the topics of this book, one might well feel it worthwhile to conduct an investigation into what sorts of pressures, or what sorts of psychological make-up, decide a woman to go in for a career as a courtesan. But, given that some amount of physical attractiveness is a prerequisite for such a career, one couldn't begin without first sorting out the various problems in relationship to the notion of beauty. To come right back to some of the examples with which I began this book – Jack Kemp, Cecil Parkinson, Giovanni Goria, etc. – are we indeed in an era, as ex-governor Brown declared, of two-dimensional and packaged politics? What do we think of this report from Washington on the possible Presidential aspirations of Jeane Kirkpatrick: 'She does not fit into the familiar mold of presidential candidates, having an acerbic style, no measurable wit and lacking good looks'? [29]

To grapple with these, or other similar questions, one requires a solid definition of 'beauty'. Maybe beauty entails no more than 'society's sex-specific definitions of physical attractiveness' or 'targets defined by the culture as attractive'.[30] Yet, even if standards do greatly change from age to age (which I don't accept), it is still clear that the pursuit of beauty has gone on throughout the ages: thus, even if arguing that beauty itself changes, one has to explain why, whatever it is, it has such a profound appeal. I believe it is more in keeping with the facts as we know them from the sources left by the past to see beauty as a relative universal, but a relative universal in many varieties. Throughout this book I could just about have substituted the contemporary social scientist's phrase 'physical attractiveness' for 'beauty' – but not quite, since physical attractiveness can involve other physical attributes than the beauty of face and form of which I am speaking.

Few people today, I believe, have difficulty in recognizing the special, and purely physical, quality I call 'beauty', even if in ordinary conversations they may slide from beauty as a physical attribute to employing the word in respect of qualities of character or personality. This sort of slide is not acceptable in serious academic analysis. Accordingly I have made it absolutely clear how I am using the word 'beauty'; even if readers prefer to reserve the word for something more noble, I hope that my rigid adherence to the one definition has enabled my points to come over with clarity. Actually I believe that this 'mere' beauty, this physical beauty, this autonomous beauty, is of great importance in human affairs. Of course, many other qualities come into play, strength of character, intelligence, thoughtfulness, etc., etc. In one-to-one relationships, many other considerations may weigh more heavily, not least of them being the force of love, which can often be founded in attributes other than physical beauty. While it has been interesting and important, where the evidence exists, to look at the private lives of ordinary people, my major concern has to be the attitudes of people en masse, and of the powerful individuals who make social mobility possible for others. There are all sorts of personal idiosyncracies and subjective judgments, but the beauty I speak of, the beauty which is useable as a variable in scholarly study, is the beauty perceived by the majority. I have tried to show the way in which beauty, conceived as an autonomous characteristic, was, in different ages, evaluated against other characteristics, particularly social status and wealth. I have suggested that, at least before the nineteenth century, a wealthy woman could do well in the sexual marketplace even though only personable; for a poor woman, I have argued, beauty was essential if significant upward mobility was to be achieved. I have tried to show something of the strategies by which women in different circumstances exploited their gift of beauty. I have tried to bring out that beauty could also be important for men, though usually in less dramatic and less overtly sexual ways. I have also indicated that there is absolutely no guarantee that those who are beautiful will enjoy success; but the chances are that they will lead more than usually eventful lives. (The nemesis fallen upon Gary Hart may be seen as the nemesis which attended other beautiful men, including the Marquis de Cinq-Mars and James, Duke of Monmouth).

This book has linked the emergence of what I have called the 'modern', 'autonomous' concept of beauty to the processes summarized, in shorthand fashion, as 'modernization'. In 'traditional' societies beauty was perceived as a powerful and disturbing influence; but the prejudices and confusions of traditional society resulted in beauty being distrusted and given a relatively low evaluation. While insisting that the development is not a simple linear one, I have charted the slow emergence of the modern, high evaluation of beauty, demonstrating that it was only with the cultural revolution of the 1960s that open acknowledgment was made of the power of beauty. Many, no doubt, will continue to prefer the traditional rejection of 'mere' (carnal) beauty, in favour of a beauty associated with the divine. Among them, I suspect, will be many who are also opposed to the developments associated with modernization; that, of course, would help to confirm my overall thesis. For more compelling confirmation, one need only turn to the Iran of the Ayatollahs: here we have a conscious and explicit anti-modernization programme which, among other things, has resulted in the concealment of all the attributes of feminine beauty – these are designated dangerous and shameful.

If you tell a man that, despite the evidence of his own mirror, or of the reactions of the very women he desires most, he, because he is kind, and tolerant, and sensitive, is a truly beautiful person, you may not greatly comfort him. If you say the same sort of thing to a woman who is miserable because constantly made aware that most men do not find her physically attractive, it will probably not comfort her. It would seem to me better to recognize that beauty is a physical quality which, like many other qualities, such as mathematical skills, musical, artistic or literary talent, or deep instinctive sensitivity to the feelings and needs of others, is most unequally and unfairly shared around. It seems to me silly and futile to try to denigrate this quality of beauty as being merely a facet of passing fashion or something contrived by men to put down women, or simply a provoker of lust. Beautiful people give pleasure (to the generality of beholders: I am not here speaking of the sexual embrace). Of course, cheerful and charming people give pleasure as well, but that does not detract from the special appeal of purely physical beauty. One has only to reflect on one's own experience: any gathering is instantly improved if joined by a beautiful person, even if that person is utterly inaccessible. A few pages back I cited a woman journalist's reaction to a beautiful male model in a TV commercial, a commercial she recognized as essentially silly.

Beauty *is* very highly valued by our modern society, and not for reasons which are entirely bogus or entirely commercial. But having given beauty its true value, we should not then confuse matters by attributing to beauty other desirable qualities, such as moral or intellectual worth. Beauty is important but limited. Once one has cleared that up, one can then go on and look at all the other highly desirable qualities which human beings possess: talent of one sort or another, friendliness, integrity, strength of character, etc., etc. I am, on the whole, in favour of a person making the most of their personal appearance, but that should be an individual decision. What is important is that we should value each individual, and each individual should be encouraged to value himself or herself, for their total range of qualities. It should be possible to say, with genuine warmth and enthusiasm, and without offence, 'you are not very beautiful, but you are wonderfully stimulating to be with, and entirely loveable'. Maybe that is not possible either. Some aspects of life are painful and are likely to remain so; among them, for men as well as women, the fact of not being as sexually desirable as we would like to be. But this book is not concerned with homilies or policies. It started and finished with how we are today, and merely addressed itself to the humble task of showing how we got here.

# Notes

## CHAPTER 1

1 Private information.

2 See chapter nine.

3 See, for example, Erica Jong, *Fanny* (1980) and *Fear of Flying* (1975); Lisa Alter, *Kinflicks* (1976) and *Original Sins* (1981); Fay Weldon, *The Life and Loves of a She Devil* (1983); Sandra Harmon, *A Girl Like Me* (1975); Susan Fromberg Schaeffer, *The Madness of a Seduced Woman* (1983).

4 See, for example, Anita Brookner, *Providence* (1982).

5 *New Society*, 22 March 1984. The research is discussed briefly in chapter two and more extensively in chapter eight.

6 Joseph Berger, *Status Characteristics and Social Interaction: An Expectation States Approach* (New York, 1977); Murray Webster, Jr and James E. Driskell, Jr, 'Beauty as status', *American Journal of Sociology*, vol.89, no.1 (1983), pp.140–65.

7 K. J. Dover, *Greek Homosexuality* (1978), p.12, footnote.

8 S. N. Eisenstadt, *Modernization: Protest and Change* (New Jersey, 1966), p.1.

9 See, for example, Mustafa O. Attir, Burkart Holzner and Zdenek Suda, *Directions of Change: Modernization Theory, Research and Realities* (Boulder, Colorado, 1981), esp. pp.xi and 5.

10 The literature on the social and sexual facts is immense, and often highly complex; the inferences in regard to beauty are my own. Reference may be made to Philippe Ariès, *Centuries of Childhood: A Social History of Family Life* (1962); J. Kirshner and S. F. Wemple, *Women of the Medieval World* (1985); M. W. Labarge, *Women in Medieval Life* (1986); R. A. Houlbrooke, *The English Family 1485–1700* (1984); Michael Anderson, *Approaches to the History of the Western Family 1500–1914* (1980); M. Segalen, *Love and Power in the Seventeenth Century* (1984); M. Slater, *Family Life in the Seventeenth Century* (1984); Edward Shorter, *The Making of the Modern Family* (New York, 1976); Lawrence Stone, *The Family, Sex and Marriage in England 1500–1800* (1977); Peter M. Stearns, *European Society in Upheaval* (New York, 1975); Paul Robinson, *The Modernization of Sex* (New York, 1976); Peter Laslett, *The World We Have Lost* (3rd edition, 1983); A. Macfarlane, *Marriage and Love in England 1300–1840* (1986); E. A. Wrigley and R. Schofield, *The Population History of England 1541–1871* (1981); Ferdinand Mount, *The Subversive Family* (2nd edition, 1983); Jeffrey Weeks, *Sexuality* (1986); Georges Duby, *Le Chevalier, la femme et le prêtre: le mariage dans la France féodale* (Paris, 1981); Jean Louis Flandrin, *Familles: parenté, maison, sexualité dans l'ancienne société* (Paris, 1976); Jean Louis Flandrin, *Le Sexe et l'occident: l'évolution des attitudes at des comportements* (Paris, 1981); François Lebrun, *La Vie conjugale sous l'ancien régime* (Paris, 1975); Natalie Zemon Davis, *The Return of Martin Guerre* (Cambridge, Mass., 1983); A. L. Rowse, *Simon Forman: Sex and Society in Shakespeare's Age* (1974).

11 For a standard example see Madge Garland, *The Changing Face of Beauty: Four Thousand Years of Beautiful Women* (New York, 1957). An exception is Kenneth Clark, *Feminine Beauty* (1980). I do not, however, derive great comfort from his company.

12 Peter L. Berger and Thomas Luckmann, *The Social Construction of Reality* (New York, 1966, 1967 edition), p.67. This book is the classic exposition of an approach against which I pose my own notion of the relative universality of beauty.

13 Jeffrey Weeks, *Sex, Politics and Society: The Regulation of Sexuality since 1800* (1981), p.11. In general: Jeffrey Weeks, *Sexuality and its Discontents: Meanings, Myths and Modern Sexuality* (1985), and *Sexuality* (1986); Michel Foucault, *Histoire de la sexualité* (Paris, 3 vols., 1976–84); J. H. Gagnon and William Simon, *Sexual Conduct: The Social Sources of Sexuality* (1973); Sue Cartledge and Joanna Ryan (eds.), *Sex and Love: New Thoughts and Old Contradictions* (1983); Rosalind Coward, *Female Desire: Women's Sexuality Today* (1984); Berger and Luckmann, *Social Construction*, p.202.

## CHAPTER 2

1 Ford Madox Brown's description of his painting *Work* is contained in F. Madox Heuffer, *Ford Madox Brown* (1896), pp. 189–95.

2 J. H. Lupton (ed.), *The Utopia of Sir Thomas More: in Latin from the Edition of March 1518, and in English from the first Edition of Ralph Robynson's Translation in 1551* (Oxford, 1895), book two, chapter seven, p.232.

3 *Ibid.*, pp.226–27, 232.

4 *Ibid.*, p.225.

5 *Ibid.*, p.232.

6 T. Bell, *Kalogynomia or the Laws of Female Beauty* (1821), pp.312–17; repeated in slightly expanded form in Alexander Walker, *Beauty, Illustrated Chiefly by an Analysis and Classification of Beauty in Women* (1836), pp.386–90. See chapter five.

7 Alphonse Karr, *Les Femmes* (Paris, 1855), p.209; H. T. Finck, *Romantic Love and Personal Beauty* (New York, 1887), vol.2, pp.178, 374–75. See chapter five.

8 Marcel Braunschvig, *La Femme et la beauté* (Paris, 1919), p.135.

9 Theodore Zeldin, *France 1848–1945*, vol.2 (Oxford, 1977), p.44.

10 Anne Hollander, *Seeing Through Clothes* (New York, 1978), p.86.

11 *Ibid.*, p.331. See also Bernard Rudolfsky, *The Unfashionable Human Body* (Garden City, NY, 1981), esp. pp.12–15; Michael Batterberry, *Fashion, The Mirror of History* (New York, 1982); Alison Lurie, *The Language of Clothes* (New York, 1981); Fernand Braudel, 'Les costumes et la mode', in *Civilisation matérielle et capitalisme* (*'XV*ᵉ*–XVIII*ᵉ *siècle'*), vol.1 (Paris, 1967), pp.233–49; Neil McKendrick, 'The commercialization of fashion', in *The Birth of a Consumer Society: The Commercialization of Eighteenth-Century England* (ed. Neil McKendrick, John Brewer, J. H. Plumb, 1982), pp.34–99.

12 I have been specially helped in formulating these thoughts by Valerie Steele's brilliant *Fashion and Eroticism: Ideals of Feminine Beauty from the Victorian Era to the Jazz Age* (New York, 1985), though I do not share the notion that ideals of beauty (as distinct from conventions of self-presentation) change from era to era.

13 Hollander, *Seeing Through Clothes*, p.360.

14 Susan Brownmiller, *Femininity* (New York, 1984).

15 Simone de Beauvoir, *Le Deuxième Sexe* (Paris, 1947), vol.2, p.345.

16 Dr Vernon Coleman with Margaret Coleman, *Face Values: How the Beauty Industry Affects You* (1981), p.xi.

17 *Ibid.*, pp.xiii–xiv.

18 *San Francisco Chronicle*, 11 January 1985.

19 *Théorie de la figure humaine, considérée dans ses principes, soit en repos ou en mouvement, ouvrage traduit du Latin de Pierre-Paul Rubens* (Paris, 1773), p.50.

20 *Dr Salter of Tolleshunt D'Arcy: Diary and Reminiscences 1849–1932* (ed. J. O. Thompson, 1933), 29 December 1859.

21 H. T. Finck, *My Adventures in the Golden Age of Music* (New York, 1926), p.272. The photograph is on page 270.

22 For a most useful summary of the different experiments, see E. Berscheid and E. Walster, 'Physical attractiveness', in *Advances in Experimental Social Psychology*, vol.7 (New York, 1974), pp.157–215; see also Donald Symons, *The Evolution of Human Sexuality* (New York, 1979), p.267.

23 Robin Tolmach Lakoff and Raquel L. Scherr, *Face Value: The Politics of Beauty* (Boston, 1984), p.56; another important feminist work, Nancy C. Baker, *The Beauty Trap* (New York, 1984), is discussed in chapter nine.

24 Lakoff and Scherr, *Face Value*, p.57.

25 *Ibid.*

26 *Ibid.*, p.59.

27 *Ibid.*, p.66.

28 *Ibid.*, p.148.

29 *New York Times*, 25 November 1984.

30 Lakoff and Scherr, *Face Value*, p.20.

31 *Ibid.*

32 *Ibid.*, p.296.

33 William Shakespeare, Sonnets 1 (c. 1593).

34 Charles Darwin, *The Descent of Man and Selection in Relation to Sex* (1871, revised and augmented edition, New York, 1879), pp.573–87.

35 Finck, *Romantic Love*, vol.2, pp.377ff.

36 Lucien Bray, *Du beau: essai sur l'origine et l'évolution du sentiment esthétique* (Paris, 1902), p.291.

37 Sigmund Freud, *Three Essays on the Theory of Sexuality* (originally published Vienna, 1905; 4th edition, Vienna, 1920; first English edition, London, 1949), p.35, note 1, and p.87.

38 *Ibid.*, *Civilization and its Discontents* (1930), in J. Strachey and A. Freud (eds.), *The Standard Edition of the Complete Psychological Works of Sigmund Freud*, vol.21 (1964), p.140.

39 Stendhal (Henri Beyle), *De l'amour* (1822; Paris 1853 edition), pp.33–34.

40 See references in chapter nine.

41 Havelock Ellis, *Studies in the Psychology of Sex: IV Sexual Selection in Man* (Philadelphia, 1906), pp.136–37.

42 Rémy de Gourmont, *Physique le l'amour: essai sur l'instinct sexuel* (Paris, 1903), pp.69–70.

43 W. Stroebe, C. A. Insko, V. D. Thompson and B. D. Layton, 'Effects of physical attractiveness, attitude similarity, and sex on various aspects of interpersonal attraction', *Journal of Personality and Social Psychology*, vol.18 (1971), pp.79–91. See discussion in chapter eight.

44 Donald Symons, *The Evolution of Human Sexuality* (New York, 1979), p.27.

45 *Ibid.*, p.143.

46 *Ibid.*

47 Georges Bataille, *Death and Sensuality: A study of Eroticism and the Taboo* (New York, 1957), pp.142–43.

48 *Ibid.*, p.143.

49 Darwin, *Descent*; Ellis, *Studies*; H. Stratz, *Die Schönheit des Weiblichen Körpers* (14th

edition, Berlin, 1903); de Gourmont, *Physique*, p.70; Emile Bayard, *L'Art de reconnaître la beauté du corps humain* (Paris, 1926), pp.240ff. Finck, *Romantic Love*, vol.1, pp.100–01.

50 Anton Chekov, *Uncle Vanya* (1899), act III.

51 Finck, *Romantic Love*, vol.2, pp.136–37.

52 *Ibid.* (drawing on the extensive contemporary literature), vol.1, p.283.

53 Symons, *Evolution*, p.166.

54 Braunschvig, *La Femme*, p.221; Bayard, *L'Art de reconnaître*, p.10, citing Stratz; Bernard Bosanquet, 'The aesthetic theory of ugliness', *Proceedings of the Aristotelian Society*, vol.1, no.3 (1891), p.36.

55 I am particularly indebted to my colleague Professor Erika Langmuir for her helpful comments here; in the end I have gone my own way, though, thanks to her guidance, with great caution.

56 Rubens, *Théorie*, pp.1 and 9.

57 *Ibid.*, pp.14–15.

58 *Ibid.*, pp.49–50.

59 Rubens to Pierre Dupuy, 15 July 1626, *The Letters of Peter Paul Rubens*, translated and edited by Ruth Saunders Magurn (Cambridge, Mass., 1955), p.136.

60 Jacqueline Bouchot-Saupique, *Helena Fourment Rubens* (1948), pp.1–2.

61 Quoted in Christopher White, *Rubens and his World* (1968), p.101.

62 Keith Roberts, *Rubens* (1977), p.3.

63 *Ibid.*, p.4.

64 Jan Marsh, *The Pre-Raphaelite Sisterhood* (1985), pp.15–34, 117–23.

65 Arthur Marwick, *The Nature of History* (2nd edition, 1981).

# CHAPTER 3

1 Flandrin, *Familles*, pp.80–81, writes: 'in a society where the overwhelming majority of families drew their subsistence from assets, small or large, which bore fruit or not, depending on their own labour, it was

criminal with respect to children yet to be born to marry without having the capital necessary to maintain a family'. In general, see works cited in note 10 to chapter one.

2 See, generally, Anthony Andrewes, *The Greeks* (1967, republished 1971 as *Greek Society*); K. J. Dover, *Greek Popular Morality in the Time of Plato and Aristotle* (1974).

3 Plato, *Greater Hippias*, 287e. Throughout I use the accepted method of citation, common to all editions and translations. My English versions (I do not read Greek) are drawn from *The Dialogues of Plato translated by Benjamin Jowett* (Oxford, 1871; 4th edition, revised, 1964) and J. S. Blackie, *On Beauty: Three Discourses . . . with an Exposition of the Doctrine of the Beautiful according to Plato* (Edinburgh, 1858) – more the latter than the former.

4 *Greater Hippias*, 289b, 295c.

5 *Phaedras*, 250de, 251a.

6 Dover, *Greek Homosexuality*, pp.12–13, 161, note 11.

7 Plato, *Symposium*, 210, 211, 212a.

8 Plato, *Charmides*, 154de, 155de.

9 Dover, *Greek Homosexuality*, p.115.

10 See the exhibits, and the supporting text, in the Roman section of the Museum of London.

11 Walter C. Curry, *The Middle English Ideal of Personal Beauty* (Baltimore, 1916), p.3; but see also Jacqueline Boucher, *Société et mentalités autour de Henri III* (Lille/Paris, 1981), p.3.

12 Curry, *Middle English Ideal*, pp.4–5.

13 *Ibid.*, p.3.

14 E. Rodocanachi, *La Femme italienne à l'époque de la Renaissance* (Paris, 1907), p.90.

15 Curry, *Middle English Ideal*, p.7.

16 *Ibid.*, p.6.

17 'Certeyne Rewles of Phisnomy', from British Library MS Sloan 213, fols.118v–121v, reprinted by M. A. Manzalaoui, *Secretum Secretorum: Nine English Versions* (Early English Text Society, Oxford, 1977), vol.1, pp.10–17.

18 Curry, *Middle English Ideal*, p.5.

19 Gabriel de Minut, *De la beauté, discours divers . . . voulans signifier, que ce qui est naturellement beau, est aussi naturellement bon* (Paris, 1587), pp.210–12.

20 David de Flurance Rivault, *L'Art d'embellir* (Paris, 1608), book 1, fols. 2–3.

21 Minut, *De la beauté*, p.214.

22 *Ibid.*, p.213.

23 *Ibid.*, pp.255ff.

24 *Ibid.*, pp.261–62.

25 *Ibid.*, p.270.

26 Jefferson Butler Fletcher, *The Relations of Beauty in Women, and Other Essays on Platonic Love in Poetry and Society* (New York, 1911), p.3.

27 Joan Kelly-Gadol, 'Did women have a Renaissance?', in Renata Bridenthal and Claudia Koonz (eds.), *Becoming Visible: Women in European History* (Boston, 1977), pp.137–64.

28 A. G. Dickens, *The Age of Humanism and Reformation* (Englewood Cliffs, NJ, 1972), p.125.

29 Agnolo Firenzuola, 'Dialogo delle bellezze delle donne', in *Prose di M. Agnolo Firenzuola Fiorentino* (Florence, 1548), fol.51.

30 See J. R. Woodhouse, *Baldesar Castiglione* (Edinburgh, 1977), Robert W. Hanning and David Rostand (eds.), *Castiglione: The Ideal and the Real in Renaissance Culture* (New Haven, 1983), and George Bull, *The Book of the Courtier: Baldesar Castiglione* (1967), Introduction, p.23. The original edition, *Il libro de cortegiano del Conte Baldesar Castiglione* (Venice, 1528) has no folio or page numbers, and this is also true of *The Book of the Courtier. From the Italian of Count Baldessare Castiglione done into English by Sir Thomas Hoby* (1561). My page references, therefore, are to the 1900 re-printing of the latter, now cited as *The Courtier*; the Italian phrases can, without too much difficulty, be tracked down in the original Venetian edition.

31 *The Courtier*, p.343.

32 *Ibid.*, p.348.

33 *Ibid.*, p.349.

34 Michel de Montaigne, *Essais*, vol.3 (1588), no.12, 'De la phisionomie', p.467: 'I cannot say how much I estime beauty . . . it places itself out in front, seduces and pre-empts our judgments . . .' See Appendix 1.

35 Introduction, by Theodore Child, to the abbreviated English translation, *Dialogue on the Beauty of Women* (1892).

36 Nicoló Franco, *Dialogo dove si ragiona delle bellezze* (Venice, 1542); Lodovico Domenichi, *La nobiltà dell donne* (Venice, 1549); Federigo Luigini, *Il libro della bella donna* (Venice, 1554; English translation, 1909); Nicoló Campani, *Bellezze della donna* (Venice, 1566). In general, see the still authoritative Ruth Kelso, *Doctrine for the Lady of the Renaissance* (Urbana, 1956), especially chapter six, 'Love and Beauty', pp.136–209; my interpretations are slightly different from hers.

37 'I ritratti di Giovan Giorgio Trissino', in *Tutti le opere di Giovan Giorgio Trissino*, vol.2 (Verona, 1729), pp.269–77. For a splendid survey of theoretical treatises aimed at painters and sculptors, see Elizabeth Cropper, 'On beautiful women, Parmigianino, *Petrarchismo*, and the vernacular style', in *The Art Bulletin*, vol.58, no.3 (1976), pp.374–94.

38 Firenzuola, *Dialogue*, fol.75.

39 *The Courtier*, p.216.

40 Firenzuola, *Dialogue*, fols.67–71.

41 *Ibid.*, fol.74.

42 Franco, fol.23.

43 Firenzuola, fol.99.

44 Franco, fol.43.

45 *Ibid.*, fols.75ff.

46 Domenichi, fol.24.

47 Firenzuola, fol.70.

48 *Ibid.*, fol.63.

49 *Ibid.*, fol.106.

50 *Ibid.*, fol.65.

51 *Ibid.*, fol.62.

52 *Ibid.*, fol.64 (misprinted as 74).

53 Campani, *Bellezze della donna*, and Mario Equicola d'Areto, *Di natura d'amore*, as quoted in Rodocanachi, *La Femme italienne*, p.103.

54 Shakespeare, *As You Like It*, act 1, scene 3.

55 Discussed further in chapter four.

56 Rodocanachi, *La Femme italienne*, p.103.

57 Henry Fielding, *History of Tom Jones* (1749), book 1, chapter twelve.

58 *Ibid.*, 'To a Friend on choosing a Wife', in *Miscellanies*, vol.1 (1743), pp.27ff.

59 Quoted in R. B. Outhwaite (ed.), *Marriage and Society: Studies in the Social History of Marriage* (1981), p.10. A recently published collection of family letters in which attitudes to marriage and wealth, status and beauty emerge most distinctly is *Barrington Family Letters 1628–1632* (edited for the Royal Historical Society by Arthur Searle, Camden Fourth Series, vol.28, 1983).

60 Quoted in Outhwaite, *Marriage and Society*, p.10.

61 Roger Thompson, *Women in Stuart England and America* (1974), p.117.

62 Lawrence Stone, *The Family, Sex and Marriage in England 1500–1800* (1977), pp.281–315; Mary Astell, *Some Reflections on Marriage* (1700), pp.10, 13, 18, 19, 21; *Memoirs of Her Life, by Mrs Catherine Cappe* (1822), p.133.

63 Kathleen M. Davies, 'Continuity and change in literary advice on marriage', in Outhwaite, *Marriage and Society*, pp.58–80; Stone, *The Family, Sex and Marriage*, p.188.

64 Peter Borsay, 'The English urban renaissance: the development of provincial urban culture, c.1680–c.1760', *Social History* (May 1977), p.595.

65 Edward Shorter, *The Making of the Modern Family* (New York, 1976), p.144; Charles Perron, *Les Franc-Comtois: leur caractère national, leurs moeurs, leurs usages* (Besançon, 1892), p.85.

66 Olwen Hufton, in Outhwaite, *Marriage and Society*, pp.198–99.

67 'Journal of a tour in France, Switzerland, Italy and part of Germany in the year 1824', anonymous holograph in Stanford University Library Special Collections, M290, Box 6, Item 31.

68 *The World*, 2 January 1755, reprinted in *Miscellaneous Works of the late Philip Dormer Stanhope, Earl of Chesterfield*, vol.1 (1777–78), pp.175–76.

69 *Mundus Muliebris: or The Lady's Dressing Room Unlock'd* (1690, edited with an Introduction by T. L. Newton, 1977).

70 Minut, especially title preface ('*épistre*'), and p.270.

71 Flurance Rivault, *épistre*, fols.3–4.

72 *Ibid.*, esp. 1st, 2nd, 3rd and 5th discourses.

73 *Les Vies des dames galantes, tirées des mémoires de Messire Pierre de Bourdeilles, Seignieur de Brantôme* (after the original edition of 1666, Paris, 1879), vol.2, 2nd Discourse, p.26.

74 Jean de la Bruyère, *Les Caractères de Théophraste traduits du grec: avec les caractères ou les moeurs de ce siècle* (Paris, 1688), p.142.

75 *Ibid.*, p.134.

76 *Ibid.*, p.132.

77 *Discours de m. le chevalier de Méré à Madame XXX* (Paris, 1677), pp.98, 100.

78 *Aubrey's Brief Lives, edited from the Original Manuscripts by Oliver Lawson Dick* (1958 edition), p.252.

79 Anthony Ashley Cooper, Lord Shaftesbury, *Characteristics*, vol.2, treatise v, 'The moralists' (1709), p.395.

80 *Ibid.*, pp.398, 211, 423, 400–01, 399.

81 *Ibid.*, p.399.

82 Edmund Burke, *A Philosophical Enquiry into the Origin of our Ideas on the Sublime and Beautiful* (1756), pp.103–04.

83 *Ibid.*, p.424.

84 Voltaire, *Dictionnaire philosophique portatif* (1764), 'Beau, beauté', p.47.

85 Friedrich Schiller, *Aesthetical and Philosophical Essays* (original German edition,

1792), edited by Nathan Haskell Dole, vol.1 (Boston, 1902), pp.43–45.

86 Henry Home, *Elements of Criticism* (Edinburgh, 1761; 6th edition, 1785), vol.1, p.209.

87 Sir Harry Beaumont (i.e. Rev. Joseph Spence), *Crito: or A Dialogue on Beauty* (1752).

88 Dr Cosens, *The Economy of Beauty; in a Series of Fables Addressed to the Ladies* (1777); Dr Cozens (*sic*), *Fables Addressed to the Ladies* (Philadelphia, 1788), lines 48, 78–81.

89 *The Ladies Dictionary, Being a General Entertainment for the Fair Sex: A WORK never attempted before in English* (1694), p.57.

90 *The Art of Beauty* (1760), pp.iii–iv; the phrasing is almost identical in *Beautie's Treasury: or The Ladies' Vade Mecum* (1705).

91 *The Art of Beauty*, p.1.

92 *Ibid.*, p.2.

93 *Ibid.*, p.iv.

94 *Ibid.*, pp.2–4.

95 *Beauty's Triumph or the Superiority of the Fair Sex invincibly proved* (1751), title page.

## CHAPTER 4

1 Jacqueline Boucher, *Société et mentalités autour de Henri III* (Lille/Paris, 1981), p.3.

2 Philippe Erlanger, *Diane de Poitiers* (Paris, 1972).

3 Raymond Ritter, *Charmante Gabrielle* (Paris, 1947), esp. chapter three (the drawing of Gabrielle is reproduced as plate 4); David Buisseret, *Henry IV* (1984), esp. pp.38, 64, 79; Henri Carré, *Gabrielle d'Estrées, presque reine* (Paris, 1936).

4 Cited by Buisseret, *Henry IV*, p.88.

5 *Ibid.*, p.64.

6 Michel Carmona, *Marie de Médicis* (Paris, 1981), p.10.

7 Quoted by Buisseret, *Henry IV*, pp.86–87.

8 *Souvenirs et correspondance de Madame de Caylus* (annotated edition, Paris, 1881), *pas-*

sim; Henri Carré, *Mademoiselle de la Vallière* (Paris, 1938), and *Madame de Montespan* (Paris, 1939); Pierre Gaxotte, *La France de Louis XIV* (Paris, 1974), chapter five; Lucy Norton, *The Sun King and his Loves* (1982).

9 The portraits not reproduced here are: French School of the seventeenth century, 'Madame de Montespan' (Museé de Versailles); Henri Gascard, 'Mme de Montespan in her gallery at Clagny' (private collection); Jean Petitot, 'Mlle de la Vallière', and 'Mlle de la Vallière as Flora' (both in the Bibliothèque Nationale) – all four paintings are reproduced in Gaxotte, *Louis XIV*.

10 Quoted by Carré, *Montespan*, p.24.

11 *Ibid.*, p.21.

12 Carré, *La Vallière*, chapters one to four.

13 *Ibid.*, p.45.

14 *Journal d'Olivier Lefèvre d'Ormesson, Tome 2 1661–1672* (Paris, 1861), p.422, entry for Wednesday 27 Jan. 1666.

15 *Ibid.*, p.603, entry for 14 Dec. 1670.

16 G. Braux, *Louise de la Vallière de sa Touraine natale au Carmel de Paris* (Chambray-les-Tours, 1981), p.52.

17 This comes out strongly in the sources: see note 7.

18 Portraits are reproduced in Gaxotte, *Louis XIV* and Norton, *The Sun King.*

19 Quoted by Norton, *ibid.*, p.105.

20 *Souvenirs de Mme de Caylus*, p.27.

21 R. B. Beckett, *Lely* (1951), p.16.

22 Reresby and Boyer respectively, quoted by Brian Masters, *The Mistresses of Charles II* (1979), p.53.

23 *The Diary of Samuel Pepys* (edited by Robert Latham and William Mathews, 11 vols., 1970–83), vol.3, p.175 (23 August 1662); vol.4, p.63 (1 March 1662); vol.6, p.191 (15 August 1665); vol.3, p.139 (16 July 1662).

24 Masters, *Mistresses of Charles II*, p.51.

25 Quoted in *ibid.*, p.10.

26 Pepys, *Diary*, vol.4, p.230 (14 July

1663); vol.5, p.139 (2 May 1664).

27 Beckett, *Lely*, pp.14–27, esp. pp.19 and 23.

28 *Memoirs of the Life of Eleanor Gwinn* (1752); *Dictionary of Natural Biography* (*DNB*), vol.23 (1890), pp.401–03.

29 Sir Oliver Miller, *Sir Peter Lely* (1978), p.62; but see Beckett, *Lely*, p.25 and Brian Bevan, *Nell Gwyn* (1969). On the various portraits, see David Piper, *Catalogue of Seventeenth-Century Portraits in the National Portrait Gallery* (Cambridge, 1963), pp.148–49; Richard Ormond and Malcolm Rogers (eds.), *Dictionary of British Portraiture*, vol.1 (1979), p.55; and Geffrye Museum, *Nell Gwyn* (1973). Though neither is in any way responsible for my conclusion, I would like to record how much I have been assisted by the expert advice of John Jacob, curator of Kenwood House, and Tony Coulson, Liaison Librarian (Arts) at the Open University.

30 Aphra Behn, *The Feign'd Curtizans, or, a Nights Intrigue* (1679), Dedication.

31 Madame D. . . (i.e. D'Aulnoy), *Mémoires de la cour d'Angleterre* (Paris, 1695), vol.2, pp.225–27.

32 Masters, *Mistresses of Charles II*, p.133.

33 This paragraph is based on Masters, *Mistresses of Charles II*, chapter four and Emile Henriot, *Portraits de femmes* (Paris, 1950), pp.57ff.

34 *DNB*, vol.23 (1890) p.403.

35 See Antonia Fraser, *The Weaker Vessel: Woman's Lot in Seventeenth-Century England* (1984), p.401; V. de Sola Pinto, *Sir Charles Sedley 1639–1701* (1927), pp.132–40.

36 Quoted in J. P. Kenyon, *The Stuarts* (1958, 1966 paperback edn), p.51. In general, see Roger Lockyer, *Buckingham* (1981).

37 Philippe Erlanger, *Le Mignon du roi* (Paris, 1967), p.51. My account is based mainly on this book. *Conjuration de Cinq-Mars* (Paris, 1853) is a brief selection of primary texts.

38 D'Aulnoy, *Mémoires*, pp.3–6.

39 Charles Chenevix Trench, *The Western Rising* (1969), p.20.

40 Dryden, *Absalom and Achitophel* (1681), lines 17–18.

41 For the account of Monmouth and his Rebellion given here I have used W. Mac-Donald Wigfield, *The Monmouth Rebellion* (Bradford-on-Avon, 1980); Peter Earle, *Monmouth's Rebels* (1977); Robin Clifton, *The Last Popular Rebellion* (1984); Trench, *The Western Rising*; J. R. Jones, *Country and Court: England 1658-1714* (1978), pp.227–29; and David Ogg, *England in the Reigns of James II and William III* (Oxford, 1955, 1984 reprint), pp.145–50.

42 Bryan Bevan, *Marlborough the Man* (1975), p.15; see also George Malcolm Thomson, *The First Churchill* (1979).

43 Quoted by Bevan, *Marlborough*, p.29.

44 *The Letters of Philip Dormer Stanhope, 4th Earl of Chesterfield*, ed. Bonamy Dobrée (6 vols., 1932), vol.4, pp.1261–62, letter to his son, 18 Nov. 1748.

45 The basic information (including the visual) is, as always, beautifully and lucidly set out by Sir J. H. Plumb, *The First Four Georges* (1956; paperback, 1966).

46 *Ibid.*, p.97.

47 Jacques Levron, *La Vie quotidienne à la cour de Versailles au XVII<sup>e</sup> et XVIII<sup>e</sup> siècle* (Paris, 1965), p.163. My discussions of Louis XV and his mistresses are based on: Levron, *ibid.*; Edmond and Jules de Goncourt, *Les Maîtresses de Louis XV* (2 vols., Paris, 1860); Jacques Levron, *Madame de Pompadour: l'amour et la politique* (Paris, 1961, 1975); Duc de Castries, *La Pompadour* (Paris, 1983); Jean Nicolle, *Madame de Pompadour et la société de son temps* (Paris, 1980); Nancy Mitford, *Madame de Pompadour* (1954); Alfred Leroy, *Madame de Pompadour et son temps* (Paris, 1936); Jacques Levron, *Madame Du Barry: ou la fin d'une courtisane* (Paris, 1961, 1974); Stanley Loomis, *Du Barry: A Biography* (Philadelphia, 1959); and the various primary sources cited separately.

48 Pierre Gaxotte, 'Madame de Pompadour', *Les Oeuvres Libres*, March 1953, p.8.

49 Or the Nattier in Leroy, *Pompadour*, p.96.

50 Anne de Marnhac, *Femmes au bain: les métamorphoses de la beauté* (Paris, 1986), p.60.

51 *Mémoires et journal inédits du Marquis d'Argenson publiés et annotés par M. le Marquis d'Argenson*, vol.2 (Paris, 1857), p.341.

52 *Mémoires du Duc de Luynes* (Paris, 1861), p.382.

53 *Correspondance complète de la Marquise du Deffand*, vol.1 (Paris, 1865), p.70.

54 J. N. Duffort, Comte de Cheverny, *Mémoires sur les règnes de Louis XV et Louis XVI* (1886), vol.1, p.68.

55 'Portrait de la Marquise de Pompadour' (for the years 1745–48; she was twenty-four in 1745) by Georges Leroy, lieutenant of the hunt at Versailles, in *Correspondance de Mme de Pompadour*, ed. M.A.P.-Malassis (Paris, 1878), pp.xxv–xxvi.

56 Cheverny, *Mémoires*, vol.1, p.68.

57 De Castries, *Pompadour*, p.49.

58 Pidonsat de Maurobat, *Anecdotes sur Madame la Comtesse Dubarré* (Amsterdam, 1776), p.22.

59 Cited by Levron, *Du Barry*, p.31.

60 *Mémoires du Prince de Ligne* (Paris and Brussels, 1860), p.243.

61 *Journal d'émigration du Comte d'Espinchal, publié d'après les manuscrits originaux* (Paris, 1912), pp.147–48.

62 Levron, *Du Barry*, p.56.

63 My account is based on Robert Coughlan, *Elizabeth and Catherine* (1974); Joan Haslip, *Catherine the Great* (1977); Gertrude Aretz, *The Empress Catherine* (1947); *The Memoirs of Catherine the Great* (1955), ed. Dominique Maroger, translated by Moura Budberg, with an introduction by G. P. Gooch; and on other primary sources individually cited.

64 *Memoirs of Catherine the Great*, pp.60, 70.

65 *Ibid.*, p.200.

66 *Mémoires secrets et inédits de Stanislas Auguste, Comte Poniatowski* (Leipzig, 1862), p.7.

67 *Memoirs of Catherine the Great*, p.215.

68 Haslip, *Catherine the Great*, p.273.

69 Convenient editions of the letters are *Lettres de Mme de Sévigné, de sa famille et de ses amis* (2 vols., Paris, 1836, reprinted 1938); *Lettres de Mme de Sévigné, de sa famille et de ses amis* (14 vols., Paris, 1862–76);

*Lettres de Mme de Sévigné* (3 vols., Paris, 1953–57); *Correspondance de Mme de Sévigné* (12 vols., Paris, 1972–78). In general, see Roger Duchêne, *Madame de Sévigné, ou la chance d'être femme* (Paris, 1982).

70 Quoted by Duchêne, *Madame de Sévigné*, p.190. My account of Mlle de Sévigné is based on Duchêne, *ibid.*, pp.189–205.

71 Quotations in *ibid.*, pp.189–92.

72 *Ibid.*, p.200.

73 Mme de Sévigné, letter to Bussy, 4 Dec. 1668, in *ibid.*, p.203.

74 Quoted in *ibid.*, p.201.

75 Henriot, *Portraits*, pp.41ff. My account is based on Henriot, together with: Marie Dormoy, *La Vraie Marion de Lorne* (Paris, 1934); Georges Montgrédien, *Marion de Lorne et ses amours* (Paris, 1940); and other sources cited individually.

76 Tallement de Réaux, *Historiettes* (1662, published Paris, 1854), vol.2, p.34.

77 Montgrédien, *Marion de Lorne*, p.186; Dormoy, *La Vraie Marion de Lorne*, p.25.

78 Montgrédien, *Marion de Lorne*, p.172.

79 Emile Magne, *Ninon de Lanclos: édition définitive* (Paris, 1948), pp.124–26.

80 Tallement, *Historiettes*, vol.2, p.34; Somaize, *Dictionnaire des précieuses* (Paris, 1661), p.100.

81 Cited by Magne, *Ninon de Lanclos*, pp.124–26. My account of Ninon is based on: Roger Duchêne, *Ninon de Lanclos: la courtisane du grand siècle* (Paris, 1964); Magne, *Ninon de Lanclos*; Henriot, *Portraits*, pp.48ff.; and Edgar H. Cohen, *Mademoiselle Libertine: A Portrait of Ninon de Lanclos* (Toronto, 1970).

82 Dreux de Radier, *Récréations historiques* (Paris, 1767), vol.1, pp.58–82.

83 De Beauvoir, *Le Deuxième Sexe*, vol.2, p.345.

84 Claude Ferral, *Madame du Deffand* (1933), in the manner of many uncritical biographers, assumes, pp.19–23, that she was. Gérard Doscot, *Madame du Deffand* (Lausanne, 1967) is altogether more scholarly. The only known portrait, by Carmontelle, shows her as a blind old lady.

85 Quoted by Doscot, *ibid.*, p.55.

86 Doscot presents a convenient gallery of reproductions of paintings of the important hostesses.

87 Janct Aldis, *Madame Geoffrin: Her Salon and her Times, 1750–1777* (1905), esp. pp.3–17. A portrait by Nattier shows her, at thirty-eight, an agreeable-looking woman. In the famous and powerful Chardin she is a severely plain old lady.

88 Aldis, *ibid.*, pp.267ff.

89 *Lettres de Mlle de Lespinasse précédées d'une notice de Sainte Beuve et suivies des autres écrits de l'auteur et des principaux documents qui le concernent* (Paris, 1893). The main biography is PMMH de Ségur, *Julie de Lespinasse* (Paris, 1905). See also Camilla Jebb, *A Star of the Salons: Julie de Lespinasse* (1908).

90 *Lettres . . . documents*, p.393.

91 Jebb, *Julie de Lespinasse*, p.85.

92 Jebb, *ibid.*, p.216.

93 *Ibid.*, p.212.

94 *Ibid.*, p.239.

95 *Lettres . . . documents*, pp.ixff.

96 *Ibid.*, p.405.

97 *Correspondance entre Mlle de Lespinasse et le Comte de Guibert*, ed. Comte de Villeneuve-Guibert (Paris, 1906), p.100.

98 John Christopher Herold, *Mistress to an Age: A Life of Madame de Staël* (New York, 1958), p.26.

99 In general, see the full and scholarly biography, *Madame de Staël*, by Ghislain de Diesback (Paris, 1983).

100 Herold, *Madame de Staël*, p.51.

101 Comtesse Jean de Pauge, *Monsieur de Staël* (Paris, 1932), pp.40, 41.

102 Irving Wallace, *The Nymphs and other Maniacs* (New York, 1971), p.67.

103 My account is based on that of Duc de Castries, *Madame Récamier* (Paris, 1971).

104 *Ibid.*, p.331.

105 J. Steven Watson, *The Reign of George III 1760-1815* (Oxford, 1960), p.275, n.1.

106 Brian Masters, *Georgiana, Duchess of Devonshire* (1981), p.34, in fact repeating the nineteenth-century view enshrined in the *DNB*, vol.9 (1887), p.348. See also Hugh Stokes, *The Devonshire Home Circle* (1917), esp. pp.73–76; and II. Palmer, *The Face Without a Frown: Georgiana, Duchess of Devonshire* (1944).

107 Nathaniel Wraxall, *Historical and Post-humous Memoirs* (1884), vol.3, p.342.

108 *The Letters of Horace Walpole* (9 vols., 1857–59), vol.6, p.186.

109 *Diary and Letters of Madame D'Arblay* (Fanny Burney) (1891), vol.3, p.369 (20 August 1791).

110 *Letters of David Garrick* (ed. D. M. Little and G. M. Kahrl, 1963), p.1035.

111 *The Autobiography and Correspondence of Mary Granville, Mrs Delany* (ed. Lady Llan-over), 2nd series (1862), vol.2, p.98; Wal-pole, *Letters*, vol.6, p.70.

112 The cartoons are in the Department of Prints and Drawings, British Museum, between nos. 6484 and 6720. See *Catalogue of Political and Personal Satires Preserved in the Department of Prints and Drawings in the British Museum*, vols.5 and 6 (1978). For the songs, see *DNB*, vol.4, p.348.

113 David Green, *Sarah, Duchess of Marl-borough* (1967); *Memoirs of Sarah, Duchess of Marlborough* (ed. William King, 1950).

114 Bevan, *Nell Gwyn*, p.22.

115 Pepys, *Diary*, vol.6, p.73 (3 April 1665); vol.8, p.193 (1 May 1667); p.463 (5 October 1667); vol.8, p.91 (2 March 1667).

116 Henriot, *Portraits*, pp.63ff.

117 Quoted in Henriot, *Portraits*, p.65.

118 Macklin and Richard Cumberland respectively, quoted in Carola Oman, *David Garrick* (1958), pp.25, 93.

119 *Ibid.*, p.330.

120 *The Life of Mrs Abington (Formerly Miss Barton) Celebrated Comic Actress . . . by the Editor of the 'Life of Quin'* (1888), p.6. My account is based, felicitously I hope, on this Victorian source.

121 'A modern writer', quoted in *ibid.*

122 *Life of Mrs Abington*, p.32.

123 *Ibid.*, p.37.

124 Thomas Davies, *Memoirs of the Life of David Garrick* (1780), vol.1, p.188, vol.2, pp.169, 171.

125 Petronius Arbiter, *Memoirs of the Present Countess of Derby (Late Miss Farren)* (1797), p.10; *The Testimony of Truth to Exalted Memory: or A Biographical Sketch of the Right Honourable the Countess of Derby in Refutation of a False and Scandalous Libel* (1797), p.2.

126 Quoted in *Testimony of Truth*, p.23.

127 *Memoirs*, p.17.

128 *Ibid.*, p.20.

129 *Thalia to Eliza* (1798).

130 Quoted by Roger Manvell, *Sarah Siddons: Portrait of an Actress* (1970), p.23. In general, see Yvonne French, *Mrs Siddons* (1936) and Linda Kelly, *The Kemble Era: John Philip Kemble, Sarah Siddons and the London Stage* (1980).

131 Edwige Feuillère, *Moi La Clairon* (Paris, 1984).

132 Edward Ward, *The London Spy – The Vanities and Vices of the Town Exposed to View* (1703), cited by Alison Adburgham, *Shopping in Style* (1979), pp.14–21.

133 Pepys, *Diary*, vol.5, p.264 (6 September 1664).

134 James Peller Malcolm, *Anecdotes of the Manners and Customs of London during the Eighteenth Century* (1808), p.133.

135 Adburgham, *Shopping in Style*, pp.42–43.

136 Pierre Nouvion and Emile Liez, *Minis-tre de modes sous Louis XVI: Mademoiselle Bertin, marchande de modes de la reine 1747–1813* (Paris, 1971), pp.8–13. My account is drawn from this book.

137 Mme Campan, *Mémoires sur la vie privée de Marie Antoinette* (3 vols., Paris, 1822), p.95.

138 *Ibid.*, pp.95–96.

139 Jean-Pierre Gutton, *Domestiques et ser-*

*viteurs dans la France de l'ancien régime* (Paris, 1981), pp.73, 164. Two interesting autobiographies are: *Mémoires de monsieur de Gourville, conseiller d'état, concernant les affaires aux quelles il a été employé par en couer, depuis 1642 jusqu'en 1698* (Paris, 1792) – Gourville began his career as a personal manservant – and 'Souvenirs de Legrain, valet de chambre de Mirabeau', in *Nouvelle Revue Rétrospective*, 2nd series, vols.15 and 16 (1901).

140 Merlin Waterson, *The Servants' Hall: A Domestic History of Erodig* (1980), p.170.

141 Cissie Fairchilds, *Domestic Enemies: Servants and their Masters in Old Regime France* (Baltimore, 1984), pp.91–92.

142 *Ibid.*, p.91.

143 Sarah C. Maza, *Servants and Masters in Eighteenth-Century France* (Princeton, NJ, 1983), pp.35–36.

144 Henry Fielding, 'A journey from this world to the next', *Miscellanies*, vol.2 (1743), p.48.

145 Quoted by Flora Fraser, *Beloved Emma: The Life of Emma, Lady Hamilton* (1986), p.57. My account is based on this excellent biography, which authoritatively dismisses many well-known myths.

146 Horace Bleackley, *The Beautiful Duchess, being an account of the Life and Times of Elizabeth Gunning, Duchess of Hamilton and Argyll* (1927), pp.6–7. My account is largely based on this book.

147 *Life and Character of the Late Illustrious Duchess of Kingston . . . collected from Authentic Sources* (1788), p.15.

148 Anon. [K. Hamilton, 6th Duke of Hamilton], *The Charms of Beauty or The Grand Contest between the Fair Hibernians, and the English Toasts, A Poem occasioned by the Marriage of his Grace the Duke of Hamilton with Miss Elizabeth Gunning; and the expected Marriage of her elder sister with a certain noble Earl* (1752).

149 Cited by Ernest John Knapton, *Empress Josephine* (Cambridge, Mass., 1963), p.18, on which my discussion is based.

150 *Ibid.*, p.19.

151 *Ibid.*, p.25.

152 *Ibid.*, pp.127–28.

153 *Ibid.*, p.113.

154 Nina Epton, *Josephine: The Empress and her Children* (1975), p.1.

155 Sebastien Mercier, *Tableau de Paris* (Paris, 1781), vol.2, p.7.

156 *Ibid.*, p.11.

157 Antonia Fraser, *Weaker Vessel*, p.410.

158 *Harris's List of Covent Garden Ladies* (1793), p.24.

159 *Ibid.*, p.35.

160 *Ibid.*, p.25.

161 *Ranger's Impartial List of the Ladies of Pleasure in Edinburgh* (Edinburgh, 1775) (Miss Fraser, Miss Cobb).

162 Harris, *Covent Garden Ladies*, pp.30, 93.

163 *Ibid.*, pp.31, 40; Ranger (Miss Nairn, Mrs Dingwell, Miss Smith).

164 Antonia Fraser, *Weaker Vessel*, p.413.

165 Harris, *Covent Garden Ladies*, p.25.

166 Roy Porter, *English Society in the Eighteenth Century* (1982), p.282.

167 Quoted in *ibid.*, p.280.

168 James R. Childs, *Casanova: A Biography based on New Documents* (1961); Bonamy Dobrée, *Giacomo Casanova, Chevalier de Seingalt* (1933); Giacomo Casanova, *History of my Life* (translated W. R. Trask, 6 vols., 1967–72).

169 Pat Rogers, *An Introduction to Pope* (1975), p.2.

170 *The Diary of Thomas Turner 1754–1765*, ed. David Vaizey (Oxford, 1984), 30 Aug. 1755 (p.13); 1 Jan. 1756 (p.21).

171 *Ibid.*, 10 Feb., 15 Oct. 1756 (pp.27–28, 66).

172 *Ibid.*, 17 Jan. 1762 (p.243).

173 *Ibid.*, 23 June 1763 (p.274).

174 *Ibid.*, 13 Aug. 1764 (p.300).

175 *Ibid.*, 10 Nov. 1763, 17 Jan. 1762 (pp.281, 243).

176 *Ibid.*, p.288; 24 March 1765 (p.317).

177 *Ibid.*, p.318 (5 April, 6 April 1765).

178 *Ibid.*, p.318 (14 April 1765).

179 *Ibid.*, pp.318–19 (14 April 1765).

180 *Ibid.*, p.320 (24 April 1765).

181 *Ibid.*, p.321 (11 May 1765).

182 *Ibid.*, p.323 (31 July 1765).

183 Nicolas-Edme Rétif de la Breton, *La Vie de mon père* (Paris, 1779, ed. Gilbert Rouger, Paris, 1970), pp.19, 33–48; *Daily Advertiser*, 1750, quoted in Derek Jarrett, *England in the Age of Hogarth* (1976), p.103.

184 *Tableau*, vol.2, p.164.

185 *The Diary of Dudley Ryder 1715–1716*, ed. William Mathews (1959), 4 and 11 April 1716 (pp.213–14).

186 *Ibid.*, 22 May 1716 (p.240); 3 April 1716 (p.211).

187 *Ibid.*, 23 May 1716 (p.241).

188 E. L. Mossner, *The Life of David Hume* (Edinburgh, 1954), pp.566–67. I am heavily indebted to Dr Mossner's brilliant and thorough biography.

189 Lord Charlemont's 'Anecdotes of Hume', quoted by Mossner, *ibid.*, pp.213–14.

190 Mossner, *ibid.*, p.280.

191 Descriptions and quotations in *ibid.*, pp.214–16.

192 *Ibid.*, pp.441–45, 508.

193 *Ibid.*, p.567.

194 Ralph M. Wardle, *Oliver Goldsmith* (Lawrence, Kansas, 1957), pp.12–13, 20–21, 70–71, 90–91, 118–19, 184–85, 292–93.

195 Oman, *David Garrick*, p.16.

196 *Diary of Dudley Ryder*, 1 Dec. 1715 (p.143).

197 *Nancy Shippen: Her Journal Book*, edited by Ethel Armes (Philadelphia, 1935),

Introduction, p.15. Biographical information from editorial comments.

198 *Nancy Shippen*, pp.143–44.

199 *DNB*, vol.45 (1896), pp.258–59, 365.

200 Quoted by Louis Kronenberger, *The Extraordinary Mr. Wilkes* (New York, 1974), p.4.

201 Quoted by Audrey Williamson, *Wilkes: 'A Friend to Liberty'* (1974), p.72.

202 *Ibid.*, p.18. My account is drawn from Kronenberger and Williamson.

203 Donald Nicholas, *The Portraits of Bonnie Prince Charlie* (1973), p.1, *passim*; Hugh Douglas, *Charles Edward Stuart: The Man, the King, the Legend* (1975); Margaret Forster, *The Rash Adventurer: The Rise and Fall of Charles Edward Stuart* (1975).

204 *DNB*, vol.44 (1895), p.419. My summary is based on the *DNB* entry.

205 *Ibid.*, p.418.

## CHAPTER 5

1 The key article on this point is Carl N. Degler, 'What ought to have been and what was: women's sexuality in the nineteenth century', *American Historical Review*, December 1974. More detail has been provided by, among others, Peter Gay, *The Bourgeois Experience: Victoria to Freud*, vol.1, *The Education of the Senses* (New York, 1984).

2 See especially the discussion of Emily Wharton in Anthony Trollope, *The Prime Minister* (1875–76), chapters two to five, ten, twenty-three and twenty-four.

3 *Chester Chronicle*, 1796, quoted in Mass Observation, *Browns and Chester: Portrait of a Shop 1780–1946* (1947), p.84.

4 James P. Malcolm, *Anecdotes of the Manners and Customs of London during the Eighteenth Century, with a Review of the State of Society in 1807* (1808), pp.448–49.

5 *Chester Chronicle*, 1817, quoted in *Browns and Chester*, p.86.

6 Adburgham, *Shops and Shopping*, p.54.

7 Charles Dickens, *American Notes* (1842), in *Pictures from Italy: American Notes* (1892

edition), pp.239, 279, 344.

8 *Pictures from Italy* (1849) in *ibid.*, pp.30, 38, 50, 52, 57, 63, 70, 119.

9 Thomas Hamilton, *Men and Manners in America* (2 vols., Edinburgh, 1833).

10 *Ibid.*, vol.1, pp.14–15.

11 *Ibid.*, p.33.

12 *Ibid.*, vol.2, pp.206–07.

13 *Ibid.*, p.375.

14 *Ibid.*, vol.1, pp.40–41.

15 Captain James E. Bouldu Diary, Stanford University Libraries, Special Collections and University Archives, M84, entry for 28 January 1850.

16 Robert Stephen Harlin Diaries, Stanford Libraries, Special Collections and University Archives, M86, entry for 5 April 1849.

17 Mary Hallock to Helena de Kay, undated (1869): Mary Hallock Foote Papers, Stanford University Libraries, Special Collections and University Archives, M115, Box 1, letter no.7.

18 M. Hallock to H. de Kay Gilder, undated (1870?): Mary Hallock Foote Papers, Box 1, letter no.14.

19 *Ibid.*, 7 December 1876: Mary Hallock Foote Papers, Box 8, letter no.130.

20 *The Journal of Katherine Mansfield*, ed. J. Middleton Murry (1954), p.5.

21 Anne-Marie and Charles Lalo, *La Faillite de la beauté* (Paris, 1923), pp.110–38.

22 Louis de Saint-Ange, *Le Secret de triompher des femmes, et de les fixer* (Paris, 1825), p.2.

23 *Ibid.*, pp.10–17.

24 *Ibid.*, pp.18–21.

25 *Ibid.*, pp.135–44.

26 Horace Raisson, *Code de la toilette, manuel complet d'élégance et d'hygiène contenant les lois, règles, applications et exemples de l'art de soigner sa personne, et de s'habiller avec goût et méthode* (Paris, 1829), pp.5–9.

27 *Ibid.*, p.24.

28 *Ibid.*, pp.25–26, 59.

29 *Ibid.*, p.41.

30 *Ibid.*, pp.65–69.

31 *Ibid.*, pp.71–84.

32 *Ibid.*, pp.166–283.

33 *The Book of Health and Beauty or the Toilette of Rank and Fashion* (1837), pp.xii–xiii, chapter sixteen; *The Toilette: or A Guide to the Improvement of Personal Appearance and the Preservation of Health* (1854), pp.3, 15.

34 Mrs A. Walker, *Female Beauty, as Preserved and Improved by Regimen, Cleanliness and Dress* (1857), p.vii.

35 *The Toilette: A Dressing-Table Companion* (1839), pp.1–2.

36 Robert Dick, MD, *The Connections of Health and Beauty* (1857), p.3.

37 *The Art of Beautifying and Improving the Face and Figure comprising Instructions, Hints and Advice, together with Numerous New and Infallible Recipes in connection with the Skin, Complexion, Hair, Teeth, Eyes, Eyebrows, Eyelids, Lips, Ears, Hands, Feet, Figure, etc.* (1858), p.1.

38 Arnold J. Cooley, *The Toilet and Cosmetic Arts in Ancient and Modern Times* (1866), pp.1–2, 126–27.

39 *Finden's Tableaux of National Character, Beauty and Costume* (1843), title page.

40 *Ibid.*, pp.1, 49; see also E. and W. Finden, *Portraits of the Female Aristocracy* (1849); W. Finden, *Gallery of the Graces* (1850), etc., Mrs Caroline M. G. Kirkland, *The Book of Home Beauty* (New York, 1851).

41 Throne Crick, *Sketches from the Life of a Commercial Traveller* (1847), pp.53–54.

42 Mrs Susan D. Power, *The Ugly Girl Papers: or Hints for the Toilet* (New York, 1874), p.110.

43 Eugénie de Guérin, *Journal [1834–1841]* (Paris, 1934), p.6.

44 Annie Kethrol to Charlena Van Vleck, 23 April 1865, Anderson Papers, Box 60, Stanford University Libraries, Special Collections, M51.

45 Graeme Tytler, *Physiognomy in the European Novel: Faces and Fortunes* (Princeton, 1982), p.82. See, e.g., Thomas Cooke, *A Practical and Familiar View of the Science of Physiognomy* (1819); Alexander Walker, *Physiognomy founded on Physiology* (1834).

46 Tytler, *Physiognomy*, pp.96, 318; Henry Murger, *Scènes de la Bohême* (Brussels, 1851), vol.2, p.94, vol.3, p.69, vol.1, p.90.

47 Roy Porter, 'Making faces: physiognomy and fashion in eighteenth-century England', *Etudes Anglaises*, tome XXXVIII, 1985, pp.395–96.

48 *Gentleman's Magazine*, vol.78 (1808), p.1083.

49 *The Art of Beauty or the Best Methods of Improving and Preserving the Shape, Carriage, and Complexion together with the Theory of Beauty* (1825), pp.382–83.

50 T. Bell, *Kalogynomia, or the Laws of Female Beauty* (1821), p.v.

51 *Ibid.*, p.312.

52 Alexander Walker, *Beauty, Illustrated Chiefly by an Analysis and Classification of Beauty in Women* (1836), pp.4, 386–90.

53 Keats to the George Keats's, 24 October 1818, *The Letters of John Keats*, ed. Hyder Edward Rollins (Cambridge, Mass., 1958), vol.1, p.403.

54 Shelley, 'Hymn to intellectual beauty', stanza 2, Shelley, *Poems* (Penguin Poetry Library, 1956), p.71.

55 See Walter Jackson Bates, *John Keats* (1967), pp.516–20.

56 Keats to Fanny Brawne, 8 July 1819, *Letters*, vol.2, p.177. See Joanna Richardson, *Fanny Brawne* (1952), pp.15–21.

57 P. B. Shelley, 'A discourse on the manners of the ancient Greeks relative to the subject of love', in *Plato's Banquet & C* (1931), p.14.

58 Leigh Hunt, 'Criticism on female beauty', in *Men, Women and Books*, vol.1 (1847), pp.233, 284–85.

59 Both quotations are in Bernard Grebanier, *The Uninhibited Byron* (1970), p.199; see also Leslie A. Marchand, *Byron: A Biography* (1957), vol.1, p.370.

60 *Ibid.*, pp.13–14, 199; Elizabeth Longford, *Byron* (1976), p.14.

61 There are seldom sudden and total changes in human behaviour. Even in the era I have, for the purposes of this book, termed 'traditional' there were many examples of romantic, individualistic love. For 'The growth of affective individualism', see Stone, *Family*, pp.221–68. In general, see Flandrin, *Familles*, chapter three.

62 Lord Monson to his son, 30 November 1850, Monson Papers, Lincoln County Record Office, Mon. 25/10/2/4/8.

63 Shorter, *Making of Modern Family*, p.65.

64 Karr, *Les Femmes*, p.37, pp.39ff.

65 Paul Diffloth, *La Beauté s'en va: des méthodes propres à la rénovation de la beauté féminine* (Paris, 1905), p.71.

66 Le Comte de Gobineau, *Essai sur l'inégalité des races humaines* (1854, 6th edition, Paris, 1933), p.214.

67 Karl Pearson, *Life of Francis Galton* (4 vols., 1914), vol.2, p.341.

68 *Dictionary of American Biography*, vol.6 (New York, 1931), pp.383ff.; Henry Theophilus Finck, *My Adventures in the Golden Age of Music* (New York, 1926), pp.270–72.

69 Finck, *ibid.*, p.270.

70 *Ibid.*, pp.271–72.

71 H. T. Finck, *Romantic Love and Personal Beauty* (New York, 1887), vol.1, p.93.

72 *Ibid.*, pp.283–95.

73 *Ibid.*, p.52.

74 *Ibid.*, vol.2, p.122.

75 H. T. Finck, *Primitive Love and Love Stories* (New York, 1899), pp.272–73.

76 *Romantic Love*, vol.2, p.259.

77 *Primitive Love*, p.284.

78 *Romantic Love*, vol.2, p.223; Stratz, *Die Schönheit des Weiblichen Körpers* (14th edn, Berlin, 1903), p.200; Havelock Ellis, *Sexual Selection*, p.164.

79 Guérin, *Journal*, p.6.

80 *DAB.*, vol.6 (1931), p.138; *DNB*, supplement, vol.3 (1901), p.305.

81 *The Complete Work of Ralph Waldo Emerson* (New York, 1929), p.24.

82 John Ruskin, *Modern Painters*, part 4, 'Of many things', chapter six, 'Of modern landscape' (1856, new edition in small format, 1897), p.270.

83 Anon., *The Beauty and Her Plain Sister* (Edinburgh, 1865).

84 Mrs Caroline M. G. Kirkland, *The Book of Home Beauty* (New York, 1851), title page.

85 *Ibid.*, pp.37–38.

86 *Ibid.*, pp.51, 145.

87 Anton Chekov, *Uncle Vanya*, act II.

88 William Morris, *News from Nowhere* (1893), p.19.

89 *Ibid.*, pp.24–25, 54–55.

90 *Ibid.*, p.88.

91 A good statement of that position (rather similar to that of Havelock Ellis quoted in chapter two) is contained in *The Sense of Beauty* (New York, 1896) by the American philosopher George Santayana, p.59:
The attraction of sex could not become efficient unless the senses were first attracted. The eye must be fascinated and the ear charmed by the object which nature intends should be pursued . . . The colour, the grace, the form, which become the stimuli of sexual passion and the guides of sexual selection, acquire, before they can fulfill that office, a certain intrinsic charm. This charm is not only present for reasons which, in an admissible sense, we may call teleological, on account, that is, of its past utility in reproduction, but its intensity and power are due to the simultaneous stirring of profound sexual impulses.

92 Ignoring articles, guides, 'hints', etc., in periodicals, and confining the count strictly to guides and manuals separately published and dealing explicitly with 'beauty' (rather than etiquette) at least seventy were published in Britain, France and the USA in the period under review, compared with about a dozen in the first seventy-five years of the nineteenth century.

93 Comtesse de Norville, *Les Coulisses de la beauté; comment la femme séduit* (Paris, 1894), p.152, recommends careful attention to intimate hygiene. British and American works do not.

94 Ella Adelin Fletcher, *The Woman Beautiful* (New York, 1899), p.1.

95 *Ibid.*, pp.36, 2.

96 *Ibid.*, p.26.

97 *Ibid.*, p.20.

98 Mrs H. R. Haweis, *The Art of Beauty* (1878), p.3.

99 *Ibid.*, p.9.

100 *Ibid.*, p.195. For interesting thoughts on the notion of 'moral cosmetics', see Karen Halttunen, *Confidence Men and Painted Women: A Study of Middle-Class Culture in America 1830-1870* (New Haven, Conn., 1982), pp.89, 159.

101 Harriet Hubbard Ayer, *Harriet Hubbard Ayer's Book: A Complete and Authentic Treatise on the Laws of Health and Beauty* (Springfield, Mass., 1899 and 1902), p.57.

102 *Ibid.*, p.48.

103 *Ibid.*, p.46.

104 *Ibid.*, p.29. The photographs are on pp.37–38.

105 Prof. Boyd Laynard, *Secrets of Beauty, Health, and a Long Life* (1900), p.8.

106 *The Lady's Dressing Room, translated from the French of Baroness Staffe, by Lady Colin Cambell* (1892), pp.179–80.

107 Annie Wolf, *The Truth about Beauty* (New York, 1892), p.8.

108 Mrs C. E. Humphry, *How to be Pretty though Plain* (1899), pp.9, 15.

109 Fletcher, *Woman Beautiful*, p.2.

110 *Harriet Hubbard Ayer's Book*, p.35.

111 Haweis, *Art of Beauty*, p.3.

112 Dr P. Marrin, *La Beauté chez l'homme et la femme: les moyens de l'acquérir et de l'augmenter* (Paris, 1891), p.13.

113 Haweis, *Art of Beauty*, p.3.

114 Teresa H. Dean, *How to be Beautiful* (1890), preface.

115 Haweis, *Art of Beauty*, pp.3, 257.

116 *Ibid.*, p.5.

117 H. Ellen Browning, *Beauty Culture* (1898), p.13.

118 Laynard, *Secrets of Beauty*, pp.6–7.

119 Haweis, *Art of Beauty*, p.256.

120 *Sylvia's Book of the Toilet: A Ladies' Guide to Dress and Beauty with a Fund of Information of Importance to Gentlemen* (1886), p.5.

121 Arthur Lefèbvre, *L'Art d'être belle* (Paris, 1901), p.9.

122 *Lady's Dressing Room*, p.12.

123 *Ibid.*, pp.14–16.

124 Marquise de Garches, *Les Secrets de beauté d'une parisienne* (Paris, 1894), p.2.

125 Docteur Monin, *L'Hygiène et la beauté* (Paris, 1886), pp.1–2; *Beauty: How To Get It and How to Keep It* (1885), p.5; 'Hygiène', *The Lady Beauty Book* (1900), p.11; Madame Bayard, *Toilet Hints or How to Preserve Beauty and How to Acquire It* (1883), p.13; O. de Jalin, *Les Secrets de la beauté* (Paris, 1904), p.5; Comtesse de Norville, *Les Coulisses de la beauté*, p.v.; *Beauty and How to Keep It, by a Professional Beauty* (New York and London, 1889), p.19; Haweis, *Art of Beauty*, p.4; Fletcher, *Woman Beautiful*, p.3; Browning, *Beauty Culture*, p.10; Lefèbvre, *L'Art d'être belle*, p.7.

126 Power, *Ugly Girl Papers*, p.10.

127 *Beauty and How to Keep It*, p.19.

128 Bayard, *Toilet Hints*, p.13.

129 Humphry, *How to be Pretty*, p.12.

130 C. Sherman Big, *Face and Figure* (1879), p.21.

131 *Harriet Hubbard Ayer's Book*, chapter three, pp.50ff.

132 Femina-Bibliothèque (preface by Henri Duvernois), *Pour être belle* (Paris, 1913), pp.i–ix; Lefèbvre, *L'Art d'être belle*, p. 7; Humphry, *How to be Pretty*, p.14 ('work well done has made many a plain face beautiful'); Comtesse de Traver, *Que veut la femme: être jolie, être aimée, et dominer* (Paris, 1911), p.9; Alice M. Long, *My Lady Beautiful* (Chicago, 1906), *passim*.

133 Gordon Stables, MD, *The Girls' Own Book of Health and Beauty* (1892), p.vii; Laynard, *Secrets of Beauty*, p.8; Jalin, *Les Secrets de la beauté*, pp.5–6; *Beauty and How to Keep It*, pp.45, 62–63; Isobel Handbooks, no.7, *The Art of Beauty: A Book for Women and Girls* (1899), pp.1–2; *Beauty and the Preservation of Health*, by MD (1903), p.7.

134 Fletcher, *Woman Beautiful*, p.6; Dean, *How to be Beautiful*, p.3; Laynard, *Secrets of Beauty*, p.6.; *Beauty and How to Keep It*, p.19.

135 *Sylvia's Book*, pp.10–12.

136 Laynard, *Secrets of Beauty*, p.7.

137 *Beauty and How to Keep It*, pp.7–12.

138 MD, pp.4–5.

139 Haweis, *Art of Beauty*, p.120.

140 Laynard, *Secrets of Beauty*, p.18.

141 *Beauty: How to Get It and How to Keep It*, p.18.

142 Mathilde Pokitonoff, *La Beauté par l'hygiène* (Paris, 1892), p. 145; Marquise de Garches, *Les Secrets de beauté d'une parisienne*, p.31; Power, *Ugly Girl Papers*, p.123; *Pour être belle*, p.220.

143 *Beauty and How to Keep It*, pp.7–9.

144 *Ibid.*, p.46.

145 *Ibid.*

146 Jalin, *Les Secrets de la beauté*, pp.89–90.

147 *Sylvia's Book*, p.33; *Beauty and How to Keep It*, p.39.

148 *Beauty and How to Keep It*, p.40.

149 *Ibid.*, p.42.

150 *Beauty and How to Keep It*, p.45.

151 *Ibid.*, p.49.

152 *Ibid.*, p.47; Garches, *Les Secrets de beauté d'une parisienne*, p.75; Humphry, *How to be Pretty*, p.102; see also Jalin, *Les Secrets de la beauté*, p.11: 'Nothing is uglier than an obese woman.'

153 Marrin, *La Beauté chez l'homme et la femme*, p.235.

154 Wolf, *The Truth about Beauty*, p.60.

155 *The Times*, 22 December 1869; advertisements and leaflets in 'Beauty Parlour', 4 boxes in John Johnson Collection, Bodleian Library.

156 *Sylvia's Book*, p.47; *The Lady Beauty Book*, p.12.

157 *Harriet Hubbard Ayer's Book*, p.55.

158 Haweis, *Art of Beauty*, p.196.

159 *Beauty and How to Keep It*, p.18.

160 Isobel Handbooks, p.88.

161 *Beauty and How to Keep It*, p.20.

162 *Harriet Hubbard Ayer's Book*, p.49.

163 Jalin, *Les Secrets de la beauté*, p.36.

164 *Beauty and How to Keep It*, p.56.

165 *Ibid.*, p.51.

166 E.g. Marie Christine, *Boudoir Gossip on Health and Appearance* (1892); Mrs Anna Ruppert, *Book of Beauty* (n.d.). See also materials in 'Beauty Parlour'.

167 Bayard, *Toilet Hints*, p.15.

168 *Pour être belle*, p.1.

169 Dean, *How to be Beautiful*, preface.

170 *Beauty: How to Get It and How to Keep It*, p.27.

171 *Sylvia's Book*, pp.14, 16.

172 *Ibid.*, p.57.

173 *Beauty: How to Get It and How to Keep It*, p.30.

174 *The Art of Being Beautiful: A Series of Interviews with a Society Beauty* (1902), p.81; Marrin, *La Beauté chez l'homme et la femme*, p.9.

175 *Sylvia's Book*, p.5.

176 *Harriet Hubbard Ayer's Book*, p.40.

177 Marrin, *La Beauté chez l'homme et la femme*, pp.12–13; Fletcher, *Woman Beautiful*, pp.3–4; Wolf, *The Truth about Beauty*, pp.15, 186.

178 Wolf, *ibid.*, pp.72–73.

179 *Ibid.*, p.72.

180 *Ibid.*, pp.187–193.

181 *Beauty and Power* (London and New York, 1871), pp.138–40.

182 *Ibid.*, pp.8–10.

## CHAPTER 6

1 *Appleton's Cyclopaedia of American Biography* (New York, 1888–89), vol.1, p.28.

2 *Dictionary of American Biography (DAB)*, vol.10 (New York, 1933), pp.17–18.

3 *Ibid.*, vol.12 (1933), p.190.

4 *Ibid.*, vol.18 (1936), p.353. For an engraving of Harrison, see *Cyclopaedia*, vol.3, p.97.

5 *DAB*, vol.9 (1932), p.529; vol.19 (1926), pp.152, 91; vol.14 (1934), p.38; *Cyclopaedia*, vol.6, pp.283, 233.

6 *DAB*, vol.14, p.577; *Cyclopaedia*, vol.5, p.9.

7 *Cyclopaedia*, vol.3, p.726; *DAB*, vol.11 (1933), pp.246–47.

8 Quoted by Stephen B. Oates, *Abraham Lincoln: The Man Behind the Myths* (New York, 1984), pp.50–51. See also Richard N. Current, *The Lincoln Nobody Knows* (New York, 1958), pp.1–6.

9 Dwight C. Anderson, *Abraham Lincoln* (New York, 1982); Cullom Davis (ed.), *The Public and the Private Lincoln* (1979); Oates, *Abraham Lincoln*; Current, *The Lincoln Nobody Knows*.

10 Cited by Oates, *Abraham Lincoln*, p.35.

11 Current, *The Lincoln Nobody Knows*, pp.4–5, 2.

12 *DNB*, vol.56 (1898), p.17.

13 'Memoirs from Lord Shaftesbury', The Hon. Evelyn Ashley, MP, *The Life of Henry John Temple, Viscount Palmerston 1846–1865* (1876), vol.2, p.316.

14 Kenneth Bourne, *Palmerston: The Early Years* (1982), pp.185, 434.

15 Ashley, *Viscount Palmerston*, vol.2, p.288.

16 *DNB*, vol.15 (1888), p.10.

17 Robert Blake, *Disraeli* (1966), p.473.

18 *DNB 1941–1950* (1959), p.528.

19 W. P. R. George, *My Brother and I* (1976), pp.94–95. In general, see John Grigg, *The Young Lloyd George* (1973), esp. pp.58–59, *Lloyd George: The People's Champion 1902–1911* (1978), esp. p.189.

20 David Duff, *Eugénie and Napoleon* (1978), p.98.

21 *Ibid.*, p.72; see also Jasper Ridley, *Napoleon III and Eugénie* (1979), p.157.

22 E.g. *Cyclopaedia*, vol.4, p.271; *DAB*, vol.10, p.18.

23 Banner, *American Beauty*, pp.32–33.

24 Louis Fissner Journals, 14 April 1854, Stanford University Libraries, Special Collections, M89.

25 Henry Mayhew, *The Shops and Companies of London* (1865), p.86.

26 John Bird Thomas, *Shop Boy: An Autobiography* (1920), p.163.

27 *Pick-me-up*, 1 December 1888, reproduced in Alison Adburgham, *Shops and Shopping*, p.169.

28 Merlin Waterson, *The Servant's Hall* (1980), p.170.

29 Pamela Horn, *The Rise and Fall of the Victorian Servant* (Dublin, 1975), p.84.

30 Donald E. Sutherland, *Americans and their Servants: Domestic Service in the United States from 1800 to 1920* (Baton Rouge, 1981), p.42.

31 See, in particular, Gordon Grimmet in Rosina Harrison (ed.), *Gentlemen's Gentlemen* (1976), p.33.

32 George Washington in *ibid.*, p.176. In general, see Anne Martin-Fugier, *La Place des bonnes: la domesticité féminine à Paris en 1900* (Paris, 1979).

33 Andrew Roth, *Heath and the Heathmen* (1972), pp.18–19.

34 Adburgham, *Shops and Shopping*, p.236.

35 Mayhew, *Shops and Companies*, p.52.

36 Banner, *American Beauty*, p.131.

37 Cited in Joanna Richardson, *The Courtesans: The Demi-Monde in Nineteenth-Century France* (1967), p.100.

38 Walker, *Beauty*, p.249.

39 Edith Saunders, *The Age of Worth* (1954), p.22. See also Diana de Marly, *Worth: Father of Haute Couture* (1980), esp. p.23 and chapter three; and J. P. Worth, *A Century of Fashion* (1928), on which this and the previous paragraph are based.

40 Gay, *Bourgeois Experience*, vol.1, p.281; Stanley Weintraub, *Victoria, Biography of a Queen* (1987).

41 The factual information is taken from Jan Marsh, *The Pre-Raphaelite Sisterhood* (1985), *passim*.

42 *Ibid.*, pp.15–32.

43 *Ibid.*, p.25.

44 *Ibid.*, pp.16–17, 26,

45 Jan Marsh, 'Pre-Raphaelite women', *New Society*, 23 February 1984, pp.279–82.

46 *Pre-Raphaelite Sisterhood*, pp.117–20. In general, see 'Models', chapter seven of William Gaunt and F. Gordon Row, *Etty and the Nude* (1943).

47 *Pre-Raphaelite Sisterhood*, p.140.

48 Derek Hudson, *Munby, Man of Two Worlds: The Life and Diaries of Arthur J. Munby 1828–1910* (1972), pp.40–41.

49 Céleste Mogador, *Mémoires* (Paris, 1858–59), vol.1, pp.240–41.

50 *Ibid.*, p.173.

51 *Ibid.*

52 Quoted in Hilary Evans, *The Oldest Profession: An Illustrated History of Prostitution* (Newton Abbot, 1979), p.121.

53 *Ibid.*

54 B. Pierce Egan, *Life in London* (1869), pp.88–90.

55 William Acton, *Prostitution Considered in its Moral, Social, and Sanitary Aspects* (2nd edition, 1870), pp.19–20.

56 E.g. Curtis Cate, *George Sand* (1975); Ruth Jordan, *George Sand* (1976); Renée Winegarten, *The Double Life of George Sand* (New York, 1978); Francine Mallet, *George Sand* (Paris, 1976); Patricia Thomson, *George Sand and the Victorians* (1977); Gordon S. Haight, *George Eliot: A Biography* (Oxford, 1968, 1978); Ruby Redinger, *George Eliot* (1976).

57 See Winegarten, *Double Life of George Sand*, p.207; also introduction by Dan Hofstadter to G. Sand, *Story of my Life* (1979).

58 George Sand, *Indiana* (Paris, 1832), p.56.

59 George Sand, *Journal intime* (Paris, 1981 edition), p.19.

60 *Ibid.*, p.85.

61 Haight, *Biography*, p.115.

62 'John Chapman's diaries', 30 May 1851, in Gordon S. Haight, *George Eliot and John Chapman* (New Haven, 1940), p.172.

63 George Eliot to the Brays, 20 August 1849, *The George Eliot Letters* (ed. G. S. Haight, 9 vols., 1954–78), vol.1, p.298.

64 Herbert Spencer, 'Personal beauty', *Leader*, 15 April 1854, pp.356–57.

65 Haight, *George Eliot*, p.115.

66 *Ibid*, pp.112ff.

67 *Ibid.*, p.128.

68 *Ibid.*, pp.133ff.

69 *Letters*, vol.5, p.9; vol.7, p.241.

70 George Sand, *Histoire de ma vie* (Paris, 1909 edition), vol.4, p.485.

71 Cited by Hofstadter in introduction to G. Sand, *Story of my Life*.

72 *Journal d'Edmond Got* (Paris, 1910), entry for 20 Dec. 1840, p.7.

73 James Gall, 'Journal 1809–1813', January 1809, National Library of Scotland (NLS), Acc.8874.

74 Diary of E. E. Graham, 1872–1932, 12 March 1875, Robert Graham Diaries, NLS, Acc.9077.

75 *Ibid.*, entries for 7, 11, 12, 13, 16 April, 5 August.

76 Anderson Papers, Boxes 1, 2, 6, 7, 60, Stanford University Libraries, Special Collection and University Archives, M51.

77 From the private papers of Mabel Loomis Todd, cited by Peter Gay, *The Bourgeois Experience*, vol.1, *Education of the Senses*, pp.78, 101.

78 *A Victorian Diarist: Extracts from the Journals of Mary, Lady Monkswell, 1873–1895*, ed. Hon. E. C. F. Collier (1944).

79 *Ibid.*, entries for 7 July 1874, 17 Oct. 1873, 7 March, 2/3 July 1874.

80 William Etty, 'Letters addressed to a relative', *The Art Journal*, vol.11 (1849), p.40.

81 T. F. Thiselton-Dyer, *The Loves and Marriages of Some Eminent Persons* (1890), vol.1, p.279; Gaunt and Rose, *Etty*, p.42.

82 Joseph-Emile Muller, *Toulouse-Lautrec* (Paris, 1975); Guido Sari, *Boldini a Parigi* (Alghero, 1980); Max Beerbohm, *Zuleika Dobson* (1911, 1983 paperback), p.17.

83 Musée Jacquemart André, *Giovanni Boldini 1842–1931* (Exhibition Catalogue) (Paris, 1963), p.8; see also Cléo de Mérode, *Le Ballet de ma vie* (Paris, 1955), p.142.

84 E. Cardona, *La Vie de Jean Boldini* (Paris, 1931); Enrico Piceni, *Boldini: l'uomo e l'opera* (Busto Arsizio, 1981) seeks to rehabilitate Boldini as an artist and as a man.

85 Cornelia Otis Skinner, *Elegant Wits and Grand Horizontals* (1963), pp.188ff.

86 *Ibid.*, p.188.

87 Biographical information from Joanna

Richardson, *The Courtesans: The Demi-Monde in Nineteenth-Century France* (1967); Skinner, *Elegant Wits and Grand Horizontals*; Henry Blyth, *Skittles, the Last Victorian Courtesan: The Life and Times of Catherine Walters* (1977); Charles Castle, *La Belle Otero: The Last Great Courtesan* (1981).

88 Richardson, *The Courtesans*, chapter five.

89 Cited by Richardson, *ibid.*, p.52.

90 'Zed', *Le Demi-Monde sous le second empire: souvenirs d'un sybarite* (Paris, 1892), p.53.

91 *Ibid.*, p.14.

92 For reproductions of portraits of 'Skittles', see Blyth, *Skittles, the Last Victorian Courtesan*; for other reproductions, see the works by Richardson and Skinner, and Rebecca West, *1900* (1982).

93 Paul Gsell, *Mémoires de Mme. Judith de la Comédie Française* (Paris, 1911), p.221.

94 This account is based on Poiret-Dalpach, *Marie Duplessis: 'La dame aux camélias'* (Paris, 1981).

95 Mogador, *Mémoires*, vol.2, p.38.

96 Richardson, *The Courtesans*, chapter one.

97 Blyth, *Skittles, the Last Victorian Courtesan*, pp.21–22.

98 See Ishbel Ross, *The Uncrowned Queen: The Life of Lola Montez* (New York, 1972).

99 R. P. Pzewaski, preface to Liane de Pougy, *My Blue Notebooks* (1979), p.14.

100 See Jean-Louis Vaudoyer, *Alice Ozy ou l'aspasie moderne* (Paris, 1930), pp.77ff.

101 Ross, *Life of Lola Montez*, pp.273ff.; Lola Montez, *Memoirs* (New York, 1860), *The Arts and Secrets of Beauty* (New York, 1853).

102 Rebecca West, *1900*, p.154.

103 Pzewaski, preface to Liane de Pougy, *My Blue Notebooks*, p.14.

104 This account is based on Fred Kupferman, *Mata Hari: songes et mensonges* (Brussels, 1982) and on the photographs reproduced there.

105 For Castiglione, see Jasper Ridley, *Napoleon III and Eugénie* (1979), p.402; for de Mérode and Savatier, see, respectively, de Mérode, *Le Ballet de ma vie* and Richardson, *The Courtesans*, chapter eleven.

106 Banner, *American Beauty*, chapters six to eight.

107 *Ibid.*, p.128.

108 *Ibid.*, p.135.

109 *Ibid.*

110 *Ibid.*, p.136.

111 Clarence Day, quoted in *ibid.*, p.136.

112 *Ibid.*, plate 19 and caption.

113 *Ibid.*, p.136.

114 *Ibid.*, p.257.

115 *Ibid.*, p.258.

116 *Ibid.*, p.138.

117 *Ibid.*

118 *Spirit of the Times*, 15 Nov. 1882, quoted in *ibid.*, p.138.

119 James Brough, *The Prince and the Lily* (New York, 1975), pp.141–42. My account is based on Brough.

120 See Tom Prideaux, *Love or Nothing: The Life and Times of Ellen Terry* (New York, 1975), and Ellen Terry, *My Life* (1910).

121 Prideaux, *Life and Times of Ellen Terry*, p.113.

122 Philippe Jullian, *Sarah Bernhardt* (Paris, 1977), p.34. My account is based on this excellent biography, amplified by André Castelot, *Ensourcelante Sarah Bernhardt* (Paris, 1961, 1973), *Ma double vie: mémoires de Sarah Bernhardt* (Paris, 1907), and Pierre Spirakoff, *Sarah Bernhardt vue par les Nadar* (Paris, 1982).

123 De Mérode, *Le Ballet de ma vie*, pp.88–89.

124 René Jeanne, Charles Ford, *Histoire du cinéma* (Paris, 1947–55), vol.1, pp.208, 468, vol.2, pp.29–30, vol.3, pp.107, 405.

## CHAPTER 7

1 E. Charles-Roux, *Chanel* (Paris, 1976), pp.151–53.

2 Arthur Marwick, *War and Social Change in the Twentieth Century: A Comparative Study of Britain, France, Germany, Russia, and the United States* (1974); for the 'psychological dimension', see p.13; see also my 'Problems and consequences of organizing society for total war', in N. F. Dreisziger (ed.), *Mobilization for Total War: The Canadian, American and British Experience 1914–1918, 1939–1945* (Waterloo, Ontario, 1981), pp.3–21; see also Neil A. Wynn, *From Progressivism to Prosperity: World War I and American Society* (New York, 1986).

3 Marwick, *The Deluge: British Society and the First World War* (1965), pp.140–43. Nicholas Reeves, *Official British Film Propaganda during the First World War* (1986), esp. pp.157–64, 227, 243–47.

4 René Jeanne, *Les Grandes Vedettes du cinéma: beauté masculine* (Paris, 1929), p.3.

5 Madame Athena, *Pour se faire aimer* (Paris, n.d., *c.*1920), p.11.

6 Hortense Odlum, *A Woman's Place* (New York, 1939), pp.218–20.

7 US War Department Education Manual, EM982, *Establishing and Operating a Beauty Shop* (Madison, Wisconsin, n.d., *c.*1944), p.2.

8 *Ibid.*, pp.2–3.

9 Louis Léon-Martin, *L'Industrie de la beauté* (Paris, 1930), p.230.

10 See in particular the four boxes of advertisements, leaflets, hand bills, etc., entitled 'Beauty Parlour', in the John Johnson Collection, Bodleian Library, Oxford.

11 Nose machine, and supporting advertisements, etc., in Museum of London.

12 Mme Vriac-Lecot, *Pour être belle à tout âge* (Paris, 1929), p.7.

13 Allied Newspapers, *Beauty for Every Woman* (Manchester, 1929), p.7.

14 S. Simson, *La Beauté pour toutes* (Paris, 1933), p.5.

15 *Beauty for Every Woman*, p.8.

16 Vriac-Lecot, *Pour être belle à tout âge*, pp.24–25.

17 Paula S. Fass, *The Damned and the Beautiful: American Youth in the 1920s* (New York, 1977), p.281.

18 Vriac-Lecot, *Pour être belle à tout âge*, pp.20–1.

19 Fass, *Damned and the Beautiful*, p.284.

20 Letter to *Le Petit Parisien* quoted by Léon-Martin, *L'Industrie de la beauté*, pp.236–38.

21 Banner, *American Beauty*, p.269. In general, see Frank Deford, *There She Is: The Life and Times of Miss America* (New York, 1971).

22 Robert Roberts, *The Classic Slum* (1971), p.181.

23 Jane Russell, *Success and Happiness through Charm* (1939), part seven.

24 *Ibid.*, part four.

25 *Ibid.*, parts one and two.

26 Herbert Andrews; General Manager Screen Advertising Inc., to Hon. Ernest Lundeen, 23 Jan. 1918, Ernest Lundeen Papers, Box 91, Hoover Institution Archives.

27 *New York Tribune*, 7 December 1923, clipping in Mark Sullivan Papers, Box 2, Hoover Archives.

28 Edward Pessen, *The Log Cabin Myth: The Social Background of the Presidents* (New Haven, Conn., 1984), p.156.

29 W. E. Leuchtenberg, *The Perils of Prosperity 1914–1932* (Chicago, 1958), p.89.

30 Mark Sullivan Diary, 12 Sept. 1923, Mark Sullivan Papers, Box 1, Hoover Institution Archives.

31 *New York Tribune*, 7 December 1923, Mark Sullivan Papers, Box 2, Hoover Institution Archives.

32 *Kansas City Journal*, 14 Sept. 1932: Mark Sullivan Papers, Box 233; *New York Times*, 6 Nov. 1932, clippings in Raymond Moley Papers, Boxes 5, 11, Hoover Institution Archives.

33 *New York Times Magazine*, 6 Nov. 1932.

34 *Seattle Star*, 26 Sept. 1932; *Chicago Sunday Tribune*, 21 August 1932; *Cleveland Plain Dealer*, 21 August 1932; *Cleveland Sunday News*, 21 Aug. 1932; clippings in Moley Papers, Boxes 5, 4, 11.

35 Friends of Franklin Roosevelt, *Franklin D. Roosevelt: Who He Is and . . . What He Has Done* (1932), Moley Papers, Box 11.

36 *World Telegram*, 23 Aug. 1932, Moley Papers, Box 4.

37 *Chicago Sunday Tribune*, 21 Aug. 1932, Moley Papers, Box 4.

38 *Ibid.*

39 See *DNB 1931–1940* (Oxford, 1949), p.569.

40 See David Marquand, *Ramsay MacDonald* (1977), pp.285–87.

41 Marquand, *ibid.*, pp.69, 6.

42 Arthur Marwick, *Class in the Twentieth Century* (Brighton, 1986), p.23.

43 Cited in Robert Heussler, *Yesterday's Rulers: The Making of the British Colonial Service* (Syracuse, NY, 1963), pp.74–75.

44 *Report of the Royal Commission on the Civil Service* (1931), paras. 250–56.

45 H. W. Nevinson, *Running Accompaniments* (1936), p.124.

46 Ben Pimlott, *Hugh Dalton* (1985), p.37.

47 *Ibid.*, p.115.

48 *Ibid.*, p.31.

49 See John Colville, *The Fringes of Power: Downing Street Diaries 1939–1955* (1985).

50 Yale University, *The Class of 1913* (New Haven, 1914), p.17.

51 Fass, *Damned and the Beautiful*, pp.155, 157, 201, 230, 240–41.

52 Gordon Grimmett, 'The lamp boy's story', in Rosina Harrison (ed.), *Gentleman's Gentlemen* p.16.

53 *Ibid.*, p.31.

54 *Ibid.*, p.37.

55 *Ibid.*, p.79–80.

56 Edwin Lee, 'The page boy's story', in *ibid.*, p.110.

57 Grimmett in Harrison, *Gentlemen's Gentlemen*, p.33.

58 Charles-Roux, *Chanel*, p.31.

59 *Ibid.*, p.62. My account is based on this authoritative biography.

60 Quoted in Frederick Sands and Sven Bromen, *The Divine Garbo* (1979), p.30. My account is drawn from this book.

61 Boston Herndon, *Mary Pickford and Douglas Fairbanks* (1977), p.68. My account is based on this book.

62 *Ibid.*, p.1.

63 The standard biography is Joe Morella and Edward Z. Epstein, *The 'It' Girl: The Incredible Story of Clara Bow* (New York, 1976).

64 Noel Botham and Peter Donnelly, *Valentino: The Love God* (1976), pp.30–83.

65 Charles Higham, *Bette: The Life of Bette Davis* (New York, 1981), p.31.

66 *Ibid.*

67 *Ibid.*, p.32.

68 *Ibid.*, pp.57–58, 66–67.

69 *Ibid.*, p.87.

70 Gary Carey, *Katharine Hepburn* (New York, 1983), p.23.

71 Helen Lawrenson, 'Hepburn reconsidered', *The Dial*, March 1981. I am indebted to Professor Dan Leab for this reference.

72 Laurence Olivier, *Confessions of an Actor* (1982), p.108.

73 Claude Anet, *Suzanne Lenglen* (Paris, 1927).

74 The light-hearted words are those of Robert Graves and Alan Hodge, *The Long Weekend* (1940; 1985 reprint), p.282. There is a contemporary 'popular life', Hubert S. Banner, *Amy Johnson* (1933), and a good biography, *Amy Johnson* (1967) by Constance Babbington Smith.

75 Karl H. von Wiegand Papers, Hoover Archives: Box 8, correspondence between von Wiegand and Lady Grace Drummond-Hay; Box 55, clippings from *Evening Standard*, 28 May 1928, *Daily Chronicle*, 29 May 1928, *Manchester Guardian*, 29 May 1928; Box 56, clippings from *The Sphere*.

76 *Cincinnati Enquirer*, 22 Oct. 1928, Box 55; clippings from *The Sphere*, Box 56; photograph of her at breakfast in *New York Times*, 2 Oct. 1928, Box 51.

77 Radio Obituary Script, Box 55.

78 Joseph P. Lash, *Eleanor and Franklin* (New York, 1971), pp.28, 46.

79 *Ibid.*, p.101.

80 *Ibid.*, p.220.

81 War Diary of Ann Meader, typescript in Imperial War Museum, London (there is also a copy in the Hoover Archives), 23 September 1939.

82 *Ibid.*, 4 October 1939; 14 January 1940.

83 *Ibid.*, 8 October 1939.

84 *Ibid.*, 5 November 1939.

85 *Ibid.*, 15 January 1940, 4 March, 10 May, 16 May, 25 July, 20 August, 16 September 1941.

86 *Ibid.*, 10 May 1943.

87 J. B. Priestley, *English Journey* (1933), pp.310, 311.

88 Helen Forrester, *Twopence to Cross the Mersey* (1974, 1981 edition).

89 *Ibid.*, p.137.

90 *Ibid.*, p.169.

91 Walter Greenwood, *Love on the Dole* (1932).

92 Olivier, *Confessions*, pp.32, 86.

93 Douglas T. Miller and Marion Nowak, *The Fifties: The Way We Really Were* (Garden City, NY, 1977), p.8.

94 *Ibid.*, p.129.

95 Alfred Kinsey, *Sexual Behavior in the Human Male* (New York, 1948); *Sexual Behavior in the Human Female* (New York, 1954).

96 Miller and Nowak, *The Fifties*, p.8.

97 Lindsay Anderson in Tom Maschler (ed.), *Declaration* (1957), p.155.

98 *Paris Match*, 8 Sept. 1962.

99 Mildred Freely Hart and Charlotte Wright Wilkinson, *A Wonderful You! A Modern Woman's Guide to Poise, Charm and Beauty* (New York, 1947), pp.1, 23.

100 Elsie Archer, *Let's Face It: A Guide to Good Grooming for Negro Girls* (Phila., 1959), p.12.

101 *Ibid.*, p.55.

102 Peter Noble and Yvonne Saxon, *Glamour: Film Fashion and Beauty* (1953), pp.4, 16–17, 54–55.

103 Florence Picard, *Voulez-vous être belle?* (Paris, 1952), p.14.

104 *Ibid.*, p.11.

105 Dr Charles Mayer, *La Médecine au service de la beauté* (Paris, 1955), p.174.

106 *Ibid.*, pp.161–68, 174.

107 Clifford Bax, *The Beauty of Women* (1946), p.95.

108 Robert K. Riedel to Ingrid Bergman, 9 February 1947. Joseph Henry Steele Papers, Stanford University Libraries, Special Collections, M167, Box 2, Folder 7.

109 *Ibid.*

110 *Marty* (United Artists/Hecht-Hill-Lancaster, 1955).

111 Anthony Summers, *Goddess: The Secret Lives of Marilyn Monroe* (1985), pp.6–11.

112 Quotations in *ibid.*, p.26–38.

113 Quoted in *ibid.*, pp.35–61.

114 Quoted in *ibid.*, p.177.

115 *Ibid.*, pp.221–22.

116 I have followed the careful and persuasive account given in *ibid.*, pp.301–68.

## CHAPTER 8

1 Ken Jameson in Ronald Weber (ed.),

*America in Change: Reflections on the 60's and 70's* (Notre Dame, 1972), p.18.

2 E. H. Lacombe (ed.), *Les Changements de la société française* (Paris, 1971); Arthur Marwick, *British Society since 1945* (1982), part two.

3 *Paris Match*, 27 April 1963.

4 *Ibid.*, 30 November 1963.

5 Elizabeth Kendall, *Good Looks, Good Grooming* (New York, 1963), p.25.

6 *Paris Match*, 4 September 1965.

7 *Life*, 11 April 1960.

8 *Ibid.*, 28 January 1966.

9 *Time*, 3 June 1966.

10 The phrase was first used by the London-based American Melvyn Lasky, in an article in *Time*, 16 April 1966.

11 *Paris Match*, 20 May 1967.

12 On the general question, see Neil A. Wynn, *The Afro-American and the Second World War* (New York, 1974). For *Ebony's* views on its own foundation, see *Ebony*, November 1965.

13 *Harper's Magazine*, November 1959.

14 *Ibid.*

15 *American Mercury*, September 1958.

16 *Paris Match*, 4 April 1964.

17 Rudi Gernreich in Peter Joseph, *Good Times: An Oral History of America in the Nineteen Sixties* (New York, 1973), p.61.

18 *Harper's Magazine*, October 1967.

19 See Paul Robinson, *The Modernization of Sex* (New York, 1976).

20 As quoted in *American Mercury*, January 1960.

21 *Ibid.*; *Paris Match*, 26 November 1960.

22 See my 'Room at the Top, Saturday Night and Sunday Morning, and the cultural revolution in Great Britain', in *Journal of Contemporary History*, January 1984.

23 *Life*, 29 February 1960.

24 Quoted in *Ibid.*

25 Quoted in Marilyn Bender, *The Beautiful People* (New York, 1967), p.189.

26 Geoffrey Gorer, *Exploring English Character* (1952), *Sex and Marriage in England Today* (1971).

27 M. Schofield, *Sexual Behaviour of Young People* (1965).

28 Figures from CSO, *Annual Abstract of Statistics*, for relevant years.

29 Conveniently collected in Françoise Giraud, *Une poignée d'eau* (Paris, 1973).

30 *L'Express*, November 1966.

31 Kingsley Amis, *Take a Girl Like You* (1960), p.20.

32 John Braine, *Room at the Top* (1957).

33 Richard Todd, 'Turned-on and super-sincere in California', *Harper's Magazine*, January 1967.

34 See William Meyers, *The Image-Makers: Power and Persuasion on Madison Avenue* (New York, 1984).

35 Bender, *Beautiful People*, p.23.

36 *Life*, 26 December 1969.

37 *Ebony*, July 1956, November 1965.

38 *Ibid.*, November 1958.

39 *Ibid.*, June 1964, June 1965.

40 *Ibid.*, December 1965.

41 *Ibid.*, October 1961.

42 *Ibid.*, September 1958.

43 *Ibid*, July 1965.

44 *Ibid.*, January 1966.

45 *Ibid.*, February 1966.

46 *Ibid.*, April 1966.

47 *Ibid.*, June 1966.

48 *Ibid.*, August 1966.

49 *Ibid.*, March 1964.

50 Arthur Marwick, 'The upper class in Britain, France, and the USA since World War I', in Marwick (ed.), *Class in the Twentieth Century*, pp.17–61.

51 Jean Shrimpton, *The Truth about Modelling* (1964), p.12.

52 *Ibid.*, p.153.

53 *Ibid.*, pp.16ff.

54 *Ibid.*, p.17.

55 *Ibid.*, p.20.

56 *Ibid.*, p.66.

57 *Ibid.*, p.68.

58 *Ibid.*, p.68.

59 Twiggy, *An Autobiography* (1975), p.8.

60 *Ibid.*, p.24.

61 *Ibid.*

62 *Ibid.*, p.25.

63 *Ibid.*, p.29.

64 *Ibid.*, p.36.

65 *Ibid.*, pp.53-68.

66 Joseph, *Good Times*, p.185.

67 Quoted in Michael Parkinson, *George Best: An Intimate Biography* (1975), p.69, on which this section is based.

68 *Ibid.*, p.50.

69 *Ibid.*, p.33.

70 *Ibid.*, p.54.

71 Susan Cleeve, *Growing Up in the Swinging Sixties* (1980), p.69. In general, see Jack Olsen, *Cassius Clay: A Biography* (1967).

72 *Ladies Home Journal*, August 1979.

73 *Life*, 18 March 1966.

74 *Life*, 9 January 1970.

75 *Le Figaro*, 1 December 1965.

76 Murray Webster, Jr and James E. Driskell, Jr, 'Beauty as status', *American Journal of Sociology*, vol.89, no.1 (1983), pp.163–65.

77 A most useful research tool is *Psychological Abstracts*. Elaine Berscheid and Elaine Walster, 'Physical attractiveness', in Leonard Berkowitz (ed.), *Advances in Experimental Social Psychology*, vol.7 (New York, 1974), pp.157–215, is an invaluable survey.

78 F. A. C. Perrin, 'Physical attractiveness and repulsiveness', *Journal of Experimental Psychology*, vol.4 (1921), pp.203–17.

79 *Ibid.*, pp.212, 216.

80 Wilfred Waller, 'The rating and dating complex', *American Sociological Review*, vol.2 (1937), pp.727–37.

81 A. H. Iliffe, 'A study of preferences in feminine beauty', *British Journal of Psychology*, vol.51 (1960), pp.267–73.

82 Erving Goffman, 'On calling the mark out: some aspects of adaptation to failure', *Psychiatry*, vol.15 (1952), p.456.

83 E. Walster, V. Aronson, D. Abrahams and L. Rottman, 'Importance of physical attractiveness in dating behavior', *Journal of Personality and Social Psychology*, vol.5 (1966), pp.508–16.

84 *Ibid.*, pp.513–14.

85 *Ibid.*, p.514.

86 W. Stroebe, C. A. Insko, V. D. Thompson and B. D. Layton, 'Effects of physical attractiveness, attitude similarity, and sex on various aspects of interpersonal attraction', *Journal of Personality and Social Psychology*, vol.18 (1971), pp.79–91.

87 *Ibid.*, p.84.

88 *Ibid.*, p.89.

89 E. Berscheid, K. K. Dion, E. Walster and G. W. Walster, 'Physical attractiveness and dating choice', *Journal of Experimental Social Psychology*, vol.7 (1971), pp.173–89.

90 *Ibid.*, p.179.

91 *Ibid.*, pp.180–81.

92 *Ibid.*, p.183.

93 T. L. Huston, 'Ambiguity of acceptance, social desirability, and dating choice', *Journal of Experimental Psychology*, vol.9 (1973), pp.32–42.

94 Stroebe *et al.*, 'Effects of physical attractiveness', p.89.

95 Bernard J. Murstein, 'Physical attractiveness and marital choice', *Journal of Personality and Social Psychology*, vol.22, no.1 (1972), p.11.

96 *Journal of Personality and Social Psychology*, vol.24 (1972), pp.205–90.

97 D. Krebs and A. A. Adinolfi, 'Physical attractiveness, social relations, and personality style', *Journal of Personality and Social Psychology*, vol.31 (1975), pp.245–53; M. Dermer and D. L. Thiel, 'When beauty may fail', in *ibid.*, pp.1168–76.

98 J. E. Singer, 'The use of manipulative strategies: Machiavellianism and attractiveness', *Sociometry*, vol.27 (1964), pp.128–50.

99 *L'Encyclopédie beauté bien-être* (Paris, 1964), p.5.

100 Josette Lyon, *La Femme et la beauté* (Paris, 1965), pp.9, 12; Helen Whitcombe and Rosalind Lancy, *Charm: The Career Girl's Guide to Business and Personal Success* (New York, 1964); Brigitte Baer, *Grande forme: être bien dans sa peau* (Paris, 1970), p.16.

101 Gilda Lund, *Beauty* (1963), p.7.

102 E.g. Helen M. McLachlan, *Poise, Personality and Charm* (New York, 1965); Elizabeth Kendall, *Good Looks, Good Grooming*.

103 E.g. Sophie Lamiral and Dodi Schultz, *Everyday Beauty* (New York, 1969), p.146; Baer, *Grande forme*, p.25.

104 E.g. 'Famille 2000', *Beauté et hygiène* (Paris, 1971); Pierre Desjardin, *Le Guide de la santé et de la beauté* (Paris, 1971), pp.9–11.

105 Dr Robert Schwartz, *Médecine et beauté* (Paris, 1969); Pierre Desjardin, *Guide de la santé*.

106 Schwartz, *Médecine et beauté*, pp.157ff.

107 See, e.g., Franka Guez, *Masculin quotidien: guide pratique à l'usage des hommes* (Paris, 1969), pp.7–8; 'Marabout Flash', *Le Guide Flash de l'homme* (Verviers, Belgium, 1970), pp.8–9.

108 Guez, *Masculin quotidien*, p.8.

109 *Le Guide Flash*, p.11.

110 Catherine Harlé, *Comment devenir modèle* (Paris, 1970), p.24.

111 *Life*, 12 March 1965.

112 Pierrette Sartin, *La Réussite professionnelle* (Paris, 1971), pp.37–38.

113 Jennie Lee, *This Great Journey: A Volume of Autobiography* (1963) [one portrait], *My Life with Nye* (1980) [several portraits]; Wilfred De'ath, *Barbara Castle: A Portrait from Life* (1970); Jean Choffel, *Seille une Femme . . . Alice Saunier-Seïté* (Paris, 1979), p.96; Alice Saunier-Seïté, *En première ligne: de la communale aux universités* (Paris, 1982) – the portrait on the cover shows her as very beautiful.

114 See, e.g., *Life*, 24 August 1959, cover story: 'Jackie Kennedy: a front runner's appealing wife'.

115 W. L. O'Neill, *Coming Apart: An Informal History of America in the 1960s* (Chicago, 1971), p. 387, footnote.

116 Kathleen Hall Jamieson, *Packaging the President* (New York, 1984), pp.139–41.

117 *Ibid.*, pp.153ff.

118 *Life*, 26 May 1961.

119 *Life*, 28 May 1965.

120 *Life*, 21 Jan. 1966.

121 Edmund G. Brown, *Reagan and Reality: The Two Californias* (New York, 1970), pp.40–41.

122 *Harper's Magazine*, September 1967.

123 In France and the USA there was legislation similar to the British Chronically Sick and Disabled Persons Act of 1970. A summary of French developments after 1969 and a characteristic expression of concern can be found in Rassemblement pour la République, *Le R.P.R. propose égalité pour les handicappés* (December 1977).

## CHAPTER 9

1 For 'Ugly', see Brigid Keenan, *The Women we Wanted to Look Like* (1977), p.195. In general, see 'America's obsession with beautiful people', *U.S. News and World Report*, 11 Jan. 1982.

2 *The Way We Were* (Columbia/Rostar,

1973); *Alice Doesn't Live Here Any More* (Warner, 1974).

3 Nancy C. Baker, *The Beauty Trap: How Every Woman Can Save Herself From It* (New York, 1984), p.7; Susan Brownmiller, *Femininity* (New York, 1984), p.165; John T. Molloy, *Women: Dress for Success* (New York, 1978); 'Women: what's on their minds? What do they fear? What do they hope for?', *Glamour*, Jan. 1983.

4 Sandra L. Bem, 'The measurement of pyschological androgyny', *Journal of Consulting and Clinical Psychology*, vol.42 (1974), pp.155–62.

5 Madeleine E. Heilman and Lois K. Suruwatari, 'When beauty is beastly: the effects of appearance and sex on evaluations of job applicants for managerial and nonmanagerial posts', *Organizational Behaviour and Human Performance*, vol.23 (1979), pp.360–72.

6 *Ibid.*, p.317.

7 Susan M. Anderson and Sandra L. Bem, 'Sex typing and androgyny in dyadic interaction: individual differences in responsiveness to physical attractiveness', *Journal of Personality and Social Psychology*, vol.41 (1981), pp.74-86.

8 Linda A. Jackson, 'The influence of sex, physical attractiveness, sex role, and occupational sex-linkage on perceptions of occupational suitability', *Journal of Applied Social Psychology*, vol.13 (1983), pp.33-35.

9 *Psychological Abstracts*, vol.70 (1983), p.1268.

10 Jackson, 'The influence of sex . . . on perceptions of occupational suitability', pp.41-42.

11 Thomas F. Cash and Robert N. Kilcullen, 'The aye of the beholder: susceptibility to sexism and beautyism in the evaluation of managerial applicants', *Journal of Applied Social Psychology*, vol.15 (1985), pp. 594-95, 601-03.

12 Terry A. Beehr and C. C. Gilmore, 'Applicant attractiveness as a perceived job-relevant variable in selection of management trainees', *Academy of Management Journal*, vol.25 (1982), pp.607-17.

13 Robert Baron, 'Self-presentation in job interviews: where there can be "too much of a good thing"', *Journal of Applied Social Psychology*, vol.16 (1986), pp.16–28.

14 *New York Times*, 13 January 1985.

15 See Nickie Roberts, *The Front Line: Women in the Sex Industry Speak* (1986).

16 *The Sun*, 14 July 1986.

17 Germaine Greer, *The Female Eunuch* (1970), p.261.

18 ICA, *Women's Images of Men* (1980), p.12.

19 *The Sunday Times*, 18 November 1984.

20 *Ibid.*

21 Cecily Hunt, *How to Get Work and Make Money in Commercials and Modeling* (New York, 1982), p.25.

22 W. Benoy Joseph, 'The credibility of physically attractive communicators', *Journal of Advertising*, vol.11 (1982), pp.15–24.

23 *Observer Magazine*, 4 November 1984.

24 Baker, *The Beauty Trap*, p.7.

25 Lakoff and Scherr, *Face Value*, pp.16–17.

26 *Observer*, 27 July 1986.

27 Baker, *The Beauty Trap*, p.9.

28 *Ibid.*, pp.245-49.

29 *The Independent*, 23 September 1987.

30 Anderson and Bem, 'Sex typing and androgyny', p.75.

# Appendix 1

## Aphorisms and Declarations relating to Beauty

(These demonstrate the contradictions and confusions with which the subject abounds, and show that it is certainly a fruitful one for serious discussion and debate. Some appear in my text; all relate to some attitude or aspect referred to in it.)

What is beautiful is good, and who is good will soon be beautiful
(SAPPHO, *Fragment, c.* 610 BC)

The good is beautiful
(PLATO, *Lysis,* 216d *c.* 330 BC)

Gaze not upon a maiden, lest her beauty be a stumbling block to thee
(ECCLESIASTICUS, IX, 5, *c.* 180 BC)

Lust not after her beauty in thine heart; neither let her take thee with her eyelids
(PROVERBS, VI:25 *c.* 150 BC)

Beauty is heaven's gift, and how few can boast of beauty
(OVID, Ars Amatoria, *c.* 10 BC)

Allas! too deare boughte she her beautee,
Wherefore I say al day that men may see,
That giftes of Fortune, and of Nature,
Ben cause of deth to many a creature
Her Beautee was her deth, I dar well sayn,
Allas! so piteiusly as she was slayn
(GEOFFREY CHAUCER, words of the Hoost to the Phisicien,
*Canterbury Tales, c.* 1390)

For all men be not so wise as to have respect to the virtuous condition of the party; and the endowments of the body cause the virtues of the mind to be esteemed and regarded, yea even in the marriages of wise men
(SIR THOMAS MORE, *Utopia,* 1518)

Me think well beauty is more necessary in her than in the Courtier, for (to say the truth) there is a great lack in the woman that wanteth beauty

There be also many wicked men that have the comliness of a beautiful countenance, and it seemeth that nature hath so shaped them, because they may be the readier to deceive, and that this amiable look were like a bait that covereth the hook
(BALDESAR CASTIGLIONE, *Book of the Courtier,* 1527)

His appearance is completely royal, so that without ever having seen his face or his portrait, on seeing him one would say instantly: 'it's the King. All of his movements are so noble and so majestic that no prince could equal him'
(VENETIAN REPORT on Francis I of France, 1546)

When we speak of a beautiful woman we mean one whom all alike admire, not this one or that one only

Women like looking at the beauty of men, as men like looking at the beauty
of women
(AGNOLO FIRENZUOLA, *Dialogue on the Beauties of Women*, 1548)

What is naturally beautiful is also naturally good
(GABRIEL DE MINUT, *Of Beauty*, 1587)

I cannot say enough how much I esteem beauty a powerful and advantageous
quality . . . We have absolutely no quality that surpasses it in credit, nor
which holds a higher rank in human relations; it places itself out in front, and,
with great authority and wondrous impressiveness, seduces and preempts our
judgment . . . in a face which is not too well formed, there may dwell an air
of probity and trustworthiness; as, the other way round, I have sometimes
read between two beautiful eyes menaces of a malignant and dangerous nature
(MICHEL DE MONTAIGNE, *De la phisionomie*, 1588)

When one has a beautiful wife, one has no fine pigs – Why? – Because the
pigs, instead of eating, spend all their time staring at her
(PEASANT SAYING from the Franche-Compté)

From fairest creatures we desire increase,
That thereby beauty's rose might never die
(SHAKESPEARE, Sonnet 1, *c.* 1590)

She's beautiful and therefore to be woo'd
(SHAKESPEARE, I, Henry VI, v. 1592)

Beauty itself doth of itself persuade
The eyes of men without an orator
(SHAKESPEARE, *The Rape of Lucrece*, 1594)

Beauty provoketh thieves sooner than gold
(SHAKESPEARE, *As You Like It, c.* 1599)

Beauty's but skin deep
(JOHN DAVIES OF HEREFORD, *A Select Second Husband for Sir Thomas Overburie's
Wife*, 1616)

Virtue is best in a body that is comely, though not of delicate features; and
that hath rather dignity of presence, than beauty of aspect

There is no excellent beauty that hath not some strangeness in the proportion
(FRANCIS BACON, *Of Beauty*, 1625)

Tis true, gold can do much
But beauty more
(PHILIP MASSINGER, *The Unnatural Combat, c.* 1619)

The body of a woman should be neither too thin and scrawny nor too large
and fat

For perfection of form woman takes second place to man
(PETER PAUL RUBENS, *Theory of the Human Figure*, 1620)

Beauty is a good letter of introduction
(GERMAN PROVERB)

Beauty is a letter of recommendation which has no fixed limit
(attributed to NINON DE LENCLOS, *c.* 1650)

It is worth nothing to be young without being beautiful, nor to be beautiful
without being young
(LA ROCHEFOUCAULD, *Maximes*, no.497, 1665)

Yet beauty, though injurious, hath strange power
(JOHN MILTON, *Samson Agonistes*, 1671)

Beauty stands
In the admiration of weak minds
Led captive
(JOHN MILTON, *Paradise Regained*, II, 1671)

I would have wished to be a girl, and a beautiful girl from the age of thirteen
to the age of twenty-two, and then after that to be a man

A beautiful face is of all spectacles the most beautiful
(JEAN DE LA BRUYERE, *Caractères*, 1688)

There's no great odds between his Marrying for the Love of Money, or for
the Love of Beauty, the Man does not Act according to Reason in either Case;
but is governed by irregular Appetites
(MARY ASTELL, *Some Reflections on Marriage*, 1700)

No woman can be a beauty without a fortune
(FARQUHAR, *The Beaux' Stratagem*, 1707)

'Tis not a lip, or eye, we beauty call,
But the joint force and full result of all
(ALEXANDER POPE, *An Essay on Criticism*, II, 1711)

Beauties in vain their pretty eyes may roll;
Charm strikes the sight, but merit wins the soul
(ALEXANDER POPE, *The Rape of the Lock*, V, 1712)

With scorn Clodalia's haughty face we view,
The Deadn'd aspect, and the sordid hue,
Her wealth discover'd gives her features lies
And we find charms to reconcile our eyes
(TUNBRIDGE AND BATH MISCELLANY FOR 1714)

Beauty like wit, cannot be defined, but is discern'd only by a taste or
sensation
(DAVID HUME, *Treatise of Human Nature*, 1739)

Nothing is more fortunate than handsome men, nor more unfortunate than
handsome women
(HENRY FIELDING, *A Journey from this World to the Next*, 1743)

Among the chief men of the colleges sodomy is very usual . . . it is dangerous
sending a young man who is beautiful to Oxford
(DUDLEY RYDER, *Diary*, 1744)

The Beauty of Virtue or Goodness exceeds all other Beauty, as much as the Soul does the Body
('SIR HARRY BEAUMONT', *Crito, or a Dialogue on Beauty*, 1752)

It is nearly always the ugly ones who introduce a new fashion, to which the beautiful ones have the stupidity to submit themselves
(attributed to ROUSSSEAU, *c.* 1755)

By beauty I mean, that quality or those qualities by which they cause love, or some passion similar to it
(EDMUND BURKE, *Philosophical Enquiry into the Origins of our Ideas of the Sublime and Beautiful*, 1757)

Although piety, modesty, virtue, good sense, and ingenuity ought to be the chief objects of every woman's attention, yet since the frailty of human nature inclines men rather to listen to their senses than their judgment, it must be allowed an innocent at least, if not a necessary care in the fair sex to cultivate beauty
(ART OF BEAUTY, 1760)

Ask a toad what is beauty . . . he will answer that it is his female with two huge round eyes coming out of her tiny head, large flat mouth, yellow belly and brown back. Question a negro from Guinea, beauty for him is an oily black skin, sunken eyes and squat nose
(VOLTAIRE, *Dictionnaire philosophique portatif*, 1764)

Great beauty should rather be avoided than sought in marriage . . . If extreme ugliness was not disgusting, I should prefer it to extreme beauty
(ROUSSEAU, *Thoughts on Different Subjects*, 1770)

Unfortunately, I could not help listening to him; he was handsome as the dawn
(CATHERINE THE GREAT, *Memoirs*, *c.* 1771)

Mere *beauty* is not happiness
But fatal to itself; – in power
It gleams the meteor of an hour;
For one it guides to joy and light,
It plunges ten in *Stygian night*
(DR JOHN COSENS, *Economy of Beauty*, 1777)

The sense of beauty does not tend to advance the interests of society. Love . . . arising from a sense of beauty, loses, when excessive, its sociable character: the appetite for gratification, prevailing over affection for the beloved object, is ungovernable, and tends violently to its end, regardless of the misery that must follow
(HENRY HOME, *Elements of Criticism*, 1784)

Physical beauty is the sign of an interior beauty, a spiritual and moral beauty which is the basis, the principle, and the unity of the beautiful
(FRIEDRICH SCHILLER, *Essays Aesthetical and Philosophical*, 1792)

I would gladly give half of the wit with which I am credited for half of the beauty you possess
(MADAME DE STAEL, Letter to Mme Récamier, 1790)

But *Tam* kend what was what fu' brawlie,
There was ae winsome wench and wawlie . . .
And how Tam stood, like one bewitch'd,
And thought his very een enrich'd;
Even Satan glowr'd and fidg'd fu' fain,
And hotch'd and blew wi' might and main . . .
(ROBERT BURNS, *Tam o'Shanter*, 1790)

There were very few Beauties, and such as there were, were not very
handsome
(JANE AUSTEN to her sister Cassandra, 20 Nov. 1800)

'Beauty is truth, truth beauty' – that is all
Ye know on earth, and all ye need to know
(JOHN KEATS, *Ode on a Grecian urn, c.* 1819)

Why may I not speak of your Beauty, since without that I could never have
loved you
(JOHN KEATS to Fanny Brawne, 8 July 1819)

She walks in beauty like the night
Of cloudless climes and starry skies;
And all that's best of dark and bright
Meet in her aspect and her eyes
(LORD BYRON, *She Walks in Beauty*, 1820)

As a preliminary to the following list, it may not be amiss to give a few
indications, by which the Kalogynomist, who happens to follow a female in
the street, or on the promenade, may be aided in determining whether it is
worth his while to glance at her face in passing
(T. BELL, MD, *Kalogynomia or the Laws of Female Beauty*, 1821)

Beauty is only the promise of happiness
(STENDHAL, *De l'amour*, 1822)

Fashion is gentility running away from vulgarity and afraid of being overtaken
(WILLIAM HAZLITT, *The Conversations of James Northcote*, 1830)

Beauty is the mark God sets upon virtue
(RALPH WALDO EMERSON, *Nature*, 1836)

The sensation of beauty . . . is dependent on a pure, right, and open state of
the heart
(JOHN RUSKIN, *Modern Painters*, 1852)

The saying 'that beauty is but skin-deep' is but a skin-deep saying
(HERBERT SPENCER, *'Personal beauty'*, 1854)

Listen to the questions one asks about a woman one does not know: 'Is she
beautiful?' That is the first question, and nearly always the only one
(ALPHONSE KARR, *Women*, 1855)

The romantic ideal of a forehead of ivory, eyes of sapphire, eye brows and
hair of ebony, cheeks of roses, a mouth of coral, teeth of pearl, and a swan's
neck would be more likely to arouse the desire of a robber than of a lover
(attributed to ALPHONSE KARR)

A mere notice of the influence of personal beauty alone, on individuals and on society, in all ages of the world, would embrace the whole history of the human race. It has, perhaps, owing to the lawless passions and vices of mankind, been productive of more contention than has been caused by ambition, and more misery than has been occasioned by avarice and gold
(A. J. COOLEY, *The Toilet and Cosmetic Arts in Ancient and Modern Times*, 1866)

Many persons are convinced, as it appears to me with justice, that our aristocracy, including under this term all wealthy families in which primogeniture has long prevailed, from having chosen during many generations from all classes the more beautiful women as their wives, have become handsomer, according to the European standard, than the middle classes
(CHARLES DARWIN, *The Descent of Man*, 1871)

Beauty is in the eye of the beholder
(MARGARET WOLFE HUNGERFORD, *Molly Bawn*, 1878)

Fashion is the ugly majority compelling the beautiful minority to conceal their charms
(H. T. FINCK, *Romantic Love and Personal Beauty*, 1887)

No woman has a right to be ugly, and ought to do everything in reason to make herself beautiful
('A PROFESSIONAL BEAUTY', *Beauty and How to Keep It*, 1880)

It is amazing how complete is the delusion that beauty is goodness
(TOLSTOY, *The Kreutzer Sonata*, 1889)

It is better to be beautiful than to be good, but it is better to be good than to be ugly
(OSCAR WILDE, *The Picture of Dorian Gray*, 1891)

Obesity is the enemy of beauty and incompatible with it
(MARQUISE DE GARCHES, *Les Secrets de beauté d'une parisienne*, 1894)

Oh lovely lass . . .
Oh sweetly gentle face
suffused by the awakening moon
In you I behold
The dream I'd like to dream forever*
(GIACOSA and ILLICA, *La Bohème*, music by Puccini, 1896)

As to work, it is the sweetener of daily life to both men and women . . .
Work well done has made many a plain face beautiful
(MRS HUMPHRY, *How to be Beautiful though Plain*, 1899)

In numerous walks of life, men and women discover the fact that their face has, indeed, much to do with their fortune
(PROF. BOYD LAYNARD, *Secrets of Beauty*, 1900)

There is to my mind no doubt that the concept of 'beautiful' has its roots in sexual excitation and its original meaning was 'sexually stimulating'
(SIGMUND FREUD, *Three Essays on the Theory of Sexuality*, 1905)

*But never mind the words (my translation), listen to the music.

Fashion is the defiance of beauty and the cult of the common
(E. FEYDEAU, *L'Art de plaire*, 1913)

Swann did not strive to find the women with whom he passed his time
beautiful, but to pass his time with the women he found beautiful
(MARCEL PROUST, *Du côté de chez Swann*, 1913)

What undoubtedly attracted young men of the period [the early twenties] was
legs! Far from looking male, girls, with that daring length of limb on show,
appeared not less but more delightfully feminine than ever
(ROBERT ROBERTS, *The Classic Slum*, 1971)

Harding had no qualifications for being President except that he looked like
one – which is, given the mythological role of the President in American
culture, not an unimportant consideration
(WILLIAM E. LEUCHTENBERG, *The Perils of Prosperity 1914–32*, 1958)

We like a man to be good-looking, well-built, physically plucky, socially
agreeable, 'Brooksey'
(DAILY PRINCETONIAN, 1 December 1924)

Sex and beauty are inseparable, like life and consciousness
(D. H. LAWRENCE, *Sex Versus Loveliness*, 1930)

Our inherent preference for beauty rather than sensationalism is the real secret
of your popularity. To us, the audience, you represent that high degree of
beauty and virtue to which we all aspire, however failingly
(FAN LETTER TO INGRID BERGMAN, 1947)

In the ideal figure, the largest part of the bust is supposed to be equal to the
largest part of the hips, and the waist should be ten inches smaller than either.
If your bust is 35, then your hips should be 35 and your waist should be 25.
A variation of two inches one way or the other still gives you a nice figure
(ELEANORE KING, *Glorify Yourself*, 1948)

It is ugliness that is immoral
(FLORENCE PICARD, *Voulez-vous être belle*, 1952)

In assessing the beauty of a man or woman, the further removed from the
animal is their appearance, the more beautiful they are reckoned
(GEORGES BATAILLE, *Death and Sensuality*, 1953)

There is a guy for every doll, if that doll knows what she wants and knows
what to look for in the guy of her life. Too many girls are influenced only by
good looks, or achievement in sports, or the way a boy dances, or the line he
hands her . . . These things impress you because you want to be seen with a
boy that you can be proud of
(ELSIE ARCHER, *Let's Face It: A Guide to Good Grooming for Negro Girls*, 1959)

It is difficult to be certain why the effects of physical beauty have not been
studied more systematically. It may be that, at some level, we would hate to
find evidence indicating that beautiful women are better liked than homely
women – somehow this seems undemocratic
(psychologist E. ARONSON, *'Some antecedents of interpersonal attraction'*, 1969)

Is it too much to ask that women be spared the daily struggle for super human beauty in order to offer it to the caresses of a sub-humanly ugly mate?
(GERMAINE GREER, *The Female Eunuch*, 1970)

A beautiful woman generally leads a vastly different life from a plain one
(STEPHEN KERN, *Anatomy and Destiny*, 1975)

Dress is a form of visual art, a creation of images with the visible self as its medium
(ANNE HOLLANDER, *Seeing through Clothes*, 1978)

To praise someone's beauty is (whether we like it or not) a sexual act
(SIR KENNETH DOVER, *Greek Homosexuality*, 1978)

Women employers are likely to be no less concerned than men about the physical attractiveness of their female employees, since they recognize that beauty is a tangible economic asset. Of course this is true also of male employees, but to a markedly lesser extent
(DONALD SYMONS, *Evolution of Human Sexuality*, 1979)

I have always believed the male form is equally as beautiful than [sic] the female but in photographing the male body, you must approach it leaving all preconceived thoughts behind, using intuition as guide. Many photographs of men destroy the male mystique. Posing and looking directly into the camera's eye immediately loses the picture's erotic appeal. Most male models take up female gestures, posing through conditioning, which also makes the photograph look ridiculously wrong
(ROBERTA JUZEFA in *Women's Images of Men*, 1980)

To work hard, as I've worked, to accomplish anything and then have some yo-yo come up and say 'Take-off those dark glasses and let's have a look at those blue eyes' is really discouraging
(PAUL NEWMAN, 1986)

# Appendix 2

Extracts from *La Cousine Bette* by Honoré de Balzac

All historical texts are complex, extracts from works of creative literature particularly so. From these fairly extended passages from one of Balzac's pair of final novels, published in 1846/47, and set in 1838, with many references back to the beginning of the century, readers may care to judge for themselves how far my general points about the significance of beauty, and how far the particular points I was making in the first sections of chapter five, seem to be supported. Can one, for example, say that in estimating the eligibility for marriage of a woman 'traditional' society placed the greatest emphasis on her dowry, while 'modern' society places a great emphasis on her beauty?

Crivel (aged fifty-one) is a very wealthy retired vendor of perfumes; the text itself makes very clear the origins of both Baron and Baronne Hulot – Hortense is their daughter.

'One cannot today arrange the marriage of a daughter as beautiful as Mademoiselle Hortense without a dowry', replied Crivel, reassuming his pinched expression. 'Your daughter is one of those beauties terrifying for husbands; it's like one of those thoroughbred horses which require too much costly attention to have many purchasers. Can a man go about with such a woman on his arm? Everybody looks at you, follows you, desires your wife. Such success upsets many people who don't want to have lovers to kill; for after all, one never kills more than one. In the situation you are in, you can only marry your daughter in three ways; with my help, which you will not accept; by finding an old man of sixty, very rich, without children, who wants to have them – difficult, but it happens . . . The last way is the easiest.'

Madame Hulot lifted her head, looking anxiously at the former perfumer.

'Paris is a city where all the energetic, growing like wild flowers across the land of France, come together; it swarms with the talented, possessed of neither house nor home, but with daring capable of anything, even of making a fortune . . . Well, one of these condottierri, as one says, of the stock market, of the pen, or of the paintbrush, is the sole being in Paris capable of marrying a beautiful girl without a sou, because they have every type of courage. These people are mad! They believe in love as they believe in their fortune and their talents. Look for a man of energy who will fall in love with your daughter and he will marry her without a thought for present circumstances . . .'

From the first day of her marriage right up to this moment, the Baronne had loved her husband, as Josephine had finished by loving Napoleon . . . If she was unaware of the details which Crivel had just given her, she still knew well enough that for twenty years the Baron had had his infidelities; but she had put a heavy veil across her eyes and wept in silence, and never allowed a word of reproach to escape . . .

Now it is necessary to explain the extraordinary devotion of this beautiful and noble woman: and here is the history of her life in a few words. In a village situated on the furthest boundaries of Lorraine, at the foot of the Vosges mountains, three brothers, of the name of Fischer, simple labourers, were conscripted by the Republic into what was called the Army of the Rhine. In 1799 the second of the brothers, André, a widower and father of Madame Hulot, left his daughter in the care of his elder brother, Pierre Fischer, who had been rendered incapable of military service by a wound received in 1787, and who had several employments in the Military Transport,

work which he owed to the patronage of the Commissioner Hulot d'Evry. By
a perfect natural turn of fortune, Hulot, visiting Strasbourg, saw the Fischer
family. Adeline's father and his younger brother were at that time sub-
commissioners for forage in Alsace.

Adeline, then seventeen, could have been compared to the famous Madame
Du Barry, like her, a daughter of Lorraine. She was one of those total
beauties, whose beauty strikes like the crash of thunder.

Adeline Fischer, one of the most beautiful of this divine tribe, possessed the
sublime characteristics, the sinuous lines, the devastating ensemble of these
women born queens. The blond hair which our mother Eve took from the
hand of God, the figure of an empress, an air of dignity, an august profile and
a rustic modesty stopped every man in his tracks, enchanted as art lovers are
in front of a Raphael; seeing her, the Commissioner, in the shortest legal time,
made Adeline Fischer his wife, to the great astonishment of the Fischers . . .

This marriage was for the peasant girl like an Assumption. The beautiful
Adeline passed straight from the mud of her village into the paradise of the
imperial court. In fact, at that time, the Commissioner, one of the most
honest and most active in his corps, was named baron, called to the side of
the Emperor, and attached to the imperial guard. The beautiful village girl,
through love of her husband, with whom she was quite simply intoxicated,
had the spirit to seek out an education for herself. The Chief Commissioner
besides was, as a man, a replica of Adeline as a woman. He belonged to the
elite corps of beautiful men. Tall, well made, blond, with irresistible blue
eyes, spirited and playful, and an elegant figure, he was remarked upon
among the d'Orsays, the Forbins, the Ouvrards, and finally in the battalion of
the beaux of the Empire . . .

Hortense resembled her mother, but she had golden hair, curling and
abundant to an astonishing degree. Her appeal was that of mother of pearl.
One could clearly see in her the fruit of an honest marriage, of a pure and
noble love in all its force. There was a passionate expressiveness in her face, a
liveliness in her features, a spirited youthfulness, a freshness of life, a richness
of health which sent electric vibrations all around her. Hortense commanded
attention. When her ultramarine eyes, redolent of innocence, lighted upon a
passer-by, he would shiver involuntarily . . . Tall, plump without being fat,
with a lithe figure whose nobility equalled that of her mother, she fully
merited that title of goddess so over-used by the ancient authors . . .

Lizbeth Fischer [Cousin Bette], five years younger than Madame Hulot,
though nevertheless the daughter of the elder of the Fischers, was very far
from being beautiful like her cousin; thus she had been prodigiously jealous of
Adeline. This jealousy formed the base of her character full of *eccentricities*, a
word used by the English for the follies not of small, but of great houses. A
peasant from the Vosges, in the fullest meaning of the term, thin, brown,
with shining black hair, thick eyebrows, joined together in a tuft of hair, long
strong arms, thick feet, several warts on her long and simian face, such is the
concise portrait of this virgin.

The families who lived together had sacrificed the common daughter to the
pretty one, the bitter fruit to the lovely flower. Lizbeth worked on the land,
while her cousin was cosseted; thus one day, finding Adeline alone, she was
seized by an irresistible urge to pull her nose, a true Greek nose which the
older women admired. Even though beaten for this crime, she continued to
tear the gowns and spoil the collars of the privileged daughter.

(Honoré de Balzac, *La Cousine Bette*, Livre de Poche edition, Paris, 1984,
pp. 36–48)

# SOURCES

(Even bibliographies have tongues: the choice of broad categories is deliberate, as is the allocation within them – some striking juxtapositions result; so too with the overall heading 'sources'. Place of publication is London unless otherwise stated, save that I do not give place of publication for learned journals.)

## A. PRIMARY SOURCES

### 1 Museums and Archives

Bodleian Library, Oxford:
John Johnson Collection: 'Beauty Parlour' (4 boxes)

British Museum, London
Department of Prints and Drawings:
Political and Personal Satires
5373–6720

Hoover Institution Archives, Stanford University:
George Barr Baker Collection
Mrs Edsall P. Ford: Diary
Ernest Lundeen Papers
Raymond Moley Papers
Ronald Reagan Papers (understandably most of this collection is closed, but the press releases, clippings and other printed material proved invaluable)
Mark Sullivan Papers
Karl H. von Wiegand Papers

Imperial War Museum:
War Diary of Ann Meader
Brinton-Lee Diary, 1940–41

Museum of London:
Various artifacts, leaflets, etc.

Lincoln County Record Office
Monson Papers

National Library of Scotland:
James Gall, 'Journal 1809–1813' (Acc.8874)
Diary of E. E. Graham, 1872–1932,
Robert Graham Diaries (Acc.9077)
Diary of E. C. Batten, 1837 (Acc.8129)

Stanford University Libraries, Special Collections and University Archives
Anderson Papers (M51)
James E. Bouldu Diary (M84)

Bound Manuscripts: Two Commonplace Books 1779–82 (Box 4, Item 6) and 1837 (Box 2, Item 10) (M290)
Louis Fissner Journals (M89)
Mary Hallock Foote Papers (M115)
Robert Stephen Harlin Diaries (M86)
'Journal of a Tour in France, Switzerland, Italy and a part of Germany in the year 1824': anonymous holograph (M290, Box 6, Item 31)
Joseph Henry Steel Papers (M167)

### 2 Art Galleries

(I have tried, wherever possible, to study originals of the portraits discussed in the text, though at times I have had to use reproductions; complete details on provenance are given elsewhere.)

Principal Galleries Visited:
City Art Gallery, Birmingham
City Art Gallery, Manchester
Dulwich Art Gallery, London
Frick Collection, New York
Kenwood House, London
Louvre, Paris
Musée des Beaux Arts, Orléans
Musée Carnavalet, Paris
Musée Cognacq-Jay, Paris
Museo Correr, Venice
Museum of Brussels
National Gallery of Art, Washington
National Gallery of Scotland
National Portrait Gallery
Palazzo Bianco, Genoa
Scottish National Portrait Gallery
Uffizi Gallery, Florence
Vatican Museum, Rome
Wallace Collection, London

### 3 Guides, Treatises, Surveys and other Contemporary Printed Materials

ACTON, William, *Prostitution Considered in its Moral, Social, and Sanitary Aspects* (1857, 1870)
A LADY, *Beauty: What It Is, and How to Retain It* (1873)
ALLIED NEWSPAPERS, *Beauty for Every Woman* (Manchester, 1929)
ALQ, Louise d', *Les Secrets du cabinet de toilette, conseils et recettes par une femme du monde* (Paris, 1881)
AMERICA'S, 'America's obsession with beautiful people', *U.S. News and World Report* (New York, 11 Jan. 1982)
ANDERSON, Lindsay, 'Coming back to

nanny', in Tom Maschler (ed.),
    *Declaration* (1957)
ANDREWS, J., *Remarks on the French and
    English Ladies* (Dublin, 1783)
ANON. *Reflections on Marriage* (1703)
ARBAUD, Michel and AUBRY, Fernand,
    *et al., Paris et la beauté féminine* (Paris,
    1944)
'ARBITER, Petronius', *Memoirs of the
    Present Countess of Derby (Late Miss
    Farren)* (1797)
ARCHER, Elsie, *Let's Face It: A Guide to
    Good Grooming for Negro Girls*
    (Philadelphia, 1959)
ART, *The Art of Attracting Men* (St Louis,
    1922)
ART, *The Art of Beauty* (1760)
ART, *The Art of Beautifying and Improving
    the Face and Figure* (1858)
ART, *The Art of Beauty or the Best Methods
    of Improving and Preserving the Shape,
    Carriage, and Complexion together with the
    Theory of Beauty* (1825)
ART, *The Art of Dress, or Guide to the
    Toilette, with Directions for Adapting the
    Various Parts of the Female Costume to the
    Complexion and Figure* (1834)
ASSOCIATION GENERALE DES
    ETUDIANTS, *La Beauté* (Paris, 1963)
ASTELL, Mary, *A Serious Proposal to the
    Ladies* (1694)
ASTELL, Mary, *Some Reflections on
    Marriage* (1700)
ATHENA, Madame, *Pour se faire aimer*
    (Paris, n.d., c. 1920)
AUBIGNY, Madame Estelle d', *The
    Woman Beautiful in the Twentieth Century*
    (New York, 1902)
AUBREY, John, *Aubrey's Brief Lives, edited
    from the Original Manuscripts by Oliver
    Lawson Dick* (1958)
AUCLAIR, Marcelle, *Toute la beauté* (Paris,
    1937)
AUTEUIL, Dr Jean d', *A travers la beauté*
    (Paris, n.d.)
AYER, Harriet Hubbard, *Harriet Hubbard
    Ayer's Book: A Complete and Authentic
    Treatise on the Laws of Health and Beauty*
    (Springfield, Mass., 1899 and 1902)

BACON, Francis, 'Of beauty', no.43 in
    *The Essays or Counsels, Civill and Morall,
    of Francis Lo. Verulam, Viscount St.
    Albans. Newly written* (1625)
BAER, Brigitte, *Grande forme: être bien dans
    sa peau* (Paris, 1970)
BAKER, Nancy C., *The Beauty Trap: How
    Every Woman Can Save Herself From It*
    (New York, 1984)
BANNER, Hubert S., *Amy Johnson* (1933)
BARRY, Kathleen, *Female Sexual Slavery*
    (1979)
BATAILLE, Georges, *Death and Sensuality:*

*A Study of Eroticism and the Taboo* (New
    York, 1957)
BAX, Clifford, *The Beauty of Women* (1946)
BAYARD, Emile, *L'Art du bon goût: étude
    théorique et pratique de la beauté mise à
    porteé de tous* (Paris, 1908)
BAYARD, Emile, *L'Art de reconnaître la
    beauté du corps humain* (Paris, 1926)
BAYARD, Madame, *Toilet Hints or How to
    Preserve Beauty and How to Acquire It*
    (1883)
BEAUMONT, Sir Harry (i.e. Rev. Joseph
    Spence), *Crito: or A Dialogue on Beauty*
    (1752)
BEAUTY, *Beauty: How to Get It and How
    to Keep It* (1885)
BEAUTY, *Beauty and Power* (London and
    New York, 1871)
BEAUTY, *Beauty's Treasury: or The Ladies'
    Vade Mecum* (1705)
BEAUTY, *Beauty's Triumph or the
    Superiority of the Fair Sex invincibly
    proved* (1751)
BELL, T., *Kalogynomia, or the Laws of
    Female Beauty* (1821)
BENDER, Marilyn, *The Beautiful People*
    (New York, 1967)
BERKELEY, Bishop, *The New Alciphron*
    (1732)
BIG, C. Sherman, *Face and Figure* (1879)
BLACK, Elsa, *Beauty for Every Woman*
    (1935)
BOLDINI, Giovanni (1842–1931),
    *Esposition* (Musée Jacquemart André,
    Paris, 1963) (catalogue)
BOOK, *The Book of Health and Beauty or the
    Toilette of Rank and Fashion* (1837)
BOSANQUET, Bernard, 'The aesthetic
    theory of ugliness', *Proceedings of the
    Aristotelian Society*, vol.1, no.3 (1891)
BRANTOME, *Les Vies des dames galantes,
    tirées des mémoires de Messire Pierre de
    Bourdeille, Seigneur de Brantôme* (after the
    original edition of 1666, Paris, 1879)
BRAUNSCHVIG, Marcel, *La Femme et la
    beauté* (Paris, 1919)
BRAY, Lucien, *Du beau: essai sur l'origine et
    l'évolution du sentiment esthétique* (Paris,
    1902)
BRINTON, D. G. and NAPHEYS,
    George H., *Personal Beauty: How to
    Cultivate and Preserve It* (Springfield,
    Mass., 1870)
BROWN, Edmund G., *Reagan and Reality:
    The Two Californias* (New York, 1970)
BROWNING, H. Ellen, *Beauty Culture*
    (1898)
BROWNMILLER, Susan, *Femininity*
    (New York, 1984)

CAMPANI, Nicoló, *Bellezze della donna*
    (Venice, 1566)
CARON-MIALARET, Nelly, *Forge ton*

destin (Paris, 1945)

CASTIGLIONE, Baldesar, *Il libro de cortegiano del Conte Baldesar Castiglione* (Venice, 1528)

CASTIGLIONE, Baldesar, *The Book of the Courtier. From the Italian of Count Baldessare Castiglione done into English by Sir Thomas Hoby* (1561)

CAUFEYNON, Dr, *Les Secrets de la beauté* (Paris, n.d.)

CAVE, Marie-Elizabeth, *Beauté physique de la femme* (Paris, n.d., 1868?)

CERTEYNE REWLES, 'Certayne Rewles of Phisnomy', from British Library MS Sloan 213, fols. 118v–121v, reprinted by M. A. Manzalaoui, *Secretum Secretorum: Nine English Versions* (Early English Text Society, Oxford, 1977)

CHAPUS, Eugénie, *L'Homme et la femme comme il faut* (Paris, 1862)

CHAUCHARD, Dr Paul, *Médecine de la beauté* (Paris, n.d.)

CHAVANT, Jeanne, *Créez votre beauté* (Paris, 1958)

CHAVANT, Jeanne, *Le Plaisir d'être belle* (Paris, 1971)

CHESTERFIELD, *Miscellaneous Works of the late Philip Dormer Stanhope, Earl of Chesterfield* (1777–78)

CHEVASSE, P. H., *Man's Strength and Woman's Beauty* (Chicago, 1880)

CHRISTINE, Marie, *Boudoir Gossip on Health and Appearance* (1892)

COBBETT, William, *Advice to Young Men* (1829)

COLEMAN, Dr Vernon (with Margaret Coleman), *Face Values: How the Beauty Industry Affects You* (1981)

COOKE, Thomas, *A Practical and Familiar View of the Science of Physiognomy* (1819)

COOLEY, Arnold J., *The Toilet and Cosmetic Arts in Ancient and Modern Times* (1866)

COSENS, Dr (John), *The Economy of Beauty; in a Series of Fables Addressed to the Ladies* (1777)

COZENS (sic), Dr, *Fables Addressed to the Ladies* (Philadelphia, 1788) (a new version of the above)

COSMOPOLITAN, *Cosmopolitan's Guide to Marvelous Men* (by J. D. Sanderson, 1975)

COURTNEY, Florence, *Physical Beauty: How to Develop and Preserve It* (New York, 1922)

COUSIN, Fabienne, *La Beauté féminine* (Paris, 1973)

COUSIN, Fabienne and GRANT-VEILLARD, S., *L'Encyclopédie beauté, bien-être* (Paris, 1968)

DARWIN, Charles, *The Descent of Man and Selection in Relation to Sex* (1871, revised and augmented edn., New York, 1879)

DARWIN, Leonard, *The Necessity for Eugenics Reform* (1926)

DAVIS, Adelle, *Let's Have Healthy Children* (1951)

DAYOT, Armand, *L'Image de la femme* (Paris, 1899)

DEAN, Teresa H., *How to be Beautiful* (1890)

DE BEAUVOIR, Simone, *Le Deuxième Sexe* (2 vols., Paris, 1947)

DEFOE, Daniel, *Conjugal Lewdness, or Matrimonial Whoredom* (1727)

DESBONNET, Professeur, *Pour devenir belle* (Paris, 1911)

DESJARDIN, Pierre, *Le Guide de la santé et de la beauté* (Paris, 1971)

DICK, Robert, MD, *The Connections of Health and Beauty* (1857)

DICTIONNAIRE, *Dictionnaire de la beauté féminine* (Paris, 1977)

DIFFLOTH, Paul, *La Beauté s'en va: des méthodes propres à la rénovation de la beauté féminine* (Paris, 1905)

DOMENICHI, Lodovico, *La nobiltà delle donne* (Venice, 1549)

DUBAN, Dr Pierre, *Les Hommes préfèrent les rondes* (Paris, 1981)

DU BLED, Victor, *La Femme dans la nature, dans les moeurs, dans la légende, dans la societé* (Paris, 1896–1900)

DUNLAP, Knight, *Personal Beauty and Racial Betterment* (St Louis, 1920)

DUVERNOIS, Henri, see Femina-Bibliothèque

ECRITS, *Ecrits sur la beauté* (Paris, 1945)

EGAN, B. Pierce, *Life in London* (1869)

EMERSON, Ralph Waldo, *The Complete Works of Ralph Waldo Emerson* (New York, 1929)

L'ENCYCLOPEDIE, *L'Encyclopédie beauté bien-être* (Paris, 1964)

EQUICOLA D'ARETO, Mario, *Libro de natura d'amore* (1525)

EVERY WOMAN, *Every Woman's Book of Health and Beauty* (1935)

'FAMILLE 2000', *Beauté et hygiène* (Paris, 1971)

FEMINA-BIBLIOTHEQUE (preface by Henri Duvernois), *Pour être belle* (Paris, 1913)

FEYDEAU, Ernest, *L'Art de plaire: études d'hygiène, de goût et de toilettes, dédiées aux jolies femmes de tous les pays du monde* (Paris, n.d., 1913?)

FINCK, Henry T., *Romantic Love and Personal Beauty* (New York, 1887)

FINCK, Henry T., *Primitive Love and Love Stories* (New York, 1899)

FINDEN, *Finden's Illustrations of the Works of Lord Byron* (1833)

FINDEN, *Finden's Tableaux of National Character, Beauty and Costume* (1843, 1845)

FINDEN, E. and W., *Portraits of the Female Aristocracy of the Court of Queen Victoria* (1849)

FINDEN, W., *Gallery of the Graces* (1850)

FINOT, Jean, *Problems of the Sexes* (New York, 1887)

FIRENZUOLA, Agnolo, 'Dialogo delle bellezze delle donne', *Prose di M. Agnolo Firenzuola Fiorentino* (Florence, 1548)

FIRENZUOLA, see Child, Theodore (under Secondary Sources)

FLETCHER, Ella Adelin, *The Woman Beautiful* (New York, 1899)

FLURANCE RIVAULT, David de, *L'Art d'embellir* (Paris, 1608)

FOUQUET, C. and KNIBSEHLER, T., *La Beauté pour quoi faire* (Paris, 1982)

FRANCO, Nicoló, *Dialogo dove si ragiona delle bellezze* (Venice, 1542)

FREUD, Sigmund, *Three Essays on the Theory of Sexuality* (Vienna, 1905; 4th edition, Vienna, 1920. First English edition, 1949)

FREUD, Sigmund, *Civilization and Its Discontents* (1930), in J. Strachey and A. Freud (eds.), *The Standard Edition of the Complete Psychological Works of Sigmund Freud*, vol.21 (1964)

GALLICHAN, Walter M., *The Psychology of Marriage* (New York, 1918)

GARCHES, Marquise de, *Les Secrets de beauté d'une parisienne* (Paris, 1894)

GAUTIER, Dr J., *Les Glandes: beauté et charme de la femme* (Paris, 1978)

GOBINEAU, Comte de, *Essai sur l'inégalité des races humaines* (1854; 6th edition, Paris, 1933)

GOURMONT, Rémy de, *Physique de l'amour: essai sur l'instinct sexuel* (Paris, 1903)

GRAVES, Robert and HODGE, Alan, *The Long Week-End: A Social History of Great Britain 1918–1939* (1940)

GREENBIE, Marjorie B., *Personality and the Diverse Methods by which Some Men and Here and There a Woman Have Achieved It* (New York, 1932)

GREER, Germaine, *The Female Eunuch* (1970)

GRIVEAU, Maurice, *La Sphère de la beauté* (Paris, 1901)

GUEZ, Franka, *Masculin quotidien: guide pratique à l'usage des hommes* (Paris, 1969)

HAMILTON, K. (published anonymously), *The Charms of Beauty or the Grand Contest between the Fair Hibernians, and the English Toasts, A Poem occasioned by the Marriage of his Grace the Duke of Hamilton with Miss Elizabeth Gunning; and the expected Marriage of her older sister with a certain noble Earl* (1752)

HAMILTON, Thomas, *Men and Manners in America* (2 vols., Edinburgh, 1833)

HARLE, Catherine, *Comment devenir modèle* (Paris, 1970)

HARRIS, *Harris's List of Covent Garden Ladies* (1793)

HART, Hornell, *Personality of the Family* (New York, 1935)

HART, Mildred Freely and WILKINSON, Charlotte Wright, *A Wonderful You! A Modern Woman's Guide to Poise, Charm and Beauty* (New York, 1947)

HAUSER, Gayelord, *Mirror, Mirror on the Wall* (New York, 1960)

HAVELOCK ELLIS, Henry, *A Study of British Genius* (1904)

HAVELOCK ELLIS, Henry, *Studies in the Psychology of Sex; IV Sexual Selection in Man* (Philadelphia, 1906)

HAWEIS, Mrs H. R., *The Art of Beauty* (1878)

HERMANN, Georges, *Santé et beauté par des moyens très simples* (Paris, 1937)

HOGARTH, William, *Analysis of Beauty* (1753)

HOLMES, Samuel J., *The Trend of the Race* (New York, 1921)

HOME, Henry (Lord Kames), *Elements of Criticism* (Edinburgh, 1761, 6th edition, 1785)

HOW, *How to be Beautiful* (Edinburgh, 1866)

HUME, David, *A Treatise of Human Nature* (1739)

HUMPHRY, Mrs C. E., *How to be Pretty though Plain* (1899)

HUNT, Cecily, *How to Get Work and Make Money in Commercials and Modeling* (New York, 1982)

HUNT, Leigh, 'Criticism on female beauty', in *Men, Women and Books*, vol.1 (1847)

'HYGIENE', *The Lady Beauty Book* (1900)

INSTITUTE OF CONTEMPORARY ARTS, *Women's Images of Men* (1980)

ISOBEL, Isobel Handbooks, no.7., *The Art of Beauty: A Book for Women and Girls* (1899)

JALIN, O. de, *Les Secrets de la beauté* (Paris, 1904)

JEANNE, René, *Les Grandes Vedettes du cinéma: beauté féminine* (Paris, 1929)

JEANNE, René, *Les Grandes Vedettes du cinéma: beauté masculine* (Paris, 1929)

JOHNSON, A., *Closet for Ladies and Gentlemen* (1654)

JOHNSON, Rosewell H., *An Address on Marriage Selection at the First National Conference on Race Betterment* (New York, 1916)

JONGEWARD, Dorothy and SCOTT, Dru, *Women as Winners: Transactional Analysis for Personal Growth* (Reading, Mass., 1976)

JOSEPH, Peter, *Good Times: An Oral History of America in the 1960s* (New York, 1973)

KARR, Alphonse, *Les Femmes* (Paris, 1855)

KEENAN, Brigid, *The Women we Wanted to Look Like* (1977)

KEIFFER, Betsy, *McCall's Guide to Teenage Beauty and Glamour* (New York, 1959)

KENDALL, Elizabeth, *Good Looks, Good Grooming* (New York, 1963)

KENYON, Lesley, *The Joy of Beauty* (1983)

KING, Eleanore, *Glorify Yourself* (1948)

KIRKLAND, Mrs Caroline M. G., *The Book of Home Beauty* (New York, 1851)

LADIES, *The Ladies Dictionary, Being a General Entertainment for the Fair Sex* (1694)

LADIES, *The Ladies Handbook of the Toilet* (1842)

LADIES, *The Ladies Handbook of the Toilet: A Manual of Elegance and Fashion* (1813)

LADY'S, *The Lady's Toilette; containing a Critical Examination of the Nature of Beauty* (1808)

LAKOFF, Robin Tolmach and SCHERR, Raquel L., *Face Value: The Politics of Beauty* (Boston, 1984)

LALO, Anne-Marie and Charles, *La Faillite de la beauté* (Paris, 1923)

LALO, Charles, *La Beauté et l'instinct sexuel* (Paris, 1922)

LAMIRAL, Sophie and SCHULTZ, Dodi, *Everyday Beauty* (New York, 1969)

LANNOY, Josine, *Savoir être belle* (Paris, 1966)

LAUWICK, Hervé, *L'Art d'attraper les hommes* (Paris, 1972)

LAVATER, Johan, *Physiognomische Fragmente* (Zurich, 1775)

LAWRENCE, D. H., *Sex Versus Loveliness* (1930)

LAYNARD, Prof. Boyd, *Secrets of Beauty, Health, and a Long Life* (1900)

LEFEBVRE, Arthur, *L'Art d'être belle* (Paris, 1901)

LEON-MARTIN, Louis, *L'Industrie de la beauté* (Paris, 1930)

LIVINGSTONE, Helen and MARONI, Ann, *Everyday Beauty Culture* (Bloomington, Ill., 1945)

LOBEL, Sali, *Glamour and How to Achieve It* (1938)

LONG, Alice M., *My Lady Beautiful* (Chicago, 1906)

LOUGEE, Carolyn C., *Le Paradis des femmes* (Paris, 1976)

LUIGINI, Federigo, *Il libro della bella donna* (Venice, 1554; English translation, 1909)

LUND, Gilda, *Beauty* (1963)

LYON, Josette, *La Femme et la beauté* (Paris, 1965)

MALAIT, Gine, *Guide intime du bonheur de la femme* (Paris, 1939)

MALCOLM, James P., *Anecdotes of the Manners and Customs of London during the Eighteenth Century, with a Review of the State of Society in 1807* (1808)

'MARABOUT FLASH', *Le Guide Flash de l'homme* (Verviers, Belgium, 1970)

MARIETTE, Pauline, *L'Art de la toilette* (Paris, 1866)

MARRIN, Dr P., *La Beauté chez l'homme et la femme: les moyens de l'acquérir et de l'augmenter* (Paris, 1891)

MAURIN, Dr Robert, *40 consultations d'esthétique* (Paris, 1972)

MAYER, Dr Charles, *La Médecine au service de la beauté* (Paris, 1955)

MAYHEW, Henry, *The Shops and Companies of London* (1865)

McLACHLAN, Helen, M., *Poise, Personality and Charm* (New York, 1965)

McNALLY, Fiona, *Women for Hire: A Study of the Female Office Worker* (1979)

MD, *Beauty and the Preservation of Health* (1903)

MERCIER, Sebastien, *Tableau de Paris* (2 vols., Paris, 1781)

MINUT, Gabriel de, *De la beauté, discours divers, . . . voulans signifier, que ce qui est naturellement beau, est aussi naturellement bon* (Paris, 1587)

MIROIR, *Miroir des dames et de la tendresse* (Paris, n.d., c. 1790?)

MIRROR, *The Mirror of the Graces* (1811)

MOLLOY, John T., *Women: Dress for Success* (New York, 1978)

MONIN, Dr, *L'Hygiène et la beauté* (Paris, 1886)

MONTAIGNE, Michel de, 'De la phisionomie', *Essais*, vol.3 (1588), no.12

MONTEMAYOR, George de, *Les Sept Livres de la Diane de Georges de Montemayor, traduit d'espagnol en français* (Rheims, 1578)

MONTEZ, Lola, *The Arts and Secrets of Beauty* (New York, 1853)

MORE, Sir Thomas, *The Utopia of Sir Thomas More: in Latin from the Edition of March 1518, and in English from the first Edition of Ralph Robynson's Translation of 1551* (ed. J. H. Lupton, Oxford, 1895)

MORRIS, William, *News from Nowhere* (1893)
MORTON, Grace M., *The Arts and Costume of Personal Appearance* (New York, 1943)
MUNDUS, *Mundus Muliebris: or The Lady's Dressing Room Unlock'd* (1690, edited with an Introduction by T. L. Newton, 1977)
'MYRENE', *The Lady Beauty Book* (1900)

NEVINSON, H. W., *Running Accompaniments* (1936)
NOBLE, Peter and SAXON, Yvonne, *Glamour: Film Fashion and Beauty* (1953)
NOCKER, Jean, *En direct avec vous* (Paris, 1963) (radio broadcasts)
NOELLAT, Gabrielle, *Pour plaire et rester jeune* (Paris, 1928)
NORVILLE, Comtesse de, *Les Coulisses de la beauté; comment la femme séduit* (Paris, 1894)
NOUVEAU, *Le Nouveau Bréviaire de la beauté* (Paris, n.d., 1925?)

PAILLERY, Georges, *Les Produits de beauté modernes* (Paris, 1948)
PERRON, Charles, *Les Franc-Comtois: leur caractère national, leurs moeurs, leurs usages* (Besançon, 1892)
PERUTZ, Kathrin, *Beyond the Looking Glass: Life in the Beauty Culture* (New York, 1970)
PICARD, Florence, *Voulez-vous être belle?* (Paris, 1952)
PLAIRE, *Plaire et séduire* (Paris, 1946)
PLAT, Sir H., *Delightes for Ladies* (1643)
PLATO, *The Dialogues of Plato translated by Benjamin Jowett* (Oxford, 1871, 4th edition, revised, 1964)
PLATO, *On Beauty*, see BLACKIE, J. S.
POKITONOFF, Mathilde, *La Beauté par l'hygiène* (Paris, 1892)
POPENOE, Paul and JOHNSON, Rosewell H., *Applied Eugenics* (New York, 1927)
POWER, Mrs Susan D., *The Ugly Girl Papers: or Hints for the Toilet* (New York, 1874)
POWERS, Ron, *Face Value* (1981)
PREVOT, Floriane, *Belle en travaillant* (Paris, 1972)
PREVOT, Floriane, *Dictionnaire de la beauté féminine* (Paris, 1972)
PRIESTLEY, J. B., *English Journey* (1933)
'PROFESSIONAL BEAUTY', *Beauty and How to Keep It, by a Professional Beauty* (New York and London, 1889)

RAISSON, Horace, *Code de la toilette, manuel complet d'élégance et d'hygiène* (Paris, 1829)

RANGER, *Ranger's Impartial List of the Ladies of Pleasure in Edinburgh* (Edinburgh, 1775)
REGNAL, Mme G., *Conquête et culture de la beauté* (Paris, 1972)
RIPAULT, Christine, *Pense-belle* (Paris, 1972)
ROBERTS, Nickie, *The Front Line: Women in the Sex Industry Speak* (1986)
ROCHER, Yvres, *Restez vraie* (Paris, 1977)
ROUET, Marcel, *Plaire* (Paris, 1949)
ROUET, Marcel, *Santé et beauté plastique de la femme* (Paris, 1971)
ROUSSEAU, Jean-Jacques, *Discours: si le rétablissement des sciences et des arts a pu contribuer à épurer les moeurs* (Grenoble, 1750)
ROUSSEAU, Jean-Jacques, *Discours sur l'inégalité des hommes* (Paris, 1755)
ROUSSEAU, Jean-Jacques, *Thoughts on Different Subjects* (Glasgow, 1770)
RUBENS, Peter Paul, *Théorie de la figure humaine, considérée dans ses principes, soit en repos ou en mouvement, ouvrage traduit du Latin de Pierre-Paul Rubens* (Paris, 1773)
RUBINSTEIN, Helena, *Pour la beauté* (Paris, 1939)
RUPPERT, Mrs Anna, *Book of Beauty* (n.d., c. 1890)
RUSKIN, John, *Modern Painters* (complete edition, 1888)
RUSSELL, Jane, *Success and Happiness through Charm* (1939)

SAINT-ANGE, Louis de, *Le Secret de triompher des femmes, et de les fixer* (Paris, 1825)
SANTAYANA, George, *The Sense of Beauty* (New York, 1896)
SANTE, *Santé–Beauté* (Paris, 1952)
SARTIN, Pierrette, *La Réussite professionnelle* (Paris, 1971)
SAVY, André, *Secrets de beauté et charme personnelle* (Paris, 1971)
SCHILLER, Friedrich, *Aesthetical and Philosophical Essays* (original German edition, 1792, English translation edited by Nathan Haskell Dole, Boston, 1902)
SCHOPENHAUER, Arthur, 'On the metaphysics of the beautiful and on aesthetics' and 'On women', in *Selected Essays of Arthur Schopenhauer* (ed. E. Belfort Bax, 1891)
SCHWARTZ, Dr Robert, *Médecine et beauté* (Paris, 1969)
SEM, *Le Vrai et le Faux Chic* (Paris, n.d., 1913?)
SHAFTESBURY, Anthony Ashley Cooper, Lord Shaftesbury, 'The moralists', *Characteristics*, vol.2, treatise V (1709)

SHELLEY, Percy Byshe, 'A discourse on the manners of the ancient Greeks relative to the subject of love', in *Plato's Banquet & C* (1931)

SIMSON, S., *La Beauté pour toutes* (Paris, 1933)

'SOCIETY BEAUTY', *The Art of Being Beautiful: A Series of Interviews with a Society Beauty* (1902)

SOURIAU, Paul, *La Beauté rationnelle* (Paris, 1904)

SPENCER, Herbert, 'Personal beauty', *Leader* (15 April 1854)

STABLES, Gordon, MD, *The Girls Own Book of Health and Beauty* (1892)

STAFFE, Baroness, *The Lady's Dressing Room, translated from the French of Baroness Staffe, by Lady Colin Campbell* (1892)

STENDHAL (Henri Beyle), *De l'amour* (Paris, 1822, 1853)

STRATZ, H., *Die Schönheit des Weiblichen Körpers* (14th edition, Berlin, 1903)

SWETNAM, J., *The Arraignment of Lewd, Idle, Froward and Unconstant Women* (1616)

SYLVIA, *Sylvia's Book of the Toilet: A Ladies' Guide to Dress and Beauty with a Fund of Information of Importance to Gentlemen* (1886)

SYLVIA OF HOLLYWOOD (Sylvia Ullbach), *Pull Yourself Together, Baby* (New York, 1936)

TESTIMONY, *The Testimony of Truth to Exalted Memory: or A Biographical Sketch of the Right Honourable the Countess of Derby in Refutation of a False and Scandalous Libel* (1797)

'THALIA', *Thalia to Eliza* (1798)

THIMM, P., *Lehre und Pflege der Schönheit des menschlichen Körpers für Gebildete von Dr med P. Thimm* (Berlin, 1898)

TOILET, *The Toilet* (1821)

TOILET, *The Toilet: A Dressing-Table Companion* (1839)

TOILETTE, *The Toilette: A Dressing-Table Companion* (1839)

TOILETTE, *The Toilette: or A Guide to the Improvement of Personal Appearance and the Preservation of Health* (1854)

TRAVER, Comtesse de, *Que veut la femme: être jolie, être aimée, et dominer* (Paris, 1911)

TRISSINO, Giorgio, 'I ritratti di Giovan Giorgio Trissino', in *Tutti le opere di Giovan Giorgio Trissino* (Verona, 1729)

US WAR DEPARTMENT Education Manual, EM982, *Establishing and Operating a Beauty Shop* (Madison, Wis., n.d., c. 1944)

UZANNE, Louis, *L'Art et les artifices de la beauté* (Paris, 1902)

VERNI, Maria, *Modern Beauty Culture* (1934)

VOLTAIRE, 'Grace', in *L'Encyclopédie* (Paris, 1752)

VOLTAIRE, *Dictionnaire philosophique portatif* (Paris, 1764)

VRIAC-LECOT, Madame, *Pour être belle à tout âge* (Paris, 1929)

WALKER, Alexander, *Beauty, Illustrated Chiefly by an Analysis and Classification of Beauty in Women* (1836)

WALKER, Alexander, *Physiognomy founded on Physiology* (1834)

WALKER, Mrs Alexander, *Female Beauty, as Preserved and Improved by Regimen, Cleanliness and Dress* (1857)

WANDERING WHORE, *The Wandering Whore: A Dialogue between Magdalena a Crafty Bawd, Julietta an Exquisite Whore, Francis a lascivious Gallant, and Gusman a Pimping Hector* (5 issues, 1660–61, reprinted *The Rota*, University of Exeter, 1977)

WARD, Edward, *The London Spy – The Vanities and Vices of the Town Exposed to View* (1703)

WARD, Edward, *The London Spy Compleat in Eighteen Parts* (1705)

WEININGER, Otto, *Sex and Character* (authorized translation from the 6th German edition, 1906)

WHEELER-BENNETT, Joan, *Women at the Top* (1977)

WHITCOMBE, Helen and LANCY, Rosalind, *Charm: The Career Girl's Guide to Business and Personal Success* (New York, 1964)

WIGGAM, Albert E., *The Fruit of the Family Tree* (Indianapolis, 1924)

WOLF, Annie, *The Truth about Beauty* (New York, 1892)

WOLLSTENCROFT, Mary, *A Vindication of the Rights of Women* (1792)

WOOLLEY, Hannah, *The Ladies Delight* (1672)

WOOLLEY, Hannah, *The Gentleman's Companion* (1675)

WOMEN, 'Women: what's on their minds? What do they fear? What do they hope for?', *Glamour* (New York, January 1983)

YALE UNIVERSITY, *History of the Class of 1913* (New Haven, Conn., 1914)

ZETTERBERG, Hans L., 'The secret ranking', in Marcello Truzzi (ed.), *The Sociology of Everyday Life* (Garden City, NJ, 1968)

## 4 Published Diaries, Letters, Memoirs and other Biographical Material of a Primary Character

ARGENSON, *Mémoires et journal inédits du Marquis d'Argenson publiés et annotés par M. le Marquis d'Argenson* (2 vols., Paris, 1857)

ASHLEY, Hon. Evelyn, MP, *The Life of Henry John Temple, Viscount Palmerston 1846–1865* (1876)

AUSTEN, Jane, *Austen Papers* (ed. R. A. Austen-Leigh, 1942)

AUSTEN, Jane, *Jane Austen's Letters to her Sister Cassandra and Others* (collected and edited by R. W. Chapman, 2nd edition, 1952)

BARRINGTON, *Barrington Family Letters 1628–1632* (edited for the Royal Historical Society by Arthur Searle, Camden Fourth Series, vol.28, 1983)

BERGEN, Candice, *Knock on Wood* (New York, 1984)

BERNHARDT, Sarah, *Ma double vie: mémoires de Sarah Bernhardt* (Paris, 1907)

BURNEY, Fanny, *Diary and Letters of Madame D'Arblay* (Fanny Burney) (1891)

CAMPAN, Madame, *Mémoires sur la vie privée de Marie Antoinette* (3 vols., Paris, 1822)

CAPPE, Catherine, *Memoirs of her Life, by Mrs Catherine Cappe* (1822)

CASANOVA, Giacomo, *History of my Life* (translated W. R. Trask, 6 vols., 1967–72)

CATHERINE THE GREAT, *The Memoirs of Catherine the Great*, translated by Moura Budberg, edited by Dominique Maroger (1955)

CAYLUS, *Souvenirs et correspondance de Madame de Caylus* (Paris, 1881)

CHAPMAN, John, 'John Chapman's diaries', in G. S. Haight, *George Eliot and John Chapman* (New Haven, 1940)

CHESTERFIELD, *The Letters of Philip Dormer Stanhope, 4th Earl of Chesterfield*, ed. Bonamy Dobrée (6 vols., 1932)

CHEVERNY, J. N. Dufort, Comte de, *Mémoires sur les règnes de Louis XV et Louis XVI* (ed. R. de Crèvecoeur, 2 vols., Paris, 1886)

CINQ-MARS, *Conjuration de Cinq-Mars* (collection of primary texts ) (Paris, 1853)

COLE, William, *The Bletcheley Diary of the Reverend William Cole 1765–67* (ed. F. C. Stokes, 1931)

COLVILLE, John, *The Fringes of Power: Downing Street Diaries 1939–1955* (1985)

CRICK, Throne, *Sketches from the Life of a Commercial Traveller* (1847)

CUMBERLAND, G. and R., *Cumberland Letters 1771–84* (ed. C. Black, 1912)

D'AULNOY, Madame, *Mémoires de la cour d'Angleterre* (2 vols., Paris, 1695)

DAVIES, Thomas, *Memoirs of the Life of David Garrick* (1780)

DEFFAND, *Correspondance complète de la Marquise du Deffand* (Paris, 1865)

DELANY, *The Autobiography and Correspondence of Mary Granville, Mrs Delany*, ed. Lady Hanover, 2nd series (1862)

DE POUGY, Liane, *My Blue Notebooks* (edited R. P. Pzewaski, 1979)

DERVAL, Paul, *The Folies Bergère* (1955)

DREUX DE RADIER, *Récréations historiques* (Paris, 1767)

ELIOT, George, *The George Eliot Letters* (edited G. S. Haight, 9 vols., 1954–78)

ESPINCHAL, *Journal d'émigration du Comte d'Espinchal, publié d'après les manuscrits originaux* (Paris, 1912)

ETTY, William, 'Letters addressed to a relative', *Art Journal*, vol.11 (1849)

FINCK, Henry T., *My Adventures in the Golden Age of Music* (New York, 1926)

FORRESTER, Helen, *Twopence to Cross the Mersey* (1974)

GARRICK, David, *Letters of David Garrick* (ed. D. M. Little and G. M. Kahol, 1963)

GEORGE, W. P. R., *My Brother and I* (1976)

GOT, Edmond, *Journal d'Edmond Got* (Paris, 1910)

GOURVILLE, *Mémoires de monsieur de Gourville, conseiller d'état, concernant les affaires aux quelles il a été employé par en couer, depuis 1642 jusqu'en 1698* (Paris, 1792)

GUERIN, Eugénie de, *Journal [1834–1841]* (Paris, 1934)

HARRISON, Rosina (ed.), *Gentlemen's Gentlemen* (1976)

HAUSSET, Madame de, *Mémoires de Madame de Hausset: femme de chambre de Madame de Pompadour* (Paris, 1824)

HEROARD, Jean, *Journal de Jean Héroard sur l'enfance et la jeunesse de Louis XIII (1601–1628)* (2 vols., Paris, 1868)

HOOKE, Robert, *Diary of Robert Hooke, 1677–1680* (1935)

JOUBERT, Joseph, *Les Carnets de Joseph Joubert: journal intime de Joubert 1784–1824* (Paris, 1938)

JUDITH, Mme, *Mémoires de Mme Judith de la Comédie Française* (ed. Paul Gsell, 1911)

KEATS, John, *The Letters of John Keats* (ed. Hyder Edward Rollins, Cambridge, Mass., 1958)
KEPPEL, Sonia, *Edwardian Daughter* (1958)
KINGSTON, *Life and Character of the Late Illustrious Duchess of Kingston . . . collected from Authentic Sources* (1788)

LEE, Jennie, *This Great Journey: A Volume of Autobiography* (1963)
LEE, Jennie, *My Life with Nye* (1980)
LEFEVRE d'ORMESSON, *Journal d'Olivier Lefèvre d'Ormesson* (Paris, 1861)
LEGRAIN, 'Souvenirs de Legrain, valet de chambre de Mirabeau', *Nouvelle Revue Rétrospective,* 2nd series, vols. 15 and 16 (Paris, 1901)
LENCLOS, Ninon de, *Lettres de Ninon de Lenclos au marquis de Sévigné précédées d'une notice historique . . . augmentées de 'la Coquette vengée', pièce attribuée à Ninon, de la correspondance . . . avec Saint-Evremond et Mme de Maintenon . . . etc, et terminées par l'histoire de Marion de Lorne, amie intime de Ninon* (Paris, 1806)
LESPINASSE, Julie de, *Lettres de Mlle de Lespinasse précédées d'une notice de Sainte-Beuve et suivies des autres écrits de l'auteur et des principaux documents qui le concernent* (Paris, 1893)
LESPINASSE, Julie de, *Correspondance entre Mlle de Lespinasse et le Comte de Guibert,* ed. Comte de Villeneuve-Guibert (Paris, 1906)
LIGNE, *Mémoires du Prince de Ligne* (Paris and Brussels, 1860)
LISLE, *The Lisle Letters: An Abridgement* (edited by Muriel St Clare Bryne, 1983)
LUYNES, *Mémoires du Duc de Luynes* (Paris, 1861)

MANSFIELD, Katherine, *The Journal of Katherine Mansfield* (1954)
MARLBOROUGH, Sarah, Duchess of, *Memoirs of Sarah, Duchess of Marlborough* (ed. William King, 1950)
MARMONTEL, J.-F., *Mémoires* (Paris, 1809, ed. John Renwick, 2 vols., Paris, 1972)
MERE, *Discours de m. le chevalier de Méré à Madame XXX* (Paris, 1677)
MERODE, Cléo de, *Le Ballet de ma vie* (Paris, 1955)
MOGADOR, Céleste, *Mémoires* (Paris, 1858–59)
MONKSWELL, Lady, *A Victorian Diarist: Extracts from the Journals of Mary, Lady Monkswell, 1873–1895* (ed. Hon. E. C. F. Collier, 1944)

MONTEZ, Lola, *Memoirs* (New York, 1860)
MUNBY, Arthur J., *Munby, Man of Two Worlds: The Life and Diaries of Arthur J. Munby 1828–1910* (by Derek Hudson, 1972)

ODLUM, Hortense, *A Woman's Place: An Autobiography* (New York, 1939)
OLIVIER, Laurence, *Confessions of an Actor* (1982)

PASTON, *The Paston Letters* (ed. John Warrington, 2 vols., 1924)
PEPYS, *The Diary of Samuel Pepys* (edited by Robert Latham and William Mathews, 11 vols., 1970–83)
PIDONSAT de MAUROBAT, *Anecdotes sur Madame la Comtesse Dubarré* (Amsterdam, 1776)
POMPADOUR, *Correspondance de Mme de Pompadour,* ed. M. A. P.-Malassis (Paris, 1878)
PONIATOWSKI, *Mémoires secrets et inédits de Stanislas Auguste, Comte Poniatowski* (Leipzig, 1862)

ROBERTS, Robert, *The Classic Slum* (1971)
RUBENS, Peter Paul, *The Letters of Peter Paul Rubens,* translated and edited by Ruth Saunders Magurn (Cambridge, Mass., 1955)

SALTER, Dr, *Dr Salter of Tolleshunt D'Arcy: Diary and Reminiscences 1849–1932* (ed. J. O. Thompson, 1933)
SAND, George, *Correspondance* (Paris, 1892)
SAND, George, *Histoire de ma vie* (Paris, 1859, 1909)
SAND, George, *Journal intime* (Paris, 1981)
SAUNIER-SEITE, Alice, *En première ligne: de la communale aux universités* (Paris, 1982)
SEVIGNE, *Lettres de Mme de Sévigné, de sa famille et de ses amis* (14 vols., Paris, 1862–76)
SEVIGNE, *Lettres de Mme de Sévigné, de sa famille et de ses amis* (2 vols., Paris, 1836, 1938)
SEVIGNE, *Lettres de Mme de Sévigné* (3 vols., Paris, 1953–57)
SEVIGNE, *Correspondance de Mme de Sévigné* (12 vols., Paris, 1972–78)
SEWELL, Samuel, *Diary of Samuel Sewell 1674–1729. Newly edited from the Manuscript at the Massachusetts Historical Society by M. Halsey Thomas* (2 vols., New York, 1973)
SHRIMPTON, Jean, *The Truth about Modelling* (1964)
SOMAIZE, *Dictionnaire des précieuses*

(Paris, 1661)

STONOR, *The Stonor Letters and Papers 1290–1483* (edited by Charles Lethbridge Kingsford, 2 vols., 1919, Camden 3rd series, vols.29, 30)

TALLEMENT DE REAUX, *Historiettes* (Paris, 1662, 1854)

TERRY, Ellen, *My Life* (1910)

THOMAS, John Bird, *Shop Boy: An Autobiography* (1920)

TURNER, Thomas, *The Diary of Thomas Turner 1754–1765* (ed. David Vaizey, Oxford, 1984)

TWIGGY, *An Autobiography* (1975)

VERNEY, *Memoirs of the Verney Family during the Seventeenth Century* (ed. F. P. and M. M. Verney, 1907)

VERNEY, *Verney Letters of the Eighteenth Century* (ed. Lady M. Verney, 1930)

WALPOLE, Horace, *The Letters of Horace Walpole* (9 vols., 1857–59)

WEETON, E., *Miss Weeton's Journal as a Governess* (ed. J. J. Bagley, Newton Abbot, 1969)

WORTH, J. P., *A Century of Fashion* (1928)

WRAXALL, Nathaniel, *Historical and Posthumous Memoirs* (1884)

'ZED' (i.e. Count Albert de Maugny), *Le Demi-Monde sous le second empire: souvenirs d'un sybarite* (Paris, 1892)

## 5 Research and Survey Reports

ABBOT, Aaron A. and SEBASTIEN, Richard J., 'Physical attractiveness and expectation of success', *Personality and Social Psychology Bulletin*, vol.6 (1981)

ANDERSON, S. M. and BEM, S. L., 'Sex typing and androgyny in dyadic interaction: individual differences in responsiveness to physical attractiveness', *Journal of Personality and Social Psychology*, vol.41 (1981)

BARON, R., 'Self-presentation in job interviews: where there can be "too much of a good thing"', *Journal of Applied Social Psychology*, vol.16 (1986)

BEEHR, T. and GILMORE, C. C., 'Applicant attractiveness as a perceived job-relevant variable in selection of management trainees', *Academy of Management Journal*, vol.25 (1982)

BEM, Sandra L., 'The measurement of psychological androgyny', *Journal of Consulting and Clinical Psychology*, vol.42 (1974)

BERCHEID, E., DION, K. K., WALSTER, E. and WALSTER, G. W., 'Physical attractiveness and dating choice', *Journal of Experimental Social Psychology*, vol.7 (1971)

BERSCHEID, Elaine and WALSTER, Elaine, 'Physical attractiveness', in *Advances in Experimental Social Psychology*, vol.7 (New York, 1974)

BYRNE, D. O. and REEVES, K., 'The effects of physical attractiveness, sex, and attitude similarity on interpersonal attraction', *Journal of Personality*, vol.36 (1968)

CAMPBELL, D. P.,'Vocational interests of beautiful women', *Personality and Guidance Journal* (1967)

CASCIO, W. F. (ed.), *Applied Psychology in Personnel Management* (1982)

CASH, T. F., GILLEN, B. and BURNS, S. D., 'Sexism and "beautyism" in personnel consultant decision-making', *Journal of Applied Psychology*, vol.62 (1977)

CASH, T. F. and KILCULLEN, R. N., 'The aye of the beholder: susceptibility to sexism and beautyism in the evaluation of managerial applicants', *Journal of Applied Social Psychology*, vol.15 (1985)

CROSS, John F. and CROSS, Jane, 'Age, sex, race, and the perception of facial beauty', *Developmental Psychology*, vol.5 (1971)

DICKEY-BRYANT, Le Anne, LAUTENSCHLAGER, Gary J., MENDOZA, Jorge L. and ABRAHAMS, Norman, 'Facial attractiveness and its relation to occupational success', *Journal of Applied Psychology*, vol.71 (1986)

DION, K., BERSCHEID, E. and WALSTER, E., 'What is beautiful is good', *Journal of Personality and Social Psychology*, vol.24 (1972)

DION, K., 'Young children's stereotyping of facial attractiveness', *Developmental Psychology*, vol.9 (1973)

DION, K. and BERSCHEID, E., 'Physical attractiveness and peer perception among children', *Sociometry*, vol.37 (1974)

DIPBOYE, R. L., FROMKIN, H. L. and WIBACK, K., 'Relative importance of applicant: sex, attractiveness and scholastic standing in evaluation of job applicant résumés', *Journal of Applied Psychology*, vol.60 (1975)

ELDER, Glenis H., Jr, 'Appearance and education in marriage mobility',

*American Journal of Sociology*, vol.34 (1967)

GAGNON, J. H. and SIMON, William, *Sexual Conduct: The Social Sources of Sexuality* (1973)

GILLEN, Barry, 'Physical attractiveness as a determinant of two types of goodness', *Personality and Social Psychology Bulletin*, vol.7 (1981)

GIRARD, A., *Le Choix du conjoint* (Paris, 1966)

GOFFMAN, Erving, 'On calling the mark out: some aspects of adaptation to failure', *Psychiatry*, vol.15 (1952)

GORER, Geoffrey, *Exploring English Character* (1952)

GORER, Geoffrey, *Sex and Marriage in England Today* (1971)

GROSS, Alan E. and CROFTON, Christine, 'What is good is beautiful', *Sociometry*, vol.40 (1977)

HATCH, Clara E., 'The relationship between beauty and intelligence', MA Dissertation in Zoology, U.C. Berkeley (1933)

HEILMAN, M. E. and SURUWATARI, L. K., 'When beauty is beastly: the effects of appearance and sex on evaluations of job applicants for managerial and nonmanagerial posts', *Organizational Behaviour and Human Performance*, vol.23 (1979)

HUSTON, T. L., 'Ambiguity of acceptance, social desirability, and dating choice', *Journal of Experimental Psychology*, vol.9 (1973)

HUSTON, T. L. (ed.), *Foundations of Interpersonal Attractions* (New York, 1974)

ILLIFFE, A. H., 'A study of preferences in feminine beauty', *British Journal of Psychology*, vol.51 (1960)

JACKSON, L. A., 'The influence of sex, physical attractiveness, sex role, and occupational sex-linkage on perceptions of occupational suitability', *Journal of Applied Social Psychology*, vol.13 (1983)

JONES, Randy M. and ADAMS, Gerald R., 'Assessing the importance of physical attractiveness across the life-span', *Journal of Social Psychology*, vol.117 (1982)

JOSEPH, W. B., 'The credibility of physically attractive communicators', *Journal of Advertising*, vol.11 (1982)

KINSEY, Alfred, *Sexual Behavior in the Human Male* (New York, 1948)

KINSEY, Alfred, *Sexual Behavior in the Human Female* (New York, 1954)

KREBS, D. and ADINOLFI, A. A., 'Physical attractiveness, social relations, and personality style', *Journal of Personality and Social Psychology*, vol.31 (1975)

LANDY, David and SIGALL, Harold, 'Beauty is talent: task evaluation as a function of the performer's physical attractiveness', *Journal of Personality and Social Psychology*, vol.29 (1974)

MAJOR, B. and DEAUX, K., 'Physical attractiveness and masculinity and femininity', *Personality and Social Psychology Bulletin*, vol.7 (1981)

MASTERS, William and JOHNSON, Virginia, *Human Sexual Response* (Boston, 1966)

MILLER, A. C., 'Raw and physical attractiveness in impression formation', *Psychonomic Science*, vol.19 (1970)

MILLER, H. L. and RIBENBARK, W. H., 'Sexual differences in physical attractiveness as a determinant of heterosexual likings', *Psychological Reports*, vol.27 (1970)

MURSTEIN, Bernard J., 'Physical attractiveness and marital choice', *Journal of Personality and Social Psychology*, vol.22, no.1 (1972)

PERRIN, F. A. C., 'Physical attractiveness and repulsiveness', *Journal of Experimental Psychology*, vol.4 (1921)

ROKEACH, Milton, 'Some determinants of the perceptions of beauty in women', MA Dissertation in Psychology, U.C. Berkeley (1942)

SCHOFIELD, M., *Sexual Behaviour of Young People* (1965)

SINGER, J. E., 'The use of manipulative strategies: Machiavellianism and attractiveness', *Sociometry*, vol.27 (1964)

SOLOMON, M. (ed.), *The Psychology of Fashion* (1985)

STROEBE, W., INSKO, C. A., THOMPSON, V. D. and LAYTON, B. D., 'Effects of physical attractiveness, attitude similarity, and sex on various aspects of interpersonal attractiveness', *Journal of Personality and Social Psychology*, vol.18 (1971)

WALLER, Wilfred, 'The rating and dating complex', *American Sociological Review*, vol.2 (1937)

WALSTER, E., ARONSON, V., ABRAHAMS, D. and ROTTMAN, L., 'Importance of physical attractiveness in dating behavior',

*Journal of Personality and Social Psychology*, vol.5 (1966)
WEBSTER, Murray, Jr and DRISKELL, James E., Jr, 'Beauty as status', *American Journal of Sociology*, vol.89 (1983)

## 6 Newspapers and Periodicals

(None of these have been studied systematically, save, in some cases, for the particular period of the 1960s; many were used simply through clippings. However, it seemed useful to set out the range of materials coming within the scope of this study.)

*American Mercury* (New York)
*Chester Chronicle* (1796, 1817)
*Cincinnati Enquirer*
*Cleveland Plain Reader*
*Cleveland Sunday News*
*Cosmopolitan* (London)
*Daily Chronicle* (London
*Ebony* (Chicago, 1945– )
*Evening Standard* (London)
*L'Express* (Paris)
*Female Tatler* (London)
*Le Figaro* (Paris)
*Gentleman's Magazine* (London)
*Glamour* (New York)
*Harper's Magazine* (New York)
*Kansas City Journal*
*Ladies' Home Journal* (New York)
*Life* (New York)
*Manchester Guardian*
*Marie-Claire* (Paris)
*Marie-France* (Paris)
*New York Times*
*New York Tribune*
*Observer* (London)
*Paris Match* (Paris)
*Pick-Me-Up* (London)
*Punch* (London)
*San Francisco Chronicle*
*The Sun* (London)
*Seattle Star*
*The Sphere* (London)
*Time* (New York)
*Woman's Own* (London)
*The World* (1755–56) (London)
*World Telegram* (New York)

## 7 Novels, Plays, Poems and Stories

(There is scarcely a novel or play written that does not, even if only negatively, comment on beauty; this is a strictly functional list related to the main issues of this work.)

ALTER, Lisa, *Kinflicks* (New York, 1976)
ALTER, Lisa, *Original Sins* (New York, 1981)

AMIS, Kingsley, *Take a Girl Like You* (1960)
ANON., *The Beauty and her Plain Sister* (Edinburgh, 1865)

BALZAC, Honoré de, *Le Père Goriot* (Paris, 1827)
BALZAC, Honoré de, *La Cousine Bette* (Paris, 1846)
BEERBOHM, Max, *Zuleika Dobson* (1911, paperback, 1983)
BRAINE, John, *Room at the Top* (1957)
BROOKNER, Anita, *Providence* (1982)
BUCK, Joan Juliet, *The Only Place to Be* (New York, 1982)
BURNEY, Fanny, *Evelina* (1778)
BURNS, Robert, *Tam O'Shanter* (1790)

CHAUCER, Geoffrey, *Canterbury Tales* (c. 1387–c. 1400)
CHEKOV, Anton, *Uncle Vanya* (Moscow, 1899; English translation by Constance Garnett, 1923)
COLETTE, *Chéri* (Paris, 1920)
COLETTE, *La Chatte* (Paris, 1933)

DEFOE, Daniel, *Moll Flanders* (1722)
DICKENS, Charles, *David Copperfield* (1849–50)
DICKENS, Charles, *Great Expectations* (1861)
DICKENS, Charles, *Our Mutual Friend* (1864–65)
DRYDEN, John, *Absalom and Achitophel* (1681)

ELIOT, George, *The Mill on the Floss* (1860)
ELIOT, George, *Felix Holt Radical* (1866)
ELIOT, George, *Daniel Deronda* (1876)

FIELDING, Henry, *History of Tom Jones* (1749)
FIELDING, Henry, 'Advice to a friend on choosing a wife', *Miscellanies*, vol.1 (1743)
FIELDING, Henry, 'A journey from this world to the next', *Miscellanies*, vol.2 (1743)

GREENWOOD, Walter, *Love on the Dole* (1932)

HARMON, Sandra, *A Girl Like Me* (New York, 1975)
HARDY, Thomas, *A Pair of Blue Eyes* (1873)
HARDY, Thomas, *The Hand of Ethelberta* (1876)
HARDY, Thomas, *A Laodicean* (1881)
HARDY, Thomas, *The Woodlanders* (1887)
HARDY, Thomas, *Tess of the d'Urbervilles* (1891)

JAMES, Henry, *Washington Square* (1887)
JONG, Erica, *Fear of Flying* (New York, 1975)
JONG, Erica, *Fanny* (New York, 1980)

LESSING, Doris, *The Golden Note-Book* (1962)

MILLER, Alice Duer, *The Beauty and the Bolshevik* (New York, 1920)
MURGER, Henry, *Scènes de la Bohême* (Paris, 1851)

POPE, Alexander, *The Rape of the Lock* (1714)
POPE, Alexander, *Essay on Criticism* (1711)
PROUST, Marcel, *Du Côté de chez Swann* (Paris, 1913)

RIHOIT, Catherine, *La Favorite* (Paris, 1982)

SAND, George, *Indiana* (Paris, 1832)
SAND, George, *Un Hiver à Majorque* (Paris, 1842)
SCHAEFFER, Susan Fromberg, *The Madness of a Seduced Woman* (1983)
SCOTT, Sir Walter, *Quentin Durward* (1823)
SHAKESPEARE, William, *The Sonnets* (1593–1600)
SHAKESPEARE, William, *As You Like It* (1596–1600)
SHELLEY, Percy Byshe, 'Hymn to intellectual beauty' (1820)
STENDHAL, *Le Rouge et le noir* (Paris, 1830)
STENDHAL, *La Chartreuse de Parme* (Paris, 1839)

THACKERAY, William Makepeace, *The Newcomes* (1854–55)
TROLLOPE, Anthony, *Barchester Towers* (1857)
TROLLOPE, Anthony, *The Eustace Diamonds* (1873)
TROLLOPE, Anthony, *The Prime Minister* (1875–76)

WELDON, Fay, *The Life and Loves of a She Devil* (1983)
WILDE, Oscar, *Picture of Dorian Gray* (1890–91)

ZOLA, Emile, *Thérèse Raquin* (Paris, 1867)

## 8 Operas

(Many opera stars are not beautiful – see chapter one. Can music portray physical beauty, or is it more accurately love or passion that music conveys? – subject for another book. Again, a strictly functional list.)

Cosí fan tutte (Mozart, 1790)
Die Zauberflöte (Mozart, 1791)
La Traviata (Verdi, 1853)
Parsifal (Wagner, 1882)
Don Carlos (Verdi, 1867)
Carmen (Bizet, 1875)
Cavalleria Rusticana (Mascagni, 1890)
I Pagliacci (Leoncavallo, 1892)
La Bohème (Puccini, 1897)
Tosca (Puccini, 1900)
Turandot (Puccini, 1926)

## 9 Filmography

(Functional select list.)

*Birth of a Nation* (Epoch, 1915, dir. D. W. Griffith, with Lillian Gish)
*The Poor Little Rich Girl* (Epoch, 1917, with Mary Pickford)
*The Sheik* (Famous Players, Lasky, 1921, with Rudolf Valentino)
*A Woman of Affairs* (MGM, 1928, with Greta Garbo)
*Grand Hotel* (MGM, 1932, with Greta Garbo)
*Of Human Bondage* (RKO, 1934, with Leslie Howard, Bette Davis)
*Gone with the Wind* (MGM, 1939, dir. David O. Selznick, with Vivian Leigh, Clark Gable)
*The Philadelphia Story* (MGM, 1940, with Katharine Hepburn, Cary Grant)
*The Heiress* (Paramount, 1949, dir. William Wyler, with Olivia de Havilland)
*Gentlemen Prefer Blondes* (Twentieth Century Fox, 1953, with Marilyn Monroe, Jane Russell)
*The Seven Year Itch* (Twentieth Century Fox, 1955, with Marilyn Monroe)
*Marty* (United Artists/Hecht-Hill-Lancaster, 1955, with Betsy Blair, Ernest Borgnine)
*And God Created Woman* (Iena/VCIL/Cocinor, 1956, dir. Roger Vadim, with Brigitte Bardot)
*Some Like it Hot* (United Artists/Mirisch, 1959, dir. Billy Wilder, with Marilyn Monroe, Tony Curtis)
*Room at the Top* (Remus, 1959, with Laurence Harvey, Simone Signoret)
*Let's Make Love* (Twentieth Century Fox, 1960, with Marilyn Monroe, Yves Montand)
*L'Avventura* (Cino del Duca/PCE/Lyre, 1960, dir. Antonioni, with Monica Vitti)
*The Misfits* (United Artists/Seven Arts, 1961, with Marilyn Monroe, Clark Gable)

*Dr No* (United Artists/Eon, 1962, with Sean Connery, Ursula Andress)

*The Leopard* (Titanus, 1963, dir. Visconti, with Claudia Cardinale and Alain Delon)

*Georgie Girl* (Columbia/Everglades, 1966, with Lynne Redgrave, Charlotte Rampling)

*Blow-Up* (MGM/Carlo Ponti, 1966, dir. Antonioni, with Vanessa Redgrave, David Hemmings)

*Guess Who's Coming to Dinner* (Columbia/ Stanley Kramer, 1967, with Sidney Poitier)

*Funny Girl* (Columbia/Rostar, 1968, dir. William Wyler, with Barbra Streisand)

*The Way We Were* (Columbia/Rostar, 1973, with Robert Redford, Barbra Streisand)

*Alice Doesn't Live Here Any More* (Warner, 1974, dir. Martin Scorsese)

# B. SECONDARY SOURCES

## 1 Reference Works

*Annuaire statistique de la France*

*Annual Abstracts of Statistics* (Central Office of Information, UK)

*Appleton's Cyclopaedia of American Biography*

*Benham's Book of Quotations* (1948)

*Cassell's Classified Quotations* (by W. Gurney Benham, 1920)

*Catalogue of Seventeenth-Century Portraits in the National Portrait Gallery* (by David Piper, Cambridge, 1963)

*Dictionary of American Biography*

*Dictionary of British Portraiture* (Richard Ormond and Malcolm Rogers (eds.), 1979)

*Dictionary of National Biography*

*Dictionnaire de biographie français*

*Familiar Quotations* (15th edition, Boston, 1980)

*Halliwell's Film Guide* (5th edition, 1985)

*The Home Book of Quotations* (10th edition, New York, 1967)

*A New Dictionary of Quotations* (ed. H. L. Mencken, New York, 1982)

*The New Encyclopedia of the Opera* (by David Ewen, New York, 1971)

*Nouvelle Biographie générale* (Paris and Copenhagen, 1965– )

*Oxford Companion to Literature* (ed. Margaret Drabble, Oxford, 1985)

*Oxford Dictionary of Quotations* (3rd edition, 1979)

*Psychological Abstracts*

*Statistical Abstracts of the United States* (US Bureau of Census)

## 2 Biographies, General Accounts and other Secondary Materials

'ABINGTON', *The Life of Mrs Abington (Formerly Miss Barton) Celebrated Comic Actress . . . by the Editor of the 'Life of Quin'* (1888)

ABLEMAN, Paul, *Anatomy of Nakedness* (1982)

ADBURGHAM, Alison, *Shopping in Style* (1979)

ADBURGHAM, Alison, *Shops and Shopping 1800–1914* (1964, 1981)

ALDIS, Janet, *Madame Geoffrin: Her Salon and her Times 1750–1777* (1905)

ANANOFF, Alexandre, *François Boucher* (2 vols., Lausanne, 1976)

ANDERSON, Dwight C., *Abraham Lincoln* (New York, 1982)

ANDERSON, Michael, *Approaches to the History of the Western Family 1500–1914* (1980)

ANDREWES, Anthony, *The Greeks* (1967; republished 1971 as *Greek Society*)

ANET, Claude, *Suzanne Lenglen* (Paris, 1927)

ARETZ, Gertrude (translated by James Laver), *The Elegant Woman* (1932)

ARETZ, Gertrude, *The Empress Catherine* (1947)

ARIES, Philippe, *Centuries of Childhood: A Social History of Family Life* (1962)

ATTIR, Mustafa O., HOLZNER, Burkart and SUDA, Zdenek, *Directions of Change: Modernization Theory, Research and Realities* (Boulder, Colo., 1981)

BANNER, Lois W., *American Beauty* (New York, 1983, Chicago, 1984)

BATES, Walter Jackson, *John Keats* (1967)

BATTERBERRY, Michael, *Fashion, The Mirror of History* (New York, 1982)

BECKETT, R. B., *Lely* (1951)

BERGER, Joseph, *et al.*, *Status Characteristics and Social Interaction: An Expectation States Approach* (New York, 1977)

BEVAN, Bryan, *Marlborough the Man* (1975)

BLACKIE, J. S., *On Beauty: Three Discourses . . . with an Exposition of the Doctrine of the Beautiful according to Plato* (Edinburgh, 1858)

BLAKE, Robert, *Disraeli* (1966)

BLEAKLEY, Horace, *The Beautiful Duchess, being an Account of the Life and Times of Elizabeth Gunning, Duchess of Hamilton and Argyll* (1927)

BLYTH, Henry, *Skittles, the Last Victorian Courtesan: The Life and Times of Catherine Walters* (1977)

BORSAY, Peter, 'The English urban renaissance: the development of provincial urban culture *c.*1680–*c.*1760', *Social History* (May 1977)

BOTHAM, Noel and DONNELLY,

Peter, *Valentino: The Love God* (1976)

BOUCHER, Jacqueline, *Société et mentalités autour de Henri III* (Lille/Paris, 1981)

BOUCHOT-SAUPIQUE, Jacqueline, *Helena Fourment Rubens* (1948)

BOURNE, Kenneth, *Palmerston: The Early Years* (1982)

BOUTET DE MONVEL, Roger, *Beau Brummel and his Times* (1908)

BRAUDEL, Fernand, *Civilisation matérielle et capitalisme* (tome I, Paris, 1967)

BRAUX, G., *Louise de la Vallière de sa Touraine au Carmel de Paris* (Chambray-les-Tours, 1981)

BROOKNER, Anita, *Greuze: The Rise and Fall of an Eighteenth-Century Phenomenon* (1972)

BROUGH, James, *The Prince and the Lily* (New York, 1975)

BROWN, Judith C., *Immodest Acts: The Life of a Lesbian Nun in Renaissance Italy* (New York, 1985)

BUISSERET, David, *Henri IV* (1984)

BULL, George, 'Introduction' to *The Book of the Courtier: Baldesar Castiglione* (1967)

BYRD, Penelope, *The Male Image: Men's Fashions in Britain, 1300–1970* (1979)


CAMDEN, Carroll, *The Elizabethan Woman* (New York, 1975)

CARDONA, E., *La Vie de Jean Boldini* (Paris, 1931)

CAREY, Gary, *Katharine Hepburn* (New York, 1983)

CARMONA, Michel, *Marie de Médicis* (Paris, 1981)

CARRE, Henri, *Gabrielle d'Estrées, presque reine* (Paris, 1936)

CARRE, Henri, *Mademoiselle de la Vallière* (Paris, 1938)

CARRE, Henri, *Madame de Montespan* (Paris, 1939)

CARRITT, E. F., *Philosophies of Beauty: From Socrates to Robert Bridges* (readings) (1931)

CARTLIDGE, Sue and RYAN, Joanna (eds.), *Sex and Love: New Thoughts and Old Contradictions* (1983)

CASTELOT, André, *Ensorcelante Sarah Bernhardt* (Paris, 1961, 1973)

CASTLE, Charles, *La Belle Otero: The Last Great Courtesan* (1981)

CASTLE, Charles, *The Folies Bergère* (1982)

CASTLE, Charles, *Model Girl* (1982)

CASTRIES, Duc de, *La Pompadour* (Paris, 1983)

CASTRIES, Duc de, *Madame Récamier* (Paris, 1971)

CATE, Curtis, *George Sand* (1975)

CHARLES-ROUX, E., *Chanel* (Paris, 1976)

CHENEVIX TRENCH, Charles, *The Western Rising* (1969)

CHILD, Theodore, 'Introduction' to Firenzuola, *Dialogue on the Beauty of Women* (1892)

CHILDS, James R., *Casanova: A Biography based on New Documents* (1961)

CHOFFEL, Jean, *Seille une femme . . . Alice Saunier-Seité* (Paris, 1979)

CLARK, Kenneth, *Feminine Beauty* (1980)

CLEEVE, Susan, *Growing Up in the Swinging Sixties* (1980)

CLIFTON, Robin, *The Last Popular Rebellion* (1984)

COHEN, Edgar H., *Mademoiselle Libertine: A Portrait of Ninon de Lanclos* (Toronto, 1970)

COUGHLAN, Robert, *Elizabeth and Catherine* (1974)

CROPPER, Elizabeth, 'On beautiful women, Parmigianino, *Petrarchismo*, and the vernacular style', *Art Bulletin*, vol. 58 (1976)

CURRENT, Richard N., *The Lincoln Nobody Knows* (New York, 1958)

CURRY, Walter C., *The Middle English Ideal of Personal Beauty* (Baltimore, 1916)


DAUGE, Abbé C., *Le Marriage et la famille en Gascogne d'après proverbes et chansons* (Paris, 1916)

DAVIDOFF, Leonora, *The Best Circles: Society Etiquette and the Season* (1973)

DAVIS, Cullom (ed.), *The Public and the Private Lincoln* (1979)

DAVIS, Natalie Zemon, *The Return of Martin Guerre* (Cambridge, Mass., 1983)

DE'ATH, Wilfred, *Barbara Castle: A Portrait from Life* (1970)

DEFORD, Frank, *There She Is: The Life and Times of Miss America* (New York, 1971)

DEGLER, Carl N., 'What ought to have been and what was: women's sexuality in the nineteenth century', *American Historical Review* (December 1974)

DE SOLA PINTO, V., *Sir Charles Sedley 1639–1701* (1927)

DOUGLAS, Hugh, *Charles Edward Stuart: The Man, the King, the Legend* (1975)

DOVER, Sir Kenneth J., *Greek Popular Morality in the Time of Plato and Aristotle* (1974)

DOVER, Sir Kenneth J., *Greek Homosexuality* (1978)

DUBY, Georges, *Le Chevalier, la femme et le prêtre: le mariage dans la France féodale* (Paris, 1981)

DUCHENE, Roger, *Ninon de Lanclos: la courtisane du grand siècle* (Paris, 1964)

DUCHENE, Roger, *Madame de Sévigné, ou la chance d'être femme* (Paris, 1982)

DUFF, David, *Eugénie and Napoleon* (1978)

EARLE, Peter, *Monmouth's Rebels* (1977)

EISENSTADT, S. N., *Modernization: Protest and Change* (Englewood Cliffs, NJ, 1966)

EPTON, Nina, *Josephine: The Empress and her Children* (1975)

ERLANGER, Philippe, *Le Mignon du roi* (Paris, 1967)

ERLANGER, Philippe, *Diane de Poitiers* (Paris, 1972)

EVANS, Hilary, *The Oldest Profession: An Illustrated History of Prostitution* (Newton Abbot, 1979)

FAIRCHILDS, Cissie, *Domestic Enemies: Servants and their Masters in Old Regime France* (Baltimore, 1984)

FARR, Denis L. A., *William Etty* (1958)

FASS, Paula S., *The Damned and the Beautiful: American Youth in the 1920s* (New York, 1977)

FERGUSON, Marjorie, *Forever Feminine: Women's Magazines and the Cult of Femininity* (1983)

FERRAL, Claude, *Madame du Deffand* (1933)

FEUILLERE, Edwige, *Moi La Clairon* (Paris, 1984)

FLANDRIN, Jean Louis, *Familles: parenté, maison, sexualité dans l'ancienne société* (Paris, 1976)

FLANDRIN, Jean Louis, *Le Sexe et l'occident: l'évolution des attitudes et des comportements* (Paris, 1981)

FLETCHER, Jefferson Butler, *The Relation of Beauty in Women, and Other Essays on Platonic Love in Poetry and Society* (New York, 1911)

FORSTER, Margaret, *The Rash Adventurer: The Rise and Fall of Charles Edward Stuart* (1975)

FOUCAULT, Michel, *Histoire de la sexualité* (Paris, 3 vols., 1976–84)

FOXON, D., 'Libertine literature in England 1660–1675', *Book Collector*, vol. 11 (1963)

FRASER, Antonia, *The Weaker Vessel: Women's Lot in Seventeenth-Century England* (1984)

FRASER, Flora, *Beloved Emma: The Life of Emma, Lady Hamilton* (1986)

FRENCH, Yvonne, *Mrs Siddons* (1936)

GARLAND, Madge, *The Changing Face of Beauty: Four Thousand Years of Beautiful Women* (New York, 1957)

GAUNT, William and ROW, F. Gordon, *Etty and the Nude* (1943)

GAXOTTE, Pierre, *La France de Louis XIV* (Paris, 1953)

GAXOTTE, Pierre, 'Madame de Pompadour', *Les Oeuvres Libres* (March 1953)

GAY, Peter, *The Bourgeois Experience: Victoria to Freud,* vol. I, *The Education of the Senses* (New York, 1984)

GEORGE, M. D., *Catalogue of Political and Personal Satires Preserved in the Department of Prints and Drawings in the British Museum,* vols. 5 and 6 (1978)

GIES, F. and J., *Women in the Middle Ages* (1970)

GIRARD, Alain, *Le Choix du conjoint* (Paris, 1964)

GONCOURT, Edmond and Jules de, *Les Maîtresses de Louis XV* (2 vols., Paris, 1860)

GONCOURT, Edmond de, *Mlle Clairon* (Paris, 1890)

GREBANIER, Bernard, *The Uninhibited Byron* (1970)

GREEN, David, *Sarah, Duchess of Marlborough* (1967)

GRIGG, John, *The Young Lloyd George* (1973)

GRIGG, John, *Lloyd George: The People's Champion 1902–1911* (1978)

GUIRAL, Pierre and THUILLIER, Guy, *La Vie quotidienne des domestiques en France au XIXᵉ siècle* (Paris, 1978)

GUTTON, Jean-Pierre, *Domestiques et serviteurs dans la France de l'ancien régime* (Paris, 1981)

'GWINN', *Memoirs* [i.e. a later anonymous biography] *of the Life of Eleanor Gwinn* (1752)

HAIGHT, Gordon S., *George Eliot: A Biography* (Oxford, 1968, 1978)

HALTUNNEN, Karen, *Confidence Men and Painted Women: A Study of Middle-Class Culture in America 1830–1870* (New Haven, Conn., 1982)

HAMILTON, Charles and OSTENDORF, Lloyd, *Lincoln in Photographs: An Album of Every Known Pose* (Norman, Okla., 1963)

HANNING, Robert W. and ROSTAND, David, *Castiglione: The Ideal and the Real in Renaissance Culture* (New Haven, Conn., 1983)

HARRIS, Janet, *The Prime of Ms America* (New York, 1975)

HASLIP, Joan, *Catherine the Great* (1977)

HELMHOLZ, R. H., *Marriage Litigation in Medieval England* (Cambridge, 1974)

HENRIOT, Emile, *Portraits de femmes* (Paris, 1950)

HERNDON, Boston, *Mary Pickford and Douglas Fairbanks* (1977)

HEROLD, John Christopher, *Mistress to an Age: A Life of Madame de Staël* (New York, 1958)

HEUFFER, Ford Madox, *Ford Madox Brown* (1896)

HEUSSLER, Robert, *Yesterday's Rulers: The Making of the British Colonial Service* (Syracuse, NY, 1963)

HIGHAM, Charles, *Bette: The Life of Bette Davis* (New York, 1981)

HOFSTADTER, Dan, Introduction to G. Sand, *Story of My Life* (1979)

HOLLANDER, Anne, *Seeing Through Clothes* (New York, 1978)

HORN, Pamela, *The Rise and Fall of the Victorian Servant* (Dublin, 1975)

HOULBROOKE, R. A., *The English Family 1485–1700* (1984)

JALLAND, Pat, *Women, Marriage and Politics 1860–1914* (Oxford, 1986)

JAMIESON, Kathleen Hall, *Packaging the President* (New York, 1984)

JEBB, Camilla, *A Star of the Salons: Julie de Lespinasse* (1908)

JONES, J. R., *Country and Court: England 1658–1714* (1978)

JORDAN, Ruth, *George Sand* (1976)

JUDD, Dennis, *Palmerston* (1975)

JULLIAN, Philippe, *Sarah Bernhardt* (Paris, 1977)

JUNOR, Penny, *Margaret Thatcher: Wife, Mother, Politician* (1983)

KAMM, J., *John Stuart Mill in Love* (1977)

KELLY, Linda, *The Kemble Era: John Philip Kemble, Sarah Siddons and the London Stage* (1980)

KELLY-GADOL, Joan, 'Did women have a Renaissance?', in Renata Bridenthal and Claudia Koonz (eds.), *Becoming Visible: Women in European History* (Boston, 1977)

KELSO, Ruth, *Doctrine for the Lady of the Renaissance* (Urbana, 1956)

KENYON, J. P., *The Stuarts* (1958)

KIRSHNER, J. and WEMPLE, S. F., *Women of the Medieval World* (1985)

KNAPTON, Ernest J., *Empress Josephine* (Cambridge, Mass., 1963)

KOENIG, René, *A la Mode: On the Social Psychology of Fashion* (translated by F. Bradley, New York, 1973)

KUNZLE, David, *Fashion and Fetishism: A Social History of the Corset, Tight-Lacing and other Forms of Body Sculpture in the West* (Totowa, NJ, 1982)

KUPFERMAN, Fred, *Mata Hari: songes et mensonges* (Brussels, 1982)

LABARGE, M. W., *Women in Medieval Life* (1986)

LACOMBE, E. H. (ed.), *Les Changements de la société française* (Paris, 1971)

LASH, Joseph P., *Eleanor and Franklin* (New York, 1971)

LASLETT, Peter, *The World We Have Lost* (3rd edition, 1983)

LAWRENSON, Helen, 'Hepburn reconsidered', *The Dial* (March 1981)

LEBRUN, François, *La Vie conjugale sous l'ancien régime* (Paris, 1975)

LEROY, Alfred, *Madame de Pompadour et son temps* (Paris, 1936)

LEUCHTENBERG, W. E., *The Perils of Prosperity 1914–1932* (Chicago, 1958)

LEVRON, Jacques, *Madame Du Barry: ou la fin d'une courtisane* (Paris, 1961, 1974)

LEVRON, Jacques, *Madame de Pompadour: l'amour et la politique* (Paris, 1961, 1975)

LOCKYER, Roger, *Buckingham: the life and political career of George Villiers, first Duke of Buckingham 1592–1628* (1981)

LONGFORD, Elizabeth, *Byron* (1976)

LOOMIS, Stanley, *Du Barry: A Biography* (Philadelphia, 1959)

LUCAS, A. M., *Women in the Middle Ages* (1983)

LURIE, Alison, *The Language of Clothes* (New York, 1981)

MACCOBY, E. E. and JACKLIN, C. E., *The Psychology of Sex Differences* (Stanford, 1974)

MACFARLANE, Alan, *The Family Life of Ralph Josselin* (Cambridge, 1970)

MACFARLANE, Alan, *Marriage and Life in England 1300–1840* (1986)

MAGNE, Emile, *Ninon de Lanclos: édition définitive* (Paris, 1948)

MAILLARD, Claude, *Les Prostituées* (Paris, 1975)

MALLET, Francine, *George Sand* (Paris, 1976)

MANVELL, Roger, *Sarah Siddons: portrait of an actress* (1970)

MARCHAND, Leslie A., *Byron: A Biography* (1957)

MARLY, Diana de, *Worth: Father of Haute Couture* (1980)

MARNHAC, Anne de, *Femmes au bain: les métamorphoses de la beauté* (Paris, 1986)

MARQUAND, David, *Ramsay MacDonald* (1977)

MARSH, Jan, 'Pre-Raphaelite women', *New Society* (23 February 1984)

MARSH, Jan, *The Pre-Raphaelite Sisterhood* (1985)

MARSH, Jan, *Jane and May Morris: A Biographical Story 1839–1938* (1986)

MARTIN-FUGIER, Anne, *La Place des bonnes: la domesticité féminine à Paris en 1900* (Paris, 1979)

MARWICK, Arthur, *The Deluge: British Society and the First World War* (1965)

MARWICK, Arthur, *War and Social Change in the Twentieth Century* (1974)

MARWICK, Arthur, *The Nature of History* (2nd edition, 1981)

MARWICK, Arthur, *British Society since 1945* (1982)

MARWICK, Arthur, 'Room at the Top, Saturday Night and Sunday Morning, and the cultural revolution in Great Britain', *Journal of Contemporary History* (Jan. 1984)

MARWICK, Arthur (ed.), *Class in the Twentieth Century* (Brighton, 1986)

MARWICK, Arthur, 'Problems and consequences of organizing society for total war', in N. F. Dreiziger (ed.), *Mobilization for Total War* (Waterloo, Ontario, 1981)

MASS OBSERVATION, *Browns and Chester: Portrait of a Shop 1780–1946* (1947)

MASTERS, Brian, *The Mistresses of Charles II* (1979)

MASTERS, Brian, *Georgiana, Duchess of Devonshire* (1981)

MASTERS, Brian, *Great Hostesses* (1982) (refers to Britain and the USA in the twentieth century)

MASTERS, Brian, *The Swinging Sixties* (1985)

MATUSOW, Barbara, *The Evening Stars: The Rise of the Network News Anchor* (New York, 1983)

MAZA, Sarah C., *Servants and Masters in Eighteenth-Century France* (Princeton, NJ, 1983)

McKENDRICK, Neil, BREWER, John and PLUMB, J. H., *The Birth of a Consumer Society: The Commercialization of Eighteenth-Century England* (1982)

MEYERS, William, *The Image-Makers: Power and Persuasion on Madison Avenue* (New York, 1984)

MILLER, Douglas T. and NOWAK, Marion, *The Fifties: The Way We Really Were* (Garden City, NY, 1977)

MILLER, Sir Oliver, *Sir Peter Lely* (1978)

MITFORD, Nancy, *Madame de Pompadour* (1954)

MOERS, Ellen, *The Dandy: Brummel to Beerbohm* (New York, 1960)

MOLLAT, Michel, *Les Pauvres au moyen âge* (Paris, 1978)

MONGREDIEN, Georges, *Marion de Lorne et ses amours* (Paris, 1940)

MORAVIA, Alberto, *Claudia Cardinale* (Rome, 1963)

MORELLA, Joe and EPSTEIN, Edward Z., *The 'It' Girl: The Incredible Story of Clara Bow* (New York, 1976)

MOUNT, Ferdinand, *The Subversive Family: An Alternative History of Love and Marriage* (2nd edition, 1983)

MULLER, Joseph-Emile, *Toulouse Lautrec* (Paris, 1981)


NICHOLAS, Donald, *The Portraits of Bonnie Prince Charlie* (1973)

NICOLLE, Jean, *Madame de Pompadour et la société de son temps* (Paris, 1980)

NORTON, Lucy, *The Sun King and his Loves* (1982)

NOUVION, Pierre and LIEZ, Emile, *Ministre de modes sous Louis XVI: Mademoiselle Bertin, marchande de modes de la reine 1747–1813* (Paris, 1971)


OATES, Stephen B., *Abraham Lincoln: The Man Behind the Myths* (New York, 1984)

OGG, David, *England in the Reigns of James II and William III* (Oxford, 1955)

OLSEN, Jack, *Cassius Clay: A Biography* (1967)

OMAN, Carola, *David Garrick* (1958)

O'NEILL, W. L., *Coming Apart: An Informal History of America in the 1960s* (Chicago, 1971)

OUTHWAITE, R. B. (ed.), *Marriage and Society: Studies in the Social History of Marriage* (1981)


PALEOLOGUE, Maurice, 'Une patricienne de la Renaissance: Jeanne d'Aragon', *La Revue de Paris*, vol.2 (1896)

PALMER, I. I., *The Face Without a Frown: Georgiana, Duchess of Devonshire* (1944)

PARKINSON, Michael, *George Best: An Intimate Biography* (1975)

PAUGE, Comtesse J. de, *Monsieur de Staël* (Paris, 1932)

PEARSON, Karl, *Life of Francis Galton* (4 vols., 1914)

PERROT, Philippe, *Le Travail des apparences: ou les transformations du corps féminin XVIIIᵉ–XIXᵉ siècle* (Paris, 1984)

PESSEN, Edward, *The Log Cabin Myth: The Social Background of the Presidents* (New Haven, Conn., 1984)

PICENI, Enrico, *Boldini: l'uomo e l'opera* (Busto Arsizio, 1981)

PIMLOTT, Ben, *Hugh Dalton* (1985)

PLUMB, Sir J. H., *The First Four Georges* (1956)

POIROT-DALPACH, *Marie Duplessis: 'La dame aux camélias'* (Paris, 1981)

PORTER, Roy, *English Society in the Eighteenth Century* (1982)

PORTER, Roy, 'Making faces: physiognomy and fashion in eighteenth-century England', *Etudes Anglaises*, tome XXXVIII (1985)

POWERS, Ron, *The News Business as Show Business* (New York, 1977)

PRIDEAUX, Tom, *Love or Nothing: The Life and Times of Ellen Terry* (New York, 1975)


REDINGER, Ruby, *George Eliot* (1976)

REES, Joan, *Jane Austen: Woman and Writer* (1976)

REEVES, Nicholas, *Official British Film Propaganda during the First World War* (1986)

RICHARDSON, Joanna, *Fanny Brawne* (1952)

RICHARDSON, Joanna, *The Courtesans: The Demi-Monde in Nineteenth-Century France* (1967)

RIDLEY, Jasper, *Napoleon III and Eugénie* (1979)

RIESE, Laure, *Les Salons littéraires parisiens: du second empire à nos jours* (Paris, 1962)

RITTER, Raymond, *Charmante Gabrielle* (Paris, 1947)

ROBERTS, Keith, *Rubens* (1977)

ROBINSON, Paul, *The Modernization of Sex* (New York, 1976)

RODOCANACHI, Emanuel, *La Femme italienne à l'époque de la Renaissance* (Paris, 1907)

ROGERS, Pat, *An Introduction to Pope* (1975)

ROSS, Ishbel, *The Uncrowned Queen: The Life of Lola Montez* (New York, 1972)

ROTH, Andrew, *Heath and the Heathmen* (1972)

ROUSSELOT, Jean, *Rubens: la couleur et la femme* (Paris, 1972)

ROWSE, A. L., *Simon Forman: Sex and Society in Shakespeare's Age* (1974)

RUDOLFSKY, Bernard, *The Unfashionable Human Body* (Garden City, NY, 1981)

SAINT-ANDRE, Claude, *La Vie de Mme Du Barry* (Paris, 1930)

SANDS, Frederick and BROMEN, Sven, *The Divine Garbo* (1979)

SARI, Guido, *Boldini a Parigi* (Alghero, 1980)

SAUNDERS, Edith, *The Age of Worth* (1954)

SCOTT, George Ryley, *A History of Prostitution from Antiquity to the Present Day* (1936, 1940, 1954)

SEGALEN, M., *Love and Power in the Seventeenth Century* (1984)

SEGUR, P. M. M. H. de, *Julie de Lespinasse* (Paris, 1905)

SHORTER, Edward, *The Making of the Modern Family* (New York, 1976)

SKINNER, Cornelia Otis, *Elegant Wits and Grand Horizontals* (1963)

SLATER, M., *Family Life in the Seventeenth Century* (1984)

SMITH, Constance Babbington, *Amy Johnson* (1967)

SPIRAKOFF, Pierre, *Sarah Bernhardt par les Nadar* (Paris, 1982)

STEARNS, Peter M., *European Society in Upheaval* (New York, 1975)

STEELE, Valerie, *Fashion and Eroticism: Ideals of Feminine Beauty from the Victorian Era to the Jazz Age* (New York, 1985)

STOKES, Hugh, *The Devonshire Home Circle* (1917)

STONE, Lawrence, *The Family, Sex and Marriage in England 1500–1800* (1977)

SULEMAN, Susan Ribin (ed.), *The Female Body in Western Culture* (1986)

SUMMERS, Anthony, *Goddess: The Secret Lives of Marilyn Monroe* (1985)

SUTHERLAND, Donald E., *Americans and their Servants: Domestic Service in the United States from 1800 to 1920* (Baton Rouge, 1981)

SYMONS, Donald, *The Evolution of Human Sexuality* (New York, 1979)

THIRSK, Joan, 'The fantastical folly of fashion: the English stocking knitting industry, 1500–1700', in *Textile History and Economic History* (ed. N. G. Harte and K. G. Ponting, Manchester, 1973)

THISELTON-DYER, T. F., *The Loves and Marriages of Some Eminent Persons* (1890)

THISELTON-DYER, T. F., *Folk-lore of Women* (1905)

THOMPSON, F. M. L., *English Landed Society in the Nineteenth Century* (1963)

THOMPSON, Roger, *Women in Stuart England and America* (1974)

THOMSON, George Malcolm, *The First Churchill* (1979)

THOMSON, Patricia, *George Sand and the Victorians* (1977)

TYTLER, Graeme, *Physiognomy in the European Novel: Faces and Fortunes* (Princeton, 1982)

VAUDOYER, Jean Louis, *Alice Ozy ou l'aspasie moderne* (Paris, 1930)

WALLACE, Irving, *The Nymphs and Other Maniacs* (New York, 1971)

WARNER, Marina, *Monuments and Maidens: Allegory of the Female Form* (1985)

WATERSON, Merlin, *The Servants' Hall: A Domestic History of Erodig* (1980)

WEBER, Ronald (ed.), *America in Change: Reflections on the 60's and 70's* (Notre Dame, 1972)

WEEKS, Jeffrey, *Sex, Politics and Society: The Regulation of Sexuality since 1800* (1981)

WEEKS, Jeffrey, *Sexuality and Its Discontents: Meanings, Myths and Modern Sexuality* (1985)

WEEKS, Jeffrey, *Sexuality* (1986)

WEINTRAUB, Stanley, *Victoria, Biography of a Queen* (1987)

WEST, Rebecca, *1900* (1982)

WHEELER, K. W. and LUSSIER, V. L., *Women, the Arts, and the 1920s in Paris and New York* (New Brunswick, NJ, 1982)

WHITE, Christopher, *Rubens and his World* (1968)
WIGFIELD, W. MacDonald, *The Monmouth Rebellion* (Bradford-on-Avon, 1980)
WINEGARTEN, Renée, *The Double Life of George Sand* (New York, 1978)
WOODHOUSE, J. R., *Baldesar Castiglione* (Edinburgh, 1977)
WRIGLEY, E. A. and SCHOFIELD, R., *The Population History of England 1541–*

*1871* (1981)
WYNN, Neil A., *The Afro-American and the Second World War* (New York, 1974)
WYNN, Neil A., *From Progressivism to Prosperity: World War I and American Society* (New York, 1986)

ZELDIN, Theodore, *France 1848–1945*, vol.2 (Oxford, 1977)
ZOLLA, Elémir, *The Androgyne: Fusion of the Sexes* (1981)

# Acknowledgments

BBC Hulton Picture Library 30, 57, 59, 79, 80, 87, 89, 95, 96, 97, 114, 115, 117, 118, 119, 123; Musée du Berry, Bourges 12; Russell Cotes Art Gallery and Museum, Bournemouth 64; British Vogue © The Condé Nast Publications Ltd., photo Justin de Villeneuve 116; Musées Royaux, Brussels 33; Musée Condé, Chantilly (Giraudon) 35; Chatsworth, Devonshire Collection. Reproduced by permission of the Chatsworth Settlement Trustees 39; Chiddingstone, Kent, The Trustees of the Denys Eyre Bower Trust 18; Cino del Duca (National Film Archive) 110; Columbia Pictures Corporation (National Film Archive) 120; Château de Coppet 37; National Gallery of Ireland, Dublin 61; Eastmancolour/Cinemascope (National Film Archive) 100; National Galleries of Scotland, Edinburgh 48, 50; Spencer Museum of Art, University of Kansas, Lawrence 72; British Museum, London 17, 40, 43, 49; The Iveagh Bequest, Kenwood, London 45, 51; National Film Archive, London 101, 102, 103, 106, 111, 112, 113; National Portrait Gallery, London 15, 16, 20, 22, 23, 44, 46, 47, 53, 54, 58, 75, 91; Royal Academy of Arts, London 2; St Bride Printing Library, London 70; Tate Gallery, London 71; Wallace Collection, London 26; Prado, Madrid 5; Manchester City Art Gallery 65; Mansell Collection 62; Metro Goldwyn Mayer/United Artists Entertainment Co. (National Film Archive) 107, 108, 121; Alte Pinakothek, Munich 6; Bayerische Staatsgemäldesammlungen, Munich 7; Schloss Nymphenburg, Munich 82; Musées de Narbonne, photo J. Lepage 21; Yale Center for British Art, Paul Mellon Collection, New Haven 42; Metropolitan Museum of Art, New York 27; Ashmolean Museum, Oxford 69; Paramount Pictures (National Film Archive) 124; Bibliothèque Nationale, Paris 11, 19, 31, 92; Musée Carnavalet, Paris (Bulloz) 32, 74; Louvre, Paris (Giraudon) 3, 4, 10; Louvre, Paris (Réunion des Musées Nationaux) 1, 8, 38, 78; Private Collections 14, 24 (Bulloz) 66, 67, 68, 81, 90 (courtesy Sotheby's, London); Renn-Burrill (National Film Archive) 122; Musée de St Omer (Giraudon) 25; Anderson Family Papers (M051), Department of Special Collections and University Archives, The Stanford University Libraries, Stanford 76, 77; Hoover Institution Archives/Karl Von Wiegand Collection, Stanford 104; National Museum, Stockholm 29; Swedish Film Institute, Stockholm 98; Museo Correr, Venice (Giraudon) 9; Musée National du Château de Versailles (Giraudon) 60; Musée National du Château de Versailles (Réunion des Musées Nationaux) 13, 34; Collection Viollet 84, 85, 86, 94; Library of Congress, Washington, D.C. 88; Helen Woodburn, courtesy of the Hoover Institution Archives (Ann Meader Collection) 105.

# Index